Instant Vortex Air Fryer Oven
Cookbook for Beginners

1200+ Quick & Delicious Instant Vortex Air Fryer Recipes
and 4-Week Meal Plan for Everyone

Eleanor Pearce

Table of Contents

Chapter 4 Fish and Seafood

Chapter 6 Snack and Appetizer

Introduction

The Instant Vortex Air Fryer Oven has revolutionized modern cooking. It can do many functions and is the kitchen appliance that replaces your dehydrator, toaster, oven, and microwave as it is multipurpose, which means it has the ability to reduce the number of machines you have to buy in your kitchen and save your kitchen space. It is one of the easiest multi-cookers to operate. From breakfast to dessert, you can prepare all foods using this kitchen appliance. Therefore, Instant Vortex Air Fryer Oven is an ideal kitchen companion for gatherings, occasions, and holidays.

The microprocessor technology utilized in the appliance makes it the best for cooking because of the programmed keys. With an Instant Vortex Air Fryer Oven, you can prepare crunchy and delicious food for your family and friends. There are a lot of benefits of this appliance. For example, it saves on fat consumption. You can quickly cook your foods without worrying about the time and temperature. It cooks 70% faster than a conventional oven, and it uses less energy. It does not spread too much heat in your kitchen. It is easy to use – anyone can cook with this appliance. You can prepare restaurant-style food with this appliance. It is easy to clean. You can remove accessories from the unit and clean it. You don't have to take a lot of time to cook and clean as it is simple to use-turn the oven on, and it does all the work for you.

Instant Vortex Air Fryer Oven offers a healthier and more convenient alternative to prepare to fry, in addition to versatility to roast, bake and reheat. In this way, it is possible to fry potatoes and all kinds of food using just a few drops of oil and thus achieve frying in which the ingredients barely absorb oil. This type of frying is much less caloric than conventional frying consisting of submerging food in hot oil. As a result, you can produce healthier versions of all your favorite fried foods--- It gives you tasty, healthy, and fast food. Air frying can, in many cases, reduce cooking time, so the cooking time is also less than what you would need using a conventional convection oven.

In this book, we will cover a wide array of recipes that you can choose and enjoy a meal in the comfort of your home. You can prepare a delightful breakfast, poultry dishes, vegetables, juicy meat, delicious seafood, snack, and incredible desserts. There is something for everyone here. An air fryer prepares food easily, needs few ingredients during preparation, and is simple enough for anyone to use — from inexperienced cooks to seasoned chefs.

If you are looking for an air fryer that is more than just an air fryer, the Instant Vortex Air Fryer Oven might be the right choice for you. Try any recipe in this book, and you will see for yourself how this appliance is such a marvel.

What Is Instant Vortex Air Fryer Oven?

The Instant Vortex Air Fryer Oven utilizes advanced technology to help people cook their favorite family foods with just one touch! It runs on a simple hot air technology which allows your food to be crispy on the outside and tender on the inside using a minimal amount of oil. The Instant Vortex Air Fryer Oven has eight cooking programs: dehydrate, air fry, roast, bake, toast, broil, reheat, and proof. The appliance blows scorching air inside the oven, and the convection fan will distribute the hot air to allow the device to cook the meal effectively. This technology will enable you to cook foods well and evenly. Further, your air fryer is equipped with a digital display that shows the cooking time and temperature and various options and buttons to select smart cooking programs. The vortex air fryer usually releases heat from the heating element while cooking. It also has an exhaust fan located above the cooking chamber. This will allow circulating air required to cook the food and maintain fresh air circulation throughout the cooking process. Besides, it ensures that the air entering the oven is fresh and filtered to allow you to cook food more healthily. As for cooking accessories, the vortex air fryer comes with six accessories with two cooking trays, a rotisserie spit, a rotisserie basket, a drip pan, a rotisserie lift, and a rotisserie fork. You should place the ingredients in a cooking tray or rotisserie basket, press the desired button, and wait for your meal to get cooked. Thanks to the cooking trays incorporated in the Instant Vortex Air Fryer Oven, you can distribute a relatively large amount of food on them in a single layer. In this way, the heat distribution will be much more uniform than in a conventional air fryer, and you will achieve much faster and more homogeneous cooking!

Main Functions of Instant Vortex Air Fryer Oven

The cooking buttons are intuitive and guide you all along the cooking process. It tells you when to add food and when to remove it. Among them, the four cooking modes of Air Fry, Roast, Broil, and Bake have a preheating program before the cooking, while the other modes do not have a preheating program. The 8 smart cooking programs are simple to use:

Air Fry

This cooking mode is suitable for all your favorite deep-fried meals, like fries, cauliflower bites, wings, nuggets, and more. It cooks the food evenly, both fresh and frozen, with a crisp and crunchy outside and the inside tender.

Roast

This function is ideal for cooking vegetable dishes, beef, lamb, pork, poultry, etc. With this function, you will get a crisp on the outside.

Broil

Broiling is top-down direct heat, perfect for melting cheese on onion soup, machos, and more. This cooking function is used to give a final touch to the food

Bake

This function works well for cakes, cupcakes, muffins, etc. You can bake larger quantities as you have two cooking trays.

Dehydrate

Dehydration is a slow process. It is perfect for homemade fruit leather, jerky, dried vegetables, etc. It takes several hours to dehydrate the food, but it gives a tasty flavor to the food.

Reheat

You can easily warm up your food with this function. You can reheat leftovers and save your budget with this useful function.

Proof

To get the scrumptious, loaves and rolls, allow the dough to rest and rise and let the yeast its job with this smart program!

Toast

There are no specific temperature settings in this cooking mode, only three levels of cooking temperature. The toasting level is also affected by how close you place the cooking tray to the element.

Buttons & User Guide of Instant Vortex Air Fryer Oven

The Instant Vortex Air Fryer oven has a touch screen that allows you to choose the function you want to introduce. These functions are easy to key in and are described as follows.

Display

The vortex air fryer has a digital panel that makes your cooking convenient and easy. You can select the automatic as well as the manual function. The functions are easy to key in, and you can change them until you have found the correct function you want.

Smart Programs

The programs are automated and by using them, you will not need to set temperature or cooking time. Usually, when the air fryer goes on standby mode, it indicates "OFF". The smart programs included in the oven include: Roast, Air Fry, Bake, Broil, Dehydrate, Reheat

+/- Temp

The "+" button is used to raise the temperature, and the "-" button is used to lower the temperature.

+/- Time

This is used to adjust the time taken in cooking your food. You can use the "+" to increase the time taken to cook the food or use "-" to reduce the time taken in cooking the food depending on your taste and preference.

Rotate

This is a function key that you can use while roasting or any other process that requires a rotisserie. This button is only available when you choose to roast or air fry.

Light

The Light button is used to turn ON and OFF the oven light.

Cancel

This function is vital in stopping the cooking process. This is important, especially if you have chosen the wrong function.

Start

This function is effective in beginning the cooking process.

Clean & Maintain

Cleaning Tips

Your air fryer, like any other kitchen appliance, should be cleaned and maintained regularly. Dirty air fryers can also

accumulate grease, which can cause your fryer to smoke and lower the quality of your food. Here's how to keep your air fryer clean and to run smoothly

Step 1:

Unplug your air fryer from the wall socket and let it cool completely before attempting to clean it. Keep the door open while it cools down.

Step 2:

Remove all the trays, dripping pan, steel racks, and other accessories inside the oven. Clean them with warm soapy water. If they have stuck or burnt-on food, soak them for about 30 minutes in warm water and dish soap, then clean away the food particles with a soft cloth or sponge. Before reassembling and using your air fryer, make sure your air frying basket, pan, and other removable accessories are entirely dried out. Do not use the hard scrubber to clean them.

Step 3:

If the heating element has some oil, use a small amount of dish soap on the cloth or sponge to help remove it. And, using clean, hot water, brush away the soap. To remove any stuck-on dirt or particles, use a soft-bristle food brush. Using a soft sponge or cloth and hot water, clean the interior thoroughly. Dry the interior of the air fryer thoroughly.

Step 4:

Use a damp cloth or sponge and a mild detergent to clean the outside. Make sure never to submerge it in water.

Maintaining Tips

Below are tips for maintaining your air fryer to keep it running for a long time:
· Cleaning your air fryer after each use is the simplest way to keep it in good working order. This protects the appliance from food particles and grease accumulation.
· Enable your air fryer to dry completely before storing it in its original box or a clean, dry location (i.e., don't store it next to your stovetop or near your dishwasher).
· To prevent food from reaching the heating device, follow the directions to ensure you're using the frying basket and pan correctly.
· Most importantly, don't clutter your air fryer. When you put too much food in the basket, it won't cook properly, it'll take longer to cook, and more grease and food particles will end up on the heating unit.

4-Week Meal Plan

Week-1

Day-1

Pumpkin Seed Wheat Bread
Breaded Fish Fingers
Turmeric Brussel Sprout Chips
Coated Pork Chops
Baked Pears with Honey

Day-2

Baked Eggs with Cheeses
Chicken Wings with Sweet Chili Sauce
Crunchy Nut Pretzel Mix
Green Spiced Lamb
Vanilla Brownie with Sultanas

Day-3

Breakfast Ham Soufflé
Pecan Brownies
Tasty Kale Chips
Spicy Turkey Breast
Baked Nut and Apples

Day-4

Firm Tofu and Bell Peppers Bake
Herbed Chicken Breast in White Wine
Savory Avocado Chips
Smoked Salmon Frittatas
Maple Syrup Toast Sticks

Day-5

Veggie Frittata
Tuna-Stuffed Starchy Potatoes
Cumin Chickpeas Snack
Glossy Pork Belly
Coconut Walnut Blondies

Day-6

Nutritious Carrot Oatmeal
BBQ Steak Cubes
Old Bay Cauliflower Florets
Oat and Quinoa Burgers
Spiced Pumpkin Cupcakes

Day-7

Chicken Spring Rolls
Mayonnaise Crab Cake
Ranch Baby Potato Halves
Lamb Kofta
Vanilla Candied Walnuts

Week-2

Day-1

Sticky Rolls
Cajun Chicken Wings
Tuna Muffins with Celery
Herbed Salmon Fillets
Pistachio Cheese-Stuffed Apricots

Day-2

Peanut Butter Banana Sandwich
Spiced Catfish Fillets
Zucchini Chips
Spicy Chicken Breast Fillets
Banana Bites

Day-3

French Texas Toast Sticks
Rosemary Chicken Wings
Crunchy Cashews
Olives and Broccoli with Parmesan Cheese
Sheet Roll Oreos

Day-4

Avocado Egg Sandwich
Yummy Stuffed Mushrooms
Almond-Asparagus Fries
Salmon Croquettes
Almond Vanilla Cheesecake

Day-5

Sausage-Egg Burrito
Red Potatoes Cubes
Ginger Turkey Meatballs
Juicy Pork Chops
Allspice Donuts

Day-6

Eggs in Bread Cups with Tomato Slices
Crispy Shrimp with Lime Wedges
Almond Zucchini Fries
Beef-Sausage Meatballs
Fried Brandy Peaches

Day-7

Bacon Sausage Toasts
Chicken Croquettes
Coriander Mushroom Caps
Spicy Firm Tofu
Crispy Bananas

Week-3

Day-1

Crispy Tofu
Coconut Shrimp with Hot Sauce
Dehydrated Bacon Slices
Parmesan Turkey Meatballs
Ginger Apple Cider Donuts

Day-2

Tater Tot Bake
Cheesy Eggplant
Spicy and Sweet Walnut
Juicy Beef and Fruit
Nutmeg Bread Pudding

Day-3

Spinach-Onion Frittata
Orange Duck in Chicken Broth
Mini Pork Burgers
Easy Shrimp Cooked with Basil Pesto
Allspice Pecan Muffins

Day-4

Broccoli Stuffed Peppers
Mayo Zucchini and Carrot
Fried Basil Ravioli
Homemade Chicken Cutlets
Pumpkin Coconut Blondies

Day-5

Cheese Zucchini Noodles
Spicy Lamb Skewers
Honey Roasted Carrots
Veggies with Rice
Vanilla Coconut Pie with Monk Fruit

Day-6

Asparagus Frittata
Skin-on Salmon and Broccoli Florets
Zucchini Mushroom Pizza
Skinless Chicken Drumsticks with Cajun Seasoning
Delicious Coconut Vanilla Cake

Day-7

Mushroom Frittata with Parmesan Cheese
Avocado Fingers
Sriracha Tomato-Avocado Rolls
Rosemary Lamb Shashlik
Chocolate Macaroon

Week-4

Day-1

Chili Egg Soufflé
Air-Fried Chicken Legs
Simple-Fried Potato Fries
Butternut Squash Fries
Cranberry Bread Loaf

Day-2

Hash Browns
Glazed Carrot Sticks
Ranch Chickpeas
Aromatic Pork Chops
Vanilla Blueberry Bars

Day-3

Greek Spinach & Tomato Frittata
Cod Nuggets
Cheese Broccoli
Crusted Bone-in Chicken Thighs
Brazilian Pineapple

Day-4

Egg Avocado Tacos
Veggies Medley
Cajun Zucchini Chips
Air-Fried Paprika Chicken Drumsticks
Cream Cinnamon Rolls

Day-5

Ham Bread Cups
Baked Parmesan Chicken Breasts
BBQ Little Sausages
Cajun Ribeye Steaks
Raspberry Almond Crumble

Day-6

Tomato Bacon Cups
Stuffed Beef Burgers
Parmesan Baby Carrots
Buttermilk-Glazed Chicken Tenders
Strawberry Scones

Day-7

Scrambled Eggs
Chicken and Bell Pepper Skewers
Chinese-Style Dumplings
Tasty Cod Fillets with Pearl Onions
Cinnamon Donuts

Baked Spinach Sausage

Prep time: 10 minutes | Cook time: 35 minutes | Serves: 10

10 eggs	½-inch pieces
1 cup spinach, diced	1 teaspoon garlic powder
1 cup onion, diced	½ cup almond milk
1 cup pepper, diced	Black pepper, to taste
1-pound sausage, cut into	Salt, to taste

1. Spray a suitable 8x8-inch baking dish with cooking spray and set aside. 2. In a bowl, whisk eggs with milk and spices. 3. Add chopped vegetables and sausage and stir to combine. 4. Pour the prepared egg mixture into the prepared baking dish. 5. Select the "Bake" mode on your air fryer. 6. Use the timer (+ / − Time) arrow keys to adjust the cooking time to 35 minutes. 7. Adjust its cooking temperature to 390 degrees F, using the temp (+/- Temp) arrow keys. 8. Press the Start button to initiate preheating. 9. Transfer the egg bake baking dish to the rack of the air fryer when the screen displays "Add Food." 10. Close its door, and let the machine do the cooking. 11. Slice and serve.

Per serving: Calories 260; Fat 20.2g; Sodium 408mg; Carbs 4.9g; Fiber 1.6g; Sugars 1.3g; Protein 15.3g

Broccoli Egg Casserole with Cheddar Cheese

Prep time: 10 minutes | Cook time: 30 minutes | Serves: 12

12 eggs	1 small onion, diced
1 ½ cups cheddar cheese, shredded	1 cup milk
2 cups broccoli florets, chopped	Black pepper, to taste
	Salt, to taste

1. Spray a suitable 9x13-inch baking dish with cooking spray and set aside. 2. Whisk eggs with milk, pepper, and salt in a suitable bowl. 3. Add cheese, broccoli, and onion and stir well. 4. Pour the broccoli egg mixture into the prepared baking dish. 5. Select the "Bake" mode on your air fryer. 6. Use the timer (+ / − Time) arrow keys to adjust the cooking time to 30 minutes. 7. Adjust its cooking temperature to 375 degrees F, using the temp (+/- Temp) arrow keys. 8. Press the Start button to initiate preheating. 9. Transfer the baking dish to the air fryer when the screen displays "Add Food." 10. Close its door and let the machine do the cooking. 11. Slice and serve.

Per serving: Calories 138; Fat 9.5g; Sodium 164mg; Carbs 3.1g Fiber 0.5g; Sugars 1.8g; Protein 10.2g

Cheddar Ham Omelet

Prep time: 10 minutes | Cook time: 25 minutes | Serves: 8

8 eggs	⅓ cup milk
1 cup ham, chopped	Black pepper, to taste
1 cup cheddar cheese, shredded	Salt, to taste

1. Spray a suitable 9x9-inch baking dish with cooking spray and set aside. 2. Whisk eggs with milk, pepper, and salt in a suitable bowl. Stir in ham and cheese. 3. Pour this ham egg mixture into the prepared baking dish. 4. Select the "Bake" mode on your air fryer. 5. Use the timer (+ / − Time) arrow keys to adjust the cooking time to 25 minutes. 6. Adjust its cooking temperature to 390 degrees F using the temp (+/- Temp) arrow keys. 7. Press the Start button to initiate preheating. 8. Transfer the baking dish to the air fryer when the screen displays "Add Food." 9. Close its door and let the machine do the cooking. 10. Slice and serve.

Per serving: Calories 152; Fat 10.7g; Sodium 374mg; Carbs 1.7g; Fiber 0.2g; Sugars 0.9g; Protein 12.2g

Egg Ham Bake

Prep time: 10 minutes | Cook time: 40 minutes | Serves: 6

4 eggs	ded
20 ounces' hash browns	1 cup sour cream
1 onion, chopped	1 cup milk
2 cups ham, chopped	Black pepper, to taste
3 cups cheddar cheese, shred-	Salt, to taste

1. Spray a suitable 9x13-inch baking dish with cooking spray and set aside. 2. Whisk eggs with sour cream, milk, pepper, and salt in a suitable mixing bowl. 3. Add 2 cups cheese and stir well. 4. Cook onion and ham in a medium pan until onion is softened. 5. Add hash brown to the pan and cook for 5 minutes. 6. Add onion ham mixture into the egg mixture and mix well. 7. Pour this egg mixture into the prepared baking dish. Cover dish with foil. 8. Select the "Bake" mode on your air fryer. 9. Use the timer (+ / − Time) arrow keys to adjust the cooking time to 35 minutes. 10. Adjust its cooking temperature to 375 degrees F using the temp (+/- Temp) arrow keys. 11. Press the Start button to initiate preheating. 12. Transfer the egg bake baking dish to the rack of the air fryer when the screen displays "Add Food." 13. Close its door and let the machine do the cooking. 14. Remove foil and bake for 25 minutes more. 15. Slice and serve.

Per serving: Calories 476; Fat 27.6g; Sodium 992mg; Carbs 40.5g; Fiber 4g; Sugars 4.3g; Protein 16.8g

Cheese Potato Broccoli Frittata

Prep time: 10 minutes | Cook time: 35 minutes | Serves: 8

10 eggs	2 cups broccoli, chopped
¼ cup goat cheese, crumbled	1 tablespoon olive oil
1 onion, diced	Black pepper, to taste
1 sweet potato, diced	Salt, to taste

1. Spray a suitable baking dish with cooking spray and set it aside. 2. Set a suitable pan with oil over medium heat. 3. Add sweet potato, broccoli, and onion, and cook for 10-15 minutes or until sweet potato is tender. 4. In a suitable mixing bowl, whisk eggs with pepper and salt. 5. Transfer cooked vegetables into the baking dish. 6. Pour egg mixture over vegetables. Sprinkle with goat cheese. 7. Select the "Bake" mode on your air fryer. 8. Use the timer (+ / − Time) arrow keys to adjust the cooking time to 20 minutes. 9. Adjust its cooking temperature to 390 degrees F, using the temp (+/- Temp) arrow keys. 10. Press the Start button to initiate preheating. 11. Transfer the baking dish to the air fryer when the screen displays "Add Food." 12. Close its door and let the machine do the cooking. 13. Slice and serve.

Per serving: Calories 124; Fat 7.7g; Sodium 113mg; Carbs 6.2g Fiber 1.4g; Sugars 2.3g; Protein 8.3g

Oat Squash Muffins

Prep time: 10 minutes | Cook time: 20 minutes | Serves: 6

2 eggs	1 teaspoon vanilla
1 tablespoon pumpkin pie spice	⅓ cup olive oil
	½ cup yogurt
2 teaspoons baking powder	½ cup maple syrup
1 cup oats	1 cup butternut squash puree
1 cup all-purpose flour	½ teaspoon sea salt

1. Line 12 cups muffin pan with cupcake liners. 2. Whisk together eggs, oil, vanilla, maple syrup, yogurt, and squash puree in a suitable bowl. 3. Mix flour, pumpkin pie spice, baking powder, oats, and salt in another suitable bowl. 4. Add this flour spice mixture into the wet mixture and stir to combine. 5. Scoop the prepared muffin batter into a greased muffin pan. 6. Select the "Bake" mode on your air fryer. 7. Use the timer (+ / − Time) arrow keys to adjust the cooking time to 20 minutes. 8. Adjust its cooking temperature to 390 degrees F using the temp (+/- Temp) arrow keys. 9. Press the Start button to initiate preheating. 10. Transfer the muffin tray to the air fryer when the screen displays "Add Food." 11. Close its door and let the machine do the cooking. 12. Serve and enjoy.
Per serving: Calories 250; Fat 3g; Sodium 198mg; Carbs 48.3g Fiber 2.5g; Sugars 19.2g; Protein 7g

Hash Brown Egg Bake

Prep time: 10 minutes | Cook time: 60 minutes | Serves: 12

32 ounces frozen hash browns with onions and peppers	5 bacon slices, cooked and chopped
2 cups cheddar cheese, shredded	Black pepper, to taste
	Salt, to taste
15 eggs, lightly beaten	

1. Spray a suitable 9x13-inch casserole dish with cooking spray and set aside. 2. In a large mixing bowl, whisk eggs with pepper and salt. 3. Add 1 cup cheese, bacon, and hash browns and mix well. 4. Pour egg mixture into the prepared casserole dish and sprinkle with remaining cheese. 5. Select the "Bake" mode on your air fryer. 6. Use the timer (+ / − Time) arrow keys to adjust the cooking time to 60 minutes. 7. Adjust its cooking temperature to 350 degrees F, using the temp (+/- Temp) arrow keys. 8. Press the Start button to initiate preheating. 9. Transfer the casserole dish to the air fryer when the screen displays "Add Food." 10. Close its door and let the machine do the cooking. 11. Slice and serve.
Per serving: Calories 272; Fat 19g; Sodium 389mg; Carbs 10.4g; Fiber 0.7g; Sugars 1.1g; Protein 15.6g

Baked Eggs with Cheeses

Prep time: 10 minutes | Cook time: 20 minutes | Serves: 4

4 eggs	Black pepper, to taste
½ cup parmesan cheese, grated	Salt, to taste
2 cups marinara sauce	

1. Spray 4 small, shallow baking dishes with cooking spray and set aside. 2. Divide marinara sauce into four baking dishes. 3. Break the egg into each baking dish. 4. Sprinkle cheese, pepper, and salt on the eggs. 5. Select the "Bake" mode on your air fryer. 6. Use the timer (+ / − Time) arrow keys to adjust the cooking time to 20 minutes. 7. Adjust its cooking temperature to 390 degrees F, using the temp (+/- Temp) arrow keys. 8. Press the Start button to initiate preheating. 9. Transfer the baking dishes to the air fryer when the screen displays "Add Food." 10. Close its door and let the machine do the cooking. 11. Serve and enjoy.
Per serving: Calories 183; Fat 8.5g; Sodium 607mg; Carbs 17.7g; Fiber 3.3g; Sugars 11.4g; Protein 8.9g

Cinnamon Apple Turnovers

Prep time: 15 minutes | Cook time: 20 minutes | Serves: 4

1 cup diced apple (about 1 medium apple)	1 teaspoon all-purpose flour
	½ package (1 sheet) frozen puff pastry, thawed
1 tablespoon brown sugar	
¼ teaspoon cinnamon	1 large egg, beaten
⅛ teaspoon allspice	2 teaspoons granulated sugar
1 teaspoon lemon juice	

1. In a suitable bowl, stir together the apple, cinnamon, allspice, brown sugar, lemon juice, and flour. 2. Unfold the puff pastry sheet onto the board and roll it out. 3. Cut this dough into four squares. 4. Scoop a quarter of the apple mixture into the center of each puff pastry square. 5. Spread this filling evenly on the triangle shape over half the pastry, leaving a border of about ½ inch around the edges of the pastry. 6. Fold the pastry diagonally over the filling to form triangles. Press their edges to seal them using a fork. 7. Place the turnovers on the sheet pan, spacing them evenly. 8. Cut three slits at the top of each turnover. 9. Brush with the egg. Sprinkle evenly with the granulated sugar. 10. Select the "Bake" mode on your air fryer. 11. Use the timer (+ / − Time) arrow keys to adjust the cooking time to 20 minutes. 12. Adjust its cooking temperature to 350 degrees F using the temp (+/- Temp) arrow keys. 13. Press the Start button to initiate preheating. 14. Transfer the sheet pan to the cooking tray of the air fryer when the screen displays "Add Food." 15. Close its door and let the machine do the cooking. 16. Flip the food halfway and then resume cooking. 17. Serve.
Per serving: Calories 185; Fat 10.4g; Sodium 77mg; Carbs 20.5g; Fiber 1.9g; Sugars 7.2g; Protein 3.6g

Pumpkin Seed Wheat Bread

Prep time: 40 minutes | Cook time: 18 minutes | Serves: 2

3 ½ ounces of flour	3 ½ ounces wheat flour
1 teaspoon yeast	¼ cup pumpkin seeds
1 teaspoon salt	

1. Mix the wheat flour, yeast, salt, seeds, and plain flour in a suitable bowl. 2. Stir in ¾ cup of lukewarm water and stir until dough becomes soft. 3. Knead for another 5 minutes until the dough becomes elastic and smooth. 4. Mold into a ball and cover with a plastic bag. Set aside 30 minutes for it to rise. 5. Transfer the dough to a small pizza pan. 6. Select the "Bake" mode on your air fryer. 7. Use the timer (+ / − Time) arrow keys to adjust the cooking time to 18 minutes. 8. Adjust its cooking temperature to 390 degrees F using the temp (+/- Temp) arrow keys. 9. Press the Start button to initiate preheating. 10. Transfer the pan to the cooking tray of the air fryer when the screen displays "Add Food." 11. Close its door and let the machine do the cooking. 12. Slice and serve
Per serving: Calories 280; Fat 8.5g; Sodium 1168mg; Carbs 41.7g; Fiber 2.4g; Sugars 0.3g; Protein 10.1g

Spinach Florentine

Prep time: 10 minutes | Cook time: 15 minutes | Serves: 4

3 cups frozen spinach, thawed and drained

¼ teaspoon kosher salt or ⅛ teaspoon fine salt

4 ounces' ricotta cheese

2 tablespoons heavy (whipping) cream

2 garlic cloves, minced

⅛ teaspoon freshly ground white or black pepper

2 teaspoons unsalted butter, melted

3 tablespoons grated Parmesan or similar cheese

½ cup panko bread crumbs

4 large eggs

1. In a suitable bowl, stir together the spinach, salt, ricotta, cream, garlic, and pepper. 2. In a suitable bowl, stir together the butter, cheese, and panko. Set aside. 3. Scoop the spinach mixture into four even circles on the sheet pan. 4. Select the "Roast" mode on your air fryer. 5. Use the timer (+ / − Time) arrow keys to adjust the cooking time to 15 minutes. 6. Adjust its cooking temperature to 375 degrees F using the temp (+/- Temp) arrow keys. 7. Press the Start button to initiate preheating. 8. Transfer the sheet pan to the air fryer when the screen displays "Add Food." 9. Close its door and let the machine do the cooking. 10. After 8 minutes, press Cancel and remove the pan. 11. With the back of a spoon, make 4 indentations in the spinach for the eggs. 12. Crack the eggs into the indentations and sprinkle the panko mixture over the surface of the eggs. 13. Return the pan to the oven and press Start to resume cooking. 14. Serve the eggs with toasted English muffins.
Per serving: Calories 236; Fat 13.9g; Sodium 451mg; Carbs 13.2g; Fiber 1.2gSugars 1.4g; Protein 14.3g

Peanut Butter Banana Sandwich

Prep time: 10 minutes | Cook time: 6 minutes | Serves: 2

2 slices of whole-wheat bread

1 teaspoon sugar-free maple syrup

1 sliced banana

2 tablespoons Peanut butter

1. Evenly coat each side of the sliced bread with peanut butter. 2. Add the sliced banana and drizzle with some sugar-free maple syrup. 3. Select the "Bake" mode on your air fryer. 4. Use the timer (+ / − Time) arrow keys to adjust the cooking time to 6 minutes. 5. Adjust its cooking temperature to 330 degrees F, using the temp (+/- Temp) arrow keys. 6. Press the Start button to initiate preheating. 7. Transfer the slices to the rack of the air fryer when the screen displays "Add Food." 8. Close its door and let the machine do the cooking. 9. Serve warm.
Per serving: Calories 336; Fat 17.3g; Sodium 281mg; Carbs 38.1g; Fiber 5.3g; Sugars 17.7g; Protein 12.3g

Corned Beef Hash

Prep time: 10 minutes | Cook time: 38 minutes | Serves: 6

2 Yukon Gold potatoes, peeled, cut into ¼-inch cubes (about 3 cups)

1 medium onion, chopped (about 1 cup)

⅓ cup diced red bell pepper

3 tablespoons vegetable oil

½ teaspoon dried thyme

½ teaspoon kosher salt or ¼ teaspoon fine salt

½ teaspoon freshly ground black pepper

¾ pound corned beef, cut into ¼-inch pieces

4 large eggs

1. Mix the potatoes, onion, red pepper, oil, thyme, ¼ teaspoon of pepper, and ¼ teaspoon of salt in a suitable bowl. 2. Spread the chopped vegetables on the sheet pan in an even layer. 3. Select the "Roast" mode on your air fryer. 4. Use the timer (+ / − Time) arrow keys to adjust the cooking time to 25 minutes. 5. Adjust its cooking temperature to 375 degrees F, using the temp (+/- Temp) arrow keys. 6. Press the Start button to initiate preheating. 7. Transfer the sheet pan to the rack of the air fryer when the screen displays "Add Food." 8. Close its door and let the machine do the cooking. 9. Add the corned beef after 15 minutes of cooking. 10. Stir the mixture to incorporate the corned beef. 11. Return the pan to the air fryer and continue cooking for 5 minutes. 12. Use any spoon's back to create 4 circles in the hash to hold the eggs. 13. Crack an egg into each circle; season eggs with the remaining ¼ teaspoon salt and ¼ teaspoon of pepper. 14. Return the sheet pan to the oven. Continue cooking for 3 to 8 minutes. 15. Serve immediately.
Per serving: Calories 257; Fat 17.3g; Sodium 748mg; Carbs 12.8g; Fiber 1.3g; Sugars 1.8g; Protein 13.3g

Sticky Rolls

Prep time: 10 minutes | Cook time: 25 minutes | Serves: 4

2 teaspoons cinnamon

⅓ cup light brown sugar

1 (9-by-9-inch) frozen puff pastry sheet, thawed

All-purpose flour for dusting

6 teaspoons (2 tablespoons) unsalted butter, melted

1. In another suitable bowl, mix the cinnamon and brown sugar. 2. Unfold the puff pastry on a lightly floured surface. 3. Using a rolling pin, press the folds together and roll the dough out in one direction to measure about 9 by 11 inches. 4. Cut it in half to form two squat rectangles of about 5½ by 9 inches. 5. Brush 2 teaspoons of butter over each pastry half, then sprinkle with 2 generous tablespoons of the cinnamon sugar. 6. Pat it down lightly with the palm of your hand to help it adhere to the butter. 7. Starting with the 9-inch side of one rectangle and using your hands, carefully roll the dough into a cylinder. 8. Repeat with the other rectangle. To make slicing easier, refrigerate the rolls for 10 to 20 minutes. 9. Slice each roll into nine 1-inch pieces. 10. Transfer the rolls to the center of the sheet pan. 11. For neater rolls, turn the outside, so the seam is to the inside. 12. Add 2 teaspoons butter over the rolls and sprinkle the remaining cinnamon sugar. 13. Select the "Bake" mode on your air fryer. 14. Use the timer (+ / − Time) arrow keys to adjust the cooking time to 25 minutes. 15. Adjust its cooking temperature to 350 degrees F using the temp (+/- Temp) arrow keys. 16. Press the Start button to initiate preheating. 17. Transfer the rolls to the rack of the air fryer when the screen displays "Add Food." 18. Close its door and let the machine do the cooking. 19. Flip the rolls halfway and resume cooking. 20. Serve.
Per serving: Calories 123; Fat 9.5g; Sodium 146mg; Carbs 9.9g; Fiber 0.9g; Sugars 4.3g; Protein 0.9g

Honey Ham Sandwiches

Prep time: 10 minutes | Cook time: 5 minutes | Serves: 4

2 bagels

4 teaspoons honey mustard

4 slices of cooked honey ham

4 pieces of Swiss cheese

1. Spread honey mustard on each half of the bagel. 2. Add ham and cheese and close the bagel. 3. Select the "Bake" mode on your air fryer. 4. Use the timer (+ / − Time) arrow keys to adjust the cooking time to 5 minutes. 5. Adjust its cooking temperature to 400 degrees F, using the temp (+/- Temp) arrow keys. 6. Press the Start button to initiate preheating. 7. Transfer the sandwiches to the rack of the air fryer when the screen displays "Add Food." 8. Close its door and

let the machine do the cooking. 9. Serve.

Per serving: Calories 285; Fat 9.8g; Sodium 639mg; Carbs 31.1g; Fiber 1.2g; Sugars 5.1g; Protein 17.8g

Avocado Egg Sandwich

Prep time: 7 minutes | Cook time: 42 minutes | Serve: 1

2 eggs	1 bunch spinach
½ avocado	Pinch of salt
2 slices bread	Pinch of pepper

1. Bring a suitable pan with water to a rolling boil. 2. Place bread on a pan and toast it in the oven for 10 minutes. 3. Once the water is boiling, whisk it around in a circle until it creates a vortex. 4. Drop one egg in the hole, turn the heat low, and then poach for 2 minutes. 5. Repeat with the second egg. 6. Mash peeled and pitted avocado and spread it over the toast while the eggs poach. 7. Add the eggs to the toast and top with spinach, then transfer to a baking sheet. 8. Select the "Bake" mode on your air fryer. 9. Use the timer (+ / − Time) arrow keys to adjust the cooking time to 30 minutes. 10. Adjust its cooking temperature to 400 degrees F using the temp (+/- Temp) arrow keys. 11. Press the Start button to initiate preheating. 12. Transfer the sheet to the rack of the air fryer when the screen displays "Add Food." 13. Close its door and let the machine do the cooking. 14. Serve warm.

Per serving: Calories 229; Fat 15.1g; Sodium 338mg; Carbs 15.4g; Fiber 7.3g; Sugars 1.7g; Protein 12.1g

Bacon, Bell Pepper and Onion Casserole

Prep time: 20 minutes | Cook time: 19 minutes | Serves: 4

Salt, to taste	¾ cup shredded Cheddar cheese
Cooking oil	
Black pepper, to taste	½ cup chopped red bell pepper
½ cup chopped green bell pepper	
	6 slices bacon
6 eggs	½ cup chopped onion

1. Cook the bacon in a skillet for 5 to 7 minutes, flipping to evenly crisp over medium-high heat. 2. Drain on paper towels, crumble, and set aside. 3. In a suitable bowl, whisk the eggs. 4. Add salt and pepper to taste. 5. Spray a barrel pan with cooking oil. Make sure to cover the bottom and sides of the pan. 6. Add the beaten eggs, crumbled bacon, red bell pepper, green bell pepper, and onion to the pan. 7. Select the "Bake" mode on your air fryer. 8. Use the timer (+ / − Time) arrow keys to adjust the cooking time to 12 minutes. 9. Adjust its cooking temperature to 375 degrees F, using the temp (+/- Temp) arrow keys. 10. Press the Start button to initiate preheating. 11. Transfer the pan to the rack of the air fryer when the screen displays "Add Food." 12. Close its door and let the machine do the cooking. 13. Serve.

Per serving: Calories 235; Fat 17.1g; Sodium 590mg; Carbs 3.6g; Fiber 0.8g; Sugars 1.9g; Protein 16.5g

Grape Tomato and Spinach Frittata

Prep time: 15 minutes | Cook time: 30 minutes | Serves: 10

3 tablespoons olive oil	ach
10 large eggs	1-pint grape tomatoes
2 teaspoons kosher salt	4 scallions
½ teaspoon black pepper	8 ounces' feta cheese
1 (5-ounce) bag of baby spin-	

1. Beat eggs with black pepper and salt in a medium mixing bowl and whisk together for a minute. 2. Stir in tomatoes, spinach, and scallions to the bowl and mix well. 3. Crumble the cheese into the bowl and mix gently. 4. Select the "Bake" mode on your air fryer. 5. Use the timer (+ / − Time) arrow keys to adjust the cooking time to 30 minutes. 6. Adjust its cooking temperature to 350 degrees F using the temp (+/- Temp) arrow keys. 7. Press the Start button to initiate preheating. 8. Transfer the baking dish to the rack of the air fryer when the screen displays "Add Food." 9. Close its door and let the machine do the cooking. 10. Slice and serve warm.

Per serving: Calories 179; Fat 14.1g; Sodium 802mg; Carbs 3.7g; Fiber 0.9g; Sugars 2.5g; Protein 10.4g

Toasted Lemon Bananas

Prep time: 10 minutes | Cook time: 10 minutes | Serves: 1

1 ripe banana	2 teaspoons honey
Lemon juice	Ground cinnamon

1. Slice the ripe bananas lengthwise and place them on a greased baking sheet. 2. Brush each slice with lemon juice. 3. Drizzle honey and sprinkle cinnamon over each slice. 4. Select the "Bake" mode on your air fryer. 5. Use the timer (+ / − Time) arrow keys to adjust the cooking time to 10 minutes. 6. Adjust its cooking temperature to 350 degrees F using the temp (+/- Temp) arrow keys. 7. Press the Start button to initiate preheating. 8. Transfer the baking sheet to the rack of the air fryer when the screen displays "Add Food." 9. Close its door and let the machine do the cooking. 10. Serve warm.

Per serving: Calories 148; Fat 0.4g; Sodium 2mg; Carbs 38.5g; Fiber 3.1g; Sugars 25.9g; Protein 1.3g

Ham Jalapeños Burrito

Prep time: 20 minutes | Cook time: 30 minutes | Serves: 8

16 ounces cooked bacon ends and pieces	8 hash brown squares
	8 large soft flour tortillas
16 eggs	2 diced jalapeños
1 tablespoon butter	2 cups shredded sharp cheddar

1. Select the "Bake" mode on your air fryer. 2. Use the timer (+ / − Time) arrow keys to adjust the cooking time to 10 minutes. 3. Adjust its cooking temperature to 450 degrees F, using the temp (+/- Temp) arrow keys. 4. Press the Start button to initiate preheating. 5. Transfer the bacon to the cooking tray of the air fryer when the screen displays "Add Food." 6. Close its door and let the machine do the cooking. 7. Flip the bacon halfway and resume cooking. 8. Whisk all 16 eggs together in a bowl and set aside. 9. Melt butter into a saucepan and mix in eggs until they start to cook but are not fully hardened. 10. While eggs are cooking, microwave and cool hash brown squares. 11. Roll out tortillas and top them with hash browns, bacon, jalapeños, and cheese. 12. Wrap up the burritos and place them seam-down on a baking sheet. 13. Select the "Bake" mode on your air fryer. 14. Use the timer (+ / − Time) arrow keys to adjust the cooking time to 20 minutes. 15. Adjust its cooking temperature to 375 degrees F using the temp (+/- Temp) arrow keys. 16. Press the Start button to initiate preheating. 17. Transfer the bacon to the rack of the air fryer when the screen displays "Add Food." 18. Close its door and let the machine do the cooking. 19. Flip the rolls halfway and resume cooking. 20. Serve warm.

Per serving: Calories 363; Fat 20.5g; Sodium 583mg; Carbs 28g; Fiber 1.6g; Sugars 2.1g; Protein 18.5g

Raspberry Scones

Prep time: 10 minutes | Cook time: 10 minutes | Serves: 4

Olive oil spray
2½ tablespoons cold butter, cubed
1½ teaspoons baking powder
¼ teaspoon salt
1 cup all-purpose flour
½ cup milk
½ cup fresh raspberries
1 tablespoon granulated sugar

1. Place a parchment liner in the cooking tray. 2. Combine the sugar, flour, baking powder, cold butter, and salt in a mixing bowl. 3. Work the ingredients with clean hands until the mixture is crumbly. 4. Create a hole in the center of the mixture, and pour in the milk. 5. Knead the combination with your hands until it forms a thick dough. 6. Transfer to a well-floured, flat work surface. 7. Add the raspberries and gently work them throughout the dough, taking care not to squash the berries. 8. Mold the prepared dough into a ball and flatten it out slightly, making sure not to crush the berries. 9. Select the "Air Fry" mode on your air fryer. 10. Use the timer (+ / − Time) arrow keys to adjust the cooking time to 10 minutes. 11. Adjust its cooking temperature to 400 degrees F using the temp (+/- Temp) arrow keys. 12. Press the Start button to initiate preheating. 13. Transfer the scones to the cooking tray of the air fryer when the screen displays "Add Food." 14. Close its door and let the machine do the cooking. 15. Flip the scones when the display says "turn Food" and resume cooking. 16. Serve warm.
Per serving: Calories 213; Fat 8.2g; Sodium 244mg; Carbs 30.6g; Fiber 1.8g; Sugars 5.1g; Protein 4.5g

Chicken Spring Rolls

Prep time: 10 minutes | Cook time: 4 minutes | Serves: 8

Filling
1 sliced celery stalk
4 ounces' chicken breast, cooked and shredded
½ cup mushrooms, sliced
1 teaspoon sugar
½ teaspoon ginger, chopped
1 teaspoon chicken stock
powder
1 carrot, sliced
Spring roll wrappers
1 teaspoon cornstarch
1 beaten egg
8 spring roll wrappers
½ teaspoon vegetable oil

1. Prepare the filling. Put the meat, carrot, mushrooms, and celery in a bowl. 2. Mix until combined. Add the chicken stock powder, sugar, and ginger. Mix well. 3. In another bowl, combine the cornstarch and egg and whisk until thick. Set aside. 4. Spoon some filling into a spring roll wrapper. Roll and seal the ends with the egg mixture. 5. Brush the prepared spring rolls with a bit of oil. 6. Select the "Bake" mode on your air fryer. 7. Use the timer (+ / − Time) arrow keys to adjust the cooking time to 4 minutes. 8. Adjust its cooking temperature to 390 degrees F using the temp (+/- Temp) arrow keys. 9. Press the Start button to initiate preheating. 10. Transfer the spring rolls to the rack of the air fryer when the screen displays "Add Food." 11. Close its door and let the machine do the cooking. 12. Serve.
Per serving: Calories 217; Fat 3.5g; Sodium 289mg; Carbs 20.2g; Fiber 0.9g; Sugars 1.1g; Protein 24.4g

Honey Pancakes

Prep time: 10 minutes | Cook time: 8 minutes | Serves: 4

2 tablespoons honey
½ cup coconut milk
¼ teaspoon baking soda
4 tablespoons brown sugar
2 whisked eggs
¼ teaspoons cinnamon pow-
der
Salt, to taste
1 cup whole wheat flour
1 teaspoon baking powder
½ cup almond flour

1. Add wheat flour, all-purpose flour, salt, baking powder, baking soda, and brown sugar in a suitable bowl, and mix well. 2. Now add eggs and milk. Whisk a little with a fork for 1-2 minutes. 3. Transfer the prepared batter into a greased baking pan. 4. When done, transfer to a serving platter and drizzle honey on top. 5. Select the "Bake" mode on your air fryer. 6. Use the timer (+ / − Time) arrow keys to adjust the cooking time to 6 minutes. 7. Adjust its cooking temperature to 400 degrees F, using the temp (+/- Temp) arrow keys. 8. Press the Start button to initiate preheating. 9. Transfer the baking dish to the cooking tray of the air fryer when the screen displays "Add Food." 10. Close its door and let the machine do the cooking. 11. Serve with berries.
Per serving: Calories 344; Fat 14.9g; Sodium 227mg; Carbs 43.4g; Fiber 4g; Sugars 8.8g; Protein 9.7g

French Texas Toast Sticks

Prep time: 10 minutes | Cook time: 9 minutes | Serves: 4

1 teaspoon vanilla extract
1 tablespoon butter
1 teaspoon ground cinnamon
1 egg
1 teaspoon stevia
¼ cup milk
Cooking oil
4 slices of Texas toast

1. Divide the bread slices into 3 pieces each. 2. Melt butter in a bowl by heating in the microwave for 15 seconds. 3. Whisk in stevia, egg, cinnamon, milk, and vanilla extract. Whisk until thoroughly combined. 4. Coat each of the breadsticks in the egg mixture. 5. Select the "Bake" mode on your air fryer. 6. Use the timer (+ / − Time) arrow keys to adjust the cooking time to 8 minutes. 7. Adjust its cooking temperature to 375 degrees F, using the temp (+/- Temp) arrow keys. 8. Press the Start button to initiate preheating. 9. Transfer the toasts to the cooking tray of the air fryer when the screen displays "Add Food." 10. Close its door and let the machine do the cooking. 11. Flip the French toasts halfway and resume cooking. 12. Allow cooking until the French toast sticks are crisp. 13. Cool before serving.
Per serving: Calories 153; Fat 5.3g; Sodium 253mg; Carbs 20.4g; Fiber 1.3g; Sugars 2.9g; Protein 4.9g

Chicken Wings and Waffles

Prep time: 10 minutes | Cook time: 25 minutes | Serves: 8

8 whole chicken wings
1 teaspoon garlic powder
Chicken seasoning or rub
Black pepper, to taste
½ cup all-purpose flour
Cooking oil
8 frozen waffles
Maple syrup, to taste

1. Rub the chicken with the chicken seasoning, garlic powder, and pepper in a sizable bowl. 2. Set the chicken in a sealable plastic bag and add the flour to coat evenly. 3. Grease the cooking tray with cooking oil and put it inside the air fryer. 4. Select the "Air Fry" mode on your air fryer. 5. Use the timer (+ / − Time) arrow keys to adjust the cooking time to 20 minutes. 6. Adjust its cooking temperature to 400 degrees F using the temp (+/- Temp) arrow keys. 7. Press the Start button to initiate preheating. 8. Transfer the coated chicken wings to the cooking tray of the air fryer when the screen displays "Add Food." 9. Close its door and let the machine do the cooking. 10. Toss the chicken wing when the display says "turn Food" and resume cooking. 11. Decrease the temperature of the air fryer to 370 degrees F. 12. Transfer the waffles to the rack of the air fryer

and cook on "Toast" mode on L2 settings. 13. Enjoy the waffles with the chicken and a touch of maple syrup.

Per serving: Calories 200; Fat 11.1g; Sodium 350mg; Carbs 12.2g; Fiber 1.2g; Sugars 0.1g; Protein 12.9g

Onion Omelet Frittata

Prep time: 10 minutes | Cook time: 6 minutes | Serves: 3

3 eggs, lightly beaten	¼ small onion, chopped
2 tablespoons cheddar cheese, shredded	¼ bell pepper, diced
	Black pepper, to taste
2 tablespoons heavy cream	Salt, to taste
2 mushrooms, sliced	

1. Whisk eggs with cream, vegetables, pepper, and salt in a bowl. 2. Pour egg mixture into a suitable baking pan. 3. Add shredded cheese on top of the frittata. 4. Select the "Bake" mode on your air fryer. 5. Use the timer (+ / − Time) arrow keys to adjust the cooking time to 6 minutes. 6. Adjust its cooking temperature to 375 degrees F using the temp (+/- Temp) arrow keys. 7. Press the Start button to initiate pre-heating. 8. Transfer the baking dish to the rack of the air fryer when the screen displays "Add Food." 9. Close its door and let the machine do the cooking. 10. Serve and enjoy.

Per serving: Calories 124; Fat 9.7g; Sodium 96mg; Carbs 2.4g; Fiber 0.4g; Sugars 1.3g; Protein 7.5g

Seasoned Potatoes Bake

Prep time: 5 minutes | Cook time: 40 minutes | Serves: 2

2 russet potatoes, scrubbed	blend seasoning
½ tablespoon butter, melted	½ teaspoon garlic powder
½ teaspoon garlic and herb	Salt, to taste

1. In a bowl, mix all of the spices and salt. 2. With a fork, prick the potatoes. 3. Coat the russet potatoes with butter and sprinkle with spice mixture. 4. Select the "Bake" mode on your air fryer. 5. Use the timer (+ / − Time) arrow keys to adjust the cooking time to 40 minutes. 6. Adjust its cooking temperature to 400 degrees F using the temp (+/- Temp) arrow keys. 7. Press the Start button to initiate preheating. 8. Transfer the potatoes to the rack of the air fryer when the screen displays "Add Food." 9. Close its door and let the machine do the cooking. 10. Toss the potatoes halfway and resume cooking. 11. Serve hot.

Per serving: Calories 175; Fat 3.1g; Sodium 33mg; Carbs 34g; Fiber 5.2g; Sugars 2.6g; Protein 3.7g

Breakfast Ham Soufflé

Prep time: 15 minutes | Cook time: 8 minutes | Serves: 4

6 eggs	parsley
⅓ cup milk	½ cup chopped ham
½ cup shredded mozzarella cheese	1 teaspoon salt
	1 teaspoon black pepper
1 tablespoon freshly chopped	½ teaspoon garlic powder

1. Grease 4 ramekins with a nonstick cooking spray. 2. Using a suitable bowl, add and stir all the ingredients until it mixes properly. 3. Pour the egg mixture into the greased ramekins. 4. Then, carefully remove the soufflé from your air fryer and al-low it to cool off. 5. Select the "Bake" mode on your air fryer. 6. Use the timer (+ / − Time) arrow keys to adjust the cooking time to 8 minutes. 7. Adjust its cooking temperature to 350 degrees F, using the temp (+/- Temp) arrow keys. 8. Press the Start button to initiate preheating. 9. Transfer the ramekins to

the rack of the air fryer when the screen displays "Add Food." 10. Close its door and let the machine do the cooking. 11. Serve and enjoy!

Per serving: Calories 143; Fat 8.9g; Sodium 925mg; Carbs 3g; Fiber 0.4g; Sugars 1.7g; Protein 12.9g

Italian Frittata

Prep time: 5 minutes | Cook time: 10 minutes | Serves: 6

⅓ cup of milk	½ cup feta cheese, grated
6 eggs	1 zucchini, chopped
4 ounces' Italian sausage, chopped	1 tablespoon of basil, chopped
3 cups kale, stemmed and chopped	1 teaspoon garlic powder
	1 teaspoon onion powder
1 red bell pepper, deseeded and chopped	1 teaspoon salt
	1 teaspoon black pepper

1. Add the Italian sausage to a suitable greased pan. 2. Mix eggs, kale, and the rest of the ingredients in a bowl until mixed properly. 3. Add the egg mixture to the same pan. 4. Select the "Bake" mode on your air fryer. 5. Use the timer (+ / − Time) arrow keys to adjust the cooking time to 10 minutes. 6. Adjust its cooking temperature to 360 degrees F using the temp (+/- Temp) arrow keys. 7. Press the Start button to ini-tiate preheating. 8. Transfer the baking pan to the rack of the air fryer when the screen displays "Add Food." 9. Close its door and let the machine do the cooking. 10. Serve and enjoy!

Per serving: Calories 176; Fat 12.7g; Sodium 740mg; Carbs 3.5g; Fiber 0.5g; Sugars 2.3g; Protein 12g

Sausage-Egg Burrito

Prep time: 15 minutes | Cook time: 15 minutes | Serves: 6

6 eggs	chopped
Black pepper, to taste	8 ounces' chicken sausage, ground
Salt, to taste	
Cooking oil to grease	½ cup salsa
½ cup red bell pepper, chopped	6 (8-inch) flour tortillas
	½ cup Cheddar cheese, shred-ded
½ cup green bell pepper,	

1. Beat eggs with black pepper and salt in a bowl. 2. Set a skillet with cooking oil on medium-high heat. 3. Pour in eggs, scramble for 3 minutes until the eggs are fluffy, then transfer to a plate. 4. Add the chopped bell peppers to the same skil-let. 5. Cook for 3 minutes; once the peppers are soft, add the ground sausage to the skillet. 6. Crumble the sausage while cooking into smaller pieces using a spatula or spoon. 7. Cook for 4 minutes until the sausage is brown. 8. Stir in salsa and scrambled eggs. 9. Spoon the mixture evenly onto the tor-tillas. 10. Fold the sides of the tortilla towards the middle and then roll up from the bottom; secure each burrito with a toothpick. 11. Select the "Bake" mode on your air fryer. 12. Use the timer (+ / − Time) arrow keys to adjust the cooking time to 8 minutes. 13. Adjust its cooking temperature to 375 degrees F using the temp (+/- Temp) arrow keys. 14. Press the Start button to initiate preheating. 15. Transfer the burritos to the rack of the air fryer when the screen displays "Add Food." 16. Close its door and let the machine do the cooking. 17. Flip the burritos halfway and resume the cooking. 18. Sprinkle the Cheddar cheese over the burritos. 19. Serve.

Per serving: Calories 331; Fat 18.3g; Sodium 623mg; Carbs 14.4g; Fiber 2.4g; Sugars 2.4g; Protein 26.6g

Cheese Bacon Muffins

Prep time: 5 minutes | Cook time: 15 minutes | Serves: 4

1 ½ cups all-purpose flour	slices
2 teaspoons of baking powder	1 thinly chopped onion
½ cup milk	½ cup shredded cheddar
2 eggs	cheese
1 tablespoon freshly chopped parsley	½ teaspoon onion powder
	1 teaspoon salt
4 cooked and chopped bacon	1 teaspoon black pepper

1. Using a suitable bowl, add and stir all the ingredients until it mixes properly. 2. Then, grease the muffin cups with a nonstick cooking spray or line them with parchment paper. 3. Pour the batter proportionally into each muffin cup. 4. Select the "Bake" mode on your air fryer. 5. Use the timer (+ / − Time) arrow keys to adjust the cooking time to 15 minutes. 6. Adjust its cooking temperature to 360 degrees F using the temp (+/- Temp) arrow keys. 7. Press the Start button to initiate preheating. 8. Transfer the muffin tray to the rack of the air fryer when the screen displays "Add Food." 9. Close its door and let the machine do the cooking. 10. Serve and enjoy!
Per serving: Calories 335; Fat 10.4g; Sodium 1084mg Carbs 42.7g; Fiber 2.3g; Sugars 3g; Protein 17.1g

Cheddar Chicken Burrito with Bell Pepper

Prep time: 10 minutes | Cook time: 9 minutes | Serves: 2

4 chicken breast slices; cooked and shredded	2 eggs; whisked
2 tortillas	2 tablespoons mild salsa
1 avocado; peeled, pitted, and sliced	2 tablespoons cheddar cheese; grated
1 green bell pepper; sliced	Black pepper, to taste
	Salt, to taste

1. In a bowl, whisk the eggs with salt and pepper and pour them into a pan. 2. Select the "Bake" mode on your air fryer. 3. Use the timer (+ / − Time) arrow keys to adjust the cooking time to 5 minutes. 4. Adjust its cooking temperature to 400 degrees F, using the temp (+/- Temp) arrow keys. 5. Press the Start button to initiate preheating. 6. Transfer the pan to the rack of the air fryer when the screen displays "Add Food." 7. Close its door and let the machine do the cooking. 8. Place the tortillas on a working surface and divide the eggs, chicken, bell peppers, avocado, and the cheese; roll the burritos. 9. Line your air fryer rack with tin foil, add the burritos and cook them at 300 degrees F for 3-4 minutes. 10. Serve.
Per serving: Calories 385; Fat 23.2g; Sodium 1098mg; Carbs 25g; Fiber 9.3g; Sugars 2.9g; Protein 23.4g

Vanilla Oatmeal with Milk

Prep time: 10 minutes | Cook time: 17 minutes | Serves: 2

1 cup steel-cut oats	2 teaspoons vanilla extract
1 cup milk	2 tablespoons brown sugar
2½ cups water	

1. Mix all ingredients and stir well in a pan that fits your air fryer. 2. Select the "Bake" mode on your air fryer. 3. Use the timer (+ / − Time) arrow keys to adjust the cooking time to 17 minutes. 4. Adjust its cooking temperature to 360 degrees F, using the temp (+/- Temp) arrow keys. 5. Press the Start button to initiate preheating. 6. Transfer the pan to the rack of the air fryer when the screen displays "Add Food." 7. Close its door and let the machine do the cooking. 8. Divide into bowls and serve.
Per serving: Calories 296; Fat 5.2g; Sodium 99mg; Carbs 37.2g; Fiber 4.1g; Sugars 6.4g; Protein 9.4g

Herbed Omelet with Heavy Cream

Prep time: 10 minutes | Cook time: 15 minutes | Serves: 6

6 eggs; whisked	chopped.
2 tablespoons parmesan cheese; grated	2 tablespoons chives; chopped.
4 tablespoons heavy cream	Black pepper, to taste
1 tablespoon parsley; chopped.	Salt, to taste
1 tablespoon tarragon;	

1. In a bowl, mix all ingredients except the parmesan and whisk well. 2. Pour this into a pan that fits your air fryer. 3. Select the "Bake" mode on your air fryer. 4. Use the timer (+ / − Time) arrow keys to adjust the cooking time to 15 minutes. 5. Adjust its cooking temperature to 350 degrees F, using the temp (+/- Temp) arrow keys. 6. Press the Start button to initiate preheating. 7. Transfer the pan to the rack of the air fryer when the screen displays "Add Food." 8. Close its door and let the machine do the cooking. 9. Divide the omelet between plates and serve with the parmesan sprinkled on top.
Per serving: Calories 125; Fat 8.7g; Sodium 186mg; Carbs 1.6g; Fiber 0.1g; Sugars 0.4g; Protein 10.4g

Parmesan Potato Frittata

Prep time: 10 minutes | Cook time: 20 minutes | Serves: 6

1-pound small potatoes; chopped.	2 red onions; chopped.
1-ounce parmesan cheese; grated	8 eggs; whisked
	1 tablespoon olive oil
½ cup heavy cream	Black pepper, to taste
	Salt, to taste

1. In a bowl, mix all ingredients except the potatoes and oil; stir well. 2. Toss the potatoes with oil in a suitable baking pan. 3. Select the "Bake" mode on your air fryer. 4. Use the timer (+ / − Time) arrow keys to adjust the cooking time to 5 minutes. 5. Adjust its cooking temperature to 320 degrees F, using the temp (+/- Temp) arrow keys. 6. Press the Start button to initiate preheating. 7. Transfer the pan to the rack of the air fryer when the screen displays "Add Food." 8. Close its door and let the machine do the cooking. 9. Add the egg mixture, spread, and bake for 15 minutes more. 10. Divide the frittata between plates and serve.
Per serving: Calories 138; Fat 7.1g; Sodium 96mg; Carbs 11.4g   Fiber 0.7g; Sugars 2.7g; Protein 7.2g

Cheese Butter Toast

Prep time: 10 minutes | Cook time: 8 minutes | Serves: 4

4 bread slices	4 teaspoons butter; softened
4 cheddar cheese slices	

1. Spread the softened butter over each slice of bread. 2. Place 2 cheese slices each on 2 bread slices, then top with the other 2 slices; cut each in half. 3. Select the "Bake" mode on your air fryer. 4. Use the timer (+ / − Time) arrow keys to adjust the cooking time to 8 minutes. 5. Adjust its cooking temperature to 370 degrees F, using the temp (+/- Temp) arrow keys. 6. Press the Start button to initiate preheating. 7. Transfer the sandwiches to the rack of the air fryer when the screen displays "Add Food." 8. Close its door and let the machine do the cooking. 9. Serve hot and enjoy!
Per serving: Calories 170; Fat 13.4g; Sodium 262mg; Carbs 4.9g; Fiber 0.2g; Sugars 0.5g; Protein 7.7g

Air Fried Carrots and Cauliflower

Prep time: 10 minutes | Cook time: 20 minutes | Serves: 4

1 cauliflower head; florets separated and steamed	steamed
2 ounces' milk	3 eggs
2 ounces' cheddar cheese; grated	2 teaspoons cilantro; chopped.
3 carrots; chopped and	Black pepper, to taste
	Salt, to taste

1. In a bowl, mix the eggs with the milk, parsley, salt, and pepper; whisk. 2. Put the cauliflower and the carrots in your cooking tray, add the egg mixture, and spread. 3. Then sprinkle the cheese on top. 4. Select the "Air Fry" mode on your air fryer. 5. Use the timer (+ / − Time) arrow keys to adjust the cooking time to 20 minutes. 6. Adjust its cooking temperature to 350 degrees F using the temp (+/- Temp) arrow keys. 7. Press the Start button to initiate preheating. 8. Transfer the cooking tray to the air fryer when the screen displays "Add Food." 9. Close its door and let the machine do the cooking. 10. Serve.

Per serving: Calories 311; Fat 22.4g; Sodium 461mg; Carbs 8.2g; Fiber 2.4g; Sugars 4.7g; Protein 19.6g

Onion and Fish Tacos

Prep time: 10 minutes | Cook time: 14 minutes | Serves: 4

4 big tortillas	and boneless
1 yellow onion; chopped	A handful of mixed romaine lettuce; spinach, and radicchio
1 cup corn	
1 red bell pepper; chopped	4 tablespoons parmesan; grated
½ cup salsa	
4 white fish fillets; skinless	

1. Select the "Bake" mode on your air fryer. 2. Use the timer (+ / − Time) arrow keys to adjust the cooking time to 6 minutes. 3. Adjust its cooking temperature to 350 degrees F, using the temp (+/- Temp) arrow keys. 4. Press the Start button to initiate preheating. 5. Transfer the fish to the rack of the air fryer when the screen displays "Add Food." 6. Close its door and let the machine do the cooking. 7. Meanwhile, heat a pan over medium-high heat, add bell pepper, onion, and corn; stir and cook for 1 - 2 minutes 8. Arrange tortillas on a working surface, divide fish fillets, spread salsa over them; divide mixed veggies and mixed greens, and spread parmesan on each at the end. 9. Select the "Bake" mode on your air fryer. 10. Use the timer (+ / − Time) arrow keys to adjust the cooking time to 6 minutes. 11. Adjust its cooking temperature to 350 degrees F using the temp (+/- Temp) arrow keys. 12. Press the Start button to initiate preheating. 13. Roll your tacos; transfer them to the rack of the air fryer when the screen displays "Add Food." 14. Close its door and let the machine do the cooking. 15. Divide fish tacos between plates and serve for breakfast.

Per serving: Calories 264; Fat 7.4g; Sodium 583mg; Carbs 25.7g; Fiber 4.3g; Sugars 5.8g; Protein 27.6g

Mustard Tuna Sandwiches

Prep time: 10 minutes | Cook time: 10 minutes | Serves: 6

16 ounces canned tuna; drained	¼ cup mayonnaise
6 bread slices	2 tablespoons mustard
6 provolone cheese slices	1 tablespoon lime juice
2 spring onions; chopped.	3 tablespoons butter; melted

1. Spread butter over the bread slices. 2. Transfer the toasts to the rack of the air fryer and close its door. 3. Select the "Toast" mode on your air fryer. 4. Adjust its cooking temperature to L2 settings using the temp (+/- Temp) arrow keys. 5. Let the machine do the cooking. 6. In a bowl, mix the tuna, mayo, lime juice, mustard, and spring onions; stir until combined. 7. Spread tuna mix on half of the bread slices and top with the cheese and the other bread slices. 8. Select the "Bake" mode on your air fryer. 9. Use the timer (+ / − Time) arrow keys to adjust the cooking time to 5 minutes. 10. Adjust its cooking temperature to 375 degrees F using the temp (+/- Temp) arrow keys. 11. Press the Start button to initiate preheating. 12. Transfer the sandwiches to the rack of the air fryer when the screen displays "Add Food." 13. Close its door and let the machine do the cooking. 14. Divide between plates and serve.

Per serving: Calories 298; Fat 18.3g; Sodium 447mg; Carbs 9.8g; Fiber 0.9g; Sugars 1.7g; Protein 23.5g

Firm Tofu and Bell Peppers Bake

Prep time: 10 minutes | Cook time: 10 minutes | Serves: 1

3 ounces' firm tofu; crumbled	1 green bell pepper; cut into strips
1 green onion; chopped.	
1 yellow bell pepper; cut into strips	2 tablespoons parsley; chopped.
1 orange bell pepper; cut into strips	Black pepper, to taste
	Salt, to taste

1. In a pan that fits your air fryer, place the bell pepper strips and mix 2. Then add all remaining ingredients, and toss well. 3. Select the "Bake" mode on your air fryer. 4. Use the timer (+ / − Time) arrow keys to adjust the cooking time to 10 minutes. 5. Adjust its cooking temperature to 400 degrees F, using the temp (+/- Temp) arrow keys. 6. Press the Start button to initiate preheating. 7. Transfer the pan to the rack of the air fryer when the screen displays "Add Food." 8. Close its door and let the machine do the cooking. 9. Divide between plates and serve.

Per serving: Calories 181; Fat 5.7g; Sodium 68mg; Carbs 23.1g; Fiber 8.1g; Sugars 13.8g; Protein 13.8g

Cheese Egg Puffs

Prep time: 10 minutes | Cook time: 15 minutes | Serves: 4

1 (8-ounce) frozen puff pastry sheet, thawed	4 large eggs
¾ cup Monterey Jack cheese, shredded	1 tablespoon fresh chives, minced

1. Unfold the puff pastry and arrange it onto a lightly floured surface. 2. Cut the pastry into 2 equal-sized squares. Arrange 2 squares onto a cooking tray. 3. Select the "Bake" mode on your air fryer. 4. Use the timer (+ / − Time) arrow keys to adjust the cooking time to 10 minutes. 5. Adjust its cooking temperature to 390 degrees F, using the temp (+/- Temp) arrow keys. 6. Press the Start button to initiate preheating. 7. Transfer the cooking tray to the rack of the air fryer when the screen displays "Add Food." 8. Close its door and let the machine do the cooking. 9. Press down the center of each pastry with a metal spoon to make a nest. 10. Place ¼ of the cheese into each nest and carefully push it to the sides. 11. Carefully crack an egg into each nest and return the tray to the cooking chamber, then Bake for 5 minutes. 12. Repeat with the remaining pastry squares, cheese, and eggs. 13. Serve warm. 14. Garnish with chives and serve warm.

Per serving: Calories 171; Fat 11.7g; Sodium 219mg; Carbs 4.3g; Fiber 0.3g; Sugars 0.8g; Protein 12g

Ham Patties with Mozzarella Cheese

Prep time: 10 minutes | Cook time: 10 minutes | Serves: 4

8 ham slices; chopped.   1 puff pastry sheet
4 handfuls of mozzarella   4 teaspoons mustard
cheese; grated

1. Roll out puff pastry on a working surface and cut it into 12 squares. 2. Divide cheese, ham, and mustard on half of them, top with the other halves and seal the edges. 3. Select the "Bake" mode on your air fryer. 4. Use the timer (+ / − Time) arrow keys to adjust the cooking time to 10 minutes. 5. Adjust its cooking temperature to 370 degrees F, using the temp (+/- Temp) arrow keys. 6. Press the Start button to initiate preheating. 7. Transfer the patties to the rack of the air fryer when the screen displays "Add Food." 8. Close its door and let the machine do the cooking. 9. Divide the patties between plates and serve.
Per serving: Calories 243; Fat 14.8g; Sodium 935mg; Carbs 9.4g; Fiber 1.4g; Sugars 0.6g; Protein 17.9g

Lime Pepper Lettuce Salad

Prep time: 10 minutes | Cook time: 10 minutes | Serves: 2

2 ounces rocket leaves   1 tablespoon lime juice
4 red bell peppers   3 tablespoons heavy cream
1 lettuce head; torn   Black pepper, to taste
2 tablespoons olive oil   Salt, to taste

1. Select the "Bake" mode on your air fryer. 2. Use the timer (+ / − Time) arrow keys to adjust the cooking time to 10 minutes. 3. Adjust its cooking temperature to 400 degrees F, using the temp (+/- Temp) arrow keys. 4. Press the Start button to initiate preheating. 5. Transfer the bell peppers to the rack of the air fryer when the screen displays "Add Food." 6. Close its door and let the machine do the cooking. 7. Transfer the bell peppers to a serving bowl. 8. Add all remaining ingredients, toss and serve.
Per serving: Calories 296; Fat 23.2g; Sodium 16mg; Carbs 21g   Fiber 3.3g; Sugars 12.5g; Protein 5.3g

Oregano Artichoke Omelet

Prep time: 10 minutes | Cook time: 15 minutes | Serves: 2

3 artichoke hearts; canned,   ½ teaspoon oregano; dried
drained, and chopped.   Black pepper, to taste
6 eggs; whisked   Salt, to taste
2 tablespoons avocado oil

1. In a bowl, mix all ingredients; stir well, then transfer to a baking pan. 2. Select the "Bake" mode on your air fryer. 3. Use the timer (+ / − Time) arrow keys to adjust the cooking time to 15 minutes. 4. Adjust its cooking temperature to 320 degrees F, using the temp (+/- Temp) arrow keys. 5. Press the Start button to initiate preheating. 6. Transfer the baking pan to the rack of the air fryer when the screen displays "Add Food." 7. Close its door and let the machine do the cooking. 8. Serve warm.
Per serving: Calories 102; Fat 2.2g; Sodium 135mg; Carbs 8.7g; Fiber 5.8g; Sugars 1.4g; Protein 12.7g

Nutritious Carrot Oatmeal

Prep time: 10 minutes | Cook time: 15 minutes | Serves: 2

½ cup steel cut oats   1 cup carrots; shredded
2 cups almond milk   2 teaspoons sugar

1 teaspoon cardamom; ground   Cooking spray

1. Toss oats with milk, carrots, sugar, and cardamom in a greased pan. 2. Select the "Bake" mode on your air fryer. 3. Use the timer (+ / − Time) arrow keys to adjust the cooking time to 15 minutes. 4. Adjust its cooking temperature to 365 degrees F, using the temp (+/- Temp) arrow keys. 5. Press the Start button to initiate preheating. 6. Transfer the pan to the rack of the air fryer when the screen displays "Add Food." 7. Close its door and let the machine do the cooking. 8. Divide into bowls and serve
Per serving: Calories 128; Fat 2.7g; Sodium 75mg; Carbs 23.1g; Fiber 2.5g; Sugars 7.6g; Protein 3.3g

Eggs in Bread Cups with Tomato Slices

Prep time: 10 minutes | Cook time: 12 minutes | Serves: 4

½ teaspoon butter   ⅛ teaspoons maple syrup
2 bread slices   ⅛ teaspoons balsamic vinegar
1 pancetta slice, chopped   ¼ teaspoon fresh parsley
4 tomato slices   chopped
1 tablespoon mozzarella   Black pepper, to taste
cheese, shredded   Salt, to taste
2 eggs

1. Grease 2 ramekins. Line each prepared ramekin with 1 bread slice. 2. Divide bacon and tomato slices over bread slices evenly in each ramekin. 3. Top with the cheese evenly. Crack 1 egg in each ramekin over cheese. 4. Drizzle with maple syrup and balsamic vinegar, then sprinkle with parsley, salt, and black pepper. 5. Arrange the ramekins on top of a cooling rack. 6. Select the "Air Fry" mode on your air fryer. 7. Use the timer (+ / − Time) arrow keys to adjust the cooking time to 12 minutes. 8. Adjust its cooking temperature to 320 degrees F using the temp (+/- Temp) arrow keys. 9. Press the Start button to initiate preheating. 10. Transfer the cooking rack to the air fryer when the screen displays "Add Food." 11. Close its door and let the machine do the cooking. 12. Serve warm.
Per serving: Calories 112; Fat 6.1g; Sodium 218mg; Carbs 7.2g; Fiber 0.3g; Sugars 4.2g; Protein 7g

Veggie Frittata

Prep time: 10 minutes | Cook time: 15 minutes | Serves: 4

4 eggs   4 tablespoons fresh spinach,
3 tablespoons heavy cream   chopped
Salt, to taste   3 grape tomatoes, halved
4 tablespoons cheddar cheese   2 tablespoons fresh mixed
grated   herbs, chopped
4 fresh mushrooms, sliced   1 scallion, sliced

1. Add the eggs, cream, and salt to a bowl and beat well. 2. Add the remaining ingredients and stir to combine. 3. Place the egg mushroom mixture into a greased baking dish that will fit the air fryer. 4. Arrange the drip pan at the bottom of the air fryer cooking chamber. 5. Select the "Bake" mode on your air fryer. 6. Use the timer (+ / − Time) arrow keys to adjust the cooking time to 15 minutes. 7. Adjust its cooking temperature to 350 degrees F, using the temp (+/- Temp) arrow keys. 8. Press the Start button to initiate preheating. 9. Transfer the dish to the rack of the air fryer when the screen displays "Add Food." 10. Close its door and let the machine do the cooking. 11. Serve warm.
Per serving: Calories 245; Fat 17.6g; Sodium 315mg; Carbs 7.2g; Fiber 2.4g; Sugars 3.3g; Protein 15g

Delicious Turkey & Spinach Cups

Prep time: 10 minutes | Cook time: 23 minutes | Serves: 4

1 tablespoon unsalted butter	chopped
1-pound fresh baby spinach	4 teaspoons milk
4 eggs	Black pepper, to taste
7 ounces cooked turkey,	Salt, to taste

1. In a suitable skillet, melt the butter over medium heat and cook the spinach for about 2-3 minutes or until just wilted. 2. Remove this skillet from the heat and transfer the spinach into a bowl. 3. Set aside to cool slightly. Divide the spinach into 4 greased ramekins, followed by the turkey. 4. Crack 1 egg into each ramekin and drizzle with milk. 5. Sprinkle with salt and black pepper. Arrange the ramekins on top of a cooling rack. 6. Select the "Air Fry" mode on your air fryer. 7. Use the timer (+ / − Time) arrow keys to adjust the cooking time to 20 minutes. 8. Adjust its cooking temperature to 355 degrees F using the temp (+/- Temp) arrow keys. 9. Press the Start button to initiate preheating. 10. Transfer the ramekins to the rack of the air fryer when the screen displays "Add Food." 11. Close its door and let the machine do the cooking. 12. Serve warm.
Per serving: Calories 206; Fat 10.5g; Sodium 214mg; Carbs 5.2g; Fiber 2.5g; Sugars 1.5g; Protein 23.8g

Bacon Sausage Toasts

Prep time: 5 minutes | Cook time: 20 minutes | Serves: 4

8 sausages	1 (16-ounce) can of baked
8 bacon slices	beans
4 eggs	8 slices of toast

1. Select the "Bake" mode on your air fryer. 2. Use the timer (+ / − Time) arrow keys to adjust the cooking time to 10 minutes. 3. Adjust its cooking temperature to 320 degrees F, using the temp (+/- Temp) arrow keys. 4. Press the Start button to initiate preheating. 5. Transfer the bacon and sausage to the rack of the air fryer when the screen displays "Add Food." 6. Close its door and let the machine do the cooking. 7. Add the baked beans to a ramekin, then whisk the eggs in another ramekin. 8. Select the "Bake" mode on your air fryer. 9. Use the timer (+ / − Time) arrow keys to adjust the cooking time to 10 minutes. 10. Adjust its cooking temperature to 290 degrees F using the temp (+/- Temp) arrow keys. 11. Press the Start button to initiate preheating. 12. Transfer the pan to the rack of the air fryer when the screen displays "Add Food." 13. Close its door and let the machine do the cooking. 14. Top the bread slices with baked beans, eggs, sausages, and bacon. 15. Serve.
Per serving: Calories 340; Fat 17.8g; Sodium 952mg; Carbs 25.4g; Fiber 5.4g; Sugars 1.6g; Protein 19.6g

Fried Chicken Rice with Cauliflower and Carrots

Prep time: 15 minutes | Cook time: 20 minutes | Serves: 4

3 cups cooked brown rice cold	soy sauce
1 cup cooked chicken diced	1 tablespoon avocado oil
1 cup cauliflower and carrots	½ cup onion diced
6 tablespoons low; sodium	

1. Put the cooked brown rice in the bowl, add the avocado oil and soy sauce and mix well. 2. Put the peas and carrots, the diced onion, and the diced chicken, and mix well. 3. Put the rice mixture into the non-stick pan. 4. Select the "Air Fry" mode on your air fryer. 5. Use the timer (+ / − Time) arrow keys to adjust the cooking time to 20 minutes. 6. Adjust its

cooking temperature to 360 degrees F using the temp (+/- Temp) arrow keys. 7. Press the Start button to initiate preheating. 8. Transfer the baking pan to the rack of the air fryer when the screen displays "Add Food." 9. Close its door, and let the machine do the cooking. 10. Serve and enjoy!
Per serving: Calories 147; Fat 1.3g; Sodium 437mg; Carbs 9.1g; Sugar 1.1g; Fiber 0.7g; Protein 10.1g

Crusted Pork Chops with Parmesan Cheese

Prep time: 15 minutes | Cook time: 12 minutes | Serves: 2

1 ½ pounds boneless pork chops
⅓ cup almond flour
¼ cup grated parmesan cheese
1 teaspoon garlic powder
1 teaspoon paprika

1. Mix all the ingredients, excluding pork chops, in a large airtight bag. 2. Place the pork chops in the bag, close them, and shake to cover the pork chops. 3. Discard from the bag and put 1 layer on a cooking tray. 4. Select the "Air Fry" mode on your air fryer. 5. Use the timer (+ / − Time) arrow keys to adjust the cooking time to 12 minutes. 6. Adjust its cooking temperature to 350 degrees F using the temp (+/- Temp) arrow keys. 7. Press the Start button to initiate preheating. 8. Transfer the tray to the rack of the air fryer when the screen displays "Add Food." 9. Close its door, and let the machine do the cooking. 10. Serve.
Per serving: Calories 204; Fat 7.2g; Sodium 442mg; Carbs 1.9g; Fiber 2.3g; Sugars 0.5g; Protein 31.4g

Chicken Pesto Casserole

Prep time: 5 minutes | Cook time: 33 minutes | Serves: 4

Chicken Casserole	5 ounces diced feta cheese
1½ lbs. boneless chicken thighs	1 clove of garlic, finely chopped
Black pepper, to taste	For Serving
Salt, to taste	5 ounces' leafy greens
2 tablespoons butter	4 tablespoons coconut oil
3 ounces' pesto	Black pepper, to taste
1¼ cups coconut cream	Salt, to taste
3 ounces' green olives	

1. Spray a 6-inch soufflé dish with nonstick cooking spray; set aside. 2. Put the butter in a large saucepan. 3. Heat the pan until the butter is melted, then sauté the chicken pieces until golden. 4. Combine pesto and cream in a container to make the sauce. 5. Put the chicken, olives, feta, garlic, and pesto sauce in a casserole dish. 6. Select the "Bake" mode on your air fryer. 7. Use the timer (+ / − Time) arrow keys to adjust the cooking time to 30 minutes. 8. Adjust its cooking temperature to 305 degrees F using the temp (+/- Temp) arrow keys. 9. Press the Start button to initiate preheating. 10. Transfer the food to a casserole dish to the air fryer when the screen displays "Add Food." 11. Close its door and let the machine do the cooking. 12. Sauté greens with oil, black pepper, and salt in a pan for 3 minutes. 13. Add the sautéed greens to the chicken. 14. Serve warm.
Per serving: Calories 465; Fat 40.2g; Sodium 644mg; Carbs 7.4g; Fiber 0.5g; Sugars 2.8g; Protein 18.3g

Salmon Toast

Prep time: 10 minutes | Cook time: 5 minutes | Serves: 4

1 garlic clove, minced	Ground black pepper, as required
8 ounces' ricotta cheese	4 bread slices
1 teaspoon lemon zest grated finely	4 ounce smoked salmon

1. In a food processor, add the garlic, ricotta, lemon zest, and black pepper and pulse until smooth. 2. Spread the ricotta garlic mixture over each bread slice evenly. 3. Arrange the bread slices onto the lightly greased cooking tray. 4. Transfer the tray to the air fryer and close its door. 5. Select the "Toast" mode on your air fryer. 6. Adjust its cooking temperature to L2 settings using the temp (+/- Temp) arrow keys. 7. Let the machine do the cooking. 8. Top each toast with smoked salmon and serve warm.
Per serving: Calories 138; Fat 6g; Sodium 699mg; Carbs 8.1g; Fiber 0.3g; Sugars 0.9g; Protein 12.4g

Bacon Sausage Omelet

Prep time: 10 minutes | Cook time: 10 minutes | Serves: 4

4 eggs	1 onion, chopped
Black pepper, to taste	1 teaspoon fresh parsley minced
1 bacon slice, chopped	
2 sausages, chopped	

1. Catch the eggs and black pepper in a bowl and beat well. 2. Add the remaining ingredients and gently stir to combine. 3. Place the mixture into a baking dish that will fit the air fryer. 4. Select the "Bake" mode on your air fryer. 5. Use the timer (+ / − Time) arrow keys to adjust the cooking time to 10 minutes. 6. Adjust its cooking temperature to 320 degrees F using the temp (+/- Temp) arrow keys. 7. Press the Start button to initiate preheating. 8. Transfer the baking dish to the rack of the air fryer when the screen displays "Add Food." 9. Close its door and let the machine do the cooking. 10. Serve warm.
Per serving: Calories 122; Fat 8.2g; Sodium 221mg; Carbs 3g; Fiber 0.6g; Sugars 1.5g; Protein 8.9g

Herbed Skinless Chicken Thighs

Prep time: 10 minutes | Cook time: 25 minutes | Serves: 2

1 ½-pound skinless, boneless chicken thighs	½ teaspoon garlic powder
¼ cup coconut flour	½ teaspoon stevia powder
⅓ cup almond flour	¼ teaspoon ground paprika
2 ½ teaspoons Cajun seasoning	⅛ teaspoon cayenne pepper
	¼ teaspoon salt

1. Mix coconut flour, almond flour, Cajun spice, garlic powder, salt, stevia powder, paprika, and cayenne pepper in a dish. 2. Coat the chicken thighs with the seasoned flour mixture. 3. Select the "Bake" mode on your air fryer. 4. Use the timer (+ / − Time) arrow keys to adjust the cooking time to 25 minutes. 5. Adjust its cooking temperature to 360 degrees F, using the temp (+/- Temp) arrow keys. 6. Press the Start button to initiate preheating. 7. Transfer to chicken thighs to the rack of the air fryer when the screen displays "Add Food." 8. Close its door and let the machine do the cooking. 9. Flip the chicken halfway and resume cooking. 10. Sprinkle the lemon juice over each leg. 11. Serve warm.
Per serving: Calories 337; Fat 20.5g; Sodium 385mg; Carbs 15g; Fiber 8.3g; Sugars 0.3g; Protein 25.2g

Bang-Bang Chicken Breast

Prep time: 10 minutes | Cook time: 30 minutes | Serves: 2

1 cup Greek yogurt	1-pound chicken breast tenderloins, diced
½ cup sweet chili sauce	1 ½ cups panko bread crumbs
2 tablespoons hot sauce	2 green onions, chopped
⅓ cup coconut flour	

1. Whisk Greek yogurt, sweet chili sauce, and hot sauce in a large container. 2. Set aside ¾ cup of the batter with a spoon and put the coconut flour in a plastic bag with a large seal. 3. Add the chicken, close the bag, and mix well to cover. 4. Place the coated chicken pieces with the yogurt mixture in a large container and stir. 5. Place the panko breadcrumbs in another big plastic bag with a zipper. 6. Work in batches, place chicken pieces in panko, mix well and coat well. 7. Select the "Air Fry" mode on your air fryer. 8. Use the timer (+ / − Time) arrow keys to adjust the cooking time to 30 minutes. 9. Adjust its cooking temperature to 400 degrees F, using the temp (+/- Temp) arrow keys. 10. Press the Start button to initiate preheating. 11. Transfer to chicken to the rack of the air fryer when the screen displays "Add Food." 12. Close its door and let the machine do the cooking. 13. Flip the fried chicken when the display says "turn Food," then resume cooking. 14. Transfer the fried chicken to a large container and put the reaming sauce over it. 15. Sprinkle with spring onions and cover and stir. 16. Serve immediately.
Per serving: Calories 269; Fat 2.8g; Sodium 570mg; Carbs 26.8g; Fiber 4.5g; Sugars 14.5g; Protein 29.5g

Breaded Pork Chops

Prep time: 15 minutes | Cook time: 23 minutes | Serves: 4

Cooking spray	(7-½ ounces)
2 large eggs	¼ cup coconut flour
¼ cup coconut milk	2 tablespoons stevia
1 cup panko bread crumbs	2 tablespoons raspberry
1 cup chopped walnuts	1 tablespoon fresh orange juice
4 smoked bone-in pork chops	

1. Mix the eggs and coconut milk in a flat bowl. 2. Mix the panko breadcrumbs with walnuts in another flat bowl and cover the pork chops with the flour. 3. Dip into the egg mixture and then into the crumb mixture and tap on it to help it stick. 4. Select the "Air Fry" mode on your air fryer. 5. Use the timer (+ / − Time) arrow keys to adjust the cooking time to 15 minutes. 6. Adjust its cooking temperature to 400 degrees F using the temp (+/- Temp) arrow keys. 7. Press the Start button to initiate preheating. 8. Transfer the chops to the rack of the air fryer when the screen displays "Add Food." 9. Close its door, and let the machine do the cooking. 10. In the meantime, put the remaining ingredients in a small saucepan. Bring to a boil. Boil and stir until it gets a little thick, 6-8 minutes. 11. Serve with chops.
Per serving: Calories 542; Fat 31.2g; Sodium 348mg; Carbs 24.9g; Sugar 1.4g; Fiber 0.7g; Protein 41.3g

Asparagus Steak Bundles

Prep time: 15 minutes | Cook time: 10 minutes | Serves: 4

2 ½ pounds flank steak, cut into 6 pieces	3 bell peppers, seeded and sliced
Kosher salt and black pepper, to taste	⅓ cup beef broth
2 cloves garlic, crushed	2 tablespoons unsalted butter
1-pound asparagus, trimmed	Olive oil spray

1. Season the fillets with salt and black pepper and place them in a large zippered bag. 2. Add garlic. Close the bag and massage the fillets so that they are entirely covered. 3. Put in the fridge and marinate for at least 1 hour overnight. 4. When done, remove the marinade fillets and place them on a chopping board or sheet. 5. Spread the mass evenly and place the asparagus and peppers in the middle of each steak. 6. Roll the steak around the vegetables and secure them. 7. Select the "Air Fry" mode on your air fryer. 8. Use the timer (+ / − Time) arrow keys to adjust the cooking time to 10 minutes. 9. Adjust its cooking temperature to 390 degrees F, using the temp (+/- Temp) arrow keys. 10. Press the Start button to initiate preheating. 11. Transfer the steak rolls to the rack of the air fryer when the screen displays "Add Food." 12. Close its door, and let the machine do the cooking. 13. Heat in a small to medium-hot pan: balsamic vinegar, broth, and butter over medium heat. 14. Mix and continue cooking until the sauce thickens and halves. 15. Season it with salt and black pepper, and pour the sauce over the meat packets before serving. 16. Serve.

Per serving: Calories 220; Fat 10g; Sodium 348mg; Carbs 3.8g; Sugar 0.4g; Fiber 0.7g; Protein 27.6g

Strawberry Tarts

Prep time: 15 minutes | Cook time: 10 minutes | Serves: 4

2 refrigerated piecrusts	room temperature
½ cup strawberry preserves	3 tablespoons confectioners'
1 teaspoon cornstarch	sugar
Cooking oil spray	Rainbow sprinkles for decorating
½ cup low-fat vanilla yogurt	
1-ounce cream cheese, at	

1. Place the piecrusts on a flat surface. 2. Cut each pie crust into 3 rectangles using a knife or pizza cutter, for 6. Discard any unused dough from the piecrust edges. 3. In a small bowl, stir together the preserves and cornstarch. 4. Mix well, ensuring there are no lumps of cornstarch remaining. 5. Scoop 1 tablespoon of the strawberry mixture onto the top half of each piece of pie crust. 6. Fold the bottom of each piece up to enclose the filling. 7. Press along the edges of each tart to seal using the back of a fork. 8. Select the "Air Fry" mode on your air fryer. 9. Use the timer (+ / − Time) arrow keys to adjust the cooking time to 10 minutes. 10. Adjust its cooking temperature to 375 degrees F using the temp (+/- Temp) arrow keys. 11. Press the Start button to initiate preheating. 12. Transfer the tarts to the rack of the air fryer when the screen displays "Add Food." 13. Close its door, and let the machine do the cooking. 14. In a small bowl, stir together the yogurt, cream cheese, and confectioners' sugar. 15. Spread the breakfast tarts with the frosting and top with sprinkles. 16. Serve.

Per serving: Calories 408; Fat 20.5g; Sodium 613mg; Carbs 56g; Sugar 1g; Fiber 0.7g; Protein 1g

Lemon Chicken Thighs

Prep time: 10 minutes | Cook time: 24 minutes | Serves: 4

¼ cup lemon juice	⅛ teaspoon ground black pepper
2 tablespoons coconut oil	
1 teaspoon Dijon mustard	4 skin-on, bone-in chicken
2 cloves garlic, minced	thighs
¼ teaspoon salt	4 lime wedges

1. Put lemon juice, coconut oil, Dijon mustard, garlic, salt, and pepper in a container and mix well. 2. Reserve the marinade and put the chicken legs in a large plastic bag with a zipper. 3. Put the marinade over the chicken and close the bag. Make sure all chicken bits are covered. 4. Put in the freezer for at most 120 minutes. 5. Take the chicken out of the marinade and dry it with a kitchen towel. 6. Transfer the chicken to a cooking tray. 7. Select the "Roast" mode on your air fryer. 8. Use the timer (+ / − Time) arrow keys to adjust the cooking time to 24 minutes. 9. Adjust its cooking temperature to 390 degrees F, using the temp (+/- Temp) arrow keys. 10. Press the Start button to initiate preheating. 11. Transfer the baking pan to the rack of the air fryer when the screen displays "Add Food." 12. Close its door, and let the machine do the cooking. 13. Press a lime wedge on each slice before serving. 14. Serve.

Per serving: Calories 222; Fat 16.8g; Sodium 388mg; Carbs 1.5g; Sugar 0.1g; Fiber 0.7g; Protein 15.9g

Breakfast Potatoes with Bell Peppers

Prep time: 10 minutes | Cook time: 20 minutes | Serves: 6

1½ teaspoons olive oil, plus more for misting	1 teaspoon minced garlic
4 large potatoes, skins on, cut into cubes	2 large green or red bell peppers, cut into 1-inch chunks
2 teaspoons seasoned salt	½ onion, diced

1. Lightly mist the fryer basket with olive oil. 2. In a medium bowl, toss the potatoes with ½ teaspoon olive oil. 3. Sprinkle with 1 teaspoon of seasoned salt and ½ teaspoon of minced garlic. Stir to coat. 4. Place the seasoned potatoes in a cooking tray. 5. Select the "Air Fry" mode on your air fryer. 6. Use the timer (+ / − Time) arrow keys to adjust the cooking time to 15 minutes. 7. Adjust its cooking temperature to 390 degrees F, using the temp (+/- Temp) arrow keys. 8. Press the Start button to initiate preheating. 9. Transfer the cooking tray to the rack of the air fryer when the screen displays "Add Food." 10. Close its door, and let the machine do the cooking. 11. Meanwhile, toss the bell peppers and onion in a medium bowl with the remaining ½ teaspoon of olive oil. 12. Sprinkle the peppers and onions with the remaining 1 teaspoon of seasoned salt and ½ teaspoon of minced garlic. Stir to coat. 13. Add the seasoned peppers and onions to the potatoes. Cook for 5 minutes. 14. Serve.

Per serving: Calories 199; Fat 1g; Sodium 315mg; Carbs 43g; Sugar 1g; Fiber 0.7g; Protein 5g

Tasty Zucchini Muffin

Prep time: 10 minutes | Cook time: 20 minutes | Serves: 6

6 eggs	¾ cup coconut flour
4 drops stevia	¼ teaspoon ground nutmeg
¼ cup Swerve	1 teaspoon ground cinnamon
⅓ cup coconut oil, melted	½ teaspoon baking soda
1 cup zucchini, grated	

1. Add all ingredients, except for the zucchini, to a bowl and mix well. 2. Add zucchini and stir well. 3. pour batter into the silicone muffin molds and place it into the cooking tray. 4. Select the "Air Fry" mode on your air fryer. 5. Use the timer (+ / − Time) arrow keys to adjust the cooking time to 20 minutes. 6. Adjust its cooking temperature to 325 degrees F using the temp (+/- Temp) arrow keys. 7. Press the Start button to initiate preheating. 8. Transfer the cooking tray to the rack of the air fryer when the screen displays "Add Food." 9. Close its door, and let the machine do the cooking. 10. Serve and enjoy.

Per serving: Calories 136; Fat 12g; Sodium 305mg; Carbs 1g; Sugar 1g; Fiber 0.7g; Protein 4 g

Beef Sirloin Steak with Mushrooms

Prep time: 5 minutes | Cook time: 20 minutes | Serves: 2

1-pound beef sirloin steak, cut into 1-inch cubes	1 tablespoon olive oil
8 ounces' button mushrooms, sliced	1 teaspoon parsley flakes
¼ cup Worcestershire sauce	1 teaspoon paprika
	1 teaspoon crushed chili flakes

1. Mix steak, mushrooms, Worcestershire sauce, coconut oil, parsley, paprika, and chili flakes in a big bowl. 2. Cover and freeze for at least 4 hours or overnight. 3. Remove from fridge 30 minutes before cooking. 4. Dry out the marinade of the meat mixture and throw it away. 5. Place the steak and mushrooms in a baking pan. 6. Select the "Air Fry" mode on your air fryer. 7. Use the timer (+ / − Time) arrow keys to adjust the cooking time to 10 minutes. 8. Adjust its cooking temperature to 400 degrees F using the temp (+/- Temp) arrow keys. 9. Press the Start button to initiate preheating. 10. Transfer the baking pan to the rack of the air fryer when the screen displays "Add Food." 11. Close its door, and let the machine do the cooking. 12. Mix and cook for another 5 minutes. 13. Place the steak and mushrooms on a plate and let them rest for 5 minutes
Per serving: Calories 269; Fat 10.8g; Sodium 438mg; Carbs 5.2g; Sugar 1.2g; Fiber 0.7g; Protein 36.3g

Erythritol Jalapeno Muffins

Prep time: 10 minutes | Cook time: 15 minutes | Serves: 6

5 eggs	¼ cup unsweetened coconut milk
⅓ cup coconut oil, melted	
2 teaspoons baking powder	⅔ cup coconut flour
3 tablespoons erythritol	¾ teaspoon sea salt
3 tablespoons jalapenos, sliced	

1. Mix coconut flour, baking powder, erythritol, and sea salt in a large bowl. 2. Stir in eggs, jalapenos, coconut milk, and coconut oil until well combined. 3. pour batter into the silicone muffin molds and place it into a cooking tray. 4. Select the "Air Fry" mode on your air fryer. 5. Use the timer (+ / − Time) arrow keys to adjust the cooking time to 15 minutes. 6. Adjust its cooking temperature to 325 degrees F using the temp (+/- Temp) arrow keys. 7. Press the Start button to initiate preheating. 8. Transfer the cooking tray to the rack of the air fryer when the screen displays "Add Food." 9. Close its door, and let the machine do the cooking. 10. Serve and enjoy.
Per serving: Calories 125; Fat 12g; Sodium 298mg; Carbs 7g; Sugar 1.2g; Fiber 0.7g; Protein 3 g

Crispy Tofu

Prep time: 5 minutes | Cook time: 16 minutes | Serves: 4

¼ cup chickpea flour	1 (15-ounce) package tofu, firm or extra-firm
¼ cup arrowroot	
1 teaspoon sea salt	Cooking oil spray (sunflower, safflower, or refined coconut)
1 teaspoon granulated garlic	
½ teaspoon black pepper	

1. Mix flour, arrowroot, salt, garlic, and pepper in a medium bowl. Stir well to combine. 2. Cut the tofu into cubes. 3. Place the cubes into the flour mixture. Toss well to coat. Spray the tofu with oil and toss again. 4. Spray the baking pan with oil. 5. Place the tofu in a single layer in the baking pan and spray the tops with oil. Fry for 8 minutes. 6. Remove the baking pan and spray again with oil. 7. Select the "Air Fry" mode on your air fryer. 8. Use the timer (+ / − Time) arrow keys to adjust the cooking time to 8 minutes. 9. Adjust its cooking tempera-

ture to 350 degrees F using the temp (+/- Temp) arrow keys. 10. Press the Start button to initiate preheating. 11. Transfer the baking pan to the rack of the air fryer when the screen displays "Add Food." 12. Close its door, and let the machine do the cooking. 13. Serve immediately.
Per serving: Calories 148; Fat 5g; Sodium 258mg; Carbs 14g; Sugar 0.4g; Fiber 0.7g; Protein 11g

Fried Potatoes with Bell Peppers

Prep time: 5 minutes | Cook time: 24 minutes | Serves: 4

3 large russet potatoes	Black pepper, to taste
1 tablespoon canola oil	1 cup chopped onion
1 tablespoon olive oil	1 cup chopped red bell pepper
1 teaspoon paprika	1 cup chopped green bell pepper
Salt, to taste	

1. Cut the potatoes into ½-inch cubes. 2. Place the potatoes in a large bowl of cold water and allow them to soak for at least 30 minutes. 3. Dry out the potatoes and wipe thoroughly with paper towels. Return them to the empty bowl. 4. Add the canola, olive oils, paprika, salt, and black pepper to flavor. Toss to coat the potatoes thoroughly. 5. Select the "Air Fry" mode on your air fryer. 6. Use the timer (+ / − Time) arrow keys to adjust the cooking time to 20 minutes. 7. Adjust its cooking temperature to 350 degrees F, using the temp (+/- Temp) arrow keys. 8. Press the Start button to initiate preheating. 9. Transfer the baking pan to the rack of the air fryer when the screen displays "Add Food." 10. Close its door, and let the machine do the cooking. 11. Put the onion and red and green bell peppers in the baking pan. 12. Fry for 3 to 4 minutes until the potatoes are cooked thoroughly, and the peppers are soft. 13. Cool before serving. 14. Serve.
Per serving: Calories 279; Fat 8g; Sodium 464mg; Carbs 50g; Sugar 1.1g; Fiber 0.7g; Protein 6g

Cherry Tarts

Prep time: 15 minutes | Cook time: 10 minutes | Serves: 4

For the tarts:	For the frosting:
2 refrigerated piecrusts	½ cup vanilla yogurt
⅓ cup cherry preserves	1-ounce cream cheese
1 teaspoon cornstarch	1 teaspoon stevia
Cooking oil	Rainbow sprinkles

To make the tarts: 1. Place the piecrusts on a flat surface. 2. Use a knife or pizza cutter; cut each piecrust into 3 rectangles, for 6 in total. 3. In a small bowl, combine the preserves and cornstarch. Mix well. 4. Scoop 1 tablespoon of the preserved mixture onto the top half of each piece of pie crust. 5. Fold the bottom of each piece up to close the tart. Press along the edges of each tart to seal using the back of a fork. 6. Sprinkle the breakfast tarts with cooking oil and place them in a baking pan. 7. Select the "Air Fry" mode on your air fryer. 8. Use the timer (+ / − Time) arrow keys to adjust the cooking time to 10 minutes. 9. Adjust its cooking temperature to 390 degrees F, using the temp (+/- Temp) arrow keys. 10. Press the Start button to initiate preheating. 11. Transfer the baking pan to the rack of the air fryer when the screen displays "Add Food." 12. Close its door, and let the machine do the cooking. 13. Allow the breakfast tarts to cool fully before removing them from the air fryer. 14. If needed, repeat steps 5 and 6 for the remaining breakfast tarts.
To make the frosting: 1. Mix the yogurt, cream cheese, and stevia in a small bowl. Mix well. 2. Spread the breakfast tarts with frosting and top with sprinkles, and serve.
Per serving: Calories 119; Fat 4g; Sodium 528mg; Carbs 19g; Sugar 0.1g; Fiber 0.7g; Protein 2g

Broccoli Stuffed Peppers

Prep time: 10 minutes | Cook time: 40 minutes | Serves: 4

4 eggs	1 teaspoon dried thyme
½ cup cheddar cheese, grated	¼ cup feta cheese, crumbled
2 bell peppers, cut in half and remove seeds	½ cup broccoli, cooked
	¼ teaspoon pepper
½ teaspoon garlic powder	½ teaspoon salt

1. Stuff feta and broccoli into the bell peppers halved. 2. Beat egg in a bowl with seasoning and pour egg mixture into the pepper halved over feta and broccoli. 3. Place bell pepper halved into the cooking tray. 4. Select the "Air Fry" mode on your air fryer. 5. Use the timer (+ / − Time) arrow keys to adjust the cooking time to 40 minutes. 6. Adjust its cooking temperature to 325 degrees F using the temp (+/- Temp) arrow keys. 7. Press the Start button to initiate preheating. 8. Transfer the cooking tray to the rack of the air fryer when the screen displays "Add Food." 9. Close its door, and let the machine do the cooking. 10. Top with grated cheddar cheese and cook until cheese melts. 11. Serve and enjoy.
Per serving: Calories 340; Fat 22g; Sodium 344mg; Carbs 12g; Sugar 0.4g; Fiber 0.7g; Protein 22 g

Asparagus Frittata

Prep time: 10 minutes | Cook time: 15 minutes | Serves: 4

6 eggs	1 cup mozzarella cheese, shredded
3 mushrooms, sliced	
10 asparagus, chopped	1 teaspoon pepper
¼ cup half and half	1 teaspoon salt
2 teaspoon butter, melted	

1. Toss mushrooms and asparagus with melted butter and add to the cooking tray. 2. Select the "Air Fry" mode on your air fryer. 3. Use the timer (+ / − Time) arrow keys to adjust the cooking time to 10 minutes. 4. Adjust its cooking temperature to 350 degrees F, using the temp (+/- Temp) arrow keys. 5. Press the Start button to initiate preheating. 6. Transfer the cooking tray to the rack of the air fryer when the screen displays "Add Food." 7. Close its door, and let the machine do the cooking. 8. Meanwhile, whisk together eggs, half and half, pepper, and salt in a bowl. Transfer cook mushrooms and asparagus into the air fryer baking dish. Pour egg mixture over mushrooms and asparagus. 9. Place dish in the air fryer and cook at 350 degrees F for 5 minutes or until eggs are set. 10. Slice and serve.
Per serving: Calories 211; Fat 13g; Sodium 286mg; Carbs 4g; Sugar 1.2g; Fiber 0.7g; Protein 16 g

Fried Chicken Wings

Prep time: 10 minutes | Cook time: 26 minutes | Serves: 4

8 whole chicken wings	½ cup all-purpose flour
1 teaspoon garlic powder	Cooking oil
Chicken seasoning or rub	8 frozen waffles
Pepper	Maple syrup (optional)

1. In a medium bowl, spice the chicken with garlic powder and chicken seasoning, and pepper to flavor. 2. Put the chicken in a sealable plastic bag and add the flour. Shake to coat the chicken thoroughly. 3. Sprinkle the baking pan with cooking oil. 4. Use tongs, and put the chicken from the bag on the cooking tray. 5. Select the "Air Fry" mode on your air fryer. 6. Use the timer (+ / − Time) arrow keys to adjust the cooking time to 20 minutes. 7. Adjust its cooking temperature to 370 degrees F, using the temp (+/- Temp) arrow keys. 8. Press the Start

button to initiate preheating. 9. Transfer the cooking tray to the rack of the air fryer when the screen displays "Add Food." 10. Close its door, and let the machine do the cooking. 11. Put the frozen waffles in the air fryer. 12. Sprinkle the waffles with cooking oil. Cook for 6 minutes. 13. If necessary, remove the cooked waffles from the air fryer, then repeat step 9 for the leftover waffles. 14. Serve the waffles with the chicken.
Per serving: Calories 461; Fat 22g; Sodium 338mg; Carbs 45g; Sugar 0.6g; Fiber 0.7g; Protein 28g

Zucchini Cauliflower Rice

Prep time: 10 minutes | Cook time: 23 minutes | Serves: 2

1 cauliflower head, cut into florets	1 zucchini, trimmed and cut into cubes
½ teaspoon cumin	½ teaspoon paprika
½ teaspoon chili powder	½ teaspoon garlic powder
6 onion spring, chopped	½ teaspoon cayenne pepper
2 jalapenos, chopped	½ teaspoon pepper
4 tablespoons olive oil	½ teaspoon salt

1. Add cauliflower florets into the food processor and process until it looks like rice. 2. Transfer cauliflower rice to a cooking tray and drizzle with half oil. 3. Select the "Air Fry" mode on your air fryer. 4. Use the timer (+ / − Time) arrow keys to adjust the cooking time to 12 minutes. 5. Adjust its cooking temperature to 370 degrees F, using the temp (+/- Temp) arrow keys. 6. Press the Start button to initiate preheating. 7. Transfer the baking pan to the rack of the air fryer when the screen displays "Add Food." 8. Close its door, and let the machine do the cooking. 9. Heat the remaining oil in a small pan over medium heat. 10. Add zucchini and cook for 5-8 minutes. 11. Add onion and jalapenos and cook for 5 minutes. 12. Add spices and stir well. Set aside. 13. Add cauliflower rice into the zucchini mixture and stir well. 14. Serve and enjoy.
Per serving: Calories 254; Fat 28g; Sodium 346mg; Carbs 12.3g; Sugar 1g; Fiber 0.7g; Protein 4.3 g

Bacon Egg Casserole

Prep time: 20 minutes | Cook time: 17 minutes | Serves: 6

6 slices bacon	per
6 eggs	½ cup chopped green bell pepper
Salt, to taste	
Pepper, to taste	½ cup chopped onion
Cooking oil	¾ cup shredded Cheddar cheese
½ cup chopped red bell pep-	

1. In a pan, over medium-high heat, cook the bacon 5 to 7 minutes, flipping to evenly crisp. 2. Dry out on paper towels, crumble, and set aside. In a medium bowl, whisk the eggs. 3. Add salt and black pepper to taste. 4. Spray a barrel pan with cooking oil. Make sure to cover the bottom and sides of the pan. 5. Add the beaten eggs, crumbled bacon, red bell pepper, green bell pepper, and onion to the pan. 6. Select the "Air Fry" mode on your air fryer. 7. Use the timer (+ / − Time) arrow keys to adjust the cooking time to 8 minutes. 8. Adjust its cooking temperature to 390 degrees F using the temp (+/- Temp) arrow keys. 9. Press the Start button to initiate preheating. 10. Transfer the baking pan to the rack of the air fryer when the screen displays "Add Food." 11. Close its door, and let the machine do the cooking. 12. Sprinkle the cheese over the casserole. Cook for an additional 2 minutes. Cool before serving. 13. Serve.
Per serving: Calories 348; Fat 26g; Sodium 589mg; Carbs 4g; Sugar 0.5g; Fiber 0.7g; Protein 25g

Chili Egg Soufflé

Prep time: 5 minutes | Cook time: 8 minutes | Serves: 2

2 eggs
¼ teaspoon chili pepper
2 tablespoons heavy cream
¼ teaspoon pepper
1 tablespoon parsley, chopped
Salt, to taste

1. In a bowl, whisk eggs with remaining gradients. 2. Spray two ramekins with cooking spray. 3. Pour the egg mixture into the prepared ramekins and place them on the cooking tray. 4. Select the "Air Fry" mode on your air fryer. 5. Use the timer (+ / − Time) arrow keys to adjust the cooking time to 8 minutes. 6. Adjust its cooking temperature to 390 degrees F using the temp (+/- Temp) arrow keys. 7. Press the Start button to initiate preheating. 8. Transfer the cooking tray to the rack of the air fryer when the screen displays "Add Food." 9. Close its door, and let the machine do the cooking. 10. Serve and enjoy.
Per serving: Calories 116; Fat 10g; Sodium 338mg; Carbs 1.1g; Sugar 1g; Fiber 0.7g; Protein 6 g

Onion Radish Browns

Prep time: 10 minutes | Cook time: 17 minutes | Serves: 2

1-pound radishes washed and cut off roots
1 tablespoon olive oil
½ teaspoon paprika
½ teaspoon onion powder
½ teaspoon garlic powder
1 medium onion
¼ teaspoon pepper
¾ teaspoon sea salt

1. Slice onion and radishes using a mandolin slicer. 2. Add sliced onion and radishes to a large mixing bowl and toss with olive oil. 3. Transfer onion and radish slices to the baking pan. 4. Select the "Air Fry" mode on your air fryer. 5. Use the timer (+ / − Time) arrow keys to adjust the cooking time to 13 minutes. 6. Adjust its cooking temperature to 400 degrees F using the temp (+/- Temp) arrow keys. 7. Press the Start button to initiate preheating. 8. Transfer the baking pan to the rack of the air fryer when the screen displays "Add Food." 9. Close its door, and let the machine do the cooking. 10. Return onion and radish slices to a mixing bowl and toss with seasonings. 11. Again, cook onion and radish slices in the baking pan for 5 minutes at 400 degrees F. 12. Shake the basket halfway through. 13. Serve and enjoy.
Per serving: Calories 62; Fat 3.7g; Sodium 208mg; Carbs 7.1g; Sugar 1.1g; Fiber 0.7g; Protein 1.2 g

Egg Vegetable Cups

Prep time: 10 minutes | Cook time: 16 minutes | Serves: 4

4 eggs
1 tablespoon cilantro, chopped
4 tablespoons half and half
1 cup cheddar cheese, shredded
1 cup vegetables, diced
Pepper, to taste
Salt, to taste

1. Sprinkle four ramekins with cooking spray and set them aside. 2. Whisk eggs with cilantro, half and half, vegetables, ½ cup of cheese, pepper, and salt in a mixing bowl. 3. Pour the egg mixture into the four ramekins. 4. Place ramekins in the cooking tray. 5. Select the "Air Fry" mode on your air fryer. 6. Use the timer (+ / − Time) arrow keys to adjust the cooking time to 14 minutes. 7. Adjust its cooking temperature to 300 degrees F, using the temp (+/- Temp) arrow keys. 8. Press the Start button to initiate preheating. 9. Transfer the cooking tray to the rack of the air fryer when the screen displays "Add Food." 10. Close its door, and let the machine do

the cooking. 11. Top with remaining ½ cup cheese and cook for 2 minutes more at 400 degrees F. 12. Serve and enjoy.
Per serving: Calories 194; Fat 11.5g; Sodium 341mg; Carbs 6g; Sugar 0.1g; Fiber 0.7g; Protein 13 g

Vanilla Blueberry Oatmeal

Prep time: 10 minutes | Cook time: 25 minutes | Serves: 6

1½ cups quick oats
1¼ teaspoons ground cinna-mon
½ teaspoon baking powder
Pinch salt
1 cup unsweetened vanilla al-mond milk
¼ cup honey
1 teaspoon vanilla extract
1 egg, beaten
2 cups blueberries
Olive oil
1½ teaspoons sugar
6 tablespoons low-fat whipped topping

1. Mix the oats, 1 teaspoon of cinnamon, baking powder, and salt in a large bowl. 2. Whisk the almond milk, honey, vanilla, and egg in a medium bowl. 3. Pour the liquid ingredients into the oats mixture and stir to combine. Fold in the blueberries. 4. Lightly spray around an air fryer–friendly pan with oil. 5. Add half the blueberry mixture to the pan. 6. Sprinkle ⅛ teaspoon of cinnamon and ½ teaspoon of sugar over the top. 7. Cover the pan with aluminum foil. 8. Select the "Air Fry" mode on your air fryer. 9. Use the timer (+ / − Time) arrow keys to adjust the cooking time to 25 minutes. 10. Adjust its cooking temperature to 350 degrees F using the temp (+/- Temp) arrow keys. 11. Press the Start button to initiate preheating. 12. Transfer the baking pan to the rack of the air fryer when the screen displays "Add Food." 13. Close its door, and let the machine do the cooking. 14. Transfer the mixture to a shallow bowl. 15. Repeat with the remaining blueberry mixture, ½ teaspoon sugar, and ⅛ teaspoon cinnamon. 16. To serve, spoon into bowls and top with whipped topping.
Per serving: Calories 170; Fat 3g; Sodium 399mg; Carbs 34g; Sugar 0.6g; Fiber 0.7g; Protein 4g

Spinach-Onion Frittata

Prep time: 5 minutes | Cook time: 8 minutes | Serves: 2

3 eggs
1 cup spinach, chopped
1 small onion, minced
2 tablespoon mozzarella
cheese, grated
Pepper, to taste
Salt, to taste

1. Spray a baking pan with cooking spray. 2. In a bowl, whisk eggs with the remaining ingredients until well combined. 3. Pour the egg mixture into the prepared pan and place the pan on the cooking tray. 4. Select the "Air Fry" mode on your air fryer. 5. Use the timer (+ / − Time) arrow keys to adjust the cooking time to 8 minutes. 6. Adjust its cooking temperature to 350 degrees F using the temp (+/- Temp) arrow keys. 7. Press the Start button to initiate preheating. 8. Transfer the cooking tray to the rack of the air fryer when the screen displays "Add Food." 9. Close its door, and let the machine do the cooking. 10. Serve and enjoy.
Per serving: Calories 384; Fat 23.3g; Sodium 238mg; Carbs 10.7g; Sugar 0.4g; Fiber 0.7g; Protein 34.3 g

Cheese Tartar Soufflés

Prep time: 10 minutes | Cook time: 20 minutes | Serves: 4

6 large eggs, separated
¾ cup heavy cream
¼ teaspoon cayenne pepper
½ teaspoon xanthan gum
½ teaspoon pepper
¼ teaspoon cream of tartar

2 tablespoons chives, chopped	ded
2 cups cheddar cheese, shred-	1 teaspoon salt

1. Spray 8 ramekins with cooking spray. Set aside. 2. Whisk together almond flour, cayenne, pepper, salt, and xanthan gum in a bowl. 3. Slowly add heavy cream and mix to combine. 4. Whisk in egg yolks, chives, and cheese until well combined. 5. In a large bowl, add egg whites and cream of tartar and beat until stiff peaks form. 6. Fold the egg white mixture into the almond flour mixture until combined. 7. Pour mixture into the prepared ramekins. 8. Place the ramekins into the cooking tray. 9. Select the "Air Fry" mode on your air fryer. 10. Use the timer (+ / − Time) arrow keys to adjust the cooking time to 20 minutes. 11. Adjust its cooking temperature to 325 degrees F using the temp (+/- Temp) arrow keys. 12. Press the Start button to initiate preheating. 13. Transfer the cooking tray to the rack of the air fryer when the screen displays "Add Food." 14. Close its door, and let the machine do the cooking. 15. Serve and enjoy.
Per serving: Calories 210; Fat 16g; Sodium 434mg; Carbs 1g; Sugar 0.8g; Fiber 0.7g; Protein 12 g

Cheese Zucchini Noodles

Prep time: 10 minutes | Cook time: 39 minutes | Serves: 2

1 egg	2 medium zucchinis, trimmed
½ cup parmesan cheese, grated	and spiralized
½ cup feta cheese, crumbled	2 tablespoons olive oil
1 tablespoon thyme	1 cup mozzarella cheese, grated
1 garlic clove, chopped	½ teaspoon pepper
1 onion, chopped	½ teaspoon salt

1. Add spiralized zucchini and salt to a colander and set aside for 10 minutes. 2. Wash zucchini noodles and pat dry with a paper towel. 3. Heat the oil in a pan over medium heat. Add garlic and onion and sauté for 3-4 minutes. 4. Add zucchini noodles and cook for 4-5 minutes or until softened. 5. Add the zucchini mixture to the cooking tray. Add egg, thyme, and cheeses. Mix well and season. 6. Select the "Air Fry" mode on your air fryer. 7. Use the timer (+ / − Time) arrow keys to adjust the cooking time to 35 minutes. 8. Adjust its cooking temperature to 350 degrees F using the temp (+/- Temp) arrow keys. 9. Press the Start button to initiate preheating. 10. Transfer the cooking tray to the rack of the air fryer when the screen displays "Add Food." 11. Close its door, and let the machine do the cooking. 12. Serve and enjoy.
Per serving: Calories 435; Fat 29g; Sodium 543mg; Carbs 10.4g; Sugar 1.1g; Fiber 0.7g; Protein 25 g

Mushroom Frittata with Parmesan Cheese

Prep time: 10 minutes | Cook time: 10 minutes | Serves: 2

1 cup egg whites	2 tablespoons parmesan
1 cup spinach, chopped	cheese, grated
2 mushrooms, sliced	Salt, to taste

1. Sprinkle pan with cooking spray and heat over medium heat. 2. Add mushrooms and sauté for 2-3 minutes. Add spinach and cook for 1-2 minutes or until wilted. 3. Transfer the mushroom-spinach mixture to the cooking tray. 4. Beat egg whites in a mixing bowl until frothy. Season it with a pinch of salt. 5. Pour the egg white mixture into the spinach and mushroom mixture and sprinkle with parmesan cheese. 6. Select the "Air Fry" mode on your air fryer. 7. Use the timer (+ / − Time) arrow keys to adjust the cooking time to 8 minutes. 8. Adjust its cooking temperature to 350 degrees F using the temp (+/- Temp) arrow keys. 9. Press the Start button to initi-

ate preheating. 10. Transfer the cooking tray to the rack of the air fryer when the screen displays "Add Food." 11. Close its door, and let the machine do the cooking. 12. Slice and serve.
Per serving: Calories 176; Fat 3g; Sodium 251mg; Carbs 4g; Sugar 0.1g; Fiber 0.7g; Protein 31 g

Cinnamon Granola

Prep time: 5 minutes | Cook time: 35 minutes | Serves: 2

1 cup rolled oats	oil
3 tablespoons pure maple syr-	¼ teaspoon sea salt
up	¼ teaspoon ground cinnamon
1 tablespoon sugar	¼ teaspoon vanilla extract
1 tablespoon neutral-flavored	

1. In a medium bowl, stir together the oats, maple syrup, sugar, oil, salt, cinnamon, and vanilla until thoroughly combined. 2. Transfer the granola to a 6-by-2-inch round baking pan. 3. Select the "Air Fry" mode on your air fryer. 4. Use the timer (+ / − Time) arrow keys to adjust the cooking time to 35 minutes. 5. Adjust its cooking temperature to 390 degrees F, using the temp (+/- Temp) arrow keys. 6. Press the Start button to initiate preheating. 7. Transfer the baking pan to the rack of the air fryer when the screen displays "Add Food." 8. Close its door, and let the machine do the cooking. 9. Place the granola on a plate to cool when the cooking is complete. It will become crisp as it cools. Store the completely cooled granola in an airtight container in a cool, dry place for 1 to 2 weeks.
Per serving: Calories 165; Fat 5g; Sodium 364mg; Carbs 27g; Sugar 0.4g; Fiber 0.7g; Protein 3g

Tater Tot Bake

Prep time: 5 minutes | Cook time: 13 minutes | Serves: 4

4 eggs	12 ounces ground chicken
1 cup milk	sausage
1 teaspoon onion powder	1-pound frozen tater tots
Salt, to taste	¾ cup shredded Cheddar
Pepper, to taste	cheese
Cooking oil	

1. In a medium bowl, whisk the eggs. 2. Add the milk, onion powder, salt, and black pepper to taste. Stir to combine. 3. Spray a skillet with cooking oil and set over medium-high heat. 4. Add the ground sausage. Using a spatula or spoon, break the sausage into smaller pieces. 5. Cook for 3 to 4 minutes until the sausage is brown. Remove from heat and set aside. 6. Spray a barrel pan with cooking oil. Make sure to cover the bottom and sides of the pan. 7. Place the tater tots in the barrel pan. 8. Select the "Air Fry" mode on your air fryer. 9. Use the timer (+ / − Time) arrow keys to adjust the cooking time to 4 minutes. 10. Adjust its cooking temperature to 390 degrees F using the temp (+/- Temp) arrow keys. 11. Press the Start button to initiate preheating. 12. Transfer the baking pan to the rack of the air fryer when the screen displays "Add Food." 13. Close its door, and let the machine do the cooking. 14. Add the egg mixture and cooked sausage to the pan. Cook for an additional 6 minutes. 15. Open the air fryer and sprinkle the cheese over the tater to bake. Cook for an additional 2 to 3 minutes. 16. Cool before serving. 17. Serve.
Per serving: Calories 518; Fat 30g; Sodium 658mg; Carbs 31g; Sugar 0.4g; Fiber 0.7g; Protein 30g

Simple Vegetable Soufflé

Prep time: 10 minutes | Cook time: 20 minutes | Serves: 4

4 large eggs
1 teaspoon onion powder
1 teaspoon garlic powder
1 teaspoon red pepper, crushed

½ cup broccoli florets, chopped
½ cup mushrooms, chopped

1. Sprinkle four ramekins with cooking spray and set them aside. 2. Whisk eggs with onion powder, garlic powder, and red pepper in a bowl. 3. Add mushrooms and broccoli and stir well. 4. Pour egg mixture into the prepared ramekins and place ramekins into the cooking tray. 5. Select the "Air Fry" mode on your air fryer. 6. Use the timer (+ / − Time) arrow keys to adjust the cooking time to 20 minutes. 7. Adjust its cooking temperature to 350 degrees F, using the temp (+/- Temp) arrow keys. 8. Press the Start button to initiate preheating. 9. Transfer the cooking tray to the rack of the air fryer when the screen displays "Add Food." 10. Close its door, and let the machine do the cooking. 11. Serve and enjoy.
Per serving: Calories 91; Fat 5.1g; Sodium 231mg; Carbs 4.7g; Sugar 1.1g; Fiber 0.7g; Protein 7.4 g

Sweet Berry Muffins

Prep time: 15 minutes | Cook time: 17 minutes | Serves: 8

1⅓ cups 1 tablespoon all-purpose flour
¼ cup granulated sugar
2 tablespoons light brown sugar

2 teaspoons baking powder
2 eggs
⅔ cup whole milk
⅓ cup safflower oil
1 cup mixed fresh berries

1. In a medium bowl, stir together 1⅓ cups of flour, the granulated sugar, brown sugar, and baking powder until mixed well. 2. In a small bowl, whisk the eggs, milk, and oil until combined. 3. Mix the egg mixture into the dry ingredients just until combined. 4. In another small bowl, toss the mixed berries with the leftover 1 tablespoon of flour until coated. Gently stir the berries into the batter. 5. Two times the 16 foil muffin cups to make 8 cups. 6. Select the "Air Fry" mode on your air fryer. 7. Use the timer (+ / − Time) arrow keys to adjust the cooking time to 17 minutes. 8. Adjust its cooking temperature to 315 degrees F using the temp (+/- Temp) arrow keys. 9. Press the Start button to initiate preheating. 10. Transfer the baking cups to the rack of the air fryer when the screen displays "Add Food." 11. Close its door, and let the machine do the cooking. 12. Let the muffins cool for 10 minutes before serving. 13. Serve.
Per serving: Calories 230; Fat 11g; Sodium 467mg; Carbs 30g; Sugar 1.2g; Fiber 0.7g; Protein 4g

Greek Bagels

Prep time: 10 minutes | Cook time: 10 minutes | Serves: 2

½ cup self-rising flour
½ cup plain Greek yogurt
1 egg
1 tablespoon water

4 teaspoons of everything bagel spice mix
Cooking oil spray
1 tablespoon butter, melted

1. In a large bowl, using a wooden spoon, stir together the flour and yogurt until a tacky dough forms. 2. Transfer the dough to a lightly floured work surface and roll the dough into a ball. 3. Cut the dough into 2 pieces and roll each piece into a log. 4. Form each log into a bagel shape, pinching the ends together. 5. Beat the egg and water in a small bowl. Brush the egg wash on the bagels. 6. Sprinkle 2 teaspoons of the spice mix on each bagel and gently press it into the dough. 7. Select the "Air Fry" mode on your air fryer. 8. Use the timer (+ / − Time) arrow keys to adjust the cooking time to 10 minutes. 9. Adjust its cooking temperature to 330 degrees F, using the temp (+/- Temp) arrow keys. 10. Press the Start button to initiate preheating. 11. Transfer the bagels to the rack of the air fryer when the screen displays "Add Food." 12. Close its door, and let the machine do the cooking.
Per serving: Calories 271; Fat 13g; Sodium 237mg; Carbs 28g; Sugar 1.1g; Fiber 0.7g; Protein 10g

Maple Doughnuts

Prep time: 10 minutes | Cook time: 14 minutes | Serves: 4

1 (8-count) can of jumbo flaky refrigerator biscuits
Cooking oil spray
½ cup light brown sugar

¼ cup butter
3 tablespoons milk
2 cups confectioners' sugar
2 teaspoons pure maple syrup

1. Remove the biscuits from the tube and cut out the center of each biscuit with a small, round cookie cutter. 2. Select the "Air Fry" mode on your air fryer. 3. Use the timer (+ / − Time) arrow keys to adjust the cooking time to 5 minutes. 4. Adjust its cooking temperature to 350 degrees F, using the temp (+/- Temp) arrow keys. 5. Press the Start button to initiate preheating. 6. Transfer the biscuits to the rack of the air fryer when the screen displays "Add Food." 7. Close its door, and let the machine do the cooking. 8. Mix brown sugar, butter, and milk in a small saucepan over medium heat. Heat them until the butter is melted, and the sugar is dissolved for about 4 minutes. 9. Remove the pan from the heat and whisk in the confectioners' sugar and maple syrup until smooth. 10. Dip the slightly cooled doughnuts into the maple glaze. 11. Place them on a wire rack and dust with confectioners' sugar. 12. Let rest just until the glaze sets. 13. Enjoy the doughnuts warm.
Per serving: Calories 219; Fat 10g; Sodium 344mg; Carbs 30g; Sugar 0.5g; Fiber 0.7g; Protein 2g

Tasty Jam-Filled Doughnut

Prep time: 10 minutes | Cook time: 12 minutes | Serves: 12

1 (8-count) can of refrigerated biscuits
Cooking oil spray
1 cup raspberry jam

3 tablespoons melted unsalted butter
¼ cup confectioners' sugar

1. Separate the biscuits and cut each biscuit into thirds for 24 pieces. 2. Flatten each biscuit piece slightly and put 1 teaspoon jam in the center. 3. Wrap the dough around the chocolate and seal the edges well. 4. Select the "Air Fry" mode on your air fryer. 5. Use the timer (+ / − Time) arrow keys to adjust the cooking time to 12 minutes. 6. Adjust its cooking temperature to 330 degrees F using the temp (+/- Temp) arrow keys. 7. Press the Start button to initiate preheating. 8. Transfer the biscuits to the rack of the air fryer when the screen displays "Add Food." 9. Close its door, and let the machine do the cooking. 10. Serve warm.
Per serving: Calories 393; Fat 17g; Sodium 438mg; Carbs 55g; Sugar 1g; Fiber 0.7g; Protein 5g

Hash Browns

Prep time: 15 minutes | Cook time: 20 minutes | Serves: 4

4 russet potatoes, peeled
1 teaspoon paprika
Salt, to taste

Black pepper, to taste
Cooking oil spray

1. Using a box grater or food processor, shred the potatoes. If your grater has different hole sizes, use the most significant holes. 2. Place the shredded potatoes in a large bowl of cold water. Let it sit for 5 minutes. 3. Dry out the potatoes and pat them with paper towels until the potatoes are dry. 4. Season the potatoes with paprika, salt, and pepper. 5. Spray the crisper plate with cooking oil. 6. Spray the potatoes with the cooking oil and place them on a cooking tray. 7. Select the "Air Fry" mode on your air fryer. 8. Use the timer (+ / − Time) arrow keys to adjust the cooking time to 20 minutes. 9. Adjust its cooking temperature to 360 degrees F, using the temp (+/- Temp) arrow keys. 10. Press the Start button to initiate preheating. 11. Transfer the cooking tray to the rack of the air fryer when the screen displays "Add Food." 12. Close its door, and let the machine do the cooking. 13. When the cooking is complete, remove the hash browns from the basket and serve warm. 14. Serve.
Per serving: Calories 150; Fat 0g; Sodium 266mg; Carbs 34g; Sugar 1.2g; Fiber 0.7g; Protein 4g

Egg Avocado Tacos

Prep time: 5 minutes | Cook time: 15 minutes | Serves: 2

1 peeled avocado, sliced	Salt, to taste
1 beaten egg	2 tortillas and toppings
½ cup panko bread crumbs	

1. Using a bowl, add the egg. 2. Using a separate bowl, set in the breadcrumbs. 3. Dip the avocado into the bowl with the beaten egg and coat it with the breadcrumbs. 4. Sprinkle the coated wedges with a bit of salt. 5. Arrange them in the cooking tray in a single layer. 6. Select the "Air Fry" mode on your air fryer. 7. Use the timer (+ / − Time) arrow keys to adjust the cooking time to 15 minutes. 8. Adjust its cooking temperature to 390 degrees F using the temp (+/- Temp) arrow keys. 9. Press the Start button to initiate preheating. 10. Transfer the cooking tray to the rack of the air fryer when the screen displays "Add Food." 11. Close its door, and let the machine do the cooking. 12. Put them on tortillas with your preferred toppings. 13. Serve.
Per serving: Calorie 140; Fat 8.8g; Sodium 218mg; Carbs 12g; Sugar 1.2g; Fiber 0.7g; Protein 6g

Italian Egg Cups with Basil

Prep time: 5 minutes | Cook time: 12 minutes | Serves: 4

Olive Oil	cheese
1 cup marinara sauce	Salt, to taste
4 eggs	Black pepper, to taste
4 tablespoons shredded mozzarella cheese	Chopped fresh basil for garnish
4 teaspoons grated Parmesan	

1. Lightly spray four individual ramekins with olive oil. 2. Pour ¼ cup of marinara sauce into each ramekin. 3. Crack one egg into each ramekin on top of the marinara sauce. 4. Sprinkle 1 tablespoon mozzarella and 1 tablespoon of Parmesan cheese on top of each egg. 5. Season it with salt and black pepper. 6. Cover each ramekin with aluminum foil. 7. Select the "Air Fry" mode on your air fryer. 8. Use the timer (+ / − Time) arrow keys to adjust the cooking time to 12 minutes. 9. Adjust its cooking temperature to 350 degrees F, using the temp (+/- Temp) arrow keys. 10. Press the Start button to initiate preheating. 11. Transfer the ramekins to the rack of the air fryer when the screen displays "Add Food." 12. Close its door, and let the machine do the cooking. 13. Garnish with basil and serve.
Per serving: Calories 135; Fat 8g; Sodium 387mg; Carbs 6g; Sugar 0.5g; Fiber 0.7g; Protein 10g

Puffed Tarts

Prep time: 10 minutes | Cook time: 20 minutes | Serves: 4

⅓ sheet frozen puff pastry, thawed	2 eggs
	¼ teaspoon salt
Cooking oil spray	1 teaspoon minced fresh parsley
½ cup shredded Cheddar cheese	

1. Lay the puff pastry sheet on a piece of parchment paper and cut it in half. 2. Transfer the two squares of pastry to a cooking tray, keeping the parchment paper on. 3. Select the "Air Fry" mode on your air fryer. 4. Use the timer (+ / − Time) arrow keys to adjust the cooking time to 20 minutes. 5. Adjust its cooking temperature to 390 degrees F, using the temp (+/- Temp) arrow keys. 6. Press the Start button to initiate preheating. 7. Transfer the cooking tray to the rack of the air fryer when the screen displays "Add Food." 8. Close its door, and let the machine do the cooking. 9. After 10 minutes, use a metal spoon to press down the center of each pastry square to make a well. 10. Divide the cheese equally between the baked pastries. 11. Carefully crack an egg on top of the cheese, and sprinkle each with the salt. 12. Resume cooking for 7 to 10 minutes until the eggs are cooked through. 13. Sprinkle each with parsley and serve.
Per serving: Calories 322; Fat 24g; Sodium 668mg; Carbs 12g; Sugar 0.4g; Fiber 0.7g; Protein 15g

Strip Steak with Eggs

Prep time: 10 minutes | Cook time: 10 minutes | Serves: 4

Cooking oil spray	1 teaspoon salt
4 (4-ounce) New York strip steaks	1 teaspoon black pepper
	4 eggs
1 teaspoon granulated garlic	½ teaspoon paprika

1. Select the "Air Fry" mode on your air fryer. 2. Use the timer (+ / − Time) arrow keys to adjust the cooking time to 10 minutes. 3. Adjust its cooking temperature to 360 degrees F, using the temp (+/- Temp) arrow keys. 4. Press the Start button to initiate preheating. 5. Once the unit is preheated, spray the crisper plate with cooking oil. 6. Place two steaks into a baking pan. 7. Transfer the baking pan to the rack of the air fryer when the screen displays "Add Food." 8. Close its door, and let the machine do the cooking. 9. Sprinkle each with ¼ teaspoon of granulated garlic, ¼ teaspoon salt, and ¼ teaspoon of pepper. 10. Resume cooking until the steaks register at least 145 degrees F on a food thermometer. 11. When the cooking is complete, transfer the steaks to a plate and tent with aluminum foil to keep warm. 12. Repeat steps 2, 3, and 4 with the remaining steaks. 13. Spray 4 ramekins with olive oil. Crack one egg into each ramekin. 14. Sprinkle the eggs with the paprika and the remaining ½ teaspoon of salt and black pepper. 15. Work in batches, and place two ramekins into the basket. 16. Serve the eggs with the steaks.
Per serving: Calories 304; Fat 19g; Sodium 423mg; Carbs 2g; Sugar 0.6g; Fiber 0.7g; Protein 31g

Spinach Muffins

Prep time: 10 minutes | Cook time: 21 minutes | Serves: 12

9 eggs
½ cup onion, sliced
1 tablespoon olive oil
8 ounces ground sausage
¼ cup coconut milk

½ teaspoon oregano
1 ½ cups spinach
¾ cup bell peppers, chopped
Pepper, to taste
Salt, to taste

1. Add ground sausage to a pan and sauté over medium heat for 5 minutes 2. Add olive oil, oregano, bell pepper, and onion, and sauté until onion is translucent. 3. Put spinach in the pan and cook for 30 seconds. 4. Remove pan from heat and set aside. 5. Whisk together eggs, coconut milk, pepper, and salt in a mixing bowl until well beaten. 6. Add sausage and vegetable mixture into the egg mixture and mix well. 7. Pour the egg mixture into the silicone muffin molds and place it into the cooking tray. 8. Select the "Air Fry" mode on your air fryer. 9. Use the timer (+ / − Time) arrow keys to adjust the cooking time to 15 minutes. 10. Adjust its cooking temperature to 325 degrees F using the temp (+/- Temp) arrow keys. 11. Press the Start button to initiate preheating. 12. Transfer the cooking tray to the rack of the air fryer when the screen displays "Add Food." 13. Close its door, and let the machine do the cooking. 14. Serve and enjoy.
Per serving: Calories 135; Fat 11g; Sodium 358mg; Carbs 1.5g; Sugar 1g; Fiber 0.7g; Protein 8 g

Vanilla Blueberry Cobbler

Prep time: 5 minutes | Cook time: 15 minutes | Serves: 4

⅓ cup whole-wheat pastry flour
¾ teaspoon baking powder
Dash sea salt
½ cup 2% milk
2 tablespoons pure maple syr-

up
½ teaspoon vanilla extract
Cooking oil spray
½ cup fresh blueberries
¼ cup Granola or plain store-bought granola

1. Whisk the flour, baking powder, and salt in a medium bowl. Add the milk, maple syrup, and vanilla and gently whisk until thoroughly combined. 2. Spray a 6-by-2-inch round cooking tray with cooking oil and pour the batter into the pan. 3. Top evenly with the blueberries and granola. 4. Select the "Air Fry" mode on your air fryer. 5. Use the timer (+ / − Time) arrow keys to adjust the cooking time to 15 minutes. 6. Adjust its cooking temperature to 350 degrees F using the temp (+/-Temp) arrow keys. 7. Press the Start button to initiate preheating. 8. Transfer the cooking tray to the rack of the air fryer when the screen displays "Add Food." 9. Close its door, and let the machine do the cooking. 10. Serve.
Per serving: Calories 112; Fat 1g; Sodium 523mg; Carbs 23g; Sugar 0.6g; Fiber 0.7g; Protein 3g

Bacon Potato Boats

Prep time: 10 minutes | Cook time: 15 minutes | Serves: 2

2 large russet potatoes, scrubbed
Olive oil
Salt, to taste
Black pepper, to taste

4 eggs
2 tablespoons chopped, cooked bacon
1 cup shredded cheddar cheese

1. Poke holes in the potatoes with a fork and microwave on full power for 5 minutes. 2. Turn potatoes over and cook for 3 to 5 minutes, or until the potatoes are fork-tender. 3. Cut the potatoes in half lengthwise and use a spoon to scoop out the inside of the potato. 4. Be careful to leave a layer of potato so

that it makes a sturdy "boat." 5. Lightly spray a cooking tray with olive oil. 6. Spray the skin side of the potatoes with oil and sprinkle with salt and black pepper to taste. 7. Place the potato skins in the cooking tray skin side down. Crack one egg into each potato skin. 8. Sprinkle ½ tablespoon of bacon pieces and ¼ cup of shredded cheese on top of each egg. 9. Sprinkle with salt and black pepper to taste. 10. Select the "Air Fry" mode on your air fryer. 11. Use the timer (+ / − Time) arrow keys to adjust the cooking time to 10 minutes. 12. Adjust its cooking temperature to 350 degrees F using the temp (+/- Temp) arrow keys. 13. Press the Start button to initiate preheating. 14. Transfer the baking pan to the rack of the air fryer when the screen displays "Add Food." 15. Close its door, and let the machine do the cooking. 16. Serve.
Per serving: Calories 338; Fat15g; Sodium 383mg; Carbs 35g; Sugar 1.2g; Fiber 0.7g; Protein 17g;

Greek Spinach & Tomato Frittata

Prep time: 10 minutes | Cook time: 22 minutes | Serves: 4

Olive oil
5 eggs
¼ teaspoon salt
⅛ teaspoon black pepper

1 cup baby spinach leaves, shredded
½ cup halved grape tomatoes
½ cup crumbled feta cheese

1. Spray a small round baking pan with olive oil. 2. Whisk together eggs, salt, and pepper in a medium bowl, and whisk to combine. 3. Add the spinach and stir to combine. 4. Pour ½ cup of the egg mixture into the pan. 5. Sprinkle ¼ cup of the tomatoes and ¼ cup feta on top of the egg mixture. 6. Cover the pan with aluminum foil and secure it around the edges. 7. Select the "Air Fry" mode on your air fryer. 8. Use the timer (+ / − Time) arrow keys to adjust the cooking time to 12 minutes. 9. Adjust its cooking temperature to 350 degrees F, using the temp (+/- Temp) arrow keys. 10. Press the Start button to initiate preheating. 11. Transfer the baking pan to the rack of the air fryer when the screen displays "Add Food." 12. Close its door, and let the machine do the cooking. 13. Remove the foil from the pan and cook until the eggs are set, 5 to 7 minutes. 14. Transfer the frittata to a serving platter. Repeat with the remaining ingredients. 15. Serve.
Per serving: Calories 146; Fat 10g; Sodium 369mg; Carbs 3g; Sugar 1.1g; Fiber 0.7g; Protein 11g

Ricotta Shrimp Frittata

Prep time: 15 minutes | Cook time: 20 minutes | Serves: 4

1 teaspoon olive oil, plus more for spraying
½ small red bell pepper, diced
1 teaspoon minced garlic
1 (4-ounce) can of tiny

shrimp, Dry out
Salt, to taste
Black pepper, to taste
4 eggs, beaten
4 teaspoons ricotta cheese

1. Spray four ramekins with olive oil. Preheat 1 teaspoon of olive oil in the skillet over medium-low heat. Add the bell pepper, garlic, and sauté for 5 minutes or until the pepper is soft. 2. Add the shrimp, season with salt and black pepper, and cook until warm, 1 to 2 minutes. Remove from the heat. 3. Add the eggs and stir to combine. Pour one-quarter of the mixture into each ramekin. 4. Select the "Air Fry" mode on your air fryer. 5. Use the timer (+ / − Time) arrow keys to adjust the cooking time to 15 minutes. 6. Adjust its cooking temperature to 350 degrees F using the temp (+/- Temp) arrow keys. 7. Press the Start button to initiate preheating. 8. Transfer the ramekins to the rack of the air fryer when the screen displays "Add Food." 9. Close its door, and let the ma-

chine do the cooking. 10. Top each frittata with 1 teaspoon of ricotta cheese. 11. Return the pan to the air fryer and cook until eggs are set and the top is lightly browned 4 to 5 minutes. 12. Serve.

Per serving: Calories 114; Fat 7g; Sodium 373mg; Carbs 1g; Sugar 0.8g; Fiber 0.7g; Protein 12g

Spinach Mushroom Quiche with Cheeses

Prep time: 10 minutes | Cook time: 15 minutes | Serves: 4

1 teaspoon olive oil, plus more for spraying	½ cup shredded Cheddar cheese
1 cup coarsely chopped mushrooms	½ cup shredded mozzarella cheese
1 cup fresh baby spinach, shredded	¼ teaspoon salt
4 eggs, beaten	¼ teaspoon black pepper

1. Spray four silicone baking cups with olive oil and set them aside. 2. In a medium sauté pan over medium heat, warm 1 teaspoon of olive oil. 3. Add the mushrooms and sauté until soft, 3 to 4 minutes. 4. Add the spinach, and sauté them for 1 to 2 minutes until wilted. Set aside. 5. Whisk together the eggs, Cheddar cheese, mozzarella cheese, salt, and pepper in a medium bowl. Gently fold the mushrooms and spinach into the egg mixture. 6. Pour ¼ of the mixture into each silicone baking cup. 7. Select the "Air Fry" mode on your air fryer. 8. Use the timer (+ / − Time) arrow keys to adjust the cooking time to 10 minutes. 9. Adjust its cooking temperature to 350 degrees F, using the temp (+/- Temp) arrow keys. 10. Press the Start button to initiate preheating. 11. Transfer the baking cups to the rack of the air fryer when the screen displays "Add Food." 12. Close its door, and let the machine do the cooking. 13. Serve.

Per serving: Calories 183; Fat 13g; Sodium 427mg; Carbs 3g; Sugar 0.4g; Fiber 0.7g; Protein 14g

Cheese Bacon with English Muffins

Prep time: 5 minutes | Cook time: 8 minutes | Serves: 4

4 English muffins	4 slices cheese
8 slices of Canadian bacon	Cooking oil

1. Split each English muffin. Assemble the breakfast sandwiches by layering two slices of Canadian bacon and one slice of cheese onto each English muffin bottom. 2. Put it on top of the other half of the English muffin. 3. Select the "Air Fry" mode on your air fryer. 4. Use the timer (+ / − Time) arrow keys to adjust the cooking time to 8 minutes. 5. Adjust its cooking temperature to 390 degrees F, using the temp (+/- Temp) arrow keys. 6. Press the Start button to initiate preheating. 7. Transfer the baking pan to the rack of the air fryer when the screen displays "Add Food." 8. Close its door, and let the machine do the cooking. 9. Spray the top of each with cooking oil. Cook for 4 minutes. 10. Open the air fryer and flip the sandwiches halfway. Cook for an additional 4 minutes. 11. Cool before serving.

Per serving: Calories 333; Fat 14g; Sodium 1219mg; Carbs 27g; Fiber 2g; Sugars 1.3g; Protein 24g

Homemade Mexican Pepper Rings

Prep time: 5 minutes | Cook time: 10 minutes | Serves: 4

Olive oil	¾-inch rings
1 large red, yellow, or orange bell pepper, cut into four	4 eggs
	Salt, to taste

Black pepper, to taste   2 teaspoons salsa

1. Lightly spray a small round baking pan with olive oil. 2. Place two bell pepper rings on the pan. 3. Crack one egg into each bell pepper ring. Season it with salt and black pepper. 4. Spoon ½ teaspoon of salsa on top of each egg. 5. Select the "Air Fry" mode on your air fryer. 6. Use the timer (+ / − Time) arrow keys to adjust the cooking time to 10 minutes. 7. Adjust its cooking temperature to 350 degrees F, using the temp (+/- Temp) arrow keys. 8. Press the Start button to initiate preheating. 9. Transfer the baking pan to the rack of the air fryer when the screen displays "Add Food." 10. Close its door, and let the machine do the cooking. 11. Repeat with the remaining two pepper rings. Serve hot. 12. Serve.

Per serving: Calories 84; Fat 5g; Sodium 413mg; Carbs 3g; Sugar 1g; Fiber 0.7g; Protein 7g

Cajun Muffins

Prep time: 10 minutes | Cook time: 10 minutes | Serves: 4

Olive oil	1 cup diced ham
4 eggs, beaten	½ cup shredded Cheddar cheese
2¼ cups frozen hash browns, thawed	½ teaspoon Cajun seasoning

1. Lightly spray 12 silicone muffin cups with olive oil. 2. Mix the eggs, hash browns, ham, Cheddar cheese, and Cajun seasoning in a medium bowl. 3. Spoon 1½ tablespoons of hash brown mixture into each muffin cup. 4. Select the "Air Fry" mode on your air fryer. 5. Use the timer (+ / − Time) arrow keys to adjust the cooking time to 10 minutes. 6. Adjust its cooking temperature to 350 degrees F using the temp (+/- Temp) arrow keys. 7. Press the Start button to initiate preheating. 8. Transfer the muffin cups to the rack of the air fryer when the screen displays "Add Food." 9. Close its door, and let the machine do the cooking. 10. Serve.

Per serving: Calories 178; Fat 9g; Sodium 369mg; Carbs 13g; Sugar 0.1g; Fiber 0.7g; Protein 11g

Cheese Sausage Biscuits

Prep time: 5 minutes | Cook time: 15 minutes | Serves: 4

12 ounces' chicken breakfast sausage	1 (6-ounce) can of biscuits
	⅛ cup cream cheese

1. Form the sausage into five small patties. 2. Place the sausage patties on a cooking tray. 3. Select the "Air Fry" mode on your air fryer. 4. Use the timer (+ / − Time) arrow keys to adjust the cooking time to 5 minutes. 5. Adjust its cooking temperature to 350 degrees F, using the temp (+/- Temp) arrow keys. 6. Press the Start button to initiate preheating. 7. Transfer the baking pan to the rack of the air fryer when the screen displays "Add Food." 8. Close its door, and let the machine do the cooking. 9. Open the air fryer. Flip the patties. Cook for an additional 5 minutes. 10. Remove the cooked sausages from the air fryer. 11. Separate the biscuit dough into five biscuits and cook for 5 minutes. 12. Remove the cooked biscuits from the air fryer. 13. Split each biscuit in half. 14. Spread 1 teaspoon of cream cheese onto the bottom of each biscuit. 15. Top with a sausage patty and the other half of the biscuit, and serve.

Per serving: Calories 249; Fat 13g; Sodium 556mg; Carbs 20g; Sugar 1.1g; Fiber 0.7g; Protein 9g

Cinnamon Pancake with Cream Cheese

Prep time: 15 minutes | Cook time: 5 minutes | Serves: 2

2 eggs
2 cups low-fat cream cheese
½ teaspoon cinnamon
1 pack Stevia

1. Combine cream cheese, cinnamon, eggs, and stevia in a blender. 2. Pour a quarter of the mixture into the cooking tray. 3. Let cook for 2 minutes on both sides. 4. Select the "Air Fry" mode on your air fryer. 5. Use the timer (+ / − Time) arrow keys to adjust the cooking time to 5 minutes. 6. Adjust its cooking temperature to 330 degrees F using the temp (+/- Temp) arrow keys. 7. Press the Start button to initiate preheating. 8. Transfer the cooking tray to the rack of the air fryer when the screen displays "Add Food." 9. Close its door, and let the machine do the cooking. 10. Repeat the process with the rest of the mixture. 11. Serve.

Per serving: Calories 106; Fat 3.2g; Sodium 247mg; Carbs 10g; Sugar 1.2g; Fiber 0.7g; Protein 9g

Cheese Scallion Sandwich

Prep time: 10 minutes | Cook time: 10 minutes | Serves: 2

2 slices of wheat bread
2 teaspoons low-fat butter
2 sliced scallions
1 tablespoon grated parmesan
cheese
¾ cup low-fat, grated cheddar cheese

1. Apply butter to a slice of bread. 2. Place it inside the cooking tray with the butter side facing down. 3. Place cheese and scallions on top. 4. Spread the rest of the butter on the other slice of bread. 5. Then, put it on top of the sandwich and sprinkle it with parmesan cheese. 6. Select the "Air Fry" mode on your air fryer. 7. Use the timer (+ / − Time) arrow keys to adjust the cooking time to 10 minutes. 8. Adjust its cooking temperature to 356 degrees F using the temp (+/- Temp) arrow keys. 9. Press the Start button to initiate preheating. 10. Transfer the cooking tray to the rack of the air fryer when the screen displays "Add Food." 11. Close its door, and let the machine do the cooking. 12. Let it cook for 10 minutes. 13. Serve.

Per serving: Calories 154; Fat 2.5g; Sodium 269mg; Carbs 9g; Sugar 1.2g; Fiber 0.7g; Protein 8.6g

Simple Fried Egg

Prep time: 5 minutes | Cook time: 4 minutes | Serve: 1

1 pastured egg
⅛ teaspoon salt
⅛ tablespoon cracked black pepper

1. Grease a baking pan with olive oil, then crack the egg. 2. Select the "Air Fry" mode on your air fryer. 3. Use the timer (+ / − Time) arrow keys to adjust the cooking time to 4 minutes. 4. Adjust its cooking temperature to 370 degrees F, using the temp (+/- Temp) arrow keys. 5. Press the Start button to initiate preheating. 6. Transfer the baking pan to the rack of the air fryer when the screen displays "Add Food." 7. Close its door, and let the machine do the cooking. 8. After 3 minutes, open the air fryer to check if the egg needs more cooking. 9. Serve the egg. Add salt and black pepper to season it.

Per serving: Calories 90; Fat 7g; Sodium 351mg; Carbs 0.6g; Sugar 1.1g; Fiber 0.7g; Protein 6.3 g

Tomato Scrambled Egg

Prep time: 5 minutes | Cook time: 10 minutes | Serves: 2

2 eggs
1 chopped tomato
dash of salt
1 teaspoon butter
¼ cup cream

1. Put the eggs in a bowl, then add salt and cream. Whisk until fluffy. 2. Add butter to a cooking tray and stir in the egg mixture. 3. Select the "Air Fry" mode on your air fryer. 4. Use the timer (+ / − Time) arrow keys to adjust the cooking time to 10 minutes. 5. Adjust its cooking temperature to 300 degrees F, using the temp (+/- Temp) arrow keys. 6. Press the Start button to initiate preheating. 7. Transfer the cooking tray to the rack of the air fryer when the screen displays "Add Food." 8. Close its door, and let the machine do the cooking. 9. Serve warm.

Per serving: Calories 105; Fat 8g; Sodium 254mg; Carbs 2.3g; Sugar 0.4g; Fiber 0.7g; Protein 6.4g

Ham Bread Cups

Prep time: 6 minutes | Cook time: 15 minutes | Serves: 2

2 eggs
2 tablespoons grated cheddar cheese
Salt and black pepper to taste
1 ham slice cut into 2 pieces
4 bread slices flat with a rolling pin

1. Spray both sides of the ramekins with cooking spray. 2. Place two slices of bread into each ramekin. 3. Add the ham slice pieces into each ramekin. 4. Crack an egg in each ramekin, then sprinkle with cheese. 5. Season with salt and black pepper. 6. Select the "Air Fry" mode on your air fryer. 7. Use the timer (+ / − Time) arrow keys to adjust the cooking time to 15 minutes. 8. Adjust its cooking temperature to 300 degrees F using the temp (+/- Temp) arrow keys. 9. Press the Start button to initiate preheating. 10. Transfer the ramekins to the rack of the air fryer when the screen displays "Add Food." 11. Close its door, and let the machine do the cooking. 12. Serve warm.

Per serving: Calories 162; Fat 8g; Sodium 246mg; Carbs 10g; Sugar 0.1g; Fiber 0.7g; Protein11g

Fried Potatoes with Onion

Prep time: 10 minutes | Cook time: 30 minutes | Serves: 2

2 russet potatoes
1 red bell pepper
1 white onion
Cooking spray
Salt and black pepper to taste

1. Cut the potatoes into 1-inch small cubes. 2. Put them in a baking pan, spray with cooking spray, and sprinkle with a bit of salt and black pepper. 3. Select the "Air Fry" mode on your air fryer. 4. Use the timer (+ / − Time) arrow keys to adjust the cooking time to 15 minutes. 5. Adjust its cooking temperature to 400 degrees F, using the temp (+/- Temp) arrow keys. 6. Press the Start button to initiate preheating. 7. Transfer the baking pan to the rack of the air fryer when the screen displays "Add Food." 8. Close its door, and let the machine do the cooking. 9. Stir in the onions and peppers with the potatoes. Season with salt and black pepper. 10. Cook at 400 degrees F for another 15 minutes, shaking a few times and checking to ensure the potatoes aren't being overcooked. 11. Serve.

Per serving: Calories 376; Fat 0.8g; Sodium 33 mg; Carbs 86.2g; Sugar 0.6g; Fiber 0.7g; Protein 9.6g.

Individual Cheese Egg Sandwich

Prep time: 3 minutes | Cook time: 6 minutes | Serve: 1

1 egg
2 slices of cheddar or Swiss cheese

A bit of butter
1 roll of either an English muffin or Kaiser Bun, halved

1. Butter the sliced rolls on both sides. 2. Whisk the eggs in an oven-safe dish. 3. Place the cheese, egg dish, and rolls on a cooking tray. 4. Select the "Air Fry" mode on your air fryer. 5. Use the timer (+ / − Time) arrow keys to adjust the cooking time to 6 minutes. 6. Adjust its cooking temperature to 390 degrees F using the temp (+/- Temp) arrow keys. 7. Press the Start button to initiate preheating. 8. Transfer the cooking tray to the rack of the air fryer when the screen displays "Add Food." 9. Close its door, and let the machine do the cooking. 10. Place the egg and cheese between the pieces of roll. 11. Serve warm.
Per serving: Calories 212; Fat 11.2g; Sodium 349mg; Carbs 9.3g; Sugar 1g; Fiber 0.7g; Protein 12.4g

Cheese Sausage Wraps

Prep time: 5 minutes | Cook time: 3 minutes | Serves: 4

8 pre-cooked sausages
2 pieces of American cheese

1 can of 8 counts refrigerated crescent roll dough

1. Cut each of the cheese slices into corners. 2. Unroll the crescent roll. 3. At the crescent roll's wide end, put ¼ of cheese and 1 sausage. 4. Starting at the wide end, roll the crescent up and tuck in the ends to cover the sausage and cheese. 5. Select the "Air Fry" mode on your air fryer. 6. Use the timer (+ / − Time) arrow keys to adjust the cooking time to 3 minutes. 7. Adjust its cooking temperature to 380 degrees F, using the temp (+/- Temp) arrow keys. 8. Press the Start button to initiate preheating. 9. Transfer the wraps to the rack of the air fryer when the screen displays "Add Food." 10. Close its door, and let the machine do the cooking. 11. Serve.
Per serving: Calories 325; Fat 24.7g; Sodium 783 mg; Carbs 7.9g; Sugar 0.5g; Fiber 0.7g; Protein 16.7 g.

Tomato-Sausage Frittata

Prep time: 5 minutes | Cook time: 15 minutes | Serves: 6

6 eggs
8 halved cherry tomatoes
2 tablespoons shredded par-

mesan cheese
1 Italian sausage, diced
Salt and black pepper to taste

1. Add the tomatoes and sausage to the cooking tray. 2. Select the "Air Fry" mode on your air fryer. 3. Use the timer (+ / − Time) arrow keys to adjust the cooking time to 10 minutes. 4. Adjust its cooking temperature to 390 degrees F, using the temp (+/- Temp) arrow keys. 5. Press the Start button to initiate preheating. 6. Transfer the cooking tray to the rack of the air fryer when the screen displays "Add Food." 7. Close its door, and let the machine do the cooking. 8. Meanwhile, add eggs, cheese, salt, oil, and pepper into the mixing bowl, then whisk properly. 9. Remove the baking dish from the air fryer and pour the egg mixture on top. Ensure you spread it evenly. 10. Place the dish back into the air fryer and air fry for an additional 5 minutes. 11. Serve.
Per serving: Calories 273; Fat 8.2g; Sodium 338mg; Carbs 7g; Sugar 1.2g; Fiber 0.7g; Protein 14.2g

Cheeseburger Sliders

Prep time: 5 minutes | Cook time: 10 minutes | Serves: 6

1 pound of ground beef
6 slices of cheddar cheese

6 dinner rolls
Salt and black pepper to taste

1. Mix beef with salt and black pepper in a bowl, then make six patties. 2. Select the "Air Fry" mode on your air fryer. 3. Use the timer (+ / − Time) arrow keys to adjust the cooking time to 10 minutes. 4. Adjust its cooking temperature to 390 degrees F, using the temp (+/- Temp) arrow keys. 5. Press the Start button to initiate preheating. 6. Transfer the baking pan to the rack of the air fryer when the screen displays "Add Food." 7. Close its door, and let the machine do the cooking. 8. Remove the burger patties from the air fryer; place the cheese on top of the burgers, return to the air fryer, and cook for another minute. 9. Serve.
Per serving: Calories 262; Fat 9.4g; Sodium 432mg; Carbs 8.2g; Sugar 0.6g; Fiber 0.7g; Protein 16.2g

Cheese Toasts

Prep time: 4 minutes | Cook time: 5 minutes | Serves: 2

4 slices of brown bread
½ cup shredded sharp cheddar

cheese
¼ cup melted butter

1. In separate bowls, place cheese and butter. 2. Melt butter and brush it onto the four slices of bread. 3. Place cheese on two sides of bread slices. 4. Put sandwiches together and place them into a baking pan. 5. Select the "Air Fry" mode on your air fryer. 6. Use the timer (+ / − Time) arrow keys to adjust the cooking time to 5 minutes. 7. Adjust its cooking temperature to 390 degrees F, using the temp (+/- Temp) arrow keys. 8. Press the Start button to initiate preheating. 9. Transfer the baking pan to the rack of the air fryer when the screen displays "Add Food." 10. Close its door, and let the machine do the cooking. 11. Serve warm.
Per serving: Calories 214; Fat 11.2g; Sodium 377mg; Carbs 9.4g; Sugar 1.2g; Fiber 0.7g; Protein 13.2g

Bacon Muffins

Prep time: 3 minutes | Cook time: 6 minutes | Serves: 2

2 whole-wheat English muffins
4 slices bacon

Pepper, to taste
2 eggs

1. Crack an egg each into ramekins, then season with pepper. 2. Add bacon and muffins alongside the ramekins. 3. Select the "Air Fry" mode on your air fryer. 4. Use the timer (+ / − Time) arrow keys to adjust the cooking time to 6 minutes. 5. Adjust its cooking temperature to 390 degrees F, using the temp (+/- Temp) arrow keys. 6. Press the Start button to initiate preheating. 7. Transfer the baking pan to the rack of the air fryer when the screen displays "Add Food." 8. Close its door, and let the machine do the cooking. 9. When the bacon and eggs are cooked, add two pieces of bacon and one egg to each egg muffin. 10. Serve when hot.
Per serving: Calories 276; Fat 12g; Sodium 531mg; Carbs 10.2g; Sugar 1g; Fiber 0.7g; Protein 17.3g

Paprika Zucchini Hash

Prep time: 15 minutes | Cook time: 25 minutes | Serves: 4

2 zucchinis	Salt, to taste
2 potatoes	Pepper, to taste
1 teaspoon paprika	Cooking oil

1. Peel the zucchinis and potatoes using a vegetable peeler. 2. Using a cheese grater, shred the zucchinis and potatoes. 3. Place the grated zucchini and potatoes in a large bowl with cold water. Let it sit for 5 minutes. 4. The cold water helps remove excess starch from the potatoes. Stir to help dissolve the starch. 5. Drain the potatoes and zucchini, then dry them with paper towels or napkins. Make sure the potatoes are completely dry. 6. Season the potatoes and zucchini with paprika and salt and black pepper to taste. 7. Spray the potatoes and zucchini with cooking oil and transfer them to a cooking tray. 8. Select the "Air Fry" mode on your air fryer. 9. Use the timer (+ / − Time) arrow keys to adjust the cooking time to 20 minutes. 10. Adjust its cooking temperature to 350 degrees F using the temp (+/- Temp) arrow keys. 11. Press the Start button to initiate preheating. 12. Transfer the cooking tray to the rack of the air fryer when the screen displays "Add Food." 13. Close its door, and let the machine do the cooking. 14. Cool before serving. 15. Serve.

Per serving: Calories 150; Fat 0g; Sodium 52mg; Carbs 34g; Sugar 0.4g; Fiber 0.7g; Protein 4g

Ham Egg Breads

Prep time: 10 minutes | Cook time: 15 minutes | Serves: 2

2 eggs	Melted butter
4 slices of bread	Salt and black pepper to taste
1 slice of ham	

1. Grease the inside of the ramekin with melted butter. 2. Toast bread and flatten it with a rolling pin. 3. Press one piece of toast into the bottom of the ramekin to create a bread bowl. 4. Press another piece of toast onto the first 1 to create a double layer. 5. Cut the ham into four slices, then line the inside of the toast cups with two strips of ham each. 6. Crack an egg into the middle of each cup and season with salt and black pepper. 7. Select the "Air Fry" mode on your air fryer. 8. Use the timer (+ / − Time) arrow keys to adjust the cooking time to 15 minutes. 9. Adjust its cooking temperature to 320 degrees F, using the temp (+/- Temp) arrow keys. 10. Press the Start button to initiate preheating. 11. Transfer the ramekins to the rack of the air fryer when the screen displays "Add Food." 12. Close its door, and let the machine do the cooking. 13. Serve.

Per serving: Calories 202; Fat 2.6g; Sodium 488 mg; Carbs 16g; Sugar 1g; Fiber 0.7g; Protein 9.2 g

Homemade Donut Holes

Prep time: 10 minutes | Cook time: 10 minutes | Serves: 2

1 (8-count) can of refrigerated biscuits	chocolate chips
	3 tablespoons melted butter
1 bag of semi-sweet white	¼ cup powdered sugar

1. Cut each biscuit into thirds. 2. Flatten each third with your hands and put a small dimple in the center with your thumb. 3. Place 2 – 3 chocolate chips inside each dimple and wrap the dough around the chocolate chips, creating a ball. 4. Brush each ball with butter and place them in a baking pan. 5. Select the "Air Fry" mode on your air fryer. 6. Use the timer (+ / −

Time) arrow keys to adjust the cooking time to 10 minutes. 7. Adjust its cooking temperature to 320 degrees F, using the temp (+/- Temp) arrow keys. 8. Press the Start button to initiate preheating. 9. Transfer the baking pan to the rack of the air fryer when the screen displays "Add Food." 10. Close its door, and let the machine do the cooking. 11. Mix powdered sugar in a bowl and drizzle over the donuts. 12. Serve.

Per serving: Calories 297; Fat 15.5g; Sodium 705 mg; Carbs 35.4g; Sugar 1g; Fiber 0.7g; Protein 4.7g.

Breakfast Bacon and Egg Sandwich

Prep time: 1 minute | Cook time: 5 minutes | Serves: 1

1 egg	1 slice of cheddar cheese
1 English muffin	Salt and black pepper to taste
2 pieces' bacon	

1. Break an egg in a ramekin and add salt and black pepper. 2. Select the "Air Fry" mode on your air fryer. 3. Use the timer (+ / − Time) arrow keys to adjust the cooking time to 5 minutes. 4. Adjust its cooking temperature to 400 degrees F, using the temp (+/- Temp) arrow keys. 5. Press the Start button to initiate preheating. 6. Transfer the ramekin to the rack of the air fryer when the screen displays "Add Food." 7. Close its door, and let the machine do the cooking. 8. Assemble the sandwich with the bottom of the muffin, egg, cheese, bacon, and the top of the muffin orderly. 9. Serve.

Per serving: Calories 404; Fat 21.6g; Sodium 745 mg; Carbs 32.5g; Sugar 1.1g; Fiber 0.7g; Protein 18.6g.

Bacon Eggroll

Prep time: 15 minutes | Cook time: 10 minutes | Serves: 4

4 eggs	cheese
4 slices bacon	5 egg roll wrappers
½ cup shredded cheddar	

1. In a big pan, fry the bacon until crispy and set aside. 2. Drain the bacon; Fat, but leave a little left behind in the skillet. 3. Using the bacon, Fat, scramble your eggs. 4. Roll out your eggroll wrappers. 5. In a separate bowl, crumble the bacon into tiny pieces, then mix the eggs and the cheese. 6. Scoop in equal amounts of the mixture to the center of each wrapper. 7. Pull the bottom left corner of the wrapper over the mixture, then fold each side in. 8. Wet the remaining edge and roll the eggroll shut. 9. Select the "Air Fry" mode on your air fryer. 10. Use the timer (+ / − Time) arrow keys to adjust the cooking time to 10 minutes. 11. Adjust its cooking temperature to 360 degrees F using the temp (+/- Temp) arrow keys. 12. Press the Start button to initiate preheating. 13. Transfer the rolls to the rack of the air fryer when the screen displays "Add Food." 14. Close its door, and let the machine do the cooking. 15. Serve.

Per serving: Calories 302; Fat 18.5g; Sodium 483 mg; Carbs 19.2g; Sugar 0.1g; Fiber 0.7g; Protein 13.8g.

Vanilla Banana Bites

Prep time: 10 minutes | Cook time: 10 minutes | Serves: 2

3 bananas	1 egg
1 cup dry pancake mix	1 teaspoon vanilla
1 cup milk	

1. Combine the egg, milk, vanilla, and pancake mix in a medium bowl. 2. Cut every single banana into ½-inch slices. 3. Use a fork to dip each banana slice in the pancake mix, allow-

ing the extra batter to drip off. 4. Place the coated bananas in a baking pan. 5. Select the "Air Fry" mode on your air fryer. 6. Use the timer (+ / − Time) arrow keys to adjust the cooking time to 10 minutes. 7. Adjust its cooking temperature to 320 degrees F, using the temp (+/- Temp) arrow keys. 8. Press the Start button to initiate preheating. 9. Transfer the baking pan to the rack of the air fryer when the screen displays "Add Food." 10. Close its door, and let the machine do the cooking. 11. Serve with a side of maple syrup for dipping.
Per serving: Calories 114; Fat 1.9g; Sodium 60 mg; Carbs 22.3g; Sugar 0.4g; Fiber 0.7g; Protein 3.1g.

Almond Sausage Balls

Prep time: 10 minutes | Cook time: 15 minutes | Serves: 2

1-pound breakfast sausage	1 cup sharp cheddar cheese
1 egg	2 teaspoons baking powder
1 cup almond meal	

1. Put all ingredients in a bowl and mix it well. 2. Spoon out small scoops, roll them into balls, and place them in a baking pan. 3. Select the "Air Fry" mode on your air fryer. 4. Use the timer (+ / − Time) arrow keys to adjust the cooking time to 15 minutes. 5. Adjust its cooking temperature to 350 degrees F, using the temp (+/- Temp) arrow keys. 6. Press the Start button to initiate preheating. 7. Transfer the baking pan to the rack of the air fryer when the screen displays "Add Food." 8. Close its door, and let the machine do the cooking. 9. Serve.
Per serving: Calories 262; Fat 21.8g; Sodium 533 mg; Carbs 2.7g; Sugar 1g; Fiber 0.7g; Protein 14.2g.

Simple Fried Bacon

Prep time: 11 minutes | Cook time: 12 minutes | Serves: 11

11 slices of bacon

1. Select the "Air Fry" mode on your air fryer. 2. Use the timer (+ / − Time) arrow keys to adjust the cooking time to 12 minutes. 3. Adjust its cooking temperature to 400 degrees F, using the temp (+/- Temp) arrow keys. 4. Press the Start button to initiate preheating. 5. Transfer the bacon to the rack of the air fryer when the screen displays "Add Food." 6. Close its door, and let the machine do the cooking. 7. Serve.
Per serving: Calories 80; Fat 7g; Sodium 344 mg; Carbs 1g; Sugar 1.2g; Fiber 0.7g; Protein 5.2g

Little Bacon Smokies

Prep time: 10 minutes | Cook time: 10 minutes | Serves: 6

14 ounces of little smokies	tute
⅔ ounce of bacon	Toothpicks
⅓ cup of brown sugar substi-	

1. Cut Bacon tips into thirds, and put the brown sugar substitute into a shallow dish that is enough to fit the bacon thirds. 2. Place a slice of bacon into the brown sugar substitute and coat on both sides. 3. Wrap one little smokie with a slice of brown sugar-coated bacon and pin it with a Toothpick. 4. Repeat with the rest of the little smokies and place them in a baking pan. 5. Select the "Air Fry" mode on your air fryer. 6. Use the timer (+ / − Time) arrow keys to adjust the cooking time to 10 minutes. 7. Adjust its cooking temperature to 350 degrees F, using the temp (+/- Temp) arrow keys. 8. Press the Start button to initiate preheating. 9. Transfer the baking pan to the rack of the air fryer when the screen displays "Add Food." 10. Close its door, and let the machine do the cooking. 11. Serve.

Per serving: Calories 680; Fat 27g; Sodium 745mg; Carbs 41g; Sugar 1.4g; Fiber 0.7g; Protein 15 g

East-to-Make Hard Eggs

Prep time: 1 minute | Cook time: 15 minutes | Serves: 4

6 large eggs

1. Place eggs in a baking pan. 2. Select the "Air Fry" mode on your air fryer. 3. Use the timer (+ / − Time) arrow keys to adjust the cooking time to 15 minutes. 4. Adjust its cooking temperature to 270 degrees F, using the temp (+/- Temp) arrow keys. 5. Press the Start button to initiate preheating. 6. Transfer the baking pan to the rack of the air fryer when the screen displays "Add Food." 7. Close its door, and let the machine do the cooking. 8. When the time is up, remove it from the baking pan and place it in a bowl filled with ice water for 5 minutes. 9. Remove and peel. 10. Serve.
Per serving: Calories 80; Fat 2g; Sodium 243mg; Carbs 1g; Sugar 1.1g; Fiber 0.7g; Protein 5 g

Cheese Sandwich

Prep time: 1 minute | Cook time: 8 minutes | Serves: 2

1 tablespoon butter	2 cheddar cheese slices
4 frozen bread slices	

1. Evenly spread butter on each bread slice evenly. 2. Place one cheese slice between two bread slices. 3. Transfer sandwiches to a baking pan. 4. Select the "Air Fry" mode on your air fryer. 5. Use the timer (+ / − Time) arrow keys to adjust the cooking time to 8 minutes. 6. Adjust its cooking temperature to 360 degrees F using the temp (+/- Temp) arrow keys. 7. Press the Start button to initiate preheating. 8. Transfer the baking pan to the rack of the air fryer when the screen displays "Add Food." 9. Close its door, and let the machine do the cooking. 10. Serve with coffee or tea or with vegetables.
Per serving: Calories 272; Fat 16.56g; Sodium 383mg; Carbs 20.3g; Sugar 1.2g; Fiber 0.7g; Protein 10.39 g

Air Fried Brussels Sprouts

Prep time: 5 minutes | Cook time: 15 minutes | Serves: 2

1 pound Brussels sprouts	5 teaspoons olive oil
½ teaspoon kosher salt	

1. Remove outer leaves with bruises and trim the stems. 2. Slice vertically into 2. Rinse them and shake off excess liquid. Put them in a dish. 3. Stir in olive oil and salt to coat evenly. 4. Arrange the prepared sprouts in the baking pan. 5. Select the "Air Fry" mode on your air fryer. 6. Use the timer (+ / − Time) arrow keys to adjust the cooking time to 15 minutes. 7. Adjust its cooking temperature to 390 degrees F, using the temp (+/- Temp) arrow keys. 8. Press the Start button to initiate preheating. 9. Transfer the baking pan to the rack of the air fryer when the screen displays "Add Food." 10. Close its door, and let the machine do the cooking. 11. Serve.
Per serving: Calories 198; Fat 12.4g; Sodium 362mg; Carbs 20.6g; Sugar 1.2g; Fiber 0.7g; Protein 7.7g

Mayonnaise Baguettes

Prep time: 10 minutes | Cook time: 10 minutes | Serves: 2

2 stale French baguettes
4 tablespoons crushed or crumpled garlic

1 cup mayonnaise
Powdered grated parmesan
1 tablespoon olive oil

1. Mix mayonnaise with garlic and set aside. 2. Cut the baguettes into slices, but without separating them. 3. Fill the cavities of equals, then brush with olive oil and sprinkle with grated cheese. 4. Select the "Air Fry" mode on your air fryer. 5. Use the timer (+ / − Time) arrow keys to adjust the cooking time to 10 minutes. 6. Adjust its cooking temperature to 350 degrees F using the temp (+/- Temp) arrow keys. 7. Press the Start button to initiate preheating. 8. Transfer the baking pan to the rack of the air fryer when the screen displays "Add Food." 9. Close its door, and let the machine do the cooking. 10. Serve.

Per serving: Calories 151; Fat 7.1g; Sodium 342mg; Carbs 17.9g; Sugar 1.1g; Fiber 0.7g; Protein 3.6g

Cinnamon Pancake

Prep time: 7 minutes | Cook time: 6 minutes | Serves: 2

2 eggs
2 cups reduced-fat cream cheese

½ teaspoon cinnamon
1 pack Stevia

1. Mix cream cheese, cinnamon, eggs, and stevia in a blender. 2. Pour a quarter of the mixture into the cooking tray. 3. Select the "Air Fry" mode on your air fryer. 4. Use the timer (+ / − Time) arrow keys to adjust the cooking time to 4 minutes. 5. Adjust its cooking temperature to 330 degrees F, using the temp (+/- Temp) arrow keys. 6. Press the Start button to initiate preheating. 7. Transfer the cooking tray to the rack of the air fryer when the screen displays "Add Food." 8. Close its door, and let the machine do the cooking. 9. Cook for 2 minutes on all sides. 10. Repeat the process with the remaining portion of the mixture. 11. Serve.

Per serving: Calories 140; Fat 10.6g; Sodium 341mg; Carbs 5.4g; Sugar 1g; Fiber 0.7g; Protein 22.7g

Fried Sweet Potatoes

Prep time: 2 minutes | Cook time: 15 minutes | Serves: 2

½ chopped onion
3 cubed sweet potatoes
2 chopped red bell peppers

1 teaspoon olive oil
Salt and black pepper to taste

1. Sprinkle salt and black pepper on potatoes and drizzle olive oil; toss to combine. 2. Place potatoes on the cooking tray. 3. Select the "Air Fry" mode on your air fryer. 4. Use the timer (+ / − Time) arrow keys to adjust the cooking time to 10 minutes. 5. Adjust its cooking temperature to 350 degrees F, using the temp (+/- Temp) arrow keys. 6. Press the Start button to initiate preheating. 7. Transfer the cooking tray to the rack of the air fryer when the screen displays "Add Food." 8. Close its door, and let the machine do the cooking. 9. Add red bell peppers and onion, and cook again for 5 minutes. 10. Serve.

Per serving: Calories 289; Fat 2.68g; Sodium 453mg; Carbs 61.24g; Sugar 0.6g; Fiber 0.7g; Protein 7.46 g

Stuffed Peppers

Prep time: 15 minutes | Cook time: 13 minutes | Serves: 2

4 eggs

1 bell pepper, halved and deseeded
Salt and black pepper to taste

1 teaspoon olive oil
¼ teaspoon sriracha flakes

1. Rub the bell pepper with olive oil around the edges. 2. Crack two eggs directly into each half of the bell pepper. 3. Drizzle all the spices over the eggs. 4. Place the bell peppers on a cooking tray. 5. Select the "Air Fry" mode on your air fryer. 6. Use the timer (+ / − Time) arrow keys to adjust the cooking time to 13 minutes. 7. Adjust its cooking temperature to 390 degrees F, using the temp (+/- Temp) arrow keys. 8. Press the Start button to initiate preheating. 9. Transfer the cooking tray to the rack of the air fryer when the screen displays "Add Food." 10. Close its door, and let the machine do the cooking. 11. Serve.

Per serving: Calories 164; Fat 10g; Sodium 236mg; Carbs 4g; Sugar 0.1g; Fiber 0.7g; Protein 11 g

Parmesan Bread

Prep time: 15 minutes | Cook time: 10 minutes | Serves: 4

1 large egg
¼ cup grated parmesan cheese
½ teaspoon garlic powder

1 cup shredded mozzarella cheese

1. Layer the baking pan with parchment paper. 2. Mix parmesan cheese, mozzarella cheese, garlic powder, and egg in a suitable bowl. 3. Set the mixture in a well-greased pan. 4. Select the "Air Fry" mode on your air fryer. 5. Use the timer (+ / − Time) arrow keys to adjust the cooking time to 10 minutes. 6. Adjust its cooking temperature to 350 degrees F using the temp (+/- Temp) arrow keys. 7. Press the Start button to initiate preheating. 8. Transfer the baking pan to the rack of the air fryer when the screen displays "Add Food." 9. Close its door, and let the machine do the cooking. 10. Slice and serve warm.

Per serving: Calories 225; Fat 14.3g; Sodium 377mg; Carbs 2.8g; Sugar 1.2g; Fiber 0.7g; Protein 28.2 g

Cream Soufflé

Prep time: 5 minutes | Cook time: 10 minutes | Serves: 4

4 eggs
¼ teaspoon red chili pepper
Chopped fresh parsley.

4 tablespoons cream
Salt and black pepper to taste

1. Grease 4 ramekin dishes with cooking spray. 2. Take a large bowl and add the eggs, whisking well to combine. 3. Add the cream, parsley, and chili and stir well to combine. 4. Transfer the egg mixture into the ramekin dishes halfway. 5. Select the "Air Fry" mode on your air fryer. 6. Use the timer (+ / − Time) arrow keys to adjust the cooking time to 10 minutes. 7. Adjust its cooking temperature to 390 degrees F, using the temp (+/- Temp) arrow keys. 8. Press the Start button to initiate preheating. 9. Transfer the ramekins to the rack of the air fryer when the screen displays "Add Food." 10. Close its door, and let the machine do the cooking. 11. Serve and enjoy.

Per serving: Calories 127; Fat 7g; Sodium 341mg; Carbs 3g; Sugar 1.4g; Fiber 0.7g; Protein 10g

Ham and Cheese

Prep time: 5 minutes | Cook time: 8 minutes | Serves: 4

4 slices of smoked country ham
4 slices bread

4 thick slices of tomato
1 teaspoon butter
4 slices of Cheddar cheese

1. Spread ½ teaspoon of butter onto one side of 2 slices of

bread. 2. Each sandwich will have one slice of bread with butter and one without butter. 3. Assemble each sandwich by layering two slices of ham, two slices of cheese, and two slices of tomato on the unbuttered pieces of bread. 4. Put it on top of the rest of the bread slices, with the buttered side up. 5. Place the sandwiches in a baking pan buttered-side down. 6. Select the "Air Fry" mode on your air fryer. 7. Use the timer (+ / − Time) arrow keys to adjust the cooking time to 8 minutes. 8. Adjust its cooking temperature to 390 degrees F using the temp (+/- Temp) arrow keys. 9. Press the Start button to initiate preheating. 10. Transfer the baking pan to the rack of the air fryer when the screen displays "Add Food." 11. Close its door, and let the machine do the cooking. 12. Cut each sandwich in half and enjoy.

Per serving: Calories 525; Fat 25g; Sodium 698mg; Carbs 34g; Sugar 0.4g; Fiber 0.7g; Protein 41g

Spaghetti Squash Fritters with Parsley

Prep time: 15 minutes | Cook time: 8 minutes | Serves: 4

2 cups cooked spaghetti squash	mond flour
2 stalks of green onion, sliced	2 tablespoons unsalted butter; softened
1 large egg	½ teaspoon garlic powder
¼ cup blanched ground al-	1 teaspoon dried parsley

1. Remove excess moisture from the squash using a cheesecloth or kitchen towel. 2. Mix all Ingredients in a large bowl. Form into four patties. 3. Cut a piece of parchment to fit a baking pan. 4. Place each patty on the parchment into the baking pan. 5. Select the "Air Fry" mode on your air fryer. 6. Use the timer (+ / − Time) arrow keys to adjust the cooking time to 8 minutes. 7. Adjust its cooking temperature to 400 degrees F, using the temp (+/- Temp) arrow keys. 8. Press the Start button to initiate preheating. 9. Transfer the baking pan to the rack of the air fryer when the screen displays "Add Food." 10. Close its door, and let the machine do the cooking. 11. Serve warm.

Per serving: Calories 131; Fat 10.1g; Sodium 362mg; Carbs 7.1g; Sugar 1.4g; Fiber 0.7g; Protein 3.8g

Bacon Bombs

Prep time: 10 minutes | Cook time: 5 minutes | Serves: 4

3 eggs	1 tablespoon fresh chives
3 bacon slices	1-ounce cream cheese
4 ounces of pizza dough	

1. Pop a pan over medium heat and cook the bacon for ten minutes until crisp. 2. Remove from the heat and crumble, then pop to 1 side. 3. Stir the eggs into the pan and cook until set. Remove from the heat. 4. Place the eggs into a bowl with cream cheese, chives, and bacon. 5. Next, take the pizza dough and carefully cut it into four pieces. 6. Roll each piece into a circle. 7. Place ¼ of the egg mixture into the middle dough, and fold over the sides of the dough to meet in the middle. 8. Select the "Air Fry" mode on your air fryer. 9. Use the timer (+ / − Time) arrow keys to adjust the cooking time to 5 minutes. 10. Adjust its cooking temperature to 350 degrees F using the temp (+/- Temp) arrow keys. 11. Press the Start button to initiate preheating. 12. Transfer the bacon bombs to the rack of the air fryer when the screen displays "Add Food." 13. Close its door, and let the machine do the cooking. 14. Serve.

Per serving: Calories 305; Fat 15g; Sodium 327mg; Carbs 23g; Sugar 0.8g; Fiber 0.7g; Protein 19g

Tomato Bacon Cups

Prep time: 10 minutes | Cook time: 9 minutes | Serves: 2

3 eggs, beaten	2 bacon slices, cooked and crumbled
4 tomato slices	
4 teaspoons cheddar cheese, shredded	Black pepper, to taste
	Salt, to taste

1. Spray silicone muffin molds with cooking spray. 2. In a small bowl, whisk the egg with pepper and salt. 3. Pour eggs into the silicone muffin molds. Divide cheese and bacon into molds. 4. Top each with a tomato slice and place in a baking pan. 5. Select the "Air Fry" mode on your air fryer. 6. Use the timer (+ / − Time) arrow keys to adjust the cooking time to 9 minutes. 7. Adjust its cooking temperature to 350 degrees F, using the temp (+/- Temp) arrow keys. 8. Press the Start button to initiate preheating. 9. Transfer the baking pan to the rack of the air fryer when the screen displays "Add Food." 10. Close its door, and let the machine do the cooking. 11. Serve and enjoy.

Per serving: Calories 67; Fat 4g; Sodium: 634; Carbs 1g; Sugar 0.7g; Sugar 1.2g; Fiber 0.7g; Protein 5.1 g

Easy Pumpkin Pancakes

Prep time: 15 minutes | Cook time: 12 minutes | Serves: 2

1 square puff pastry	1 small egg, beaten
3 tablespoons pumpkin filling	

1. Roll out a puff pastry square and layer it with pumpkin pie filling, leaving about ¼-inch space around the edges. 2. Cut it into eight equal-sized square pieces and coat the edges with a beaten egg. 3. Select the "Air Fry" mode on your air fryer. 4. Use the timer (+ / − Time) arrow keys to adjust the cooking time to 12 minutes. 5. Adjust its cooking temperature to 355 degrees F, using the temp (+/- Temp) arrow keys. 6. Press the Start button to initiate preheating. 7. Transfer the baking pan to the rack of the air fryer when the screen displays "Add Food." 8. Close its door, and let the machine do the cooking. 9. Serve warm.

Per serving: Calories 109; Fat 6.7g; Sodium 87 mg; Carbs 9.8g; Fiber 0.5g; Sugar 2.6g; Protein 2.4 g

Chicken Omelet with Zucchini

Prep time: 15 minutes | Cook time: 35 minutes | Serves: 4

8 eggs	chopped
½ cup milk	1 cup Cheddar cheese, shredded
Salt and ground black pepper to taste	ded
	½ cup fresh chives, chopped
1 cup cooked chicken,	¾ cup zucchini, chopped

1. Add the eggs, milk, salt, and black pepper to a bowl and beat well. 2. Add the remaining ingredients and stir to combine. 3. Place the mixture into a greased baking pan. 4. Select the "Air Fry" mode on your air fryer. 5. Use the timer (+ / − Time) arrow keys to adjust the cooking time to 35 minutes. 6. Adjust its cooking temperature to 315 degrees F using the temp (+/- Temp) arrow keys. 7. Press the Start button to initiate preheating. 8. Transfer the baking pan to the rack of the air fryer when the screen displays "Add Food." 9. Close its door, and let the machine do the cooking. 10. Cut into equal-sized wedges and serve hot.

Per serving: Calories 209; Fat 13.3g; Sodium 252 mg; Carbs 2.3g; Fiber 0.3g; Sugar 1.8g; Protein 9.8 g

Chili BBQ Bacon

Prep time: 2 minutes | Cook time: 10 minutes | Serves: 4

1 tablespoon dark brown sugar
½ teaspoon chili powder
1 pinch of ground cumin
1 pinch of cayenne pepper
4 slices bacon, halved

1. Mix seasonings until well combined. 2. Dip the bacon in the dressing until it is completely covered. Leave aside. 3. Select the "Air Fry" mode on your air fryer. 4. Use the timer (+ / − Time) arrow keys to adjust the cooking time to 10 minutes. 5. Adjust its cooking temperature to 370 degrees F, using the temp (+/- Temp) arrow keys. 6. Press the Start button to initiate preheating. 7. Transfer the bacon to the rack of the air fryer when the screen displays "Add Food." 8. Close its door, and let the machine do the cooking. 9. Serve.
Per serving: Calories 424; Fat 72g; Sodium 562mg; Carbs 59g; Sugar 0.8g; Fiber 0.7g; Protein 49g

Potato Chips and Iberian Ham

Prep time: 5 minutes | Cook time: 30 minutes | Serves: 4

⅔ pound potatoes
Salt, to taste
1 tablespoon olive oil
3 ½ ounces Iberian Ham
4 eggs

1. Cut the elongated French fries, rinse through plenty of water and dry well with paper towels. 2. Put the potatoes in a baking pan. 3. Select the "Air Fry" mode on your air fryer. 4. Use the timer (+ / − Time) arrow keys to adjust the cooking time to 25 minutes. 5. Adjust its cooking temperature to 400 degrees F, using the temp (+/- Temp) arrow keys. 6. Press the Start button to initiate preheating. 7. Transfer the baking pan to the rack of the air fryer when the screen displays "Add Food." 8. Close its door, and let the machine do the cooking. 9. When we see that they are starting to brown, put paper under the potatoes and lay the eggs. 10. Put in the air fryer again for 5 more minutes. 11. Finally, add Iberian ham flakes. 12. If you want to go faster while the potatoes are fried in the air fryer, you can prepare the grilled eggs in a small pan and then mix them with the potatoes and ham on the plate. 13. Serve.
Per serving: Calories 162.6; Fat 12g; Sodium 466mg; Carbs 0.6g; Sugar 0.4g; Fiber 0.7g; Protein 16.6g

Pea Tortilla with Mint

Prep time: 10 minutes | Cook time: 8 minutes | Serves: 4

½ pound baby peas
4 tablespoons butter
1 ½ cups yogurt
8 eggs
½ cup mint, chopped
Salt and black pepper to the taste

1. Heat a pan that fits your air fryer with the butter over medium heat, add peas, and sauté for 1 minute. 2. Meanwhile, mix half of the yogurt with salt, pepper, eggs, and mint in a bowl and whisk well. 3. Pour this over the peas, and toss. 4. Select the "Air Fry" mode on your air fryer. 5. Use the timer (+ / − Time) arrow keys to adjust the cooking time to 7 minutes. 6. Adjust its cooking temperature to 350 degrees F using the temp (+/- Temp) arrow keys. 7. Press the Start button to initiate preheating. 8. Transfer the baking pan to the rack of the air fryer when the screen displays "Add Food." 9. Close its door, and let the machine do the cooking. 10. Spread the rest of the yogurt over your tortilla, slice, and serve. 11. Enjoy!
Per serving: Calories 192; Fat 5; Sodium 502mg; Carbs 8; Sugar 1.2g; Fiber 0.7g; Protein 7g

Almond Crusted Chicken Breasts

Prep time: 10 minutes | Cook time: 25 minutes | Serves: 2

2 chicken breasts, skinless and boneless
1 tablespoon Dijon mustard
2 tablespoon mayonnaise
¼ cup almonds
Pepper, to taste
Salt, to taste

1. Add almond into the food processor and process until ground. 2. Transfer almonds to a plate and set aside. 3. Mix mustard and mayonnaise and spread over chicken. 4. Coat chicken with almonds and place into a baking pan. 5. Select the "Air Fry" mode on your air fryer. 6. Use the timer (+ / − Time) arrow keys to adjust the cooking time to 25 minutes. 7. Adjust its cooking temperature to 350 degrees F, using the temp (+/- Temp) arrow keys. 8. Press the Start button to initiate preheating. 9. Transfer the baking pan to the rack of the air fryer when the screen displays "Add Food." 10. Close its door, and let the machine do the cooking. 11. Serve and enjoy.
Per serving: Calories 409; Fat 22g; Sodium 722g; Carbs 6g; Sugar 1.5g; Fiber 0.7g; Protein 45 g

Fish-Onion Tacos

Prep time: 10 minutes | Cook time: 14 minutes | Serves: 4

4 big tortillas
1 red bell pepper, chopped
1 yellow onion, chopped
1 cup corn
4 white fish fillets, skinless and boneless
½ cup salsa
A handful of mixed romaine lettuce, spinach, and radicchio
4 tablespoons parmesan, grated

1. Put fish fillets in a baking pan. 2. Select the "Air Fry" mode on your air fryer. 3. Use the timer (+ / − Time) arrow keys to adjust the cooking time to 6 minutes. 4. Adjust its cooking temperature to 350 degrees F, using the temp (+/- Temp) arrow keys. 5. Press the Start button to initiate preheating. 6. Transfer the baking pan to the rack of the air fryer when the screen displays "Add Food." 7. Close its door, and let the machine do the cooking. 8. Meanwhile, heat a pan over medium-high heat, add bell pepper, onion, and corn, stir and cook for 1-2 minutes. 9. Arrange tortillas on a working surface, divide fish fillets, spread salsa over them, divide mixed veggies and greens, and spread parmesan on each at the end. 10. Roll your tacos, place them in a preheated air fryer and cook at 350 degrees F for 6 minutes. 11. Divide fish tacos onto plates and serve for breakfast. 12. Enjoy.
Per serving: Calories 200; Fat 3; Fiber 7; Sodium 728mg; Carbs 9; Sugar 1.4g; Fiber 0.7g; Protein 5g

Fried Potatoes with Bacon

Prep time: 10 minutes | Cook time: 20 minutes | Serves: 4

4 potatoes, peeled and cut into medium cubes
6 garlic cloves, minced
4 bacon slices, chopped
2 rosemary springs, chopped
1 tablespoon olive oil
Salt and black pepper to the taste
2 eggs, whisked

1. Mix oil with potatoes, garlic, bacon, rosemary, salt, pepper, and eggs in a baking pan, and whisk. 2. Select the "Air Fry" mode on your air fryer. 3. Use the timer (+ / − Time) arrow keys to adjust the cooking time to 20 minutes. 4. Adjust its cooking temperature to 400 degrees F, using the temp (+/- Temp) arrow keys. 5. Press the Start button to initiate preheating. 6. Transfer the baking pan to the rack of the air fryer when the screen displays "Add Food." 7. Close its door, and

let the machine do the cooking. 8. Enjoy!

Per serving: Calories 211; Fat 3; Fiber 5; Sodium 457mg; Carbs 8; Sugar 0.1g; Fiber 0.7g; Protein 12g

Mushroom Herb Salad

Prep time: 10 minutes | Cook time: 5 minutes | Serves: 4

10 mushrooms, halved	1 tablespoon cheddar cheese, grated
1 tablespoon fresh parsley, chopped	1 tablespoon dried mixed herbs
1 tablespoon olive oil	Black pepper, to taste
1 tablespoon mozzarella cheese, grated	Salt, to taste

1. Add all ingredients into the bowl and toss well. 2. Transfer the bowl mixture to a baking dish. 3. Select the "Air Fry" mode on your air fryer. 4. Use the timer (+ / − Time) arrow keys to adjust the cooking time to 5 minutes. 5. Adjust its cooking temperature to 380 degrees F, using the temp (+/- Temp) arrow keys. 6. Press the Start button to initiate preheating. 7. Transfer the baking pan to the rack of the air fryer when the screen displays "Add Food." 8. Close its door, and let the machine do the cooking. 9. Serve and enjoy.

Per serving: Calories 90; Fat 7g; Sodium 329mg; Carbs 2g; Sugar 1g; Fiber 0.7g; Protein 5 g

Scrambled Eggs

Prep time: 5 minutes | Cook time: 7 minutes | Serves: 4

4 large eggs.	2 tablespoons unsalted butter; melted.
½ cup shredded sharp Cheddar cheese.	

1. Crack eggs into a 2-cup round baking dish and whisk. 2. Select the "Air Fry" mode on your air fryer. 3. Use the timer (+ / − Time) arrow keys to adjust the cooking time to 5 minutes. 4. Adjust its cooking temperature to 400 degrees F, using the temp (+/- Temp) arrow keys. 5. Press the Start button to initiate preheating. 6. Transfer the baking pan to the rack of the air fryer when the screen displays "Add Food." 7. Close its door, and let the machine do the cooking. 8. After 5 minutes, stir the eggs and add the butter and cheese. 9. Allow eggs to finish cooking for an additional 2 minutes or remove if they are to your desired liking. 10. Use a fork to fluff. 11. Serve warm.

Per serving: Calories 359; Fat 27.6g; Sodium 309mg; Carbs 1.1g; Sugar 0.5g; Fiber 0.7g; Protein 19.5g

Mushrooms Spread

Prep time: 5 minutes | Cook time: 20 minutes | Serves: 4

¼ cup mozzarella cheese; shredded	A pinch of salt and black pepper
½ cup coconut cream	Cooking spray
1 cup white mushrooms	

1. Put the mushrooms in a cooking tray, and grease with cooking spray. 2. Select the "Air Fry" mode on your air fryer. 3. Use the timer (+ / − Time) arrow keys to adjust the cooking time to 20 minutes. 4. Adjust its cooking temperature to 370 degrees F, using the temp (+/- Temp) arrow keys. 5. Press the start button to initiate preheating. 6. Transfer the baking pan to the rack of the air fryer when the screen displays "Add Food." 7. Close its door, and let the machine do the cooking. 8. Transfer to a blender, add the remaining ingredients, pulse well, divide into bowls and serve.

Per serving: Calories 202; Fat 12g; Sodium 244mg; Carbs 5g; Fiber; Sugars 1.3g; Protein 7g

Fennel Frittata with Cilantro

Prep time: 5 minutes | Cook time: 15 minutes | Serves: 6

1 fennel bulb; shredded	Cooking spray
6 eggs; whisked	A pinch of salt and black pepper
2 teaspoons cilantro; chopped.	
1 teaspoon sweet paprika	

1. Take a bowl and mix all the ingredients, except for the cooking spray and stir well. 2. Grease a baking pan with the cooking spray, pour the frittata mix, and spread well. 3. Select the "Air Fry" mode on your air fryer. 4. Use the timer (+ / − Time) arrow keys to adjust the cooking time to 15 minutes. 5. Adjust its cooking temperature to 370 degrees F, using the temp (+/- Temp) arrow keys. 6. Press the Start button to initiate preheating. 7. Transfer the baking pan to the rack of the air fryer when the screen displays "Add Food." 8. Close its door, and let the machine do the cooking. 9. Divide between plates and serve them for breakfast.

Per serving: Calories 200; Fat 12g; Fiber 1g; Sodium 521mg; Carbs 5g; Sugar 1.1g; Fiber 0.7g; Protein 8g

Vanilla Strawberries Oatmeal

Prep time: 5 minutes | Cook time: 15 minutes | Serves: 4

½ cup coconut; shredded	¼ teaspoon vanilla extract
¼ cup strawberries	2 teaspoons stevia
2 cups coconut milk	Cooking spray

1. Grease a baking pan with the cooking tray, add all ingredients, and toss. 2. Select the "Air Fry" mode on your air fryer. 3. Use the timer (+ / − Time) arrow keys to adjust the cooking time to 15 minutes. 4. Adjust its cooking temperature to 365 degrees F, using the temp (+/- Temp) arrow keys. 5. Press the Start button to initiate preheating. 6. Transfer the baking pan to the rack of the air fryer when the screen displays "Add Food." 7. Close its door, and let the machine do the cooking. 8. Serve.

Per serving: Calories 142; Fat 7g; Fiber 2g; Sodium 214mg; Carbs 3g; Sugar 1.2g; Fiber 0.7g; Protein 5g

Zucchini Squash Mix with Parsley

Prep time: 10 minutes | Cook time: 35 minutes | Serves: 4

1-pound zucchini, sliced	1 tablespoon olive oil
1 tablespoon parsley, chopped	Pepper, to taste
1 yellow squash, halved, deseeded, and chopped	Salt, to taste

1. Add all ingredients into the large bowl and mix well. 2. Transfer the bowl mixture to the baking pan. 3. Select the "Air Fry" mode on your air fryer. 4. Use the timer (+ / − Time) arrow keys to adjust the cooking time to 35 minutes. 5. Adjust its cooking temperature to 400 degrees F, using the temp (+/- Temp) arrow keys. 6. Press the Start button to initiate preheating. 7. Transfer the baking pan to the rack of the air fryer when the screen displays "Add Food." 8. Close its door, and let the machine do the cooking. 9. Serve and enjoy.

Per serving: Calories 49; Fat 3g; Sodium 344g; Carbs 4g; Sugar 2g; Fiber 0.7g; Protein 1.5 g

Arugula Asparagus Salad

Prep time: 5 minutes | Cook time: 10 minutes | Serves: 4

1 cup baby arugula	grated
1 bunch asparagus; trimmed	A pinch of salt and black pepper
1 tablespoon balsamic vinegar	
1 tablespoon cheddar cheese;	Cooking spray

1. Put the asparagus in a baking pan, greased with cooking spray, and season with salt and black pepper. 2. Select the "Air Fry" mode on your air fryer. 3. Use the timer (+ / − Time) arrow keys to adjust the cooking time to 10 minutes. 4. Adjust its cooking temperature to 360 degrees F, using the temp (+/- Temp) arrow keys. 5. Press the Start button to initiate preheating. 6. Transfer the baking pan to the rack of the air fryer when the screen displays "Add Food." 7. Close its door, and let the machine do the cooking. 8. Take a bowl and mix the asparagus with the arugula and the vinegar, toss, divide between plates and serve hot with cheese sprinkled on top.

Per serving: Calories 200; Fat 5g; Sodium 168mg; Carbs 4g; Sugar 0.4g; Fiber 0.7g; Protein 5g

Lemony Raspberries Bowls

Prep time: 5 minutes | Cook time: 12 minutes | Serves: 2

1 cup raspberries	2 tablespoons lemon juice
2 tablespoons butter	1 teaspoon cinnamon powder

1. Mix all the ingredients in a baking pan, and cover. 2. Select the "Air Fry" mode on your air fryer. 3. Use the timer (+ / − Time) arrow keys to adjust the cooking time to 12 minutes. 4. Adjust its cooking temperature to 350 degrees F, using the temp (+/- Temp) arrow keys. 5. Press the Start button to initiate preheating. 6. Transfer the baking pan to the rack of the air fryer when the screen displays "Add Food." 7. Close its door, and let the machine do the cooking. 8. Serve.

Per serving: Calories 208; Fat 6g; Sodium 355mg; Carbs 14g; Fiber 9g; Sugars 1.3g; Protein 3g

Zucchini Cheese Fritters

Prep time: 15 minutes | Cook time: 7 minutes | Serves: 4

10½ ounces zucchini, grated and squeezed	2 eggs
7 ounces Halloumi cheese	1 teaspoon fresh dill, minced
¼ cup all-purpose flour	Salt and ground black pepper to taste

1. In a large bowl and mix all the ingredients. 2. Make a small-sized fritter from the mixture. 3. Select the "Air Fry" mode on your air fryer. 4. Use the timer (+ / − Time) arrow keys to adjust the cooking time to 7 minutes. 5. Adjust its cooking temperature to 355 degrees F, using the temp (+/- Temp) arrow keys. 6. Press the Start button to initiate preheating. 7. Transfer the fritters to the rack of the air fryer when the screen displays "Add Food." 8. Close its door, and let the machine do the cooking. 9. Serve warm.

Per serving: Calories 253; Fat 17.2g; Sodium 333 mg; Carbs 10g; Fiber 1.1g; Sugar 2.7g; Protein 15.2 g

Cheddar Onion Omelet

Prep time: 10 minutes | Cook time: 15 minutes | Serves: 4

4 eggs	
¼ teaspoon low-sodium soy sauce	1 medium yellow onion, sliced
Ground black pepper to taste	¼ cup Cheddar cheese, grated
1 teaspoon butter	

1. In a skillet, melt the butter over medium heat, cook the onion, and cook for about 8-10 minutes. 2. Remove from the heat and set aside to cool slightly. 3. Meanwhile, in a bowl, add the eggs, soy sauce, and black pepper and beat well. 4. Add the cooked onion and gently stir to combine. 5. Place the zucchini mixture into a small baking pan. 6. Select the "Air Fry" mode on your air fryer. 7. Use the timer (+ / − Time) arrow keys to adjust the cooking time to 5 minutes. 8. Adjust its cooking temperature to 355 degrees F using the temp (+/- Temp) arrow keys. 9. Press the Start button to initiate preheating. 10. Transfer the baking pan to the rack of the air fryer when the screen displays "Add Food." 11. Close its door, and let the machine do the cooking.

12. Cut the omelet into two portions and serve hot.

Per serving: Calories 222; Fat 15.4g; Sodium 264 mg; Carbs 6.1g; Fiber 1.2g; Sugar 3.1g; Protein 15.3 g

Chapter 2 Poultry

Cheese Farrita and Chicken

Prep time: 25 minutes | Cook time: 20 minutes | Serves: 4

1 (1-pound) fillet chicken breast	4 eggs
Sea salt to taste	½ teaspoon cayenne pepper
ground black pepper to taste	½ cup Mascarpone cream
1 tablespoon olive oil	¼ cup Asiago cheese, freshly grated

1. Using a meat mallet, flatten the chicken breast. Salt & pepper to taste. 2. In a cooking tray, heat the olive oil over medium heat. 3. Select the Air Fry function. Set timer to 12 minutes and temperature to 400 degrees F. 4. Cook for 10 to 12 minutes, then slice into tiny pieces and set aside. 5. Then, in a mixing bowl, whisk the eggs and cayenne pepper until thoroughly combined; season with salt to taste. 6. Stir in the cheese until everything is well combined. 7. Return the chicken to the pan. After that, pour the mixture into a lightly oiled pan and place it in the cooking basket. 8. Cook for 10 minutes at 355 degrees F in a preheated air fryer, turning halfway through.

Per serving: Calories 329; Fat 25.3g; Sodium 220mg; Carbs 3.4g; Fiber 1g; Sugar 2.3g; Protein 21.1g

Parmesan Chicken Breast

Prep time: 3 minutes | Cook time: 12 minutes | Serves: 4

2 eggs	breast halves
½ cup Parmesan cheese, grated	2 sprigs rosemary, chopped
1 cup seasoned bread crumbs	Salt and ground black pepper to taste
1 pound (454 g) chicken	

1. Heat the air fryer to 400 degrees F ahead of time. Using cooking spray, spray the cooking tray. 2. In a separate dish, beat the egg and season with salt and black pepper. In the second bowl, combine the Parmesan and bread crumbs. 3. Dredge the chicken in the first basin to thoroughly coat it, then shake off the excess in the second bowl. 4. Select Air Fry function. Set timer to 12 minutes and temperature to 400 degrees F. Cook the chicken for 12 minutes in a preheated air fryer or until the internal temperature reaches 165 degrees F (74°C). Halfway through the cooking time, flip the chicken. 5. Place the chicken on a dish and garnish it with rosemary.

Per serving: Calories 430; Fat 25g; Sodium 335mg; Carbs 21.5g; Fiber 5g; Sugar 5.4g; Protein 48g

Easy Chicken Paprika

Prep time: 7 minutes | Cook time: 18 minutes | Serves: 4

4 chicken breasts	chopped
1 tablespoon paprika	Salt and ground black pepper to taste
¼ teaspoon garlic powder	
2 tablespoons fresh thyme,	2 tablespoons butter, melted

1. Heat the air fryer to 400 degrees F in advance. Using cooking spray, spray the cooking tray. 2. Rub the chicken breasts with paprika, garlic powder, salt, and black pepper on a clean work surface, then brush with butter. 3. Select the Air Fry function. Set timer to 18 minutes and temperature to 400 degrees F. 4. Cook the chicken for 18 minutes until the internal temperature reaches 165 degrees F (74°C). Halfway through

the cooking time, flip the chicken using tongs. 5. Serve the cooked chicken on a platter garnished with thyme.

Per serving: Calories 368; Fat 14.1g; Sodium 420mg; Carbs 2.3g; Fiber 1g; Sugar 1g; Protein 57.9g

Stuffed Chicken Breasts

Prep time: 3 minutes | Cook time: 12 minutes | Serves: 4

1 cup spinach, chopped	ing
4 tablespoons cottage cheese	Juice of ½ lime
2 chicken breasts	2 or 4 toothpicks, soaked for
2 tablespoons Italian season-	at least 30 minutes

1. Heat the air fryer to 400 degrees F in advance. Using cooking spray, spray the cooking tray. 2. In a large mixing basin, combine the chopped spinach and cheese. Remove from the equation. 3. Flatten the chicken breasts with a rolling pin after butterflying them. Wrap the spinach and cheese mixture in the butterflied chicken breasts and season with Italian seasoning. Toothpicks are used to keep everything together. 4. Spray the chicken with cooking spray and place it on the cooking tray. 5. Select Air Fry function. Set time to 12 minutes and temperature to 400 degrees F. 6. Cook for 12 minutes until the internal temperature reaches 165 degrees F (74 degrees Celsius). Halfway through the cooking time, flip the chicken. 7. Take the chicken out of the cooking tray and set it aside. Remove the toothpicks and sprinkle with lemon juice before serving.

Per serving: Calories 248; Fat 11g; Sodium 370mg; Carbs 4.1g; Fiber 1g; Sugar 1g; Protein 31g

Spiced Bacon-Wrapped Chicken

Prep time: 5 minutes | Cook time: 15 minutes | Serves: 4

2 chicken breasts	Juice from ½ lemon
8 ounces (227 g) onion and	1 tablespoon butter
chive cream cheese	Salt to taste
6 slices of turkey bacon	2 or 4 toothpicks, soaked for
1 tablespoon fresh parsley, chopped	at least 30 minutes

1. Preheat the air fryer to 380 degrees F. Using cooking spray, spray the cooking tray. 2. Brush both sides of the chicken breasts with cream cheese and butter on a clean work surface. Season with salt. 3. Wrap three pieces of bacon around each chicken breast and fasten with 1 or 2 toothpicks. 4. Select the Roast function. Set timer to 14 minutes and temperature to 380 degrees F. 5. Cook the bacon-wrapped chicken for 14 minutes in a preheated air fryer, or until the bacon is nicely browned and a meat thermometer placed in the chicken reads at least 165 degrees F (74 C). Halfway through the cooking time, flip them. 6. Take them out of the cooking tray and garnish them with parsley and lemon juice.

Per serving: Calories 437; Fat 28.6g; Sodium 450mg; Carbs 5.2g; Fiber 1g; Sugar 1.2g; Protein 39.8g

Texas Chicken Thighs

Prep time: 10 minutes | Cook time: 20 minutes | Serves: 8

8 chicken thighs	chopped
2 teaspoons Texas BBQ Jerky	1 tablespoon olive oil
seasoning	Salt and ground black pepper
2 tablespoons cilantro,	to taste

1. Preheat the air fryer to 380 degrees F (193 degrees Celsius). Using cooking spray, spray the cooking tray. 2. Place the chicken thighs in the cooking tray and brush all sides with olive oil. BBQ seasoning, salt, and black pepper to taste. 3. Select Air Fry function. Set time to 20 minutes and temperature to 400 degrees F. 4. Cook for 20 minutes, or until the thighs achieve an internal temperature of 165 degrees F (74°C). During the cooking period, flip the thighs three times. 5. Remove the chicken thighs from the cooking tray and garnish them with cilantro.
Per serving: Calories 444; Fat 33.8g; Sodium 540mg; Carbs 1g; Fiber 0g; Sugar 0g; Protein 31.9g

Roasted Spicy Chicken

Prep time: 10 minutes | Cook time: 40 minutes | Serves: 4

1 (3 pound / 1.4 kg) chicken,	1 lemon, cut into wedges
rinsed and patted dry	2 tablespoons butter, melted
1 garlic bulb	Salt and ground black pepper
1 sprig of fresh tarragon	to taste

1. Preheat the air fryer to 380 degrees F (193 degrees Celsius). Using cooking spray, spray the cooking tray. 2. Brush the chicken with butter and season with salt and black pepper on a clean work surface. Garlic, tarragon, and lemon wedges should be stuffed into the chicken. 3. Place the chicken in the cooking tray and select Roast function, and set the timer to 40 minutes and temperature to 380 degrees F; then roast for 40 minutes, or until an instant-read thermometer inserted in the thickest section of the chicken registers at least 165 degrees F (74 degrees Celsius). 4. Place the chicken on a big plate after removing it from the tray. To serve, carve the chicken and slice it.
Per serving: Calories 440; Fat 15g; Sodium 440mg; Carbs 2.6g; Fiber 1g; Sugar 1g; Protein 69.7g

Chicken Thighs with Marina Sauce

Prep time: 10 minutes | Cook time: 10 minutes | Serves: 4

2 tablespoons grated Parmesan cheese	Jack cheese
	½ cup marinara sauce
½ cup Italian bread crumbs	From the Cupboard:
4 chicken thighs	1 tablespoon butter, melted
½ cup shredded Monterrey	

1. Heat the air fryer to 400 degrees F in advance. Using cooking spray, spray the cooking tray. 2. In a mixing dish, combine the Parmesan and bread crumbs. 3. Brush the chicken thighs with butter on a clean work surface, then coat them with the Parmesan mixture. 4. Select Air Fry function. Set timer to 10 minutes and temperature to 400 degrees F. 5. Cook for 5 minutes in a hot air fryer, then top with Monterrey Jack cheese and marinara sauce and cook for another 4 minutes until the thighs are golden brown and the cheese has melted. 6. Place the thighs on a platter and serve immediately.
Per serving: Calories 617; Fat 42.1g; Sodium 540mg; Carbs 17.7g; Fiber 3.1g; Sugar 1.9g; Protein 39.6g

Chicken Thighs with Honey Dijon Sauce

Prep time: 5 minutes | Cook time: 25 minutes | Serves: 4

8 bone-in and skinless chicken	¼ cup Dijon mustard
thighs	2 garlic cloves, minced
Chicken seasoning or rub to	Salt and ground black pepper
taste	to taste
½ cup honey	

1. Heat the air fryer to 400 degrees F in advance (205 degrees Celsius). Using cooking spray, spray the cooking tray. 2. Rub the chicken thighs with chicken seasoning, salt, and black pepper on a clean work surface. 3. Select Air Fry function. Set timer to 15 minutes and temperature to 400 degrees F. 4. Cook the chicken thighs for 15 minutes in a preheated air fryer or until they reach an internal temperature of 165 degrees F (74°C). Halfway through the cooking time, flip the thighs. To minimize congestion, you may need to work in bunches. 5. Meanwhile, mix the honey, Dijon mustard, and garlic in a saucepan and simmer for 3 to 4 minutes over medium-high heat until the sauce is reduced by one-third. 6. Throughout the cooking process, keep stirring. 7. Remove the chicken thighs from the cooking tray and put them on a dish. 8. Baste the thighs with the cooked sauce and serve warm.
Per serving: Calories 382; Fat 18g; Sodium 470mg; Carbs 36g; Fiber 7g; Sugar 7.5g; Protein 21g

Honey-Glazed Cornish Game Hen

Prep time: 10 minutes | Cook time: 20 minutes | Serves: 2

1 (2 pound/907g) Cornish	thyme leaves
game hen, split in half	1 tablespoon olive oil
¼ teaspoon dried thyme	Salt and ground black pepper
Juice and zest of 1 lemon	to taste
¼ cup honey	½ teaspoon soy sauce
1½ teaspoon chopped fresh	

1. Heat the air fryer to 400 degrees F in advance. Using cooking spray, spray the cooking tray. 2. Brush the game hen halves with olive oil on a clean work surface, then season with dried thyme, salt, and black pepper. 3. Select Air Fry function. Set timer to 20 minutes and temperature to 400 degrees F. 4. Cook for 15 minutes in a preheated air fryer or until the hen is gently browned. Halfway through, flip the hen. 5. In a separate bowl, combine the lemon juice, zest, honey, thyme leaves, soy sauce, and black pepper. 6. Cook for another 4 minutes, or until the game hen is thoroughly glazed and a meat thermometer in the bird reads at least 165 degrees F (74 degrees C). 7. Remove the game hen from the cooking tray. Allow to cool for a few minutes and slice to serve.
Per serving: Calories 724; Fat 22g; Sodium 680mg; Carbs 37.5g; Fiber 5g; Sugar 6.9g; Protein 91.3g

Chicken Stuffed with Spinach

Prep time: 20 minutes | Cook time: 25 minutes | Serves: 4

1 (10 ounce/284g) package	Salt and ground black pepper
frozen spinach, thawed and	to taste
drained well	Special Equipment:
1 cup feta cheese, crumbled	4 or 8 toothpicks, soaked for
4 boneless chicken breasts	at least 30 minutes

1. Heat the air fryer to 400 degrees F in advance. Using cooking spray, spray the cooking tray. 2. To make the filling, follow these steps: Chop the spinach and combine it with the feta cheese and 12 teaspoons of ground black pepper in a large mixing dish. Stir everything together thoroughly. 3. Cut

a 1-inch horizontal incision on the thicker side of each chicken breast on a clean work surface using a knife. Make a 3-inch long pocket from the incision, keeping the sides and bottom intact. 4. Using 1 or 2 toothpicks, secure the chicken pockets with the filling. 5. Place the filled chicken breasts in the air fryer that has been warmed. Spritz with cooking spray and season with salt and black pepper. To minimize congestion, you may need to work in bunches. 6. Select Air Fry function. Set timer to 12 minutes and temperature to 400 degrees F. 7. Cook chicken for 12 minutes in the air fryer or until the chicken reaches an internal temperature of 165 degrees F (74°C). Halfway through the cooking time, flip the chicken. 8. Take the chicken out of the cooking tray and set it aside. Remove the toothpicks and set them aside to cool for 10 minutes before serving.

Per serving: Calories 648; Fat 38.7g; Sodium 440mg; Carbs 4.5g; Fiber 1g; Sugar 1g; Protein 68.2g

Dijon Turkey Sandwich

Prep time: 5 minutes | Cook time: 5 minutes | Serves: 1

2 slices of whole-grain bread	cheese
2 teaspoons Dijon mustard	3 strips roasted red bell pepper
2 ounces (57 g) cooked turkey breast, thinly sliced	Salt and ground black pepper to taste
2 slices of low-fat Swiss	

1. At 400 degrees F, preheat the air fryer. Using cooking spray, spray the cooking tray. 2. Assemble the sandwich: Place a slice of bread on a plate, then spread 1 teaspoon of Dijon mustard evenly over the bread with a knife. 3. Using your chosen arrangement, layer the turkey, Swiss cheese slices, and red pepper strips on the toast. Add the remaining teaspoon of Dijon mustard and the last slice of bread. 4. Spray the sandwich with cooking spray and place it in the preheated air fryer. Season the sandwich with salt and black pepper to taste. 5. Select the Air Fry function. Set timer to 5 minutes and temperature to 400 degrees F, then cook for 5 minutes, or until the cheese has melted and the bread has browned somewhat. Halfway through the cooking time, flip the sandwich. 6. Serve the sandwich as soon as possible.

Per serving: Calories 328; Fat 5g; Sodium 470mg; Carbs 38g; Fiber 5.7g; Sugar 4.9g; Protein 29g

Spicy Turkey Breast

Prep time: 5 minutes | Cook time: 40 minutes | Serves: 4

2-pound (907 g) turkey breast	1 teaspoon red pepper flakes
2 teaspoon taco seasonings	Salt and ground black pepper to taste
1 teaspoon ground cumin	

1. Heat the air fryer to 400 degrees F in advance. Spray the cooking tray. 2. Rub the turkey breast with taco seasoning, ground cumin, red pepper flakes, salt, and black pepper on a clean work surface. 3. Select Air Fry function. Set timer to 40 minutes and temperature to 400 degrees F. 4. Place the turkey in the preheated air fryer and cook for 40 minutes, or until the internal temperature of the turkey reaches 165 degrees F (74 degrees C). 5. Halfway through the cooking time, flip the turkey breast. 6. Take the turkey out of the tray and set it aside. Allow 15 minutes to cool before slicing to serve.

Per serving: Calories 235; Fat 5.6g; Sodium 444mg; Carbs 6.6g; Fiber 1g; Sugar 1.4g; Protein 37.3g

Chicken and Pepper Kabobs

Prep time: 1 hour and 5 minutes | Cook time: 15-20 minutes | Serves: 4

⅓ cup raw honey	diced
2 tablespoons sesame seeds	⅓ cup soy sauce
2 boneless chicken breasts, cut into cubes	Salt and ground black pepper to taste
6 white mushrooms, cut in halves	4 wooden skewers, soaked for at least 30 minutes
3 green or red bell peppers,	

1. Mix the honey, soy sauce, sesame seeds, salt, and black pepper in a large mixing bowl. Stir everything together thoroughly. 2. Place the chicken cubes in this bowl, cover with plastic wrap, and refrigerate for at least an hour to marinate. 3. Preheat the air fryer to 400 degrees F. Spray the cooking tray. 4. Remove the chicken cubes from the marinade and alternately thread the skewers through the chicken, mushrooms, and bell peppers. 5. Place the chicken, mushrooms, and bell peppers in the preheated air fryer and baste them with the marinade. 6. Select Air Fry function. Set timer to 20 minutes and temperature to 400 degrees F. 7. Cook for 15 to 20 minutes, or until the mushrooms and bell peppers are soft and the chicken cubes are nicely browned, after spraying them with cooking spray. Halfway through the cooking time, flip them. 8. Place the skewers on a large dish and serve immediately.

Per serving: Calories 380; Fat 16g; Sodium 560mg; Carbs 26.1g; Fiber 3g; Sugar 3.6g; Protein 34g

Zucchini Chicken Cubes

Prep time: 30 minutes | Cook time: 20 minutes | Serves: 6

¼ cup olive oil	2 chicken breast fillets, sliced into cubes
1 tablespoon lemon juice	
2 tablespoons red wine vinegar	1 zucchini, sliced
1 teaspoon oregano	1 red onion, sliced
1 tablespoon garlic, chopped	1 cup cherry tomatoes, sliced
	Salt and pepper to taste

1. Combine the olive oil, lemon juice, vinegar, oregano, and garlic in a mixing bowl. 2. Pour half the mixture into another bowl, and toss another half with the chicken. Cover and set aside for 15 minutes to marinate. 3. Toss the vegetables with the remaining ingredients. 4. Season the chicken and the vegetables with salt and pepper. 5. In the cooking tray, place the chicken. 6. Arrange the vegetables on top. 7. Select the Air Fry function. Set time to 20 minutes and temperature 400 degrees F. 8. Cook for 20 minutes.

Per serving: Calories 281; Fat 19.04g; Sodium 340mg; Carbs 5.31g; Fiber 1g; Sugar 1g; Protein 21.87g

Air Fried Chicken Wings with Buffalo Sauce

Prep time: 15 minutes | Cook time: 30 minutes | Serves: 4

2 pound. chicken wings	½ cup Buffalo sauce
2 tablespoon oil	

1. Using a brush, coat the chicken wings in oil. 2. Place in a cooking tray. 3. Select the Air Fry function. Set timer to 30 minutes and temperature to 400 degrees F. 4. Cook for 15 minutes. Cook for another 15 minutes after shaking. 5. Before serving, coat in Buffalo sauce.

Per serving: Calories 376; Fat 16.4g; Sodium 343mg; Carbs 2.18g; Fiber 0.1g; Sugar 0.1g; Protein 51.93g

Spicy Chicken Breast Fillets

Prep time: 15 minutes | Cook time: 50 minutes | Serves: 4

4 chicken breast fillets
2 tablespoons vegetable oil

Salt and pepper to taste
1 cup barbecue sauce

1. In the air fryer, select the Bake function. 2. Preheat the air fryer to 365 degrees F for 25 minutes. 3. Start by pressing the Start button. 4. Using a brush, coat the chicken breasts in oil. 5. Season it with salt and pepper on both sides. 6. Set timer to 30 minutes and temperature to 365 degrees F. 7. Cook for 10 minutes after adding the chicken. 8. Cook for another 10 minutes on the other side. 9. Brush the barbecue sauce on the chicken. 10. Cook for 5 minutes in the air fryer. 11. Cook for another 5 minutes after brushing the other side.
Per serving: Calories 707; Fat 35.61g; Sodium 540mg; Carbs 30.21g; Fiber 3.6g; Sugar 5.4g; Protein 62.88g

Baked Chicken with Cabbage and Potatoes

Prep time: 30 minutes | Cook time: 40 minutes | Serves: 8

1 cup apple cider vinegar
2 pounds of chicken thigh fillets
6 oz. barbecue sauce

2 pounds' cabbage, sliced into wedges and steamed
1 pound of potatoes, roasted
Salt and pepper to taste

1. Place the chicken on the cooking tray. 2. Season it with salt and pepper on both sides. 3. Select the Bake function. Set timer to 40 minutes and temperature to 365 degrees F. 4. Bake the chicken thigh fillets for 15 to 20 minutes per side. 5. Brush the barbecue sauce all over the chicken. 6. Serve the chicken with potatoes and cabbage as a side dish.
Per serving: Calories 385; Fat 19.97g; Sodium 340mg; Carbs 28.03g; Fiber 5.1g; Sugar 7.5g; Protein 22.59g

Chicken Glazed with Honey and Soy Sauce

Prep time: 15 minutes | Cook time: 45 minutes | Serves: 8

1 tablespoon olive oil
½ tablespoon apple cider vinegar
3 teaspoons garlic, minced

1 tablespoon honey
¼ cup light brown sugar
⅓ cup soy sauce
8 chicken thigh fillets

1. Except for the chicken, combine all ingredients in a mixing bowl. 2. Save ¼ cup of the mixture for later use. 3. Marinate the chicken for 30 minutes in the remaining mixture. 4. To your air fryer, add a cooking tray. 5. Press the Bake button. 6. Set the timer for 25 minutes. 7. Set temp to 365 degrees F. 8. Place the chicken on the tray. 9. Pull the hood over your head. 10. Cook for 10 minutes before serving. 11. Cook for another 5 minutes on the other side. 12. Brush the remaining mixture on top. 13. Cook for an additional 5 minutes.
Per serving: Calories 518; Fat 36.41g; Sodium 540mg; Carbs 12.36g; Fiber 4g; Sugar 3.75g; Protein 33.52g

Parmesan Turkey Meatballs

Prep time: 10 minutes | Cook time: 13 minutes | Serves: 4

2 pounds' lean ground turkey
¼ cup onion, minced
2 cloves garlic, minced
2 tablespoons parsley, chopped
2 eggs

1½ cup parmesan cheese, grated
½ teaspoon red pepper flakes
½ teaspoon Italian seasoning
Salt and black pepper to taste

1. In a mixing basin, combine all meatball ingredients and stir thoroughly. Make tiny meatballs with the ingredients and cook them on a cooking tray. 2. Choose the "Air Fry" mode, and press the +/- Time arrows to adjust the cooking time to 13 minutes. To adjust the temperature, press the +/- Temp arrows to set the temperature to 400 degrees F. 3. Place the cooking tray into the preheated air fryer and close the door. 4. When the meatballs are halfway done, flip them. Serve warm.
Per serving: Calories 472; Fat 25.8g; Sodium 550mg; Carbs 1.7g; Fiber 0.1g; Sugar 0.1g; Protein 59.6g

Herbed Chicken Thighs with Onion

Prep time: 10 minutes | Cook time: 35 minutes | Serves: 8

2 tablespoons unsalted butter
1 medium yellow onion (to be peeled and chopped)
½ pound poblano peppers (to be seeded and roughly chopped)
½ pound Anaheim peppers (to be seeded and roughly chopped)
½ pound tomatillos (to be husked and quartered)
2 small jalapeño peppers (to be seeded and roughly

chopped)
2 garlic cloves (to be peeled and minced)
1 teaspoon. ground cumin
6 bone-in, skin-on chicken thighs (2 ½ pounds in total)
2 cups chicken stock
2 cups water
⅓ cup roughly chopped fresh cilantro
3 cans Great Northern beans (to be drained and rinsed, 15 oz. cans)

1. When the air fryer is heated, press the "Broil" button and add butter to melt. When the butter has melted, add the onion and simmer for 3 minutes, or until it has softened. 2. Toss in the poblano and Anaheim peppers, followed by the tomatillos and jalapeño. Cook for another 3 minutes before adding the garlic and cumin. 3. Select the Broil option. Set the timer for 30 minutes and the temperature to 400 degrees F after adding the thighs, stock, and water to the saucepan. 4. Transfer the chicken to a chopping board after the cooking time. Shred the meat with two forks after gently removing the skin. 5. Purée the sauce in a blender until smoothened. 6. Serve warm with the meat, cilantro, and beans.
Per serving: Calories 304; Fat 10g; Sodium 240mg; Carbs 19g; Fiber 1.9g; Sugar 2.75g; Protein 33g

Super Spicy Chicken Wings

Prep time: 10 minutes | Cook time: 45 minutes | Serves: 8

½ teaspoon celery salt
½ teaspoon bay leaf powder
½ teaspoon ground black pepper
½ teaspoon paprika

¼ teaspoon dry mustard
¼ teaspoon cayenne pepper
¼ teaspoon allspice
2 pounds of chicken wings

1. Heat the air fryer to 400 degrees F in advance, and grease the cooking tray. Celery salt, bay leaf powder, black pepper, paprika, dry mustard, cayenne pepper, and allspice are combined in a basin. Coat the wings with this mixture thoroughly. 2. In the cooking tray, arrange the wings in an equal layer. 3. Select Air Fry function. Set timer to 36 minutes and temperature to 400 degrees F. 4. Cook for 30 minutes until the chicken is no longer pink around the bone, then cook for another 6 minutes, or until crispy on the exterior.
Per serving: Calories 332; Fat 10.1g; Sodium 720mg; Carbs 31.3g; Fiber 1.9g; Sugar 2.57g; Protein 12g

Sesame-Glazed Chicken Wings

Prep time: 10 minutes | Cook time: 40 minutes | Serves: 4

1-pound chicken wings
1 cup soy sauce, divided

½ cup brown sugar
½ cup apple cider vinegar

2 tablespoons fresh ginger, minced	pepper
2 tablespoons fresh garlic, minced	2 tablespoons cornstarch
1 teaspoon finely ground black	2 tablespoons cold water
	1 teaspoon sesame seeds

1. Pour half a cup of soy sauce into a dish with chicken wings. Refrigerate for 20 minutes; remove from refrigerator and pat dry. 2. Select Air Fry function. Set the timer to 30 minutes and temp 400 degrees F. Cook the wings in the air fryer for 30 minutes, rotating halfway through. To avoid overcooking, make sure to check them towards the finish. 3. Stir sugar, half cup soy sauce, vinegar, ginger, garlic, and black pepper in a pan over medium heat. 4. Select Air Fry function. Set timer to 6 minutes and temp 400 degrees F. 5. Cook for 4 to 6 minutes, or until the sauce has somewhat reduced. 6. In a bowl, dissolve 2 tablespoons of cornstarch in cold water, then whisk the slurry into the sauce until it thickens, about 2 minutes. 7. Drizzle the sauce over the wings and top with sesame seeds.

Per serving: Calories 413; Fat 8.3g; Sodium 670mg; Carbs 7g; Fiber 1g; Sugar 1.3g; Protein 8.3g

Simple Roasted Turkey Breast

Prep time: 6 minutes | Cook time: 60 minutes | Serves: 10

4 pounds' turkey breast, with skin on the bone (ribs removed)	1 tablespoon olive oil
	2 teaspoons kosher Seasoning

1. Rub ½ tablespoon of oil all over the turkey breast. Season with salt and turkey seasoning on all sides, then brush with the remaining half a tablespoon of oil on the skin side. 2. Preheat the air fryer to 380 degrees F, select Roast function, and set time to 60 minutes and temperature to 380 degrees F. 3. Cook the skin side down for 20 minutes, then flip and cook for another 30 to 40 minutes, depending on the breast size, until the internal temperature reaches 160 degrees F, using an instant-read thermometer. 4. Take a ten-minute break before serving.

Per serving: Calories 226; Fat 10g; Sodium 470mg; Carbs 1g; Fiber 0g; Sugar 0g; Protein 4g

Spicy Roasted Chicken

Prep time: 30 minutes | Cook time: 1 hour and 10 minutes | Serves: 6

1 whole chicken	2 tablespoons butter
½ teaspoon onion powder	¼ cup flour
1 teaspoon garlic powder	2 cups chicken broth
1 teaspoon paprika	Basting Butter
Salt and pepper to taste	2 tablespoons butter
2 drops of liquid smoke	Dash garlic powder
1 cup water	

1. Combine onion powder, garlic powder, paprika, salt, and pepper in a mixing bowl. 2. In the cooking tray, place the chicken. 3. Combine liquid smoke and butter in a mixing bowl. 4. Pour into your air fryer's cooking tray. 5. Select Air Fry and set the timer to 45 minutes with temp 400 degrees F. 6. Cook for 45 minutes. 7. Drain out all the water. 8. Butter the chicken and dust it with flour. 9. Select Air Fry function. Set timer to 15 minutes and temperature to 400 degrees F. 10. Cook the chicken for 15 minutes in the air fryer. 11. Baste with a combination of the ingredients for the basting butter. 12. Cook for an additional ten minutes.

Per serving: Calories 410; Fat 18.64g; Sodium 730mg; Carbs 6.05g; Fiber 1g; Sugar 1.4g; Protein 51.61g

Turkey Breast with Lemon and Pepper

Prep time: 6 minutes | Cook time: 60 minutes | Serves: 6

3 pounds uncooked turkey breast de-boned	sauce
2 teaspoons of oil	1 teaspoon of lemon pepper or herb-dried seasoning
1 tablespoon Worcestershire	½ teaspoon salt, or for taste

1. Dry the turkey with a paper towel. 2. Combine Worcestershire sauce, oil, lemon pepper or spices, and salt in a cup or plastic bag. Place the turkey breast in a marinade and make sure it is completely covered. If required, marinate for 1-2 hours. 3. An air fryer's basket should be lightly oiled. Take the turkey breast out of the marinade and lay it on the cooking tray. 4. Select Air Fry function. Set time to 60 minutes and temperature to 400 degrees F. 5. Cook for 25 minutes. Flip the turkey breast over to the skin side and continue to Air Fry for another 25-35 minutes, or until the interior turkey temperature in the thickest portion reaches 165° F. 6. Cook bone-in turkey breast for an estimated 5-10 minutes if feasible.

Per serving: Calories 400; Fat 21g; Sodium 210mg; Carbs 1g; Fiber 0g; Sugar 0g; Protein 50g

Parmesan Chicken Meatballs

Prep time: 7 minutes | Cook time: 25 minutes | Serves: 4

1-pound chicken ground	1 tablespoon parsley
1 medium beaten egg	½ teaspoon salt
½ cup grated parmesan	½ teaspoon black pepper
2 cloves finely chopped garlic	1 cup sauce marinara
1 thin, finely chopped onion	1 cup grated mozzarella
1 tablespoon oregano	

1. Combine the meatball ingredients in a mixing basin and well combine. 2. To form the chicken mixture into wide walnut-sized balls, use clean wet hands or a cookie scoop. 3. Using a gentle spray, lightly coat the cooking tray. 4. Spray the chicken balls from the fryer carefully to ensure they do not strike. 5. Select the Air Fry function. Set timer to 15 minutes and temp 400 degrees F. 6. Cook for 12-14 minutes, or until golden. 7. Drizzle a tablespoon of marinara sauce over each meatball and top with mozzarella cheese. 8. Cook for 1-2 minutes, or until the cheese has melted. 9. Enjoy yourself as you eat.

Per serving: Calories 339; Fat 20g; Sodium 420mg; Carbs 8g; Fiber 1g; Sugar 1g; Protein 33g

Paprika Chicken Wings

Prep time: 15 minutes | Cook time: 24 minutes | Serves: 6

1 ½ pound chicken wings	½ teaspoon smoked paprika
¼ teaspoon sea salt	½ teaspoon garlic powder
½ teaspoon black pepper	

1. In a small bowl, combine smoked paprika, black pepper, salt, garlic powder, baking powder, and onion powder. 2. Add all of the chicken wings to a large mixing bowl, and pour the spice mixture over them. 3. Toss the wings well and place them in a cooking tray. 4. Return the cooking tray to its original position in the air fryer. 5. Preheat the air fryer to 400 degrees F and Set the time to 24 minutes and the temperature to 400 degrees F, then bake for 24 minutes in the Air Fry mode. 6. Once the wings are halfway cooked, toss them. 7. Warm the dish before serving.

Per serving: Calories 220; Fat 1.7g; Sodium 70mg; Carbs 1.7g; Fiber 0.1g; Sugar 0.1g; Protein 32.9g

Air Fried Dijon Chicken Pieces

Prep time: 20 minutes | Cook time: 50 minutes | Serves: 4

¼ cup Dijon mustard
¼ cup cooking oil
Salt and pepper to taste
2 tablespoons honey
1 tablespoon dry oregano

2 teaspoons dry Italian seasoning
1 tablespoon lemon juice
6 chicken pieces

1. In a mixing dish, combine all ingredients except the chicken. 2. Mix thoroughly. 3. With a large mixing bowl, toss the chicken in the mixture. Add it to the cooking tray. 4. Select the Roast function. 5. Preheat the air fryer to 380 degrees F. 6. Set time to 50 minutes and temperature to 380 degrees F for cooking. 7. Cook for 30 minutes. 8. Cook for another 15 to 20 minutes after flipping.
Per serving: Calories 1781; Fat 54.33g; Sodium 1048mg; Carbs 11.71g; Fiber 4g; Sugar 3.7g; Protein 293.44g

Rosemary Chicken Wings

Prep time: 15 minutes | Cook time: 35 minutes | Serves: 6

1 teaspoon paprika
Salt to taste
½ teaspoon baking powder
2 pounds of chicken wings
¼ cup honey

1 tablespoon lemon juice
1 tablespoon garlic, minced
1 tablespoon rosemary, chopped

1. In your air fryer, select the Air Fry setting. 2. Preheat the air fryer to 400 degrees F. 3. Start the healing process by pressing the start button. 4. Mix the paprika, salt, and baking powder in a bowl as you wait. 5. Place the chicken wings in the cooking tray. 6. Set the timer for 35 minutes and temperature to 400 degrees F. 7. Cook for 15 minutes with the lid closed. Cook for another 15 minutes on the opposite side. 8. Combine the remaining ingredients in a mixing dish. 9. Cook for another 5 minutes after coating the wings with the sauce.
Per serving: Calories 251; Fat 6.44g; Sodium 360mg; Carbs 12.56g; Fiber 1.9g; Sugar 2.3g; Protein 34.49g

Baked Chicken Thighs and Legs

Prep time: 20 minutes | Cook time: 25 minutes | Serves: 2

2 chicken thighs and legs
2 tablespoons oil, divided
Salt and pepper to taste
1 onion, diced
¼ cup mushrooms, sliced
1 cup potatoes, diced

1 tablespoon lemon juice
1 tablespoon honey
4 sprigs fresh thyme, chopped
2 cloves garlic, crushed and minced

1. Select the Bake function and set the temperature to 365 degrees F. 2. Preheat by pressing the Start button. 3. Half of the oil should be brushed on the chicken. 4. Salt & pepper to taste. 5. In the remaining oil, toss the onion, mushrooms, and potatoes. 6. Season it with salt and pepper. 7. Place the chicken on the cooking tray. 8. Fill the cooking tray with the potato mixture. 9. Set timer to 25 minutes and temp 365 degrees F. 10. Cook for 10 to 15 minutes with the hood closed. 11. Toss the potatoes and flip the chicken. 12. Cook for an additional ten minutes.
Per serving: Calories 715; Fat 48.89g; Sodium 990mg; Carbs 31.05g; Fiber 4.7g; Sugar 5g; Protein 37.93g

Garlic Chicken Thigh Fillets

Prep time: 10 minutes | Cook time: 20 minutes | Serves: 8

3 pounds' chicken thigh fillets
Garlic salt to taste

1. Preheat the air fryer to 365 degrees F. 2. On both sides, season the chicken with garlic salt. 3. Select Bake function. 4. Set timer to 17 minutes and temperature to 365 degrees F. 5. Cook for a total of 8 to 10 minutes. 6. Cook for another 7 minutes on the opposite side.
Per serving: Calories 386; Fat 29.01g; Sodium 440mg; Carbs 0.43g; Fiber 0g; Sugar 0g; Protein 28.9g

Baked Chicken Breast Fillets

Prep time: 45 minutes | Cook time: 45 minutes | Serves: 4

¼ cup olive oil
2 tablespoons balsamic vinegar
3 teaspoons garlic, minced
3 tablespoons soy sauce

1 tablespoon Worcestershire sauce
¼ cup brown sugar
Salt and pepper to taste
4 chicken breast fillets

1. Combine all ingredients, except the chicken, in a mixing bowl. 2. Save ¼ cup of the mixture for later use. 3. Marinate the chicken breast for 30 minutes in the remaining marinade. 4. In the air fryer, add the chicken to a cooking tray. 5. Select the Bake function. 6. Set the timer for 25 minutes and the temperature to 365 degrees F. 7. Close the hood and add the chicken breast. 8. Cook for 10 minutes before serving. 9. Cook for another 5 minutes on the other side. 10. Using the leftover sauce, baste the chicken. Cook for an additional 5 minutes. 11. If there is any leftover sauce, serve with it.
Per serving: Calories 716; Fat 44.04g; Sodium 610mg; Carbs 13.16g; Fiber 1.75g; Sugar 2.1g; Protein 63.31g

Air-Fried Chicken Legs

Prep time: 20 minutes | Cook time: 24 minutes | Serves: 6

12 chicken legs
2 tablespoons seasoned salt

4 tablespoons olive oil
1 bag of chicken breading

1. Toss the drumsticks in olive oil and season with salt and pepper. 2. Toss in the breadcrumbs and cover the drumsticks thoroughly. 3. Spray the coated drumsticks with cooking oil and place them on the cooking tray. 4. Return the cooking tray to its original position in the air fryer. 5. Preheat the air fryer to 400 degrees F. 6. Select Air Fry mode and set the timer to 24 minutes and the temperature to 400 degrees F. then bake for 24 minutes. 7. After the drumsticks have been cooked halfway through, flip them and continue cooking. 8. Warm the dish before serving.
Per serving: Calories 380; Fat 29g; Sodium 340mg; Carbs 34.6g; Fiber 2g; Sugar 2.6g; Protein 30g

Spicy Chicken Breasts

Prep time: 15 minutes | Cook time: 22 minutes | Serves: 4

4 boneless skinless chicken breasts
½ teaspoon garlic powder

½ teaspoon salt
⅛ teaspoon black pepper
½ teaspoon dried oregano

1. In a small bowl, combine garlic powder, oregano, black pepper, and salt. 2. Using frying spray, coat the chicken breasts. 3. Season the chicken generously with the spice mix. 4. In the cooking tray, place the seasoned chicken breasts. 5.

Return the cooking tray to its original position in the air fryer. 6. Select Air Fry mode and set time to 22 minutes and temperature to 400 degrees F, then cook for 22 minutes. 7. Once the chicken is halfway done, flip it and sprinkle the remaining spice on top. 8. Return to the stove and cook until the chicken is golden brown. 9. Warm the dish before serving.

Per serving: Calories 268; Fat 10.4g; Sodium 270mg; Carbs 0.4g; Fiber 0g; Sugar 0g; Protein 40.6g

Tangy Chicken Drumstick

Prep time: 15 minutes | Cook time: 20 minutes | Serves: 4

1 teaspoon paprika	1 teaspoon of sea salt
8 chicken drumsticks	1 teaspoon fresh cracked pepper
2 tablespoons olive oil	

1. Mix all the spices and herbs in a small bowl. 2. In a mixing dish, toss the drumsticks with the olive oil and spice mixture to coat well. 3. Preheat your air fryer on Air Fry setting to 400 degrees F. 4. In the cooking tray, spread out the drumsticks. 5. Return the cooking tray to its original position in the air fryer. 6. Set timer to 20 minutes and temperature to 400 degrees F, then bake for 20 minutes in the Air Fry mode. 7. Once the drumsticks are halfway cooked, flip them. 8. Warm the dish before serving.

Per serving: Calories 220; Fat 13g; Sodium 170mg; Carbs 0.9g; Fiber 0g; Sugar 0.1g; Protein 25.6g

Turkey Leg with Poultry Spice

Prep time: 10 minutes | Cook time: 27 minutes | Serves: 2

1 pound. turkey leg	1 teaspoon garlic salt
1 teaspoon poultry seasoning	

1. Season the turkey leg with garlic salt and poultry spice. 2. In the cooking tray, place the turkey leg. 3. Return the cooking tray to its original position in the air fryer. 4. Preheat the air fryer to 365 degrees F. 5. Set timer to 27 minutes and temperature to 365 degrees F for cooking, then bake for 27 minutes in the Bake mode. 6. Once the turkey leg is halfway done, flip it. 7. Warm the dish before serving.

Per serving: Calories 502; Fat 25g; Sodium 370mg; Carbs 1.5g; Fiber 0.1g; Sugar 0.1g; Protein 64.1g

Lemony Chicken Thighs

Prep time: 15 minutes | Cook time: 14 minutes | Serves: 4

4 boneless skinless chicken thighs	¼ cup coarse ground mustard
¼ cup lemon juice	¼ cup balsamic vinaigrette
	1 teaspoon kosher salt

1. In a bowl, combine the lemon juice, mustard, vinaigrette, salt, rosemary, and black pepper. 2. Toss in the chicken thighs and coat well. 3. To marinate, cover and refrigerate for 2 hours. 4. Spray the seasoned chicken with frying oil and place it on the cooking tray. 5. Return the cooking tray to its original position in the air fryer. 6. Preheat the air fryer to 365 degrees F 7. Set timer to 14 minutes and temperature to 365 degrees F for cooking, then bake for 14 minutes in the Bake mode. 8. Halfway through cooking, flip the chicken. And then get back to cooking. 9. Warm the dish before serving.

Per serving: Calories 331; Fat 17g; Sodium 470mg; Carbs 1.7g; Fiber 1g; Sugar 0.1g; Protein 41g

Buttermilk-Glazed Chicken Tenders

Prep time: 10 minutes | Cook time: 20 minutes | Serves: 6

1 cup buttermilk	1 cup all-purpose flour
½ teaspoon hot sauce	1 ½ teaspoons Stone House Seasoning
2 pounds of chicken tenders	

1. In a large mixing basin, combine buttermilk and spicy sauce. 2. Add the chicken tenders, toss thoroughly, and chill overnight. 3. In a small dish, combine flour and stone house seasoning. 4. 14 cups buttermilk marinade, whisked together until creamy 5. Coat the chicken tenders in the batter that has been made. 6. Spray the coated chicken tenders with frying oil and place them on the cooking tray. 7. Return the cooking tray to its original position in the air fryer. 8. Preheat the air fryer to 365 degrees F and select Bake function 9. Set timer to 20 minutes and temperature to 365 degrees F, then bake for 20 minutes. 10. After the tenders have been cooked halfway through, flip them and continue frying. 11. Warm the dish before serving.

Per serving: Calories 379; Fat 12g; Sodium 470mg; Carbs 18g; Fiber 1.9g; Sugar 1.67g; Protein 47.2g

Chicken Wings with Ranch

Prep time: 15 minutes | Cook time: 20 minutes | Serves: 4

1 tablespoon Ranch seasoning mix	2 tablespoons mayonnaise
1 tablespoon garlic powder	1 pound of chicken wings

1. Wash the chicken wings and dry them with a paper towel. 2. In a large mixing bowl, combine mayonnaise and seasonings. 3. Toss in the chicken wings and coat well. 4. Refrigerate the chicken for 15 minutes after concealing it. 5. Spray the chicken wings with cooking oil and place them on the cooking tray. 6. Return the cooking tray to its original position in the air fryer. 7. Preheat the air fryer to 400 degrees F 8. Select Air Fry function. Set timer to 20 minutes and temperature to 400 degrees F, then bake for 20 minutes in the air fryer. 9. Once the wings are halfway done, flip them and continue to cook. 10. Warm the dish before serving.

Per serving: Calories 251; Fat 11g; Sodium 150mg; Carbs 3.3g; Fiber 0.2g; Sugar 1g; Protein 33.2g

Turkey Cutlets with Parsley

Prep time: 10 minutes | Cook time: 25 minutes | Serves: 4

1 egg	¼ cup parmesan cheese, grated
1 ½ pounds turkey cutlets	
½ teaspoon garlic powder	½ cup almond flour
½ teaspoon onion powder	salt and pepper
½ teaspoon dried parsley	

1. Season the turkey cutlets with salt and pepper. 2. In a small dish, mix the eggs. 3. Combine parmesan cheese, garlic powder, onion powder, parsley, and almond flour in a shallow dish. 4. Each turkey cutlet should be dipped in the egg and coated in the parmesan cheese mixture. 5. Place the coated turkey cutlets on a baking sheet lined with parchment paper. 6. Select Bake mode, then set the temperature to 365 degrees F and the duration to 25 minutes before pressing the start button. 7. Place the frying pan in the air fryer when the display says Add Food. 8. While cooking, flip the cutlet. 9. Serve and have fun.

Per serving: Calories 405; Fat 17.8g; Sodium 270mg; Carbs 3.8g; Fiber 1g; Sugar 1g; Protein 56.1g

Baked Parmesan Chicken Breasts

Prep time: 10 minutes | Cook time: 45 minutes | Serves: 4

4 chicken breasts, skinless & boneless	½ cup parmesan cheese, grated
5 plain Greek yogurts	½ teaspoon pepper
1 teaspoon garlic powder	1 teaspoon salt

1. Season the chicken breasts with salt and pepper before placing them in the baking dish. 2. Pour a mixture of yogurt, garlic powder, and parmesan cheese over chicken breasts. Wrap foil around the dish. 3. Select Bake mode, then set the temperature to 365 degrees F and the duration to 45 minutes before pressing the start button. 4. Place the baking dish in the air fryer when the display says Add Food. 5. Serve and have fun.

Per serving: Calories 347; Fat 13.3g; Sodium 430mg; Carbs 13.3g; Fiber 1.7g; Sugar 2.3g; Protein 49.3g

Spicy Chicken Drumsticks

Prep time: 10 minutes | Cook time: 45 minutes | Serves: 6

2 pounds' chicken drumsticks	1 teaspoon paprika
1 teaspoon parsley, chopped	2 tablespoons olive oil
1 teaspoon onion powder	½ teaspoon pepper
1 teaspoon garlic powder	½ teaspoon salt

1. Seal the zip-lock bag with the chicken drumsticks and other ingredients and shake vigorously to coat. 2. Place the chicken drumsticks on the baking sheet. 3. Select Bake mode, then set the temperature to 365 degrees F and the duration to 40-45 minutes before pressing the start button. 4. Place the frying pan in the air fryer when the display says Add Food. 5. Serve and have fun.

Per serving: Calories 300; Fat 13.4g; Sodium 370mg; Carbs 1g; Fiber 0.1g; Sugar 0.1g; Protein 41.8g

Mayonnaise Chicken Strips

Prep time: 10 minutes | Cook time: 20 minutes | Serves: 4

3 chicken breasts, cut into strips	½ cup parmesan cheese, grated
2 teaspoons Italian seasoning	½ cup mayonnaise
½ cup pork rinds, crushed	

1. Add mayonnaise to a small mixing bowl. 2. Combine pork rinds, parmesan cheese, and Italian seasoning in a small dish. 3. After dipping the chicken strip in mayonnaise, slather it with the pork rind mixture. 4. Place the coated chicken strips on a baking sheet lined with parchment paper. 5. Select Bake mode, then set the temperature to 365 degrees F and the duration to 20 minutes before pressing the Start button. 6. Place the frying pan in the air fryer when the display says Add Food. 7. Serve and have fun.

Per serving: Calories 376; Fat 21.7g; Sodium 270mg; Carbs 7.7g; Fiber 0.6g; Sugar 1g; Protein 36.7g

Crusted Bone-in Chicken Thighs

Prep time: 10 minutes | Cook time: 45 minutes | Serves: 4

1 ½ pounds chicken thighs, bone-in	½ teaspoon garlic powder
¼ teaspoon pepper	½ teaspoon paprika
½ teaspoon onion powder	1 tablespoon olive oil
	½ teaspoon salt

1. Place the chicken thighs in a zip-lock bag with the other ingredients, seal the bag, and shake well to coat. 2. Place the chicken thighs on the baking sheet. 3. Select Bake mode, then set the temperature to 365 degrees F and the duration to 34-45 minutes before pressing the start button. 4. Place the cooking tray in the air fryer when the display says Add Food. 5. Serve and have fun.

Per serving: Calories 356; Fat 16.1g; Sodium 540mg; Carbs 0.7g; Fiber 0.1g; Sugar 0.1g; Protein 49.4g

Ground Turkey Zucchini Meatballs

Prep time: 10 minutes | Cook time: 18 minutes | Serves: 6

2 eggs, lightly beaten	2 tablespoons fresh oregano, chopped
1 medium zucchini, grated	1 tablespoon garlic, minced
1-pound ground turkey	1 tablespoon nutritional yeast
1 teaspoon cumin	⅓ cup coconut flour
1 tablespoon dried onion flakes	½ teaspoon salt
1 tablespoon basil, chopped	

1. In a mixing bowl, add all ingredients and stir until thoroughly mixed. 2. Form tiny balls out of the beef mixture and lay them on a parchment-lined cooking tray. 3. Select Bake mode, then set the temperature to 365 degrees F and the duration to 18 minutes before pressing the Start button. 4. Place the cooking tray in the air fryer when the display says Add Food. 5. Serve and have fun.

Per serving: Calories 194; Fat 10.3g; Sodium 400mg; Carbs 4.7g; Fiber 1g; Sugar 1.3g; Protein 24.2g

Easy Baked Chicken Breasts

Prep time: 10 minutes | Cook time: 22 minutes | Serves: 6

6 chicken breasts, boneless & skinless	2 tablespoons olive oil
¼ teaspoon paprika	¼ teaspoon pepper
1 teaspoon Italian seasoning	½ teaspoon salt

1. Combine paprika, Italian seasoning, pepper, and salt in a small bowl. 2. Rub the spice mixture into the chicken breasts after brushing them with oil. 3. Place the chicken breasts on the cooking tray. 4. Select Bake mode, then set the temperature to 365 degrees F and the duration to 22 minutes before pressing the Start button. 5. Place the cooking tray in the air fryer when the display says Add Food. 6. Serve and have fun.

Per serving: Calories 320; Fat 15.7g; Sodium 450mg; Carbs 0.2g; Fiber 0; Sugar 0; Protein 42.3g

Garlicky Chicken Wings

Prep time: 10 minutes | Cook time: 04 minutes | Serves: 4

2 pounds of chicken wings	1 teaspoon onion powder
⅛ teaspoon cayenne pepper	2 tablespoons butter, melted
¼ teaspoon pepper	1 teaspoon sea salt
1 teaspoon garlic powder	

1. Combine cayenne pepper, pepper, garlic powder, onion powder, and salt in a small bowl. 2. Brush melted butter on the chicken wings and then massage with the spice mixture. 3. Place the chicken wings on the cooking tray. 4. Select Bake mode, then set the temperature to 365 degrees F and the duration to 40 minutes before pressing the Start button. 5. Place the frying pan in the air fryer when the display says Add Food. 6. Serve and have fun.

Per serving: Calories 487; Fat 22.6g; Sodium 340mg; Carbs 1.1g; Fiber 0.1g; Sugar 0.1g; Protein 65.9g

Greek-Style Chicken Breasts

Prep time: 10 minutes | Cook time: 30 minutes | Serves: 4

1 ½ pounds of chicken breasts, skinless & boneless	2 garlic cloves, crushed
1 tablespoon olive oil	1 lemon zest, grated
½ tablespoon dried oregano	¼ teaspoon salt

1. Combine the oil, oregano, garlic, lemon zest, and salt in a small bowl. 2. Brush the chicken breasts with the oil mixture. Place the chicken breasts on the cooking tray. 3. Select Bake mode, then set the temperature to 365 degrees F and the duration to 30 minutes before pressing the start button. 4. Place the cooking tray in the air fryer when the display says Add Food. 5. Serve and have fun.

Per serving: Calories 358; Fat 16.2g; Sodium 450mg; Carbs 1g; Fiber 0g; Sugar 0g; Protein 49.4g

Simple Air Fried Chicken Legs

Prep time: 15 minutes | Cook time: 25 minutes | Serves: 6

2-½ pounds of chicken legs	1 teaspoon garlic powder
2 tablespoons olive oil	½ teaspoon ground cumin
1 teaspoon smoked paprika	Salt and ground black pepper

1. Combine all ingredients in a large mixing basin and stir thoroughly. 2. Arrange the chicken legs evenly on two baking pans. 3. Place the pan in the cooking chamber of the air fryer. 4. Choose Air Fry and set the temperature to 400 degrees F. 5. Press the Start button after setting the timer for 25 minutes. 6. Insert one tray in the top and the other in the bottom when the display says Add Food. 7. When the display says Flip Food, don't turn the food; instead, move the cooking trays around. 8. Remove the trays from the air fryer after the cooking time is over. 9. Serve immediately

Per serving: Calories 402; Fat 18.8g; Sodium 440mg; Carbs 0.6g; Fiber 0g; Sugar 0g; Protein 54.8g

Herbed Chicken Thighs

Prep time: 15 minutes | Cook time: 20 minutes | Serves: 4

1 teaspoon ground cumin	Salt and ground black pepper
1 teaspoon garlic powder	4 chicken thighs
½ teaspoon smoked paprika	2 tablespoons olive oil
½ teaspoon ground coriander	

1. Combine the spices, salt, and black pepper in a large mixing basin and stir well. 2. Rub the chicken thighs with the spice mixture after coating them in oil. 3. Place the chicken thighs on the cooking tray. 4. Place the drip pan in the bottom of the air fryer cooking chamber. 5. Choose Air Fry and set the temperature to 400 degrees F. 6. Press the Start button after setting the timer for 20 minutes. 7. Place the cooking tray in the center when the display says Add Food. 8. Turn the chicken thighs when the display says turn Food. 9. Remove the chicken pieces when the cooking time is over. 10. Serve immediately.

Per serving: Calories 334; Fat 17.7g; Sodium 234mg; Carbs 0.9g; Fiber 0g; Sugar 0.1g; Protein 41.3g

Breaded Chicken Breasts

Prep time: 15 minutes | Cook time: 12 minutes | Serves: 6

1 cup breadcrumbs	¼ cup fresh parsley, minced
½ cup Parmesan cheese, grated	Salt and ground black pepper
	1½ pounds boneless, skinless chicken breasts
3 tablespoons olive oil	Olive oil cooking spray

1. Combine the breadcrumbs, Parmesan cheese, parsley, salt, and black pepper in a shallow dish. 2. Coat the chicken breasts with the breadcrumb mixture after rubbing them with oil. 3. Spray the chicken breasts with cooking spray and place them on the cooking tray. Place the pan in the air fryer's cooking chamber's bottom. 4. Choose Air Fry and set the temperature to 400 degrees F. 5. Press the Start button after setting the timer for 12 minutes. 6. Place the cooking tray in the center when the display says Add Food. 7. Turn the chicken breasts when the display says Turn Food. 8. Remove the chicken breasts from the pan when the cooking time is over. 9. Serve immediately.

Per serving: Calories 371; Fat 18g; Sodium 390mg; Carbs 13.1g; Fiber 2.1g; Sugar 1.9g; Protein 38g

Spicy Chicken Wings and Drumettes

Prep time: 20 minutes | Cook time: 25 minutes | Serves: 4

2 pounds of chicken wings and drumettes	2 tablespoons molasses
½ cup ketchup	½ teaspoon liquid smoke
3 tablespoons white vinegar	¼ teaspoon paprika
2 tablespoons honey	¼ teaspoon garlic powder
	Pinch of cayenne pepper

1. Arrange the wings in a single layer on two cooking trays. 2. Place the drip pan in the bottom of the air fryer cooking chamber. 3. Choose Air Fry and set the temperature to 400 degrees F. 4. Press the Start button after setting the timer for 25 minutes. 5. Insert one tray in the top and the other in the bottom when the display says Add Food. 6. When the display says turn Food, don't turn the food; instead, move the cooking trays around. 7. Meanwhile, boil the other ingredients in a small saucepan over medium heat for about 10 minutes, stirring periodically. 8. Remove the trays from the air fryer when the cooking time is up. 9. Add the chicken wings and honey mixture to a large bowl and toss to coat well. 10. Serve immediately.

Per serving: Calories 524; Fat 16.9g; Sodium 430mg; Carbs 24g; Fiber 3g; Sugar 2.75g; Protein 66.2g

Easy Turkey Breast

Prep time: 10 minutes | Cook time: 45 minutes | Serves: 8

1 turkey breast	to taste
Salt and ground black pepper	

1. Season both sides of the turkey breast with salt and black pepper. 2. Tie the turkey breast with kitchen twines to keep it compact. 3. Attach the cover to the rotisserie basket and place the turkey breast inside. 4. Place the drip pan in the bottom of the air fryer cooking chamber. 5. Choose Air Fry and set the temperature to 400 degrees F. Set the time to 45 minutes. 6. Press the Start button to begin. 7. Then, close the door and press the Rotate button. 8. Place the rotisserie basket on the rotisserie spit when the display says Add Food. 9. Then close the door and press the Rotate button. 10. To release the spit, press the red lever after the cooking time is up. 11. Remove the turkey breast from the air fryer and set it aside for 5-10 minutes before slicing. 12. Cut the turkey breast into desired-sized pieces with a sharp knife and serve.

Per serving: Calories 153; Fat 1.5g; Sodium 170mg; Carbs 3g; Fiber 1g; Sugar 1g; Protein 31.9g

Roasted Whole Chicken

Prep time: 10 minutes | Cook time: 40 minutes | Serves: 4

1 teaspoon dried oregano
1 teaspoon dried rosemary
1 teaspoon paprika
1 teaspoon garlic powder
Salt and ground black pepper
1 whole chicken, neck, and
giblets removed
1 lemon, quartered
3 garlic cloves, halved
2 fresh rosemary sprigs
2 tablespoons olive oil

1. Combine the dried herbs, spices, salt, and black pepper in a small bowl. 2. Fill the bird's cavity with lemon, garlic, and rosemary sprigs. 3. Tie the bird with kitchen twine. 4. Apply a thin layer of oil to the chicken and then massage in the herb mixture. 5. Through the chicken, insert the rotisserie spit. 6. To attach the rod to the bird, use one rotisserie fork on each side of the spit. 7. Place the drip pan in the bottom of the air fryer cooking chamber. 8. Adjust the temperature to 380 degrees F after selecting Roast. 9. Press the Start button after setting the timer for 40 minutes. 10. Press the red lever down and load the left side of the rod into the air fryer when the display says Add Food. 11. Now, slip the spit's left side into the metal bar's groove to keep it from moving. 12. Then close the door and press the Rotate button. 13. To release the spit, press the red lever after the cooking time is up. 14. Set the chicken on a dish for 5-10 minutes before cutting. 15. Cut the chicken into appropriately sized pieces with a sharp knife and serve.
Per serving: Calories 584; Fat 17.5g; Sodium 350mg; Carbs 2.3g; Fiber 0.1g; Sugar 0.1g; Protein 99g

Turkey Breasts Air-Fried with Herbs

Prep time: 15 minutes | Cook time: 1 hour | Serves: 8

2 tablespoons olive oil
2 tablespoons lemon juice
1 tablespoon garlic, minced
2 teaspoons ground mustard
Salt and ground black pepper
1 teaspoon ground sage
1 teaspoon dried thyme
1 teaspoon dried rosemary
1 turkey breast

1. Combine all ingredients in a small mixing basin, except the turkey breast, and stir until thoroughly mixed. 2. Apply a liberal amount of the oil mixture to the exterior of the turkey breast and beneath any loose skin. 3. Place the turkey breast skin side up on a cooking tray. 4. Place the drip pan in the bottom of the air fryer cooking chamber. 5. Choose Air Fry and set the temperature to 400 degrees F. Set the time to 60 minutes. 6. Press the Start button. 7. Place the cooking tray in the center when the display says Add Food. 8. To release the spit, press the red lever after the cooking time is up. 9. Remove the turkey breast from the air fryer and set it aside for 5-10 minutes before slicing. 10. Cut the turkey breast into desired-sized pieces with a sharp knife and serve.
Per serving: Calories 214; Fat 6.6g; Sodium 470mg; Carbs 8.1g; Fiber 1g; Sugar 1g; Protein 29.4g

Mozzarella Boneless Chicken Breasts

Prep time: 5 minutes | Cook time: 24 minutes | Serves: 6

6 chicken breasts, skinless, boneless, and halved
Salt and black pepper
2 tablespoons olive oil
1-pound mozzarella, sliced
2 cups baby spinach
1 teaspoon Italian seasoning
2 tomatoes, sliced
1 tablespoon basil, chopped

1. Make slits in reach chicken breast half and fill with mozzarella, spinach, and tomatoes. Season with salt, pepper, and Italian seasoning. 2. Select Air Fry function. Set timer to 25 minutes and temperature to 400 degrees F. 3. Drizzle the oil over the filled chicken, place it on the cooking tray, and cook for 12 minutes on each side. 4. Serve with basil sprinkled over the top, divided across plates.
Per serving: Calories 285; Fat 12g; Sodium 270mg; Carbs 7g; Fiber 1g; Sugar 1g; Protein 15g

Air Fried Duck Breasts with Soy Sauce

Prep time: 5 minutes | Cook time: 15 minutes | Serves: 2

2 duck breasts
2 garlic cloves, minced
6 tarragon sprigs
1 tablespoon. butter
¼ cup sherry wine
1 cup white wine
¼ cup soy sauce
Salt and black pepper to the taste

1. Stir duck breasts with white wine, soy sauce, garlic, tarragon, salt, and pepper in a basin, toss well, and chill for one day. 2. Select Air Fry function. Set timer to 10 minutes and temperature to 400 degrees F. 3. Cook the duck breasts in a preheated air fryer for 10 minutes, turning halfway through. 4. Meanwhile, pour the marinade into a skillet and heat over medium heat, then add the butter and sherry and combine. 5. Bring to a low simmer and cook for 5 minutes before turning off the heat. 6. Serve the duck breasts on plates with the sauce drizzled over them.
Per serving: Calories 475; Fat 12g; Sodium 370mg; Carbs 10g; Fiber 1g; Sugar 1g; Protein 48g

Turkey Breasts and Peas Casserole

Prep time: 10 minutes | Cook time: 20 minutes | Serves: 4

2 pounds' turkey breasts, skinless, boneless
1 yellow onion, chopped
1 celery stalk, chopped.
½ cup peas
1 cup chicken stock
1 cup cream, mushrooms soup
1 cup bread cubes
Salt and black pepper

1. Select Air Fry function. Set timer to 20 minutes and temperature to 400 degrees F. 2. Combine turkey, salt, pepper, onion, celery, peas, and stock in a pan that fits your air fryer, then transfer to your air fryer and cook for 15 minutes. 3. Stir in the bread cubes and cream of mushroom soup, then cook for another 5 minutes. 4. Serve immediately, divided among plates.
Per serving: Calories 271; Fat 9g; Sodium 370mg; Carbs 16g; Fiber 1.8g; Sugar 1.75g; Protein 7g

Lemon Chicken Drumsticks

Prep time: 10 minutes | Cook time: 30 minutes | Serves: 4

8 chicken drumsticks
¼ teaspoon cayenne pepper
1 tablespoon onion powder
1 tablespoon garlic powder
1 ½ tablespoons honey
1 ½ tablespoons fresh lemon juice
1 tablespoon Worcestershire sauce
¼ cup soy sauce, low-sodium
1 tablespoon sesame oil
2 tablespoons olive oil
½ teaspoon kosher salt

1. In a large mixing basin, combine all ingredients except the chicken and stir thoroughly. 2. Toss in the chicken drumsticks and toss until fully coated. 3. Select Air Fry function. Set timer to 30 minutes and temperature to 400 degrees F. 4. Place the chicken drumsticks on the cooking tray and air dry for 15 minutes at 400 degrees F. 5. Cook for another 15 minutes on the opposite side of the chicken drumsticks. 6. Serve and have fun.

Per serving: Calories 296; Fat 15.8g; Sodium 570mg; Carbs 11.6g; Fiber 4g; Sugar 8.7g; Protein 26.9g

Gluten-Free Chicken Drumsticks

Prep time: 10 minutes | Cook time: 25 minutes | Serves: 6

6 chicken drumsticks, rinse and pat dry with a paper towel	1 cup buttermilk
1 teaspoon ginger	¼ cup brown sugar
1 teaspoon onion powder	½ cup breadcrumbs
1 teaspoon garlic powder	1 cup all-purpose flour
1 teaspoon paprika	½ teaspoon pepper
	1 teaspoon salt

1. Preheat the air fryer to 365 degrees F in the bake mode. 2. Mix the breadcrumbs, spices, and flour in a zip-lock bag. 3. Combine the chicken and buttermilk in a mixing dish and set aside for 2 minutes. 4. Place a single piece of chicken in the zip-lock bag and shake it until the breadcrumb mixture is equally distributed. Repeat with the remaining chicken pieces. 5. Spray the chicken that has been coated with cooking spray. 6. Select the Bake function. Set timer to 25 minutes and temperature to 365 degrees F. 7. Bake for 25 minutes with the chicken in the bottom tray of the air fryer. 8. Serve and have fun.

Per serving: Calories 234; Fat 3.8g; Sodium 570mg; Carbs 31.5g; Fiber 5.1g; Sugar 8.7g; Protein 17.6g

Garlicky Chicken Wings with Parmesan

Prep time: 10 minutes | Cook time: 21 minutes | Serves: 4

1 pound of chicken wings	ed
1 teaspoon parsley	1 tablespoon butter, melted
2 tablespoons garlic, minced	¼ teaspoon pepper
¾ cup parmesan cheese, grat-	1 teaspoon salt

1. Select Air Fry function. Set timer to 21 minutes and temperature to 400 degrees F. 2. Place chicken wings on a cooking tray and air dry for 7 minutes at 400 degrees F. 3. Turn the chicken wings over and air fry for another 7 minutes. 4. Turn the chicken wings over and cook for another 7 minutes in the air fryer. 5. Combine the cheese, butter, parsley, garlic, pepper, and salt in a mixing bowl. 6. When the chicken wings are done, place them in a mixing basin and toss them with the cheese mixture until well covered. 7. Serve and have fun.

Per serving: Calories 398; Fat 20.3g; Sodium 440mg; Carbs 1.5g; Fiber 0.1g; Sugar 0.1g; Protein 45.2g

Chicken Popcorns

Prep time: 10 minutes | Cook time: 10 minutes | Serves: 6

1-pound chicken breast, skinless, boneless, and cut into 1-inch pieces	1 cup buttermilk
	1 teaspoon baking powder
1 egg, lightly beaten	1 cup all-purpose flour
½ tablespoon Tabasco sauce	½ teaspoon pepper
	1 teaspoon salt

1. Season the chicken pieces with salt and pepper. 2. Combine all-purpose flour and baking powder in a medium mixing basin. 3. Combine the egg, buttermilk, and Tabasco sauce in a separate mixing dish. 4. Coat the chicken in flour, dip it in the egg mixture, and coat it again. 5. Place the chicken pieces on a cooking tray that has been greased. Cooking spray the covered chicken pieces. 6. Select Air Fry function. 7. Preheat the air fryer to 400 degrees F and then set cooking time to 10 minutes and temperature to 400 degrees F. 8. Air fry the chicken popcorn for several minutes. Turn the chicken popcorn over and air fried for another 5 minutes. 9. Serve and

have fun.

Per serving: Calories 285; Fat 4.8g; Sodium 450mg; Carbs 27.6g; Fiber 4g; Sugar 3.1g; Protein 30.7g

Rotisserie Whole Chicken

Prep time: 10 minutes | Cook time: 50 minutes | Serves: 6

3 pounds of whole chicken	2 cups buttermilk
¾ teaspoon garlic powder	Pepper and salt
¼ cup olive oil	

1. In a large zip-lock bag, combine garlic powder, olive oil, buttermilk, pepper, and salt. 2. Place the whole chicken in the bag. Marinate the chicken in the bag overnight. 3. Remove the chicken from the bag and season with salt and pepper. 4. Place the marinated chicken on the rotisserie spit inside the air fryer. 5. Select Air Fry function. Set cooking time to 50 minutes and temperature to 400 degrees F. 6. Heat the air fryer to 400 degrees F in advance and air fried the chicken for 50 minutes, or until the internal temperature reaches 165 degrees F. 7. Serve and have fun.

Per serving: Calories 537; Fat 25.9g; Sodium 340mg; Carbs 4.2g; Fiber 1g; Sugar 1g; Protein 68.4g

Adobo Chicken Wings

Prep time: 10 minutes | Cook time: 35 minutes | Serves: 4

12 chicken wings	1 tablespoon adobo seasoning
2 tablespoon water	1 teaspoon salt
1 tablespoon sazon seasoning	

1. In a large mixing dish, place the chicken wings. 2. Toss with the other ingredients until the chicken is completely covered. 3. Place the rotisserie basket in the air fryer and add the chicken. 4. Select Air Fry function. Set timer to 35 minutes and temperature to 400 degrees F. 5. Air fry the chicken for 35 minutes. 6. Serve and have fun.

Per serving: Calories 476; Fat 32.1g; Sodium 370mg; Carbs 16.1g; Fiber 2g; Sugar 0g; Protein 29.2g

Chicken Breasts with Italian Seasoning

Prep time: 10 minutes | Cook time: 8 minutes | Serves: 4

1-pound chicken breasts, skinless and boneless	3 tablespoons butter, melted
	1 teaspoon Italian seasoning
2 tablespoons fresh lemon juice	1 tablespoon olive oil
	½ teaspoon pepper
1 teaspoon garlic, minced	1 teaspoon salt

1. Combine lemon juice, garlic, butter, Italian seasoning, olive oil, pepper, and salt in a mixing bowl. 2. Toss the chicken in the mixing bowl and coat well. 3. Using cooking spray, coat the cooking tray. 4. Select Air Fry function. Set timer to 8 minutes and temperature to 400 degrees F. 5. Place chicken on a tray and air dry for 4 minutes at 400 degrees F. 6. Cook for another 4 minutes on the opposite side of the chicken. 7. Serve and have fun.

Per serving: Calories 329; Fat 21g; Sodium 349mg; Carbs 0.7g; Fiber 0g; Sugar 0.3g; Protein 33g

Lemon Skinless Chicken Breasts

Prep time: 10 minutes | Cook time: 30 minutes | Serves: 2

2 chicken breasts, boneless &
skinless
1 lemon juice

2 tablespoons olive oil
2 sprigs thyme
Pepper and salt

1. Place the chicken breasts in the baking dish and top with the other ingredients. 2. Select Bake mode, then set the temperature to 365 degrees F and the duration to 30 minutes before pressing the Start button. 3. Place the baking dish in the air fryer when the display says Add Food. 4. Cut into slices and serve.
Per serving: Calories 415; Fat 25.3g; Sodium 450mg; Carbs 3.3g; Fiber 1g; Sugar 0.1g; Protein 42.8g

Air Fried Turkey Breast with Lemon Zest

Prep time: 10 minutes | Cook time: 50 minutes | Serves: 6

3 pounds of turkey breast
3 garlic cloves, minced
1 tablespoon fresh sage leaves,
chopped
1 tablespoon rosemary leaves,
chopped

1 tablespoon fresh thyme
3 tablespoons butter
1 teaspoon lemon zest, grated
½ teaspoon pepper
1 teaspoon kosher salt

1. Combine butter, garlic, sage, rosemary, thyme, lemon zest, pepper, and salt in a mixing bowl. 2. Rub the butter mixture all over the turkey breast. 3. Select Air Fry function. Set timer to 50 minutes and temperature to 400 degrees F. 4. Place the turkey breast on the bottom rack of the air fryer and cook for 20 minutes. 5. Cook for another 30 minutes, or until the internal temperature of the turkey breast reaches 160 degrees F. 6. Cut into slices and serve.
Per serving: Calories 294; Fat 9.7g; Sodium 320mg; Carbs 11.1g; Fiber 2g; Sugar 8g; Protein 39g

Lemon Pepper Air Fried Chicken Breast

Prep time: 10 minutes | Cook time: 30 minutes | Serves: 4

1 chicken breast, boneless &
skinless
1 ½ teaspoon granulated garlic

1 tablespoon lemon pepper
seasoning
1 teaspoon salt

1. Heat the air fryer to 400 degrees F in advance. 2. Lemon pepper spice, granulated garlic, and salt are used to season chicken breasts. 3. Select Air Fry function. Set timer to 30 minutes and temperature to 400 degrees F. 4. Cook for 30 minutes with the chicken on the cooking tray. Halfway through cooking, flip the chicken. 5. Serve and have fun.
Per serving: Calories 285; Fat 10.9g; Sodium 244mg; Carbs 1.8g; Fiber 0.1g; Sugar 0.1g; Protein 42.6g

Jalapeno Air Fried Chicken

Prep time: 10 minutes | Cook time: 15 minutes | Serves: 2

Chicken breasts, boneless and
skinless
½ cup cheddar cheese, shredded
1 tablespoon pickled jalape-

nos, chopped
1-ounce cream cheese softened
1 bacon slice, cooked and
crumbled

1. Slit the tops of the chicken breasts five to six times. 2. Add ½ cheddar cheese, pickled jalapenos, cream cheese, and bacon to a mixing bowl. 3. Fill the slits with the cheddar cheese mixture. 4. Select Air Fry function. Set timer to 14 minutes and temperature to 400 degrees F. 5. Place the chicken in the cooking tray and cook for 14 minutes. 6. Sprinkle the remain-

ing cheese on top of the chicken and cook in the air fryer for another minute. 7. Serve and have fun.
Per serving: Calories 736; Fat 49g; Sodium 450mg; Carbs 3.7g; Fiber 1g; Sugar 1g; Protein 65.5g

Simple Hassel-back Chicken Breast

Prep time: 10 minutes | Cook time: 18 minutes | Serves: 2

1 chicken breast, boneless and
skinless
½ cup sauerkraut, squeezed,
and remove excess liquid
1 thin Swiss cheese slice, tear

into pieces
1 thin deli corned beef slice,
tear into pieces
Salt and Pepper

1. Cut five incisions through the tops of the chicken breasts. Season the chicken with salt and pepper. 2. Make a slit in each slit and stuff it with meat, sauerkraut, and cheese. 3. Select Air Fry function. Set timer to 18 minutes and temperature to 400 degrees F. 4. Cook the chicken in the cooking tray after spraying it with cooking spray. 5. Preheat the air fryer to 400 degrees F and bake the chicken for 18 minutes. 6. Serve and have fun.
Per serving: Calories 724; Fat 39.9g; Sodium 346mg; Carbs 3.6g; Fiber 0.1g; Sugar 1g; Protein 83.6g

Western Style Turkey Breast

Prep time: 10 minutes | Cook time: 40 minutes | Serves: 8

1-pound turkey breast, boneless
1 tablespoon olive oil

1 ½ teaspoons paprika
1 ½ teaspoons garlic powder
Salt and pepper

1. Heat the air fryer to 400 degrees F in advance. 2. Combine paprika, garlic powder, pepper, and salt in a mixing bowl. 3. Using your hands, rub the oil and spice mixture over the turkey breast. 4. Select Air Fry function. Set timer to 40 minutes and temperature to 400 degrees F. 5. Cook for 25 minutes with the turkey breast skin on the cooking tray. 6. Cook for 15-20 minutes more, or until the internal temperature of the turkey reaches 160 degrees F. Turn the turkey breast and cover with foil. 7. Allow 10 minutes for the turkey breast to cool after removing it from the air fryer. 8. Cut into slices and serve.
Per serving: Calories 254; Fat 5.6g; Sodium 370mg; Carbs 10.4g; Fiber 1g; Sugar 1g; Protein 38.9g

Turkey Breast with Worcestershire Sauce

Prep time: 10 minutes | Cook time: 30 minutes | Serves: 6

1-pound turkey breast, de-
boned
1 teaspoon lemon pepper seasoning

1 tablespoon Worcestershire
sauce
1 tablespoon olive oil
½ teaspoon salt

1. In a zip-lock bag, combine the olive oil, Worcestershire sauce, lemon pepper spice, and salt. Add the turkey breast to the marinade, coat thoroughly, and set aside for 10 minutes to marinate. 2. Place the turkey breast in the cooking tray after removing it from the marinade. 3. Select Air Fry function. Preheat the air fryer to 365 degrees F. 4. Set cooking time to 40 minutes and temperature to 365 degrees F. Bake for 25 minutes. Cook for another 15 minutes, or until the internal temperature of the turkey breast reaches 165 degrees F. 5. Cut into slices and serve.
Per serving: Calories 279; Fat 8.4g; Sodium 460mg; Carbs 10.3g; Fiber 1.8g; Sugar 3g; Protein 38.8g

Tender Turkey Legs

Prep time: 10 minutes | Cook time: 27 minutes | Serves: 4

Turkey legs	1 tablespoon butter
¼ teaspoon oregano	Salt and Pepper
¼ teaspoon rosemary	

1. Season the turkey legs with salt and pepper. 2. Combine butter, oregano, and rosemary in a small basin. 3. Rub the butter mixture all over the turkey legs. 4. Select Air Fry function. 5. Preheat the air fryer to 400 degrees F. 6. Set time to 27 minutes and temperature to 400 degrees F. 7. Cook the turkey legs for 27 minutes on the cooking tray. 8. Serve and have fun.

Per serving: Calories 182; Fat 9.9g; Sodium 630mg; Carbs 1.9g; Fiber 0.1g; Sugar 0.1g; Protein 20.2g

Air Fried Chicken Breasts

Prep time: 10 minutes | Cook time: 15 minutes | Serves: 4

1-pound chicken breasts, skinless and boneless	1 teaspoon olive oil
1 teaspoon poultry seasoning	1 teaspoon salt

1. Season the chicken breasts with poultry seasoning and salt after drizzling them with oil. 2. Select the Air Fry function. Set time to 15 minutes and temperature to 400 degrees F. 3. Place the chicken breasts in the cooking tray and cook for 10 minutes. Cook for another 5 minutes after flipping the chicken. 4. Serve and have fun.

Per serving: Calories 237; Fat 10.8g; Sodium 370mg; Carbs 0.3g; Fiber 0g; Sugar 0g; Protein 32.9g

Chicken Wings with Ranch Seasoning Mix

Prep time: 10 minutes | Cook time: 25 minutes | Serves: 4

1 pound of chicken wings	1 tablespoon ranch seasoning mix
4 garlic cloves, minced	
¼ cup butter, melted	

1. Place the chicken wings in a zip-lock bag. 2. Combine the butter, garlic, and ranch seasoning in a mixing bowl and pour over the chicken wings. Refrigerate overnight after sealing the bag and shaking it carefully. 3. Select Air Fry function. Set timer to 25 minutes and temperature to 400 degrees F. 4. Place the marinated chicken wings in the cooking tray and cook for 20 minutes. Twice shake the cooking tray. 5. Cook the chicken wings for another 5 minutes. 6. Serve and have fun.

Per serving: Calories 552; Fat 28.3g; Sodium 440mg; Carbs 1.3g; Fiber 0.1g; Sugar 0.1g; Protein 66g

Chicken Thighs with Ranch Seasoning

Prep time: 10 minutes | Cook time: 23 minutes | Serves: 4

4 chicken thighs, bone-in & skin-on	½ tablespoon ranch dressing mix

1. Toss the chicken thighs with the ranch dressing mix in a mixing basin. Toss well to coat. 2. Cook the chicken thighs in the cooking tray after spraying them. 3. Select Air Fry function. Set timer to 23 minutes and temperature to 400 degrees F. 4. Cook for 23 minutes. Flip the chicken halfway through cooking. 5. Serve and have fun.

Per serving: Calories 558; Fat 21.7g; Sodium 280mg; Carbs 0.5g; Fiber 0g; Sugar 0g; Protein 84.6g

Taco Ranch Chicken Wings

Prep time: 10 minutes | Cook time: 30 minutes | Serves: 4

1 pound of chicken wings	1 ½ teaspoons taco seasoning
1 teaspoon ranch seasoning	1 teaspoon olive oil

1. Heat the air fryer to 400 degrees F in advance. 2. Combine the chicken wings, ranch seasoning, taco seasoning, and oil in a mixing dish and toss well to coat. 3. Select Air Fry function. Set timer to 30 minutes and temperature to 400 degrees F. 4. Cook for 15 minutes in the cooking tray with chicken wings. 5. Cook for another 15 minutes on the opposite side of the chicken wings. 6. Serve and have fun.

Per serving: Calories 444; Fat 18g; Sodium 170mg; Carbs 0g; Fiber 0g; Sugar 0g; Protein 65.6g

Cajun Chicken Wings

Prep time: 10 minutes | Cook time: 25 minutes | Serves: 4

2 pounds of chicken wings	1 tablespoon + ½ teaspoon Cajun seasoning
⅓ cup ranch dressing	

1. Apply the Cajun spice to the chicken wings. 2. Select Air Fry function. Set the timer to 25 minutes to temp to 400 degrees F. 3. Cook the chicken wings in the cooking tray for 25 minutes at 400 degrees F. Halfway through the cooking time, flip the chicken wings. 4. Meanwhile, whisk together ranch dressing and 1 teaspoon of Cajun spice in a small dish. 5. Enjoy the chicken wings with a Cajun ranch sauce.

Per serving: Calories 437; Fat 16.9g; Sodium 370mg; Carbs 1.1g; Fiber 0g; Sugar 0.1g; Protein 65.9g

Almond Chicken

Prep time: 10 minutes | Cook time: 10 minutes | Serves: 4

8 oz. chicken, skinless and boneless	½ teaspoon salt
½ teaspoon black pepper	½ cup almond meal
	1 egg, beaten

1. Heat the air fryer to 400 degrees F in advance. 2. In a mixing bowl, whisk the egg until it is foamy, then season with pepper and salt. 3. Combine almond meal and salt in a small dish. 4. After dipping the chicken in the egg mixture, coat it with an almond meal. 5. Select Air Fry function. Set timer to 10 minutes and temperature to 400 degrees F. 6. Cook for 10 minutes in a cooking tray with breaded chicken. 7. Serve and have fun.

Per serving: Calories 285; Fat 12.8g; Sodium 440mg; Carbs 3.7g; Fiber 1g; Sugar 1g; Protein 38.1g

Lime Chicken Wings with Honey

Prep time: 10 minutes | Cook time: 30 minutes | Serves: 6

3 pounds of chicken wings	¼ teaspoon white pepper powder
1 tablespoon fresh lime juice	
Salt and black pepper to taste	1 tablespoon honey

1. Combine all ingredients in a mixing bowl and toss to combine. 2. Refrigerate the chicken wings for 10 minutes after marinating them. 3. Preheat the air fryer to 400 degrees F. 4. Select Air Fry function. Set timer to 15 minutes and temperature to 400 degrees F. 5. Cook for 15 minutes in the cooking tray with marinated chicken wings. Shake the cooking tray halfway through. 6. Serve and have fun.

Per serving: Calories 311; Fat 11.2g; Sodium 440mg; Carbs 6.1g; Fiber 0.1g; Sugar 0.1g; Protein 43.8g

Chicken Drumsticks with Chicken Seasoning

Prep time: 10 minutes | Cook time: 16 minutes | Serves: 4

1 ½ pounds chicken drum-sticks
1 tablespoon chicken season-ing
1 teaspoon black pepper
1 tablespoon olive oil
1 teaspoon salt

1. Combine the chicken seasoning, olive oil, pepper, and salt in a small bowl. 2. Using your hands, rub the spice mixture over the chicken. 3. Select Air Fry function. Set timer to 16 minutes and temperature to 400 degrees F. 4. Cook for 10 minutes in the cooking tray with seasoned chicken, flipping drumsticks halfway through. 5. Serve and have fun.

Per serving: Calories 319; Fat 13.2g; Sodium 540mg; Carbs 0.3g; Fiber 0g; Sugar 0g; Protein 46.8g

Super Easy Chicken Wings

Prep time: 10 minutes | Cook time: 25 minutes | Serves: 4

2 pounds of chicken wings
1 tablespoon pepper
1 tablespoon garlic powder
1 tablespoon seasoning salt

1. Except for the chicken wings, combine all ingredients in a mixing dish. 2. Toss the chicken wings in a basin until fully coated. 3. Preheat the air fryer for 5 minutes at 400 degrees F. 4. Select Air Fry function. Set timer to 20 minutes and temperature to 400 degrees F. 5. Cook for 20 minutes in the air fryer's basket with the chicken wings. Halfway through cooking, give the basket a good shake. 6. Serve and have fun!

Per serving: Calories 442; Fat 16.9g; Sodium 390mg; Carbs 2.6g; Fiber 0.1g; Sugar 1g; Protein 66.1g

Chicken Thighs with Curry Paste

Prep time: 10 minutes | Cook time: 20 minutes | Serves: 4

1-pound chicken thighs, bone-less and skinless
1 teaspoon ginger, minced
2 garlic cloves, chopped
½ cup coconut milk
1 tablespoon curry paste

1. In a zip-lock bag, combine all ingredients and shake thoroughly before placing them in the refrigerator overnight. 2. On a pie plate, combine the marinated chicken and the sauce. 3. Select Air Fry function. Set timer to 20 minutes and temperature to 400 degrees F. 4. Cook for 20 minutes in the air fryer. 5. Serve and have fun.

Per serving: Calories 341; Fat 20g; Sodium 430mg; Carbs 5.2g; Fiber 1g; Sugar 1g; Protein 34.1g

Air Fried Chicken Patties

Prep time: 10 minutes | Cook time: 13 minutes | Serves: 8

3 pounds of ground chicken
1 cup homemade salsa
½ small onion, chopped
1 ½ cups egg whites
Salt and Pepper

1. Blend the egg whites, salsa, and onion until smooth. 2. In a large mixing bowl, combine the ground chicken and egg mixture. Mix in the pepper and salt until everything is thoroughly mixed. 3. Form tiny patties out of the meat mixture. 4. Using cooking spray, coat the cooking tray. 5. Select Air Fry function. Set timer to 13 minutes and temperature to 400 degrees F. 6. Cook for 12-13 minutes in an air fryer with chicken patties. Cook in batches if possible. 7. Serve and have fun.

Per serving: Calories 357; Fat 12.7g; Sodium 520mg; Carbs 2.8g; Fiber 0g; Sugar 0g; Protein 54.7g

Skinless Chicken Drumsticks with Cajun Seasoning

Prep time: 5 minutes | Cook time: 15 minutes | Serves: 2

4 chicken drumsticks, skinless
1 tablespoon Cajun seasoning
1 teaspoon olive oil

1. In a zip-lock bag, combine all of the ingredients. Refrigerate for 30 minutes after thoroughly shaking the bag. 2. Select Air Fry function. Set timer to 15 minutes and temperature to 400 degrees F. 3. Cook for 15 minutes at 400 degrees F/ 204 degrees C in a cooking tray with marinated chicken drumsticks. 4. Serve and have fun.

Per serving: Calories 118; Fat 7.3g; Sodium 450mg; Carbs 0g; Fiber 0g; Sugar 0g; Protein 12.7g

Chicken Drumsticks with Garlic and Honey

Prep time: 10 minutes | Cook time: 15 minutes | Serves: 2

4 chicken drumsticks, skinless
½ teaspoon garlic, minced
1 teaspoon honey
1 teaspoon olive oil

1. In a mixing bowl, combine all ingredients and stir until thoroughly combined. 2. Refrigerate the chicken for 30 minutes. 3. Select Air Fry function. Set timer to 15 minutes and temperature to 400 degrees F. 4. Cook for 15 minutes at 400 degrees F/204 degrees C in the air fryer with marinated chicken. 5. Serve and have fun.

Per serving: Calories 140; Fat 7.3g; Sodium 440mg; Carbs 6g; Fiber 0g; Sugar 0g; Protein 12.7g

Chicken Wings with Sriracha Sauce

Prep time: 10 minutes | Cook time: 35 minutes | Serves: 2

1 pound of chicken wings
½ lime juice
1 tablespoon grass-fed butter
1 tablespoon sriracha sauce
¼ cup honey

1. Heat the air fryer to 400 degrees F in advance. 2. Select Air Fry function. Set timer to 30 minutes and temperature to 400 degrees F. 3. Cook for 30 minutes in a cooking tray with chicken wings. 4. Meanwhile, combine all remaining ingredients in a saucepan and bring to a boil for 3 minutes. 5. When the chicken wings are finished, mix them with the sauce and serve.

Per serving: Calories 711; Fat 32.6g; Sodium 564mg; Carbs 35.9g; Fiber 4g; Sugar 3.7g; Protein 65.8g

Sweet and Spicy Chicken Wings

Prep time: 10 minutes | Cook time: 20 minutes | Serves: 8

3 pounds of chicken wings
1 tablespoon honey
½ cup buffalo sauce
1 tablespoon grass-fed butter, melted
salt and pepper to taste

1. Select the Air Fry function. Set timer to 20 minutes and temperature to 400 degrees F. 2. Cook the chicken wings in the cooking tray for 20 minutes at 400 degrees F/204 degrees C. During the frying process, shake the cooking tray twice. 3. Combine the honey, buffalo sauce, butter, pepper, and salt in a large mixing basin. 4. Toss the cooked chicken wings in the bowl with the sauce until completely covered. 5. Serve and have fun.

Per serving: Calories 262; Fat 11.7g; Sodium 345mg; Carbs 4.6g; Fiber 0.1g; Sugar 0.1g; Protein 32.9g

Breaded Turkey Breast

Prep time: 5 minutes | Cook time: 20 minutes | Serves: 4

4 oz. turkey breast
1 egg, beaten
1 cup breadcrumbs
½ teaspoon dried thyme
Salt and black pepper to taste

1. Heat the air fryer to 400 degrees F using the Air Fry function. Transfer the turkey to a bowl after pulsing it in a food processor. Add the thyme, salt, and pepper and mix well. 2. Form nugget-sized balls out of the turkey mixture and coat them with breadcrumbs, eggs, and breadcrumbs. Place the nuggets in the baking pan on a greased cooking tray. 3. Set the time to 10 minutes and the temperature to 400 degrees F. Cook for 10 minutes, or until golden brown, shaking once. 4. Warm the dish before serving.
Per serving: Calories 285; Fat 12.8g; Sodium 440mg; Carbs 3.7g; Fiber 0g; Sugar 0.1g; Protein 38.1g

Chicken Cubes with Fruit and BBQ Sauce

Prep time: 5 minutes | Cook time: 20 minutes | Serves: 2

1 chicken breast, cubed
1 green bell pepper, sliced
½ onion, sliced
1 can drain pineapple chunks
½ cup barbecue sauce

1. Preheat the air fryer to 365 degrees F on the Bake setting. 2. On the skewers, thread the green bell peppers, chicken pieces, onions, and pineapple chunks. 3. Set the time to 20 minutes and the temperature to 365 degrees F. 4. Brush with barbecue sauce and cook for 20 minutes in your air fryer, until slightly crispy. 5. Serve.
Per serving: Calories 296; Fat 10g; Sodium 310mg; Carbs 5g; Fiber 0g; Sugar 1g; Protein 34g

Honey-Glazed Chicken Drumsticks

Prep time: 35 minutes | Cook time: 20 minutes | Serves: 4

8 chicken drumsticks, skin removed
2 tablespoons olive oil
2 tablespoons honey
½ tablespoon garlic, minced

1. In a sealable zip bag, combine the garlic, olive oil, and honey. 2. Set aside 30 minutes after adding the chicken and tossing it to coat it. 3. Place the coated chicken in the basket and place it on the baking sheet; cook for 15 minutes on the Air Fry function at 400 degrees F, flipping once. 4. Serve and have fun!
Per serving: Calories 364; Fat 8g; Sodium 340mg; Carbs 5g; Fiber 0g; Sugar 1g; Protein 32g

Hot Chicken Wings

Prep time: 5 minutes | Cook time: 20 minutes | Serves: 2

1 pound of chicken wings
1 tablespoon water
1 tablespoon potato starch
1 tablespoon hot curry paste
½ tablespoon baking powder

1. Combine the hot curry paste and the water in a bowl. Toss in the wings to coat them. Refrigerate for 30 minutes after covering the bowl with plastic wrap. 2. Preheat the air fryer to 400 degrees F using the Air Fry function. Combine the baking powder and potato starch in a mixing dish. Take the wings out of the refrigerator and coat them in the starch mixture. 3. Set the air fryer in air fry mode. Set time to 14 minutes and temperature to 400 degrees F. 4. Cook for 7 minutes in your air fryer on a lined baking dish. Cook for another 5 minutes on the other side. 5. Remove from the air fryer and serve.
Per serving: Calories 283; Fat 12g; Sodium 540mg; Carbs 3.8g; Fiber 0g; Sugar 0.1g; Protein 29g

Sweet Chicken Drumsticks

Prep time: 35 minutes | Cook time: 20 minutes | Serves: 2

1-pound chicken drumsticks, skin removed
1 tablespoon olive oil
1 tablespoon honey
½ tablespoon garlic, minced

1. In a re-sealable bag, combine all ingredients and massage until thoroughly covered. Refrigerate the chicken for 30 minutes to allow it to marinade. 2. Preheat to 400 degrees F using the Air Fry function. After removing the chicken drumsticks from the fridge, place them in the oiled basket. 3. Set timer to 15 minutes and temperature to 400 degrees F. Cook for 15 minutes, shaking once, on the cooking tray. 4. Serve immediately.
Per serving: Calories 245; Fat 9g; Sodium 370mg; Carbs 8g; Fiber 1g; Sugar 1g; Protein 34g

Spicy Buffalo Chicken Wings

Prep time: 5 minutes | Cook time: 25 minutes | Serves: 4

2 pounds of chicken wings
½ cup cayenne pepper sauce
½ cup coconut oil
1 tablespoon Worcestershire sauce
1 tablespoon kosher salt

1. Set aside a bowl containing cayenne pepper sauce, coconut oil, Worcestershire sauce, and salt. 2. Place the chicken in the cooking tray and the baking pan. 3. Set the time to 25 minutes and the temperature to 400 degrees F using the Air Fry function. Then cook in the air fryer. 4. To serve, transfer to a large dish and sprinkle with the prepared sauce.
Per serving: Calories 285; Fat 12.8g; Sodium 270mg; Carbs 3.7g; Fiber 0g; Sugar 1g; Protein 38.1g

Rosemary Chicken Breasts

Prep time: 5 minutes | Cook time: 15 minutes | Serves: 4

1 chicken breasts
salt and black pepper to taste
½ cup dried rosemary
1 tablespoon butter, melted

1. Preheat to 400 degrees F using the Air Fry function. 2. On a level surface, place a sheet of foil. Drizzle the butter over the breasts and sprinkle with rosemary, tarragon, salt, and pepper. 3. Select the Air Fry function. Set time to 12 minutes and temperature to 400 degrees F. 4. Wrap the foil around the breasts and secure it in place. 5. Cook for 12 minutes with the covered chicken in the cooking tray. Remove the wrapper and carefully unwrap it. 6. Serve with steamed vegetables and the sauce extract.
Per serving: Calories 312; Fat 7.5g; Sodium 470mg; Carbs 6g; Fiber 1g; Sugar 1g; Protein 42g

Chicken Thighs with Ketchup

Prep time: 10 minutes | Cook time: 30 minutes | Serves: 2

1 pound of chicken thighs, skinless and boneless
½ teaspoon ground ginger
1 garlic clove, minced
1 tablespoon ketchup
½ cup honey

1. Cut the chicken thighs into tiny pieces and set them in the cooking tray. 2. Select the Air Fry function. Cook by setting time to 25 minutes and temperature to 400 degrees F/204 degrees C. 3. Meanwhile, combine honey, ketchup, garlic, and ground ginger in a skillet and cook for 4-5 minutes. 4. After the chicken is done, place it in a mixing dish. 5. Toss the chicken in the honey mixture until completely covered. 6. Serve and have fun.
Per serving: Calories 554; Fat 16.3g; Sodium 365mg; Carbs 37.2g; Fiber 4g; Sugar 3.8g; Protein 63.7g

Chicken Drumsticks Roasted with Herbs

Prep time: 5 minutes | Cook time: 20 minutes | Serves: 4

1-pound chicken drumsticks
1 tablespoon lemon juice
1 teaspoon garlic salt
1 teaspoon chili powder
1 ½ teaspoon mixed herbs

1. Heat the air fryer to 400 degrees F for 5 minutes. 2. Combine garlic salt, chili powder, and mixed herbs in a small bowl. 3. Rub the chicken with lemon juice and garlic salt mixture. 4. Select the Air Fry function. Set timer to 15 minutes and temperature to 400 degrees F. 5. Cook the chicken on the cooking tray. 6. Serve and have fun.
Per serving: Calories 86; Fat 2.8g; Sodium 70mg; Carbs 1.3g; Fiber 0g; Sugar 0g; Protein 13g

Honey Chicken Thighs

Prep time: 5 minutes | Cook time: 25 minutes | Serves: 4

2 pounds of chicken thighs, skin-on
1 tablespoon honey
1 tablespoon Dijon mustard
½ tablespoon garlic powder
Salt and black pepper to taste

1. Combine honey, mustard, garlic, salt, and black pepper in a mixing bowl. 2. Coat the thighs with the sauce and place them in the oiled basket. 3. Fit into the baking pan, select Bake function, and bake for 16 minutes on the Air Fry setting at 365 degrees F, flipping halfway through. 4. Warm the dish before serving.
Per serving: Calories 285; Fat 12.8g; Sodium 334mg; Carbs 3.7g; Fiber 0.1g; Sugar 0.1g; Protein 38.1g

Butter Air-Fried Chicken Tenderloins

Prep time: 5 minutes | Cook time: 10 minutes | Serves: 4

2 pounds of chicken tenderloins
1 tablespoon butter, softened
1 oz. breadcrumbs
1 large egg, whisked

1. Preheat on Air Fry function at 380 degrees F. 2. In a mixing dish, combine the butter and breadcrumbs. Continue to combine and stir until the mixture becomes crumbly. Dip the chicken in the egg, then in the crumb mixture. 3. Select the Air Fry function. Set timer to 10 minutes and temperature to 400 degrees F. 4. Cook for 10 minutes, turning once, until crispy, in the oiled basket and fitted on the baking tray. 5. For a crispier flavor, use the Broil function. Serve.
Per serving: Calories 245; Fat 11g; Sodium 290mg; Carbs 4.8g; Fiber 1g; Sugar 1g; Protein 28.5g

Chicken Breast with Avocado and Radish

Prep time: 5 minutes | Cook time: 15 minutes | Serves: 2

1 chicken breasts
1 avocado, sliced
1 radish, sliced
1 tablespoon chopped parsley
Salt and black pepper to taste

1. Heat the air fryer to 400 degrees F using the Air Fry function. Cut the chicken into tiny pieces. 2. In a mixing bowl, combine all ingredients and put them on the cooking tray. 3. Set the time to 14 minutes and temp 400 degrees F. Cook for 14 minutes, shaking once halfway through. 4. Serve with fried red kidney beans or boiled rice.
Per serving: Calories 285; Fat 12g; Sodium 370mg; Carbs 3.6g; Fiber 0g; Sugar 1g; Protein 35.7g

Chinese Style Wings

Prep time: 5 minutes | Cook time: 10 minutes | Serves: 4

1 pound of chicken wings
3 tablespoons lime juice
2 tablespoons soy sauce
2 tablespoons honey
salt and black pepper to the taste

1. Whisk together honey, soy sauce, salt, black pepper, and lime juice in a mixing bowl. Add chicken pieces, toss to coat, and chill for 20 minutes. 2. Select the Air Fry function. Set time to 15 minutes and temperature to 400 degrees F. 3. Cook for 6 minutes on each side in your air fryer, then cook for 3 minutes more. 4. Serve immediately.
Per serving: Calories 372; Fat 9g; Sodium 370mg; Carbs 37g; Fiber 10g; Sugar 3g; Protein 24g

Chicken Wings with Asparagus

Prep time: 5 minutes | Cook time: 25 minutes | Serves: 4

2 asparagus spears
1-pound chicken wings, halved.
1 tablespoon rosemary,
chopped.
1 teaspoon cumin, ground.
salt and pepper to the taste

1. Season the chicken wings with salt, pepper, cumin, and rosemary before placing them on the cooking tray. 2. Select the Air Fry function and set the time to 20 minutes and the temperature to 400 degrees F. Then cook. 3. Meanwhile, heat a skillet over medium heat, add the asparagus, cover with water, and steam for a few minutes; move to a basin of cold water, drain, and serve. 4. Serve with chicken wings on the side.
Per serving: Calories 270; Fat 8g; Sodium 330mg; Carbs 24g; Fiber 12g; Sugar 2g; Protein 22g

Mustard Duck Breast with Tomato Paste

Prep time: 5 minutes | Cook time: 30 minutes | Serves: 2

1 smoked duck breast, halved.
1 tablespoon mustard
1 teaspoon tomato paste
½ tablespoon apple vinegar
1 teaspoon honey

1. Whisk together the honey, tomato paste, mustard, and vinegar in a mixing bowl. 2. Add the duck breast pieces and toss to coat thoroughly. 3. Select the Air Fry function. Set time to 25 minutes and temperature to 400 degrees F. Transfer to the air fryer and cook for 15 minutes. 4. Remove the duck breast from the air fryer, combine with the honey mixture, return to the air fryer, and cook for another 6 minutes. 5. Serve with a side salad and divide among plates.
Per serving: Calories 274; Fat 11g; Sodium 440mg; Carbs 22g; Fiber 13g; Sugar 4g; Protein 13g

Creamy Coconut Chicken

Prep time: 20 minutes | Cook time: 25 minutes | Serves: 4

4 big chicken legs
4 tablespoons coconut cream
2 tablespoons ginger, grated.
5 teaspoons turmeric powder
salt and pepper for taste

1. Whisk together the cream, turmeric, ginger, salt, and pepper in a mixing bowl. 2. Add the chicken pieces, stir well, and set aside for 20 minutes. 3. Select the Air Fry function. Set time to 25 minutes and temperature to 400 degrees F. 4. Cook for 25 minutes in a preheated air fryer; divide among plates and serve with a side salad.
Per serving: Calories 300; Fat 4g; Sodium 300mg; Carbs 22g; Fiber 12g; Sugar 1.9g; Protein 20g

Buttermilk-Marinated Whole Chicken

Prep time: 10 minutes | Cook time: 25 minutes | Serves: 6

3 pounds of whole chicken
1 tablespoon salt
1-pint buttermilk

1. Place the entire chicken in a large mixing basin and season with salt. 2. In a large mixing bowl, pour the buttermilk over the chicken and soak it overnight. 3. Refrigerate the chicken bowl overnight, covered. 4. Remove the chicken from the marinade and place it on the air fryer's rotisserie spit. 5. Select the "Roast" mode. 6. Adjust the cooking time to 25 minutes. 7. Adjust the temperature to 380 degrees F. 8. Allow the chicken to roast with the cover closed. 9. Warm the dish before serving.
Per serving: Calories 284; Fat 7.9g; Sodium 704mg; Carbs 46g; Fiber 3.6g; Sugar 5.5g; Protein 17.9g

Roasted Mayonnaise Turkey Breast

Prep time: 10 minutes | Cook time: 40 minutes | Serves: 6

3 pounds of boneless turkey breast
¼ cup mayonnaise
1 tablespoon poultry seasoning
Salt and black pepper
½ teaspoon garlic powder

1. Mix all ingredients, including the turkey, and coat it thoroughly in a mixing bowl. 2. In the cooking tray, place the boneless turkey breast. 3. Select the "Air Fry" mode. 4. Adjust the time to 40 minutes. 5. Adjust the temperature to 400 degrees F. 6. Place the cooking tray in the air fryer and close the cover to bake after it has been warmed. 7. Cut into slices and serve.
Per serving: Calories 322; Fat 11.8g; Sodium 321mg; Carbs 14.6g; Fiber 4.4g; Sugar 8g; Protein 17.3g

Chicken Breasts with Diced Tomatoes

Prep time: 10 minutes | Cook time: 25 minutes | Serves: 6

¾ pounds chicken breasts
3 tablespoons pesto sauce
½ (14 oz.) can of tomatoes, diced
1 cup Mozzarella cheese, shredded
2 tablespoons fresh basil, chopped

1. In a cooking tray, place the flattened chicken breasts and cover them with pesto. 2. Top each chicken piece with tomatoes, mozzarella, and basil. 3. To choose the "Bake" mode, press the "Start" on the air fryer. 4. Adjust the cooking time to 25 minutes. 5. Press the +/- Temp arrows to set the temperature to 365 degrees F. 6. Place the cooking tray inside and close the door after warming the air fryer. 7. Warm the dish before serving.
Per serving: Calories 537; Fat 19.8g; Sodium 719mg; Carbs 25.1g; Fiber 1g; Sugar 1.4g; Protein 37.8g

Garlic Chicken Breast Fillet

Prep time: 15 minutes | Cook time: 40 minutes | Serves: 4

1 chicken breast fillet
1 tablespoon lemon juice
1 tablespoon melted butter
1 teaspoon garlic powder
Salt and pepper to taste

1. In a mixing dish, combine lemon juice and melted butter. 2. Brush the mixture on both sides of the chicken. 3. Add garlic powder, salt, and pepper to taste. Select the Air Fry function. 4. Preheat your air fryer to 400 degrees F. 5. Place the chicken on the cooking tray. 6. Pull the hood over your head. 7. Set timer to 20 minutes and temperature to 400 degrees F 8. Cook for 15 to 20 minutes per side at 400 degrees F.
Per serving: Calories 553; Fat 31.26g; Sodium 470mg; Carbs 1.89g; Fiber 0g; Sugar 0g; Protein 62.46g

Roasted Chicken with Ranch Dressing

Prep time: 30 minutes | Cook time: 45 minutes | Serves: 6

6 chicken thigh fillets
4 tablespoons ranch dressing
garlic, salt, and pepper

1. Spread the ranch dressing on all sides of the chicken. 2. Garlic salt and pepper to taste. 3. Select the Roast function. 4. Preheat the air fryer to 380 degrees F. 5. Place the chicken on the cooking tray. 6. Set time to 30 minutes and temperature to 380 degrees F. 7. Cook each side for 15 minutes.
Per serving: Calories 475; Fat 36.43g; Sodium 440mg; Carbs 1.66g; Fiber 0g; Sugar 0g; Protein 33.16g

Sweet & Sour Chicken Thigh Pieces

Prep time: 15 minutes | Cook time: 15 minutes | Serves: 4

¾ pound boneless, skinless chicken thighs, cut into 1-inch pieces
1 small red onion, sliced
1 yellow bell pepper, cut into 1½-inch pieces
1 tablespoon cornstarch
¼ cup chicken stock
1 tablespoon olive oil
1 to 3 teaspoon curry powder
1 tablespoon honey
¼ cup orange juice

1. Drizzle olive oil over the red onion, chicken thighs, and pepper in the cooking tray. 2. Select the Air Fry function. Set time to 15 minutes and temperature to 400 degrees F. 3. Place the cover on the air fryer and cook for 12 to 14 minutes at 400 degrees F in a preheated air fryer. When the lid screen reads 'turn food', flip the chicken thighs. 4. In a 6-inch metal bowl, combine the chicken and veggies. 5. Mix the chicken stock, curry powder, honey, orange juice, and cornstarch in a mixing dish. Mix everything up thoroughly. 6. Place the metal bowl within the cooking tray and close the cover. Cook for another 3 minutes. 7. Take the bowl out of the basket. Allow 3 minutes to cool before serving.
Per serving: Calories 746; Fat 22.98g; Sodium 471mg; Carbs 25.2g; Fiber 2.1g; Sugar 14.48g; Protein 12.61g

Lime Chicken Pieces

Prep time: 5 minutes | Cook time: 30 minutes | Serves: 6

1 whole chicken; cut into medium pieces	ons
Grated Lemon Zest of 2 lem-	Juice from 2 lemons
	1 tablespoon olive oil

1. Season the chicken with salt and pepper, rub with oil and lemon zest, and sprinkle with lemon juice. 2. Select the Air Fry function. Set time to 30 minutes and temperature to 400 degrees F. Cook for 30 minutes, turning midway through. 3. Serve with a side salad and divide among plates.

Per serving: Calories 334; Fat 24g; Sodium 440mg; Carbs 26g; Fiber 12g; Sugar 5g; Protein 20g

Avocado Chicken Breast

Prep time: 15 minutes | Cook time: 10 minutes | Serves: 4

1 boneless, skinless chicken breast, sliced	½ cup spicy ranch salad dressing
1 avocado, peeled and chopped	½ teaspoon dried oregano
1 small red onion, sliced	1 corn tortillas
1 red bell pepper, sliced	1 cup torn butter lettuce

1. Combine the onion, chicken, and pepper in the cooking tray. Drizzle 1 tablespoon of salad dressing over the top and season with oregano. 2. Select the Air Fry function. Set timer to 15 minutes and temperature to 400 degrees F. 3. Place the cover on the air fryer and cook for 10 to 14 minutes at 400 degrees F in a preheated air fryer. 4. Halfway through the cooking period, flip the chicken when the lid panel displays 'Turn Food' or until the chicken is browned and slightly scorched. 5. Transfer the veggies and chicken to a serving plate from the basket. Drizzle the remaining salad dressing over the top. 6. Warm the dish before serving.

Per serving: Calories 887; Fat 34.25g; Sodium 2841mg; Carbs 14.29g; Fiber 7.3g; Sugar 4.2g; Protein 22.2g

Spicy Chicken Breast in Veggie Soup

Prep time: 5 minutes | Cook time: 20 minutes | Serves: 4

1 chicken breast, cubed	1 cup mushroom soup
1 ½ cup onion soup mix	½ cup heavy cream

1. Preheat your air fryer to 365 degrees F on the Bake setting. 2. Combine the mushrooms, onion mixture, and heavy cream in a cooking tray. 3. Heat it for 1 minute on low heat. Allow approximately 25 minutes of resting time after pouring the heated liquid over the chicken. 4. Set the time to 15 minutes and the temperature to 365 degrees F. Cook for 15 minutes after placing the marinated chicken in the basket and fitting it into the air fryer. 5. Serve and have fun!

Per serving: Calories 246; Fat 11.3g; Sodium 330mg; Carbs 4.3g; Fiber 0g; Sugar 1g; Protein 31g

Butter Turkey Breast Halves

Prep time: 5 minutes | Cook time: 20 minutes | Serves: 4

1-pound turkey breast, halved	½ teaspoon cayenne pepper
½ cup panko breadcrumbs	1 stick butter, melted
salt and black pepper to taste	

1. Combine the breadcrumbs, salt, cayenne, and black pepper in a mixing bowl. Brush the turkey breast with butter, then roll it into the crumb mixture. 2. Select the Bake function.

Set timer to 15 minutes and temperature to 365 degrees F. 3. Place in a baking dish that has been lined with parchment paper. Cook for 15 minutes at 365 degrees F in your air fryer. Warm the dish before serving.

Per serving: Calories 282; Fat 12.4g; Sodium 440mg; Carbs 3.4g; Fiber 0g; Sugar 0g; Protein 36.2g

Asian-Style Turkey Meatballs

Prep time: 24 minutes | Cook time: 13 minutes | Serves: 4

1-pound ground turkey	1 tablespoon low-sodium soy sauce
1 small onion, minced	½ teaspoon ground ginger
1 tablespoon peanut oil	¼ cup panko bread crumbs
¼ cup water chestnuts, finely chopped	1 egg, beaten

1. Combine the onion and peanut oil in a 6×6×2-inch baking pan. Stir everything together thoroughly. 2. Arrange the baking pan in the air fryer and cover it with the lid. Cook for 1 to 2 minutes in a preheated air fryer at 365 degrees F until the onion is tender and transparent. Place the sautéed onion in a large mixing basin. 3. Toss the onion with the water chestnuts, soy sauce, ground ginger, and bread crumbs. 4. In a separate bowl, mix the beaten egg and the turkey. Toss until everything is thoroughly mixed. 5. Scoop the mixture onto the cutting board and roll into 1-inch meatballs. 6. Drizzle the oil over the meatballs and arrange them in the pan. 7. Arrange the baking pan in the air fryer and cover it with the lid. 8. Select the Bake function. Bake for 10 to 12 minutes in batches at 365 degrees F. 9. Transfer the meatballs to a dish from the pan. Allow 3 minutes to cool before serving.

Per serving: Calories 683; Fat 33.29g; Sodium 342mg; Carbs 3.23g; Fiber 0.6g; Sugar 1.17g; Protein 24.77g

Spiced Chicken Pieces

Prep time: 15 minutes | Cook time: 15 minutes | Serves: 4

4 chicken pieces: drumsticks, breasts, and thighs	2 eggs, beaten
⅓ cup buttermilk	1½ cups bread crumbs
1 cup flour	2 tablespoons olive oil
2 teaspoons paprika	Freshly ground black pepper
	Salt to taste

1. Use a paper towel and thoroughly dry the chicken on your cutting board. Combine the flour, paprika, salt, and pepper in a small basin. 2. Mix the eggs and buttermilk in a separate dish until thoroughly blended. 3. Combine the bread crumbs and olive oil in a separate bowl. 4. Dredge the chicken in the flour, then in the eggs, and finally in the bread crumbs. To cover the chicken pieces thoroughly, gently yet firmly press the crumbs onto the skin. 5. In the cooking tray, place the breaded chicken. 6. Select the Air Fry function. Set time to 15 minutes and temperature to 400 degrees F. 7. Cook for 15 minutes in a preheated air fryer at 375 degrees F with the lid closed. 8. Transfer the chicken to a serving dish. Let cool for 5 minutes before serving.

Per serving: Calories 651; Fat 22.34g; Sodium 1257mg; Carbs 27.54g; Fiber 2.2g; Sugar 6.14g; Protein 14.38g

Crispy Parmigiana Chicken

Prep time: 15 minutes | Cook time: 15 minutes | Serves: 4

4 ounces boneless, skinless chicken breasts	1 teaspoon Italian seasoning
½ cup grated Parmesan cheese	Salt and pepper to taste
1 cup Italian bread crumbs	2 egg whites
	¾ cup marinara sauce

½ cup shredded mozzarella cheese   Cooking spray

1. Pound the chicken into ¼-inch chunks on a level work surface. 2. Combine the bread crumbs, Parmesan cheese, Italian seasoning, salt, and pepper in a large mixing basin. 3. Stir until everything is thoroughly mixed. Pour the egg whites into a separate basin. Remove from the equation. 4. By using cooking spray, spray the cooking tray. 5. To coat the chicken cutlets, dredge them in the egg whites and the bread crumb mixture. 6. Spray the cooking tray with cooking spray and place the breaded cutlets in it. 7. Select the Air Fry function. Set time to 7 minutes and temperature to 400 degrees F. 8. Cover the air fryer and cook for 7 minutes at 400 degrees F in a prepared air fryer. 9. Place the fried chicken cutlets on a platter to serve. 10. Drizzle the marinara sauce over the top and top with mozzarella cheese. 11. Cook for an additional 3 minutes until the cheese is bubbly. 12. Let cool for 3 minutes and serve.

Per serving: Calories 944; Fat 70g; Sodium 593mg; Carbs 220g; Fiber 1g; Sugar 4g; Protein 105g

Whole Chicken Roasted with Creamer Potatoes

Prep time: 15 minutes | Cook time: 15 minutes | Serves: 4

1 broiler-fryer whole chicken (2½ to 3 pounds)	½ teaspoon garlic salt
16 creamer potatoes, scrubbed	1 slice of lemon
4 cloves garlic, peeled	½ teaspoon dried thyme
2 tablespoons olive oil	½ teaspoon dried marjoram

1. Clean the chicken by rinsing it and patting it dry with paper towels. 2. Combine 1 tablespoon of olive oil and salt in a small bowl. Coat half of the olive mixture evenly on all sides of the chicken. 3. In the chicken, stuff the lemon slice and garlic cloves. On top, sprig the thyme and marjoram. 4. Place the chicken in the cooking tray and the cleaned potatoes. Pour the rest of the olive oil mixture on top. Select the Roast function. Set time to 25 minutes and temperature to 380 degrees F. 5. Cover the air fryer and roast for 25 minutes, or until a meat thermometer inserted into the thickest portion of the chicken reads 165 degrees F. 6. Return the chicken to the basket if it isn't entirely done, and roast for another 5 minutes. 7. Place the chicken and potatoes on a serving dish. Allow for a 5-minute rest period before serving.

Per serving: Calories 1523; Fat 22.77g; Sodium 1013mg; Carbs 24.16g; Fiber 1.5g; Sugar 0.24g; Protein 13.35g

Chicken Breast and Pita Sandwich

Prep time: 20 minutes | Cook time: 10 minutes | Serves: 4

1 boneless, skinless chicken breast cut into 1-inch cubes	½ teaspoon dried thyme
1 pita pocket split in half	1 cup cherry tomatoes, chopped
1 red bell pepper, sliced	1 cups butter lettuce, tear into slices
1 small red onion, sliced	
⅓ cup Italian salad dressing	Cooking spray

1. In the cooking tray, combine the chicken, bell pepper, and onion—1 tablespoon Italian salad dressing and thyme. To taste by using cooking spray, spritz the surface. 2. Select the Air Fry function. Set time to 11 minutes and temperature to 400 degrees F. 3. Place the cover on the air fryer and bake for 9 to 11 minutes in a preheated air fryer. When the air fryer lid panel displays "turn Food" halfway through cooking time, or until the chicken is cooked, shake the basket once. 4. Pour the remaining salad dressing over the chicken in a mixing bowl.

Mix everything up thoroughly. 5. Begin by layering the pita halves, butter lettuce pieces, and cherry tomatoes. 6. Serve right away.

Per serving: Calories 1493; Fat 146.77g; Sodium 1611mg; Carbs 36.38g; Fiber 3.7g; Sugar 9.78g; Protein 46.36g

Air-Fried Chicken Tenders

Prep time: 27 minutes | Cook time: 12 minutes | Serves: 4

4 chicken tenders	½ cup dry bread crumbs
½ cup all-purpose flour	1 tablespoon vegetable oil
1 egg	

1. Place the flour in a mixing basin. Remove from the equation. 2. Whisk the egg in a separate dish. Remove from the equation. 3. Combine the bread crumbs and oil in a separate bowl. Remove from the equation. 4. To coat the chicken tenders well, dredge them in flour, then in the whisked egg, and finally in the crumb mixture. 5. Select the Air Fry function. Set timer to 1 minute and temperature to 400 degrees F. 6. In the cooking tray, place the tenders. Cook for 12 minutes in a preheated air fryer. 7. Take the chicken tenders out of the basket and place them on a serving dish.

Per serving: Calories 253; Fat 11.4g; Sodium 171mg; Carbs 9.8g; Fiber 1g; Sugar 1g; Protein 26.2g

Lemon Pepper Chicken Wings

Prep time: 10 minutes | Cook time: 16 minutes | Serves: 4

1-pound chicken wings	1 tablespoon. olive oil
1 teaspoon lemon pepper	1 teaspoon salt

1. In a large mixing dish, place the chicken wings. 2. Toss the remaining ingredients over the chicken to evenly coat it. 3. In the cooking tray, place chicken wings. 4. Select the Air Fry function. Set time to 16 minutes and temperature to 400 degrees F. 5. Heat the air fryer to 400 degrees F ahead of time, and cook the chicken wings for 8 minutes. 6. Cook for another 8 minutes on the opposite side of the chicken wings. 7. Serve and have fun.

Per serving: Calories 247; Fat 11g; Sodium 290mg; Carbs 0.3g; Fiber 0g; Sugar 0g; Protein 32g

Whole Pekin Duck Roast

Prep time: 15 minutes | Cook time: 15 minutes | Serves: 4

6 pounds whole Pekin duck	½ cup balsamic vinegar
Salt	1 lemon, juiced
5 garlic cloves chopped	¼ cup honey
1 lemon, chopped	

1. Put the Pekin duck on a baking sheet and cover it with garlic, lemon, and salt. 2. In a mixing bowl, combine the honey, vinegar, and honey. 3. Using a brush, generously coat the duck in this glaze. Refrigerate the marinade overnight. 4. Remove the duck from the marinade and place it in the air fryer. 5. Select the "Roast" mode. 6. Adjust the cooking time to 3 hours. 7. Push the +/- Temp arrows to adjust the temperature to 380 degrees F. 8. Allow the duck to roast with the cover closed. 9. Warm the dish before serving.

Per serving: Calories 387; Fat 6g; Sodium 154mg; Carbs 37.4g; Fiber 2.9g; Sugar 15.3g; Protein 14.6g

Chicken Strips with Greek Yogurt and Buffalo Sauce

Prep time: 36 minutes | Cook time: 15 minutes | Serves: 4

1-pound skinless, boneless chicken breasts cut into 1-inch strips	1 tablespoon sweet paprika
	1 tablespoon cayenne pepper
	1 tablespoon garlic pepper
½ cup plain fat-free Greek yogurt	¼ cup egg substitute
	1 tablespoon hot sauce
1 cup panko bread crumbs	1 teaspoon hot sauce

1. Combine the bread crumbs, sweet paprika, cayenne pepper, and garlic in a mixing bowl. Remove from the equation. 2. Whisk together the Greek yogurt, egg replacement, and 1 tablespoon + 1 teaspoon spicy sauce in a separate dish. 3. Dip the chicken strips in the buffalo sauce before coating them in the bread crumb mixture. 4. Select the Air Fry function. Set time to 15 minutes and temperature to 400 degrees F. 5. In the cooking tray, arrange the well-coated chicken strips. Cook for 15 minutes in a preheated air fryer at 400 degrees F or until thoroughly browned with the air fry cover. 6. Flip the strips when the lid screen says "turn Food" halfway through. 7. Take the chicken out of the basket and place it on a dish to serve.

Per serving: Calories 234; Fat 4.6g; Sodium 696mg; Carbs 22.1g; Fiber 1.9g; Sugar 2g; Protein 31.2g

Spicy Meatballs

Prep time: 10 minutes | Cook time: 20 minutes | Serves: 6

1.5-pound turkey mince	4 tablespoons parsley, minced
1 red bell pepper, deseeded and chopped	1 tablespoon cilantro, minced
	Salt, to taste
1 large egg, beaten	Black pepper, to taste

1. In a mixing basin, combine all meatball ingredients and stir thoroughly. 2. In the cooking tray, form tiny meatballs from this mixture. 3. To choose the "Air Fry" mode, press the "Start" on the air fryer. 4. Adjust the cooking time to 20 minutes. 5. Adjust the temperature to 400 degrees F. 6. Place the cooking tray into the preheated air fryer and close the door. 7. Warm the dish before serving.

Per serving: Calories 338; Fat 9.7g; Sodium 245mg; Carbs 32.5g; Fiber 0.3g; Sugar 1.8g; Protein 10.3g

Mustard Chicken Thighs

Prep time: 10 minutes | Cook time: 30 minutes | Serves: 4

4 large chicken thighs, bone-in	1 clove of minced garlic
	½ teaspoon dried marjoram
2 tablespoons French mustard	2 tablespoons maple syrup
2 tablespoons Dijon mustard	

1. Toss the chicken with everything in a mixing basin and coat it thoroughly. 2. Place the chicken in the cooking tray with the marinade. 3. To choose the "Bake" mode, press the "Start" on the air fryer. 4. Adjust the cooking time to 30 minutes. 5. Adjust the temperature to 365 degrees F. 6. Place the cooking tray inside and close the door after warming the air fryer. 7. Warm the dish before serving.

Per serving: Calories 301; Fat 15.8g; Sodium 189mg; Carbs 31.7g; Fiber 0.3g; Sugar 0.1g; Protein 28.2g

Chicken Thighs with Orange Rice

Prep time: 10 minutes | Cook time: 55 minutes | Serves: 4

3 tablespoons olive oil	chicken thighs
1 medium onion, chopped	Black pepper, to taste
1 ¾ cups chicken broth	2 tablespoons fresh mint, chopped
1 cup brown basmati rice	
Zest and juice of 2 oranges	2 tablespoons pine nuts, toasted
Salt to taste	
4 (6-oz.) boneless, skinless	

1. Place the chicken on top of the rice in a casserole dish. 2. In a mixing basin, combine the other ingredients and generously pour over the chicken. 3. To choose the "Bake" mode, press the "Start" on the air fryer. 4. Adjust the cooking time to 55 minutes. 5. Adjust the temperature to 365 degrees F. 6. Place the casserole dish inside and close the top after it has been warmed. 7. Warm the dish before serving.

Per serving: Calories 231; Fat 20.1g; Sodium 941mg; Carbs 30.1g; Fiber 0.9g; Sugar 1.4g; Protein 14.6g

Chicken Thighs and Rice Casserole

Prep time: 10 minutes | Cook time: 40 minutes | Serves: 6

2 pounds' bone-in chicken thighs	paprika
	1 teaspoon hot Hungarian paprika
Salt and black pepper	
1 teaspoon olive oil	2 tablespoons tomato paste
5 cloves garlic, chopped	2 cups chicken broth
2 large onions, chopped	3 cups brown rice, thawed
2 large red bell peppers, chopped	2 tablespoons parsley, chopped
1 tablespoon sweet Hungarian	6 tablespoons sour cream

1. Combine the broth, tomato paste, and spices in a mixing dish. 2. Toss in the chicken and toss well to coat. 3. Spread the rice in a casserole dish and top with the chicken and marinade. 4. Finish by layering the remaining ingredients on top of the dish. 5. To choose the "Bake" mode, press the "Start" on the air fryer. 6. Adjust the cooking time to 40 minutes. 7. Push the +/- Temp arrows to adjust the temperature to 365 degrees F. 8. Place the cooking tray inside and close the door after warming the air fryer. 9. Warm the dish before serving.

Per serving: Calories 440; Fat 7.9g; Sodium 581mg; Carbs 21.8g; Fiber 2.6g; Sugar 7.1g; Protein 37.2g

Devil Chicken with Parmesan Cheese

Prep time: 10 minutes | Cook time: 40 minutes | Serves: 8

2 tablespoons butter	ed
2 cloves garlic, chopped	¼ cup chives, chopped
1 cup Dijon mustard	2 teaspoons paprika
½ teaspoon cayenne pepper	8 small bone-in chicken thighs, skin removed
1 ½ cups panko breadcrumbs	
¾ cup Parmesan, freshly grat-	

1. Mix the chicken thighs, crumbs, cheese, chives, butter, and seasonings in a mixing bowl, and toss well to coat. 2. Place the chicken in a cooking tray with the spice mixture. 3. To choose the "Air Fry" mode, press the "Start" on the air fryer. 4. Adjust the cooking time to 40 minutes. 5. Push the +/- Temp arrows to adjust the temperature to 400 degrees F. 6. Place the baking pan inside and close the lid after warming the air fryer. 7. Warm the dish before serving.

Per serving: Calories 380; Fat 20g; Sodium 686mg; Carbs 33g; Fiber 1g; Sugar 1.2g; Protein 21g

Marinated Chicken Breast Halves

Prep time: 10 minutes | Cook time: 20 minutes | Serves: 4

2 cups breadcrumbs
1 teaspoon dried oregano
½ teaspoon garlic powder
4 teaspoons paprika
½ teaspoon salt
½ teaspoon black pepper
2 egg whites
½ cup skim milk
½ cup flour
4 (6 oz.) chicken breast halves
Cooking spray
1 jar marinara sauce
¾ cup mozzarella cheese, shredded
2 tablespoons Parmesan, shredded

1. Whisk together the flour and spices in one dish, and beat the eggs in another. 2. Using flour, coat the pounded chicken and then dip it in the egg whites. 3. Dredge the chicken breast in the crumbs well. 4. Place the breaded chicken on the marinara sauce on a cooking tray. 5. Drizzle the cheese over the chicken. 6. To choose the "Bake" mode, press the "Start" on the air fryer. 7. Adjust the cooking time to 20 minutes. 8. Adjust the temperature to 365 degrees F. 9. Place the cooking tray inside and close the door after warming the air fryer. 10. Warm the dish before serving.

Per serving: Calories 361; Fat 16.3g; Sodium 515mg; Carbs 19.3g; Fiber 0.1g; Sugar 18.2g; Protein 33.3g

Rosemary Chicken with Onion and Lemon

Prep time: 10 minutes | Cook time: 45 minutes | Serves: 8

4 pounds of chicken, cut into pieces
salt and black pepper, to taste
flour for dredging
3 tablespoons olive oil
1 large onion, sliced
peel of ½ lemons
2 large garlic cloves, minced
1 ½ teaspoons rosemary leaves
1 tablespoon honey
¼ cup lemon juice
1 cup chicken broth

1. Place the chicken in the cooking tray after dredging it in flour. 2. In a mixing dish, combine the broth and the remaining ingredients. 3. Pour this mixture over the dredged chicken in the cooking tray. 4. To choose the "Bake" mode, press the "Start" on the air fryer. 5. Adjust the cooking time to 45 minutes. 6. Adjust the temperature to 365 degrees F. 7. Place the cooking tray inside and close the door after warming the air fryer. 8. Every 15 minutes, baste the chicken with the sauce. 9. Warm the dish before serving.

Per serving: Calories 405; Fat 22.7g; Sodium 227mg; Carbs 26.1g; Fiber 1.4g; Sugar 0.9g; Protein 45.2g

Chicken and Potatoes

Prep time: 10 minutes | Cook time: 25 minutes | Serves: 4

4 potatoes, diced
1 tablespoon garlic, minced
1.5 tablespoons olive oil
⅛ teaspoon salt
⅛ teaspoon pepper
1½ pounds' boneless skinless chicken
¾ cup mozzarella cheese, shredded
Parsley chopped

1. In a cooking tray, toss the chicken and potatoes with spices and oil. 2. Pour the cheese over the chicken and potatoes. 3. To choose the "Bake" mode, press the "Start" on the air fryer. 4. Adjust the cooking time to 25 minutes. 5. Adjust the temperature to 365 degrees F. 6. Place the cooking tray inside and close the door after warming the air fryer. 7. Warm the dish before serving.

Per serving: Calories 695; Fat 17.5g; Sodium 355mg; Carbs 26.4g; Fiber 1.8g; Sugar 0.8g; Protein 117.4g

Baked Chicken Breasts and Red Potatoes

Prep time: 10 minutes | Cook time: 30 minutes | Serves: 4

2 pounds. red potatoes, quartered
3 tablespoons olive oil
½ teaspoon cumin seeds
salt and black pepper, to taste
4 garlic cloves, chopped
2 tablespoons brown sugar
1 lemon (½ juiced and ½ cut into wedges)
pinch of red pepper flakes
4 skinless, boneless chicken breasts
2 tablespoons cilantro, chopped

1. In a cooking tray, combine the chicken, lemon, garlic, and potatoes. 2. Mix the spices, herbs, oil, and sugar in a mixing dish. 3. Toss the chicken and vegetables in this mixture to cover them evenly. 4. To choose the "Bake" mode, press the "Start" on the air fryer. 5. Adjust the cooking time to 30 minutes. 6. Adjust the temperature to 365 degrees F. 7. Place the cooking tray inside and close the lid after warming the air fryer. 8. Warm the dish before serving.

Per serving: Calories 545; Fat 36.4g; Sodium 272mg; Carbs 40.7g; Fiber 0.2g; Sugar 0.1g; Protein 42.5g

Chicken Thighs with Spinach and Onion

Prep time: 10 minutes | Cook time: 25 minutes | Serves: 4

½ onion, quartered
½ red onion, quartered
½ pound of potatoes, quartered
4 garlic cloves
4 tomatoes, quartered
⅛ cup chorizo
¼ teaspoon paprika powder
4 chicken thighs, boneless
¼ teaspoon dried oregano
½ green bell pepper, julienned
Salt
Black pepper

1. In a cooking tray, combine the chicken, vegetables, and remaining ingredients. 2. To choose the "Bake" mode, press the "Start" on the air fryer. 3. Adjust the cooking time to 25 minutes. 4. Adjust the temperature to 365 degrees F. 5. Place the cooking tray inside and close the door after warming the air fryer. 6. Warm the dish before serving.

Per serving: Calories 301; Fat 8.9g; Sodium 340mg; Carbs 24.7g; Fiber 1.2g; Sugar 1.3g; Protein 15.3g

Baked Chicken Penne

Prep time: 10 minutes | Cook time: 22 minutes | Serves: 4

9 oz. penne, boiled
1 onion, roughly chopped
3 chicken breasts cut into strips
2 tablespoons olive oil
1 tablespoon paprika
Salt and black pepper
Sauce
1¾ oz. butter
1¾ oz. plain flour
1 pint 6 oz. hot milk
1 teaspoon Dijon mustard
3½ oz. Parmesan cheese, grated
2 large tomatoes, deseeded and cubed

1. Toss chicken, pasta, onion, oil, paprika, salt, and black pepper in a casserole dish with butter. 2. In a suitable pan, make the sauce. Melt the butter in another saucepan on low heat. 3. Stir in the flour for 2 minutes while whisking constantly, then pour in the hot milk. 4. Combine the tomatoes, mustard, and cheese in a blender until smooth. 5. Toss well and pour over the chicken mixture in the casserole dish. 6. To choose the "Bake" mode, press the "Start" on the air fryer. 7. Adjust the cooking time to 20 minutes. 8. Adjust the temperature to 365 degrees F. 9. Serve warm.

Per serving: Calories 548; Fat 22.9g; Sodium 350mg; Carbs 17.5g; Fiber 6.3g; Sugar 10.9g; Protein 40.1g

Air-Fried Paprika Chicken Drumsticks

Prep time: 10 minutes | Cook time: 20 minutes | Serves: 8

8 chicken drumsticks
2 tablespoons olive oil
1 teaspoon salt
1 teaspoon pepper
1 teaspoon garlic powder
1 teaspoon paprika
½ teaspoon cumin

1. Add olive oil, salt, black pepper, garlic powder, paprika, and cumin to a bowl. 2. Apply this mixture liberally to all of the drumsticks. 3. In the cooking tray, place these drumsticks. 4. Select the "Air Fry" mode. 5. Adjust the time to 20 minutes. 6. Adjust the temperature to 400 degrees F. 7. Place the cooking tray into the air fryer after it has been warmed. 8. When the drumsticks are halfway done, flip them. 9. Continue air frying for the remaining 10 minutes. 10. Warm the dish before serving.

Per serving: Calories 212; Fat 11.8g; Sodium 321mg; Carbs 14.6g; Fiber 4.4g; Sugar 8g; Protein 17.3g

Creamy Chicken Casserole

Prep time: 10 minutes | Cook time: 45 minutes | Serves: 6

Chicken and Mushroom Casserole:
2 ½ pounds of chicken breasts cut into strips
1 ½ teaspoons salt
¼ teaspoon black pepper
1 cup all-purpose flour
6 tablespoons olive oil
1-pound white mushrooms, sliced
1 medium onion, diced
3 garlic cloves, minced
For Sauce
3 tablespoons unsalted butter
3 tablespoons all-purpose flour
1 ½ cups chicken broth
1 tablespoon lemon juice
1 cup half and half cream

1. Toss the chicken with the mushrooms and the rest of the casserole ingredients in a casserole dish with butter. 2. In a suitable pan, make the sauce. Melt the butter in a saucepan on low heat. 3. Pour in the milk, lemon juice, and cream after whisking in the flour for 2 minutes. 4. Mix thoroughly, then pour the sauce over the chicken mixture in the casserole dish. 5. To choose the "Bake" mode, press the "Start" on the air fryer. 6. Adjust the cooking time to 45 minutes. 7. Push the +/- Temp arrows to adjust the temperature to 365 degrees F. 8. Place the casserole dish inside. 9. Serve warm.

Per serving: Calories 409; Fat 50.5g; Sodium 463mg; Carbs 9.9g; Fiber 1.5g; Sugar 0.3g; Protein 29.3g

Baked Chicken Breasts with Basil Pesto

Prep time: 10 minutes | Cook time: 35 minutes | Serves: 3

3 chicken breasts
1 (6 oz.) jar basil pesto
2 medium fresh tomatoes,
sliced
6 mozzarella cheese slices

1. In a casserole dish, arrange the tomato slices and top with chicken. 2. Spread the pesto and cheese evenly over the chicken. 3. To choose the "Air Fry" mode, press the "Start" on the air fryer. 4. Adjust the cooking time to 30 minutes. 5. Push the +/- Temp arrows to adjust the temperature to 400 degrees F. 6. Place the casserole dish inside and close the top after it has been warmed. 7. Switch the air fryer to broil setting and broil for 5 minutes after it has finished baking. 8. Warm the dish before serving.

Per serving: Calories 452; Fat 4g; Sodium 220mg; Carbs 23.1g; Fiber 0.3g; Sugar 1g; Protein 26g

Orange Duck in Chicken Broth

Prep time: 10 minutes | Cook time: 60 minutes | Serves: 6

1 tablespoon salt
1 teaspoon ground coriander
½ teaspoon ground cumin
1 teaspoon black pepper
1 (5- to 6-pound) duck, skinned
1 juice orange, halved
4 fresh thyme sprigs
4 fresh marjoram sprigs
2 parsley sprigs
1 small onion, cut into wedges
½ cup dry white wine
½ cup chicken broth
½ carrot
½ celery rib

1. Place the Pekin duck in a cooking tray and combine the remaining ingredients in a mixing dish. 2. Brush the herb sauce liberally all over the duck. 3. To choose the "Air Fry" mode, press the "Start" on the air fryer. 4. Adjust the cooking time to 1 hour. 5. Push the +/- Temp arrows to adjust the temperature to 380 degrees F. 6. Place the casserole dish inside and close the top after it has been warmed. 7. Continue basting the duck throughout the baking process. 8. Warm the dish before serving.

Per serving: Calories 301; Fat 15.8g; Sodium 389mg; Carbs 11.7g; Fiber 0.3g; Sugar 0.1g; Protein 28.2g

Duck Baked with Piper Potatoes

Prep time: 10 minutes | Cook time: 20 minutes | Serves: 6

1 ½ sprig of fresh rosemary
½ nutmeg
Black pepper
Juice from 1 orange
1 whole duck
4 cloves garlic, chopped
1 ½ red onions, chopped
a few stalks of celery
1 ½ carrot
2 cm piece of fresh ginger
1 ½ bay leaves
2 pounds of Piper potatoes
4 cups chicken stock

1. Place the duck in a large boiling saucepan with the stock and the remaining ingredients. 2. Cook for 2 hours on low heat before transferring to a cooking tray. 3. To choose the "Air Fry" mode, press the "Start" on the air fryer and spin the dial. 4. Adjust the cooking time to 20 minutes. 5. Push the +/- Temp arrows to adjust the temperature to 400 degrees F. 6. Place the cooking tray inside and close the door after warming the air fryer. 7. Warm the dish before serving.

Per serving: Calories 308; Fat 20.5g; Sodium 688mg; Carbs 40.3g; Fiber 4.3g; Sugar 1.4g; Protein 49g

Roasted Goose with Onion

Prep time: 10 minutes | Cook time: 40 minutes | Serves: 12

8 pounds' goose
Juice of a lemon
Salt and pepper
½ yellow onion, peeled and chopped
1 head garlic, peeled and chopped
½ cup wine
1 teaspoon dried thyme

1. Place the goose in a cooking tray and whisk the remaining ingredients in a mixing basin. 2. Brush a generous amount of this rich sauce over the geese. 3. To choose the "Air Fry" mode, press the "Start" on the air fryer and spin the dial. 4. Adjust the cooking time to 40 minutes. 5. Adjust the temperature to 365 degrees F. 6. Place the casserole dish inside and close the top after it has been warmed. 7. Warm the dish before serving.

Per serving: Calories 231; Fat 20.1g; Sodium 941mg; Carbs 20.1g; Fiber 0.9g; Sugar 1.4g; Protein 14.6g

Christmas Style Goose

Prep time: 10 minutes | Cook time: 60 minutes | Serves: 12

2 goose	½ handful sprigs, chopped
2 lemons, sliced	½ handful thyme, chopped
1 ½ lime, sliced	½ handful sage, chopped
½ teaspoon Chinese five-spice powder	1 ½ tablespoons clear honey
½ handful parsley, chopped	½ tablespoons thyme leaves

1. Brush the geese with honey and place it in a cooking tray. 2. On top of the geese, arrange the lemon and lime wedges. 3. Over the lemon slices, sprinkle all herbs and spice powder. 4. To choose the "Air Fry" mode, press the "Start" on the air fryer. 5. Adjust the cooking time to 60 minutes. 6. Push the +/- Temp arrows to adjust the temperature to 380 degrees F. 7. Place the cooking tray inside and close the door after warming the air fryer. 8. Warm the dish before serving.
Per serving: Calories 472; Fat 11.1g; Sodium 749mg; Carbs 19.9g; Fiber 0.2g; Sugar 0.2g; Protein 13.5g

Chicken, Onion and Bell Pepper Kebabs

Prep time: 10 minutes | Cook time: 20 minutes | Serves: 2

16 oz. skinless chicken breasts, cubed	salt and pepper to taste
2 tablespoons soy sauce	½ green pepper sliced
½ zucchini sliced	½ red pepper sliced
1 tablespoon chicken seasoning	½ yellow pepper sliced
1 teaspoon BBQ seasoning	¼ red onion sliced
	4 cherry tomatoes
	cooking spray

1. In a mixing dish, combine the chicken and vegetables with the spices and seasonings. 2. Alternatively, skewer them and set them on the cooking tray. 3. To choose the "Air Fry" mode, press the "Start" on the air fryer and spin the dial. 4. To adjust the cooking time to 20 minutes, press the +/- Time arrows. 5. To adjust the temperature to 400 degrees F, push the +/- Temp arrows. 6. Place the cooking tray inside and close the door after warming the air fryer. 7. When the skewers are halfway done, flip them and continue frying. 8. Warm the dish before serving.
Per serving: Calories 327; Fat 3.5g; Sodium 142mg; Carbs 33.6g; Fiber 0.4g; Sugar 0.5g; Protein 24.5g

Asian Style Chicken and Mushroom Kebabs

Prep time: 10 minutes | Cook time: 12 minutes | Serves: 6

2 pounds. chicken breasts, cubed	½ cup golden sweetener
½ cup soy sauce	1 red pepper, chopped
6 cloves garlic, crushed	½ red onion, chopped
1 teaspoon fresh ginger, grated	8 mushrooms, halved
	2 cups zucchini, chopped

1. In a mixing dish, combine the chicken and vegetables with the spices and seasonings. 2. Alternatively, skewer them and set them on the cooking tray. 3. To choose the "Air Fry" mode, press the "Start" on the air fryer. 4. Adjust the cooking time to 12 minutes. 5. Adjust the temperature to 400 degrees F. 6. Place the baking dish inside and close the door after warming the air fryer. 7. When the skewers are halfway done, flip them and continue frying. 8. Warm the dish before serving.
Per serving: Calories 353; Fat 7.5g; Sodium 297mg; Carbs 10.4g; Fiber 0.2g; Sugar 0.1g; Protein 13.1g

Creamy Chicken Thighs

Prep time: 10 minutes | Cook time: 10 minutes | Serves: 2

¼ cup plain yogurt	1 teaspoon smoked paprika
1 tablespoon garlic, minced	½ teaspoon ground cinnamon
1 tablespoon tomato paste	½ teaspoon ground black pepper
1 tablespoon olive oil	
1 tablespoon lemon juice	½ teaspoon cayenne
1 teaspoon salt	1-pound boneless skinless chicken thighs, quartered
1 teaspoon ground cumin	

1. In a mixing dish, combine the chicken, yogurt, and spices. 2. Refrigerate the yogurt chicken for 30 minutes before serving. 3. Place the skewers in the cooking tray with threaded chicken pieces. 4. To choose the "Air Fry" mode, press the "Start" on the air fryer and spin the dial. 5. Adjust the cooking time to 10 minutes. 6. Adjust the temperature to 400 degrees F. 7. Place the baking dish inside and close the lid after warming the air fryer. 8. When the skewers are halfway done, flip them and continue frying. 9. Warm the dish before serving.
Per serving: Calories 248; Fat 13g; Sodium 353mg; Carbs 1g; Fiber 0.4g; Sugar 1g; Protein 29g

Honey Chicken-Mushroom Kebabs

Prep time: 10 minutes | Cook time: 15 minutes | Serves: 4

⅓ cup honey	6 mushrooms chop in half
⅓ cup soy sauce	3 bell peppers, cubed
Salt, to taste	2 chicken breasts diced

1. In a mixing dish, combine the chicken, mushrooms, and vegetables with honey and spices. 2. Alternatively, skewer them and set them on the cooking tray. 3. To choose the "Air Fry" mode, press the "Start" on the air fryer. 4. Adjust the cooking time to 15 minutes. 5. Adjust the temperature to 400 degrees F. 6. Place the baking dish inside and close the door after warming the air fryer. 7. When the skewers are halfway done, flip them and continue frying. 8. Warm the dish before serving.
Per serving: Calories 457; Fat 19.1g; Sodium 557mg; Carbs 18.9g; Fiber 1.7g; Sugar 1.2g; Protein 32.5g

Chicken and Bell Pepper Skewers

Prep time: 10 minutes | Cook time: 8 minutes | Serves: 2

1-pound chicken breasts, diced	1 teaspoon garlic powder
1 tablespoon lemon juice	1 large red onion, cut into squares
1 teaspoon chili powder	1 teaspoon salt
1 teaspoon cumin	1 teaspoon ground black pepper
1 orange bell pepper, cut into squares	
1 red bell pepper, cut into squares	1 teaspoon oregano
2 tablespoons olive oil	1 teaspoon parsley flakes
	1 teaspoon paprika

1. In a mixing dish, combine the chicken and vegetables with the spices and seasonings. 2. Alternatively, skewer them and set them on the cooking tray. 3. To choose the "Air Fry" mode, press the "Start" on the air fryer. 4. Adjust the cooking time to 8 minutes. 5. Adjust the temperature to 400 degrees F. 6. Place the baking dish inside and close the door after warming the air fryer. 7. When the skewers are halfway done, flip them and continue cooking. 8. Serve warm.
Per serving: Calories 392; Fat 16.1g; Sodium 466mg; Carbs 13.9g; Fiber 0.6g; Sugar 0.6g; Protein 48g

Boneless Turkey Breast Roast

Prep time: 15 minutes | Cook time: 50 minutes | Serves: 6

3 pounds of boneless turkey breast
¼ cup mayonnaise
2 teaspoons poultry seasoning
1 teaspoon salt
½ teaspoon garlic powder
¼ teaspoon black pepper

1. Mix all ingredients, including the turkey, and coat it thoroughly in a mixing bowl. 2. In the cooking tray, place the boneless turkey breast. 3. Select the "Air fry" mode. 4. Adjust the cooking time to 50 minutes. 5. Adjust the temperature to 400 degrees F. 6. Place the cooking tray in the air fryer and close the cover to bake after it has been warmed. 7. Cut into slices and serve.

Per serving: Calories 322; Fat 11.8g; Sodium 321mg; Carbs 14.6g; Fiber 4.4g; Sugar 8g; Protein 17.3g

Chicken, Zucchini and Grape Tomato Kebabs

Prep time: 10 minutes | Cook time: 16 minutes | Serves: 4

1 large zucchini, cut into squares
2 chicken breasts boneless, skinless, cubed
1 onion yellow, cut into squares
1.5 cup grape tomatoes
1 clove garlic minced
1 lemon juiced
¼ c olive oil
1 tablespoon olive oil
2 tablespoons red wine vinegar
1 teaspoon oregano

1. In a mixing dish, combine the chicken and vegetables with the spices and seasonings. 2. Alternatively, skewer them and set them on the cooking tray. 3. To choose the "Air Fry" mode, press the "Start" on the air fryer. 4. Adjust the cooking time to 16 minutes. 5. Press the +/- Temp arrows to adjust the temperature to 400 degrees F. 6. Place the baking dish inside and close the lid after warming the air fryer. 7. When the skewers are halfway done, flip them and continue cooking. 8. Serve warm.

Per serving: Calories 321; Fat 7.4g; Sodium 353mg; Carbs 19.4g; Fiber 2.7g; Sugar 6.5g; Protein 37.2g

Chicken Tender Skewers with Soy Sauce

Prep time: 10 minutes | Cook time: 7 minutes | Serves: 4

1-pound boneless chicken tenders, diced
½ cup soy sauce
½ cup pineapple juice
¼ cup sesame seed oil
4 garlic cloves, chopped
4 scallions, chopped
1 tablespoon grated ginger
2 teaspoons toasted sesame seeds
Black pepper

1. In a cooking tray, toss the chicken with sauces and spices. 2. To choose the "Air Fry" mode, press the "Start" on the air fryer. 3. Adjust the cooking time to 7 minutes. 4. Adjust the temperature to 400 degrees F. 5. Place the baking dish inside and close the lid after warming the air fryer. 6. Warm the dish before serving.

Per serving: Calories 248; Fat 15.7g; Sodium 94mg; Carbs 31.4g; Fiber 0.4g; Sugar 3.1g; Protein 24.9g

Baked Alfredo Chicken

Prep time: 10 minutes | Cook time: 25 minutes | Serves: 6

1 tablespoon olive oil
3 chicken breasts, cubed
Salt, to taste
Black pepper, to taste
4 cloves garlic, minced
2 ½ cups chicken broth
2 ½ cups heavy cream
1 cup penne pasta, uncooked

2 cups parmesan cheese
2 cups mozzarella cheese
1 handful of fresh parsley, chopped

1. Combine the cream, broth, chicken, pasta, and remaining ingredients in a casserole dish. 2. To choose the "Bake" mode, press the "Start" on the air fryer. 3. To adjust the cooking time to 25 minutes, press the +/- Time arrows. 4. Adjust the temperature to 365 degrees F. 5. Place the baking dish inside and close the door after warming the air fryer. 6. Warm the dish before serving.

Per serving: Calories 378; Fat 21g; Sodium 146mg; Carbs 7.1g; Fiber 0.4g; Sugar 0.1g; Protein 23g

Fajita Chicken Breasts

Prep time: 5 minutes | Cook time: 20 minutes | Serves: 4

1-pound boneless, skinless chicken breasts, cut into strips
2 tablespoons olive oil
1 teaspoon Dijon mustard
2 bell peppers, seeded and sliced
2 garlic cloves, sliced
1 teaspoon ground cumin
Sea salt
Ground black pepper to taste
1 teaspoon chili powder
1 red onion, cut into wedges
4 whole-wheat tortillas

1. Select the Roast function and set the temperature to 380 degrees F. To begin, press the "Start" key. 2. Combine the chicken strips, mustard, bell peppers, garlic, cumin, salt, black pepper, and chili powder in a mixing bowl. 3. In a baking pan, combine the chicken and peppers. Cover the drip pan with aluminum foil. 4. Place the baking pan on the cooking tray when the display says "Add Food." 5. In a preheated air fryer, roast the chicken and peppers for 15 minutes, or the internal temperature is reached 165 degrees F on a meat thermometer. 6. Assemble your fajitas with tortillas and onion wedges. Enjoy!

Per serving: Calories 413; Fat 21.6g; Sodium 470mg; Carbs 25.7g; Fiber 5.4g; Sugar 2g; Protein 28.8g

Turkey Tenderloin in Chicken Stock

Prep time: 6 minutes | Cook time: 45 minutes | Serves: 6

6 tablespoons butter, softened
2 cloves garlic, minced
1 tablespoon Italian seasoning
Coarse sea salt and ground black pepper, to taste
2 pounds of turkey tenderloin
1 teaspoon spicy brown mustard
¼ cup white wine
½ cup chicken stock

1. Select the "Roast" function and set the temperature to 380 degrees F. To begin, press the "Start" key. 2. In a baking pan, combine the turkey and the remaining ingredients. Cover the drip pan with aluminum foil. 3. Roast the turkey for 20 minutes, then turn it over and cook for another 15 minutes, or until an internal temperature of 170 degrees F is reached on a meat thermometer. 4. Allow 10 minutes for the turkey to rest before slicing and serving. Enjoy!

Per serving: Calories 421; Fat 35.6g; Sodium 270mg; Carbs 2.2g; Fiber 0.4g; Sugar 0.1g; Protein 0.6g

Spicy Turkey Meatballs

Prep time: 5 minutes | Cook time: 20 minutes | Serves: 4

1 tablespoon olive oil
1-pound ground turkey
½ cup Pecorino cheese, grated
¼ cup breadcrumbs
2 tablespoons parsley, chopped
2 tablespoons basil, chopped
2 tablespoons chives, chopped
Kosher salt and ground black pepper, to taste
1 teaspoon garlic, minced
1 teaspoon cayenne pepper

1 medium egg

1. Select the air fry function and set the temperature to 400 degrees F. To begin, press the "Start" key. 2. In the cooking tray, place a layer of parchment paper. 3. Combine the remaining ingredients in a mixing basin and stir well. Then, by using a tiny scoop, place mounds of the mixture in a single layer onto the prepared tray. 4. Cook the meatballs in the air fryer for 10 minutes at 400 degrees F. To brown the outsides of the meatballs, air fried for another 5 minutes, or until they reach an internal temperature of 165 degrees F. 5. Bon appétit!

Per serving: Calories 291; Fat 18.6g; Sodium 440mg; Carbs 3.3g; Fiber 0.5g; Sugar 0.1g; Protein 0.9g

Simple Air Fried Chicken Thighs

Prep time: 5 minutes | Cook time: 20 minutes | Serves: 4

1-pound boneless, skinless chicken thighs, quartered crosswise	mix
	½ teaspoon cayenne pepper
	Sea salt
1 tablespoon olive oil	Ground black pepper to taste
1 teaspoon poultry seasoning	

1. Select the air fry function and set the temperature to 400 degrees F. To begin, press the "Start" key. 2. In the cooking tray, place a layer of parchment paper. Toss the chicken thighs with the other ingredients in a large mixing bowl. 3. In the cooking tray, arrange the chicken thighs in a single layer. Set time to 15 minutes and temperature to 400 degrees F. 4. Cook the chicken thighs in the air fryer for 10 minutes, then flip them and cook for another 5 minutes, or until they reach an internal temperature of 165 degrees F. 5. Bon appétit!

Per serving: Calories 289; Fat 22.3g; Sodium 240mg; Carbs 1.7g; Fiber 0.3g; Sugar 0g; Protein 0.6g

Turkey Breast Tenderloin Salad

Prep time: 5 minutes | Cook time: 45 minutes | Serves: 5

1-pound turkey breast tenderloin	1 teaspoon honey
½ cup mayonnaise	1 small red onion, thinly sliced
4 tablespoons Greek-style yogurt	1 medium cucumber, diced
1 teaspoon yellow mustard	2 bell peppers, seeded and sliced
1 tablespoon white vinegar	1 cup baby spinach

1. Select the Roast function and set the temperature to 380 degrees F. To begin, press the "Start" key. 2. Place the turkey in a cooking tray that has been gently greased. Cover the drip pan with aluminum foil. 3. Set the time to 35 minutes and the temperature to 380 degrees F. Roast the turkey for 20 minutes, then turn it over and cook for another 15 minutes, or until an internal temperature of 170 degrees F is reached on a meat thermometer. 4. Allow 10 minutes for the turkey to rest before slicing and serving. Slice the turkey into strips and combine with the other ingredients. 5. Toss well to mix and serve cold. Enjoy!

Per serving: Calories 331; Fat 23.1g; Sodium 470mg; Carbs 6.2g; Fiber 1g; Sugar 1g; Protein 4.1g

Chicken Tenders with Pecorino Cheese

Prep time: 5 minutes | Cook time: 20 minutes | Serves: 4

1 tablespoon olive oil	1 tablespoon fresh parsley leaves, chopped
1 large egg	
1 tablespoon butter, melted	2 garlic cloves, minced

Sea salt
Ground black pepper to taste
1 ½ pounds of chicken tenders
1 cup breadcrumbs
¼ cup Pecorino cheese, grated

1. Select the Air Fry function and set the temperature to 400 degrees F. To begin, press the "Start" key. Using olive oil, lightly lubricate the perforated cooking tray. 2. Whisk together the egg, butter, parsley, garlic, salt, and black pepper in a small basin. Toss the chicken tenders in the bowl until they are well coated on both sides. 3. Combine the breadcrumbs and cheese in a small basin. Roll the chicken tenders in the breadcrumb mixture until they are completely covered. 4. Set the time to 15 minutes and the temperature to 400 degrees F. Place the tenders in the cooking tray when the display says "Add Food." Cook for 15 minutes in the air fryer. 5. Bon appétit!

Per serving: Calories 422; Fat 25.6g; Sodium 340mg; Carbs 39.4g; Fiber 0.3g; Sugar 0.1g; Protein 0.6g

Louisiana-Style Chicken Fillets

Prep time: 5 minutes | Cook time: 25 minutes | Serves: 4

1 ½ pound chicken fillets	8 ounces smoked pork sausage, crumbled
Sea salt	
Ground black pepper to taste	6 ounces' parmesan cheese, grated
1 teaspoon cayenne pepper	
2 tablespoons Louisiana-style hot sauce	1 cup breadcrumbs

1. Select the Air Fry function and set the temperature to 400 degrees F. To begin, press the "Start" key. 2. Season the chicken with salt, black pepper, and cayenne after patting it dry. 3. Combine the spicy sauce, sausage, and cheese in a mixing dish and stir well. Roll up the chicken fillets with the filling in between. 4. Roll them in breadcrumbs and tuck them in with toothpicks. 5. Set time to 20 minutes and temp 400 degrees F. 6. Air fry the filled chicken for approximately 10 minutes, then turn it and cook for another 10 minutes, or until the internal temperature of the chicken hits 160 degrees F on a meat thermometer. 7. Bon appétit!

Per serving: Calories 602; Fat 34.6g; Sodium 340mg; Carbs 13.3g; Fiber 0.8g; Sugar 1g; Protein 1.6g

Spicy Duck Breast

Prep time: 5 minutes | Cook time: 15 minutes | Serves: 5

1 teaspoon olive oil	1 tablespoon butter
2 pounds' duck breast	1 sprig of fresh rosemary, chopped
2 cloves garlic, chopped	
Coarse sea salt and ground black pepper, to taste	2 sprigs of fresh thyme, chopped

1. Select the Air Fry function and set the temperature to 400 degrees F. To begin, press the "Start" key. 2. Using olive oil, lightly lubricate the perforated air fryer cooking tray. Cover the drip pan with aluminum foil. 3. Toss the remaining ingredients with the duck breast. 4. Set time to 13 minutes and temperature to 400 degrees F. 5. Place the duck breast on the cooking tray when the display says "Add Food." 6. Cook the duck breasts in the air fryer for approximately 8 minutes, then turn and cook for another 5 minutes, or until cooked through. 7. Bon appétit!

Per serving: Calories 419; Fat 30.6g; Sodium 344mg; Carbs 1.3g; Fiber 0.2g; Sugar 0g; Protein 0.4g

Chicken Wings with Parmesan Cheese

Prep time: 5 minutes | Cook time: 25 minutes | Serves: 4

1 ½ pounds of chicken wings
Sea salt and ground black pepper to season
1 teaspoon cayenne pepper
¼ cup butter
2 cloves garlic, pressed
½ cup parmesan cheese, preferably freshly grated

1. Select the Air Fry function and set the temperature to 400 degrees F. To begin, press the "Start" key. 2. In the cooking tray, place a layer of parchment paper. Toss the remaining ingredients with the chicken wings. 3. In the cooking tray, arrange the chicken wings in a single layer. 4. Set time to 20 minutes and temperature to 400 degrees F. 5. Air fry the chicken wings for 10 minutes, flip them, and air fry for another 10 minutes, or until crispy and golden. 6. Bon appétit!

Per serving: Calories 487; Fat 37.6g; Sodium 270mg; Carbs 3.5g; Fiber 0.3g; Sugar 0.1g; Protein 0.6g

Chicken Breast with Red Pepper Flakes

Prep time: 5 minutes | Cook time: 25 minutes | Serves: 5

1 teaspoon olive oil
2 pounds of chicken breast, skinless and boneless
1 tablespoon coarse-ground mustard
1 tablespoon honey
Salt and ground black pepper to taste
1 teaspoon red pepper flakes, crushed
½ teaspoon garlic powder

1. Select the Roast function and set the temperature to 380 degrees F. To begin, press the "Start" key. 2. In a cooking tray, toss the chicken with the additional ingredients. Cover the drip tray with aluminum foil. 3. Set the time to 20 minutes and the temperature to 380 degrees F. 4. Roast the chicken for about 10 minutes, then turn it and cook for another 10 minutes, or until an internal temperature of 160 degrees F is reached on a meat thermometer. 5. Bon appétit!

Per serving: Calories 344; Fat 18.2g; Sodium 340mg; Carbs 5g; Fiber 0.3g; Sugar 0.1g; Protein 4g

Easy Turkey Burgers

Prep time: 5 minutes | Cook time: 20 minutes | Serves: 4

1 tablespoon olive oil
1-pound ground chicken
½ cup crackers, crushed
1 small onion, chopped
2 cloves garlic, minced
1 egg, beaten
Sea salt
Ground black pepper to taste

1. Select the Air Fry function and set the temperature to 400 degrees F. To begin, press the "Start" key. 2. In the air fryer, place a layer of parchment paper. 3. Combine all ingredients in a large mixing bowl and stir thoroughly. Form the ingredients into four patties and arrange them in a single layer in a perforated air fryer. 4. Set time to 15 minutes and temperature to 400 degrees F. 5. The turkey burgers should be air fried for 15 minutes or until they reach a temperature of 165 degrees F on the inside. 6. Bon appétit!

Per serving: Calories 322; Fat 23.2g; Sodium 340mg; Carbs 3.6g; Fiber 0.5g; Sugar 1.5g; Protein 23.8g

Mediterranean Chicken Salad

Prep time: 7 minutes | Cook time: 45 minutes | Serves: 4

1 ½ pounds skinless, boneless chicken breast
3 tablespoons olive oil
2 tablespoons freshly squeezed lemon juice
1 tablespoon white vinegar

1 teaspoon yellow mustard
2 tablespoons fresh cilantro, chopped
2 tablespoons fresh basil, chopped
1 teaspoon dried oregano
2 garlic cloves, pressed
1 bell pepper, seeded and diced
Sea salt
Ground black pepper to taste
2 cups Romaine lettuce leaves, torn into leaves
1 cucumber, diced
1 cup cherry tomatoes, halved
1 red onion, thinly sliced
3 ounces Kalamata olives pitted and sliced

1. Select the Roast function and set the temperature to 380 degrees F. To begin, press the "Start" key. 2. Place the chicken on the parchment-lined cooking tray when the display says "Add Food." 3. Set timer to 40 minutes and temperature to 380 degrees F. 4. Roast the chicken for 20 minutes, then turn it and cook for another 20 minutes, or until an internal temperature of 160 degrees F is reached on a meat thermometer. 5. Allow 10 minutes for the chicken breast to rest on a cutting board before slicing into strips. 6. Refrigerate the salad until ready to serve by tossing the chicken strips with the other ingredients. 7. Bon appétit!

Per serving: Calories 475; Fat 32g; Sodium 434mg; Carbs 11.8g; Fiber 2.8g; Sugar 7.2g; Protein 36.6g

Chicken Croquettes

Prep time: 5 minutes | Cook time: 20 minutes | Serves: 4

2 tablespoons unsalted butter
1-pound ground chicken
2 ounces of bacon
Sea salt
Ground black pepper
1 cup breadcrumbs
¼ cup whole milk
2 medium eggs

1. Select the Air Fry function and set the temperature to 400 degrees F. To begin, press the "Start" key. 2. In the cooking tray, place a layer of parchment paper. 3. Combine all ingredients in a mixing dish and stir well. Then, by using a tiny scoop, place mounds of the mixture in a single layer onto the prepared pan. 4. Set time to 15 minutes and temperature to 400 degrees F. 5. Cook the croquettes in the air fryer for 10 minutes before turning them over and air frying for another 5 minutes. 6. Bon appétit!

Per serving: Calories 397; Fat 28.1g; Sodium 445mg; Carbs 8.5g; Fiber 0.7g; Sugar 2.6g; Protein 27.1g

Simple Chicken Drumsticks

Prep time: 5 minutes | Cook time: 30 minutes | Serves: 4

1 ½ pounds chicken drumstick
2 tablespoons olive oil
1 teaspoon brown sugar
1 teaspoon paprika
1 teaspoon onion powder
1 teaspoon garlic powder
Sea salt
Ground black pepper to taste

1. Select the Air Fry function and set the temperature to 400 degrees F. To begin, press the "Start" key. 2. Using olive oil, lightly lubricate the perforated cooking tray. 3. Toss the remaining ingredients with the chicken drumsticks. 4. Set timer to 25 minutes and temperature to 400 degrees F. 5. Place the drumsticks in the cooking tray when the display says "Add Food." 6. Cook the chicken drumsticks in the air fryer for about 25 minutes, turning halfway through. 7. Bon appétit!

Per serving: Calories 419; Fat 26.3g; Sodium 344mg; Carbs 2.2g; Fiber 0.5g; Sugar 0.9g; Protein 43.9g

Lemon Chicken Bites with Parsley

Prep time: 5 minutes | Cook time: 20 minutes | Serves: 5

1 ½ pounds chicken breasts, boneless, skinless, cut into strips
2 tablespoons olive oil
¼ cup freshly squeezed lime juice
¼ cup fresh parsley leaves, chopped
1 jalapeno pepper, minced
2 cloves garlic, pressed
1 teaspoon honey
1 tablespoon brown mustard
Sea salt
Ground black pepper to taste

1. Select the Roast function and set the temperature to 380 degrees F. To begin, press the "Start" key. 2. Toss the chicken strips with the other ingredients until evenly coated. In a baking pan, place the chicken. 3. Place the baking pan on the cooking tray when the display says "Add Food." 4. Set timer to 15 minutes and temperature to 380 degrees F. 5. Roast the chicken for 15 minutes in a preheated air fryer or until an internal temperature of 165 degrees F is reached using a meat thermometer. 6. Bon appétit!

Per serving: Calories 295; Fat 18.1g; Sodium 230mg; Carbs 3g; Fiber 0.4g; Sugar 1.5g; Protein 28.7g

Homemade Chicken Cutlets

Prep time: 5 minutes | Cook time: 25 minutes | Serves: 4

1 ½ pounds chicken breasts, sliced
1 tablespoon butter, melted
2 eggs, whisked
½ teaspoon cayenne pepper
Kosher salt and ground black pepper, to taste
1 cup seasoned breadcrumbs

1. Select the Air Fry function and set the temperature to 400 degrees F. To begin, press the "Start" key. 2. Toss the chicken with the other ingredients in a large mixing bowl. 3. Place the chicken tenders in the parchment-lined air fryer pan when the display says "Add Food." 4. Set timer to 20 minutes and temperature to 400 degrees F. 5. Cook for 10 minutes on one side, then turn and cook for another 10 minutes until the chicken reaches an internal temperature of 160 degrees F on a meat thermometer. 6. Bon appétit!

Per serving: Calories 465; Fat 20.7g; Sodium 324mg; Carbs 21.1g; Fiber 4.8g; Sugar 4.4g; Protein 40.7g

Air-Fried Chicken Legs in Fish Sauce

Prep time: 5 minutes | Cook time: 30 minutes | Serves: 5

2 pounds of chicken legs
2 tablespoons coconut sugar
2 tablespoons soy sauce
2 tablespoons fish sauce
2 tablespoons rice wine vinegar
2 tablespoons fish sauce
2 tablespoons coconut oil
1 teaspoon garlic powder
1 teaspoon curry powder
Kosher salt and ground black pepper, to taste

1. Select the Air Fry function and set the temperature to 400 degrees F. To begin, press the "Start" key. 2. Using olive oil, lightly lubricate the perforated cooking tray. 3. Toss the chicken legs with the other ingredients in a large mixing bowl. 4. Set timer to 25 minutes and temperature to 400 degrees F. 5. Place the legs in the cooking tray when the display says "Add Food." 6. Cook the chicken legs in the air fryer for about 25 minutes, turning halfway through. 7. Bon appétit!

Per serving: Calories 476; Fat 35.6g; Sodium 334mg; Carbs 6.3g; Fiber 0.4g; Sugar 4.9g; Protein 31.5g

Dijon Chicken Muffins

Prep time: 5 minutes | Cook time: 20 minutes | Serves: 6

1 ½ pounds ground chicken
1 tablespoon olive oil
2 eggs
½ cup tomato paste
1 cup instant oats
1 teaspoon paprika
1 teaspoon Dijon mustard
Sea salt
Ground black pepper to taste
1 teaspoon chili powder
2 garlic cloves, minced
2 tablespoons scallions, chopped

1. Adjust the temperature to 365 degrees F and the time to 15 minutes using the "Bake" feature. To begin, press the "Start" key. 2. Brush silicone muffin cups with nonstick cooking oil in the meantime. Combine all of the ingredients in a large mixing bowl and stir thoroughly. Evenly apportion the batter evenly among the muffin cups. 3. Set timer to 20 minutes and temperature to 365 degrees F. 4. Place the muffin cups on the cooking sheet when the display says "Add Food." 5. Bake the muffins until done in the preheated air fryer. 6. Bon appétit!

Per serving: Calories 330; Fat 14.8g; Sodium 224mg; Carbs 23.3g; Fiber 4.2g; Sugar 3.2g; Protein 27.3g

Rotisserie Savory Whole Chicken

Prep time: 5 minutes | Cook time: 50 minutes | Serves: 7

3 pounds' whole chicken, tied
2 tablespoons olive oil
1 teaspoon smoked paprika
1 teaspoon garlic powder
1 teaspoon onion powder
1 teaspoon dried thyme
Kosher salt
Freshly ground black pepper, to taste

1. Push the rotisserie spit through the bird and secure the rotisserie forks with the rotisserie forks. 2. Select the Roast function and set the temperature to 380 degrees F. Set the timer for 1 hour. Press the Start key and set the air fryer to "Rotate." 3. Place the prepared chicken in the air fryer when the display says "Add Food." 4. Set timer to 40 minutes and temperature to 380 degrees F. 5. Roast the chicken for 40 minutes or until the breasts are 165 degrees F and the thighs are 185 degrees F. 6. Allow 10 minutes for the chicken to rest before cutting and serving. 7. Bon appétit!

Per serving: Calories 456; Fat 33.1g; Sodium 320mg; Carbs 0.8g; Fiber 0.2g; Sugar 0.1g; Protein 36.3g

Easy Turkey Festive Style

Prep time: 5 minutes | Cook time: 40 minutes | Serves: 5

2 pounds' turkey, giblet removed, rinsed, and pat dry
Kosher salt ground black pepper, to taste
1 teaspoon dried thyme
1 teaspoon ground rosemary
Sea salt and freshly ground black pepper
1 teaspoon paprika
1 tablespoon agave syrup
2 tablespoons olive oil

1. Set the temperature to 380 degrees F and select the "Roast" function. Set the timer for 35 minutes. Press the Start key to begin. Set the air fryer to "Rotate." 2. Place the turkey legs in the rotisserie basket when the display says "Add Food." 3. Roast the turkey until an internal temperature of 165 degrees F is reached using a meat thermometer. 4. Bon appétit!

Per serving: Calories 440; Fat 34.3g; Sodium 443mg; Carbs 4.5g; Fiber 0.3g; Sugar 3.8g; Protein 24.3g

Chicken Sausage with Italian Seasoning Mix

Prep time: 5 minutes | Cook time: 15 minutes | Serves: 4

1-pound chicken sausage, sliced
4 bell peppers, sliced
1 teaspoon garlic powder
2 tablespoons olive oil

1 teaspoon Italian seasoning mix
Kosher salt
Freshly ground black pepper, to taste

1. Select the Air Fry function and set the temperature to 400 degrees F. To begin, press the "Start" key. 2. Toss the remaining ingredients with the chicken sausage and peppers. Using parchment paper, line the perforated pan in the air fryer. 3. Set the time to 13 minutes and temp 400 degrees F. 4. Place the chicken sausage and peppers in the cooking tray when the display says "Add Food." 5. Cook the sausage and peppers for 5 minutes, then toss the pan and cook for another 5 to 7 minutes, or until well cooked. 6. Bon appétit!
Per serving: Calories 340; Fat 27.3g; Sodium 343mg; Carbs 4.8g; Fiber 0.5g; Sugar 1.2g; Protein 18.1g

Turkey Breast Cutlets

Prep time: 5 minutes | Cook time: 20 minutes | Serves: 5

1 ½ pounds turkey breast cutlets
2 medium eggs, beaten
1 teaspoon poultry seasoning

Kosher salt and ground black pepper, to taste
1 cup bread crumbs

1. Select the Air Fry function and set the temperature to 400 degrees F. To begin, press the "Start" key. 2. Combine the turkey breast cutlets, eggs, and seasonings in a mixing bowl. Roll them in bread crumbs and lay them on the perforated cooking tray with parchment paper. 3. Set the time to 15 minutes and the temperature to 400 degrees F. 4. Air-fried, the turkey cutlets for 8 minutes, then flip and cook for another 7 minutes, or until cooked through. 5. Bon appétit!
Per serving: Calories 267; Fat 11.7g; Sodium 440mg; Carbs 5.6g; Fiber 0.4g; Sugar 1.1g; Protein 33g

Simple Chicken Onion Burgers

Prep time: 5 minutes | Cook time: 20 minutes | Serves: 4

1-pound ground chicken
1 tablespoon olive oil
1 egg, whisked
1 cup bread crumbs
½ cup parmesan cheese, grated

1 small onion, finely chopped
2 garlic cloves, minced
1 teaspoon cayenne pepper
Kosher salt and ground black pepper, to taste

1. Select the Air Fry feature and set the temperature to 400 degrees F. To begin, press the "Start" key. 2. In the cooking tray, place a layer of parchment paper. 3. Combine all ingredients in a large mixing bowl and stir thoroughly. Form the ingredients into four patties and arrange them in a single layer in a perforated air fryer pan. 4. Set time to 15 minutes and temp 400 degrees F. 5. The chicken burgers should be air fried for 15 minutes or until they reach a temperature of 165 degrees F on the inside. 6. Bon appétit!
Per serving: Calories 305; Fat 26.7g; Sodium 240mg; Carbs 17.5g; Fiber 1g; Sugar 2.1g; Protein 10.7g

Chicken Tacos in a Simple Way

Prep time: 5 minutes | Cook time: 20 minutes | Serves: 4

1 ½ pounds boneless skinless chicken breasts, cut into strips
2 tablespoons olive oil
1 teaspoon red chili powder
Sea salt and coarse ground black pepper to taste

1 teaspoon garlic, minced
1 teaspoon onion powder
1 teaspoon smoked paprika
1 lime, freshly squeezed
4 large tortillas
½ cup salsa

1. Select the Roast function and set the temperature to 380 degrees F. To begin, press the "Start" key. 2. Combine the chicken strips, olive oil, chili powder, salt, black pepper, garlic, onion powder, paprika, and lime juice in a large mixing bowl. 3. In a baking pan, place the chicken. 4. Set time to 15 minutes and temperature to 380 degrees F. 5. Place the baking pan on the cooking tray when the display says "Add Food." 6. Roast the chicken for 15 minutes or until an internal temperature of 165 degrees F is reached using a meat thermometer. 7. Assemble your tacos with tortillas and salsa before serving.
Per serving: Calories 420; Fat 14.2g; Sodium 340mg; Carbs 28.5g; Fiber 2.3g; Sugar 3.1g; Protein 42.7g

Herbed Chicken Breast in White Wine

Prep time: 5 minutes | Cook time: 50 minutes | Serves: 5

2 pounds' bone-in and skin-on chicken breast
4 tablespoons olive oil
2 tablespoons fresh lemon juice
2 garlic cloves, minced
½ cup white wine

½ teaspoon cumin seeds
2 sprigs of fresh rosemary
2 sprigs of fresh thyme
1 teaspoon smoked paprika
Sea salt
Ground black pepper

1. Select the Roast function and set the temperature to 380 degrees F. To begin, press the "Start" key. 2. In a cooking tray, combine the chicken and the remaining ingredients. Cover the drip pan with aluminum foil. 3. Set the time to 20 minutes and the temperature to 380 degrees F. 4. Roast the chicken for 20 minutes, then turn it and cook for another 20 minutes, or until an internal temperature of 160 degrees F is reached on a meat thermometer. 5. Allow 10 minutes for the chicken breast to rest on a cutting board before slicing and serving. 6. Bon appétit!
Per serving: Calories 416; Fat 27.7g; Sodium 370mg; Carbs 1.5g; Fiber 0.3g; Sugar 0.4g; Protein 38.1g

Juicy Turkey Breast

Prep time: 5 minutes | Cook time: 45 minutes | Serves: 5

2 pounds of turkey breasts, boneless and skinless
1 cup buttermilk
2 garlic cloves, minced
2 tablespoons olive oil
1 tablespoon Dijon mustard
1 sprig of fresh rosemary,

chopped
1 sprig of fresh thyme, chopped
Kosher salt
Freshly ground black pepper, to taste

1. In a ceramic dish, combine all ingredients and marinate for 1 hour. 2. Select the Roast function and set the temperature to 380 degrees F. To begin, press the "Start" key. 3. Place the turkey in the perforated cooking tray. Cover the drip pan with aluminum foil. Set time to 35 minutes. 4. Roast the turkey for 20 minutes, then turn it over and cook for another 15 minutes, or until an internal temperature of 170 degrees F is reached on a meat thermometer. 5. Allow 10 minutes for the turkey to rest before slicing and serving. Enjoy!

Per serving: Calories 386; Fat 18.6g; Sodium 440mg; Carbs 2.8g; Fiber 0.2g; Sugar 0.1g; Protein 42.2g

Chicken Nuggets with Tortilla Chips

Prep time: 5 minutes | Cook time: 20 minutes | Serves: 5

1 teaspoon olive oil
2 pounds boneless, skinless chicken breasts, cut into 1-inch-thick strips
1 egg, beaten

1 cup all-purpose flour
Coarse sea salt and ground black pepper, to taste
1 cup tortilla chips, crushed

1. Select the Air Fry function and set the temperature to 400 degrees F. To begin, press the "Start" key. Then, using olive oil, lubricate the perforated cooking tray. 2. Set the chicken aside after patting it dry. 3. Whisk the egg in a shallow bowl until light and foamy, then gradually add the flour, salt, and black pepper. Toss the chicken tenders in the bowl until they are well coated on both sides. 4. Place the crumbled tortilla chips in a separate shallow dish. Roll the chicken strips in the crumbled tortilla chips until they are evenly covered. 5. Set time to 15 minutes and temperature to 400 degrees F. 6. Place the tenders in the cooking tray when the display says "Add Food" after 15 minutes. 7. Warm it up and enjoy it!
Per serving: Calories 440; Fat 13.2g; Sodium 420mg; Carbs 37.5g; Fiber 2g; Sugar 0.8g; Protein 42.4g

Simple Turkey Zucchini Kebabs

Prep time: 5 minutes | Cook time: 25 minutes + marinating time | Serves: 6

1 small lemon, freshly squeezed
3 tablespoons olive oil
1 teaspoon garlic powder
1 ½ pounds turkey breasts, cut into bite-sized chunks

½ pound zucchini, cut into bite-sized chunks
1 cup grape tomatoes
Coarse sea salt and ground black pepper, to taste
6 bamboo skewers, soaked

1. Select the Roast function and set the temperature to 380 degrees F. To begin, press the "Start" key. 2. Using olive oil, lightly lubricate the perforated cooking tray. 3. Toss all ingredients in a porcelain bowl and set aside for 1 hour to marinate. 4. Add turkey, zucchini, and grape tomatoes on bamboo skewers. 5. Set time to 20 minutes and temperature to 380 degrees F. 6. Place the skewers in the cooking tray when the display says "Add Food." They should be roasted for around 20 minutes, turning once or twice. 7. Bon appétit!
Per serving: Calories 269; Fat 14.9g; Sodium 290mg; Carbs 5g; Fiber 0.7g; Sugar 0.1g; Protein 6.6g

Cajun Ribeye Steaks

Prep time: 5 minutes | Cook time: 15 minutes | Serves: 4

1 tablespoon Cajun seasoning
1 teaspoon black pepper, coarsely ground
1 teaspoon garlic powder
1 teaspoon powdered ground coffee
1 tablespoon olive oil
1 ½ pounds ribeye steaks

1. Mix the Cajun seasoning, black pepper, garlic powder, and powdered ground coffee in a small bowl. 2. Combine the spice mixture and olive oil to make a paste. 3. Apply the Cajun spice paste on both sides of the steak. 4. Select Air Fry mode and set the temperature to 400 degrees F and time to 15 minutes. 5. Put the steak in the cooking tray of the air fryer and cook for 15 minutes. 6. When the one side is done, turn the steak and cook again. 7. Take out the steaks from the air fryer and let them rest for 10 minutes. 8. Serve hot and enjoy.
Per serving: Calories 358; Fat 15.5g; Sodium 652mg; Carbs 2.4 g; Fiber 0.5g; Sugar 1g; Protein 50.0g

Skirt Steak with Sauce

Prep time: 5 minutes | Cook time: 10 minutes | Serves: 4

16-ounce skirt steak
1 cup parsley, washed and finely chopped
¼ cup mint washed and finely chopped
2 tablespoons oregano, washed and finely chopped
3 cloves garlic, finely chopped
1 teaspoon crushed red pepper
1 tablespoon ground cumin
1 teaspoon cayenne pepper
2 teaspoons smoked paprika
1 teaspoon salt
¼ teaspoon black pepper
3 tablespoons Red wine vinegar

1. In a bowl, mix all the ingredients instead of steak until well incorporated into the sauce. 2. Cut the steak into desired portions. 3. In a zip-lock bag, put the steak and the ¼ of sauce. 4. Put the marinated meat steak in the fridge for 2 hours. 5. After 2 hours, remove the steak from the zip-lock bag and let it rest for 30 minutes. 6. Select Air Fry mode, set the temperature to 350 degrees F, and time to 10 minutes. 7. Put the steak in the air fryer cooking tray and cook; turn the food when the display shows "turn Food." 8. Garnish the steak with the sauce, serve and enjoy.
Per serving: Calories 515; Fat 40g; Sodium 852mg; Carbs 3 g; Fiber 1g; Sugar 2g; Protein 37.1g

Stuffed Beef Burgers

Prep time: 10 minutes | Cook time: 30 minutes | Serves: 5

2 pounds' beef, ground
2 tablespoons Worcestershire sauce
1 tablespoon salt
½ tablespoon ground black pepper
4 slices of bacon, cooked and chopped
8 tablespoons crumbled blue cheese
¼ cup butter
4 brioche buns
8 slices tomato
4 Bibb lettuce leaves
4 pieces of red onion

1. Mix the beef, sauce, salt, and pepper in a mixing bowl. 2. Make four balls from the mixture, then divide each ball into a half. 3. Now press the meatballs from the center and add bacon and 2 tablespoons cheese. Top with the unstuffed meat and seal the edges. 4. Put the burgers on the cooking tray of the air fryer. 5. Set the air fryer at 400 degrees F on the "Air Fry" setting for 18 minutes. 6. Air fry the burgers for 18 minutes. 7. Remove the burgers from the air fryer tray and set them aside to cool. 8. Spread the butter on the buns. Place the buns on the tray, 9. Select Air Fry mode, set the cooking temperature to 400 degrees F and the cooking time to 10 minutes; cook the buns until golden brown. 10. Add the Burgers, tomatoes, lettuce leaves, and onions to the buns. 11. Serve hot and enjoy.
Per serving: Calories 590; Fat 35g; Sodium 985 mg; Carbs 33g; Fiber 10 g; Sugar 2g; Protein 34g

Flank Steak Bundles in Beef Broth

Prep time: 15 minutes | Cook time: 15 minutes | Serves: 4

2 - 2 ½ pounds Flank steak - cut into 6 pieces
Kosher salt/black Pepper
2 cloves garlic - crushed
1-pound asparagus - trimmed
3 Bell peppers - seeded and
sliced thinly
⅓ cup Beef broth
2 tablespoons unsalted butter
Olive oil spray
Balsamic Vinegar

1. In a large zip-lock bag, add spices and the fillets with salt and Pepper. 2. Add in the garlic. Seal the bag, rub the fillets, and cover them entirely in the spices. 3. Put the marinated fillet in the fridge for 1 hour. 4. When the meat is marinated, place the fillets and meat on the board, and the tenderizer spreads the meat. 5. Spread the fillets evenly and add the asparagus and peppers in the middle of each steak. 6. Roll the steak around the vegetables and secure them with toothpicks like a veggie packet. 7. Preheat the air fryer to 400 degrees F for 5 minutes on the "Roast" setting. 8. Place the vegetables in the air fryer cooking tray. 9. Grease the vegetable meat packet with olive oil. 10. Roast the meat pockets for 15 minutes, occasionally flipping until done. 11. Let the meat rest for 5 minutes before serving/cutting. 12. In a medium pan, heat balsamic vinegar, broth, and butter over medium heat. 13. Mix the ingredient well and continue cooking until the sauce thickens and halves. 14. Season the sauce with salt and Pepper as per taste, and pour the sauce over the meat packets before serving.
Per serving: Calories 220; Fat 10g; Sodium 888mg; Carbs3.8 g; Fiber 0.7g; Sugar 0.2g; Protein 27.6g

Crispy Strip Steak

Prep time: 5 minutes | Cook time: 20 minutes | Serves: 4

1-pound strip steak, 1 inch thick
Salt and Pepper
1 tablespoon butter, unsalted
¼ cup shallots, chopped
1 tablespoon garlic, minced
½ cup dry red wine
2 tablespoons beef bouillon base
3 tablespoons heavy cream

1. Sprinkle the steak with salt and pepper and put it into the air fryer cooking tray. 2. Set the Air Fryer to 400 degrees F at the "Air Fry "setting for 10 minutes. 3. Air fry the steak for 10 minutes and turn it halfway. When both sides cook evenly, place the steak on a platter and let it rest for 10 minutes. 4. In a saucepan, melt the butter over medium heat. Add in the shallots, garlic, salt, and pepper, and sauté the veggies for 1 minute. 5. In the mixture, add red wine and bring it to a boil. Stir with bouillon base until well mixed in the form of silky sauce. 6. Add heavy cream to the sauce and cook for 1 more

minute. 7. When the sauce is ready, remove it from the heat. 8. Slice the steak evenly and serve with the sauce and enjoy.

Per serving: Calories 649; Fat 34g; Sodium 145 mg; Carbs 7.5 g; Fiber 1 g; Sugar 2g; Protein 69g

Rib Eye Steak with Steak Seasoning

Prep time: 5 minutes | Cook time: 22 minutes | Serves: 1

10 ounces Rib eye steak	½ tablespoon garlic powder
1 tablespoon salt	¾ steak seasoning
¾ tablespoon pepper	

1. Mix the steak with the spices in a mixing bowl and set it aside. 2. Marinade the steak for 2 hours in a refrigerator. 3. Put the marinated steak in the air fryer cooking tray. 4. Set the Air Fryer to 390 degrees F for 12 minutes at the "Roast" setting. 5. Roast the steak for 12 minutes; turn the steak when the display shows "turn Food." 6. Place the steak on a plate, cover it with paper foil, and let it rest for 8 minutes. Serve hot with roasted potatoes on the side, and enjoy.

Per serving: Calories 651; Fat 49g; Sodium 981mg; Carbs 7.5 g; Fiber 2.1g; Sugar 1g; Protein 44g

Spicy Steak Bites

Prep time: 5 minutes | Cook time: 20 minutes | Serves: 3

1-pound steaks	Salt to taste
8 ounces' mushrooms	Black Pepper to taste
2 tablespoon butter	Minced parsley
1 tablespoon Worcestershire sauce	Melted butter
	Chili flakes
½ tablespoon garlic powder	

1. Pat dry the steak with a paper towel. 2. Coat the steak and mushrooms with butter. 3. Combine meat and mushrooms with Worcestershire sauce, garlic, salt, and Pepper. 4. Place the spiced steak and mushrooms in the air fryer cooking tray. 5. Set the Air Fryer to 400 degrees F for 18 minutes at the "Air Fry "setting. 6. Air fry the steak and mushrooms for 18 minutes, and turn the steak and mushrooms halfway for even cooking. 7. When the steak is evenly cooked, place it on the serving plate and garnish it with parsley, butter, and chili flakes. 8. Serve the steak when warm with mushrooms.

Per serving: Calories 300; Fat 21g; Sodium 605mg; Carbs 2 g; Fiber 0 g; Sugar 2g; Protein 24g

Mustard Hanger Steak

Prep time: 5 minutes | Cook time: 25 minutes | Serves: 2

7 ounces' hanger steaks	2 tablespoons butter
Salt and Pepper	1 bottle of red wine
Oil	1 cup beef stock
For the Sauce	1 tablespoon whole-grain mustard
1 shallot, thinly sliced	

1. Mix the hanger steak with salt and Pepper and transfer it into the air fryer cooking tray. 2. Set the Air Fryer to 400 degrees F for 10 minutes at the "Air Fry" setting. 3. Air fry the steak for 10 minutes and flip the steak halfway. When both sides are evenly cooked, Let the steak rest for 10 minutes. 4. Heat butter and cook shallots until translucent over medium heat in a saucepan. Add the wine to it and cook until all the wine has evaporated. 5. Pour the beef stock and cook until it is reduced by half. 6. Put in the mustard and mix until well combined. 7. Season the sauce with salt and Pepper to taste. 8. Add cold butter to the sauce and swirl the saucepan until it melts; the sauce will be silky. Serve the sauce with the hot hanger steak and enjoy.

Per serving: Calories 619; Fat 32g; Sodium 985mg; Carbs 6.5 g; Fiber 1g; Sugar 1g; Protein 63g

Beef Meatballs with Gravy

Prep time: 10 minutes | Cook time: 14 minutes | Serves: 4

For the meatballs	Pepper
1pound 93% lean ground beef	For the gravy
1 (1-ounce) packet Lipton Onion Recipe Soup & Dip Mix	1 cup beef broth
⅓ cup bread crumbs	⅓ cup heavy cream
1 egg beaten	1 tablespoon all-purpose flour
Salt	

1. Combine the ground beef, onion soup mix, bread crumbs, egg, salt, and Pepper in a large bowl. Mix the meat well. 2. Make meatballs from the spiced meat and place them in the air fryer cooking tray. 3. Set the air fryer to the "Air Fry" setting at 350 degrees F for 14 minutes. 4. Put the meatballs in the air fryer cooking tray and air fry for 14 minutes. 5. Over medium heat, add the beef broth and heavy cream to a saucepan and cook for 1 to 2 minutes. 6. Add in the flour and mix it well; cover the saucepan and let it simmer for 3 to 4 minutes until the food thicken. 7. Spread the gravy over the hot meatballs and serve hot and enjoy.

Per serving: Calories 178; Fat 14g; Sodium 765mg; Carbs 15g; Fiber 2g; Sugar 3g; Protein 9g

Bell Peppers Stuffed with Meat and Rice

Prep time: 13 minutes | Cook time: 15 minutes | Serves: 4

4 bell peppers	thawed
2 tablespoons olive oil	1 to 20 small frozen pre-cooked meatballs, thawed
1 small onion, chopped	
2 cloves garlic, minced	½ cup tomato sauce
1 cup of frozen cooked rice,	1 tablespoon Dijon mustard

1. Prepare the peppers by cutting off their top. Carefully remove the membranes and seeds from inside the peppers. 2. Mix olive oil, onion, and garlic in a small pan. 3. Set the air fryer to the "Bake" setting at 400 degrees F for 15 minutes. 4. Place the onion-garlic in the air fryer and bake for 2 to 4 minutes. 5. In a bowl, remove the vegetable mixture from the pan and set it aside. 6. Add the rice, meatballs, tomato sauce, and mustard to the vegetable mixture and stir to combine. 7. Stuff well the deseeded peppers with the meat-vegetable mixture. 8. Place the peppers in the air fryer cooking tray and bake for 9 to 13 minutes until done and Pepper are tender. 9. Serve hot and enjoy.

Per serving: Calories 487; Fat 21g; Sodium 865mg; Carbs 6 g; Fiber 0.6g; Sugar 0.3g; Protein 26g

Air-Fried Ribeye Steak

Prep time: 5 minutes | Cook time: 10 minutes | Serves: 2

2 pounds' ribeye steak	Salt and black pepper to taste
1 tablespoon olive oil	

1. Rub both sides of the steak with oil; season with salt and Pepper. 2. Select Air Fry mode and adjust the temperature to 350 degrees F. 3. Place the steak in the Air Fryer's cooking tray and cook for 8 minutes. 4. Serve hot and enjoy!

Per serving: Calories 300; Fat 19g; Sodium 235mg; Carbs 15g; Fiber 2g; Sugar 2.5g; Protein 32g

Sirloin Steak with Stir-Fried Cabbage

Prep time: 15 minutes | Cook time: 10 minutes | Serves: 4

½ pound sirloin steak, cut into strips
1teaspoon cornstarch
1 tablespoon peanut oil
1 cup chopped red or green cabbage

1 yellow bell pepper, chopped
1 green onion, chopped
2 cloves garlic, sliced
½ cup commercial stir-fry sauce

1. Set the air fryer to the "Air Fry" setting for 10 minutes at 360 degrees F. 2. Mix the steak with the cornstarch and set it aside. 3. Combine the peanut oil with the cabbage in a metal bowl. 4. Place the metal bowl in the cooking tray and air fry for 3 to 4 minutes. 5. Remove the bowl from the tray and add the steak, Pepper, onions, and garlic. 6. Return the bowl to the air fryer and cook for 3 to 5 minutes until the desired tenderness and vegetables are crispy. 7. When the steak is ready, and the vegetables are crispy, add the stir-fry sauce and cook for 2 to 4 minutes. 8. Serve over boiled rice and enjoy.
Per serving: Calories 180; Fat 7g; Sodium 562mg; Carbs 8g; Fiber 2g; Sugar 1g; Protein 20g

Cheesy Steak with White Onion

Prep time: 5 minutes | Cook time: 15 minutes | Serves: 6

Large hoagie bun, sliced in half
6 ounces of sirloin or flank steak, cut into bite-sized pieces
½ white onion, rinsed and sliced
½ red Pepper, rinsed and sliced
1slices of American cheese

1. Set the Air Fryer to 320 degrees F for 10 minutes at the "Air Fry" setting. 2. In a piece of tin foil, arrange the steak pieces, onions, and peppers and place them on the cooking tray and cook for 10 minutes. 3. Cut the hoagie-bun in half and toast it on the stove over medium heat or bake for a crispy and golden crust. Topped the bun with cheese and toast until cheese melted. 4. Gently stir the steak, onions, and peppers with a spoon in the foil to ensure even coverage. 5. When the steak and vegetables are juicy and crispy, now on the one side of the bun, place the steak, onions, and Pepper and cover it with another bun. 6. Slice it into two pieces and serve hot with sauce and enjoy.
Per serving: Calories 540; Fat 12g; Sodium 720mg; Carbs 50 g; Fiber 8.4g; Sugar 4g; Protein 32g

Classical Bolognaise Sauce

Prep time: 5 minutes | Cook time: 30 minutes | Serves: 2

13 ounces of Ground Beef
1 Carrot
1 Stalk of Celery
1-ounce Diced Tomatoes
½ onion
Salt and Pepper to taste

1. Preheat the Air Fryer to 390 degrees F on the "Air Fry" setting for 5 minutes. 2. Finely chopped carrot, celery, and onions, combine with ground beef, mix well, place into the air fry cooking tray, and cook for 12 minutes. 3. Add the diced tomatoes to the cooking tray and season with salt and Pepper as per taste, and give it a good stir. Cook the bolognaise sauce for 18 minutes more. 4. Serve over-cooked pasta and enjoy the hot meaty sauce.
Per serving: Calories 151; Fat 11.3g; Sodium 589mg; Carbs 3.1g; Fiber 0.6g; Sugar 2.5g; Protein 10.6g

Spicy Skirt Steak

Prep time: 10 minutes | Cook time: 10 minutes | Serves: 2

2 x 8-ounce skirt steak
1 cup finely chopped parsley
¼ cup finely chopped mint
2 tablespoons fresh oregano (washed & finely chopped)
3 finely chopped cloves of garlic
1 teaspoon red pepper flakes (crushed)

1 tablespoon ground cumin
1 teaspoon cayenne pepper
2 teaspoon smoked paprika
1 teaspoon salt
¼ teaspoon pepper
¾ cup oil
3 tablespoons red wine vinegar

1. Add all the ingredients besides the steak and mix well in a bowl. 2. Put ¼ cup of the mixture with the steak in a plastic bag and leave it in the fridge overnight (2–24hrs) for the marinade. 3. Preheat the air fryer to 5 to 390 degrees F before cooking. 4. Pour into the air fry cooking tray. Place the tray on the middle shelf of the Air Fryer. 5. Set the air fryer to 390 degrees F for 10 minutes at the "Air Fry" setting. 6. Air fry the steak for 8-10 minutes as per your required tenderness. In 8 minutes, the steak will be medium-rare. 7. Put 2 tablespoons of the chimichurri mix on top of each steak before serving and serve hot and enjoy.
Per serving: Calories 308.6; Fat 22.6g; Sodium 985mg; Carbs 3g; Fiber 0.4g; Sugar 0.2g; Protein 23.7g

Herbed Steak with Mint Sauce

Prep time: 30 minutes | Cook time: 35 minutes | Serves: 2

2 Beef steak
2 cloves garlic, peeled and thinly sliced into slivers
2 long sprigs of fresh rosemary, leaves removed
2 tablespoons wholegrain mustard
1 tablespoon honey
2 tablespoon mint sauce

1. With a sharp knife, cut slits on the top of the steak. 2. Add the slices of garlic and rosemary leaves in the slits and set the steak aside. 3. Whisk the mustard, honey, and mint sauce together and brush over the steak. 4. Let the meat marinate in a cool area for 20 minutes. 5. Spray the air fry cooking tray using cooking spray and place the steak in it. 6. Air fry the steak for 35 minutes at 360 degrees F on Air Fry mode, and after 15 minutes, flip and turn the meat and cook for 20 more minutes. 7. Place the cooked steak on a platter and cover with foil to sit for 10 minutes. 8. Slice the steak and serve with the sauce and enjoy.
Per serving: Calories 309; Fat 2g; Sodium 235mg; Carbs 30 g; Fiber 16g; Sugar 10g; Protein 33g

Herbed Beef Steak Slices

Prep time: 5 minutes | Cook time: 15 minutes | Serves: 2

1 teaspoon oregano
1 teaspoon coriander
1 teaspoon thyme
1 teaspoon rosemary
½ teaspoon salt
¼ teaspoon pepper
2 tablespoons lemon juice
1 tablespoon olive oil
1-pound beef steak (Sliced)

1. Mix the oregano, coriander, thyme, rosemary, salt, pepper, lemon juice, and olive oil in a zip-lock bag and shake well, so it mixes. 2. Add the steaks slices to the bag and squish around, so the meat slices are evenly mixed. Refrigerate it 1 hour. 3. Set the air fryer to 390 degrees F for 15 minutes at the "Air Fry" setting. 4. Spray the cooking oil on the air fry cooking tray, then place the steak slices in it. 5. Air fry the steaks for 15 minutes, flipping halfway for even cooking. Plate the steak slices and serve hot with sauce and enjoy.

Per serving: Calories 321; Fat 34g; Sodium 421mg; Carbs25g; Fiber 15g; Sugar6g; Protein 18g

Veggie and Steak Kebabs

Prep time: 15 minutes | Cook time: 7 minutes | Serves: 4

2 tablespoons balsamic vinegar	¾ pound round steak, cut into 1-inch pieces
2 teaspoons olive oil	1 red bell pepper, sliced
½ teaspoon dried marjoram	16 button mushrooms
⅛ teaspoon freshly ground black pepper	1 cup cherry tomatoes

1. Set the air fryer to the "Roast" setting for 7 minutes at 360 degrees F. 2. Mix the balsamic vinegar, olive oil, marjoram, and black pepper in a medium bowl. 3. Add in the steak and stir in the marinade to coat well. Let marinate the meat for 10 minutes at room temperature. 4. Thread the beef, red bell pepper, mushrooms, and tomatoes onto skewers. 5. Roast the skewers in the air fryer for 5 to 7 minutes, or until the beef is browned and reaches at least 145 degrees F on a meat thermometer and the veggies are tender and crispy. 6. Serve immediately with the sauce and enjoy.
Per serving: Calories 194; Fat 6g; Sodium 53mg; Carbs 7g; Fiber 2g; Sugar 2g; Protein 31g

Ground Beef Cooked with Tomato and Onion

Prep time: 10 minutes | Cook time: 20 minutes | Serves: 5

½ pound 96 percent lean ground beef	2 tablespoons freshly squeezed lemon juice
2 medium tomatoes, chopped	⅓ cup low-sodium beef broth
1 onion, chopped	2 tablespoon crumbled low-sodium feta cheese
2 garlic cloves, minced	
2 cups fresh baby spinach	

1. In a small metal pan, crumble the beef. 2. Set the air fryer to the "Air Fry" setting for 30 minutes at 360 degrees F. 3. Place the bowl in the air fryer cooking tray and place in the air fryer. 4. Air fry the meat in the air fryer for 3 to 7 minutes, stirring once during cooking until browned. Drain the meat to get rid of any extra fat. 5. Add the tomatoes, onion, and garlic to the meat pan. 6. Air-fry the meat and veggies for 4 to 8 minutes more, or until the onion is tender. 7. Add the spinach, lemon juice, and beef broth to the bowl and stir. 8. Air-fry for 2 to 4 minutes more, or until the spinach is wilted and crispy. 9. Sprinkle the meat with the feta cheese and serve immediately and enjoy.
Per serving: Calories 298; Fat 15g; Sodium 410mg; Carbs 4g; Fiber 0.8g; Sugar0.1g; Protein 23.6g

Light Herbed Meatballs

Prep time: 10 minutes | Cook time: 30 minutes | Serves: 5

1 medium onion, minced	3 tablespoons 1 percent milk
2 garlic cloves, minced	1 teaspoon dried marjoram
1 teaspoon olive oil	1 teaspoon dried basil
1 slice low-sodium whole-wheat bread, crumbled	1-pound 96 percent lean ground beef

1. In a small pan, combine the onion, garlic, and olive oil. 2. Set the air fryer for 30 minutes at the "Air fry" setting on 360 degrees F. 3. Air-fry the veggies for 2 to 4 minutes, or until the vegetables are crisp-tender. Place the vegetables in a medium bowl, and add the bread crumbs, milk, marjoram, and basil. Mix well until well incorporated. 4. Add the ground beef to the veggie mix. 5. Mix the mixture gently with your hand. Form the spiced meat mixture into about 24 (1-inch) meatballs. 6. Air Fry the meatballs, in batches, in the lined/oiled air fryer cooking tray for 12 to 17 minutes, or until they reach 160 degrees F on a meat thermometer. 7. Serve hot with your favorite sauce immediately.
Per serving: Calories 190; Fat 6g; Sodium 120mg; Carbs 8g; Fiber 1g; Sugar 2g; Protein 25g

Simple-Cooked Strip Steak

Prep time: 10 minutes | Cook time: 8 minutes | Serves: 2

1 (9½-ounces) New York strip steak – 1	as required
	Olive oil – 1 teaspoon
Salt and ground black pepper,	

1. Grease the steak with oil and sprinkle with salt and black Pepper evenly as per taste. 2. Arrange the steak onto the greased cooking tray. 3. Set the air fryer to 400 degrees F at the "Air Fry" setting for 8 minutes. 4. Air fry the steak for 8 minutes, flipping halfway until tender. 5. Plate the steak once cooked warp with foil and let it rest for about 10 minutes. 6. Slice the steak into the desired size and serve with your favorite sauce.
Per serving: Calories 344; Fat 22.5g; Sodium 864mg; Carbs 0g; Fiber 0g; Sugar 0g; Protein 36g

Air Fried Sirloin Steak

Prep time: 5 minutes | Cook time: 45 minutes | Serves: 2

2 pounds of sirloin steaks	3 tablespoons olive oil
3 tablespoon butter, melted	Salt and Pepper to taste

1. Grease the sirloin steaks with olive oil and season with salt and pepper. 2. Put the beef in the air fryer cooking tray. 3. Air fry the steak for 45 minutes at 350 degrees F on Air Fry mode, flipping the meat halfway until tender. 4. Serve hot, topped with butter.
Per serving: Calories 1536; Fat 123.7g; Sodium 987mg; Carbs 0g; Fiber 0g; Sugar 0g; Protein 103.4

Country Fried Sirloin Steak

Prep time: 5 minutes | Cook time: 12 minutes | Serves: 2

1 teaspoon pepper	1 teaspoon onion powder
2 cups almond milk	1 cup panko breadcrumbs
2 tablespoons almond flour	1 cup almond flour
6 ounces ground sausage meat	3 beaten eggs
1 teaspoon pepper	6 ounces' sirloin steak, pounded till thin
1 teaspoon salt	
1 teaspoon garlic powder	

1. Season the panko breadcrumbs with spices. 2. Dredge the steak in flour, egg, and season with panko mixture. 3. Put into the air fryer cooking tray. 4. Set the Air Fryer to 370 degrees F for 12 minutes at the "Air Fry" setting. 5. Air fry the steak for 12 minutes, flipping halfway for even cooking. 6. Meanwhile, in a cooking pan, cook the sausage and dry it out of fat. 7. Add the flour to the sausage and mix until incorporated. 8. Gradually add milk over medium to high heat till it becomes thick like a sauce. 9. Season mixture with Pepper as per taste and cook 3 minutes longer. 10. Serve steak topped with yummy gravy, and enjoy.
Per serving: Calories 395; Fat 11.3g; Sodium 236mg; Carbs 0g; Fiber 0g; Sugar 0g; Protein 39g

BBQ Steak Cubes

Prep time: 5 minutes | Cook time: 40 minutes | Serves: 3

1 cup red onions cut into wedges
1 tablespoon dry mustard
1 tablespoon olive oil
1-pound boneless beef sirloin, cut into cubes
Salt and Pepper to taste

1. Mix all ingredients in a bowl until everything is coated with the seasonings. 2. Place all ingredients on the cooking tray in the air fryer and roast for 40 minutes at 390 degrees F on Roast mode, until tender. Halfway through the cooking time, give a stir to cook evenly. 3. Serve hot and enjoy.
Per serving: Calories 260; Fat 10.7g; Sodium 841mg; Carbs 0g; Fiber 0g; Sugar 0g; Protein 35.5g

Flavorful Steak

Prep time: 10 minutes | Cook time: 18 minutes | Serves: 2

2 steaks, rinsed and pat dry
½ teaspoon garlic powder
1 teaspoon olive oil
Pepper
Salt

1. Rub the steaks with olive oil and season with garlic powder, Pepper, and salt. 2. Set the air fryer to 400 degrees F at the "Air Fry" setting and adjust the time to 18 minutes. 3. Put the steaks on the air fryer cooking tray and cook for 10-18 minutes, turning halfway through. 4. Serve hot with your favorite sauce and enjoy.
Per serving: Calories 361; Fat 10.9g; Sodium 325mg; Carbs 0.5g; Fiber 0.1g; Sugar 0.1g; Protein 61.6g

Juicy Sirloin Steak Bites

Prep time: 10 minutes | Cook time: 9 minutes | Serves: 4

1-pound sirloin steak, cut into bite-size pieces
1 tablespoon steak seasoning
1 tablespoon olive oil
Pepper
Salt

1. In a prominent mixing bowl, place the steak pieces. Add the steak seasoning, oil, Pepper, and salt over steak pieces and toss until well coated. 2. Select Air Fry mode, set the temperature to 390 degrees F, and time to 10 minutes. 3. Transfer the steak pieces to the air fryer cooking tray and cook for 5 minutes. 4. Flip the steak pieces to the other side when the display shows "turn Food." 5. Serve hot with sauce and enjoy.
Per serving: Calories 241; Fat 10.6g; Sodium 236mg; Carbs 0g; Fiber 0g; Sugar 0g; Protein 34.4g

Juicy Beef Burgers

Prep time: 5 minutes | Cook time: 15 minutes | Serves: 4

1 pound 93% lean ground beef
1 teaspoon Worcestershire sauce
1 tablespoon burger seasoning
Salt
Pepper
Cooking oil
4 slices cheese
Buns

1. Mix the ground beef, Worcestershire, burger seasoning, and salt and Pepper to taste in a large bowl. 2. Spray the air fryer cooking tray with cooking oil. 3. Make the 4 patties from the mixture. Place the burgers in the air fryer. Transfer it to the air fryer cooking tray. Place the tray on the middle shelf of the Air Fryer. 4. Set Air Fryer to 375 degrees F for 8 minutes on the "Air Fry" setting. 5. Air fry the patties for 8 minutes, flip them halfway and cook the other side for 3 minutes. 6. On each burger, add a slice of cheese. Cook for an additional 1 minute. 7. Serve hot on toasted buns with any additional toppings.
Per serving: Calories 556; Fat 39g; Sodium 378mg; Carbs 0g; Fiber 0g; Sugar 0g; Protein 29g

Garlicky Ribeye Steak with Blue Cheese Butter

Prep time: 10 minutes | Cook time: 10 minutes | Serves: 2

2 ribeye steaks
1 teaspoon garlic powder
½ tablespoon blue cheese butter
1 teaspoon pepper
1 teaspoon kosher salt

1. Combine the garlic powder, pepper, and salt and rub over the steaks. 2. Spray the air fryer cooking tray with cooking spray. 3. Select Air Fry mode and adjust the temperature to 400 degrees F. 4. Place the steak in the air fryer cooking tray and cook for 4-5 minutes on each side. 5. Add some blue butter cheese to the top of the steak. 6. Serve hot and enjoy.
Per serving: Calories 830; Fat 60g; Sodium 365mg; Carbs 3g; Fiber 0.4g; Sugar 0g; Protein 70g

Top Round Steak

Prep time: 10 minutes | Cook time: 20 minutes | Serves: 4

1 ½ pounds top round steak, cut into bite-sized cubes
2 tablespoons olive oil
1 tablespoon Italian seasoning
1 teaspoon cayenne pepper
Sea salt to taste
black pepper to taste
¼ cup butter
2 garlic cloves, minced
1 teaspoon fresh rosemary
1 teaspoon fresh thyme

1. In a bowl, mix all the ingredients and marinate the beef for at least 3 hours. 2. Set the air fry to 390 degrees F for 20 minutes at the "Air Fry" setting. 3. Cook the beef for about 12 minutes. 4. Increase the temperature of the air fryer to 400 degrees F; baste the beef with the reserved marinade and continue to cook for 5 to 6 minutes more. 5. Serve hot with sauce and enjoy!
Per serving: Calories 258g; Fat 14g; Sodium 356mg; Carbs 3g; Fiber 0.2g; Sugar 0.5g; Protein 30g

Mushroom Beef Bites

Prep time: 10 minutes | Cook time: 15 minutes | Serves: 6

2 pounds' beef, cut into bite-size pieces
2 pounds' mushrooms, cut into halves
2 tablespoon Worcester sauce
1 tablespoon salt
1 tablespoon pepper

1. Select Air Fry mode, set the cooking temperature to 400 degrees F and the cooking time to 15 minutes. 2. Mix the beef bites and mushroom halves in a bowl. Add the Worchester sauce, salt, and Pepper. Mix well and leave to sit for 15 minutes. 3. Add the beef and mushrooms to the air fryer cooking tray. 4. Air fry the meaty bites for 5 minutes. Toss the meat to ensure all the sides become nice and crispy. 5. Air fry for 5-7 more minutes. 6. Serve hot with your favorite sauce, and enjoy.
Per serving: Calories 300; Fat 11g; Sodium 255mg; Carbs 7g; Fiber 1g; Sugar 1g; Protein 35g

Beef, Sausage and Mushroom Meatloaf

Prep time: 10 minutes | Cook time: 20 minutes | Serves: 6

1 pound of ground beef	1 tablespoon thyme, chopped
3 tablespoons almond flour	1 onion, chopped
1 egg, lightly beaten	Pepper
2 mushrooms, sliced	Salt
2 ounces' sausage, chopped	

1. In a large bowl, add all ingredients and mix until well combined. 2. Place the meat mixture into the greased loaf pan. 3. Set the air fryer to 390 degrees F for 20 minutes at the "Air Fry" setting. 4. Air fries the meatloaf for 20 minutes until done. 5. Serve hot with sauce and enjoy.

Per serving: Calories 319; Fat 14.9g; Sodium 154mg; Carbs 4.5g; Fiber 0.9g; Sugar 1.6g; Protein 40.3g

Delicious Montreal Steak

Prep time: 10 minutes | Cook time: 7 minutes | Serves: 2

12 ounces' steaks	1 tablespoon olive oil
1 tablespoon Montreal steak seasoning	Pepper to taste
	Salt to taste

1. Brush the steaks with oil, season with steak seasoning, pepper, and salt, and place on the air fryer cooking tray. 2. Set the air fryer to 375 degrees F for 7 minutes at the "Air Fry" setting. 3. Air fry the steak for 7 minutes, flipping halfway for even cooking. 4. Serve hot with sauce and enjoy.

Per serving: Calories 409; Fat 15.5g; Sodium 236mg; Carbs 0g; Fiber 0g; Sugar 0g; Protein 61.5g

Beef-Sausage Meatballs

Prep time: 10 minutes | Cook time: 20 minutes | Serves: 4

½ pound ground beef	½ teaspoon black pepper
½ pound Italian sausage	½ teaspoon garlic powder
½ cup mozzarella cheese, shredded	½ teaspoon onion powder
	Salt to taste

1. In a large mixing bowl, add all ingredients and mix until well combined. 2. Make meatballs from the mixture and place them onto the air fryer cooking tray. 3. Set the air fryer to 370 degrees F for 20 minutes at the "Air Fry' setting. 4. Cook the meatballs for 20 minutes until done. 5. Serve hot with fresh salad on the side and enjoy.

Per serving: Calories 310; Fat 20.3g; Sodium 458mg; Carbs 0.8g; Fiber 0g; Sugar 0.2g; Protein 29.3g

Air-Fried Steak with Onion and Bell Pepper

Prep time: 10 minutes | Cook time: 15 minutes | Serves: 6

1-pound steak, sliced	gluten-free
1 tablespoon olive oil	½ cup onion, sliced
1 tablespoon fajita seasoning,	3 bell peppers, sliced

1. In a large bowl, add all ingredients and toss until well coated with spices. 2. Place the fajita mixture into the air fryer cooking tray 3. Set the air fryer to 390 degrees F for 10 minutes at the "Air Fry' setting. 4. Air fry the fajita meat for 10 minutes, stirring once for even cooking. 5. Serve hot with toasted buns and enjoy.

Per serving: Calories 199; Fat 6.3g; Sodium 124mg; Carbs 6.4g; Fiber 1g; Sugar 3.4g; Protein 28g

Marinated Sirloin Steak Kebab

Prep time: 10 minutes | Cook time: 10 minutes | Serves: 4

1-pound sirloin steak, cut into 1-inch pieces	2 tablespoon vinegar
1 red bell pepper, cut into 1-inch pieces	2 tablespoons olive oil
	¼ cup soy sauce
1 onion, cut into 1-inch pieces	1 teaspoon ginger garlic paste
For marinade:	1 teaspoon pepper

1. In the zip-lock bag, add the meat and remaining spices, seal the bag, shake well, and place in the refrigerator overnight for the marinade. 2. Thread the marinated steak pieces, bell pepper, and onion onto the skewers. 3. Put the skewers onto the air fryer cooking tray. 4. Set the air fryer to 350 degrees F for 10 minutes at the "Air Fry" setting, then press start. 5. Air fry the skewers for 10 minutes until meat is tender and veggies are crispy. 6. Serve hot with sauce and enjoy.

Per serving: Calories 309; Fat 14.5ar 3g; Sodium 341mg; Carbs 12.42g; Fiber 1.4g; Sugar 8.43g; Protein 36.3g

Mongolian Beef with Special Sauce

Prep time: 5 minutes | Cook time: 15 minutes | Serves: 6

Olive oil	1 teaspoon hoisin sauce
½ cup almond flour	½ cup water
2 pounds of beef tenderloin or beef chuck, sliced into strips	½ cup rice vinegar
	½ cup low-sodium soy sauce
Sauce:	1 tablespoon chopped garlic
½ cup chopped green onion	1 tablespoon finely chopped ginger
1 teaspoon. red chili flakes	
1 teaspoon. almond flour	2 tablespoons olive oil
½ cup brown sugar	

1. Toss beef strips in almond flour, ensuring they are coated well. 2. Add the meat to the Air fryer cooking tray. 3. Set the air fryer to 300 degrees F for 12 minutes at the "Air Fry" setting. 4. Air fry the meat for 10 minutes. 5. While the meat is cooking, mix all the sauce ingredients into the pan and bring to a boil. 6. Add the beef strips to the sauce and cook for 2 minutes over medium-high heat. 7. Serve hot with cauliflower rice and enjoy.

Per serving: Calories306; Fat 12g; Sodium 541mg; Carbs 11g; Fiber 3g; Sugar 2g; Protein 25g

Air Fried Beef Strips with Cannellini Beans

Prep time: 5 minutes | Cook time: 15 minutes | Serves: 4

4 beef steaks, trim the fat, and cut into strips	1 can cannellini beans
	¾ cup beef broth
1 cup green onions, chopped	¼ teaspoon dried basil
2 cloves garlic, minced	½ teaspoon cayenne pepper
One red bell pepper, seeded and thinly sliced	½ teaspoon sea salt
1 can of tomatoes, crushed	¼ teaspoon ground black pepper, or to taste

1. Add the steaks, green onions, and garlic to the cooking tray. 2. Place the tray on the middle shelf of the Air fryer. 3. Set the air fryer at 390 degrees F for 15 minutes at the "Air Fry" setting. 4. Cook the steak for 10 minutes. 5. Add the remaining ingredients and cook for another 5 minutes at the "Air Fry" setting. 6. Serve hot with salad and enjoy.

Per serving: Calories 148; Fat 5g; Sodium 421mg; Carbs 10g; Fiber 1g; Sugar 1g; Protein 24g

Baked Beef Hot Dogs

Prep time: 5 minutes | Cook time: 10 minutes | Serves: 4

Package of 8 All Beef Hot Dog Wieners	Package of 8 Pop Open Crescent Rolls

1. Set the air fryer on the "Bake" setting at 375 degrees F for 10 minutes. 2. Separate the crescent rolls into eight triangles. 3. Roll each triangle around each hot dog and drop them into the Air Fryer cooking tray, leaving space between them. 4. Bake the rolls for 10 minutes, serve with dipping sauce, and enjoy.

Per serving: Calories 306.6; Fat 13.5g; Sodium 411mg; Carbs 6.6g; Fiber 1g; Sugar 0.5g; Protein 37.6g

Palatable Beef Tenderloin

Prep time: 5 minutes | Cook time: 45 minutes | Serves: 8

2 pounds of beef tenderloin	1 tablespoon salt
1 tablespoon vegetable oil	½ tablespoon black pepper, cracked
1 tablespoon dried oregano	

1. Dry the tenderloin with a paper towel and place it on a platter. 2. Add the vegetable oil and sprinkle oregano, salt, and Pepper. Coat well the spices on the meat. 3. Place the roast on the air fryer cooking tray. 4. Set the air fryer at 390 degrees F for 45 minutes at the "Air Fry" setting. 5. Air fry the meat for 22 minutes. Reduce the temperature to 360⁰ F and cook for 10 minutes more. 6. Transfer the meat to a plate and allow resting for 10 minutes 7. Serve hot and enjoy.

Per serving: Calories 256; Fat 10g; Sodium 268 mg; Carbs 12 g; Fiber 2 g; Sugar 1g; Protein 42g

Barbeque Flank Steak with Sesame Seed

Prep time: 15 minutes | Cook time: 30 minutes | Serves: 4

1-pound flank steak	vinegar
¼ Cup corn starch	1 Tablespoon garlic (crushed)
1 Tablespoon Pompeian oil	½ Tablespoon sesame seeds
½ Cup soy sauce	1 Tablespoon corn starch
½ Cup brown sugar	1 Tablespoon water
2 Tablespoon Pompeian while	

1. Sliced the steak into thin pieces and rubbed with corn starch and oil. 2. Select Air Fry mode, and set the temperature to 390 degrees F. 3. Cover the air fryer tray with aluminum foil. 4. Place the steak on the air fryer cooking tray. 5. Cook steak for 20 minutes at the "Air Fry" setting with intermittent flipping. 6. Heat all other ingredients in a pan except water and cornstarch in medium heat to form the sauce. Mix the cornstarch with water into a slurry and mix in the sauce. 7. The sauce should be heated until reduced to half. 8. Pour the sauce over the steak and served with green beans and cooked rice.

Per serving: Calories 329; Fat 8g; Sodium 222 mg; Carbs 26 g; Fiber 5 g; Sugar 7g; Protein 22g

Toothsome Beef Brisket

Prep time: 10 minutes | Cook time: 1 hour and 30 minutes | Serves: 4

½ cup beef stock	1 tablespoon chili powder
1 bay leaf	1 teaspoon dry mustard
1 tablespoon garlic powder	1 tablespoon olive oil
1 tablespoon onion powder	Salt and Pepper to taste

1. Select the Bake mode and set the temperature to 400 degrees F. 2. Place all ingredients in an air fry cooking tray. 3. Bake for 1 hour and 30 minutes. 4. Stir the beef every 30 minutes to soak in the sauce. 5. Serve hot with sauce and fresh salad and enjoy.

Per serving: Calories 306; Fat 24.1g; Sodium 246mg; Carbs 12 g; Fiber 2 g; Sugar 1g; Protein 18.3g

Beef Stroganoff

Prep time: 10 minutes | Cook time: 4 hours | Serves: 4

9 ounces of Tender Beef	¾ cup Sour Cream
1 Onion, chopped	Salt and Pepper to taste
1 tablespoon Paprika	Baking Dish

1. Chop the beef and marinate it using paprika. 2. Add the chopped onions into the air fryer cooking tray and heat for about 2 minutes in the air fryer. 3. Select Air Fry mode and set the temperature to 390 degrees F. 4. Add the beef into the air fryer cooking tray when the onions are transparent, and cook for 5 minutes at the "Air Fry "setting. 5. Once the beef is starting to tender, pour in the sour cream and cook for another 7 minutes at the "Air Fry" setting. 6. When the liquid has reduced, seasoned with salt and pepper and serve hot.

Per serving: Calories 391; Fat 23g; Sodium 300 mg; Carbs 21 g; Fiber 1.3 g; Sugar 3.2g; Protein 25g

Steak with Chimichurri Sauce

Prep time: 5 minutes | Cook time: 20 minutes | Serves: 6

1 cup commercial chimichurri	Salt and Pepper to taste
1-pound steak	

1. Put all the ingredients in a Ziploc bag and marinate in the fridge for 2 hours. 2. Preheat the air fryer to 390 degrees F at the "Roast" setting for minutes. 3. Put the steak in the air fryer cooking tray and place the air fryer cooking tray in the air fryer. 4. Roast the skirt steak for 20 minutes per batch, flipping once halfway for even cooking. 5. Serve the steak with your favorite sauce and enjoy.

Per serving: Calories 507; Fat 27g; Sodium 89 mg; Carbs 436 g; Fiber 13 g; Sugar 0.2g; Protein 63g

Classical Ribeye Steak

Prep time: 10 minutes | Cook time: 40 minutes | Serves: 4

4 (8-ounce) ribeye steaks	Salt
1 tablespoon Steak Seasoning	Pepper

1. Season the steaks with the steak seasoning and salt and Pepper to taste. 2. Place 2 steaks in the air fryer cooking tray. 3. Set the air fryer to the "Air Fry" setting at 360 degrees F for 40 minutes. 4. Air fry the steak for 20 minutes, flipping halfway for even cooking. 5. Repeat the same steps to cook the remaining 2 steaks. 6. Wrap the cooked steak in foil and let them rest before slicing. 7. Serve the steak slices with creamy mashed potatoes and enjoy.

Per serving: Calories 293; Fat 22g; Sodium 450 mg; Carbs 14 g; Fiber 0 g; Sugar 0g; Protein 23g

Beef Wraps with Lettuce Leaf

Prep time: 5 minutes | Cook time: 20 minutes | Serves: 4

¼ cup soy sauce, low sodium	1 tablespoon dark brown sugar
2 tablespoons orange juice, fresh	1 tablespoon red pepper flakes

1 tablespoon garlic, minced	toasted
2 tablespoon sesame oil	Steamed white rice
1-pound sirloin steak	Kimchi
2 tablespoon sesame seeds,	Romaine Lettuce hearts

1. Mix the first 7 ingredients in a mixing bowl. Add in the steak and toss to coat well. 2. Marinate the steak with the remaining spices for at least 4 hours. 3. Transfer the steak to the air fryer cooking tray. 4. Select the "air fry" setting of the air fryer at 400⁰ F for 10 minutes. Press the start button. 5. Air fry the steak for 10 minutes. 6. When the steak is ready, wrap it with rice and kimchi in a lettuce leaf. 7. Serve hot and enjoy.
Per serving: Calories 221; Fat 11g; Sodium 502mg; Carbs 10g; Fiber 2g; Sugar 1g; Protein 36g

Tasty Beef Korma with Baby Peas

Prep time: 10 minutes | Cook time: 20 minutes | Serves: 6

½ cup yogurt	2 cloves garlic, minced
1 tablespoon curry powder	1 tomato, diced
1 tablespoon olive oil	½ cup frozen baby peas, thawed
1 onion, chopped	

1. Combine the steak, yogurt, and curry powder in a medium bowl. Stir and set aside. 2. In a metal bowl, combine the olive oil, onion, and garlic. 3. Select Air Fry mode, set the temperature to 250 degrees F, and time to 20 minutes. 4. Place the metal bowl in the cooking tray and air fry for 3-4 minutes until crispy and tender. 5. Add the steak to the onion sautéed metal bowl, yogurt, and diced tomato. 6. Air fry the meat for 12 to 13 minutes until tender. 7. Stir in the peas and air fry for 2 to 3 minutes or until hot. 8. Serve hot and enjoy.
Per serving: Calories 289; Fat 11g; Sodium 523 mg; Carbs 10 g; Fiber 2 g; Sugar 1g; Protein 38g

Beef Schnitzel with Lemon

Prep time: 5 minutes | Cook time:12 minutes | Serves: 1

2 tablespoon Oil	Soup Plate
2–3 ounces of Breadcrumbs	1 Beef Schnitzel
Whisked Egg in a Saucer/	1 Freshly Picked Lemon

1. Set the air fryer to the "Air Fry" setting at 350 degrees F for 12 minutes. 2. In a bowl, mix the oil and breadcrumbs until loose and crumbly. 3. Dip the meat into the egg and then into the crumbs. Make sure that it is evenly covered. 4. Gently place in the air fryer tray, and air fry for 12 minutes until done. 5. The timing will depend on the thickness of the schnitzel, but for a relatively thin one, it should take roughly 12 min. 6. Serve with a lemon half and a garden salad and serve.
Per serving: Calories 234.8; Fat 15.7g; Sodium 88.7 mg; Carbs 4.4 g; Fiber 0.2 g; Sugar 0.2g; Protein 18.8g

Homemade Beef Schnitzel

Prep time: 5 minutes | Cook time: 12 minutes | Serves: 1

1 beef schnitzel	1tablespoon olive oil
Salt and ground black pepper to taste	⅓ cup breadcrumbs
	1 egg whisked

1. Season the schnitzel with salt and black Pepper. 2. Combine the oil and breadcrumbs in a mixing bowl. 3. In another shallow bowl, beat the egg until frothy. 4. Dip the schnitzel in the egg. 5. Then, dip it in the oil mixture. 6. Set the air fryer on the "Air Fry" setting for 12 minutes at 350 degrees F. 7. Put into the Air Fryer cooking tray. Place the tray on the middle shelf of the Air Fryer. Air fry the meat for 12 minutes, flipping halfway for even cooking. 8. Serve hot, and enjoy!
Per serving: Calories 220; Fat 10g; Sodium 589 mg; Carbs 3.8 g; Fiber 0 g; Sugar 1g; Protein 27.6g

Lean Steak with Kidney Beans and Tomato

Prep time: 10 minutes | Cook time: 13 minutes | Serves: 8

12 ounces' lean steak	1 teaspoon fresh thyme, chopped
1 onion, sliced	
1 can of chopped tomatoes	1 can of red kidney beans
¾ cup beef stock	salt and Pepper to taste

1. Cut the meat into thin 1cm strips. Add onion slices to the heat-safe bowl and place them in the air fryer. 2. Pour meat into the metal bowl and place the air fryer cooking tray. 3. Place the tray on the middle shelf of the Air Fryer. 4. Set the air fryer to the "Air Fry" setting for 13 minutes for 390 degrees F. 5. Air fry the meat with onion in a bowl and then add the tomatoes and their juice, beef stock, thyme, and the beans and cook for an additional 5 minutes. 6. Season with black pepper to taste on top and serve hot and enjoy.
Per serving: Calories 264; Fat 9.6g; Sodium 1083 mg; Carbs 34 g; Fiber 8.4 g; Sugar 4.2g; Protein 16g

Herbed Roast Beef

Prep time: 5 minutes | Cook time: 20 minutes | Serves: 6

½ teaspoon. fresh rosemary	1 teaspoon salt
1 teaspoon dried thyme	4-pound top round roast beef
¼ teaspoon pepper	1 teaspoon olive oil

1. Grease the beef with olive oil all over. 2. Mix the rosemary, thyme, Pepper, and salt in a small bowl and rub the spices on all sides of the beef. 3. Place the meat into the air fryer cooking tray. Place the tray on the middle shelf of the air fryer. 4. Select Air Fry mode, adjust the temperature to 360 degrees F, and set the cooking time to 20 minutes. 5. Air fry the meat for 20 minutes until tender, and don't forget to flip the meat when the display shows "turn Food." 6. Allow roast to rest 10 minutes before slicing to serve. 7. Serve hot with sauce and fresh salad and enjoy.
Per serving: Calories 390; Fat 22g; Sodium 958 mg; Carbs 36 g; Fiber 10g; Sugar 5g; Protein 12g

Goya Empanada Discs

Prep time: 5 minutes | Cook time: 10 minutes | Serves: 6

1teaspoon. water	Goya empanada discs (thawed)
1 egg white	
1 cup picadillo	

1. Spray tray the air fryer cooking tray with olive oil. 2. Place 2 tablespoons of picadillo into the center of each disc. Fold the disc in half and use a fork to seal the edges. Repeat with all discs. 3. Mix the egg white with water and brush the tops of empanadas with egg wash. 4. Add 2-3 empanadas to the air fryer. 5. Select Air Fry mode, set the temperature to 325 degrees F, and time to 8 minutes. 6. Air fry the empanadas for 8 minutes, and cook until golden. 7. Repeat till all filled empanadas are cooked. 8. Serve hot with sauce and enjoy
Per serving: Calories 183; Fat 5g; Sodium 1023 mg; Carbs 2 g; Fiber 0 g; Sugar 0g; Protein 11g

Easy Baked Beef Tenderloin

Prep time: 10 minutes | Cook time: 40 minutes | Serves: 4

1 (3-pound) Beef tenderloin, trimmed	Salt and ground black pepper, as required
2 tablespoons Olive oil	

1. Grease tenderloin with oil and season with salt and black Pepper evenly as per taste. 2. Arrange the tenderloin onto the greased air fryer cooking tray. 3. Select the "Bake" setting of the air fryer to 400 degrees F and set the time to 40 minutes; press "Start" to begin preheating. 4. When the display shows "Add Food," places the cooking tray. 5. Bake the meat for 40 minutes, flipping halfway for even cooking. 6. Cover the tenderloin with the foil and rest for 10 minutes. 7. With a sharp knife, cut the tenderloin into desired slices, serve warm with sauce, and enjoy.
Per serving: Calories 380; Fat 19g; Sodium 1010 mg; Carbs 0 g; Fiber 0 g; Sugar 0g; Protein 49.2g

Beef Cheese Casserole

Prep time: 10 minutes | Cook time: 25 minutes | Serves: 6

2 pounds of Ground beef	1 cup Cottage cheese
2 tablespoon taco seasoning	1 cup Salsa
1 cup Cheddar cheese	

1. Add the beef and taco seasoning to a bowl and mix well. 2. Add in the cheeses and salsa and stir to combine. Place the mixture into a baking dish that will fit in the air fryer. 3. Set the air fryer to 370 degrees F at the "Air Fry" setting and cook for 25 minutes. 4. Serve warm and enjoy.
Per serving: Calories 412; Fat 16.5g; Sodium 856 mg; Carbs 11 g; Fiber 2 g; Sugar 3g; Protein 56.4g

Beef Meatballs in Tomato Sauce

Prep time: 5 minutes | Cook time: 12 minutes | Serves: 3

11-ounces of minced beef	1 egg
1 onion, chopped finely	Salt and Pepper to taste
1 tablespoon fresh parsley, chopped	1 tablespoon fresh thyme, chopped
1 cup tomato sauce	

1. In a mixing bowl, mix all the ingredients, except the tomato sauce. 2. Make 11 balls from the meat mixture. 3. Set the time to 12 minutes and the temperature to 390 degrees F on Air Fry mode. 4. Add the meatballs to the air fryer cooking tray and cook for 7 minutes. 5. Transfer the meatballs to a dish and pour the tomato sauce. 6. Put the dish in the air fryer cooking tray and air fry for an additional 5-minute until tender and the sauce is well absorbed in the meatball. 7. Serve hot with the sauce and enjoy.
Per serving: Calories 275; Fat 16g; Sodium 589 mg; Carbs 2 g; Fiber 0.1 g; Sugar 0.2g; Protein 20g

Medium-Rare Traditional Steak

Prep time: 5 minutes | Cook time: 6 minutes | Serves: 4

1-3cm thick beef steak	Salt and Pepper to taste
1 tablespoon olive oil	

1. Grease the steak with olive oil and season both sides with salt and Pepper. 2. Place the steak into the cooking tray of the air fryer. 3. Set the temperature to 350 degrees F on the Air Fry program. 4. Air fry the steak for 3-minutes per side until

tender and cooked. 5. Serve hot with sauce and enjoy
Per serving: Calories 233; Fat 10g; Sodium 247 mg; Carbs 15 g; Fiber 2 g; Sugar 1g; Protein 27g

Beef Cubes with Roasted Broccoli and Mushroom

Prep time: 5 minutes | Cook time: 20 minutes | Serves: 4

2 tablespoons cornstarch	1 onion, chopped
½ cup low-sodium beef broth	1 cup sliced cremini mushrooms
1 teaspoon low-sodium soy sauce	1 tablespoon grated fresh ginger
12 ounces' sirloin strip steak, cut into 1-inch cubes	Brown rice, cooked (optional)
2½ cups broccoli florets	

1. Mix the cornstarch, beef broth, and soy sauce in a medium bowl. 2. Add in the beef and toss to coat well. Let stand for 5 minutes at room temperature. 3. With a slotted spoon, transfer the beef from the broth mixture into a medium metal bowl. Reserve the broth for later use. 4. Add the broccoli, onion, mushrooms, and ginger to the beef. 5. Set the air fryer to the "Air Fry" setting for 20 minutes at 350 degrees F. 6. Place the bowl into the air fryer and cook for 12 to 15 minutes. 7. Add the reserved broth to the meat bowl and cook for 2 to 3 minutes, or until the sauce boils. 8. Serve immediately over hot cooked brown rice, if desired.
Per serving: Calories 240; Fat 6g; Sodium 107 mg; Carbs 11 g; Fiber 2 g; Sugar 3g; Protein 19g

Juicy Beef and Fruit

Prep time: 15 minutes | Cook time: 15 minutes | Serves: 4

12 ounces' sirloin tip steak, thinly sliced	served
1 tablespoon freshly squeezed lime juice	1 teaspoon low-sodium soy sauce
1 cup canned mandarin orange segments, drained, liquid reserved	1 tablespoon cornstarch
	1 teaspoon olive oil
	2 scallions, white and green parts, sliced
1 cup canned pineapple chunks, drained, liquid re-	Brown rice, cooked (optional)

1. Mix the steak with lime juice in a medium bowl. Set aside. 2. In a small bowl, thoroughly mix 3 tablespoons of mandarin orange juice, 3 tablespoons of reserved pineapple juice, soy sauce, and cornstarch, and mix well. 3. Drain the beef and transfer it to a medium metal bowl, reserving the juice. 4. Stir the reserved juice into the mandarin-pineapple juice mixture. Set aside. 5. Set the air fryer to 350 degrees F for 15 minutes on the "Air Fry" setting. 6. Add the olive oil and scallions to the steak. Place the metal bowl in the air fryer and cook for 3 to 4 minutes at the "Air Fry" setting. 7. Stir in the mandarin oranges, pineapple, and juice mixture. Cook for 3 to 7 minutes more, or until the sauce is bubbling and the beef is tender and reaches at least 145 degrees F on a meat thermometer. 8. Stir and serve over hot cooked brown rice, if desired.
Per serving: Calories 387; Fat 22g; Sodium 301 mg; Carbs 0 g; Fiber 0 g; Sugar 0g; Protein 42g

Tender Beef in Red Cooking Wine

Prep time: 5 minutes | Cook time:12 minutes | Serves: 4

9 ounces' tender beef, chopped	2 cloves garlic, smashed
½ cup leeks, chopped	2 tablespoons red cooking wine
½ cup celery stalks, chopped	

¾ cup cream of celery soup
2 sprigs rosemary, chopped
¼ teaspoon smoked paprika

¾ teaspoon salt
¼ teaspoon black pepper, or to taste

1. Set the air fryer to the "Air Fry" setting for 12 minutes at 390 degrees F. 2. Add the beef, leeks, celery, and garlic to the air fryer cooking tray; air fry the meat and veggies for about 5 minutes. 3. After 5 minutes, pour in the wine and cream of celery soup. Season with rosemary, smoked paprika, salt, and black pepper, and stir well. 4. Now, cook the meat in the soup for additional 7 minutes until the soup boils and the meat is tender. 5. Serve hot with toasted bread and enjoy.
Per serving: Calories 364; Fat 9g; Sodium 390 mg; Carbs 39 g; Fiber 12 g; Sugar 8g; Protein 32g

Beef Veggie Spring Rolls

Prep time: 5 minutes | Cook time: 30 minutes | Serves: 10

2-ounce Asian rice noodles
1 teaspoon sesame oil
7-ounce ground beef
1 small onion, chopped
2 garlic cloves, crushed

1 cup fresh mixed vegetables
1 tsp soy sauce
1 packet spring roll skins
2 teaspoons water
Olive oil, as required

1. In a warm water bowl, soak the noodles until soft. 2. Dry out noodles and cut them into small lengths. 3. Heat the oil in a pan and add the onion, garlic, and sauté for about 4-5 minutes. 4. Add the beef and cook for about 4-5 minutes. 5. Add the vegetables and cook for about 5-7 minutes or till cooked through. 6. Stir in soy sauce and remove from the heat. 7. Stir in the noodles until all the juices have been absorbed. 8. Select Air Fry mode, set the cooking temperature to 350 degrees F. 9. Place the spring rolls skin onto a smooth surface. 10. Fold the top point over the filling and then fold in both sides. 11. On the final point, brush it with water before rolling to seal. 12. Brush the spring rolls with oil. 13. Place the rolls in batches in the air fryer and air fry for about 8 minutes until crispy and golden brown. Shake the rolls once for even cooking. Serve hot with mint or light soy sauce, and enjoy.
Per serving: Calories 364; Fat 9g; Sodium 441 mg; Carbs 39 g; Fiber 12 g; Sugar 8g; Protein 32g

Beef Top Roast

Prep time: 10 minutes | Cook time: 45 minutes | Serves: 10

2 pounds' beef top roast
1 tablespoon olive oil

2 tablespoons steak seasoning

1. Brush the roast with oil and then rub with the steak seasoning. 2. Place the roast onto the cooking tray. 3. Place the cooking tray in the bottom of the air fryer cooking chamber. 4. Set the air fryer to 360 degrees F at the "Air Fry" setting for 45 minutes. 5. Air fry the meat for 45 minutes. When the display shows "turn Food," turn the meat for even cooking. 6. Remove the cooking tray from Air Fryer and place the roast onto a platter for about 10 minutes in a foil wrap before slicing. 7. With a sharp knife, cut the roast into desired slices, serve with sauce, and enjoy.
Per serving: Calories 269; Fat 9.9g; Sodium 538 mg; Carbs 5 g; Fiber 1 g; Sugar 1g; Protein 38g

Lamb Meatballs with Zucchini and Red Onion

Prep time: 10 minutes | Cook time: 15 minutes | Serves: 4

1-pound ground lamb
Avocado oil spray
½ tablespoon garlic ghee
1 red bell pepper diced
⅓ cup red onion diced
⅓ cup cilantro diced
⅓ cup zucchini diced

1 tablespoon gyro seasoning
½ teaspoon turmeric
½ teaspoon cumin
½ teaspoon coriander
2 garlic cloves, minced
Salt and black pepper, to taste

1. Add lamb mince with all the meatball ingredients in a large mixing bowl. Mix well. 2. Make meatballs as per your desired size out of spiced meat mixture and place them on the cooking tray. 3. Select the "Air Fry" setting of the air fryer at 370 degrees F for 15 minutes. 4. Air fry the meatballs until tender. 5. Remove from the air fryer once done and serve with the sauce.
Per serving: Calories 302; Fat 12g; Sodium 1574mg; Carbs 5g; Fiber 0.2g; Sugar 0.2g; Protein 38g

Beef Burgers with Dijon Topping

Prep time: 15 minutes | Cook time: 18 minutes | Serves: 4

For Burgers:
1-pound ground beef
½ cup panko breadcrumbs
¼ cup onion, chopped finely
1 tablespoon Dijon mustard
2 teaspoons low-sodium soy sauce
2 teaspoons fresh rosemary,

chopped finely
Salt to taste
For Topping:
2 tablespoons Dijon mustard
1 tablespoon brown sugar
1 teaspoon soy sauce
Gruyere cheese slices

1. Add all the burger ingredients and mix until well combined in a large bowl. 2. Make 4 equal-sized patties from the spiced meat mixture. 3. Arrange the patties onto the air fryer cooking tray. 4. Arrange the cooking tray at the bottom of the air fryer cooking chamber. 5. Set the air fryer to 370 degrees F at the "Air Fry" setting and set the time to 18 minutes. 6. Air fry the burger patties for 15 minutes, flipping halfway until tender and juicy. 7. While the patties are cooking, make a sauce in a small bowl, add the mustard, brown sugar, and soy sauce, and mix well. 8. When cooking time is complete, remove the tray from the air fryer and coat the burgers with the mustard sauce. 9. Add the cheese slice to each burger. 10. Put the cooking tray in the air fryer and air fry for 3 minutes until the cheese melts. 11. When cooking time is complete, remove the tray from the air fryer. 12. Place the patties between the toasted buns, with more sauce and fresh lettuce, and serve hot.
Per serving: Calories 402; Fat 18g; Sodium 651 mg; Carbs 6.3 g; Fiber 0.8 g; Sugar 3g; Protein 44.4g

Lamb Strips with Toasted Hazelnuts

Prep time: 10 minutes | Cook time: 25 minutes | Serves: 2

¼ cup hazelnuts, toasted
⅔ pound shoulder of lamb, cut into strips
1 tablespoon hazelnut oil
2 tablespoons fresh mint

leaves, chopped
½ cup frozen peas
¼ cup of water
½ cup white wine
Salt and black pepper to taste

1. In a cooking tray, toss the lamb with hazelnuts, spices, and all the ingredients. 2. Select the Bake setting of the air fryer at 370 degrees F for 25 minutes. 3. Bake the lamb for 25 minutes until tender. 4. Serve hot with a fresh salad as a side and enjoy.
Per serving: Calories 435; Fat 15g; Sodium 1540mg; Carbs 3g; Fiber 0g; Sugar 0.1g; Protein 19g

Breaded Lamb Rack

Prep time: 10 minutes | Cook time: 25 minutes | Serves: 5

1.7 pounds Frenched rack of lamb	1 teaspoon cumin seeds
salt and black pepper, to taste	1 teaspoon ground cumin
⅓-pound dry breadcrumbs	1 teaspoon oil
1 teaspoon grated garlic	½ teaspoon grated lemon rind
½ teaspoon salt	1 egg, beaten

1. In a small bowl, whisk the egg. 2. In a cooking tray, place the lamb rack and pour the whisked egg on top. 3. Whisk the rest of the crusting ingredients in another bowl and spread over the lamb. 4. Select the "Air Fry" setting of the air fryer at 350 degrees F for 25 minutes. 5. Place the cooking tray in the air fryer and air fry the lamb for 25 minutes until cooked and the top crust is golden brown. 6. Serve hot with the ketchup and enjoy with a chilled drink.

Per serving: Calories 204; Fat 8g; Sodium 624mg; Carbs 3g; Fiber 0g; Sugar 0.2g; Protein 48g

Braised Lamb Shanks in Beef Broth

Prep time: 10minutes | Cook time: 20 minutes | Serves: 4

4 lamb shanks	4 to 6 sprigs of fresh rosemary
1½ teaspoons salt	3 cups beef broth, divided
½ teaspoon black pepper	2 tablespoons balsamic vinegar
4 garlic cloves, crushed	
2 tablespoons olive oil	

1. Place the lamb shanks in a baking pan. 2. Whisk the rest of the ingredients in a bowl and pour over the shanks. 3. Place these shanks pan in the cooking tray. 4. Select the "Air Fry" setting of the air fryer at 360 degrees F for 20 minutes. 5. Air fry the shanks for 20 minutes until done. 6. Once done, remove from the air fryer and rest for 10 minutes. 7. Serve with the dipping sauce of the shanks with boiled rice and enjoy.

Per serving: Calories 334; Fat 8.9g; Sodium 904mg; Carbs 7g; Fiber 2.6g; Sugar 2g; Protein 20g

Traditional Lamb Chops with Za'atar

Prep time: 10 minutes | Cook time: 10 minutes | Serves: 8

8 lamb loin chops, bone-in	1 ¼ teaspoons salt
3 garlic cloves, crushed	1 tablespoon Za'atar
1 teaspoon olive oil	Black Pepper, to taste
½ fresh lemon	

1. In a bowl, rub the lamb chops with oil, za'atar, salt, lemon juice, garlic, and black Pepper. 2. Place spiced chops in the cooking tray. 3. Select the "Air Fry" setting of the air fryer at 400 degrees F for 10 minutes. 4. Place the chops in an air fry for 10 minutes, flipping halfway until tender and done. 5. Remove once done and serve hot with favorite sauce and enjoy.

Per serving: Calories 324; Fat 19g; Sodium 674mg; Carbs 2g; Fiber 0.36g; Sugar 0.2g; Protein 12g

Spiced Lamb Sirloin Steak with Onion

Prep time: 10 minutes | Cook time: 15 minutes | Serves: 2

½ onion	½ teaspoon cardamom ground
4 slices ginger	1 teaspoon cayenne
5 cloves garlic	1 teaspoon salt
1 teaspoon garam masala	1-pound boneless lamb sirloin steaks
1 teaspoon fennel, ground	
1 teaspoon cinnamon ground	

1. Blend all the ingredients except the steaks into a fine puree. 2. Rub the steaks with a blended mixture and marinate for 30 minutes. 3. Transfer the steaks to the cooking tray. 4. Select the "Air Fry" setting of the air fryer at 330 degrees F for 15 minutes. 5. Place the cooking tray in the air fryer and close its door. 6. Air fry the steaks flipping halfway until tender and fully cooked. 7. Serve warm with sauce and enjoy.

Per serving: Calories 354; Fat 7.9g; Sodium 704mg; Carbs 6g; Fiber 3.6g; Sugar 6g; Protein 18g

Lemony Lamb Chops

Prep time: 10 minutes | Cook time: 25 minutes | Serves: 2

2 medium lamb chops	Salt to taste
¼ cup lemon juice	

1. Rub the lamb chops with lemon juice and salt. 2. Place the lemony chops in the cooking tray. 3. Select Air Fry mode, adjust the temperature to 350 degrees F, and set the time to 25 minutes. 4. Place the cooking tray in the air fryer and close its door. 5. Air fry the chops flipping halfway until done. 6. Serve warm with a chilled drink.

Per serving: Calories 444; Fat 15g; Sodium 754mg; Carbs 4g; Fiber 0.4g; Sugar 0.2g; Protein 28g

Herbed Lamb Chops

Prep time: 10 minutes | Cook time: 12 minutes | Serves: 4

4 lamb chops	2 garlic cloves, minced
2 teaspoons olive oil	2 teaspoons garlic puree
1 teaspoon fresh rosemary	Salt & black pepper

1. Rub the lamb chops with olive oil, rosemary, garlic, garlic puree, salt, and black Pepper. 2. Place lamb chops in a cooking tray. 3. Preheat the air fryer to 350 degrees F for 5 minutes at the "Air Fry" setting. 4. Once preheated, turn the timer to 12 minutes, place the cooking tray in the air fryer, and close its door. 5. Flip the chops when cooked halfway through, then resume cooking. 6. Serve warm and enjoy.

Per serving: Calories 424; Fat 9.9g; Sodium 325mg; Carbs 2g; Fiber 0.6g; Sugar 0.6g; Protein 18g

Baked Lean Lamb with White Sauce

Prep time: 10 minutes | Cook time: 35 minutes | Serves: 6

25 ounces of potatoes, boiled	Sauce
14 ounces' lean lamb mince	12 ounces' white sauce
1 teaspoon cinnamon	1 tablespoon olive oil
23 ounces jar of tomato pasta	

1. In a bowl, mash the potatoes and stir in white sauce and cinnamon. 2. In a frying pan, sauté lamb mince with olive oil until brown. 3. Layer a casserole dish with tomato pasta sauce. 4. Top the tomato sauce with cooked lamb mince. 5. Spread the white sauce potato mash over the lamb in an even layer. 6. Preheat the air fryer to the "Bake" setting at 350 degrees F for 5 minutes. 7. Once preheated, turn the timer to 35 minutes, place the casserole dish in the air fryer, and close its door. Bake the food for 35 minutes until the top is golden brown. 8. Serve warm and enjoy.

Per serving: Calories 304; Fat 25g; Sodium 1504mg; Carbs 7g; Fiber 2g; Sugar 1g; Protein 19g

Baked Lamb Shoulder Chops with Tomato Paste

Prep time: 10 minutes | Cook time: 1 hour 40 minutes | Serves: 8

8 lamb shoulder chops, trimmed	diced
	2 tablespoons tomato paste
¼ cup plain flour	2 ½ cups beef stock
1 tablespoon olive oil	2 dried bay leaves
1 large brown onion, chopped	1 cup frozen peas
2 garlic cloves, crushed	3 cups potato gems
3 medium carrots, peeled and	

1. Dredge the lamb chops lightly with flour. 2. In the cooking pan, sear the chops with olive oil for 4 minutes per side until brown. 3. Transfer the seared chops to a cooking tray. 4. Add onion, garlic, and carrot to the cooking pan and sauté for 5 minutes. 5. Stir in tomato paste, stock, and all other ingredients. 6. Stir and cook for 4 minutes, then pours this sauce over the chops in a cooking tray. 7. Preheat the air fryer to 350 degrees F for 5 minutes at the "Bake" setting. 8. Once preheated, place the cooking tray in the air fryer, set the timer to 1 hour 30 minutes, and close its door. Bake the chops. 9. Remove from cooking when done. 10. Serve warm.

Per serving: Calories 414; Fat 18g; Sodium 1254mg; Carbs 6g; Fiber 0.3g; Sugar 0.2g; Protein 21g

Curry Lamb and Mashed Potato

Prep time: 10 minutes | Cook time: 25 minutes | Serves: 4

½ pound minced lamb	1-pound potato cooked, mashed
1 tablespoon parsley chopped	
2 teaspoons curry powder	1-ounce cheese grated
1 pinch of salt and black pepper	1 ½ ounces potato chips crushed

1. Mix lamb with curry powder, seasoning, and parsley in a bowl. 2. Spread the spiced lamb mixture in a casserole dish. 3. Top the lamb mixture with potato mash, grated cheese, and crushed potato chips. 4. Select the "Bake" setting of the air fryer at 350 degrees F for 20 minutes. 5. Place the casserole dish in the cooking tray of the air fryer and bake it for 20 minutes until the top is golden brown and crispy. 6. Serve warm and enjoy.

Per serving: Calories 487; Fat 25g; Sodium 1254mg; Carbs 13g; Fiber 0.8g; Sugar 0.1g; Protein 29g

Lean Lamb Macaroni Bake

Prep time: 10 minutes | Cook time: 56 minutes | Serves: 6

1 tablespoon olive oil	1 tablespoon dried oregano
1 large onion, chopped finely	14 ounces' macaroni, boiled
2 garlic cloves, minced	9 ounces Tub ricotta
1-pound lean lamb mince	2 tablespoons parmesan, grated
1 teaspoon ground cinnamon	
1 beef or lamb stock cube	2 tablespoons milk
2 cups tomatoes, chopped	Bread, to serve optional

1. In a frying pan, sauté onion with oil for 10 minutes. 2. Stir in garlic and cook for 1 minute, then remove it from heat. 3. Toss in the lamb mince, then sautés until brown. 4. Stir in cinnamon, tomatoes, oregano, and stock cubes. 5. Cook this mixture on a simmer for 15 minutes. 6. While meat is cooking, blend ricotta with parmesan, milk, and garlic in a blender. Spread the lamb tomatoes mixture in a casserole dish. 7. Top the lamb tomatoes mix with ricotta mixture. 8. Set the air fryer to Bake at 350 degrees F. Bake the casserole for 30 minutes until the crust is golden brown and fully cooked. 9. Serve

warm and enjoy.

Per serving: Calories 245; Fat 14g; Sodium 704mg; Carbs 2g; Fiber 0g; Sugar 2g; Protein 34g

Minced Lamb and Mushrooms Casserole

Prep time: 10 minutes | Cook time: 30 minutes | Serves: 4

2 tablespoons olive oil	2 cups bottled marinara sauce
1 medium onion, chopped	1 teaspoon butter
½ pound ground lamb	4 teaspoons flour
4 fresh mushrooms, sliced	1 cup milk
1 cup small pasta shells, cooked	1 egg, beaten
	1 cup cheddar cheese, grated

1. Heat oil in a wok and sauté onions until soft. 2. Stir in mushrooms and lamb, and then cook until meat is brown. 3. Add marinara sauce to the lamb and cook it to a simmer. 4. Stir in pasta, then spread this mixture in a casserole dish. 5. For the sauce, melt butter in a saucepan over setting rate heat and, stir in flour and whisk well, pour in the milk. Mix the milk well. 6. Put ¼ cup of sauce in a small bowl, whisk with egg, and then return it to the saucepan. 7. Stir cook for 1 minute, then pours this sauce over the lamb. 8. Drizzle cheese over the lamb casserole. 9. Preheat the air fryer at the "Bake" setting for 5 minutes at 350 degrees F. 10. Once preheated, set the time to 30 minutes and bake the casserole for 30 minutes until the top is golden brown and the cheese is fully melted. 11. Serve warm and enjoy.

Per serving: Calories 384; Fat 9g; Sodium 804mg; Carbs 7g; Fiber 3.9g; Sugar 1.6g; Protein 38g

Baked Ground Lamb with Béchamel Sauce

Prep time: 10 minutes | Cook time: 67 minutes | Serves: 8

2 tablespoons olive oil	1 tablespoon tomato paste
1 large onion, diced	¾ pound penne pasta, boiled
2 pounds of ground lamb	Béchamel Sauce:
2 teaspoons salt	3 tablespoons olive oil
6 cloves garlic, chopped	¼ cup flour
½ cup red wine	2 ½ cups milk
6 cloves garlic, chopped	½ teaspoon ground nutmeg
3 teaspoons ground cinnamon	¾ teaspoon salt
2 teaspoons ground cumin	¼ teaspoon white pepper
2 teaspoons dried oregano	½ cup grated Parmesan cheese
1 teaspoon black pepper	½ cup plain Greek yogurt
1 can of 28-ounce crushed tomatoes	2 extra-large eggs, beaten

1. Heat oil in a wok over medium-high heat. 2. Toss onion, salt, and lamb meat, then stir to cook for 12 minutes. 3. Stir in red wine and cook for 2 minutes. 4. Add cinnamon, garlic, oregano, cumin, and Pepper to taste, then cook for 2 minutes. 5. Add tomato paste and diced tomatoes and cook for 20 minutes on a simmer until tomatoes dissolve in the form of sauce. 6. Toss in pre-boiled penne pasta, then spread this mixture in a casserole dish. 7. For the sauce, add oil to a wok to heat, stir in flour and cook for 1 minute. 8. Pour in milk and stir; cook until it thickens. 9. Stir in parmesan cheese, white pepper, nutmeg, egg, yogurt, and salt to taste. 10. Spread this sauce over the lamb Bolognese. 11. Select the "Bake" setting of the air fryer at 350 degrees F for 30 minutes. 12. Place the casserole dish in the air fryer and close its door. Bake for 30 minutes. 13. Remove the casserole once done and serve warm and enjoy.

Per serving: Calories 654; Fat 26g; Sodium 1874mg; Carbs 14g; Fiber 2.4g; Sugar 0.6g; Protein 28g

Baked Lamb Moussaka with Tomato Sauce

Prep time: 10 minutes | Cook time: 50 minutes | Serves: 6

¼ cup olive oil	2 ounces' butter
1 eggplant, diced	¼ cup flour
1 onion, diced	2 cups milk, hot
2 garlic cloves, crushed	½ cup cheese, grated
1-pound lamb mince	1 egg
½ teaspoon cinnamon	1 pinch nutmeg
¼ teaspoon ground cumin	Salt and black pepper to taste
1 teaspoon fresh rosemary	7 ounces' pasta, boiled
2 cups tomato pasta sauce	

1. Heat oil in a wok over medium-high heat. 2. Stir in eggplant and sauté for 5 minutes. 3. Add lamb, spices, rosemary, garlic, and onion, then stir and cook for 8 minutes. 4. Stir in pasta and tomato paste and cook on a simmer for 5 minutes. 5. Spread this lamb pasta mixture in a casserole dish. 6. Prepare the white sauce in a saucepan. 7. Heat oil, stir in flour and cook for 1 minute. 8. Pour in milk and stir; cook until it thickens. 9. Stir in grated cheese, egg, nutmeg, salt, and black Pepper. 10. Spread white sauce over the lamb pasta mixture in a casserole dish. 11. Preheat the air fryer to the "Bake" setting for 5 minutes at 350°F. 12. Once preheated, place the casserole dish and set a timer for 30 minutes. 13. Bake the casserole until the top is golden brown. 14. Serve warm and enjoy.
Per serving: Calories 654; Fat 23g; Sodium 1985mg; Carbs 15g; Fiber 6.6g; Sugar 2g; Protein 48g

Lamb Skewers with Cucumber Salad

Prep time: 10 minutes | Cook time: 15 minutes | Serves: 4

3 garlic cloves, minced	1 cucumber, chopped
4 tablespoons rapeseed oil	6 radishes, halved and sliced
2 tablespoons cider vinegar	1 fennel bound, sliced
1 large bunch of thyme	½ teaspoon caster sugar
1 ¼ pounds lamb leg, diced	4 tablespoons cider vinegar
For the salad	1 handful of dill sprigs

1. In a large bowl, toss the lamb with thyme, oil, vinegar, and garlic. 2. Marinate the thyme lamb for 2 hours in a closed container in the refrigerator. 3. Thread the marinated lamb on the bamboo skewers. 4. Place these skewers in an air fryer cooking tray. 5. Preheat the air fryer to the "Air Fry" setting for 5 minutes at 350 degrees F. 6. Once the air fryer is preheated, place the cooking tray in the air fryer and adjust the timer to 15 minutes. 7. Flip the skewers when cooked halfway through, then resume cooking. 8. While the skewers are air frying, toss the salad ingredients in a salad bowl. 9. Serve the skewers warm with fresh salad.
Per serving: Calories 321; Fat 7.8g; Sodium 2540mg; Carbs 12g; Fiber 6g; Sugar 2.6g; Protein 25g

Lamb-Onion Kebobs

Prep time: 10 minutes | Cook time: 15 minutes | Serves: 4

½ cup yogurt	½ small onion, cubed
1½ tablespoons mint	2 large pita bread
1 teaspoon ground cumin	2 handfuls lettuce, chopped
10.5 ounces diced lean lamb	

1. In a bowl, whisk the yogurt with mint and cumin. 2. Toss lamb cubes in the yogurt mix and mix well to coat. Marinate lamb for 30 minutes. 3. Place these lamb cubes in a cooking tray. 4. Preheat the air fryer to 370 degrees F for 5 minutes at the "Air Fry" setting. 5. Once preheated, adjust the timer to 15 minutes and air fry the lamb until tender. 6. Meanwhile,

the lamb is cooking, toss the pita bread from both sides. 7. With a sharp knife, create a pocket. Place lettuce in the pita pocket with lamb and onions. 8. Serve warm with mayo and ketchup.
Per serving: Calories 497; Fat 7.5g; Sodium 784mg; Carbs 7g; Fiber 0.6g; Sugar 3g; Protein 42g

Lamb Kebobs in Jerk Paste

Prep time: 10 minutes | Cook time: 18 minutes | Serves: 6

2 pounds of lamb steaks	lime
2 tablespoons jerk paste or marinade	1 tablespoon honey
Lemon zest and juice of 1	Handful thyme leaves, chopped

1. Mix lamb with jerk paste, lime juice, zest, honey, and thyme in a bowl. 2. Toss well to coat and marinate the lamb for 30 minutes. 3. Then again, thread the lamb on the skewers. 4. Place these lamb skewers in ta cooking tray. 5. Select the "Air Fry" setting at 360 degrees F for 5 minutes. 6. Once the air fryer is preheated, place the cooking tray and set the timer to 18 minutes. 7. Air fry the lamb skewers for 18 minutes, flipping halfway until cooked. 8. Serve warm with sauce.
Per serving: Calories 521; Fat 15g; Sodium 934mg; Carbs 12g; Fiber 3.6g; Sugar 0.2g; Protein 34g

Lamb Shoulder Cubes with Pea Salad

Prep time: 10 minutes | Cook time: 12 minutes | Serves: 4

⅔ pound lean lamb shoulder, cubed	½ cup couscous, boiled
1 teaspoon ground cumin	½ cup frozen pea
½ teaspoon cayenne pepper	1 large carrot, grated
1 teaspoon sweet smoked paprika	1 small pack of coriander, chopped
1 tablespoon olive oil	1 small pack of mint, chopped
24 cherry tomatoes	Juice 1 lemon
Salad:	2 tablespoons olive oil

1. In a bowl, toss tomatoes and lamb with oil, paprika, Pepper, and cumin. 2. Thread the lamb and tomatoes on the skewers. 3. Place these lamb skewers in a cooking tray. 4. Preheat the air fryer at the "Air Fry" setting for 5 minutes at 370 degrees F. 5. Once preheated, place the cooking tray in the air fryer and close its door. 6. Set the timer to 10 minutes and air fry the lamb, flipping halfway. 7. Flip the skewers when cooked halfway through, then resume cooking. 8. Meanwhile, the lamb is air frying, sauté carrots and peas with olive oil in a pan for 2 minutes. 9. Stir in mint, lemon juice, coriander, and cooked couscous. 10. Serve skewers hot with the warm couscous salad and enjoy.
Per serving: Calories 254; Fat 6.9g; Sodium 504mg; Carbs 18g; Fiber 6g; Sugar 2g; Protein 52g

Spicy Lamb Skewers

Prep time: 10 minutes | Cook time: 20 minutes | Serves: 4

Juice of ½ lemon	1 cucumber, chopped
2 tablespoons olive oil	1 handful of black olives, chopped
1 garlic clove, crushed	9 ounces' pack of feta cheese, crumbled
1 ¼ pounds diced lamb	
For the salad	1 bunch of mint, chopped
4 large tomatoes, chopped	

1. Whisk the lemon juice with garlic and olive oil in a bowl. 2. Toss in lamb cubes and mix well to coat. Marinate lamb for 30 minutes in the refrigerator. 3. Thread the lamb evenly on

the skewers. 4. Place these lamb skewers in a cooking tray. 5. Set the air fryer to the "Air Fry" setting at 360 degrees F for 20 minutes and air fry the meat, flipping halfway for even cooking. 6. Meanwhile, the lamb is cooking; mix the salad ingredients in a bowl. 7. Serve the skewers with prepared salad and enjoy.

Per serving: Calories 237; Fat 7.9g; Sodium 704mg; Carbs 15g; Fiber 3.6g; Sugar 0.6g; Protein 32g

Lamb Chunk Kebobs with Sauce

Prep time: 10 minutes | Cook time: 20 minutes | Serves: 6

2 ¼ pounds of lamb shoulder fat trimmed, cut into chunks	Zest and juice, 2 lemons
⅓ cup olive oil	2 garlic cloves, crushed
½ cup red wine	1 medium onion, chopped bite-size chunks
2 teaspoons dried oregano	2 bread slices, chunks

1. Whisk olive oil, red wine, oregano, lemon juice, zest, and garlic in a small bowl. 2. Toss lamb cubes in the mix and mix well to coat. Marinate for 30 minutes in the refrigerator. 3. Thread the lamb, onion, and bread on the skewers. 4. Place these lamb skewers in a cooking tray. 5. Preheat the air fryer to 370 degrees F for 5 minutes on the "Air Fry" setting. 6. Once preheated, set the timer to 20 minutes and place the cooking tray in it. 7. Air fry the lamb skewers flipping halfway until tender. 8. Remove from the air fryer once cooked, serve with your favorite sauce and enjoy.

Per serving: Calories 304; Fat 7.5g; Sodium 774mg; Carbs 4g; Fiber 2.3g; Sugar 2g; Protein 21g

Lamb Skewers with Brown Rice

Prep time: 10 minutes | Cook time: 16 minutes | Serves: 6

10.5 ounces' brown basmati rice	1 handful mint, chopped
1-pound lamb mince	¼ cup pitted black kalamata olive, quartered
1 tablespoon harissa	1 cucumber, diced
2 ounces' feta cheese	10.5 cherry tomato, halved
1 large red onion (½ sliced, ½ shredded)	1 tablespoon olive oil
1 handful parsley, chopped	Juice of 1 lemon

1. In a small bowl, add lamb mince with harissa, onion, feta, and seasoning and mix well until well combined. 2. Make 12 sausages with this lamb mixture, then thread them on the skewers. 3. Place these lamb skewers in a cooking tray. 4. Select the "Bake" setting of the air fryer and preheat at 370 degrees F for 5 minutes. 5. Once preheated, adjust the timer to 16 minutes and place the cooking tray in the air fryer. 6. Bake the lamb, flipping halfway, until tender and done. 7. In a salad bowl, add all salad ingredients and toss well. 8. Serve lamb skewers with freshly tossed tomato salad.

Per serving: Calories 254; Fat 8.9g; Sodium 706mg; Carbs 14g; Fiber 3.86g; Sugar 2g; Protein 35g

Harissa Lamb Kebobs with Carrot Yogurt

Prep time: 10 minutes | Cook time: 10 minutes | Serves: 8

2 tablespoons cumin seed	For the Yogurt
2 tablespoons coriander seed	3 carrots, grated
2 tablespoons fennel seed	2 teaspoons cumin seed, toasted
1 tablespoon paprika	9 ounces' Greek yogurt
2 tablespoons harissa	1 small handful of chopped the coriander
4 garlic cloves, finely minced	
½ teaspoon ground cinnamon	1 small handful of chopped
1 ½ pounds lean minced lamb	

mint

1. In a blender, blend all the spices and seeds with garlic, harissa, and cinnamon. Add blended harissa paste to the minced lamb in a bowl, then mix well. 2. Make 8-medium size sausages and thread on the skewers. 3. Place the lamb sausage skewers in the cooking tray. 4. Preheat the air fryer to the "Air Fry" setting for 370 degrees F for 10 minutes. 5. Once preheated, place skewers onto the cooking tray in the air fryer and air fry for 10 minutes, flipping halfway. 6. Meanwhile, when the lamb is air frying, prepare the yogurt ingredients in a bowl and place them in the fridge. 7. Serve hot skewers with the chilled yogurt mixture and enjoy.

Per serving: Calories 523; Fat 20g; Sodium 1850mg; Carbs 7g; Fiber 0.6g; Sugar 0.6g; Protein 31g

Rosemary Lamb Shashlik

Prep time: 10 minutes | Cook time: 20 minutes | Serves: 4

1 small leg of lamb, boneless and diced	20 garlic cloves, chopped
1 lemon, juiced and chopped	1 handful rosemary, chopped
3 tablespoons olive oil	3 green peppers, cubed
	2 red onions, cut into wedges

1. In a bowl, toss the lamb with skewers, veggies, and seasoning ingredients. 2. Thread the seasoned lamb, peppers, and onion on the skewers. 3. Place these lamb skewers in a cooking tray. 4. Preheat the air fryer; select the "Air Fry" setting at 370 degrees F for 20 minutes. 5. Once preheated, place a cooking tray in the air fryer and close its door. 6. Air fry the lamb skewers flipping halfway until done. 7. Serve warm with ranch sauce and enjoy.

Per serving: Calories 461; Fat 7.4g; Sodium 1233mg; Carbs 12g; Fiber 3.6g; Sugar 0.86g; Protein 24g

Smoked Lamb, Onion, and Bell Pepper Skewers

Prep time: 10 minutes | Cook time: 20 minutes | Serves: 4

2 teaspoons ground cumin	½ teaspoon black pepper
2 teaspoons ground coriander	1 tablespoon lemon juice
¼ teaspoon ground cinnamon	2 teaspoons olive oil
1/8 teaspoon ground smoked paprika	1 ½ pounds lean lamb, cubed
2 teaspoons lemon zest	½ yellow bell pepper, sliced into squares
½ teaspoon salt	1 onion, cut into pieces

1. In a bowl, toss the lamb with the rest of the skewer's ingredients and season well. 2. Thread the spiced lamb and veggies on the skewers alternately. 3. Place these lamb skewers in a cooking tray. 4. Preheat the air fryer to 370 degrees F for 20 minutes at the "Air Fry" setting. 5. Once preheated, place the seasoned lamb cooking tray in the air fryer and air fry for 20 minutes, flipping halfway until tender. 6. Serve warm with your favorite sauce.

Per serving: Calories 521; Fat 21g; Sodium 2074mg; Carbs 12g; Fiber 4.6g; Sugar 3.2g; Protein 42g

Red Pepper Lamb Mix

Prep time: 10 minutes | Cook time: 20 minutes | Serves: 4

2 cloves garlic	2 red peppers, cubed
1 teaspoon dried oregano	8 fresh bay leaves
2 tablespoons olive oil	2 lemons, juiced
4 lamb steaks, diced	Few sprigs of parsley, chopped

1. In a bowl, toss the lamb with the rest of the skewer's ingredients and season well. 2. Thread the lamb and veggies on the skewers and marinate them for 30 minutes. 3. Place these lamb skewers in a cooking tray. 4. Prepare the air fryer at the "Air Fry" setting for 20 minutes at 370 degrees F. 5. Once preheated, place the skewers in the air fryer and air fry for 20 minutes, flipping halfway. 6. Serve warm with the sauce and chilled drink, and enjoy.

Per serving: Calories 325; Fat 13g; Sodium 708mg; Carbs 4g; Fiber 0.3g; Sugar 1.2g; Protein 31g

Lamb Kebobs Tortillas with Mustard Dressing

Prep time: 10 minutes | Cook time: 20 minutes | Serves: 6

Lamb Kebabs

2 pounds' lamb loin chops, diced	1 teaspoon sumac
	For the Dressing
1 large onion, squares	1 tablespoon mayonnaise
Sea salt	1 tablespoon olive oil
For the Wrap	2 tablespoons lemon juice
6 tortillas	1 teaspoon yellow mustard
¼ cup onions, sliced	¼ teaspoon salt
½ cup tomatoes, sliced	1/8 teaspoon black pepper
1 ½ cups romaine lettuce, chopped	¼ teaspoon sumac

1. In a bowl, toss lamb and onion with salt to season them. 2. Thread the seasoned lamb and onion on the skewers. 3. Place these lamb skewers in a cooking tray. 4. Prepare the air fryer on the "Air Fry" setting for 20 minutes at 370 degrees F. 5. Air fry the lamb for 20 minutes, flipping halfway until done. 6. Meanwhile, the lamb is air frying; prepare the dressing by mixing all dressing ingredients in a bowl. 7. Toast the tortillas lightly in a pan and place the warm tortillas on the serving plates. 8. Divide the tortilla ingredients on the tortillas and top them with lamb kebabs. 9. Pour the prepared dressing on top, then roll the tortillas. 10. Serve warm and enjoy.

Per serving: Calories 344; Fat 9.2g; Sodium 1802mg; Carbs 8g; Fiber 2.1g; Sugar 2.1g; Protein 35g

Herbed Lamb Kebobs

Prep time: 10 minutes | Cook time: 20 minutes | Serves: 6

2 pounds' leg of lamb, cubed	¼ teaspoon dried thyme,
½ cup olive oil	1 teaspoon salt
1 lemon, juice only	¼ teaspoon black pepper
3 cloves garlic, minced	1 tablespoon parsley, chopped
1 onion, sliced	2 red pepper, cut into square
1 teaspoon oregano, dried	1 onion, cut into chunks

1. In a bowl, add lamb with the rest of the kebab ingredients and toss well with seasoning. 2. Cover the seasoned lamb and marinate it for 30 minutes in a refrigerator. 3. Thread the lamb and veggies on the skewers. 4. Place these lamb skewers in a cooking tray. 5. Preheat the air fryer to the "Air Fry" setting for 20 minutes at 370 degrees F. 6. Once preheated, place the cooking tray into the air fryer and close its door. 7. Air fry the lamb for 20 minutes, flipping halfway. 8. Serve warm with the

sauce and enjoy.

Per serving: Calories 194; Fat 5.9g; Sodium 1022mg; Carbs 4g; Fiber 1.1g; Sugar 1.0g; Protein 23g

Marinated Lamb Chops

Prep time: 10 minutes | Cook time: 20 minutes | Serves: 8

¼ cup olive oil,	1 teaspoon salt
¼ cup lemon juice,	1½ teaspoons black pepper
2 dried oregano	2 pounds' lamb chops,
2 teaspoons garlic, minced	

1. In a large mixing bowl, combine the olive oil, lemon juice, dried oregano, minced garlic, salt, and pepper with lamb chops and marinate for 10 minutes. 2. In the air fryer cooking tray, put the lamb chops. 3. Place them in the air fryer. 4. Select the "Air Fry" setting at 400 degrees F for 20 minutes. 5. Air fry the chops for 20 minutes, flipping halfway for even cooking. 6. Once done, remove to a serving plate, serve with sauce and enjoy.

Per serving: Calories 568; Fat 32g; Sodium 1895mg; Carbs 14g; Fiber 0.23g; Sugar 0.26g; Protein 25g

Turmeric Lamb Skewers

Prep time: 10 minutes | Cook time: 8 minutes | Serves: 4

¾ pound ground lamb	½ teaspoon turmeric
1 teaspoon cumin	½ teaspoon fennel seeds
1 teaspoon paprika	½ teaspoon coriander seed, ground
1 teaspoon garlic powder	
1 teaspoon onion powder	½ teaspoon salt
½ teaspoon cinnamon	4 bamboo skewers

1. Mix lamb mince with the spices and kebab ingredients in a bowl and season them well. 2. Make four sausages from this lamb mixture and thread them on the skewers. 3. Marinate the lamb skewers for 10 minutes in a refrigerator. 4. Place these lamb skewers in a cooking tray. 5. Select the "Air Fry" setting of the air fryer at 350 degrees F for 8 minutes and air fry the lamb skewers flipping halfway until done. 6. Serve warm with pita bread and salad, and enjoy.

Per serving: Calories 365; Fat 15g; Sodium 1402mg; Carbs 15g; Fiber 0.6g; Sugar 0.12g; Protein 26g

Lamb Kofta

Prep time: 10 minutes | Cook time: 10 minutes | Serves: 4

1-pound ground lamb	1 teaspoon cumin
1 tablespoon ras el hanout (North African spice)	2 tablespoons mint, chopped
½ teaspoon ground coriander	Salt and ground black pepper to taste
1 teaspoon onion powder	4 bamboo skewers
1 teaspoon garlic powder	

1. Mix the ground lamb, ras el hanout, coriander, onion powder, garlic powder, cumin, mint, salt, and ground black pepper in a bowl. 2. Make four medium-sized sausages from the spiced meat. Marinate the sausages for 15 minutes in a refrigerator. 3. Spritz a cooking tray with cooking spray. 4. Place the marinated lamb skewers in the cooking tray and spritz with cooking spray. 5. Put the cooking tray in the air fryer, select the "Air Fry" setting set the temperature to 380°F for 10 minutes. 6. Air fry the sausages for 10 minutes. Flip the lamb skewers halfway through. 7. When cooking is complete, the lamb should be well browned and tender. 8. Serve hot immediately with sauce.

Per serving: Calories 453; Fat 9.8g; Sodium 1004mg; Carbs 13g; Fiber 4.6g; Sugar 2g; Protein 34g

Classical Roasted Lamb Leg

Prep time: 10 minutes | Cook time: 45 minutes | Serves: 12

6 pounds of lamb leg	Stuffing Ingredients:
½ gallon milk	¼ cup feta cheese, crumbled
Spice Rub:	¼ cup spinach
1 cup olive oil	Baste Ingredients:
juice of 1 lemon	1 stick butter
1 teaspoon thyme	½ cup olive oil
5 teaspoons minced garlic	1-ounce soy sauce
salt to taste	1-ounce brown sugar
black pepper to taste	1 tablespoon black pepper

1. In a pot, soak the lamb leg in the milk and cover to marinate. 2. Marinate the lamb for 8 hours in the refrigerator and then remove it from the milk. 3. Place the lamb leg in a cooking tray. 4. In a bowl, whisk spice rub ingredients. 5. In another bowl, mix stuffing ingredients. 6. Carve a few slits in the lamb, then add the stuffing in these slits. 7. In another bowl, whisk the baste ingredients and keep them aside. 8. Preheat the air fryer to the "Roast" setting at 45 minutes to 370 degrees F. 9. Once preheated, place the lamb cooking tray in the air fryer and close its door. 10. Roast the lamb for 45 minutes 11. Baste the lamb leg with the basting mixture every 10 minutes. 12. Remove once done and serve warm with roasted veggies as the side.
Per serving: Calories 254; Fat 16g; Sodium 987mg; Carbs 14g; Fiber 1.3g; Sugar 0g; Protein 21g

Lamb Cheese Fried Sticks

Prep time: 20 minutes | Cook time: 30 minutes | Serves: 2

2 cups lamb (Cut the lamb into long strips)	1 tablespoon ginger-garlic paste
1 cup cottage cheese	For seasoning, salt and red
1 big lemon juice	chili powder as per taste
4 or 5 tablespoons of cornflour	½ teaspoon carom seeds
1 cup of water	1 or 2 poppadums

1. In a bowl, make a mixture of lemon juice, red chili powder, salt, ginger-garlic paste, and carom for the marinade. 2. Roll the lamb strips on the cottage cheese sticks like a wrap. 3. Let the lamb cheese pieces marinate in the mixture for some time, then roll them in cornflour. 4. Leave them aside for around 20 minutes for marinating. 5. Take the poppadum into a pan and roast them. Once cooked, crush them well. 6. In another big bowl, pour 100 ml water and dissolve two tablespoons of cornflour and make paste/slurry. 7. Dip the cottage cheese pieces in cornflour mix and roll them onto the pieces of crushed poppadum. The poppadum sticks to the lamb due to the liquid cornflour mix. 8. Preheat the air fryer for 10 minutes at 300 degrees F on the "Air Fry" setting. 9. Place the lamb pieces inside the cooking tray. 10. Air fry the lamb for 10 minutes at 300 degrees F and 250 degrees F for another 20 minutes. Flip the lamb sticks for even cooking. 11. Once they are done, serve them with ketchup or mint sauce and enjoy.
Per serving: Calories 374; Fat 7.4g; Sodium 798mg; Carbs 2g; Fiber 0g; Sugar 0.1g; Protein 25g

Lamb Club Sandwich with Barbeque Sauce

Prep time: 10 minutes | Cook time: 15 minutes | Serve: 1

2 slices of white bread	1 tablespoon softened butter
½ pound lamb, cut into cubes	¼ tablespoon Worcestershire sauce
¼ cup chopped onion	½ teaspoon olive oil
½ tablespoon sugar	½ flake garlic crushed
1 small capsicum	¼ tablespoon red chili sauce
For Barbeque Sauce:	

1. Remove the edges of the bread slices. 2. In a cooking pan, cook the ingredients for the sauce and wait till it thickens. 3. Add the lamb to the sauce and stir till it obtains flavors. 4. Roast the capsicum over the flame and cover in a bowl for 5 minutes. Peel the skin off of the capsicum. 5. Cut the capsicum into fine slices. 6. Mix the cooked lamb and capsicum and apply them to the bread slices. 7. Cut the slices horizontally. 8. Preheat the air fryer for 5 minutes at 300° F at the "Roast" setting. Place the sandwich in the cooking tray with spaces. 9. Toast the sandwich for 15 minutes until golden crust. Flip the sandwich halfway for even cooking. 10. Serve the BBQ Sandwiches with tomato ketchup or mint sauce as per desire.
Per serving: Calories 541; Fat 12g; Sodium 1085mg; Carbs 8g; Fiber 3g; Sugar 0g; Protein 28g

Crusted Lamb Chops

Prep time: 5 minutes | Cook time: 15 minutes | Serves: 4

1½ pounds of lamb chops	1 tablespoon shallots, finely diced
½ teaspoon salt	1 teaspoon lemon zest, freshly grated
½ teaspoon black pepper	¼ cup Parmesan cheese, freshly grated
1 tablespoon fresh tarragon, chopped	½ cup panko bread crumbs
1 tablespoon fresh mint, chopped	1 tablespoon Dijon mustard
1 tablespoon fresh parsley, chopped	1 tablespoon olive oil

1. Set the air fryer to 390° F on the "Air Fry" setting for 15 minutes. 2. In a bowl, season the lamb chops with salt and black pepper. 3. Blend the tarragon, mint, parsley, shallots, lemon zest, Parmesan cheese, and panko bread crumbs in a fine puree. 4. Add the Dijon mustard and olive oil and mix well in the puree. 5. Spread the cheesy pesto mixture on both sides of the lamb chops. 6. Place the lamb chops in the cooking tray of the air fryer. 7. Air fry for 10-12 minutes or until the desired tenderness is reached. 8. Remove the chops to a platter, and let them rest for at least 5 minutes before serving. 9. Serve with sauce and enjoy.
Per serving: Calories 546; Fat 24g; Sodium 1478mg; Carbs 12g; Fiber 1g; Sugar 0.3g; Protein 41g

Homemade Onion Lamb Burgers

Prep time: 15 minutes | Cook time: 8 minutes | Serves: 6

2 pounds of ground lamb	Salt and ground black pepper, as required
1 tablespoon onion powder	

1. Season the lamb with onion powder, salt, and pepper in a bowl and mix well. 2. Make six equal-sized patties from the seasoned lamb mixture. 3. Arrange the patties onto a cooking tray. 4. Arrange the drip pan at the bottom of the air fryer cooking chamber. 5. Select the "Air Fry" setting and adjust the temperature to 360 degrees F for 8 minutes. 6. Air fry the burger patties for 8 minutes, flipping halfway. 7. Once done, serve in between a toasted bun with salad and sauce and enjoy
Per serving: Calories 334; Fat 12g; Sodium 723mg; Carbs 12g; Fiber 1g; Sugar 0g; Protein 28g

Spicy Lamb Kebabs

Prep time: 10 minutes | Cook time: 15 minutes | Serves: 6

Lamb Kabobs
1-pound ground lamb
½ onion, finely diced
3 garlic cloves, finely minced
2 teaspoons cumin
2 teaspoons coriander
2 teaspoons sumac
1 teaspoon Aleppo Chili flakes

1 ½ teaspoons salt
2 tablespoons chopped mint
Yogurt Sauce:
1 cup Greek yogurt
2 tablespoons dill, chopped
2 garlic cloves, minced
¼ teaspoon salt

1. In a bowl, toss the lamb with the remaining kebob ingredients and season well. 2. Make six medium-sized sausages out of spiced mince and thread on the skewers. 3. Place these lamb sausage skewers in a cooking tray. 4. Select Air Fry mode and adjust the temperature to 370 degrees F. 5. When the display shows "Add Food," place the cooking tray in the air fryer and close its door. 6. Air fry the lamb for 10 minutes, flipping halfway until cooked. 7. Meanwhile, the lamb is air frying; prepare the yogurt sauce by whisking all its ingredients in a bowl. 8. Serve the skewers hot with garlicky yogurt sauce.
Per serving: Calories 548; Fat 24g; Sodium 2547mg; Carbs 14g; Fiber 1.2g; Sugar 1.6g; Protein 51g

Crispy Lamb Rack

Prep time: 10 minutes | Cook time: 25minutes | Serves: 4

1 tablespoon bread crumbs
1 garlic clove; minced
28 ounces' rack of lamb
2 tablespoons macadamia nuts, toasted and crushed

1 tablespoon olive oil
1 egg
1 tablespoon rosemary, chopped
Salt and black pepper

1. Add oil with garlic and stir well in a small bowl. 2. Season lamb with salt, pepper, and brush with garlic oil. 3. In another bowl, mix crushed nuts with breadcrumbs and rosemary. 4. In a separate bowl, crack an egg and whisk well. 5. Dip lamb in whisked egg, then in macadamia crumbs mix; place them in your air fryer's cooking tray. 6. Air fry at 360 degrees F for 20 minutes at the "Air Fry" setting; increase heat to 400 degrees F and cook for 5 minutes. 7. Divide among plates and serve right away with sauce, and enjoy the crusty crunch.
Per serving: Calories 350; Fat 10g; Sodium 1702mg; Carbs 10g; Fiber 1.6g; Sugar 0.2g; Protein 24g

Lamb Ribs in Veggie Stock

Prep time: 15 minutes | Cook time: 40 minutes | Serves: 8

8 lamb ribs
4 garlic cloves, minced
2 carrots, chopped
3 tablespoons white flour
2 cups veggie stock

1 tablespoon rosemary, chopped
2 tablespoons extra virgin olive oil
Salt and black pepper

1. Season lamb ribs with salt and pepper. 2. Rub with oil and garlic and place it on the cooking tray. 3. Preheated air fryer at 360 degrees F for 10 minutes on the "Air Fry" setting. 4. Air fry the lamb until done. 5. Mix stock with flour and whisk well in a heatproof dish that fits in the air fryer. 6. Add rosemary, carrots, and lamb ribs. 7. Place the dish in the air fryer and air fry at 350 degrees F for 30 minutes. 8. Divide lamb mix on plates and serve hot and enjoy.
Per serving: Calories 384; Fat 9g; Sodium 804mg; Carbs 7g; Fiber 2g; Sugar 2g; Protein 35g

Green Spiced Lamb

Prep time: 10 minutes | Cook time: 35 minutes | Serves: 6

2 tablespoons grated ginger
2 garlic cloves, minced
2 teaspoons cardamom, ground
½ teaspoon chili powder
1 teaspoon turmeric
2 teaspoons coriander, ground

1-pound spinach
1 red onion, chopped
1-pound lamb meat, cubed
2 teaspoons powder cumin
1 teaspoon garam masala
14 ounces canned tomatoes, chopped

1. In a heatproof dish that fits in the air fryer, mix the lamb with ginger, spinach, garlic, tomatoes, cardamom, onion, cumin, chili, turmeric, and garam masala, and coriander. Stir all ingredients well. 2. Preheat the air fryer at 360 degrees F for 35 minutes on the "Air Fry" setting. 3. Air fry the lamb until done. 4. Plate the lamb with veggies, serve and enjoy.
Per serving: Calories 454; Fat 19g; Sodium 1954mg; Carbs 2g; Fiber 0.3g; Sugar 0.1g; Protein 35g

Rosemary Lamb Chops

Prep time: 10 minutes | Cook time: 6 minutes | Serves: 4

4 lamb chops
2 tablespoons dried rosemary

¼ cup fresh lemon juice
salt and pepper

1. Mix lemon juice, rosemary, pepper, and salt in a bowl. 2. Brush herby lemon mixture over lamb chops and marinate for 10 minutes. 3. Place marinated lamb chops on the air fryer cooking tray. 4. Select the "Air Fry" setting and adjust the temperature to 400 degrees F for 6 minutes. 5. Air fry the chops for 6 minutes, flipping halfway until tender and well cooked. 6. Serve hot with sauce and enjoy.
Per serving: Calories 547; Fat 15g; Sodium 1244mg; Carbs 11g; Fiber 3g; Sugar 1g; Protein 36g

Crispy Lamb Shanks with Yellow Onion

Prep time: 15 minutes | Cook time: 45 minutes | Serves: 4

4 lamb shanks
1 yellow onion, chopped
1 tablespoon olive oil
2 teaspoons honey
5 ounces' dry sherry
2½ cups chicken stock

4 teaspoons coriander seeds, crushed
2 tablespoons white flour
4 bay leaves
Salt and pepper

1. Sprinkle salt and pepper over the lamb shanks. 2. Rub half the oil and put it in the air fryer. 3. Set the air fryer to Air Fry mode, adjust the temperature to 360 degrees F and time to 10 minutes. 4. Air fry lamb for 10 minutes. 5. Heat a pan that fits in the air fryer with the rest of the oil over medium-high heat; add onion and coriander, stir, and cook for 5 minutes. 6. Add flour, sherry, stock, honey, bay leaves, salt, and pepper. 7. Bring the sauce to simmer, add fried lamb, introduce everything to your air fryer and cook at 360 degrees F for 30 minutes more. 8. Divide everything between plates and serve and enjoy.
Per serving: Calories 324; Fat 8.5; Sodium 1357mg; Carbs 11g; Fiber 2g; Sugar 0.12g; Protein 24g

Boneless Pork Chops with Parmesan Cheese

Prep time: 10 minutes | Cook time: 12 minutes | Serves: 2

2 pork chops, boneless
1 teaspoon Cajun seasoning
1 teaspoon Herb de Provence
1 teaspoon paprika

3 tablespoons parmesan cheese, grated
⅓ cup almond flour
1 tablespoon olive oil

1. Mix parmesan cheese, almond flour, paprika, Herb de Provence, and Cajun seasoning in a shallow. 2. Grease the pork chops with oil and coat with parmesan cheese mixture. 3. Place coated pork chops onto the parchment-lined cooking tray. 4. Select the "Air Fry" setting of the air fryer to 350 degrees F for 8-12 minutes, and then press Start. 5. Place the cooking tray in the air fryer and air fry the chops until ready. 6. Plate the chops with sauce and serve and enjoy.
Per serving: Calories 457; Fat 38.4g; Sodium 12mg; Carbs 4.9g; Fiber 0.1g; Sugar 0.8g; Protein 25.5g

Herbed Bone-in Pork Chops

Prep time: 10 minutes | Cook time: 20 minutes | Serves: 4

4 pork chops, bone-in
½ teaspoon garlic and herb seasoning

2 tablespoons olive oil
salt and pepper

1. Grease the pork chops with oil and season with garlic herb seasoning, pepper, and salt. 2. Place pork chops onto the cooking tray. 3. Select the "Air Fry" setting of the air fryer to 380 degrees F for 20 minutes, and then press Start. 4. Place the cooking tray in the air fryer and air fry the chops until done. 5. Flip pork chops after 15 minutes for even cooking. 6. Serve hot and enjoy.
Per serving: Calories 316; Fat 26.9g; Sodium 69mg; Carbs 0g; Fiber 0g; Sugar 0g; Protein 18g

Arrow-Root Pork Chops

Prep time: 10 minutes | Cook time: 12 minutes | Serves: 6

1 egg
6 pork chops, boneless
1 teaspoon garlic, crushed
1 tablespoon water
1 teaspoon Dijon mustard
1 teaspoon garlic powder

1 teaspoon onion powder
2 teaspoons Italian seasoning
⅓ cup arrow-root
1 cup pecan pieces, crushed
¼ teaspoon sea salt

1. Whisk eggs with garlic, water, and Dijon mustard in a small bowl. 2. Mix crushed pecans, garlic powder, onion powder, Italian seasoning, arrowroot, and sea salt in a shallow dish. 3. Dip pork chop in egg mixture, then dredges into pecan mixture. 4. Place coated pork chops onto the cooking tray. 5. Select the "Air Fry" setting of the air fryer to 400 degrees F for 12 minutes, and then press Start. 6. Place the cooking tray in the air fryer and air fry the chops until done. 7. Flip pork chops halfway through for even cooking. 8. Serve hot with sauce and enjoy.
Per serving: Calories 296; Fat 22.8g; Sodium 97mg; Carbs 2.3g; Fiber 0.2g; Sugar 0.5g; Protein 19.6g

Ranch Pork Chops

Prep time: 10 minutes | Cook time: 35 minutes | Serves: 6

6 pork chops, boneless
2 tablespoons ranch seasoning
¼ cup olive oil

1 teaspoon dried parsley
salt and pepper

1. Season pork chops with pepper and salt as per your taste and place them into the air fryer cooking tray. 2. Mix olive oil, parsley, and ranch seasoning and pour over pork chops. 3. Select the "Bake" setting of the air fryer to 400 degrees F for 35 minutes, and then press Start. 4. Place the cooking tray into the air fryer and air fry the chops until done. 5. Serve hot and enjoy.
Per serving: Calories 338; Fat 28.3g; Sodium 69mg; Carbs 0g; Fiber 0g; Sugar 0g; Protein 18g

Paprika Fried Pork Ribs

Prep time: 10 minutes | Cook time: 20 minutes | Serves: 2

1 ½ pound pork ribs
2 ½ tablespoons olive oil

1 ½ tablespoons paprika
1 tablespoon salt

1. Grease the pork ribs with oil and season with paprika and salt as per your taste. 2. Place pork ribs onto the air fryer cooking tray. 3. Select the "Air Fry" setting of the air fryer to 350 degrees F for 20 minutes, and then press Start. 4. Place the cooking tray in the air fryer and fry the ribs until tender. 5. Serve hot and enjoy.
Per serving: Calories 1094; Fat 78.4g; Sodium 350mg; Carbs 2.9g; Fiber 0.2g; Sugar 0.6g; Protein 90.9g

Spicy Pork Chops

Prep time: 10 minutes | Cook time: 10 minutes | Serves: 4

4 pork chops
½ teaspoon black pepper
½ teaspoon ground cumin
1 teaspoon paprika

1 ½ teaspoons olive oil
½ teaspoon cayenne pepper
½ teaspoon garlic salt

1. Add pork chops and remaining ingredients to a Ziploc bag, seal the bag, and shake well to coat. 2. Place spiced pork chops onto the cooking tray. 3. Select the "Air Fry" setting of the air fryer to 400 degrees F for 10 minutes, and then press Start. 4. Place the cooking tray in the air fryer and cook the chop for 10 minutes. 5. Serve hot with ranch sauce and enjoy.
Per serving: Calories 276; Fat 21.8g; Sodium 69mg; Carbs 1g; Fiber 0g; Sugar 0.2g; Protein 18.2g

Air-Fried Pork Chops with BBQ Sauce

Prep time: 10 minutes | Cook time: 14 minutes | Serves: 2

2 pork chops
4 tablespoons BBQ sauce, sugar-free

½ tablespoon garlic, minced
½ teaspoon olive oil
salt and pepper

1. In a bowl, mix all ingredients well, and place in the refrigerator for 1 hour for marinating. 2. Place marinated pork chops onto the cooking tray. 3. Select the "Air Fry" setting of the air fryer to 390 degrees F for 14 minutes, and then press Start. 4. Place the cooking tray in the air fryer and air fry the chops for 14 minutes. 5. Flip pork chops halfway through for even cooking. 6. Serve hot and enjoy.
Per serving: Calories 316; Fat 21.2g; Sodium 69mg; Carbs 12.1g; Fiber 2g; Sugar 8.2g; Protein 18.5g

Fried Lamb with Brussels Sprouts

Prep time: 10 minutes | Cook time: 1 hour 10 minutes | Serves: 4

2 pounds of lamb leg scored	1 tablespoon lemon thyme, chopped.
1½ pounds Brussels sprouts, trimmed	1 tablespoon butter, melted
2 tablespoons olive oil	½ cup sour cream
1 tablespoon rosemary, chopped	1 garlic clove, minced
	Salt and black pepper

1. Season lamb leg with salt, pepper, thyme, and rosemary. 2. Brush the lamb with oil and place it in the air fryer's cooking tray. 3. Set the air fryer to Air Fry mode, adjust the temperature to 300 degrees F, and set the time to 1 hour. 4. Air fry the lamb for 1 hour until tender. 5. Transfer the lamb to a plate and keep it warm. 6. In a pan that fits in the air fryer, mix Brussels sprouts with salt, pepper, garlic, butter, and sour cream, toss well to mix, put in the air fryer, and cook at 400 degrees F for 10 minutes. 7. Divide lamb between plates, add Brussels sprouts on the side and serve and enjoy.

Per serving: Calories 451; Fat 12g; Sodium 605mg; Carbs 10g; Fiber 2g; Sugar 1g; Protein 28g

Spiced Pork Chops

Prep time: 10 minutes | Cook time: 20 minutes | Serves: 4

4 pork chops, boneless	ing
1 tablespoon olive oil	salt and pepper
1 tablespoon dash of season-	

1. Grease the pork chops with oil and season with a dash of seasoning, pepper, and salt. 2. Place pork chops onto the cooking tray. 3. Select the "Air Fry" setting of the air fryer to 360 degrees F for 20 minutes, and then press Start. 4. Place the cooking tray in the air fryer and air fry the chops. 5. Flip pork chops halfway through even cooking. 6. Serve hot and enjoy.

Per serving: Calories 286; Fat 23.4g; Sodium 69mg; Carbs 0g; Fiber 0g; Sugar 0g; Protein 18g

Toothsome Pork Chops

Prep time: 10 minutes | Cook time: 16 minutes | Serves: 4

4 pork chops	2 teaspoons parsley
1 tablespoon coconut oil	2 teaspoons garlic, grated
1 tablespoon coconut butter	salt and pepper

1. Mix coconut butter, oil, garlic cloves, parsley, pepper, and salt in a small bowl. 2. Coat pork chops with coconut butter mixture and place in the refrigerator for 1 hour for marinating. 3. Place pork chops onto the parchment-lined cooking tray. 4. Select the "Air Fry" setting of the air fryer to 350 degrees F for 16 minutes, and then press Start. 5. Place the cooking tray in the air fryer and air fry the chops for 16 minutes. 6. Flip pork chops halfway through for even cooking. 7. Serve hot and enjoy.

Per serving: Calories 301; Fat 23.8g; Sodium 69mg; Carbs 2.5g; Fiber 1g; Sugar 1.4g; Protein 18.3g

Coconut Pork Chops with Parmesan Cheese

Prep time: 10 minutes | Cook time: 30 minutes | Serves: 3

3 pork chops, boneless	cheese, grated
1 egg, lightly beaten	½ cup almond flour
3 tablespoons parmesan	2 tablespoons coconut milk

salt and pepper

1. Whisk the egg with milk in a shallow bowl. 2. Mix parmesan cheese, almond flour, pepper, and salt in a shallow dish. 3. Dip pork chops into the egg mixture, coat with parmesan mixture, and place coated pork chops onto the cooking tray. 4. Select the "Bake" setting of the air fryer to 350 degrees F for 30 minutes, and then press Start. 5. Place the cooking tray in the air fryer. 6. Serve and enjoy.

Per serving: Calories 422; Fat 34.1g; Sodium 127mg; Carbs 4.9g; Fiber 1g; Sugar 1.1g; Protein 25.6g

Rind Crusted Pork Chops

Prep time: 10 minutes | Cook time: 15 minutes | Serves: 2

2 pork chops, bone-in	½ teaspoon onion powder
1 tablespoon olive oil	½ teaspoon paprika
1 cup pork rinds, crushed	½ teaspoon parsley
½ teaspoon garlic powder	

1. Mix crushed pork rinds, garlic powder, onion powder, paprika, and parsley in a shallow dish and mix well. 2. Grease the pork chops with oil and coat with crushed pork rinds. 3. Place coated pork chops onto the cooking tray. 4. Select the "Air Fry" setting of the air fryer to 400 degrees F for 15 minutes, and then press Start. 5. Place the cooking tray in the air fryer and air fry the chops for 15 minutes, turning after 10 minutes for even cooking. 6. Serve hot and enjoy.

Per serving: Calories 362; Fat 29.5g; Sodium 79mg; Carbs 1.3g; Fiber 0.1g; Sugar 0.4g; Protein 22.8g

Lemon Pepper Pork Chops

Prep time: 10 minutes | Cook time: 15 minutes | Serves: 4

4 pork chops, boneless	soning
1 tablespoon olive oil	Salt
1 teaspoon lemon pepper sea-	

1. Grease the pork chops with oil and season with lemon pepper and salt. 2. Place spiced pork chops onto the cooking tray. 3. Select the "Air Fry" setting of the air fryer to 400 degrees F for 15 minutes, and then press Start. 4. Place the cooking tray in the air fryer and fry the chops until tender. 5. Serve hot with your favorite sauce and enjoy.

Per serving: Calories 287; Fat 23.4g; Sodium 69mg; Carbs 0.3g; Fiber 0g; Sugar 0g; Protein 18g

Veggie and Pork Patties

Prep time: 10 minutes | Cook time: 35 minutes | Serves: 6

2 pounds of ground pork	½ cup almond flour
1 egg, lightly beaten	1 teaspoon garlic powder
1 onion, minced	1 teaspoon paprika
1 carrot, minced	salt and pepper

1. In a mixing bowl, add ingredients and mix until well combined. 2. Make small balls from the meat mixture and place them onto the cooking tray. 3. Select the "Air Fry" setting to the air fryer to 375 degrees F for 35 minutes, then press Start. 4. Place the cooking tray in the air fryer and air fry the meat until done. 5. Turn patties after 20 minutes for even cooking. 6. Serve hot with salad as the side, and enjoy.

Per serving: Calories 294; Fat 10.8g; Sodium 138mg; Carbs 5.3g; Fiber 0.2g; Sugar 0.6g; Protein 42.9g

Goat Cheese Stuffed Pork Chops

Prep time: 10 minutes | Cook time: 35 minutes | Serves: 4

4 pork chops, boneless and thick-cut
2 tablespoons olives, chopped
1 tablespoon garlic, minced
2 tablespoons fresh parsley, chopped
2 tablespoons sundried tomatoes, chopped
½ cup goat cheese, crumbled

1. In a mixing bowl, combine feta cheese, garlic, parsley, olives, and sundried tomatoes well. 2. Stuff the cheese mixture into each pork chop. 3. Place pork chops onto the cooking tray. 4. Select the "Bake" setting of the air fryer to 375 degrees F for 35 minutes, and then press Start. 5. Place the cooking tray in the air fryer and fry the chops for 35 minutes. 6. Serve hot stuffed chops and enjoy.
Per serving: Calories 317; Fat 24.7g; Sodium 81mg; Carbs 1.5g; Fiber 0g; Sugar 0.4g; Protein 21.7g

Pork Pieces with Jerk Paste

Prep time: 10 minutes | Cook time: 20 minutes | Serves: 4

1 ½ pounds pork butt, chopped into pieces
¼ cup jerk paste
salt and pepper

1. In a mixing bowl, add meat and jerk paste and mix well; cover and place in refrigerator for marinating overnight. 2. Place marinated spiced meat onto the cooking tray. 3. Select the "Air Fry" setting of the air fryer to 390 degrees F for 20 minutes, and then press Start. 4. Place the cooking tray in the air fryer and air fry the meat for 20 minutes until tender. 5. Serve hot with sauce and enjoy.
Per serving: Calories 348; Fat 12.8g; Sodium 156mg; Carbs 1.4g; Fiber 0.3g; Sugar 1g; Protein 53.1g

Pork Chops with Basil Pesto

Prep time: 10 minutes | Cook time: 18 minutes | Serves: 4

4 pork chops
2 tablespoons parmesan cheese, grated
2 tablespoons basil pesto
salt and pepper

1. Season pork chops with spices and places them onto the cooking tray. 2. Spread pesto and grated cheese on top of pork chops evenly. 3. Select the "Air Fry" setting of the air fryer to 350 degrees F for 18 minutes, and then press Start. 4. Place the cooking tray in the air fryer and air fry the chops for 18 minutes until done. 5. Serve hot and enjoy.
Per serving: Calories 301; Fat 22.9g; Sodium 79mg; Carbs 0.6g; Fiber 0g; Sugar 0g; Protein 22.5g

Creole Pork Chops

Prep time: 10 minutes | Cook time: 12 minutes | Serves: 6

1 ½ pounds pork chops, boneless
1 teaspoon Creole seasoning
¼ cup mozzarella cheese, grated
⅓ cup almond flour
1 teaspoon paprika
1 teaspoon garlic powder

1. Add pork chops with all ingredients in a Ziploc bag, seal the bag, and shake well. 2. Place spiced pork chops onto the parchment-lined cooking tray. 3. Select the "Air Fry" setting of the air fryer to 360 degrees F for 12 minutes, and then press Start. 4. Place the cooking tray in the air fryer and air fry the chops for 12 minutes until done. 5. Serve hot with sauce and enjoy.

Per serving: Calories 404; Fat 31.6g; Sodium 98mg; Carbs 1.9g; Fiber 0g; Sugar 0.4g; Protein 27.3g

Garlicky Pork Chops

Prep time: 10 minutes | Cook time: 12 minutes | Serves: 4

4 pork chops, boneless
½ teaspoon granulated onion
½ teaspoon granulated garlic
2 teaspoons olive oil
½ teaspoon celery seeds
½ teaspoon parsley
½ teaspoon salt

1. Mix onion, garlic, celery seeds, parsley, and salt in a small bowl. 2. Greased pork chops with oil and rubbed with garlic mixture. 3. Place pork chops onto the cooking tray. 4. Select the "Air Fry" setting of the air fryer to 350 degrees F for 12 minutes, and then press Start. 5. Place the cooking tray in the air fryer. 6. Air fry the chops until tender and done. 7. Serve hot with the sauce and enjoy.
Per serving: Calories 278; Fat 22.3g; Sodium 69mg; Carbs 0.4g; Fiber 0g; Sugar 0.1g; Protein 18.1g

Taco Pork Stuffed Peppers

Prep time: 10 minutes | Cook time: 8 minutes | Serves: 12

24 jalapeno peppers, cut in half & remove seeds
1 ½ tablespoons taco seasoning
½ pound ground pork
¼ cup mozzarella cheese, shredded

1. In a pan, sauté the meat in little oil until browned. 2. Add taco seasoning to the meat, mix well, and remove from the heat. 3. Cool the meat and stuff it into each jalapeno half. 4. Place stuffed jalapeno peppers onto the cooking tray and top with cheese. 5. Select the "Air Fry" setting of the air fryer to 320 degrees F for 8 minutes, and then press Start. 6. Place the cooking tray in the air fryer. 7. Air fry the peppers for 8 minutes until cooked and the top is golden brown. 8. Serve hot and enjoy.
Per serving: Calories 34; Fat 1g; Sodium 15mg; Carbs 0.7g; Fiber 0g; Sugar 0.2g; Protein 5.4g

Asian-Style Pork Shoulder with Green Onions

Prep time: 10 minutes | Cook time: 15 minutes | Serves: 4

1-pound pork shoulder, boneless and cut into ½-inch slices
1 tablespoon sesame oil
1 tablespoon rice wine
1 tablespoon garlic, minced
1 tablespoon ginger, minced
2 tablespoons red pepper paste
1 onion, sliced
¼ cup green onions, sliced
1 tablespoon sesame seeds
1 teaspoon cayenne pepper

1. In a mixing bowl, add all ingredients, mix well, and place in the refrigerator for 1 hour to marinate. 2. Place marinated meat and onion slices onto the cooking tray. 3. Select the "Air Fry" setting of the air fryer to 400 degrees F for 15 minutes, and then press Start. 4. Place the cooking tray in the air fryer and air fry the chops until done. 5. Turn meat halfway through for even cooking. 6. Serve hot and enjoy.
Per serving: Calories 403; Fat 29g; Sodium 102mg; Carbs 7.2g; Fiber 1.2g; Sugar 2.5g; Protein 27.5g

Cajun Pork Patties

Prep time: 5 minutes | Cook time: 10 minutes | Serves: 2

1 egg, lightly beaten
½ pound ground pork
½ cup breadcrumbs

1 tablespoon Cajun seasoning
salt and pepper

1. Line the air fryer cooking tray with parchment paper. 2. In a mixing bowl, add all ingredients and mix until well incorporated. 3. Make two equal-sized patties from the meat mixture and place them in the air fryer cooking tray, then place them in the air fryer. 4. Set the air fryer to the "Air Fry" setting for 10 minutes at 360 degrees F. 5. Air fry the patties, flipping halfway for even cooking. 6. Serve hot with toasted buns and salad, and enjoy.

Per serving: Calories 300; Fat 7.6g; Sodium 165mg; Carbs 19.6g; Fiber 2.3g; Sugar 1.8g; Protein 36.1g

Simple Baked Pork Ribs

Prep time: 5 minutes | Cook time: 30 minutes | Serves: 8

2 pounds' pork ribs, boneless
1 tablespoon onion powder

1 ½ tablespoons garlic powder
salt and pepper

1. Fit the air fryer with the drop pan in position. 2. Place pork ribs in a cooking tray 3. Set the air fryer to the "Bake" setting at 350 degrees F for 35 minutes. 4. Bake the chops for 35 minutes until desired tenderness. 5. Serve hot with the sauce and enjoy.

Per serving: Calories 318; Fat 20.1g; Sodium 42mg; Carbs 1.9g; Fiber 0.2g; Sugar 0.1g; Protein 30.4g

Pork Sausage Balls

Prep time: 10 minutes | Cook time: 15 minutes | Serves: 4

6 ounces' pork sausages, sliced
Salt and black pepper to taste
1 cup onions, chopped

3 tablespoons breadcrumbs
½ teaspoon garlic puree
1 teaspoon sage

1. Take onions, sausages, sage, garlic puree, salt, and pepper in a mixing bowl and mix well. 2. Form medium-sized balls out of the mixture and roll in breadcrumbs. 3. Add the balls to the cooking tray. 4. Set the air fryer on the "Air fry" setting at 340 degrees F; air fry the balls for 15 minutes, shaking once. 5. Serve hot with ranch sauce and fresh salad, and enjoy!

Per serving: Calories 200; Fat 10g; Sodium 118mg; Carbs 12g; Fiber 3g; Sugar 1g; Protein 28g

Teriyaki Pork Ribs with Tangy Sauce

Prep time: 10 minutes | Cook time: 20 minutes | Serves: 3

1 pound of pork ribs
Salt and black pepper to taste
1 tablespoon sugar
1 teaspoon ginger juice
1 teaspoon five-spice powder
1 tablespoon teriyaki sauce

1 tablespoon soy sauce
1 garlic clove, minced
2 tablespoons honey
1 tablespoon tomato sauce
1 tablespoon olive oil

1. Mix pepper, sugar, five-spice powder, salt, ginger juice, and teriyaki sauce in a mixing bowl. 2. Add pork ribs to the spice mix and marinate for 2 hours. 3. Add ribs to the greased cooking tray. 4. Set the air fryer at the "Air Fry" setting for 8 minutes at 350 degrees F. 5. Air fry the chops for 8 minutes, flipping halfway until tender. 6. Mix soy sauce, garlic, honey, 1 tablespoon of water, and tomato sauce. 7. Heat a pan over

medium heat. Add olive oil and heat for 30 seconds. 8. Add air-fried pork ribs, sear for 1 minute, and then pour tomato sauce. 9. Stir-fry chops with tangy tomato sauce for a few minutes and serve hot. 10. You can garnish the chops with chopped dill also.

Per serving: Calories 421; Fat 29g; Sodium 1204mg; Carbs 14g; Fiber 2g; Sugar 2g; Protein 40g

Dijon Pork Tenderloin

Prep time: 5 minutes | Cook time: 10 minutes | Serves: 6

1 cup breadcrumbs
1 pinch of cayenne pepper
3 crushed garlic cloves
2 tablespoons ground ginger
2 tablespoons Dijon mustard

2 tablespoons raw honey
4 tablespoons water
2 teaspoons salt
1-pound pork tenderloin, sliced into 1-inch rounds

1. Season the tenderloin with pepper and salt. 2. In a bowl, combine cayenne pepper, garlic, ginger, mustard, honey, and water until smooth puree. 3. Dip pork rounds into the mixture and then dredge into breadcrumbs, ensuring they all get coated well. 4. Place coated pork tenderloin into the air fryer. 5. Set the air fryer to 400 degrees F for 10 minutes on the "Air fry" setting. 6. Air fry the chops for 10 minutes at 400 degrees F. 7. Flip and then cook an additional 5 minutes until golden in color. 8. Serve hot with sauce and enjoy.

Per serving: Calories 423; Fat 15g; Sodium 804mg; Carbs 12g; Fiber 2g; Sugar 3g; Protein 31g

Sweet Pork Chops

Prep time: 5 minutes | Cook time: 15 minutes | Serves: 3

3 pork chops, ½inch thick
Salt and black pepper to season

1 tablespoon maple syrup
1 ½ tablespoons minced garlic
3 tablespoons mustard

1. Mix garlic, mustard, salt, and pepper with maple syrup and mix well. Add the pork to the spice mix and toss to coat. 2. Place the chops in the cooking tray. 3. Set the air fryer to the "Air Fry" setting at 350 degrees F for 12 minutes. 4. Air fry the chops for 12 minutes, flipping halfway with a spatula. 5. Once ready, remove chops to a platter, serve with steamed asparagus, and enjoy.

Per serving: Calories 154; Fat 15g; Sodium 258mg; Carbs 10g; Fiber 1g; Sugar 2g; Protein 25g

Breaded Pork Chops with Parmesan Cheese

Prep time: 10 minutes | Cook time: 15 minutes | Serves: 4

4 pork chops, boneless
2 tablespoons olive oil
¼ teaspoon pepper
½ teaspoon garlic powder
1 teaspoon dried parsley

¼ teaspoon smoked paprika
2 tablespoons breadcrumbs
¼ cup parmesan cheese, grated

1. Fit the air fryer with the drop pan in position 2. Mix breadcrumbs, paprika, parmesan cheese, garlic powder, parsley, and pepper in a dish. 3. Grease the pork chops with oil and dredge in the breadcrumb mixture. 4. Place coated pork chops into the air fryer cooking tray. 5. Set the air fryer to the "Bake" setting at 450 degrees F for 15 minutes and air fry the pork chops. 6. Flip the chops halfway until cooked. 7. Serve hot with sauce and enjoy.

Per serving: Calories 350; Fat 28.3g; Sodium 73mg; Carbs 3.1g; Fiber 0.2g; Sugar 0.3g; Protein 20.4g

Pork Tenderloin with Roasted Mushroom and Rice

Prep time: 10 minutes | Cook time: 12 minutes | Serves: 4

3 scallions, diced (about ½ cup)	loin, diced
½ red bell pepper, diced (about ½ cup)	½ cup frozen peas, thawed
	½ cup roasted mushrooms
2 teaspoons sesame oil	½ cup soy sauce
½ pound (227 g) pork tender-	2 cups cooked rice
	1 egg, beaten

1. Place the scallions and red pepper in an air fryer cooking tray. 2. Drizzle the veggies with the sesame oil and toss well to coat them in the oil. 3. In the air fryer, spray the cooking tray and select the "Roast" setting to 375 degrees F for 12 minutes. 4. Roast the vegetables for 4 minutes, shaking once. 5. While roasting the vegetables, place the pork in a large bowl. 6. Add the peas, mushrooms, soy sauce, and rice to the bowl, and toss to coat the ingredients with the sauce. 7. After about 4 minutes, remove the cooking tray from the air fryer. 8. Place the sauced pork mixture on the pan and stir the scallions and peppers into the meat and rice. 9. Return the pan to the air fryer and continue cooking. 10. After another 6 minutes, remove from the air fryer. 11. Create an empty circle in the middle of the pan between the rice. Pour the egg into the circle. 12. Return the pan to the air fryer and continue cooking. 13. When cooking is complete, remove it from the air fryer and stir the egg to scramble. 14. Stir the egg into the fried rice mixture. 15. Serve hot immediately and enjoy.
Per serving: Calories 304; Fat 9g; Sodium 784mg; Carbs 12g; Fiber 2g; Sugar 1g; Protein 20g

Juicy Pork Chops

Prep time: 10 minutes | Cook time: 12 minutes | Serves: 2

2 pork chops	½ teaspoon onion powder
2 tablespoons brown sugar	1 teaspoon ground mustard
1 tablespoon olive oil	1 tablespoon paprika
¼ teaspoon garlic powder	salt and pepper

1. Set the air fryer for 12 minutes on the "Air Fry" setting at 400 degrees F. 2. In a small bowl, add all dry ingredients and mix well. 3. Grease the pork chops with oil and rub with spice mixture. 4. Place pork chops in the air fryer cooking tray. 5. When the air fryer is preheated, place a cooking tray into the air fryer. 6. Air fry chops at 400 degrees F for 12 minutes until done. 7. Serve with sauce and enjoy.
Per serving: Calories 371; Fat 27.8g; Sodium 904mg; Carbs 12.1g; Fiber 1.2g; Sugar 9.5g; Protein 19g

Tamarind Chops with Green Beans

Prep time: 10 minutes | Cook time: 50 minutes | Serves: 4

2 tablespoons tamarind paste	2 tablespoons molasses
½ pound green beans, trimmed	4 tablespoons southwest seasoning
1 tablespoon garlic, minced	
½ cup green mole sauce	2 tablespoons ketchup
3 tablespoons corn syrup	4 pork chops
1 tablespoon olive oil	

1. Mix all the ingredients in a bowl except for green beans, pork chops, and mole sauce. 2. Add 2 tablespoons of water and place the chops with the marinade mix. Let the pork chops marinate in the mixture for 30 minutes in the refrigerator. 3. Place pork chops in the cooking tray. 4. Set the air fryer to the "Air Fry" setting for 25 minutes at 350 degrees F. 5. Air fry the chops for 25 minutes, flipping halfway. 6. In a pot, blanch the green beans in salted water over medium heat for 23 minutes until tender. 7. Drain the beans and season with salt and pepper. 8. Serve the crispy pork chops with green beans and mole sauce, and enjoy.
Per serving: Calories 304; Fat 25g; Sodium 250mg; Carbs 12g; Fiber 2g; Sugar 1.2g; Protein 19g

Pork Chops Stuffed with Mix

Prep time: 10 minutes | Cook time: 25 minutes | Serves: 4

4 pork chops	4 garlic cloves, minced
Salt and black pepper to taste	2 tablespoons fresh sage leaves, chopped
4 cups stuffing mix	
2 tablespoons olive oil	

1. Cut a hole in pork chops and fill chops with stuffing mix. 2. Mix sage, garlic, oil, salt, and pepper in a bowl. 3. Rub the chops well with the marinade and marinate for 10 minutes. 4. Preheat the Air fryer on the "Bake" setting to 380 degrees F for 5 minutes. 5. Put the chops in the cooking tray and place them in the air fryer. 6. Air fry stuffed chops for 25 minutes until tender and crispy. 7. Serve hot and enjoy.
Per serving: Calories 112; Fat 12g; Sodium 91mg; Carbs 6.2g; Fiber 0.2g; Sugar 0.6g; Protein 28g

Coated Pork Chops

Prep time: 10 minutes | Cook time: 28 minutes | Serves: 2

2 boneless pork chops	salt and ground black pepper, as required
1 cup buttermilk	
½ cup flour	olive oil cooking spray
1 teaspoon garlic powder	

1. Place the chops and buttermilk in a mixing bowl and marinate for 12 hours in the refrigerator. 2. Remove the chops from the bowl of buttermilk. 3. Place flour, garlic powder, salt, and black pepper in a shallow dish and mix well. 4. Coat the milky chops with spiced flour mixture generously. 5. Place the pork chops onto the cooking tray and spray with the cooking spray. 6. Select the "Air Fry" setting of the air fryer to 380 degrees F for 28 minutes and press "Start." 7. Insert the cooking tray in the center position in the air fryer. 8. Air fry the chops flipping halfway for 28 minutes until crispy and golden brown. 9. Serve the chop hot with sauce and enjoy.
Per serving: Calories 246; Fat 6.4g; Sodium 1258mg; Carbs 30.7g; Fiber 7g; Sugar 2g; Protein 44.6g

Sweet Ham

Prep time: 10 minutes | Cook time: 40 minutes | Serves: 4

1 pound (10½-ounce) ham	2 tablespoons French mustard
1 cup whiskey	2 tablespoons honey

1. Grease a cooking tray of the air fryer. 2. Mix the whiskey, mustard, and honey in a bowl. 3. Place the ham in the cooking tray with half of the honey mixture and coat well. 4. Select the "Air Fry" setting of the air fryer to 320 degrees F for 40 minutes and press "Start." 5. Insert the cooking tray in the center position. 6. Air fry the ham for 40 minutes, Flipping halfway for even cooking. When flipping the ham, baste the remaining honey mixture on it and continue cooking. 7. Place the air-fried ham onto a platter for about 10 minutes before slicing. 8. Slice the ham into the desired size and serve and enjoy.
Per serving: Calories 352; Fat 9g; Sodium 754mg; Carbs 2g; Fiber 0.6g; Sugar 0.1g; Protein 28g

Herbed Bacon Slices and Potatoes

Prep time: 10 minutes | Cook time: 30 minutes | Serves: 4

2 pounds' potatoes, halved	1 tablespoon fresh rosemary, chopped
2 garlic cloves, minced	
4 bacon slices, chopped	2 tablespoons olive oil

1. Mix garlic, bacon, olive oil, and rosemary in a mixing bowl and toss potatoes. 2. Place the potatoes and bacon on a cooking tray. 3. Set the air fryer for 25-30 minutes at 400 degrees F on the "Air Fry" mode. 4. Air fry the potatoes and bacon for 25-30 minutes, stirring once until done. 5. Serve hot topped on a salad, and enjoy.
Per serving: Calories 201; Fat 23g; Sodium 112mg; Carbs 25g; Fiber 10g; Sugar 8g; Protein 18g

Minty Pork Chops

Prep time: 15 minutes | Cook time: 30 minutes | Serves: 6

4 medium-sized pork chops, approximately 3.5 ounces each	1 pinch of salt and pepper
	½ tablespoon of mint, either dried and ground; or fresh, rinsed and finely chopped
1 cup of breadcrumbs	
2 medium-sized eggs	

1. Cover the cooking tray of the air fryer with tin foil lining, leaving the edges uncovered to allow air to circulate through the cooking tray. 2. Preheat the air fryer to 350 degrees F for 5 minutes at the "Air Fry" setting. 3. Beat the eggs until fluffy in a bowl. Whisk until the yolks and whites are thoroughly combined and set aside. 4. Combine the breadcrumbs, mint, salt, and pepper in a mixing bowl and set aside. 5. Dip each pork chop into the bowl with dry ingredients, coating all sides. Dredge the chops into the bowl with wet ingredients, and then dip again into the dry ingredients. 6. Lay the coated pork chops on the foil covering tray in a single flat layer. 7. Place the cooking tray on the middle shelf of the air fryer. 8. Place the chops in the air fryer and air fry for 15 minutes, flipping halfway with the tong until golden brown. 9. After 15 minutes, reset the air fryer to 320 degrees F for 15 minutes. 10. Air fry the chops further for 15 minutes. 11. Plate the chops with the fresh salad and sauce on the side and serve hot.
Per serving: Calories 300; Fat 12g; Sodium 70mg; Carbs 5g; Fiber 0.3g; Sugar 0.6g; Protein 25g

Lime Pork Tenderloin Cubes

Prep time: 15 minutes | Cook time: 14 minutes | Serves: 24

1 (1 pound) pork tenderloin, cut into 1½-inch cubes	lime juice
¼ cup minced onion	2 tablespoons coconut milk
2 garlic cloves, minced	2 tablespoons unsalted peanut butter
1 jalapeño pepper, minced	2 teaspoons curry powder
2 tablespoons freshly squeezed	

1. Add the pork, onion, garlic, jalapeño, lime juice, coconut milk, peanut butter, and curry powder to a mixing bowl and mix until well incorporated. 2. Let rest the meat for 10 minutes at room temperature in the spice mix. 3. Remove the pork from the marinade and thread it into skewers. Reserve the marinade. 4. Set the air fryer for 9-14 minutes at 250 degrees F on the "Roast" setting. 5. Place the meat skewers in the cooking tray and roast for 9-14 minutes; flip the skewers halfway, brush the reserved marinade, and continue cooking. 6. Serve hot with sauce and enjoy.

Per serving: Calories 194; Fat 7g; Sodium 65mg; Carbs 7g; Fiber 1g; Sugar 3g; Protein 25g

Greek Pork Burgers

Prep time: 20 minutes | Cook time: 9 minutes | Serves: 4

½ cup Greek yogurt	½ teaspoon paprika
2 tablespoons low sodium mustard, divided	1 cup mixed baby lettuce greens
1 tablespoon lemon juice	2 small tomatoes, sliced
¼ cup sliced red cabbage	low sodium whole wheat sandwich buns, cut in half
¼ cup grated carrots	
1-pound lean ground pork	

1. Combine the yogurt with 1 tablespoon of mustard, lemon juice, cabbage, and carrots; mix well and refrigerate the salad. 2. In another bowl, combine the pork, 1 tablespoon of mustard, and paprika. Mix well until incorporated. Form into 8 small patties from the meat mix. 3. Put the doors into the air fryer cooking tray. 4. Set the air fryer to the "Air Fry" setting at 350 degrees F for 7 to 9 minutes, or until the doors register 165 degrees F when tested with a meat thermometer. 5. Assemble the burgers by placing some of the lettuce greens on a toasted bun bottom. 6. Top with a fresh tomato slice, pork burgers, and the cabbage mixture. 7. Add the bun top and serve immediately with the sauce and enjoy.
Per serving: Calories 472; Fat 15g; Sodium 138mg; Carbs 51g; Fiber 8g; Sugar 8g; Protein 35g

Aromatic Pork Chops

Prep time: 5 minutes | Cook time: 16 minutes | Serves: 4

4 pork chops	1 tablespoon coconut oil
1 tablespoon coconut butter	2 teaspoons parsley, chopped
2 teaspoons minced garlic cloves	Salt and pepper to taste

1. Set the air fryer to 350 degrees F for 16 minutes at the "Air Fry" setting. Press Start to begin preheating. 2. Mix the coconut oil, seasonings, and butter in a bowl. Add chops to it and coat the chops with this butter mixture. 3. When the air fryer is preheated, place the chops on the cooking tray and air fryer for 8 minutes per side. 4. Serve hot with sauce and salad and enjoy.
Per serving: Calories 356; Fat 30g; Sodium 704mg; Carbs 2.3g; Fiber 1g; Sugar 1g; Protein 19g

Honey Pork Balls with Fresh Basil

Prep time: minutes | Cook time: 15 minutes | Serves: 4

7 ounces minced pork	⅓ cup onion, diced
1 teaspoon organic honey	Salt and pepper to taste
1 teaspoon Dijon mustard	A handful of fresh basil, chopped
1 tablespoon cheddar cheese, grated	1 teaspoon garlic puree

1. Set the air fryer on the "Air Fry" setting for 15 minutes at 390 degrees F. 2. In a mixing bowl, mix the meat with the seasonings until well incorporated and form small-sized balls. 3. Place the pork balls into the cooking tray and air fry for 15 minutes until done. 4. Serve hot with the sauce and fresh salad and enjoy.
Per serving: Calories 121; Fat 6.8g; Sodium 1256mg; Carbs 2.7g; Fiber 0.2g; Sugar 0.6g; Protein 11.3g

Low-Sodium Mustard Tenderloin

Prep time: 10 minutes | Cook time: 16 minutes | Serves: 4

3 tablespoons low sodium grainy mustard
2 teaspoons olive oil
¼ teaspoon dry mustard powder
1 (1 pound) pork tenderloin,
silver skin, and excess fat trimmed and discarded
2 slices low sodium whole wheat bread, crumbled
¼ cup ground walnuts
2 tablespoons cornstarch

1. Set the air fryer for 16 minutes at 350 degrees F on the "Air Fry" setting. 2. Stir the mustard, olive oil, and mustard powder in a small bowl and spread this mixture over the pork. 3. Mix the bread crumbs, walnuts, and cornstarch on a shallow dish. 4. Dredge the mustard-coated pork into the crumb mixture to coat. 5. Place the meat in the cooking tray and air fry the pork for 12 to 16 minutes or until it registers at least 145 degrees F on a meat thermometer. 6. Slice and serve hot with your favorite sauce and enjoy.
Per serving: Calories 239; Fat 9g; Sodium 118mg; Carbs 15g; Fiber 2g; Sugar 3g; Protein 26g

Pork Tenderloin with Apple and Veggies

Prep time: 10 minutes | Cook time: 19 minutes | Serves: 4

1 (1 pound) pork tenderloin, cut into 4 pieces
1 tablespoon apple butter
2 teaspoons olive oil
2 Granny Smith apples or
Jona gold apples, sliced
3 celery stalks, sliced
1 onion, sliced
½ teaspoon dried marjoram
⅓ cup apple juice

1. Grease each piece of pork with apple butter and olive oil. 2. Mix the pork, apples, celery, onion, marjoram, and apple juice in a medium mixing bowl. 3. Place the pork on the cooking tray and the vegetables and apples. 4. Set the air fryer to the "Roast" setting for 19 minutes at 350 degrees F. 5. Roast the meat for 19 minutes, or until the pork reaches at least 145 degrees F on a meat thermometer and the apples and vegetables are tender. 6. Stir once during cooking. 7. Serve hot immediately and enjoy.
Per serving: Calories 213; Fat 5g; Sodium 88mg; Carbs 20g; Fiber 3g; Sugar 15g; Protein 24g

Worcestershire Pork Ribs

Prep time: 10 minutes | Cook time: 26 minutes | Serves: 4

¼ cup honey, divided
¾ cup BBQ sauce
2 tablespoons tomato ketchup
1 tablespoon Worcestershire sauce
1 tablespoon soy sauce
½ teaspoon garlic powder
ground white pepper, as required
1¾ pounds pork ribs

1. Mix 3 tablespoons of honey and the remaining ingredients with the pork in a mixing bowl until the meat is well coated with spices. 2. Marinate the meat for about 20 minutes in a refrigerator. 3. Arrange the ribs onto the greased cooking tray. 4. Select the "Air Fry" setting of the air fryer to 355 degrees F for 26 minutes and press "Start." 5. Insert the cooking tray in the center position. 6. Air fry the ribs for 26 minutes, flipping halfway for even cooking. Remove the ribs from the air fryer once done. 7. Transfer the ribs onto serving plates. Drizzle with the remaining honey and sesame seeds, serve hot, and enjoy.
Per serving: Calories 691; Fat 35.3g; Sodium 704mg; Carbs 37g; Fiber 12g; Sugar 3g; Protein 53.1g

Espresso Pork Tenderloin

Prep time: 15 minutes | Cook time: 11 minutes | Serves: 4

1 tablespoon packed brown sugar
2 teaspoons espresso powder
1 teaspoon ground paprika
½ teaspoon dried marjoram
1 tablespoon honey
1 tablespoon freshly squeezed lemon juice
2 teaspoons olive oil
1 (1 pound) pork tenderloin

1. Mix the brown sugar, espresso powder, paprika, and marjoram in the bowl. 2. Stir the honey, lemon juice, and olive oil in the dry spice mix and mix well until well incorporated. 3. Spread the spiced honey espresso mixture over the pork and let it rest for 10 minutes at room temperature. 4. Set the air fryer to the "Roast" setting at 350 degrees F for 11 minutes. 5. Place the tenderloin in the air fryer cooking tray and roast for 11 minutes, or until the meat thermometer shows the temperature of 145 degrees F. 6. Slice the meat to serve. 7. Serve hot and enjoy.
Per serving: Calories 177; Fat 5g; Sodium 61mg; Carbs 10g; Fiber 1g; Sugar 8g; Protein 23g

Roasted Pork in Chicken Broth

Prep time: 5 minutes | Cook time: 25 minutes | Serves: 4

2 cups creamer potatoes, rinsed and dried
2 teaspoons olive oil
1 (1 pound) pork tenderloin, cut into 1-inch cubes
1 onion, chopped
1 red bell pepper, chopped
2 garlic cloves, minced
½ teaspoon dried oregano
2 tablespoons low sodium chicken broth

1. Toss the potatoes and olive oil to coat in a mixing bowl. 2. Transfer the potatoes to the air fryer cooking tray. 3. Select the "Roast" setting of the air fryer at 300 degrees F. Roast the potatoes for 15 minutes. 4. Mix the potatoes, pork, onion, red bell pepper, garlic, and oregano in a heatproof bowl. 5. Drizzle the chicken broth on the potatoes and pork mix. 6. Put the bowl in the air fryer cooking tray. 7. Roast the pork for about 10 minutes more, shaking the cooking tray once during cooking until the pork reaches at least 145 degrees F on a meat thermometer and the potatoes are tender. 8. Serve immediately with potatoes and a chilled drink, and enjoy.
Per serving: Calories 235; Fat 5g; Sodium 66mg; Carbs 22g; Fiber 3g; Sugar 4g; Protein 26g

Pork and Fruit Kebabs

Prep time: 15 minutes | Cook time: 12 minutes | Serves: 4

⅓ cup apricot jam
2 tablespoons freshly squeezed lemon juice
2 teaspoons olive oil
½ teaspoon dried tarragon
1 (1 pound) pork tenderloin, cut into 1-inch cubes
Plums pitted and quartered
small apricots pitted and halved

1. Mix the jam, lemon juice, olive oil, and tarragon in a mixing bowl. 2. Add the pork to the sweet marinate mix and stir to coat. Let the meat sit for 10 minutes at room temperature. 3. Thread the pork, plums, and apricots onto skewers. 4. Brush with any remaining jam mixture on the skewers 5. Place the skewers on the cooking tray. 6. Set the air fryer to the "Roast" setting for 12 minutes at 320 degrees F. 7. Roast the kebabs in the air fryer for 12 minutes, or until the pork reaches 145 degrees F on a meat thermometer and the fruit is tender. 8. Serve hot and enjoy.
Per serving: Calories 256; Fat 5g; Sodium 60mg; Carbs 30g; Fiber 2g; Sugar 22g; Protein 24g

Bacon Wrapped Filet Mignon

Prep time: 10 minutes | Cook time: 15 minutes | Serves: 2

2 bacon slices
2 (4 ounces) filet mignon
salt and ground black pepper,
as required
olive oil cooking spray

1. Wrap bacon slice around fillet mignon and secure with toothpicks. 2. Season the bacon-wrapped filets with salt and black pepper lightly. 3. Arrange the filet mignon onto a cooking tray and spray with cooking spray. 4. Arrange the drip pan at the bottom of the air fryer cooking chamber. 5. Select the "Air Fry" setting of the air fryer to 375 degrees F for 15 minutes. 6. Insert the cooking tray in the center position. 7. Air fry the meat for 15 minutes, flipping halfway for even cooking. 8. Remove the tray from the air fryer and serve hot.

Per serving: Calories 360; Fat 19g; Sodium 737mg; Carbs 0.4g; Fiber 0g; Sugar 0g; Protein 42.6g

Cumin Skin-on Pork Shoulder

Prep time: 10minutes | Cook time: 55 minutes | Serves: 6

1 teaspoon ground cumin
1 teaspoon cayenne pepper
1 teaspoon garlic powder
salt and ground black pepper,
as required
2 pounds' skin-on pork shoulder

1. Place all spices, salt, and black pepper and mix well in a small bowl. 2. Arrange the pork shoulder skin side down on a cutting board. 3. Season the meat side of the pork shoulder with salt and black pepper. 4. Tie the pork with kitchen twines into a long cylinder shape. 5. Season the skin side of the pork shoulder with the spice mixture. 6. Insert the rotisserie rod through the pork shoulder. Insert the forks, one on each side of the rod, to secure the pork shoulder. 7. Place the drip pan in the bottom of the air fryer cooking chamber. 8. Select the "Roast" setting of the air fryer to 350 degrees F for 55 minutes and press "Start." 9. Push the red lever to the right and load the left side of the rod into the air fryer. Get the rod's left side into the groove along the metal bar to ensure it doesn't move. 10. Close the air fryer door and touch "Rotate." 11. Press the red lever to release the rod after cooking time is complete. 12. Transfer the pork to a platter for about 10 minutes before slicing. 13. Slice the pork shoulder into the desired size, serve with your favorite sauce, and enjoy.

Per serving: Calories 445; Fat 32.5g; Sodium 523mg; Carbs 0.7g; Fiber 0g; Sugar 2g; Protein 35.4g

Garlicky Pork Tenderloin

Prep time: 15 minutes | Cook time: 20 minutes | Serves: 5

1½ pounds of pork tenderloin
Nonstick cooking spray
2 small heads of roasted garlic
Salt and ground black pepper,
as required

1. Spray the garlic lightly with cooking oil. 2. Select the "Air Fry" setting of the air fryer to 400 degrees F for 20 minutes and roast the garlic. 3. Grease the pork with cooking spray and season with salt and black pepper. 4. Rub the pork with roasted garlic. 5. Arrange the roast onto the lightly greased cooking tray. 6. Air fry the pork for 20 minutes until tender and crispy. 7. When cooked, remove the tray from the air fryer, place the roast onto a platter, and let the food sit for about 10 minutes. 8. Slice the roast into the desired size and serve with mayo and enjoy.

Per serving: Calories 202; Fat 4.8g; Sodium 109mg; Carbs

1.7g; Fiber 0.1g; Sugar 0.1g; Protein 35.9g

Sriracha Pork Tenderloin

Prep time: 15 minutes | Cook time: 20 minutes | Serves: 3

1-pound pork tenderloin
2 tablespoons Sriracha
2 tablespoons honey
Salt, as required

1. Insert the rotisserie rod through the pork tenderloin and the rotisserie forks to secure the pork tenderloin. 2. Add the Sriracha, honey, and salt and mix well in a small bowl. 3. Brush the pork tenderloin with the honey mixture evenly. 4. Arrange the drip pan at the bottom of the air fryer cooking chamber. 5. Select the "Air Fry" setting of the air fryer to 350 degrees F for 20 minutes and press the "Start." 6. Press the red lever to the right and load the left side of the rod into the air fryer. 7. Now, slide the rod's left side into the groove along the metal bar, so it doesn't move. 8. Then, close the door of the air fryer and touch "Rotate." 9. When cooked, press the red lever to release the rod. 10. Transfer the pork to a platter for about 10 minutes before slicing. 11. Slice the roast into the desired size and serve warm and enjoy.

Per serving: Calories 269; Fat 5.3g; Sodium 207mg; Carbs 13.5g; Fiber 0g; Sugar 11g; Protein 39.7g

Montreal Pork Chops

Prep time: 10 minutes | Cook time: 20 minutes | Serves: 4

1-pound center-cut pork chops
1 tablespoon olive oil
1 teaspoon Montreal seasoning mix
1 teaspoon red pepper flakes, crushed
Sea salt to taste
Ground black pepper to taste

1. Select the "Air Fry" setting of the air fryer to 400 degrees F for 20 minutes. Press the "Start" key. 2. Grease the air fryer cooking tray with olive oil. 3. When the air fryer is preheated, place the pork chops in the air fryer cooking tray. 4. Air fry the chops for 20 minutes or until the internal temperature reaches 145 degrees F on a meat thermometer. 5. Serve warm and enjoy!

Per serving: Calories 279; Fat 15.9g; Sodium 542mg; Carbs 0.5g; Fiber 0.1g; Sugar 0.1g; Protein 29.1g

Homemade Baby Back Ribs

Prep time: 10 minutes | Cook time: 45 minutes | Serves: 4

2 pounds of baby back pork ribs
½ cup barbeque sauce
1 teaspoon ancho chile powder
¼ cup brown sugar
Sea salt and freshly ground black pepper to taste

1. Toss the pork ribs with the other ingredients in a mixing bowl. 2. Place aluminum foil onto the drip pan. 3. Place the pork ribs in the rotisserie basket. 4. Select the "Air Fry" setting of the air fryer to 350 ° F for 45 minutes. Press the "Start" key. 5. Cook the pork ribs for about 45 minutes or until they are thoroughly cooked. 6. Serve hot and enjoy!

Per serving: Calories 352; Fat 12.9g; Sodium 521mg; Carbs 8.5g; Fiber 0.6g; Sugar 7.8g; Protein 47.6g

Mustardy Pork Butt

Prep time: 10 minutes | Cook time: 35 minutes | Serves: 5

2 pounds' boneless pork butt
2 tablespoons olive oil
2 tablespoons red wine vine-
gar
1 tablespoon Dijon mustard
1 teaspoon cumin seeds

1 teaspoon fennel seeds
1 teaspoon cayenne pepper
Kosher salt and ground black
pepper, to taste
2 tablespoons brown sugar

1. In a mixing bowl, add all the ingredients and mix well. 2. Allow the meat to marinate in the refrigerator for at least 3 hours. 3. Select the "Air Fry" setting of the air fryer to 390 degrees F for 35 minutes. Press the "Start" key. Place aluminum foil onto the drip pan. 4. Place the pork in the air fryer cooking tray. 5. Reserve the marinade. Cook the pork for about 15 minutes, basting and flipping, and continue cooking for another 20 minutes until cooked. 6. Serve hot and enjoy!
Per serving: Calories 542; Fat 37.5g; Sodium 954mg; Carbs 3.1g; Fiber 0.3g; Sugar 3.3g; Protein 45.4g

Hot Pork Shoulder

Prep time: 15 minutes | Cook time: 55 minutes | Serves: 6

1 teaspoon ground cumin
1 teaspoon cayenne pepper
1 teaspoon garlic powder
Salt and ground black pepper,
as required
2 pounds' skin-on pork shoulder

1. Mix the spices, salt, and black pepper in the bowl. 2. Arrange the pork shoulder skin side down. 3. Season the meaty side of the pork shoulder with salt and black pepper. 4. Tie the pork shoulder into a long round cylinder shape with the help of kitchen twines. 5. Season the outer side of pork shoulder with spice mixture. 6. Insert the rotisserie rod through the pork shoulder and secure it with the rotisserie forks. 7. Arrange the drip pan at the bottom of the air fryer cooking chamber. 8. Select the "Roast" setting of the air fryer to 350 degrees F for 55 minutes and press the "Start." 9. Press the red lever to the right and load the left side of the rod into the air fryer. 10. Now, store the rod's left side into the groove along the metal bar, so it doesn't move. 11. Then, close the door of the air fryer and touch "Rotate." 12. When cooking time is complete, press the red lever to release the rod. 13. Place the pork on a platter for about 10 minutes before slicing. 14. Slice the pork shoulder into the desired size and serve hot and enjoy.
Per serving: Calories 445; Fat 32.5g; Sodium 131mg; Carbs 0.7g; Fiber 0.2g; Sugar 0.2g; Protein 35.4g

Flavorful Pork Burgers

Prep time: 10 minutes | Cook time: 20 minutes | Serves: 4

1-pound ground pork
1 egg, whisked
½ cup bread crumbs
½ cup Parmesan cheese, grated
1 tablespoon dried parsley flakes
Pinch of sea salt
Freshly ground black pepper
1 teaspoon cayenne pepper
4 hamburger buns, split
1 tablespoon Dijon mustard
4 large lettuce leaves
1 small onion, thinly sliced

1. In a mixing bowl, combine the ground pork, egg, bread crumbs, cheese, dried parsley, salt, black pepper, and cayenne pepper and mix well until incorporated. 2. Shape the mixture into four patties. 3. Select the "Air Fry" setting of the air fryer to 370 degrees F for 20 minutes. Press the "Start" key. Place aluminum foil onto the drip pan. 4. Place the pork burgers in the air fryer cooking tray. Cook your burgers for about 10 minutes. 5. Flip the burgers over and continue to cook them for a further 10 minutes. 6. Arrange burgers with toasted hamburger buns, warm patties, mustard, lettuce, and onion, and serve. 7. Serve hot immediately and enjoy!
Per serving: Calories 532; Fat 25.2g; Sodium 689mg; Carbs

45.5g; Fiber 10.6g; Sugar 1.8g; Protein 35.6g

Glossy Pork Belly

Prep time: 10 minutes | Cook time: 15 minutes | Serves: 4

1-pound pork belly sliced, patted dry
1 tablespoon Worcestershire sauce
2 garlic cloves, pressed
1 teaspoon onion powder
1 teaspoon cayenne pepper
Sea salt
Ground black pepper to taste
¼ cup tomato sauce

1. In a mixing bowl, add all the ingredients and allow the pork to marinate for at least 30 minutes. 2. Select the "Air Fry" setting of the air fryer to 350 degrees F for 15 minutes. Press the "Start" key. Place aluminum foil onto the drip pan. 3. Place the pork in the air fryer cooking tray. 4. Cook the pork for about 10 minutes, flip, and cook for 5 more minutes. 5. Serve immediately with your favorite sauce, and enjoy!
Per serving: Calories 619; Fat 60.2g; Sodium 2147mg; Carbs 6.5g; Fiber 1.4g; Sugar 2.8g; Protein 11.5g

Smoked Sausage with Cauliflower Florets

Prep time: 10 minutes | Cook time: 15 minutes | Serves: 5

1-pound smoked sausages
1-pound cauliflower florets
2 tablespoons soy sauce
1 teaspoon Italian seasoning
blend
Sea salt
Ground black pepper to taste

1. Select the "Air Fry" setting of the air fryer to 400 degrees F for 15 minutes. Press the "Start" key. Place aluminum foil onto the drip pan. 2. In a mixing bowl, toss all the ingredients well. 3. Place the sausage and cauliflower in the air fryer cooking tray. 4. Cook the sausage and cauliflower for about 10 minutes. 5. Flip them and continue to cook for a further 5 minutes. 6. Serve hot and Bon appétit!
Per serving: Calories 369; Fat 26.2g; Sodium 1845mg; Carbs 1g; Fiber 2.4g; Sugar 4.3g; Protein 19g

Olives Loaded Meatballs

Prep time: 10 minutes | Cook time: 25 minutes | Serves: 4

1-pound ground pork
½ cup plain breadcrumbs
1 large egg, whisked
1 garlic clove, minced
1 teaspoon dried basil
1 teaspoon dried oregano
Kosher salt and ground black pepper, to taste
1 teaspoon paprika
2 ounces' bacon bits
2 ounces' green olives, pitted and chopped

1. Select the "Air Fry" setting of the air fryer to 380 degrees F for 25 minutes and press the "Start" key. 2. Place parchment paper in the air fryer cooking tray. 3. In a large bowl, combine all the ingredients until well incorporated. With the help of a scoop, drop little meatballs on the lined cooking tray. 4. Air fry the meatballs for 10 minutes. Shake them and continue cooking for a further 15 minutes or until cooked through. 5. Serve hot with ranch sauce and Bon appétit!
Per serving: Calories 436; Fat 36.6g; Sodium 954mg; Carbs 22.6g; Fiber 1g; Sugar 2.2g; Protein 22.6g

Easy-to-Make Pork Loin

Prep time: 10 minutes | Cook time: 50 minutes | Serves: 5

2 pounds of pork loin	Ground black pepper to taste
1 tablespoon brown sugar	1 teaspoon garlic, pressed
1 teaspoon smoked paprika	1 teaspoon ground mustard
Sea salt	1 tablespoon olive oil

1. In a mixing bowl, add all the ingredients and mix well. 2. Allow meat to marinate for at least 1 hour. 3. Select the "Roast" setting of the air fryer to 360 degrees F for 50 minutes. 4. Press the "Start" key. Place aluminum foil onto the drip pan. 5. Place the pork loin in the air fryer cooking tray. Reserve the marinade. 6. Cook the pork for about 25 minutes, baste with marinade after flipping the meat and cook for more than 25 minutes. 7. Serve immediately with salad, and enjoy!
Per serving: Calories 355; Fat 18.5g; Sodium 875mg; Carbs 6.9g; Fiber 3.6g; Sugar 6g; Protein 39.1g

Thai-Style Rib Slab

Prep time: 10 minutes | Cook time: 35 minutes | Serves: 5

2 pounds of pork loin back rib slab	1 tablespoon fresh ginger, peeled and grated
1 cup sweet Thai chili sauce	¼ cup creamy peanut butter
2 tablespoons soy sauce	2 tablespoons rice vinegar
1 tablespoon Thai red curry paste	2 tablespoons lime juice
2 teaspoons fish sauce	2 tablespoons fresh cilantro leaves, chopped

1. In a mixing bowl, combine all the ingredients well; let the meat sit for about 30 minutes at room temperature. 2. Place aluminum foil onto the drip pan. 3. Place the riblets in the rotisserie basket. 4. Select the "Air Fry" setting of the air fryer to 350 degrees F for 35 minutes. 5. Press the "Start" key. 6. Cook the pork riblets for about 20 minutes or until they are thoroughly cooked. 7. Baste the ribs with the reserved marinade and continue cooking for 15 minutes or until they are thoroughly cooked. 8. Serve hot with a chilled drink and Bon appétit!
Per serving: Calories 388; Fat 17.5g; Sodium 965mg; Carbs 17.5g; Fiber 4.3g; Sugar 9.7g; Protein 42.6g

Ketchup-Glazed Meatloaf

Prep time: 10 minutes | Cook time: 45 minutes | Serves: 5

Meatloaf:	1 tablespoon Italian seasoning mix
1 ½ pounds ground pork	
1 cup seasoned bread crumbs	Kosher salt and ground black pepper to season
1 medium onion, chopped	
2 cloves garlic, chopped	Glaze:
2 eggs, beaten	½ cup ketchup
2 tablespoon Worcestershire sauce	1 tablespoon Dijon mustard
	¼ cup brown sugar

1. In a mixing bowl, combine all the ingredients for the meatloaf until well incorporated; press the meatloaf into a lightly greased baking pan. 2. Select the "Air Fry" setting to 360 degrees F for 45 minutes. Press the "Start" key. 3. Place the baking pan on the cooking tray. 4. Air fry the pork meatloaf for 40 minutes. 5. In a small bowl, mix the glaze ingredients and spread them over the top of the meatloaf. 6. Select the "Broil" setting and cook the meatloaf for 5 minutes. 7. Slice and serve hot, and Bon appétit!
Per serving: Calories 398; Fat 23.3g; Sodium 745mg; Carbs 18.3g; Fiber 0.8g; Sugar 11.4g; Protein 28g

Boneless Ham in Wine and Mustard

Prep time: 15 minutes | Cook time: 3 hours | Serves: 6

2 pounds cooked boneless ham	½ cup sherry wine
	2 tablespoons olive oil
½ cup brown sugar	2 garlic cloves, minced
2 tablespoons wholegrain mustard	2 tablespoons Worcestershire sauce

1. Pat the ham dry with a paper towel. 2. Place the prepared ham with the rotisserie spit into the air fryer. 3. Select the "Air Fry" setting of the air fryer to 250 degrees F for 1 hour. Select the "Rotate" setting. Press the "Start" key. 4. When the time is up, repeat the previous settings twice. 5. Meanwhile, in a mixing bowl, mix all the remaining ingredients to make the glaze. 6. Glaze the ham every 30 minutes. 7. Once cooked, allow it to rest for 10 minutes before slicing and serving. 8. Slice and serve warm, and Bon appétit!
Per serving: Calories 338; Fat 17.9g; Sodium 624mg; Carbs 17.3g; Fiber 2.2g; Sugar 8.8g; Protein 25.4g

Pork, Tomato and Onion Salad

Prep time: 10 minutes | Cook time: 50 minutes | Serves: 4

1-pound pork loin	¼ cup extra-virgin olive oil
3 cups mixed salad greens, torn into pieces	2 tablespoons apple cider vinegar
1 cup grape tomatoes	2 teaspoons fresh basil, minced
1 small red onion, thinly sliced	1 teaspoon fish sauce
1 bell pepper, sliced	2 garlic cloves, minced
1 small chili pepper, minced	

1. Select the "Roast" setting of the air fryer to 360 degrees F for 50 minutes. 2. Press the "Start" key. Place aluminum foil onto the drip pan. 3. Place the pork loin on a cooking tray. Cook the pork for about 25 minutes. 4. Flip the pork over and roast for about 25 minutes or until it reaches an internal temperature of 145 degrees F on a meat thermometer. 5. Slice the pork into strips and place them in a salad bowl. 6. Add in the vegetables and toss to combine. 7. In a small bowl, whisk the remaining ingredients to make the dressing. 8. Drizzle dressing on the salad and serve warm and enjoy!
Per serving: Calories 368; Fat 23.3g; Sodium 1236mg; Carbs 13.3g; Fiber 2.5g; Sugar 8.3g; Protein 26.5g

Pulled Pork Shoulder

Prep time: 5 minutes | Cook time: 50 minutes | Serves: 5

2 pounds' boneless pork shoulder	2 garlic cloves, pressed
	Sea salt
1 tablespoon Italian seasoning mix	Ground black pepper to taste
	1 teaspoon hot paprika
½ teaspoon cumin seeds	

1. In a mixing bowl, add all the ingredients and mix well. Marinate the meat for at least 3 hours. 2. Select the "Air Fry" setting of the air fryer to 360 degrees F for 50 minutes. 3. Press the "Start" key. Place aluminum foil onto the drip pan. 4. Place the pork in the air fryer cooking tray. Reserve the marinade. 5. Cook the pork for about 25 minutes, baste with marinade after 25 minutes, and flip over. 6. Continue cooking for about 25 minutes or until cooked through. 7. Shred the pork, and serve immediately with toasted buns and sauce. 8. Bon appétit!
Per serving: Calories 346; Fat 5g; Sodium 1238mg; Carbs 1.4g; Fiber 0.3g; Sugar 0.3g; Protein 31.8g

Bacon-Wrapped Shrimp

Prep time: 15 minutes | Cook time: 7 minutes | Serves: 4

1¼ pounds tiger shrimp, peeled and deveined	1-pound bacon

1. Wrap shrimp with a slice of bacon. Refrigerate for about 20 minutes. 2. Arrange the shrimp in a cooking tray. 3. Using the control panel, select Air Fry, then adjust the temperature to 350 degrees F and time to 7 minutes. Press the Start button to initiate preheating. 4. When the air fryer shows "Add Food" on display, transfer the cooking tray to the air fryer. 5. Close its door, and let the machine do the cooking. 6. Serve.

Per serving: Calories 285; Fat 9.8g; Sodium 639mg; Carbs 11.1g; Fiber 1.2g, Sugars 5.1g; Protein 27.8g

Panko Tilapia Fillets

Prep time: 15 minutes | Cook time: 15 minutes | Serves: 3

Old Bay seasoning	1 tablespoon almond flour
½ cup panko breadcrumbs	4 to 6-ounce tilapia fillets
1 egg	Frozen crinkle-cut fries

1. Add almond flour to a bowl, beat one egg in another bowl, and add panko breadcrumbs to the third bowl, mixed with Old Bay seasoning. 2. Dredge tilapia in flour, then egg, and then breadcrumbs. When the screen displays "Add Food," transfer the fish and fries to a baking pan. 3. Set the air fryer to Air Fry, then adjust the temperature to 390 degrees F and the time to 15 minutes. Touch Start to initiate preheating. 4. When the screen displays "Add Food," transfer the cooking tray into the air fryer. 5. Close its door, and let the machine do the cooking. 6. Serve warm.

Per serving: Calories 285; Fat 9.8g; Sodium 639mg; Carbs 11.1g; Fiber 1.2g, Sugars 5.1g; Protein 27.8g

Breaded Fish Fingers

Prep time: 15 minutes | Cook time: 15 minutes | Serves: 4

½ pound fish fillet	½ teaspoon paprika
1 tablespoon finely chopped fresh mint leaves or any fresh herbs	Generous pinch of black pepper
⅓ cup bread crumbs	Salt to taste
1 teaspoon ginger garlic paste or ginger and garlic powders	¾ tablespoon lemon juice
1 hot green chili finely chopped	¾ teaspoon garam masala powder
	⅓ teaspoon rosemary
	1 egg

1. Start by removing any skin on the fish, washing, and patting dry. Cut the fish into fingers. 2. In a medium bowl, mix all ingredients, except for egg, fish, mint, and bread crumbs. 3. Bury the fingers in the mixture and refrigerate for 30 minutes. 4. Remove the bowl from the fridge and mix in mint leaves. 5. In a separate bowl, beat the egg, and pour bread crumbs into a third bowl. 6. Dip the fingers in the beaten egg bowl, toss them in the bread crumbs bowl, and then transfer them to a cooking tray. 7. Set the air fryer to Air Fry, then adjust the temperature to 360 degrees F and the time to 15 minutes. Press Start to initiate preheating. 8. When the screen displays "Add Food," transfer the cooking tray into the air fryer. 9. Close its door, and let the machine do the cooking. 10. Serve

warm.

Per serving: Calories 236; Fat 13.9g; Sodium 451mg; Carbs 13.2g; Fiber 1.2g; Sugars 1.4g; Protein 14.3g

Bacon Halves-Wrapped Scallops

Prep time: 15 minutes | Cook time: 5 minutes | Serves: 4

16 sea scallops	8 toothpicks
8 slices of bacon, cut into halves	Salt
	Freshly ground black pepper

1. Using a paper towel, pat dries the scallops. 2. Wrap scallop with a half slice of bacon. Secure the bacon-wrapped scallops with a toothpick. 3. Place the scallops in a cooking tray in a single layer. 4. Spray the scallops with olive oil, and season them with salt and pepper. 5. Using the control panel, select Air Fry, then adjust the temperature to 370 degrees F and time to 5 minutes. Press the Start button to begin preheating. 6. When the screen displays "Add Food," transfer the cooking tray to the air fryer, when the screen displays "Add Food." 7. Close its door, and let the machine do the cooking. 8. Serve.

Per serving: Calories 344; Fat 14.9g; Sodium 227mg; Carbs 14g; Fiber 1g; Sugars 1.4g; Protein 25.7g

Spiced Salmon Fillets

Prep time: 15 minutes | Cook time: 10 minutes | Serves: 2

½ teaspoon salt	½ teaspoon smoked paprika
½ teaspoon garlic powder	2 salmon fillets

1. Mix spices and sprinkle onto salmon. Place seasoned salmon in a cooking tray. 2. Using the control panel, select Air Fry, adjust the temperature to 400 degrees F and the time to 10 minutes, then touch Start. To initiate preheating. 3. When the screen display shows "Add Food," transfer the cooking tray into the air fryer. 4. Close its door, and let the machine do the cooking. 5. Serve warm.

Per serving: Calories 336; Fat 17.3g; Sodium 281mg; Carbs 8.1g; Fiber 5.3g, Sugars 17.7g; Protein 32.3g

Cherry Tomato and Shrimp Kebab

Prep time: 15 minutes | Cook time: 5 minutes | Serves: 4

½ pounds jumbo shrimp, cleaned, shelled, and deveined	Ground black pepper to taste
1 pound of cherry tomatoes	½ teaspoon dried oregano
1 tablespoon butter, melted	½ teaspoon dried basil
1 tablespoon Sriracha sauce	1 teaspoon dried parsley flakes
Sea salt	½ teaspoon marjoram
	½ teaspoon mustard seeds

1. Toss all ingredients in a mixing bowl until the shrimp and tomatoes are covered on all sides. 2. Soak the wooden skewers in water for 15 minutes. 3. Thread the jumbo shrimp and cherry tomatoes onto skewers, then transfer them to a cooking tray. 4. Set the air fryer to Air Fry, then adjust the temperature to 400 degrees F and the time to 5 minutes. Touch Start to initiate preheating. 5. When the screen displays "Add Food," transfer the cooking tray into the air fryer. 6. Close its door, and let the machine do the cooking. 7. Serve warm.

Per serving: Calories 336; Fat 17.3g; Sodium 281mg; Carbs 8.1g; Fiber 5.3g, Sugars 17.7g; Protein 32.3g

Lemon Pepper Cod Fillets

Prep time: 15 minutes | Cook time: 12 minutes | Serves: 2

2 (8-ounce) cod fillets, cut to fit into the baking pan	½ teaspoon freshly ground black pepper
1 tablespoon Cajun seasoning	2 tablespoons unsalted butter, melted
½ teaspoon lemon pepper	lemon, cut into four wedges
1 teaspoon salt	

1. Spray the cooking tray with olive oil. Place the fillets in it. 2. In a small mixing bowl, combine the Cajun seasoning, lemon pepper, salt, and pepper. 3. Rub the seasoning mix over the fish. 4. Place the cod into the greased cooking tray. Brush the top of the fillet with melted butter. 5. Set the air fryer to Air Fry, then adjust the temperature to 360 degrees F and the time to 12 minutes. Press Start to initiate preheating. 6. When the screen display shows "Add Food," transfer the cooking tray. 7. Close its door, and let the machine do the cooking. 8. Squeeze fresh lemon juice over the fillets.
Per serving: Calories 351; Fat 22g; Sodium 502mg; Carbs 15.2g; Sugar 1.1g; Fiber 0.7g; Protein 26.4g

Wild Salmon Patties

Prep time: 15 minutes | Cook time: 10 minutes | Serves: 4

1 (14.75-ounce) can of wild salmon, drained	1 teaspoon dried dill
1 large egg	½ teaspoon freshly ground black pepper
¼ cup diced onion	1 teaspoon salt
½ cup bread crumbs	1 teaspoon Old Bay seasoning

1. Spray the cooking tray with olive oil. 2. Put the salmon in a medium bowl and remove any bones or skin. Add the egg, onion, bread crumbs, dill, pepper, salt, and Old Bay seasoning and mix well. 3. Form the salmon mixture into four equal patties. Place the patties in the greased cooking tray. 4. Set the air fryer to Air Fry, then adjust the temperature to 370 degrees F and the time to 10 minutes. Touch Start to initiate preheating. 5. When the screen displays "Add Food," transfer the cooking tray into the air fryer. 6. Close its door, and let the machine do the cooking. 7. Serve.
Per serving: Calories 249; Fat 13g; Sodium 556mg; Carbs 10g; Sugar 1.1g; Fiber 0.7g; Protein 31g

Crumbed Fish Fillets

Prep time: 15 minutes | Cook time: 17 minutes | Serves: 4

2 eggs, beaten	ed
½ teaspoon tarragon	1 teaspoon seasoned salt
4 fish fillets, halved	⅓ teaspoon mixed peppercorns
2 tablespoons dry white wine	
⅓ cup parmesan cheese, grat-	½ teaspoon fennel seed

1. Add the parmesan cheese, salt, peppercorns, fennel seeds, and tarragon to your food processor; blitz for about 20 seconds. 2. Drizzle fish fillets with dry white wine. Dump one egg into a shallow dish. 3. Now, coat the fish fillets with the beaten egg on all sides; then coat them with the seasoned cracker mix. 4. Place the fish in a cooking tray. 5. Set the air fryer to Air Fry, then adjust the temperature to 345 degrees F and the time to 17 minutes. 6. Press the Start button to initiate preheating. 7. When the screen displays "Add Food," transfer the cooking tray into the air fryer. 8. Close its door, and let the machine do the cooking. 9. Serve warm.
Per serving: Calories 307; Fat 11g; Sodium 477mg; Carbs 14g; Fiber 1g; Sugars 1.4g; Protein 25.7g

Cauliflower-White Fish Cakes

Prep time: 15 minutes | Cook time: 13 minutes | Serves: 4

½ pound cauliflower florets	2 tablespoons sour cream
½ teaspoon English mustard	2 ½ cups cooked white fish
2 tablespoons butter, room temperature	Salt and freshly cracked black pepper to savor
½ tablespoon cilantro, minced	

1. Boil the cauliflower until tender. Then purée the cauliflower in your blender. When the screen displays "Add Food," transfer to a mixing dish. 2. Now, stir in the fish, cilantro, salt, and black pepper. 3. Add the sour cream, English mustard, and butter; mix until everything's well incorporated. Shape them into patties. 4. Place in the refrigerator for about 2 hours, then transfer to a cooking tray. 5. Set the air fryer to Air Fry, then adjust the temperature to 395 degrees F and the time to 13 minutes. 6. Press the Start button to initiate preheating. 7. When the screen displays "Add Food," transfer the cooking tray into the air fryer. 8. Close its door, and let the machine do the cooking. 9. Serve warm.
Per serving: Calories 344; Fat 14.9g; Sodium 227mg; Carbs 14g; Fiber 1g; Sugars 1.4g; Protein 25.7g

Beer-Marinated Scallops

Prep time: 15 minutes | Cook time: 7 minutes | Serves: 4

2 pounds of sea scallops	2 sprigs rosemary, only leaves
½ cup beer	Sea salt and freshly cracked black pepper to taste
4 tablespoons butter	

1. In a ceramic dish, mix the sea scallops with beer; let it marinate for 1 hour. 2. Melt the butter and add the rosemary leaves. Stir for a few minutes. 3. Discard the marinade and transfer the sea scallops to the baking pan. Season with salt and black pepper. 4. Set the air fryer to Air Fry, then adjust the temperature to 400 degrees F and the time to 7 minutes. 5. Press the Start button to initiate preheating. 6. When the screen displays "Add Food," transfer the cooking tray into the air fryer. 7. Close its door, and let the machine do the cooking. 8. Serve warm.
Per serving: Calories 336; Fat 17.3g; Sodium 281mg; Carbs 8.1g; Fiber 5.3g; Sugars 17.7g; Protein 32.3g

Air-Fried Hake Fillets

Prep time: 15 minutes | Cook time: 15 minutes | Serves: 4

1 tablespoon avocado oil	chopped
1-pound hake fillets	½ cup cottage cheese
1 teaspoon garlic powder	½ cup sour cream
Sea salt and ground white pepper to taste	egg, well whisked
2 tablespoons shallots, chopped	1 teaspoon yellow mustard
	1 tablespoon lime juice
bell pepper, seeded and	½ cup Swiss cheese, shredded

1. Brush the bottom and sides of a casserole dish with avocado oil. 2. Add the hake fillets to the casserole dish and sprinkle with garlic powder, salt, and pepper. 3. Add the chopped shallots and bell peppers. 4. Thoroughly combine the cottage cheese, sour cream, egg, mustard, and lime juice in a mixing bowl. 5. Pour the mixture over the fish and spread evenly. 6. Set the air fryer to Air Fry, then adjust the temperature to 370 degrees F and the time to 15 minutes. 7. Press the Start button to initiate preheating. 8. When the screen displays "Add Food," transfer the casserole dish to the cooking tray into the air fryer. 9. Close its door, and let the machine do the cook-

ing. 10. Top with the Swiss cheese and cook for an additional 7 minutes. 11. Let it rest for 10 minutes before slicing and serving. 12. Serve.

Per serving: Calories 236; Fat 13.9g; Sodium 451mg; Carbs 13.2g; Fiber 1.2g; Sugars 1.4g; Protein 14.3g

Coconut Tilapia

Prep time: 15 minutes | Cook time: 6 minutes | Serves: 2

1 cup coconut milk	½ teaspoon ginger powder
1 tablespoon lime juice	½ Thai bird's eye chili, seeded
1 tablespoon soy sauce	and finely chopped
Salt and white pepper to taste	1-pound tilapia
1 teaspoon turmeric powder	2 tablespoons olive oil

1. In a mixing bowl, thoroughly combine the coconut milk with the lime juice, soy sauce, salt, pepper, turmeric, ginger, and chili pepper. 2. Add tilapia and let it marinate for 1 hour. 3. Brush a cooking tray with olive oil. Discard the marinade and place the tilapia fillets in the cooking tray. 4. Set the air fryer to Air Fry, then adjust the temperature to 400 degrees F and the time to 6 minutes. 5. Press the Start button to initiate preheating. 6. When the screen displays "Add Food," transfer the cooking tray into the air fryer. 7. Close its door, and let the machine do the cooking. 8. Serve with some extra lime wedges if desired.

Per serving: Calories 344; Fat 14.9g; Sodium 227mg; Carbs 14g; Fiber 1g; Sugars 1.4g; Protein 25.7g

Buttered Scallops with Fresh Thyme

Prep time: 15 minutes | Cook time: 5 minutes | Serves: 8

4 tablespoons butter, melted	Pinch of salt
3 pounds of sea scallops	Freshly ground black pepper
2 tablespoons fresh thyme, minced	to taste

1. Add butter, sea scallops, thyme, salt, and pepper to a bowl. Toss to coat well. 2. Place scallops in a cooking tray. 3. Set the air fryer to Air Fry, then adjust the temperature to 385 degrees F and the time to 5 minutes. 4. Press the Start button to initiate preheating. 5. When the screen displays "Add Food," transfer the cooking tray into the air fryer. 6. Close its door, and let the machine do the cooking. 7. Serve warm.

Per serving: Calories 336; Fat 17.3g; Sodium 281mg; Carbs 8.1g; Fiber 5.3g, Sugars 17.7g; Protein 32.3g

Crispy Nacho Prawns

Prep time: 15 minutes | Cook time: 8 minutes | Serves: 8

2 eggs	1½ pounds Nacho flavored
36 prawns, peeled and deveined	chips, crushed finely

1. Add nacho chips to a bowl and crush well. 2. Add two eggs to another bowl and beat well. 3. Dip the prawn in the egg mixture and then in the crushed nachos, then transfer them to a cooking tray. 4. Set the air fryer to Air Fry, then adjust the temperature to 350 degrees F and the time to 8 minutes. 5. Press the Start button to initiate preheating. 6. When the screen displays "Add Food," transfer the cooking tray into the air fryer. 7. Close its door, and let the machine do the cooking. 8. Take out and serve hot.

Per serving: Calories 236; Fat 13.9g; Sodium 451mg; Carbs 13.2g; Fiber 1.2g; Sugars 1.4g; Protein 14.3g

Spicy Tiger Shrimp

Prep time: 15 minutes | Cook time: 5 minutes | Serves: 8

2 teaspoons old bay seasoning	4 tablespoons olive oil
1 teaspoon cayenne pepper	2 pounds of tiger shrimp
1 teaspoon smoked paprika	Salt to taste

1. Add all the ingredients to a large bowl. Mix well. 2. Place shrimps in a cooking tray. 3. Set the air fryer to Air Fry, then adjust the temperature to 350 degrees F and the time to 5 minutes. 4. Press the Start button to initiate preheating. 5. When the screen displays "Add Food," transfer the cooking tray into the air fryer. 6. Close its door, and let the machine do the cooking. 7. Serve warm.

Per serving: Calories 307; Fat 11g; Sodium 477mg; Carbs 14g; Fiber 1g; Sugars 1.4g; Protein 25.7g

Sole Fillets and Vegetable Fritters

Prep time: 15 minutes | Cook time: 10 minutes | Serves: 2

½ pound sole fillets	bell pepper, finely chopped
½ pound mashed cauliflower	½ teaspoon scotch bonnet
egg, well beaten	pepper, minced
½ cup red onion, chopped	1 tablespoon olive oil
2 garlic cloves, minced	1 tablespoon coconut aminos
2 tablespoons fresh parsley,	½ teaspoon paprika
chopped	Salt and white pepper to taste

1. In a mixing bowl, mash the sole fillets into flakes. Stir in the remaining ingredients. 2. Shape the fish mixture into patties. 3. Set the air fryer to Air Fry, then adjust the temperature to 195 degrees F and the time to 10 minutes. 4. Press the Start button to initiate preheating. 5. When the screen displays "Add Food," transfer the patties to the cooking tray in the air fryer. 6. Close its door, and let the machine do the cooking. 7. Serve warm.

Per serving: Calories 351; Fat 22g; Sodium 502mg; Carbs 15.2g; Sugar 1.1g; Fiber 0.7g; Protein 26.4g

Breaded Plain Tuna

Prep time: 15 minutes | Cook time: 12 minutes | Serves: 4

1 tablespoon fresh lime juice	½ pound water-packed plain
1 egg	tuna
3 tablespoons canola oil	½ cup breadcrumbs
2 tablespoons hot sauce	Salt
2 teaspoons Dijon mustard	Freshly ground black pepper
2 tablespoons fresh parsley,	to taste
chopped	

1. Add tuna fish, parsley, mustard, crumbs, citrus juice, and hot sauce in a bowl. Mix well. 2. Add oil, salt, and two eggs to the bowl and make patties from the mixture. 3. Place the patties in a cooking tray. 4. Set the air fryer to Air Fry, then adjust the temperature to 360 degrees F and the time to 12 minutes. 5. Press the Start button to initiate preheating. 6. When the screen displays "Add Food," transfer the cooking tray into the air fryer. 7. Close its door, and let the machine do the cooking. 8. Take out and serve hot.

Per serving: Calories 254; Fat 28g; Sodium 346mg; Carbs 12.3g; Sugar 1g; Fiber 0.7g; Protein 24.3 g

Coconut Crusted Prawns

Prep time: 15 minutes | Cook time: 7 minutes | Serves: 4

½ cup unsweetened coconut, shredded
¼ teaspoon lemon zest
¼ teaspoon cayenne pepper
Vegetable oil, as required
¼ teaspoon red pepper flakes, crushed
½ cup flour
½ cup breadcrumbs
1 pound prawns, peeled and deveined
2 egg whites
Salt and black pepper to taste

1. Take a shallow dish and mix salt, flour, and pepper. 2. Crack two eggs in another shallow dish. Beat well. 3. Add coconut, breadcrumbs, lime zest, salt, and cayenne pepper to the third shallow dish. Mix well. 4. Dip shrimp into the flour mixture, then in the egg mixture, and roll them evenly into the breadcrumb mixture. 5. Place them on a cooking tray and drizzle them with vegetable oil. 6. Set the air fryer to Air Fry, then adjust the temperature to 395 degrees F and the time to 7 minutes. 7. Press the Start button to initiate preheating. 8. When the screen displays "Add Food," transfer the cooking tray into the air fryer. 9. Close its door, and let the machine do the cooking. 10. Cook for about 7 minutes and take out. 11. Serve and enjoy!
Per serving: Calories 285; Fat 9.8g; Sodium 639mg; Carbs 11.1g; Fiber 1.2g, Sugars 5.1g; Protein 27.8g

Cajun Fish Steaks

Prep time: 15 minutes | Cook time: 8 minutes | Serves: 4

4 tablespoons Cajun seasoning
4 fish steaks

1. Add Cajun seasoning to a bowl and rub fish evenly. 2. Place fish steaks in a cooking tray. 3. Set your air fryer to Air Fry, then adjust the temperature to 385 degrees F and the time to 8 minutes. 4. Press the Start button to initiate preheating. 5. When the screen displays "Add Food," transfer the cooking tray into the air fryer. 6. Close its door, and let the machine do the cooking. 7. Take out and serve hot.
Per serving: Calories 249; Fat 13g; Sodium 556mg; Carbs 10g; Sugar 1.1g; Fiber 0.7g; Protein 31g

Lemony Salmon Fillets

Prep time: 15 minutes | Cook time: 7 minutes | Serves: 8

8 salmon fillets
4 tablespoons fresh lemon
juice
Cajun seasoning, as needed

1. Season salmon fillets with Cajun seasoning and set them aside for 15 minutes. 2. Place salmon fillets in a cooking tray. 3. Set your air fryer to Air Fry, then adjust the temperature to 360 degrees F and the time to 7 minutes. 4. Press the Start button to initiate preheating. 5. When the screen displays "Add Food," transfer the cooking tray into the air fryer. 6. Close its door, and let the machine do the cooking. 7. Drizzle with lemon juice and serve.
Per serving: Calories 305; Fat 15g; Sodium 548mg; Carbs 12g; Sugar 1.2g; Fiber 0.7g; Protein 29g

Fried Coated Fish

Prep time: 15 minutes | Cook time: 14 minutes | Serves: 2

½ cup sesame seeds, toasted
½ teaspoon dried rosemary, crushed
8 tablespoons olive oil
14 frozen fish fillets (white fish of your choice)
6 eggs
½ cup breadcrumbs
8 tablespoons plain flour
Salt
Freshly ground black pepper to taste

1. Take three dishes, place flour in one, crack two eggs in the other and mix the remaining ingredients, except for fillets in the third one. 2. Now, coat fillets in the flour and dip in the beaten two eggs. 3. Then, dredge generously with the sesame seeds mixture. 4. Line the cooking tray with the foil. Arrange fillets in the cooking tray. 5. Set your air fryer to Air Fry, then adjust the temperature to 350 degrees F and the time to 14 minutes. 6. Press the Start button to initiate preheating. 7. When the screen displays "Add Food," transfer the cooking tray into the air fryer. 8. Close its door, and let the machine do the cooking 9. Take out and serve hot.
Per serving: Calories 344; Fat 14.9g; Sodium 227mg; Carbs 14g; Fiber 1g; Sugars 1.4g; Protein 25.7g

Catfish Fillets with Herbs

Prep time: 15 minutes | Cook time: 20 minutes | Serves: 4

4 catfish fillets
¼ cups Louisiana Fish fry
1 tablespoon olive oil
1 tablespoon chopped parsley
optional
lemon, sliced
Fresh herbs to garnish

1. Rinse the fish fillets and pat them try. 2. Rub the fillets with the seasoning and coat well. 3. Spray oil on top of the fillet. 4. Place the fillets in a cooking tray. 5. Set your air fryer to Air Fry, then adjust the temperature to 400 degrees F and the time to 20 minutes. 6. Press the Start button to initiate preheating. 7. When the screen displays "Add Food," transfer the cooking tray into the air fryer. 8. Close its door, and let the machine do the cooking. 9. Garnish with parsley, fresh herbs, and lemon. 10. Serve warm.
Per serving: Calories 351; Fat 22g; Sodium 502mg; Carbs 15.2g; Sugar 1.1g; Fiber 0.7g; Protein 26.4g

Herbed Salmon Fillets

Prep time: 15 minutes | Cook time: 7 minutes | Serves: 4

2 wild-caught salmon fillets, 1 ½ inch thick
2 teaspoons avocado oil or olive oil
2 teaspoons paprika
Salt to taste
Black pepper to taste
Green herbs to garnish

1. Clean the salmon and let it rest for 1 hour at room temperature. 2. Season the fish with olive oil, salt, pepper, and paprika. 3. Arrange the fish in a cooking tray. 4. Set your air fryer to Air Fry, then adjust the temperature to 390 degrees F and the time to 7 minutes. 5. Press the Start button to initiate preheating. 6. When the screen displays "Add Food," transfer the cooking tray into the air fryer. 7. Close its door, and let the machine do the cooking. 8. Garnish with fresh herbs. 9. Serve warm.
Per serving: Calories 344; Fat 14.9g; Sodium 227mg; Carbs 14g; Fiber 1g; Sugars 1.4g; Protein 25.7g

Montreal Raw Shrimp

Prep time: 15 minutes | Cook time: 8 minutes | Serves: 6

1-pound raw shrimp, peeled and deveined
1 egg white
½ cup all-purpose flour
¾ cup panko breadcrumbs
1 teaspoon paprika
1 tablespoon McCormick's Grill Mates Montreal Chicken Seasoning or to taste
Salt and black pepper to taste
Cooking spray

1. Toss the shrimp with Montreal seasonings. 2. Whisk one egg white in a medium-sized bowl. 3. Keep the breadcrumbs and flour in separate bowls. 4. Dredge the shrimp first in the flour, then dip into the one egg white, and then coat with the breadcrumbs. 5. Place the coated shrimps in a baking pan and spray the cooking oil over them. 6. Set your air fryer to Air Fry, then adjust the temperature to 400 degrees F and the time to 8 minutes. 7. Press the Start button to initiate preheating. 8. When the screen displays "Add Food," transfer the cooking tray into the air fryer. 9. Close its door, and let the machine do the cooking. 10. Continue cooking for another 4 minutes 11. Serve warm.
Per serving: Calories 336; Fat 17.3g; Sodium 281mg; Carbs 8.1g; Fiber 5.3g, Sugars 17.7g; Protein 32.3g

Shrimp and Baby Spinach Frittata

Prep time: 15 minutes | Cook time: 10 minutes | Serves: 2

3 eggs	½ cup shrimp, cooked, peeled,
½ teaspoon basil, dried	deveined, and chopped
Cooking spray	½ cup baby spinach, chopped
Salt and black pepper to the	½ cup Monterey jack cheese,
taste	grated
½ cup rice, cooked	

1. Mix two eggs with salt, pepper, and basil in a bowl and whisk. 2. Grease your cooking spray and add rice, shrimp, and spinach. 3. Add 1 egg mix, and sprinkle cheese all over. 4. Set your air fryer to Air Fry, then adjust the temperature to 350 degrees F and the time to 10 minutes. 5. Press the Start button to initiate preheating. 6. When the screen displays "Add Food," transfer the cooking tray into the air fryer. 7. Close its door, and let the machine do the cooking. 8. Divide among plates and serve for breakfast. Enjoy!
Per serving: Calories 254; Fat 28g; Sodium 346mg; Carbs 12.3g; Sugar 1g; Fiber 0.7g; Protein 24.3 g

Tiny Shrimp and Onion Sandwiches

Prep time: 15 minutes | Cook time: 5 minutes | Serves: 2

¼ cups cheddar, shredded	2 tablespoons green onions,
6 ounces canned tiny shrimp,	chopped
drained	4 whole-wheat bread slices
3 tablespoons mayonnaise	2 tablespoons butter, soft

1. Mix shrimp with cheese, green onion, and mayo in a bowl, and stir well. 2. Spread this on half of the bread slices, top with the other slices, cut into halves diagonally, and spread butter on top. 3. Place sandwiches on a cooking tray. 4. Set your air fryer to Air Fry, then adjust the temperature to 350 degrees F and the time to 5 minutes. 5. Press the Start button to initiate preheating. 6. When the screen displays "Add Food," transfer the cooking tray into the air fryer. 7. Close its door, and let the machine do the cooking. 8. Divide shrimp sandwiches onto plates and serve them for breakfast. Enjoy!
Per serving: Calories 285; Fat 9.8g; Sodium 639mg; Carbs 11.1g; Fiber 1.2g, Sugars 5.1g; Protein 27.8g

Tuna-Stuffed Starchy Potatoes

Prep time: 15 minutes | Cook time: 30 minutes | Serves: 4

1½ pounds tuna, dry out	30 minutes
2 tablespoons plain Greek yo-	1 tablespoon capers
gurt	1 teaspoon red chili powder
½ tablespoon olive oil	scallion, chopped and divided
4 starchy potatoes, soaked for	Salt

Freshly ground black pepper   to taste

1. Place the potatoes in a cooking tray. 2. Set your air fryer to Air Fry, then adjust the temperature to 355 degrees F and the time to 30 minutes. 3. Press the Start button to initiate preheating. 4. When the screen displays "Add Food," transfer the cooking tray into the air fryer. 5. Close its door, and let the machine do the cooking. 6. Take out and place on a flat surface. 7. Meanwhile, add yogurt, tuna, red chili powder, scallion, salt, and pepper to a bowl. Mix well. 8. Cut potato from the top side lengthwise and press the open side of potato halves slightly. 9. Stuff potato with tuna mixture and sprinkle with capers. 10. Dish out and serve.
Per serving: Calories 336; Fat 17.3g; Sodium 281mg; Carbs 8.1g; Fiber 5.3g, Sugars 17.7g; Protein 32.3g

Flour-Coated Cod Fillets

Prep time: 15 minutes | Cook time: 10 minutes | Serves: 4

⅓ cup all-purpose flour	1 tablespoon parmesan cheese,
ground black pepper, as re-	grated
quired	⅛ teaspoon cayenne pepper
1 egg	1-pound cod fillets
1 tablespoon water	salt, as required
⅔ cups cornflakes, crushed	

1. Add the flour and black pepper to a shallow dish and mix well. 2. Add one egg and water and beat well in a second shallow dish. 3. Add the cornflakes, cheese, and cayenne pepper to a third shallow dish and mix well. 4. Season the cod fillets with salt evenly. 5. Coat the fillets with flour mixture, dip them into the egg mixture, and coat with the cornflake mixture. 6. Arrange the cod fillets onto the greased cooking tray. 7. Set your air fryer to Air Fry, then adjust the temperature to 400 degrees F and the time to 10 minutes. Press the Start button to initiate preheating. 8. When the screen displays "Add Food," transfer the cooking tray into the air fryer. 9. Close its door, and let the machine do the cooking. 10. Serve.
Per serving: Calories 336; Fat 17.3g; Sodium 281mg; Carbs 8.1g; Fiber 5.3g, Sugars 17.7g; Protein 32.3g

Fried Cod with Spring Onion

Prep time: 15 minutes | Cook time: 12 minutes | Serves: 4

7 ounces' cod fillet, washed	1 teaspoon dark soy sauce
and dried	1 tablespoon olive oil
Spring onion, white and green	5 slices of ginger
parts, chopped	1 cup of water
1 dash of sesame oil	Salt and black pepper to taste
5 tablespoons light soy sauce	

1. Season the cod fillet with a dash of sesame oil, salt, and pepper, then place in a baking pan. 2. Select the "Air Fry" mode on your air fryer. 3. Set your air fryer to Air Fry, then adjust the temperature to 355 degrees F and the time to 12 minutes. Press the Start button to initiate preheating. 4. When the screen displays "Add Food," transfer the cooking tray into the air fryer. 5. Close its door, and let the machine do the cooking. 6. For the seasoning sauce, boil water in a pan on the stovetop, along with light and dark soy sauce, and stir. 7. In another small saucepan, heat the oil and add the ginger and white part of the spring onion. Fry until the ginger browns, then remove the ginger and onions. 8. Top the cod fillet with shredded green onion. Pour the oil over the fillet and add the seasoning sauce on top.
Per serving: Calories 236; Fat 13.9g; Sodium 451mg; Carbs 13.2g; Fiber 1.2g; Sugars 1.4g; Protein 14.3g

Tuna-Spring Onions Salad

Prep time: 15 minutes | Cook time: 15 minutes | Serves: 4

14 ounces canned tuna, drained and flaked
2 spring onions; chopped.
1 cup arugula

1 tablespoon olive oil
1 pinch of salt and black pepper

1. Whisk the tuna, onions, salt, and pepper in a bowl, then transfer to a cooking tray. 2. Set your air fryer to Air Fry, then adjust the temperature to 360 degrees F and the time to 15 minutes. Press the Start button to initiate preheating. 3. When the screen displays "Add Food," transfer the cooking tray into the air fryer. 4. Close its door, and let the machine do the cooking. 5. In a salad bowl, combine the arugula with the tuna mix, toss and serve.
Per serving: Calories 344; Fat 14.9g; Sodium 227mg; Carbs 14g; Fiber 1g; Sugars 1.4g; Protein 25.7g

Cajun Shrimp with Lime Wedges

Prep time: 15 minutes | Cook time: 5 minutes | Serves: 2

¼ teaspoon salt
¼ teaspoon smoked paprika
1 tablespoon garlic powder
1 teaspoon Italian seasoning
½ tablespoon chili powder
1 tablespoon onion powder
¼ teaspoon cayenne pepper

¼ teaspoon black pepper
1 tablespoon dried thyme
16 ounces' large shrimp, peeled and unveiled
1 cup olive oil
Lime wedges, to serve

1. Combine all seasonings in a large bowl. Set aside. 2. Mix the shrimp with olive oil until they are evenly coated. 3. Sprinkle the dressing mixture over the shrimp and stir until well coated. 4. Place the shrimp in a cooking tray. 5. Set your air fryer to Air Fry, then adjust the temperature to 400 degrees F and the time to 5 minutes. Press the Start button to initiate preheating. 6. When the screen displays "Add Food," transfer the cooking tray into the air fryer. 7. Close its door, and let the machine do the cooking. 8. Serve with pieces of lime.
Per serving: Calories 285; Fat 9.8g; Sodium 639mg; Carbs 11.1g; Fiber 1.2g, Sugars 5.1g; Protein 27.8g

Spiced Wild Salmon Fillets

Prep time: 15 minutes | Cook time: 7 minutes | Serves: 2

2 salmon fillets, wild-caught, about 1 ½ inch thick
1 teaspoon ground black pepper

1 teaspoon five-spice powder
1 teaspoon salt
2 teaspoons olive oil

1. Rub salmon fillet with oil and then season with black pepper, five-spice powder, and salt. 2. Set your air fryer to Air Fry, then adjust the temperature to 390 degrees F and the time to 7 minutes. Press the Start button to initiate preheating. 3. When the screen displays "Add Food," transfer the fish to the cooking tray of the air fryer. 4. Close its door, and let the machine do the cooking. 5. When the screen displays "End," transfer salmon onto a serving plate and serve.
Per serving: Calories 344; Fat 14.9g; Sodium 227mg; Carbs 12g; Fiber 1.2g; Sugars 1g; Protein 27g

Mayonnaise Crab Cake

Prep time: 15 minutes | Cook time: 10 minutes | Serves: 2

8 ounces' crab meat, wild-caught
2 tablespoons almond flour
¼ cup red bell pepper, cored,

chopped
1 teaspoon green onion, chopped

1 teaspoon old bay seasoning
1 tablespoon Dijon mustard
2 tablespoons mayonnaise,

1. Place all the ingredients to a bowl, stir until well combined, and then shape the mixture into four patties. 2. Set your air fryer to Air Fry, then adjust the temperature to 370 degrees F and the time to 10 minutes. Press the Start button to initiate preheating. 3. When the screen displays "Add Food," transfer the patties to the rack of the air fryer. 4. Close its door, and let the machine do the cooking. 5. Serve with lemon wedges.
Per serving: Calories 305; Fat 15g; Sodium 548mg; Carbs 12g; Sugar 1.2g; Fiber 0.7g; Protein 29g

Dijon Salmon Cakes with Zucchini

Prep time: 15 minutes | Cook time: 12 minutes | Serves: 2

½ cup almond flour
12 ounces cooked pink salmon
¼ teaspoon ground black pepper
¼ cup shredded zucchini

2 teaspoons Dijon mustard
2 tablespoons chopped fresh dill
2 tablespoons mayonnaise, egg, pastured
wedges of lemon

1. Add all the ingredients to a bowl, except for lemon wedges, stir until combined, and then shape into four patties, about 4-inches. 2. Set your air fryer to Air Fry, then adjust the temperature to 400 degrees F and the time to 12 minutes. Press the Start button to initiate preheating. 3. When the screen displays "Add Food," transfer the cooking tray into the air fryer. 4. Close its door, and let the machine do the cooking. 5. Serve warm.
Per serving: Calories 336; Fat 17.3g; Sodium 281mg; Carbs 8.1g; Fiber 5.3g, Sugars 17.7g; Protein 32.3g

Easy-to-Make Scallops

Prep time: 15 minutes | Cook time: 4 minutes | Serves: 2

12 medium sea scallops, rinsed and patted dry
1 teaspoon fine sea salt
¾ teaspoon ground black pep-

per, plus more for garnish
Fresh thyme leaves for garnish (optional)
Avocado oil spray

1. Coat the cooking tray with avocado oil spray. 2. Place the scallops in a medium bowl and spritz with avocado oil spray. 3. Sprinkle the salt and black pepper to taste to season. 4. When the screen displays "Add Food," transfer the seasoned scallops to the cooking tray, spacing them apart. 5. Set your air fryer to Air Fry, then adjust the temperature to 390 degrees F and the time to 4 minutes. Press the Start button to initiate preheating. 6. When the screen displays "Add Food," transfer the cooking tray into the air fryer. 7. Close its door, and let the machine do the cooking. 8. Sprinkle the pepper and thyme leaves on top for garnish, if desired. 9. Serve immediately.
Per serving: Calories 285; Fat 9.8g; Sodium 639mg; Carbs 11.1g; Fiber 1.2g, Sugars 5.1g; Protein 27.8g

Tilapia Fillets with Lemon Pepper

Prep time: 15 minutes | Cook time: 10 minutes | Serves: 4

1-pound tilapia fillets
1 tablespoon Italian seasoning
2 tablespoons canola oil

2 tablespoons lemon pepper
salt to taste
2 to 3 butter buds

1. Drizzle tilapia fillets with canola oil. 2. Mix salt, lemon pepper, butter buds, and Italian seasoning; spread on the fish. 3. Place the fillet on a cooking tray. 4. Set your air fryer to Air

Fry, then adjust the temperature to 400 degrees F and the time to 10 minutes. 5. Press the Start button to initiate preheating. 6. When the screen displays "Add Food," transfer the cooking tray into the air fryer. 7. Close its door, and let the machine do the cooking. 8. Serve warm.

Per serving: Calories 236; Fat 13.9g; Sodium 451mg; Carbs 13.2g; Fiber 1.2g; Sugars 1.4g; Protein 14.3g

Graham Cracker Crumbed Salmon

Prep time: 15 minutes | Cook time: 12 minutes | Serves: 4

4 salmon fillets
Salt and ground black pepper
1 cup crushed graham crackers

1. Season the salmon fillets with black pepper and salt evenly, then coat with graham crackers. 2. Arrange the fish fillets over the greased cooking tray. 3. Set your air fryer to Air Fry, then adjust the temperature to 350 degrees F and the time to 12 minutes. 4. Press the Start button to initiate preheating. 5. When the screen displays "Add Food," transfer the cooking tray into the air fryer. 6. Close its door, and let the machine do the cooking. 7. Serve hot.

Per serving: Calories 344; Fat 14.9g; Sodium 227mg; Carbs 14g; Fiber 1g; Sugars 1.4g; Protein 25.7g

Palatable Shrimp Skewers

Prep time: 15 minutes | Cook time: 10 minutes | Serves: 2

1 tablespoon lime juice
1 tablespoon honey
¼ teaspoon red pepper flakes
¼ teaspoon pepper
¼ teaspoon ginger
Nonstick cooking spray
1-pound medium shrimp, peel, devein and leave tails on
1 cups peas, drain and chop
½ green bell pepper, chopped fine
¼ cup scallions, chopped

1. Soak eight small wooden skewers in water for 15 minutes. 2. Whisk together lime juice, honey, and spices in a small bowl. 3. When the screen displays "Add Food," transfer 2 tablespoons of the mixture to a medium bowl. 4. Thread five shrimp on a skewer, brush both sides with marinade, and then place in a cooking tray. 5. Set your air fryer to Air Fry, then adjust the temperature to 400 degrees F and the time to 10 minutes. Press the Start button to initiate preheating. 6. When the screen displays "Add Food," transfer the cooking tray into the air fryer. 7. Close its door, and let the machine do the cooking. 8. Add peas, bell pepper, and scallions to the reserved honey mixture, and mix well. 9. Divide salsa evenly between serving plates and top with two skewers. 10. Serve immediately.

Per serving: Calories 254; Fat 28g; Sodium 346mg; Carbs 12.3g; Sugar 1g; Fiber 0.7g; Protein 24.3 g

Lemony Salmon in Poultry Seasoning

Prep time: 15 minutes | Cook time: 7 minutes | Serves: 2

2 salmon fillets
1 tablespoon poultry seasoning
½ teaspoon sugar
1 tablespoon fresh lemon juice

1. Sprinkle the salmon fillets with poultry seasoning and sugar evenly. 2. Arrange the salmon fillets skin-side up in the greased cooking tray. 3. Set your air fryer to Air Fry, then adjust the temperature to 355 degrees F and the time to 7 minutes. 4. Press the Start button to initiate preheating. 5. When the screen displays "Add Food," transfer the cooking tray into the air fryer. 6. Close its door, and let the machine do the cooking. 7. Drizzle with the lemon juice and serve hot.

Per serving: Calories 285; Fat 9.8g; Sodium 639mg; Carbs 11.1g; Fiber 1.2g, Sugars 5.1g; Protein 27.8g

Air Fried Cod Fillets in Soy Sauce

Prep time: 15 minutes | Cook time: 12 minutes | Serves: 2

2 cod fillets
Salt and ground black pepper
¼ teaspoon sesame oil
1 cup water
5 little squares of rock sugar
5 tablespoons light soy sauce
1 teaspoon dark soy sauce
scallions, sliced
¼ cup fresh cilantro, chopped
3 tablespoons olive oil
5 ginger slices

1. Season cod fillet evenly with salt and black pepper and drizzle with sesame oil. 2. Set aside at room temperature for about 15-20 minutes. 3. Dip the fish fillets into one egg and then coat with the breadcrumb mixture. 4. Arrange the cod fillets in the greased cooking tray. 5. Set your air fryer to Air Fry, then adjust the temperature to 355 degrees F and the time to 12 minutes. 6. Press the Start button to initiate preheating. 7. When the screen displays "Add Food," transfer the cooking tray into the air fryer. 8. Close its door, and let the machine do the cooking. 9. Meanwhile, in a small pan, add the water and bring it to a boil. 10. Add the rock sugar and soy sauces and cook until sugar is dissolved, stirring continuously. 11. Remove from the heat and set aside. 12. Remove the cod fillets from the air fryer and transfer them onto serving plates. 13. Top fillet with scallion and cilantro. 14. Heat the olive oil over medium heat in a small frying pan and sauté the ginger slices for about 2-3 minutes. 15. Remove the frying pan from heat and discard the ginger slices. 16. Carefully pour the hot oil evenly over cod fillets. 17. Top with the sauce mixture and serve.

Per serving: Calories 344; Fat 14.9g; Sodium 227mg; Carbs 14g; Fiber 1g; Sugars 1.4g; Protein 25.7g

Coconut Cod Burgers

Prep time: 15 minutes | Cook time: 7 minutes | Serves: 6

½ pound cod fillets
½ teaspoon fresh lime zest, grated finely
½ egg
½ teaspoon red chili paste
Salt, to taste
½ tablespoon fresh lime juice
3 tablespoons coconut, grated and divided
small scallion, chopped finely
1 tablespoon fresh parsley, chopped

1. Add cod filets, lime zest, egg, chili paste, salt, and lime juice in a food processor, and pulse until smooth. 2. When the screen displays "Add Food," transfer the cod mixture into a bowl. 3. Add 1 ½ tablespoons of coconut, scallion, and parsley and mix until well combined. 4. Make six equal-sized patties from the mixture. 5. In a shallow dish, place the remaining coconut. 6. Coat the patties in coconut evenly. 7. Arrange the patties in the greased cooking tray. 8. Set your air fryer to Air Fry, then adjust the temperature to 375 degrees F and the time to 7 minutes. 9. Press the Start button to initiate preheating. 10. When the screen displays "Add Food," transfer the cooking tray into the air fryer. 11. Close its door, and let the machine do the cooking. 12. Serve hot.

Per serving: Calories 285; Fat 9.8g; Sodium 639mg; Carbs 11.1g; Fiber 1.2g, Sugars 5.1g; Protein 27.8g

Boneless Cod Fillets with Grapes

Prep time: 15 minutes | Cook time: 10 minutes | Serves: 2

2 black cod fillets, boneless
1 tablespoon olive oil
1 fennel bulb, thinly sliced
1 cup grapes, halved
½ cup pecans
Salt and black pepper to the taste

1. Drizzle half of the oil over fish fillets, season with salt and pepper, rub well, and place fillets in a cooking tray. 2. Set your air fryer to Air Fry, then adjust the temperature to 400 degrees F and the time to 10 minutes. 3. Press the Start button to initiate preheating. 4. When the screen displays "Add Food," transfer the cooking tray into the air fryer. 5. Close its door, and let the machine do the cooking. 6. In a bowl, mix pecans with grapes, fennel, the rest of the oil, salt, and black pepper, toss to coat, add to a pan and cook for 5 minutes. 7. Divide cod between plates, add fennel and grapes mix on the side, and serve.
Per serving: Calories 236; Fat 13.9g; Sodium 451mg; Carbs 13.2g; Fiber 1.2g; Sugars 1.4g; Protein 14.3g

Tasty Cod Fillets with Pearl Onions

Prep time: 15 minutes | Cook time: 15 minutes | Serves: 2

14 ounces' pearl onions
8 ounces' mushrooms, sliced
2 medium cod fillets
1 tablespoon parsley, dried
1 teaspoon thyme, dried
Black pepper to the taste

1. Put fish in a heat-proof dish that fits your air fryer; add onions, parsley, mushrooms, thyme, and black pepper. 2. Set your air fryer to Air Fry, then adjust the temperature to 350 degrees F and the time to 15 minutes. 3. Press the Start button to initiate preheating. 4. When the screen displays "Add Food," transfer the fish dish on the cooking tray into the air fryer. 5. Close its door, and let the machine do the cooking. 6. Divide everything between plates and serve.
Per serving: Calories 344; Fat 14.9g; Sodium 227mg; Carbs 14g; Fiber 1g; Sugars 1.4g; Protein 25.7g

Toothsome Halibut Steaks

Prep time: 15 minutes | Cook time: 10 minutes | Serves: 3

1-pound halibut steaks
⅔ cup soy sauce
¼ teaspoon red pepper flakes, crushed
¼ cup orange juice
¼ teaspoon ginger, grated
¼ cup sugar
2 tablespoons lime juice
½ cup mirin
garlic clove, minced

1. Put soy sauce in a pan, heat up over medium heat, add mirin, sugar, lime and orange juice, pepper flakes, ginger, and garlic, stir well, bring to a boil and take off the heat. 2. Transfer half of the marinade to a bowl, add halibut, toss to coat, and leave aside in the fridge for 30 minutes. 3. When the screen displays "Add Food," transfer halibut to a cooking tray. 4. Set your air fryer to Air Fry, then adjust the temperature to 390 degrees F and the time to 10 minutes. 5. Press the Start button to initiate preheating. 6. When the screen displays "Add Food," transfer the cooking tray into the air fryer. 7. Close its door, and let the machine do the cooking. 8. Divide halibut steaks on plates, drizzle the rest of the marinade all over, and serve hot.
Per serving: Calories 305; Fat 15g; Sodium 548mg; Carbs 12g; Sugar 1.2g; Fiber 0.7g; Protein 29g

Trout Fillet with Orange Sauce

Prep time: 15 minutes | Cook time: 10 minutes | Serves: 4

4 trout fillets, skinless and boneless
4 spring onions, chopped
1 tablespoon olive oil
1 tablespoon ginger, minced
Salt and black pepper to the taste
Juice and zest from 1 orange

1. Season trout fillets with salt, and pepper, rub them with olive oil and place them in a pan that fits your air fryer. 2. Add ginger, green onions, orange zest, and juice toss well. 3. Set your air fryer to Air Fry, then adjust the temperature to 360 degrees F and the time to 10 minutes. 4. Press the Start button to initiate preheating. 5. When the screen displays "Add Food," transfer the cooking tray into the air fryer. 6. Close its door, and let the machine do the cooking. 7. Divide fish and sauce among plates and serve right away.
Per serving: Calories 285; Fat 9.8g; Sodium 639mg; Carbs 11.1g; Fiber 1.2g; Sugars 5.1g; Protein 27.8g

Air-Fried Cod Fillets with Cherry Tomatoes

Prep time: 15 minutes | Cook time: 10 minutes | Serves: 4

4 cod fillets, skinless and boneless
12 cherry tomatoes, halved
2 tablespoons olive oil
8 black olives, pitted and
roughly chopped
2 tablespoons lemon juice
Salt and black pepper
Cooking spray
1 bunch basil, chopped

1. Season cod with salt and black pepper to taste to the taste; place in a cooking tray. 2. Set your air fryer to Air Fry, then adjust the temperature to 360 degrees F and the time to 10 minutes. 3. Press the Start button to initiate preheating. 4. When the screen displays "Add Food," transfer the cooking tray into the air fryer. 5. Close its door, and let the machine do the cooking. 6. Heat a pan with the oil over medium heat, add tomatoes, olives, and lemon juice, stir, bring to a simmer, add basil, salt, and black pepper, stir well and take off the heat. 7. Divide fish among plates and serve with the vinaigrette drizzled on top.
Per serving: Calories 254; Fat 28g; Sodium 346mg; Carbs 12.3g; Sugar 1g; Fiber 0.7g; Protein 24.3 g

Cod Steaks with Plum Sauce

Prep time: 15 minutes | Cook time: 17 minutes | Serves: 2

2 big cod steaks
½ teaspoon garlic powder
½ teaspoon ginger powder
¼ teaspoon turmeric powder
Salt and black pepper to the taste
1 tablespoon plum sauce
Cooking spray

1. Season cod steaks with salt and pepper, spray them with cooking oil, add garlic powder, ginger powder, and turmeric powder, and rub well. 2. Place cod steaks in a cooking tray. 3. Set your air fryer to Air Fry, then adjust the temperature to 360 degrees F and the time to 15 minutes. 4. Press the Start button to initiate preheating. 5. When the screen displays "Add Food," transfer the cooking tray into the air fryer. 6. Close its door, and let the machine do the cooking. 7. Heat a pan over medium heat, add plum sauce; stir and cook for 2 minutes. 8. Divide cod steaks on plates, drizzle the plum sauce and serve.
Per serving: Calories 336; Fat 17.3g; Sodium 281mg; Carbs 8.1g; Fiber 5.3g; Sugars 17.7g; Protein 32.3g

Cod Carrot Parcel

Prep time: 15 minutes | Cook time: 15 minutes | Serves: 2

2 tablespoons butter, melted
1 tablespoon fresh lemon juice
½ teaspoon dried tarragon
Salt and ground black pepper
½ cup red bell peppers, seeded and thinly sliced
½ cup carrots, peeled and julienned
½ cup fennel bulbs, julienned
2 frozen cod fillets, thawed
1 tablespoon olive oil

1. Mix the butter, lemon juice, tarragon, salt, and black pepper in a large bowl. 2. Add the bell pepper, carrot, and fennel bulbs and generously coat with the mixture. 3. Arrange two large parchment squares onto a smooth surface. 4. Coat the cod fillets with oil and then sprinkle evenly with salt and black pepper. 5. Arrange cod fillets onto the parchment square and top evenly with the vegetables. 6. Top with any remaining sauce from the bowl. 7. Fold the parchment paper and crimp the sides to secure the fish and vegetables. 8. Arrange the cod parcels in the cooking tray. 9. Set your air fryer to Air Fry, then adjust the temperature to 350 degrees F and the time to 15 minutes. 10. Press the Start button to initiate preheating. 11. When the screen displays "Add Food," transfer the cooking tray into the air fryer. 12. Close its door, and let the machine do the cooking. 13. Serve hot.

Per serving: Calories 336; Fat 17.3g; Sodium 281mg; Carbs 8.1g; Fiber 5.3g, Sugars 17.7g; Protein 32.3g

Simple-Cooked Scallops

Prep time: 15 minutes | Cook time: 5 minutes | Serves: 4

8 scallops
salt and pepper

1. Arrange scallops in a cooking tray. 2. Spray scallops with cooking spray and season with pepper and salt. 3. Set your air fryer to Air Fry, then adjust the temperature to 390 degrees F and the time to 5 minutes. 4. Press the Start button to initiate preheating. 5. When the screen displays "Add Food," transfer the cooking tray into the air fryer. 6. Close its door, and let the machine do the cooking. 7. Serve and enjoy.

Per serving: Calories 344; Fat 14.9g; Sodium 227mg; Carbs 14g; Fiber 1g; Sugars 1.4g; Protein 25.7g

Crispy Shrimp

Prep time: 15 minutes | Cook time: 12 minutes | Serves: 4

1-pound shrimp, peeled and deveined
½ cup shredded coconut
1 cup breadcrumbs
1 egg white, lightly beaten
½ cup flour
salt and pepper

1. Mix flour, pepper, and salt in a shallow dish. 2. In a second shallow dish, add the egg white. 3. Mix breadcrumbs, shredded coconut, and salt in a third shallow dish. 4. Coat shrimp with flour mixture, coat with the egg mixture, and coat with breadcrumb mixture. 5. Arrange shrimp in a cooking tray. 6. Set your air fryer to Air Fry, then adjust the temperature to 400 degrees F and the time to 12 minutes. 7. Press the Start button to initiate preheating. 8. When the screen displays "Add Food," transfer the cooking tray into the air fryer. 9. Close its door, and let the machine do the cooking. 10. Serve and enjoy.

Per serving: Calories 236; Fat 13.9g; Sodium 451mg; Carbs 13.2g; Fiber 1.2g; Sugars 1.4g; Protein 14.3g

Garlic Shrimp Scampi

Prep time: 15 minutes | Cook time: 10 minutes | Serves: 4

1-pound shrimp
1 cup breadcrumbs
¼ teaspoon onion powder
¼ teaspoon paprika
¼ teaspoon cayenne pepper
¼ cup white wine
3 garlic cloves, minced
8 tablespoons butter
½ teaspoon salt

1. Mix breadcrumbs, onion powder, paprika, cayenne pepper, and salt in a bowl. Set aside. 2. Melt butter in a pan over medium heat. 3. Add white wine and garlic to melted butter and stir well. 4. Remove pan from heat. Add breadcrumbs and shrimp to the melted butter mixture, stir everything well, and transfer to a cooking tray. 5. Set your air fryer to Air Fry, then adjust the temperature to 350 degrees F and the time to 10 minutes. 6. Press the Start button to initiate preheating. 7. When the screen displays "Add Food", transfer the cooking tray into the air fryer. 8. Close its door, and let the machine do the cooking. 9. Serve and enjoy.

Per serving: Calories 305; Fat 15g; Sodium 548mg; Carbs 12g; Sugar 1.2g; Fiber 0.7g; Protein 29g

Dijon Salmon with Parsley

Prep time: 15 minutes | Cook time: 15 minutes | Serves: 4

1-pound salmon fillets
½ tablespoon Dijon mustard
1 tablespoon garlic, minced
1 tablespoon fresh lemon juice
1 tablespoon olive oil
2 tablespoons fresh parsley, chopped
⅛ teaspoon pepper
½ teaspoon salt

1. Mix Dijon mustard, garlic, lemon juice, olive oil, parsley, pepper, and salt in a small bowl. 2. Arrange salmon fillets in a cooking tray. 3. Spread marinade over salmon fillets. 4. Set your air fryer to Air Fry, then adjust the temperature to 400 degrees F and the time to 15 minutes. 5. Press the Start button to initiate preheating. 6. When the screen displays "Add Food," transfer the cooking tray into the air fryer. 7. Close its door, and let the machine do the cooking. 8. Serve and enjoy.

Per serving: Calories 336; Fat 17.3g; Sodium 281mg; Carbs 8.1g; Fiber 5.3g, Sugars 17.7g; Protein 32.3g

Sweet Salmon Fillets with Lemon Wedges

Prep time: 15 minutes | Cook time: 7 minutes | Serves: 4

1 salmon fillet
1 teaspoon Cajun seasoning
lemon wedges for serving
1 teaspoon liquid stevia
½ lemon, juiced

1. Combine lemon juice and liquid stevia, and coat salmon with this mixture. 2. Sprinkle Cajun seasoning all over salmon. 3. Place salmon on parchment paper in a cooking tray. 4. Set your air fryer to Air Fry, then adjust the temperature to 350 degrees F and the time to 7 minutes. 5. Press the Start button to initiate preheating. 6. When the screen displays "Add Food," transfer the cooking tray into the air fryer. 7. Close its door, and let the machine do the cooking. 8. Serve with lemon wedges.

Per serving: Calories 285; Fat 9.8g; Sodium 639mg; Carbs 11.1g; Fiber 1.2g, Sugars 5.1g; Protein 27.8g

Flour Coated Shrimp

Prep time: 15 minutes | Cook time: 10 minutes | Serves: 3

1 tablespoon rice flour	1 teaspoon powdered Sugar
1-pound shrimp, peeled and deveined	Salt and black pepper, as required
1 tablespoon olive oil	

1. Mix rice flour, olive oil, sugar, salt, and black pepper in a bowl. 2. Stir in the shrimp and transfer half of the shrimp to the cooking tray. 3. Set your air fryer to Air Fry, then adjust the temperature to 325 degrees F and the time to 10 minutes. 4. Press the Start button to initiate preheating. 5. When the screen displays "Add Food," transfer the cooking tray into the air fryer. 6. Close its door, and let the machine do the cooking. 7. Dish the mixture onto serving plates and repeat with the remaining mixture.

Per serving: Calories 236; Fat 13.9g; Sodium 451mg; Carbs 13.2g; Fiber 1.2g; Sugars 1.4g; Protein 14.3g

Cod Sticks

Prep time: 15 minutes | Cook time: 10 minutes | Serves: 4

1-pound cod fillet; cut into ¾-inch strips	1 large egg.
1-ounce pork rinds, finely ground	¼ cup blanched finely ground almond flour.
	1 tablespoon coconut oil

1. Place ground pork rinds, almond flour, and coconut oil into a large bowl and mix. 2. Take a medium bowl, beat egg. 3. Dip the fish stick into the egg and coat with the flour mixture. 4. Place fish sticks into the cooking tray. 5. Set your air fryer to Air Fry, then adjust the temperature to 400 degrees F and the time to 10 minutes. 6. Press the Start button to initiate preheating. 7. When the screen displays "Add Food," transfer the cooking tray into the air fryer. 8. Close its door, and let the machine do the cooking. 9. Serve immediately.

Per serving: Calories 249; Fat 13g; Sodium 556mg; Carbs 10g; Sugar 1.1g; Fiber 0.7g; Protein 31g

Buttered Salmon with Almonds

Prep time: 15 minutes | Cook time: 12 minutes | Serves: 4

1 ½ inch-thick salmon fillets: about 4 ounces	¼ cup pesto
¼ cup sliced almonds, roughly chopped	1 tablespoon unsalted butter; melted.

1. In a small bowl, mix pesto and almonds. Set aside. Place fillets into a 6-inch round baking pan. 2. Brush the fillet with butter and place half of the pesto mixture on the top of the fillet. 3. Set your air fryer to Air Fry, then adjust the temperature to 390 degrees F and the time to 12 minutes. 4. Press the Start button to initiate preheating. 5. When the screen displays "Add Food," transfer the cooking tray into the air fryer. 6. Close its door, and let the machine do the cooking. 7. Serve warm.

Per serving: Calories 344; Fat 14.9g; Sodium 227mg; Carbs 14g; Fiber 1g; Sugars 1.4g; Protein 25.7g

Old Bay Shrimp

Prep time: 15 minutes | Cook time: 6 minutes | Serves: 4

8 ounces' medium shelled and deveined shrimp	melted.
1 medium lemon.	½ teaspoon minced garlic
2 tablespoons unsalted butter;	½ teaspoon Old Bay seasoning

1. Zest lemon and then cut in half. 2. Place shrimp in a large bowl and squeeze juice from ½ lemon on top. 3. Add lemon zest to the bowl along with the remaining ingredients. Toss shrimp until fully coated. 4. Pour the bowl contents into a 6-inch round cooking tray. Place into the cooking tray. 5. Set your air fryer to Air Fry, then adjust the temperature to 400 degrees F and the time to 6 minutes. 6. Press the Start button to initiate preheating. 7. When the screen displays "Add Food," transfer the cooking tray into the air fryer. 8. Close its door, and let the machine do the cooking. 9. Serve warm with pan sauce.

Per serving: Calories 336; Fat 17.3g; Sodium 281mg; Carbs 8.1g; Fiber 5.3g, Sugars 17.7g; Protein 32.3g

Easy Crab Sticks

Prep time: 15 minutes | Cook time: 10 minutes | Serves: 4

1 package of crab sticks	Cooking oil spray: as needed

1. Arrange the crab sticks in a baking pan and lightly spritz using cooking spray. 2. Set your air fryer to Air Fry, then adjust the temperature to 350 degrees F and the time to 10 minutes. 3. Press the Start button to initiate preheating. 4. When the screen displays "Add Food," transfer the cooking tray into the air fryer. 5. Close its door, and let the machine do the cooking. 6. Serve warm.

Per serving: Calories 305; Fat 15g; Sodium 548mg; Carbs 12g; Sugar 1.2g; Fiber 0.7g; Protein 29g

Pecan Crusted Salmon in Lemon Juice

Prep time: 15 minutes | Cook time: 7 minutes | Serves: 4

4 Salmon fillets	Salt and black pepper to taste
Juice of ¼ lemon	1 cup pecan, crushed

1. Rinse and pat the salmon dry. Thoroughly coat the fish with salt and black pepper. 2. Arrange the fillet in the cooking tray and drizzle pecan on top. 3. Set your air fryer to Air Fry, then adjust the temperature to 355 degrees F and the time to 7 minutes. 4. Press the Start button to initiate preheating. 5. When the screen displays "Add Food," transfer the cooking tray into the air fryer. 6. Close its door, and let the machine do the cooking. 7. Serve with a drizzle of lemon.

Per serving: Calories 285; Fat 9.8g; Sodium 639mg; Carbs 11.1g; Fiber 1.2g, Sugars 5.1g; Protein 27.8g

Salmon Fillets with Sesame Seeds

Prep time: 15 minutes | Cook time: 5 minutes | Serves: 4

4 salmon fillets	⅓ cup water
1 tablespoon olive oil	1 tablespoon sesame seeds
⅓ cup light soy sauce	Salt and black pepper to taste

1. Season salmon fillets with salt and pepper. Mix the remaining ingredients in a bowl. 2. Allow the salmon fillets to marinate in the mixture for 2 hours, then transfer to a cooking tray. 3. Drizzle sesame seeds on top. 4. Set your air fryer to Air Fry, then adjust the temperature to 355 degrees F and the time to 5 minutes. 5. Press the Start button to initiate preheating. 6. When the screen displays "Add Food," transfer the cooking tray into the air fryer. 7. Close its door, and let the machine do the cooking. 8. Serve warm.

Per serving: Calories 254; Fat 28g; Sodium 346mg; Carbs 12.3g; Sugar 1g; Fiber 0.7g; Protein 24.3 g

Catfish Fillets in Fish Fry

Prep time: 15 minutes | Cook time: 10 minutes | Serves: 3

1 tablespoon olive oil
25 cups seasoned fish fry
4 catfish fillets

1. First, wash the fish, and dry with a paper towel. 2. Dump the seasoning into a sizeable zip-type baggie. 3. Add the fish and shake to cover the fillet. Spray with a spritz of cooking oil spray. Add to the cooking tray. 4. Set your air fryer to Air Fry, then adjust the temperature to 400 degrees F and the time to 10 minutes. 5. Press the Start button to initiate preheating. 6. When the screen displays "Add Food," transfer the cooking tray into the air fryer. 7. Close its door, and let the machine do the cooking. 8. Serve warm.

Per serving: Calories 236; Fat 13.9g; Sodium 451mg; Carbs 13.2g; Fiber 1.2g; Sugars 1.4g; Protein 14.3g

Spicy Boneless Cod Fillets

Prep time: 15 minutes | Cook time: 10 minutes | Serves: 4

4 cod fillets; boneless
2 tablespoons assorted chili peppers
1 lemon; sliced
Juice of 1 lemon
Salt and black pepper to taste

1. In your cooking tray, mix the cod with the chili pepper, lemon juice, salt, and black pepper, to taste 2. Arrange the lemon slices on top. 3. Set your air fryer to Air Fry, then adjust the temperature to 360 degrees F and the time to 10 minutes. 4. Press the Start button to initiate preheating. 5. When the screen displays "Add Food," transfer the cooking tray into the air fryer. 6. Close its door, and let the machine do the cooking. 7. Divide the fillets between plates and serve.

Per serving: Calories 285; Fat 9.8g; Sodium 639mg; Carbs 11.1g; Fiber 1.2g, Sugars 5.1g; Protein 27.8g

Buttered Lobster Tails

Prep time: 15 minutes | Cook time: 8 minutes | Serves: 2

2 tablespoons unsalted butter, melted
1 tablespoon minced garlic
1 teaspoon salt
1 tablespoon chopped fresh chives
2 (4- to 6-ounce) frozen lobster tails

1. In a bowl, mix the butter, garlic, salt, and chives. 2. Butterfly the lobster tail: starting at the meaty end of the tail, use kitchen shears to cut down the center of the top shell. 3. Carefully spread the meat and shell apart along the cut line, but keep the meat attached where it connects to the wide part of the tail. 4. Gently disconnect the meat from the bottom of the shell. 5. Lift the meat up and out of the shell. 6. Close the shell under the meat so the meat rests on top of the shell. 7. Place the lobster in a cooking tray and brush the butter mixture over the meat. 8. Set your air fryer to Air Fry, then adjust the temperature to 380 degrees F and the time to 8 minutes. 9. Press the Start button to initiate preheating. 10. When the screen displays "Add Food," transfer the cooking tray into the air fryer. 11. Close its door, and let the machine do the cooking. 12. Serve warm.

Per serving: Calories 305; Fat 15g; Sodium 548mg; Carbs 12g; Sugar 1.2g; Fiber 0.7g; Protein 29g

Sea Scallops with Thyme Leaves

Prep time: 15 minutes | Cook time: 5 minutes | Serves: 4

12 medium sea scallops
1 teaspoon fine sea salt
ground black pepper as desired
Fresh thyme leaves for garnish (optional)

1. Grease the cooking tray with avocado oil. 2. Rinse the scallops and pat them completely dry. 3. Spray avocado oil on the scallops and season them with salt and pepper. 4. Place them in a cooking tray, spacing them apart. 5. Set your air fryer to Air Fry, then adjust the temperature to 390 degrees F and the time to 5 minutes. 6. Press the Start button to initiate preheating. 7. When the screen displays "Add Food," transfer the cooking tray into the air fryer. 8. Close its door, and let the machine do the cooking. 9. Flip the scallops after cooking for 2 minutes, and cook for another 2 minutes. 10. Garnish with ground black pepper and thyme leaves, if desired. Best served fresh.

Per serving: Calories 236; Fat 13.9g; Sodium 451mg; Carbs 13.2g; Fiber 1.2g; Sugars 1.4g; Protein 14.3g

Spiced Catfish

Prep time: 15 minutes | Cook time: 10 minutes | Serves: 4

1 tablespoon chopped parsley
1 tablespoon olive oil
¼ cup seasoned fish fry
4 catfish fillets

1. Rinse off catfish fillets and pat dry. 2. Add fish fry seasoning to Ziploc baggie, then catfish. 3. Shake the bag and ensure the fish gets well coated. 4. Spray fillet with olive oil. Add fillets to the cooking tray. 5. Set your air fryer to Air Fry, then adjust the temperature to 400 degrees F and the time to 10 minutes. 6. Press the Start button to initiate preheating. 7. When the screen displays "Add Food," transfer the cooking tray into the air fryer. 8. Close its door, and let the machine do the cooking. 9. Serve warm.

Per serving: Calories 344; Fat 14.9g; Sodium 227mg; Carbs 14g; Fiber 1g; Sugars 1.4g; Protein 25.7g

Tasty Pecan-Crusted Catfish

Prep time: 15 minutes | Cook time: 12 minutes | Serves: 4

½ cup pecan meal
1 teaspoon fine sea salt
¼ teaspoon ground black pepper
4 (4 ounces) catfish fillets
Fresh oregano, optional for garnish

1. Grease the cooking tray with avocado oil. 2. Mix the pecan meal, salt, and pepper in a large bowl. 3. One at a time, dredge the catfish fillets in the mixture, coating them well. 4. Use your hands to press the pecan meal into the fillets. 5. Spray the fish with avocado oil and place them on a cooking tray. 6. Set your air fryer to Air Fry, then adjust the temperature to 375 degrees F and the time to 12 minutes. 7. Press the Start button to initiate preheating. 8. When the screen displays "Add Food," transfer the cooking tray into the air fryer. 9. Close its door, and let the machine do the cooking. 10. Garnish with oregano sprigs and pecan halves, if desired. 11. Serve warm.

Per serving: Calories 285; Fat 9.8g; Sodium 639mg; Carbs 11.1g; Fiber 1.2g, Sugars 5.1g; Protein 27.8g

Cod Tacos

Prep time: 15 minutes | Cook time: 15 minutes | Serves: 4

1-pound cod	10 ounces of Mexican beer
1 tablespoon cumin	2 eggs
½ tablespoon chili powder	Salt and pepper
1 ½ cups coconut flour	

1. Whisk beer and two eggs together in 1 bowl. 2. Mix flour, pepper, salt, cumin, and chili powder in a bowl. 3. Slice cod into large pieces and coat in 1 egg mixture, then flour. 4. Spray the bottom of your cooking tray with olive oil and add coated codpieces. 5. Set your air fryer to Air Fry, then adjust the temperature to 350 degrees F and the time to 15 minutes. 6. Press the Start button to initiate preheating. 7. When the screen displays "Add Food," transfer the cooking tray into the air fryer. 8. Close its door, and let the machine do the cooking. 9. Serve on lettuce leaves topped with homemade salsa.
Per serving: Calories 344; Fat 14.9g; Sodium 227mg; Carbs 14g; Fiber 1g; Sugars 1.4g; Protein 25.7g

Herbed Shrimp

Prep time: 15 minutes | Cook time: 5 minutes | Serves: 4

1 ¼ pounds shrimp, peeled and deveined	¼ cayenne pepper
½ teaspoon paprika	½ teaspoon Old Bay seasoning
1 tablespoon olive oil	

1. Mix all the ingredients in a bowl. Place the seasoned shrimp into the cooking tray. 2. Set your air fryer to Air Fry, then adjust the temperature to 400 degrees F and the time to 5 minutes. 3. Press the Start button to initiate preheating. 4. When the screen displays "Add Food," transfer the cooking tray into the air fryer. 5. Close its door, and let the machine do the cooking. 6. Serve warm.
Per serving: Calories 236; Fat 13.9g; Sodium 451mg; Carbs 13.2g; Fiber 1.2g; Sugars 1.4g; Protein 14.3g

Creamy Salmon

Prep time: 15 minutes | Cook time: 10 minutes | Serves: 2

¾ pound salmon, cut into six pieces	1 tablespoon dill, chopped
¼ cup plain yogurt	3 tablespoons light sour cream
	1 tablespoon olive oil

1. Flavor the salmon with salt and put it on a cooking tray. Drizzle the salmon with olive oil. 2. Set your air fryer to Air Fry, then adjust the temperature to 285 degrees F and the time to 10 minutes. 3. Press the Start button to initiate preheating. 4. When the screen displays "Add Food," transfer the cooking tray into the air fryer. 5. Close its door, and let the machine do the cooking. 6. Mix the dill, yogurt, sour cream, and salt in a bowl. 7. Place salmon on the serving dish and drizzle with creamy sauce. 8. Serve warm.
Per serving: Calories 305; Fat 15g; Sodium 548mg; Carbs 12g; Sugar 1.2g; Fiber 0.7g; Protein 29g

Lime Shrimp

Prep time: 15 minutes | Cook time: 15 minutes | Serves: 4

4 cups shrimp	1 fresh lime, cut into quarters
1 ½ cups barbeque sauce	

1. Place the shrimp in a bowl with barbeque sauce. Stir gently. 2. Allow shrimps to marinade for at least 5 minutes and place the shrimp in a cooking tray. 3. Set your air fryer to Air Fry, then adjust the temperature to 360 degrees F and the time to 15 minutes. 4. Press the Start button to initiate preheating. 5. When the screen displays "Add Food," transfer the cooking tray into the air fryer. 6. Close its door, and let the machine do the cooking. 7. Remove from air fryer and squeeze lime over shrimps. 8. Serve warm.
Per serving: Calories 285; Fat 9.8g; Sodium 639mg; Carbs 11.1g; Fiber 1.2g, Sugars 5.1g; Protein 27.8g

Cheese Tilapia Fillets

Prep time: 15 minutes | Cook time: 10 minutes | Serves: 4

1-pound tilapia fillets	2 teaspoons paprika
1 tablespoon olive oil	¾ cup parmesan cheese, grated
Salt and black pepper to taste	

1. Mix the parmesan cheese, paprika, salt, and pepper. 2. Drizzle olive oil over the tilapia fillets and coat with paprika and cheese. 3. Place the coated tilapia fillets on aluminum foil. 4. Set your air fryer to Air Fry, then adjust the temperature to 400 degrees F and the time to 10 minutes. 5. Press the Start button to initiate preheating. 6. When the screen displays "Add Food," transfer the fish to the rack of the air fryer. 7. Close its door, and let the machine do the cooking. 8. Serve warm.
Per serving: Calories 336; Fat 17.3g; Sodium 281mg; Carbs 8.1g; Fiber 5.3g, Sugars 17.7g; Protein 32.3g

Parmesan Salmon Fillets with Parsley

Prep time: 15 minutes | Cook time: 10 minutes | Serves: 6

2 pounds' salmon fillet	ed
salt and black pepper to taste	¼ cup parsley, fresh, chopped
½ cup parmesan cheese, grat-	2 garlic cloves, minced

1. Put the salmon skin side facing down on aluminum foil and cover with another piece of foil. 2. Set your air fryer to Air Fry, then adjust the temperature to 350 degrees F and the time to 10 minutes. 3. Press the Start button to initiate preheating. 4. When the screen displays "Add Food," transfer the foil to the cooking tray of the air fryer. 5. Close its door, and let the machine do the cooking. 6. Remove the salmon from the foil and top it with minced garlic, parsley, parmesan cheese, and pepper. 7. Serve warm.
Per serving: Calories 344; Fat 14.9g; Sodium 227mg; Carbs 14g; Fiber 1g; Sugars 1.4g; Protein 25.7g

Air-Fried Salmon and Asparagus

Prep time: 15 minutes | Cook time: 15 minutes | Serves: 4

4 salmon fillets	3 lemons, sliced
4 asparagus	Salt and black pepper to taste
2 tablespoons butter	

1. Take four pieces of aluminum foil. 2. Add asparagus, half lemon juice, pepper, and salt to a bowl and toss. 3. Divide seasoned asparagus evenly on four aluminum foil pieces. Put one salmon fillet asparagus. 4. Put some lemon slices on top of the salmon fillets. 5. Fold foil tightly to seal the parcel. 6. Set your air fryer to Air Fry, then adjust the temperature to 300 degrees F and the time to 15 minutes. 7. Press the Start button to initiate preheating. 8. When the screen displays "Add Food," transfer the parcels to the cooking tray of the air fryer. 9. Close its door, and let the machine do the cooking. 10. Serve warm.

Per serving: Calories 285; Fat 9.8g; Sodium 639mg; Carbs 11.1g; Fiber 1.2g, Sugars 5.1g; Protein 27.8g

Fresh Salmon Fillets with Blue Cheese

Prep time: 15 minutes | Cook time: 10 minutes | Serves: 5

2 pounds' fresh salmon fillet
Salt and black pepper to taste
½ cup blue cheese, grated
¼ cup fresh parsley, chopped
2 garlic cloves, minced

1. Put some salmon with the skin side down on foil and cover with more foil. 2. Set your air fryer to Air Fry, then adjust the temperature to 300 degrees F and the time to 10 minutes. 3. Press the Start button to initiate preheating. 4. When the screen displays "Add Food," transfer the foil pack to the cooking tray of the air fryer. 5. Close its door, and let the machine do the cooking. 6. Open the foil and top salmon with cheese, garlic, pepper, salt, and parsley. 7. Return for an additional minute in the air fryer. 8. Serve warm.
Per serving: Calories 254; Fat 28g; Sodium 346mg; Carbs 12.3g; Sugar 1g; Fiber 0.7g; Protein 24.3 g

Grilled Prawns with Rosemary Sprig

Prep time: 15 minutes | Cook time: 7 minutes | Serves: 4

8 medium prawns
Salt and black pepper to taste
3 garlic cloves, minced
1 tablespoon butter, melted
1 rosemary sprig

1. Add ingredients to a bowl and toss well. 2. Add the marinated prawns to the cooking tray. 3. Set your air fryer to Air Fry, then adjust the temperature to 300 degrees F and the time to 7 minutes. 4. Press the Start button to initiate preheating. 5. When the screen displays "Add Food," transfer the cooking tray into the air fryer. 6. Close its door, and let the machine do the cooking. 7. Serve warm.
Per serving: Calories 305; Fat 15g; Sodium 548mg; Carbs 12g; Sugar 1.2g; Fiber 0.7g; Protein 29g

Scallops with Basil Pesto

Prep time: 15 minutes | Cook time: 12 minutes | Serves: 4

1-pound Scallops
3 tablespoons heavy cream
¼ cups basil pesto
1 tablespoon olive oil
salt and pepper

1. Season scallops with pepper and salt; transfer the seasoned scallops to the cooking tray. 2. Set your air fryer to Air Fry, then adjust the temperature to 320 degrees F and the time to 12 minutes. 3. Press the Start button to initiate preheating. 4. When the screen displays "Add Food," transfer the cooking tray into the air fryer. 5. Close its door, and let the machine do the cooking. 6. Meanwhile, in a small pan, heat olive oil over medium heat. 7. Add pesto and heavy cream and cook for 2 minutes. Remove from heat. 8. Add scallops into the mixing bowl. Pour pesto sauce over scallops and toss well. 9. Serve and enjoy.
Per serving: Calories 236; Fat 13.9g; Sodium 451mg; Carbs 13.2g; Fiber 1.2g; Sugars 1.4g; Protein 14.3g

Creamy Shrimp with Salad Dressing

Prep time: 15 minutes | Cook time: 10 minutes | Serves: 4

1 pound of shrimp, deveined and cleaned
1-ounce parmesan cheese, grated
1 tablespoon garlic, minced
1 tablespoon lemon juice
¼ cup salad dressing

1. Spray a cooking tray with cooking spray. 2. Add shrimp to the cooking tray. 3. Set your air fryer to Air Fry, then adjust the temperature to 400 degrees F and the time to 6 minutes. 4. Press the Start button to initiate preheating. 5. When the screen displays "Add Food," transfer the cooking tray into the air fryer. 6. Close its door, and let the machine do the cooking. 7. When the screen displays "End," transfer shrimp into the mixing bowl. Add remaining ingredients over shrimp and stir for 1 minute. 8. Serve and enjoy.
Per serving: Calories 285; Fat 9.8g; Sodium 639mg; Carbs 11.1g; Fiber 1.2g, Sugars 5.1g; Protein 27.8g

Garlic Butter Salmon

Prep time: 15 minutes | Cook time: 7 minutes | Serves: 4

1-pound salmon fillets
2 tablespoons garlic, minced
¼ cups parmesan cheese, grated
¼ cups butter, melted
Salt and black pepper to taste

1. Season salmon with pepper and salt. 2. Mix butter, cheese, and garlic in a bowl, and brush over salmon fillets. 3. Place salmon fillets on a cooking tray. 4. Set your air fryer to Air Fry, then adjust the temperature to 400 degrees F and the time to 7 minutes. 5. Press the Start button to initiate preheating. 6. When the screen displays "Add Food," transfer the tray to the rack of the air fryer. 7. Close its door, and let the machine do the cooking. 8. Serve and enjoy.
Per serving: Calories 249; Fat 13g; Sodium 556mg; Carbs 10g; Sugar 1.1g; Fiber 0.7g; Protein 31g

Horseradish Salmon Fillets

Prep time: 15 minutes | Cook time: 7 minutes | Serves: 2

2 salmon fillets
¼ cup breadcrumbs
2 tablespoons olive oil
1 tablespoon horseradish
Salt and black pepper to taste

1. Place salmon fillets on a cooking tray. 2. Mix breadcrumbs, oil, horseradish, pepper, and salt in a small bowl and spread over salmon fillets. 3. Set your air fryer to Air Fry, then adjust the temperature to 400 degrees F and the time to 7 minutes. 4. Press the Start button to initiate preheating. 5. When the screen displays "Add Food," transfer the cooking tray into the air fryer. 6. Close its door, and let the machine do the cooking. 7. Serve and enjoy.
Per serving: Calories 336; Fat 17.3g; Sodium 281mg; Carbs 8.1g; Fiber 5.3g, Sugars 17.7g; Protein 32.3g

Chili Salmon with Lemon Slices

Prep time: 15 minutes | Cook time: 8 minutes | Serves: 3

1½ pounds salmon
½ teaspoon red chili powder
Salt and ground black pepper, as required
1 lemon, cut into slices
1 tablespoon fresh dill, chopped

1. Season the salmon with chili powder, salt, and black pepper. 2. Arrange the salmon fillets in the greased cooking tray. 3. Set your air fryer to Air Fry, then adjust the temperature to 375 degrees F and the time to 8 minutes. 4. Press the Start button to initiate preheating. 5. When the screen displays "Add Food," transfer the cooking tray into the air fryer. 6. Close its door, and let the machine do the cooking. 7. Garnish with fresh dill and serve hot.
Per serving: Calories 351; Fat 22g; Sodium 502mg; Carbs 15.2g; Sugar 1.1g; Fiber 0.7g; Protein 26.4g

Salmon and Potato Croquettes with Parsley

Prep time: 15 minutes | Cook time: 5 minutes | Serves: 4

½ pound red salmon
½ pound of potatoes, boiled and mashed
1 cup breadcrumbs

half of 1 bunch of chopped parsley
2 eggs

1. Drain and mash the salmon. Whisk and add the two eggs, potatoes, and parsley. 2. In another dish, mix the breadcrumbs and oil. 3. Prepare 16 croquettes using the breadcrumb mixture, then transfer to a cooking tray. 4. Set your air fryer to Air Fry, then adjust the temperature to 390 degrees F and the time to 5 minutes. 5. Press the Start button to initiate preheating. 6. When the screen displays "Add Food," transfer the cooking tray into the air fryer. 7. Close its door, and let the machine do the cooking. 8. Serve.

Per serving: Calories 254; Fat 28g; Sodium 346mg; Carbs 12.3g; Sugar 1g; Fiber 0.7g; Protein 24.3 g

Center-Cut Bacon-Wrapped Scallops

Prep time: 15 minutes | Cook time: 6 minutes | Serves: 4

1 tablespoon paprika
1 tablespoon lemon pepper

5 slices of center-cut bacon
20 raw sea scallops

1. Rinse and drain scallops on paper towels to soak up excess moisture. 2. Cut slices of bacon into four pieces. 3. With a piece of bacon, wrap scallop, then use toothpicks to secure. 4. Sprinkle wrapped scallops with paprika and lemon pepper, then place in a cooking tray. 5. Set your air fryer to Air Fry, then adjust the temperature to 400 degrees F and the time to 6 minutes. 6. Press the Start button to initiate preheating. 7. When the screen displays "Add Food," transfer the cooking tray into the air fryer. 8. Close its door, and let the machine do the cooking. 9. serve warm.

Per serving: Calories 351; Fat 22g; Sodium 502mg; Carbs 15.2g; Sugar 1.1g; Fiber 0.7g; Protein 26.4g

Quick Fried Catfish in Seafood Seasoning

Prep time: 15 minutes | Cook time: 15 minutes | Serves: 4

¾ cup original Bisquick™ mix
½ cup yellow cornmeal
1 tablespoon seafood season-

ing
4 catfish fillets (4-6 ounces)
½ cup ranch dressing

1. Mix the Bisquick mix, cornmeal, and seafood seasoning in a bowl. 2. Pat the filets dry and then brush them with ranch dressing. 3. Press the filets into the Bisquick mix on both sides until the filet is evenly coated. 4. Set your air fryer to Air Fry, then adjust the temperature to 360 degrees F and the time to 15 minutes. 5. Press the Start button to initiate preheating. 6. When the screen displays "Add Food," transfer the fish to the cooking tray of the air fryer. 7. Close its door, and let the machine do the cooking. 8. Serve.

Per serving: Calories 344; Fat 14.9g; Sodium 227mg; Carbs 12g; Fiber 1.2g; Sugars 1g; Protein 27g

Salmon Parcel in Champagne

Prep time: 15 minutes | Cook time: 13 minutes | Serves: 2

2 (4-ounce) salmon fillets
6 asparagus stalks
¼ cup white sauce
1 teaspoon oil

¼ cup champagne
Salt and ground black pepper, as required

1. In a bowl, mix all the ingredients. 2. Divide the salmon mixture over two pieces of foil evenly. 3. Seal the foil around the salmon mixture to form the packet. 4. Arrange the salmon parcels in the cooking tray. 5. Set your air fryer to Air Fry, then adjust the temperature to 355 degrees F and the time to 13 minutes. 6. Press the Start button to initiate preheating. 7. When the screen displays "Add Food," transfer the cooking tray into the air fryer. 8. Close its door, and let the machine do the cooking. 9. Serve hot.

Per serving: Calories 236; Fat 13.9g; Sodium 451mg; Carbs 13.2g; Fiber 1.2g; Sugars 1.4g; Protein 14.3g

Skin-on Salmon and Broccoli Florets

Prep time: 15 minutes | Cook time: 12 minutes | Serves: 2

1 ½ cups small broccoli florets
2 tablespoons vegetable oil, divided
Salt and ground black pepper, as required
(½-inch) piece fresh ginger, grated

1 tablespoon soy sauce
1 teaspoon rice vinegar
1 teaspoon light brown sugar
¼ teaspoon cornstarch
2 (6-ounce) skin-on salmon fillets
scallion, thinly sliced

1. Mix the broccoli, 1 tablespoon of oil, salt, and black pepper in a bowl. 2. Mix the ginger, soy sauce, vinegar, sugar, and cornstarch well in another bowl. 3. Coat the salmon fillets with the remaining oil and ginger mixture. 4. Arrange the broccoli florets in a greased cooking tray and top with the salmon fillets. 5. Set your air fryer to Air Fry, then adjust the temperature to 375 degrees F and the time to 12 minutes. 6. Press the Start button to initiate preheating. 7. When the screen displays "Add Food," transfer the cooking tray into the air fryer. 8. Close its door, and let the machine do the cooking. 9. Serve hot.

Per serving: Calories 305; Fat 15g; Sodium 548mg; Carbs 12g; Sugar 1.2g; Fiber 0.7g; Protein 29g

Salmon and Prawns with Pasta

Prep time: 15 minutes | Cook time: 10 minutes | Serves: 4

14 oz. pasta (of your choice)
4 tablespoons pesto, divided
4 4-ounce salmon steaks
2 tablespoons olive oil
½ pound cherry tomatoes, chopped

8 large prawns, peeled and deveined
2 tablespoons fresh lemon juice
2 tablespoons fresh thyme, chopped

1. In a large pan of salted boiling water, add the pasta and cook for about 8-10 minutes or until desired. 2. Meanwhile, on the bottom of a cooking tray, spread 1 tablespoon of pesto. 3. Place salmon steaks and tomatoes over pesto in a single layer and drizzle with the oil. 4. Arrange the prawns on top in a single layer. 5. Drizzle with lemon juice and sprinkle with thyme. 6. Set your air fryer to Air Fry, then adjust the temperature to 350 degrees F and the time to 8 minutes. 7. Press the Start button to initiate preheating. 8. When the screen displays "Add Food," transfer the cooking tray into the air fryer. 9. Close its door, and let the machine do the cooking. 10. Drain the pasta and transfer it into a large bowl. 11. Add the remaining pesto and toss to coat well. 12. Divide the pasta onto a serving plate and top with salmon mixture. 13. Serve immediately.

Per serving: Calories 344; Fat 14.9g; Sodium 227mg; Carbs 14g; Fiber 1g; Sugars 1.4g; Protein 25.7g

Salmon and Potato Patties

Prep time: 15 minutes | Cook time: 22 minutes | Serves: 6

3 large russet potatoes, peeled and cubed	2 tablespoons fresh parsley, chopped
1 (6-ounce) cooked salmon fillet	1 teaspoon fresh dill, chopped
1 egg	Salt and ground black pepper, as required
¾ cup frozen vegetables (of your choice), parboiled and drained	1 cup breadcrumbs
	¼ cup olive oil

1. In a pan of boiling water, cook the potatoes for about 10 minutes. 2. Drain the potatoes well. 3. When the screen displays "Add Food," transfer the potatoes into a bowl and mash with a potato masher. 4. Set aside to cool completely. 5. In another bowl, add the salmon and flake with a fork. 6. Add the cooked potatoes, egg, parboiled vegetables, parsley, dill, salt, and black pepper and mix until well combined. 7. Make six equal-sized patties from the mixture. 8. Coat patties with breadcrumbs evenly and then drizzle with the oil evenly. 9. Arrange the patties in the greased cooking tray. 10. Set your air fryer to Air Fry, then adjust the temperature to 355 degrees F and the time to 12 minutes. 11. Press the Start button to initiate preheating. 12. When the screen displays "Add Food," transfer the cooking tray into the air fryer. 13. Close its door, and let the machine do the cooking. 14. Flip the patties once halfway through. 15. Serve hot.
Per serving: Calories 285; Fat 9.8g; Sodium 639mg; Carbs 11.1g; Fiber 1.2g, Sugars 5.1g; Protein 27.8g

Seasoned Catfish Fillets

Prep time: 15 minutes | Cook time: 20 minutes | Serves: 4

4 4-ounce catfish fillets	as required
2 tablespoons Italian seasoning	1 tablespoon olive oil
Salt and ground black pepper,	1 tablespoon fresh parsley, chopped

1. Rub the fish fillets with seasoning, salt, and black pepper generously, and then coat with oil. 2. Arrange the fish fillets in the greased cooking tray. 3. Set your air fryer to Air Fry, then adjust the temperature to 400 degrees F and the time to 20 minutes. 4. Press the Start button to initiate preheating. 5. When the screen displays "Add Food," transfer the cooking tray into the air fryer. 6. Close its door, and let the machine do the cooking. 7. Flip the fish fillets once halfway through. 8. Serve hot with the garnishing of parsley.
Per serving: Calories 344; Fat 14.9g; Sodium 227mg; Carbs 14g; Fiber 1g, Sugars 1.4g; Protein 25.7g

Spiced Catfish Fillets

Prep time: 15 minutes | Cook time: 15 minutes | Serves: 5

5 (6-oz.) catfish fillets	¼ teaspoon red chili powder
1 cup milk	¼ teaspoon cayenne pepper
1 teaspoon fresh lemon juice	¼ teaspoon onion powder
½ cup yellow mustard	¼ teaspoon garlic powder
½ cup cornmeal	Salt and ground black pepper, as required
¼ cup all-purpose flour	Olive oil cooking spray
2 tablespoons dried parsley flakes	

1. Place the catfish fillets, milk, and lemon juice in a large bowl and refrigerate for about 15 minutes. 2. In a shallow bowl, add the mustard. 3. Mix the cornmeal, flour, parsley flakes, and spices in another bowl. 4. Remove the catfish fil-

lets from the milk mixture, and with paper towels, pat them dry. 5. Coat fish fillet with mustard and then roll into cornmeal mixture. 6. Then, spray the fillet with the cooking spray. 7. Arrange the catfish fillets in a greased cooking tray. 8. Set your air fryer to Air Fry, then adjust the temperature to 400 degrees F and the time to 15 minutes. 9. Press the Start button to initiate preheating. 10. When the screen displays "Add Food," transfer the cooking tray into the air fryer. 11. Close its door, and let the machine do the cooking. 12. After 10 minutes of cooking, flip the fillets and spray with the cooking spray. 13. Serve hot.
Per serving: Calories 336; Fat 17.3g; Sodium 281mg; Carbs 8.1g; Fiber 5.3g, Sugars 17.7g; Protein 32.3g

Cornmeal Catfish

Prep time: 15 minutes | Cook time: 15 minutes | Serves: 4

2 tablespoons cornmeal	Salt, as required
2 teaspoons Cajun seasoning	2 (6-oz.) catfish fillets
½ teaspoon paprika	1 tablespoon olive oil
½ teaspoon garlic powder	

1. Mix the cornmeal, Cajun seasoning, paprika, garlic powder, and salt in a bowl. 2. Add the catfish fillets and coat with the mixture. 3. Now, coat the fillet with oil. 4. Arrange the catfish fillets in a greased cooking tray. 5. Set your air fryer to Air Fry, then adjust the temperature to 400 degrees F and the time to 14 minutes. 6. Press the Start button to initiate preheating. 7. When the screen displays "Add Food," transfer the cooking tray into the air fryer. 8. Close its door, and let the machine do the cooking. 9. Serve hot
Per serving: Calories 285; Fat 9.8g; Sodium 639mg; Carbs 11.1g; Fiber 1.2g, Sugars 5.1g; Protein 27.8g

Lime-Glazed Haddock Steaks

Prep time: 15 minutes | Cook time: 11 minutes | Serves: 4

garlic clove, minced	½ cup cooking wine
¼ teaspoon fresh ginger, grated finely	¼ cup sugar
½ cup low-sodium soy sauce	¼ teaspoon red pepper flakes, crushed
¼ cup fresh orange juice	1-pound haddock steaks
2 tablespoons fresh lime juice	

1. In a pan, add all the ingredients except haddock steaks and bring to a boil. 2. Cook for about 3-4 minutes, stirring continuously. 3. Remove from the heat and set aside to cool. 4. In a resealable bag, add half of the marinade and haddock steaks. 5. Seal the bag and shake to coat well. 6. Refrigerate for about 30 minutes. 7. Remove the fish steaks from the bag, reserving the remaining marinade. 8. Arrange the haddock steaks in a greased cooking tray. 9. Set your air fryer to Air Fry, then adjust the temperature to 350 degrees F and the time to 11 minutes. 10. Press the Start button to initiate preheating. 11. When the screen displays "Add Food," transfer the cooking tray into the air fryer. 12. Close its door, and let the machine do the cooking. 13. When the screen displays "End," transfer the haddock steak onto a serving platter and immediately coat it with the remaining glaze. 14. Serve immediately.
Per serving: Calories 236; Fat 13.9g; Sodium 451mg; Carbs 13.2g; Fiber 1.2g, Sugars 1.4g; Protein 14.3g

Buttered Halibut Fillets with Jalapeño Peppers

Prep time: 15 minutes | Cook time: 15 minutes | Serves: 4

1-pound halibut fillets
1 tablespoon ginger paste
1 tablespoon garlic paste
Salt and ground black pepper,
as required
3 jalapeño peppers, chopped
¾ cup butter, chopped

1. Coat the halibut fillets with ginger-garlic paste, then season with salt and black pepper. 2. Arrange the halibut fillets in greased baking pan and top with green chilies, followed by the butter. 3. Set your air fryer to Air Fry, then adjust the temperature to 380 degrees F and the time to 15 minutes. 4. Press the Start button to initiate preheating. 5. When the screen displays "Add Food," transfer the cooking tray into the air fryer. 6. Close its door, and let the machine do the cooking. 7. Serve hot.

Per serving: Calories 254; Fat 28g; Sodium 346mg; Carbs 12.3g; Sugar 1g; Fiber 0.7g; Protein 24.3 g

Bread Crumb-Coated Fish Fillets

Prep time: 15 minutes | Cook time: 12 minutes | Serves: 4

1 tablespoon oil
3 ounces' breadcrumbs
1 egg, beaten
4 fresh fish fillets
fresh lemon (for serving)

1. Mix the crumbs and oil until it looks nice and loose. 2. Dip the fish in the egg and coat lightly, then move on to the crumbs. Make sure the fillet is covered evenly. 3. When the screen displays "Add Food," transfer the fish to a cooking tray. 4. Set your air fryer to Air Fry, then adjust the temperature to 350 degrees F and the time to 12 minutes. 5. Press the Start button to initiate preheating. 6. When the screen displays "Add Food," transfer the cooking tray into the air fryer. 7. Close its door, and let the machine do the cooking. 8. Serve with fresh lemon and chips to complete the duo.

Per serving: Calories 336; Fat 17.3g; Sodium 281mg; Carbs 8.1g; Fiber 5.3g, Sugars 17.7g; Protein 32.3g

Cod Nuggets

Prep time: 15 minutes | Cook time: 20 minutes | Serves: 4

1-pound cod fillet
2 eggs
4 tablespoons olive oil
1 cup almond flour
1 cup gluten-free breadcrumbs

1. Cut the cod into nuggets. 2. Beat the two eggs in a bowl. Combine the oil and breadcrumbs in another. Spread the almond flour on a plate. 3. Cover the nuggets with flour, a dip in the two eggs, and the breadcrumbs. 4. Arrange the prepared nuggets in the cooking tray. 5. Set your air fryer to Air Fry, then adjust the temperature to 390 degrees F and the time to 20 minutes. 6. Press the Start button to initiate preheating. 7. When the screen displays "Add Food," transfer the cooking tray into the air fryer. 8. Close its door, and let the machine do the cooking. 9. Serve warm.

Per serving: Calories 344; Fat 14.9g; Sodium 227mg; Carbs 14g; Fiber 1g; Sugars 1.4g; Protein 25.7g

Tuna Burgers with Tabasco Sauce

Prep time: 15 minutes | Cook time: 10 minutes | Serves: 8

2 (6-oz.) cans tuna, drained
½ cup panko breadcrumbs
1 egg
1 teaspoon Dijon mustard
1 tablespoon fresh parsley, chopped

Dash of Tabasco sauce
Salt and ground black pepper, as required
1 tablespoon fresh lemon juice
1 tablespoon olive oil

1. In a large bowl, add all ingredients and mix until well combined. 2. Make equal-sized patties from the mixture and arrange them onto a foil-lined tray. 3. Arrange the patties in a greased cooking tray. 4. Set your air fryer to Air Fry, then adjust the temperature to 355 degrees F and the time to 10 minutes. 5. Press the Start button to initiate preheating. 6. When the screen displays "Add Food," transfer the cooking tray into the air fryer. 7. Close its door, and let the machine do the cooking. 8. Serve hot.

Per serving: Calories 285; Fat 9.8g; Sodium 639mg; Carbs 11.1g; Fiber 1.2g, Sugars 5.1g; Protein 27.8g

Garlic Shrimp with Lemon Wedges

Prep time: 15 minutes | Cook time: 14 minutes | Serves: 4

1-pound shrimp, peeled and deveined,
1 tablespoon cooking oil
¼ teaspoon garlic powder
Salt, to taste
Black pepper, to taste
2 lemon wedges
1 teaspoon minced parsley

1. Toss the shrimp with oil and all other ingredients in a bowl. 2. Spread the seasoned shrimp in a baking pan. 3. Set your air fryer to Air Fry, then adjust the temperature to 400 degrees F and the time to 14 minutes. 4. Press the Start button to initiate preheating. 5. When the screen displays "Add Food," transfer the cooking tray into the air fryer when the screen displays "Add Food." 6. Close its door, and let the machine do the cooking. 7. Toss and flip the shrimp when cooked halfway through. 8. Serve warm.

Per serving: Calories 312; Fat 15g; Sodium 548mg; Carbs 12g; Sugar 1.2g; Fiber 0.7g; Protein 29g

Lemony Shrimp

Prep time: 15 minutes | Cook time: 8 minutes | Serves: 4

1 tablespoon olive oil
1 lemon, juiced
1 teaspoon lemon pepper
¼ teaspoon paprika
¼ teaspoon garlic powder
12 ounces' medium shrimp, peeled and deveined
lemon, sliced

1. Toss the shrimp with oil and all other ingredients in a bowl. 2. Spread the seasoned shrimp in a baking pan. 3. Set your air fryer to Air Fry, then adjust the temperature to 400 degrees F and the time to 8 minutes. 4. Press the Start button to initiate preheating. 5. When the screen displays "Add Food," transfer the cooking tray into the air fryer when the screen displays "Add Food" 6. Close its door, and let the machine do the cooking. 7. Toss and flip the shrimp when cooked halfway through. 8. Serve warm.

Per serving: Calories 249; Fat 13g; Sodium 556mg; Carbs 10g; Sugar 1.1g; Fiber 0.7g; Protein 31g

Coconut Shrimp with Hot Sauce

Prep time: 15 minutes | Cook time: 12 minutes | Serves: 4

Shrimp
½ cup flour
Salt
Black pepper
1 cup panko bread crumbs
½ cup sweetened coconut shredded
1 tablespoon Thai sweet chili sauce
2 eggs, beaten
1-pound large shrimp, peeled and deveined
Dipping Sauce
½ cup mayonnaise
1 tablespoon Sriracha

1. Mix flour with black pepper and salt in a bowl and dredge the shrimp through it. 2. Dip the shrimp in the egg and coat well with the breadcrumbs. 3. Place the crusted shrimp in a cooking tray. 4. Set your air fryer to Air Fry, then adjust the temperature to 400 degrees F and the time to 12 minutes. 5. Press the Start button to initiate preheating. 6. When the screen displays "Add Food," transfer the cooking tray into the air fryer. 7. Close its door, and let the machine do the cooking. 8. Toss and flip the shrimp when cooked halfway through. 9. Whisk mayonnaise with sriracha and chili sauce in a bowl. 10. Serve shrimp with mayo sauce.

Per serving: Calories 285; Fat 9.8g; Sodium 639mg; Carbs 11.1g; Fiber 1.2g, Sugars 5.1g; Protein 27.8g

Seasoned Shrimp with Cilantro

Prep time: 15 minutes | Cook time: 10 minutes | Serves: 4

11 pounds' shrimp, deveined and peeled	per
1 tablespoon olive oil	1 tablespoon lemon juice
1 teaspoon salt	6 cloves garlic, diced
1 teaspoon fresh cracked pep-	½ cup grated parmesan cheese
	¼ cup diced cilantro

1. Toss the shrimp with oil and all other ingredients in a bowl. 2. Spread the seasoned shrimp in a baking pan. 3. Set your air fryer to Air Fry, then adjust the temperature to 350 degrees F and the time to 10 minutes. 4. Press the Start button to initiate preheating. 5. When the screen displays "Add Food," transfer the cooking tray into the air fryer. 6. Close its door, and let the machine do the cooking. 7. Toss and flip the shrimp when cooked halfway through. 8. Serve warm.

Per serving: Calories 336; Fat 17.3g; Sodium 281mg; Carbs 8.1g; Fiber 5.3g, Sugars 17.7g; Protein 32.3g

Crispy Breaded Shrimp

Prep time: 15 minutes | Cook time: 14 minutes | Serves: 4

1-pound raw shrimp, peeled and deveined	salt and black pepper to taste
1 egg white	cooking spray
½ cup flour	Bang Bang Sauce
¾ cups panko bread crumbs	⅓ cup Greek yogurt
1 teaspoon paprika	2 tablespoons Sriracha
Montreal Seasoning to taste	¼ cup sweet chili sauce

1. Mix flour with salt, black pepper, paprika, and Montreal seasoning in a bowl. 2. Dredge the shrimp in the flour, then dips in the egg. 3. Coat the shrimp with the breadcrumbs and place them on a cooking tray. 4. Set your air fryer to Air Fry, then adjust the temperature to 400 degrees F and the time to 14 minutes. 5. Press the Start button to initiate preheating. 6. When the screen displays "Add Food," transfer the cooking tray into the air fryer. 7. Close its door, and let the machine do the cooking. 8. Toss and flip the shrimp when cooked halfway through. 9. Serve warm.

Per serving: Calories 344; Fat 14.9g; Sodium 227mg; Carbs 14g; Fiber 1g; Sugars 1.4g; Protein 25.7g

Taco Shrimp

Prep time: 15 minutes | Cook time: 5 minutes | Serves: 6

17 shrimp, defrosted, peeled, and deveined	1 tablespoon garlic salt
1 cup bread crumbs Italian	4 tablespoons butter melted
1 tablespoon taco seasoning	olive oil spray

1. Toss the shrimp with oil and all other ingredients in a

bowl. 2. Spread the seasoned shrimp on a cooking tray. 3. Set your air fryer to Air Fry, then adjust the temperature to 400 degrees F and the time to 5 minutes. 4. Press the Start button to initiate preheating. 5. When the screen displays "Add Food," transfer the cooking tray into the air fryer. 6. Close its door, and let the machine do the cooking. 7. Toss and flip the shrimp when cooked halfway through. 8. Serve warm.

Per serving: Calories 236; Fat 13.9g; Sodium 451mg; Carbs 13.2g; Fiber 1.2g; Sugars 1.4g; Protein 14.3g

Garlic Mussels with Herbs

Prep time: 15 minutes | Cook time: 6 minutes | Serves: 4

1-pound mussels	1 teaspoon chives
1 tablespoon butter	1 teaspoon basil
1 cup water	1 teaspoon parsley
1 teaspoon minced garlic	

1. Toss the mussels with oil and all other ingredients in a bowl. 2. Spread the seasoned shrimp on the cooking tray. 3. Set your air fryer to Air Fry, then adjust the temperature to 350 degrees F and the time to 6 minutes. 4. Press the Start button to initiate preheating. 5. When the screen displays "Add Food," transfer the baking tray to the rack of the air fryer. 6. Close its door, and let the machine do the cooking. 7. Serve warm.

Per serving: Calories 351; Fat 22g; Sodium 502mg; Carbs 15.2g; Sugar 1.1g; Fiber 0.7g; Protein 26.4g

Fresh Mussels with Saffron Sauce

Prep time: 15 minutes | Cook time: 8 minutes | Serves: 4

1 tablespoon unsalted butter	3 tablespoons heavy cream
1 tablespoon minced garlic	4 threads saffron
1 tablespoon minced shallot	1-pound fresh mussels
¼ cups dry white wine	

1. Whisk cream with saffron, shallots, white wine, and butter in a bowl. 2. Place the mussels in the cooking tray and pour the cream sauce on top. 3. Set your air fryer to Air Fry, then adjust the temperature to 370 degrees F and the time to 8 minutes. 4. Press the Start button to initiate preheating. 5. When the screen displays "Add Food," transfer the cooking tray to the rack of the air fryer. 6. Close its door, and let the machine do the cooking. 7. Serve warm.

Per serving: Calories 344; Fat 14.9g; Sodium 227mg; Carbs 12g; Fiber 1.2g; Sugars 1g; Protein 27g

Shrimp Cooked with Garlic Sauce

Prep time: 15 minutes | Cook time: 13 minutes | Serves: 4

¼ pound shrimp, peeled and deveined	Salt and black pepper to taste
¼ cups butter	⅛ teaspoon Red pepper flakes
1 tablespoon minced garlic	2 tablespoons chopped fresh parsley
1 tablespoon fresh lemon juice	

1. Toss the shrimp with oil and all other ingredients in a bowl. 2. Spread the seasoned shrimp in the baking pan. 3. Set your air fryer to Air Fry, then adjust the temperature to 350 degrees F and the time to 13 minutes. 4. Press the Start button to initiate preheating. 5. When the screen displays "Add Food," transfer the cooking tray into the air fryer. 6. Close its door, and let the machine do the cooking. 7. Serve warm.

Per serving: Calories 285; Fat 9.8g; Sodium 639mg; Carbs 11.1g; Fiber 1.2g, Sugars 5.1g; Protein 27.8g

Easy Shrimp Cooked with Basil Pesto

Prep time: 15 minutes | Cook time: 5 minutes | Serves: 6

1 pound of shrimp, defrosted | 14 ounces' basil pesto

1. Add shrimp and pesto into the mixing bowl and toss well. 2. Add shrimp into the baking pan. 3. Set your air fryer to Air Fry, then adjust the temperature to 400 degrees F and the time to 5 minutes. 4. Press the Start button to initiate preheating. 5. When the screen displays "Add Food," transfer the cooking tray into the air fryer. 6. Close its door, and let the machine do the cooking. 7. Serve and enjoy.

Per serving: Calories 285; Fat 9.8g; Sodium 639mg; Carbs 11.1g; Fiber 1.2g, Sugars 5.1g; Protein 27.8g

Shrimp Skewer with Teriyaki Sauce

Prep time: 15 minutes | Cook time: 6 minutes | Serves: 4

Shrimp Skewers:
1-pound shrimp, peeled and deveined
1 pineapple, peeled and cut into chunks
2 zucchinis, cut into thick slices

3 red and orange bell peppers, cut into 2-inch chunks
Bamboo or metal skewers
Teriyaki BBQ Sauce:
½ cup teriyaki sauce
2 tablespoon fish sauce
2 tablespoon chili garlic sauce

1. Toss the shrimp and veggies with all other ingredients in a bowl. 2. Thread shrimp and veggies on the skewers alternately. 3. Place the shrimp vegetable skewers in a cooking tray. 4. Mix the teriyaki sauce ingredients in a bowl and pour over the skewers. 5. Set your air fryer to Air Fry, then adjust the temperature to 350 degrees F and the time to 6 minutes. 6. Press the Start button to initiate preheating. 7. When the screen displays "Add Food," transfer the cooking tray into the air fryer. 8. Close its door, and let the machine do the cooking. 9. Toss and flip the shrimp when cooked halfway through. 10. Serve warm.

Per serving: Calories 336; Fat 17.3g; Sodium 281mg; Carbs 8.1g; Fiber 5.3g, Sugars 17.7g; Protein 32.3g

Savory Shrimp Skewers

Prep time: 15 minutes | Cook time: 6 minutes | Serves: 4

1-pound large shrimp peeled and deveined
¼ cup olive oil
2 tablespoons lemon juice
¾ teaspoon salt

¼ teaspoon pepper
1 teaspoon Italian seasoning
1 teaspoon garlic minced
1 tablespoon parsley chopped
lemon wedges for serving

1. Toss the shrimp with all other ingredients in a bowl. 2. Thread shrimp on the skewers. 3. Place the shrimp skewers in a baking pan. 4. Set your air fryer to Air Fry, then adjust the temperature to 350 degrees F and the time to 6 minutes. 5. Press the Start button to initiate preheating. 6. When the screen displays "Add Food," transfer the cooking tray into the air fryer. 7. Close its door, and let the machine do the cooking. 8. Serve warm.

Per serving: Calories 305; Fat 15g; Sodium 548mg; Carbs 12g; Sugar 1.2g; Fiber 0.7g; Protein 29g

Onion Prawn Burgers

Prep time: 15 minutes | Cook time: 6 minutes | Serves: 2

½ cup prawns, peeled, deveined, and chopped very finely
½ cup breadcrumbs

2-3 tablespoons onion, chopped finely
½ teaspoon ginger, minced

½ teaspoon garlic, minced
½ teaspoon red chili powder
½ teaspoon ground cumin

¼ teaspoon ground turmeric
Salt and ground black pepper, as required

1. In a bowl, add all ingredients and mix until well combined. 2. Make small-sized patties from the mixture. Arrange the patties in greased Baking pan. 3. Set your air fryer to Air Fry, then adjust the temperature to 355 degrees F and the time to 6 minutes. 4. Press the Start button to initiate preheating. 5. When the screen displays "Add Food," transfer the cooking tray into the air fryer. 6. Close its door, and let the machine do the cooking. 7. Serve hot.

Per serving: Calories 344; Fat 14.9g; Sodium 227mg; Carbs 14g; Fiber 1g; Sugars 1.4g; Protein 25.7g

Easy Fried Tilapia Filets

Prep time: 15 minutes | Cook time: 10 minutes | Serves: 4

½ pounds tilapia filets
1 tablespoon butter, softened
1 teaspoon onion powder
½ teaspoon garlic powder

½ teaspoon cayenne pepper
1 teaspoon dried parsley flakes
Kosher salt and freshly cracked black pepper, to taste

1. In a mixing bowl, toss the fish with the other ingredients, and place the fish on the cooking tray. 2. Set your air fryer to Air Fry, then adjust the temperature to 400 degrees F and the time to 10 minutes. 3. Press the Start button to initiate preheating. 4. When the screen displays "Add Food," transfer the cooking tray into the air fryer. 5. Close its door, and let the machine do the cooking. 6. Serve warm.

Per serving: Calories 344; Fat 14.9g; Sodium 227mg; Carbs 14g; Fiber 1g; Sugars 1.4g; Protein 25.7g

Homemade Tuna Cakes

Prep time: 15 minutes | Cook time: 12 minutes | Serves: 4

12 ounces canned tuna, drained
1 large egg, beaten
1 tablespoon butter, at room temperature
green onions, chopped
2 garlic cloves, minced
1 teaspoon stone-ground mustard
½ cup white bread, torn into small pieces

1 teaspoon lemon zest
½ teaspoon ginger, peeled and grated
2 tablespoons fresh parsley, chopped
2 tablespoons fresh basil, chopped
1 teaspoon cayenne pepper
Kosher salt
Freshly ground black pepper, to taste

1. Place a sheet of parchment paper on the cooking tray. Thoroughly combine all the ingredients. 2. Form the mixture into four patties and place them in a single layer on the cooking tray. 3. Set your air fryer to Air Fry, then adjust the temperature to 350 degrees F and the time to 12 minutes. 4. Press the Start button to initiate preheating. 5. When the screen displays "Add Food," transfer the cooking tray into the air fryer. 6. Close its door, and let the machine do the cooking. 7. Serve warm.

Per serving: Calories 254; Fat 28g; Sodium 346mg; Carbs 12.3g; Sugar 1g; Fiber 0.7g; Protein 24.3 g

Tuna Cutlets with Korean Chili Paste

Prep time: 15 minutes | Cook time: 13 minutes | Serves: 4

12 ounces canned tuna, drained
2 eggs, beaten
1 medium onion, chopped

2 garlic cloves, pressed
1 bell pepper, chopped
½ cup flour
½ cup instant oats

Sea salt
Ground black pepper to taste
4 tablespoons mayonnaise

1 teaspoon gochujang (Korean chili paste)

1. Place a sheet of parchment paper on the cooking tray. Thoroughly combine all the ingredients. 2. Form the mixture into equal patties and place them in a single layer on the cooking tray. 3. Set your air fryer to Air Fry, then adjust the temperature to 350 degrees F and the time to 13 minutes. 4. Press the Start button to initiate preheating. 5. When the screen displays "Add Food," transfer the cooking tray into the air fryer. 6. Close its door, and let the machine do the cooking. 7. Serve warm.

Per serving: Calories 285; Fat 9.8g; Sodium 639mg; Carbs 11.1g; Fiber 1.2g, Sugars 5.1g; Protein 27.8g

Smoked Salmon Frittatas

Prep time: 15 minutes | Cook time: 13 minutes | Serves: 4

12 ounces smoked salmon, chopped	chopped
6 eggs	2 tablespoons fresh basil, chopped
1-ounce butter softened	2 tablespoons fresh scallions, chopped
1-ounce cream cheese	
¼ cup sour cream	Sea salt and freshly ground
2 tablespoons fresh parsley,	black pepper to season

1. Brush silicon muffin cup with nonstick oil. 2. Mix all the ingredients until well combined. Divide the mixture between the muffin cup. 3. Set your air fryer to Air Fry, then adjust the temperature to 400 degrees F and the time to 13 minutes. 4. Press the Start button to initiate preheating. 5. When the screen displays "Add Food," transfer the cooking tray into the air fryer. 6. Close its door, and let the machine do the cooking. 7. Serve warm.

Per serving: Calories 336; Fat 17.3g; Sodium 281mg; Carbs 8.1g; Fiber 5.3g, Sugars 17.7g; Protein 32.3g

Shrimp Sliders

Prep time: 15 minutes | Cook time: 15 minutes | Serves: 4

12 ounces' shrimp, chopped	garlic cloves, minced
2 eggs, whisked	½ teaspoon dried oregano
Zest of 1 lemon	½ teaspoon dried dill
½ cup seasoned breadcrumbs	Kosher salt and freshly
½ cup parmesan cheese, preferably freshly grated	cracked black pepper, to taste
	2 tablespoons olive oil
1 large onion, chopped	8 dinner rolls

1. Place a sheet of parchment paper on the cooking tray. 2. Thoroughly combine all the ingredients, except for the dinner rolls. 3. Form the mixture into eight patties and place them in a single layer on the cooking tray. 4. Set your air fryer to Air Fry, then adjust the temperature to 350 degrees F and the time to 15 minutes. 5. Press the Start button to initiate preheating. 6. When the screen displays "Add Food," transfer the cooking tray into the air fryer. 7. Close its door, and let the machine do the cooking. 8. Serve warm.

Per serving: Calories 344; Fat 14.9g; Sodium 227mg; Carbs 14g; Fiber 1g; Sugars 1.4g; Protein 25.7g

Herbed Halibut Steaks

Prep time: 15 minutes | Cook time: 10 minutes | Serves: 4

½ pounds halibut steaks	1 tablespoon fresh basil, minced
1 tablespoon butter, melted	
1 tablespoon lemon juice	1 tablespoon fresh mint,

minced
1 tablespoon fresh parsley, minced
½ teaspoon garlic salt

1 teaspoon cayenne pepper
½ teaspoon ground black pepper

1. Toss the fish with the other ingredients in a mixing bowl. 2. Place the fish in the cooking tray. 3. Set your air fryer to Air Fry, then adjust the temperature to 350 degrees F and the time to 10 minutes. 4. Press the Start button to initiate preheating. 5. When the screen displays "Add Food", transfer the cooking tray into the air fryer. 6. Close its door, and let the machine do the cooking. 7. Serve.

Per serving: Calories 344; Fat 14.9g; Sodium 227mg; Carbs 14g; Fiber 1g; Sugars 1.4g; Protein 25.7g

Mayonnaise Jumbo Shrimp

Prep time: 15 minutes | Cook time: 10 minutes | Serves: 4

¼ cup mayonnaise	1 tablespoon brown mustard
½ cup all-purpose flour	1 cup seasoned breadcrumbs
Sea salt and freshly ground black pepper to taste	1-pound jumbo shrimp, peeled and deveined
1 teaspoon ancho chile pepper	

1. Mix the mayonnaise, flour, salt, black pepper, ancho chile pepper, and brown mustard in a shallow bowl. In another shallow bowl, place the seasoned breadcrumbs. 2. Dredge the shrimp in the mayo mixture. 3. Then, dip the strips in the breadcrumbs, coating them completely and shaking off any excess. 4. Arrange the shrimp in a cooking tray, ensuring not to crowd them. 5. Set your air fryer to Air Fry, then adjust the temperature to 350 degrees F and the time to 10 minutes. 6. Press the Start button to initiate preheating. 7. When the screen displays "Add Food," transfer the cooking tray into the air fryer. 8. Close its door, and let the machine do the cooking. 9. Serve warm.

Per serving: Calories 285; Fat 9.8g; Sodium 639mg; Carbs 11.1g; Fiber 1.2g, Sugars 5.1g; Protein 27.8g

Toothsome Fish Fingers

Prep time: 15 minutes | Cook time: 10 minutes | Serves: 5

Ingredients	1 teaspoon garlic salt
½ pounds cod fillets, cut into bite-sized strips	Freshly ground black pepper to season
1 tablespoon olive oil	½ cup dry pancake mix
1 egg, beaten	½ cup seasoned breadcrumbs
¼ cups milk	

1. Mix the olive oil, egg, milk, garlic salt, black pepper, and dry pancake mix in a shallow bowl. 2. In another shallow bowl, mix the remaining ingredients. 3. Dredge the fish strips in the oil/1 egg mixture. Then, dip the strips in the breadcrumb mixture, coating them completely and shaking off any excess. 4. Arrange the fish strips in a pan, making sure not to crowd them. 5. Set your air fryer to Air Fry, then adjust the temperature to 400 degrees F and the time to 10 minutes. 6. Press the Start button to initiate preheating. 7. When the screen displays "Add Food," transfer the cooking tray into the air fryer. 8. Close its door, and let the machine do the cooking. 9. Serve warm.

Per serving: Calories 336; Fat 17.3g; Sodium 281mg; Carbs 8.1g; Fiber 5.3g, Sugars 17.7g; Protein 32.3g

Air-Fried Flounder Fillets with Parmesan Cheese

Prep time: 15 minutes | Cook time: 10 minutes | Serves: 4

½ pounds flounder fillets	1 tablespoon oil
garlic cloves, minced	1 teaspoon dried parsley flakes
½ cup parmesan cheese, preferably freshly grated	1 teaspoon dried basil
1 cup crackers, crushed	1 teaspoon dried oregano
	2 eggs, well-beaten

1. Toss the fish with the other ingredients in a mixing bowl. 2. Place the fish in the parchment-lined cooking tray. 3. Set your air fryer to Air Fry, then adjust the temperature to 400 degrees F and the time to 10 minutes. 4. Press the Start button to initiate preheating. 5. When the screen displays "Add Food," transfer the cooking tray into the air fryer. 6. Close its door, and let the machine do the cooking. 7. Serve warm.
Per serving: Calories 344; Fat 14.9g; Sodium 227mg; Carbs 14g; Fiber 1g; Sugars 1.4g; Protein 25.7g

Hot Salmon Fillets

Prep time: 15 minutes | Cook time: 11 minutes | Serves: 2

1 teaspoon smoked paprika	as required
1 teaspoon cayenne pepper	2 (6-ounce) (1½-inch thick)
1 teaspoon onion powder	salmon fillets
1 teaspoon garlic powder	2 teaspoons olive oil
Salt and ground black pepper,	

1. Add the spices to a bowl and mix well. 2. Drizzle the salmon fillets with oil and then rub them with the spice mixture. 3. Arrange the salmon fillets in a greased cooking tray. 4. Set your air fryer to Air Fry, then adjust the temperature to 350 degrees F and the time to 11 minutes. 5. Press the Start button to initiate preheating. 6. When the screen displays "Add Food," transfer the cooking tray into the air fryer. 7. Close its door, and let the machine do the cooking. 8. Serve hot.
Per serving: Calories 344; Fat 14.9g; Sodium 227mg; Carbs 14g; Fiber 1g; Sugars 1.4g; Protein 25.7g

Easy Shrimp Bake with Parmesan Cheese

Prep time: 15 minutes | Cook time: 10 minutes | Serves: 4

½ pound large raw shrimp, peeled and deveined	1 teaspoon garlic powder
¼ cup melted butter	½ teaspoon crushed red pepper
1 teaspoon coarse salt	¼ cup Parmesan cheese, grated
¼ teaspoon black pepper	

1. Toss the shrimp with oil and all other ingredients in a bowl. 2. Spread the seasoned shrimp on the cooking tray. 3. Set your air fryer to Air Fry, then adjust the temperature to 400 degrees F and the time to 10 minutes. 4. Press the Start button to initiate preheating. 5. When the screen displays "Add Food," transfer the cooking tray into the air fryer. 6. Close its door, and let the machine do the cooking. 7. Serve warm.
Per serving: Calories 344; Fat 14.9g; Sodium 227mg; Carbs 14g; Fiber 1g; Sugars 1.4g; Protein 25.7g

Shrimp Pineapple Skewers

Prep time: 15 minutes | Cook time: 6 minutes | Serves: 4

½ cup coconut milk	deveined
4 teaspoons Tabasco Sauce	1¾ pounds pineapple chunks, diced
2 teaspoons soy sauce	
¼ cup orange juice	
¼ cup lime juice	
1-pound shrimp, peeled and	

1. Toss the shrimp and pineapple with all other ingredients in a bowl. 2. Thread shrimp and pineapple on the skewers. 3. Place the shrimp pineapple skewers in a cooking tray. 4. Set your air fryer to Air Fry, then adjust the temperature to 350 degrees F and the time to 6 minutes. 5. Press the Start button to initiate preheating. 6. When the screen displays "Add Food," transfer the cooking tray into the air fryer. 7. Close its door, and let the machine do the cooking. 8. Toss and flip the shrimp when cooked halfway through. 9. Serve warm.
Per serving: Calories 254; Fat 28g; Sodium 346mg; Carbs 12.3g; Sugar 1g; Fiber 0.7g; Protein 24.3 g

Sea Scallops

Prep time: 15 minutes | Cook time: 13 minutes | Serves: 4

½ pounds sea scallops patted dry	1 tablespoon fresh parsley, minced
1 large egg, whisked	2 tablespoons butter, softened
1 cup corn flakes, crushed	1 tablespoon olive oil
1 garlic clove, minced	Coarse sea salt and ground black pepper, to taste
1 tablespoon fresh chives, minced	1 teaspoon hot paprika

1. In a mixing bowl, toss the sea scallops with the other ingredients, then transfer them to a cooking tray. 2. Set your air fryer to Air Fry, then adjust the temperature to 400 degrees F and the time to 13 minutes. 3. Press the Start button to initiate preheating. 4. When the screen displays "Add Food," transfer the cooking tray into the air fryer. 5. Close its door, and let the machine do the cooking. 6. Serve warm.
Per serving: Calories 236; Fat 13.9g; Sodium 451mg; Carbs 13.2g; Fiber 1.2g; Sugars 1.4g; Protein 14.3g

Salmon Croquettes

Prep time: 15 minutes | Cook time: 12 minutes | Serves: 4

12 ounces' salmon fillets, chopped	to taste
2 garlic cloves, grated	1 teaspoon lemon juice
1 small onion, chopped	1 large egg, beaten
1 teaspoon red pepper flakes, crushed	½ cup tortilla chips, crushed
1 teaspoon dried oregano	½ cup Parmesan cheese, grated
Kosher salt and black pepper,	2 tablespoon butter

1. Place a sheet of parchment paper on the cooking tray. Thoroughly combine all the ingredients. 2. Form the mixture into equal balls and place them in a single layer on the cooking tray. 3. Set your air fryer to Air Fry, then adjust the temperature to 350 degrees F and the time to 12 minutes. 4. When the screen displays "Add Food," transfer the cooking tray into the air fryer when the screen displays "Add Food" 5. Close its door, and let the machine do the cooking. 6. Serve.
Per serving: Calories 285; Fat 9.8g; Sodium 639mg; Carbs 11.1g; Fiber 1.2g, Sugars 5.1g; Protein 27.8g

Tuna Anchovies Casserole with Broccoli Florets

Prep time: 15 minutes | Cook time: 10 minutes | Serves: 4

2 cups broccoli florets	Sea salt
8 ounces canned tuna, drained	Ground black pepper to taste
2 canned anchovies, chopped	½ cup cheddar cheese, shredded
small onion, chopped	
1 teaspoon garlic, chopped	½ cup tortilla chips, crushed
1 teaspoon cayenne pepper	

1. Grease the sides and bottom of a cooking tray with olive

oil. 2. Arrange the broccoli florets, tuna, anchovies, onion, and garlic in the prepared baking pan. 3. Season with cayenne pepper, salt, and black pepper. 4. Top your casserole with cheese and tortilla chips. 5. Set your air fryer to Air Fry, then adjust the temperature to 360 degrees F and the time to 10 minutes. 6. Press the Start button to initiate preheating. 7. When the screen displays "Add Food," transfer the cooking tray into the air fryer. 8. Close its door, and let the machine do the cooking. 9. Serve.

Per serving: Calories 344; Fat 14.9g; Sodium 227mg; Carbs 14g; Fiber 1g; Sugars 1.4g; Protein 25.7g

Honey Salmon Steaks

Prep time: 15 minutes | Cook time: 10 minutes | Serves: 4

½ pounds salmon steaks	1 lime, freshly squeezed
¼ cup unsalted butter	Sea salt
¼ cups honey	Ground black pepper to taste
2 cloves garlic, crushed	

1. In a mixing bowl, toss the salmon steaks with the other ingredients, then transfer them to a pan. 2. Set your air fryer to Air Fry, then adjust the temperature to 400 degrees F and the time to 10 minutes. 3. Press the Start button to initiate preheating. 4. When the screen displays "Add Food," transfer the cooking tray into the air fryer. 5. Close its door, and let the machine do the cooking. 6. Serve warm.

Per serving: Calories 285; Fat 9.8g; Sodium 639mg; Carbs 11.1g; Fiber 1.2g, Sugars 5.1g; Protein 27.8g

Cheese Crab-Pea Patties

Prep time: 15 minutes | Cook time: 10 minutes | Serves: 4

¾ pound lump crab meat	1 teaspoon brown mustard
1 cup canned green peas, drained	1 tablespoon ketchup
½ cup seasoned breadcrumbs	1 tablespoon cheddar cheese, shredded
¼ cups celery, diced	1 teaspoon smoked paprika
4 tablespoons green onions, chopped	1 teaspoon dried oregano
4 tablespoons mayonnaise	Kosher salt and ground black pepper, to taste

1. Place a sheet of parchment paper on the cooking tray. 2. Thoroughly combine all the ingredients in a mixing bowl. 3. Form the mixture into patties and place them in a single layer on the cooking tray. 4. Set your air fryer to Air Fry, then adjust the temperature to 370 degrees F and the time to 10 minutes. 5. Press the Start button to initiate preheating. 6. When the screen displays "Add Food," transfer the cooking tray into the air fryer. 7. Close its door, and let the machine do the cooking. 8. Serve.

Per serving: Calories 336; Fat 17.3g; Sodium 281mg; Carbs 8.1g; Fiber 5.3g, Sugars 17.7g; Protein 32.3g

Sardine-Zucchini Cakes

Prep time: 15 minutes | Cook time: 12 minutes | Serves: 4

½ pound zucchini, grated

12 ounces' sardines, drained and chopped	1 large egg, whisked
4 tablespoons scallions, chopped	red onion, minced
	1 celery stick, minced
1 teaspoon garlic, minced	½ cup breadcrumbs

1. Place a sheet of parchment paper in the baking pan. Thoroughly combine all the ingredients. 2. Form the mixture into four patties and place them in a single layer in the baking pan.

3. Set your air fryer to Air Fry, then adjust the temperature to 350 degrees F and the time to 12 minutes. 4. Press the Start button to initiate preheating. 5. When the screen displays "Add Food," transfer the cooking tray into the air fryer. 6. Close its door, and let the machine do the cooking. 7. Serve warm.

Per serving: Calories 285; Fat 9.8g; Sodium 639mg; Carbs 11.1g; Fiber 1.2g, Sugars 5.1g; Protein 27.8g

Tuna Steaks in Soy Sauce

Prep time: 15 minutes | Cook time: 10 minutes | Serves: 4

½ pounds tuna steaks	1 teaspoon ginger, peeled and minced
Sea salt	
Ground black pepper to season	2 cloves garlic, minced
1 teaspoon smoked paprika	2 tablespoons honey
1 tablespoon butter	2 tablespoons soy sauce

1. Toss the tuna steaks with the other ingredients in a mixing bowl. 2. Place the fish in the cooking tray. 3. Set your air fryer to Air Fry, then adjust the temperature to 400 degrees F and the time to 10 minutes. 4. Press the Start button to initiate preheating. 5. When the screen displays "Add Food," transfer the cooking tray into the air fryer. 6. Close its door, and let the machine do the cooking. 7. Serve warm.

Per serving: Calories 344; Fat 14.9g; Sodium 227mg; Carbs 14g; Fiber 1g; Sugars 1.4g; Protein 25.7g

Tuna Melts with Hawaiian Sweet Rolls

Prep time: 15 minutes | Cook time: 12 minutes | Serves: 4

12 ounces canned albacore tuna, drained	4 (1-ounce) slices of cheddar cheese
4 Hawaiian sweet rolls, split	2 tablespoons scallions, chopped
½ cup mayonnaise	

1. Assemble the sandwiches by laying out the rolls and adding the remaining ingredients. Spritz the sandwiches with non-stick oil. 2. Set your air fryer to Air Fry, then adjust the temperature to 400 degrees F and the time to 12 minutes. 3. Press the Start button to initiate preheating. 4. When the screen displays "Add Food," transfer the sandwiches to the cooking tray of the air fryer. 5. Close its door, and let the machine do the cooking. 6. Serve warm.

Per serving: Calories 336; Fat 17.3g; Sodium 281mg; Carbs 8.1g; Fiber 5.3g, Sugars 17.7g; Protein 32.3g

Air-Fried Salmon Steaks

Prep time: 15 minutes | Cook time: 10 minutes | Serves: 4

2 pounds of salmon steaks	2 tablespoons olive oil
1-pound cauliflower florets	Sea salt
1 teaspoon garlic powder	Ground black pepper to taste
1 teaspoon onion powder	Juice of 1 lemon
½ teaspoon turmeric powder	

1. Toss all the ingredients into the cooking tray. 2. Set your air fryer to Air Fry, then adjust the temperature to 400 degrees F and the time to 10 minutes. 3. Press the Start button to initiate preheating. 4. When the screen displays "Add Food," transfer the cooking tray into the air fryer. 5. Close its door, and let the machine do the cooking. 6. Serve.

Per serving: Calories 285; Fat 9.8g; Sodium 639mg; Carbs 11.1g; Fiber 1.2g, Sugars 5.1g; Protein 27.8g

Halibut, Bacon and Cauliflower Croquettes

Prep time: 15 minutes | Cook time: 13 minutes | Serves: 4

12 ounces' halibut, chopped
2 tablespoons bacon bits
1 cup cauliflower rice
4 tablespoons all-purpose flour
¼ cups cream of celery soup
2 garlic cloves, pressed
½ cup tortilla chips, crushed
2 tablespoons lime juice
Sea salt
Ground black pepper to season
1 teaspoon smoked paprika
1 teaspoon olive oil

1. Place a sheet of parchment paper on the cooking tray. Thoroughly combine all the ingredients. 2. Form the mixture into equal balls and place them in a single layer in the baking pan. 3. Set your air fryer to Air Fry, then adjust the temperature to 350 degrees F and the time to 13 minutes. 4. Press the Start button to initiate preheating. 5. When the screen displays "Add Food," transfer the cooking tray into the air fryer. 6. Close its door, and let the machine do the cooking. 7. Serve.
Per serving: Calories 236; Fat 13.9g; Sodium 451mg; Carbs 13.2g; Fiber 1.2g; Sugars 1.4g; Protein 14.3g

Masala Codfish Patties

Prep time: 15 minutes | Cook time: 12 minutes | Serves: 4

1-pound codfish, chopped (or any mild white fish)
¼ cup all-purpose flour
½ cup instant oats
Sea salt
Ground black pepper to taste
1 teaspoon onion powder
1 teaspoon paprika
1 teaspoon garam masala
½ teaspoon turmeric powder
2 medium eggs, beaten
2 teaspoons olive oil

1. Place a sheet of parchment paper on the cooking tray. 2. Thoroughly combine all the ingredients in a bowl. 3. Form the mixture into four patties and place them in a single layer on the cooking tray. 4. Set your air fryer to Air Fry, then adjust the temperature to 350 degrees F and the time to 12 minutes. 5. Press the Start button to initiate preheating. 6. When the screen displays "Add Food," transfer the cooking tray into the air fryer. 7. Close its door, and let the machine do the cooking. 8. Serve.
Per serving: Calories 285; Fat 9.8g; Sodium 639mg; Carbs 11.1g; Fiber 1.2g, Sugars 5.1g; Protein 27.8g

Spicy Sardine Cutlets

Prep time: 15 minutes | Cook time: 13 minutes | Serves: 4

10 ounces' sardines, drained and chopped
1 large egg, well-beaten
1 tablespoon ground chia seeds
1 medium onion, chopped
garlic cloves, minced
1 carrot, grated
2 tablespoon butter, softened
2 tablespoon mayonnaise
1 teaspoon Sriracha sauce
Kosher salt and ground black pepper to season
1 teaspoon smoked paprika
½ cup seasoned breadcrumbs

1. Place a sheet of parchment paper on the cooking tray. Thoroughly combine all the ingredients. 2. Form the mixture into equal patties and place them in a single layer on the cooking tray. 3. Set your air fryer to Air Fry, then adjust the temperature to 350 degrees F and the time to 13 minutes. 4. Press the Start button to initiate preheating. 5. When the screen displays "Add Food," transfer the cooking tray into the air fryer. 6. Close its door, and let the machine do the cooking. 7. Serve.
Per serving: Calories 305; Fat 15g; Sodium 548mg; Carbs 12g; Sugar 1.2g; Fiber 0.7g; Protein 29g

Tuna Flatbread Sandwiches

Prep time: 15 minutes | Cook time: 5 minutes | Serves: 4

4 (1-ounce) slices of Colby cheese
8 ounces canned tuna, drained
1 tablespoon Dijon mustard
4 heaping 1-tablespoon mayonnaise
½ cup dill pickles, thinly sliced
bell pepper, seeded and sliced
4 large flour tortillas

1. Divide the turn and rest of the ingredients on top of the tortilla. 2. Roll them tightly and place them on a greased cooking tray. 3. Set your air fryer to Air Fry, then adjust the temperature to 350 degrees F and the time to 5 minutes. 4. Press the Start button to initiate preheating. 5. When the screen displays "Add Food," transfer the cooking tray into the air fryer. 6. Close its door, and let the machine do the cooking. 7. Serve.
Per serving: Calories 236; Fat 13.9g; Sodium 451mg; Carbs 13.2g; Fiber 1.2g; Sugars 1.4g; Protein 14.3g

Flavorful Fish Burritos

Prep time: 15 minutes | Cook time: 10 minutes | Serves: 4

1 large egg
1 teaspoon Mexican oregano
1 cup seasoned breadcrumbs
1 teaspoon olive oil
1-pound cod fish fillet, cut
into strips
8 small flour tortillas (or corn tortillas)
½ cup guacamole sauce

1. Whisk the egg with oregano in a shallow bowl. 2. In another shallow bowl, mix the seasoned breadcrumbs and olive oil. 3. Dredge the fish strips in the egg mixture. Then, dip the strips in the breadcrumb mixture, coating them completely and shaking off any excess. 4. Arrange the fish strips in a cooking tray, making sure not to crowd them. 5. Set your air fryer to Air Fry, then adjust the temperature to 400 degrees F and the time to 10 minutes. 6. Press the Start button to initiate preheating. 7. When the screen displays "Add Food," transfer the cooking tray into the air fryer. 8. Close its door, and let the machine do the cooking. 9. Assemble your burritos with warm fish strips, tortillas, and guacamole sauce. 10. Serve immediately and enjoy!
Per serving: Calories 344; Fat 14.9g; Sodium 227mg; Carbs 14g; Fiber 1g; Sugars 1.4g; Protein 25.7g

Crunchy Coconut Shrimp

Prep time: 15 minutes | Cook time: 12 minutes | Serves: 4

½ cup all-purpose flour
Salt and ground white pepper, as required
2 egg whites
¾ cup plain breadcrumbs
½ cup unsweetened coconut,
shredded
2 teaspoons lime zest, grated finely
1-pound shrimp, peeled and deveined

1. Add the flour, salt, and white pepper to a shallow dish and mix well. 2. Add the egg white and beat lightly in a second shallow dish. 3. Mix the breadcrumbs, coconut, and lime zest in a third shallow dish. 4. Coat the shrimp with flour mixture, dip into the egg white, and then coat with the coconut mixture. 5. Arrange the coated shrimp onto two cooking trays in a single layer. 6. Set your air fryer to Air Fry, then adjust the temperature to 400 degrees F and the time to 12 minutes. 7. Press the Start button to initiate preheating. 8. When the screen displays "Add Food," transfer the tray to the cooking tray of the air fryer. 9. Close its door, and let the machine do the cooking. 10. Serve.
Per serving: Calories 236; Fat 13.9g; Sodium 451mg; Carbs 13.2g; Fiber 1.2g; Sugars 1.4g; Protein 14.3g

Air-Fried Shrimp in Lemon Juice

Prep time: 15 minutes | Cook time: 8 minutes | Serves: 3

2 tablespoons fresh lemon juice
1 tablespoon olive oil
1 teaspoon lemon pepper
¼ teaspoon paprika
¼ teaspoon garlic powder
12 ounces' medium shrimp, peeled and deveined

1. In a large bowl, add all the ingredients except the shrimp and mix until well combined. 2. Add the shrimp and toss to coat well. 3. Arrange the shrimps onto a cooking tray. 4. Set your air fryer to Air Fry, then adjust the temperature to 400 degrees F and the time to 8 minutes. 5. Press the Start button to initiate preheating. 6. When the screen displays "Add Food," transfer the cooking tray into the air fryer. 7. Close its door, and let the machine do the cooking. 8. Serve.

Per serving: Calories 285; Fat 9.8g; Sodium 639mg; Carbs 11.1g; Fiber 1.2g, Sugars 5.1g; Protein 27.8g

Butter Haddock Fillets

Prep time: 15 minutes | Cook time: 10 minutes | Serves: 4

½ pounds of haddock fillets (or any other white fish)
1 tablespoon butter, softened
1 cup bread crumbs
1 teaspoon dried oregano
1 teaspoon dried basil
1 teaspoon dried sage
1 teaspoon paprika
1 teaspoon garlic powder
1 teaspoon onion powder
Kosher salt and ground black pepper, to taste

1. Toss the fish with the other ingredients in a mixing bowl. 2. When the screen displays "Add Food," transfer the fish to a cooking tray. 3. Set your air fryer to Air Fry, then adjust the temperature to 400 degrees F and the time to 10 minutes. 4. Press the Start button to initiate preheating. 5. When the screen displays "Add Food," transfer the cooking tray into the air fryer. 6. Close its door, and let the machine do the cooking. 7. Serve.

Per serving: Calories 336; Fat 17.3g; Sodium 281mg; Carbs 8.1g; Fiber 5.3g, Sugars 17.7g; Protein 32.3g

Crispy Shrimp with Lime Wedges

Prep time: 15 minutes | Cook time: 5 minutes | Serves: 4

1-pound shrimp, remove shell and tail if desired
1½ tablespoons olive oil
1½ tablespoons lime juice
1½ tablespoons honey
2 cloves garlic, minced
⅛ teaspoon salt
Lime wedges, for serving
¼ cup chopped cilantro

1. Mix the olive oil, honey, lime juice, garlic, and salt in a bowl. 2. Add the shrimp, toss to combine, and marinate for 20-30 minutes. 3. Drip the excess marinade off the shrimp and put them in the cooking tray. 4. Set your air fryer to Air Fry, then adjust the temperature to 390 degrees F and time to 5 minutes. 5. Press the Start button to initiate preheating. 6. When the screen displays "Add Food," transfer the cooking tray into the air fryer. 7. Close its door, and let the machine do the cooking. 8. Garnish with chopped cilantro and lime wedges.

Per serving: Calories 336; Fat 17.3g; Sodium 281mg; Carbs 8.1g; Fiber 5.3g, Sugars 17.7g; Protein 32.3g

Easy Calamari

Prep time: 15 minutes | Cook time: 12 minutes | Serves: 4

1-pound squid rings
1 cup plain all-purpose flour
2 cups panko breadcrumbs
2 tablespoons salt
2 tablespoons cracked pepper
1 egg
1 cup buttermilk

1. Mix the buttermilk and 1 egg in a bowl. Mix the breadcrumbs, flour, salt, pepper, and buttermilk in another bowl. 2. Dip the squid rings into the buttermilk mix, then roll in breadcrumbs. 3. Arrange the coated calamari in a cooking tray in 1 layer. 4. Set your air fryer to Air Fry, then adjust the temperature to 400 degrees F and time to 12 minutes. 5. Press the Start button to initiate preheating. 6. When the screen displays "Add Food," transfer the cooking tray into the air fryer. 7. Close its door, and let the machine do the cooking. 8. Repeat for the rest of the calamari rings. 9. Serve with your favorite dipping sauce.

Per serving: Calories 344; Fat 14.9g; Sodium 227mg; Carbs 14g; Fiber 1g; Sugars 1.4g; Protein 25.7g

Shrimp Tempura

Prep time: 15 minutes | Cook time: 9 minutes | Serves: 4

2 pounds raw peeled shrimp medium
1 cup all-purpose flour
2 eggs
1 teaspoon water
2 ½ cups Panko bread crumbs
2 tablespoons vegetable oil
Lemon wedges, for serving

1. Whisk the two eggs and water in a bowl to make the egg wash. Put the flour in the second bowl and the breadcrumbs in the third one. 2. Dredge the shrimp in flour, shake off the excess flour, then dip into the egg wash, roll the shrimp in breadcrumbs, then spread on a cooking tray. 3. Set your air fryer to Air Fry, then adjust the temperature to 350 degrees F and time to 9 minutes. 4. Press the Start button to initiate preheating. 5. When the screen displays "Add Food," transfer the cooking tray into the air fryer. 6. Close its door, and let the machine do the cooking. 7. Garnish with lemon wedges and serve.

Per serving: Calories 351; Fat 22g; Sodium 502mg; Carbs 15.2g; Sugar 1.1g; Fiber 0.7g; Protein 26.4g

Simple Bacon-Wrapped Tiger Shrimp

Prep time: 15 minutes | Cook time: 7 minutes | Serves: 4

1¼ pounds tiger shrimp, peeled and deveined
1-pound bacon

1. Wrap shrimp with a slice of bacon. 2. Refrigerate for about 20 minutes. 3. Arrange the shrimp in a cooking tray. 4. Set your air fryer to Air Fry, then adjust the temperature to 390 degrees F and time to 7 minutes. 5. Press the Start button to initiate preheating. 6. When the screen displays "Add Food," transfer the cooking tray into the air fryer. 7. Close its door, and let the machine do the cooking. 8. Serve.

Per serving: Calories 285; Fat 9.8g; Sodium 639mg; Carbs 11.1g; Fiber 1.2g, Sugars 5.1g; Protein 27.8g

Bang Bang Scallops with Sauce Mix

Prep time: 15 minutes | Cook time: 11 minutes | Serves: 4

1 cup all-purpose flour, divided	¼ cup chopped green onion
	cooking spray
½ teaspoon fine sea salt	For the sauce:
½ cup buttermilk	½ cup mayonnaise
1 egg	¼ cup Sriracha hot sauce
1 cup panko bread crumbs	2 Tbsp. Thai sweet chili sauce
1-pound scallops	

1. Mix ¾ cup of flour with the salt in a bowl. Beat the buttermilk, ¼ cup of flour, and one egg thoroughly in a separate bowl. Put the breadcrumbs in a third bowl. 2. Dredge the scallops in flour, then dip into the buttermilk mix and drip off the excess liquid. Roll in the breadcrumbs and mix until evenly coated. 3. Then transfer to a cooking tray. 4. Mix the vinegar, shallots, mayo, mustard, and cayenne pepper. Set aside until ready to use. 5. Set your air fryer to Air Fry, then adjust the temperature to 375 degrees F and time to 11 minutes. 6. Press the Start button to initiate preheating. 7. When the screen displays "Add Food," transfer the cooking tray into the air fryer. 8. Close its door, and let the machine do the cooking. 9. Mix the mayonnaise, hot, and chili sauces in a small bowl until smooth. 10. Remove the scallop from the air fryer and place it in a bowl. Add ½ sauce and toss well to coat the scallop. 11. Garnish with chopped green onions.

Per serving: Calories 236; Fat 13.9g; Sodium 451mg; Carbs 13.2g; Fiber 1.2g; Sugars 1.4g; Protein 14.3g

Crab Legs

Prep time: 15 minutes | Cook time: 5 minutes | Serves: 4

1-pound crab legs cleaned and scrubbed	½ teaspoon garlic powder
	Olive oil, as needed
1 teaspoon old bay	

1. Mix the crab legs, old bay, olive oil, and garlic powder in a large bowl. 2. Rub the oil, old bay, and garlic powder all over the crab legs. 3. Wrap the crab legs tightly in foil and place them in a cooking tray. 4. Set your air fryer to Air Fry, then adjust the temperature to 380 degrees F and time to 5 minutes. 5. Press the Start button to initiate preheating. 6. When the screen displays "Add Food," transfer the cooking tray into the air fryer. 7. Close its door, and let the machine do the cooking. 8. Remove from the cooking tray and foil. 9. Serve immediately with your favorite dipping sauce.

Per serving: Calories 336; Fat 17.3g; Sodium 281mg; Carbs 8.1g; Fiber 5.3g, Sugars 17.7g; Protein 32.3g

Garlic White Fish

Prep time: 15 minutes | Cook time: 12 minutes | Serves: 4

12 ounces' tilapia fillets, rinsed and patted dry	½ teaspoon onion powder
	sea salt and pepper, to taste
½ teaspoon garlic powder	¼ cup fresh chopped parsley
½ teaspoon lemon pepper seasoning	Lemon wedges, for serving

1. Mix the garlic powder, lemon pepper, onion powder, salt, and pepper in a small bowl. 2. Coat the fillets with olive oil and season both sides with the prepared spice mix. 3. Coat the cooking tray with olive oil. Lay the fish on parchment paper in a cooking tray. Add some lemon wedges next to the fish. 4. Set your air fryer to Air Fry, then adjust the temperature to 360 degrees F and time to 12 minutes. 5. Press the Start button to initiate preheating. 6. When the screen displays

"Add Food," transfer the cooking tray into the air fryer when the screen displays "Add Food" 7. Close its door, and let the machine do the cooking. 8. Garnish with parsley and lemon wedges.

Per serving: Calories 305; Fat 15g; Sodium 548mg; Carbs 12g; Sugar 1.2g; Fiber 0.7g; Protein 29g

Pecan Crusted Halibut Fillets

Prep time: 15 minutes | Cook time: 8 minutes | Serves: 4

4 4-ounce halibut fillets skin removed	divided
	2 egg whites
½ cup pecan pieces	½ cup cornstarch
½ cup panko breadcrumbs	½ cup white wine
2 tablespoons lemon pepper,	

1. Mix the egg white and cornstarch in a bowl to make a dredge. 2. Add wine until you get the consistency of the pancake batter. Stir in the lemon pepper. 3. Break down the pecan in a food processor until it's similar to breadcrumbs. 4. Put in a bowl and mix with the panko. 5. Season filet with salt and pepper. 6. Dredge the filet into the egg and pecan panko mix, ensuring the halibut is well-crusted. Repeat with the remaining fish, then place in a cooking tray. 7. Set your air fryer to Air Fry, then adjust the temperature to 375 degrees F and time to 8 minutes. 8. Press the Start button to initiate preheating. 9. When the screen displays "Add Food," transfer the cooking tray into the air fryer. 10. Close its door, and let the machine do the cooking. 11. Serve with a side dish of your choice.

Per serving: Calories 254; Fat 28g; Sodium 346mg; Carbs 12.3g; Sugar 1g; Fiber 0.7g; Protein 24.3 g

Baked Salmon with Onion and Carrot

Prep time: 15 minutes | Cook time: 8 minutes | Serves: 2

½ pound (227 g) salmon fillet	sliced
1 teaspoon toasted sesame oil	⅓ cup chopped fresh flat-leaf parsley
1 onion, sliced	
1 carrot, shredded	¼ cup chopped fresh basil
1 yellow bell pepper, thinly	8 rice paper wrappers

1. Arrange the salmon in the cooking tray. Drizzle the sesame oil all over the salmon and scatter the onion on top. 2. Gill a small shallow bowl with warm water. One by one, dip the rice paper wrappers into the water for a few seconds or until moistened, then put them on a work surface. 3. When cooking is complete, the fish should flake apart with a fork. Remove from the air fryer to a plate. 4. Make the spring rolls: Place ⅛ of the salmon and onion mixture, parsley, carrot, bell pepper, and basil into the rice wrapper's center and fold the sides over the filling. Roll up the wrapper carefully and tightly like a burrito. Repeat with the remaining wrappers and filling. 5. When the screen displays "Add Food," transfer the rolls to the cooking tray. 6. Set your air fryer to Air Fry, then adjust the temperature to 370 degrees F and time to 8 minutes. 7. Press the Start button to initiate preheating. 8. When the screen displays "Add Food," transfer the cooking tray into the air fryer. 9. Close its door, and let the machine do the cooking. 10. Serve.

Per serving: Calories 344; Fat 14.9g; Sodium 227mg; Carbs 14g; Fiber 1g; Sugars 1.4g; Protein 25.7g

Authentic Catfish

Prep time: 15 minutes | Cook time: 10 minutes | Serves: 4

1 tablespoon chopped parsley
1 tablespoon olive oil
¼ cup seasoned fish fry
4 catfish fillets

1. Rinse off catfish fillets and pat dry. 2. Add fish fry seasoning to Ziploc baggie, then catfish. Shake the bag and ensure the fish gets well coated. 3. Spray fillet with olive oil. 4. Add fillets to the cooking tray. 5. Set your air fryer to Air Fry, then adjust the temperature to 400 degrees F and time to 10 minutes. 6. Press the Start button to initiate preheating. 7. When the screen displays "Add Food," transfer the cooking tray into the air fryer. 8. Close its door, and let the machine do the cooking. 9. Serve.

Per serving: Calories 236; Fat 13.9g; Sodium 451mg; Carbs 13.2g; Fiber 1.2g; Sugars 1.4g; Protein 14.3g

Air Fried White Fish Fillet

Prep time: 15 minutes | Cook time: 10 minutes | Serves: 4

12 ounces' white fish fillets
½ teaspoon lemon pepper seasoning
½ teaspoon garlic powder
½ teaspoon onion powder
Salt and black pepper to taste

1. Spray fish fillets with cooking spray and season with onion powder, lemon pepper seasoning, garlic powder, pepper, and salt. 2. Place parchment paper on the bottom of the cooking tray. 3. Place fish fillets into the cooking tray. 4. Set your air fryer to Air Fry, then adjust the temperature to 350 degrees F and time to 10 minutes. 5. Press the Start button to initiate preheating. 6. When the screen displays "Add Food," transfer the cooking tray into the air fryer when the screen displays "Add Food." 7. Close its door, and let the machine do the cooking. 8. Serve.

Per serving: Calories 298; Fat 13g; Sodium 345mg; Carbs 1.4g; Fiber 0.3g; Sugar 0.07g; Protein 42g

Herby Salmon

Prep time: 15 minutes | Cook time: 7 minutes | Serves: 2

2 (4-ounce) salmon fillets, skin removed
2 tablespoons unsalted butter; melted.
1 teaspoon paprika
⅛ teaspoon ground cayenne pepper
¼ teaspoon ground black pepper
½ teaspoon garlic powder

1. Brush fillet with butter. Combine remaining in a small bowl and then rub onto fish. 2. Place fillets into the cooking tray. 3. Set your air fryer to Air Fry, then adjust the temperature to 350 degrees F and time to 7 minutes. 4. Press the Start button to initiate preheating. 5. When the screen displays "Add Food," transfer the cooking tray into the air fryer. 6. Close its door, and let the machine do the cooking. 7. Serve.

Per serving: Calories 344; Fat 14.9g; Sodium 227mg; Carbs 12g; Fiber 1.2g; Sugars 1g; Protein 27g

Baked Potatoes

Prep time: 5 minutes | Cook time: 45 minutes | Serves: 3

3 Idaho or Russet Baking Potatoes	1 teaspoon parsley
1 to 2 tablespoons olive oil	1 tablespoon garlic
	1 tablespoon salt

1. Thoroughly clean the potatoes. 2. With a fork, poke numerous holes in the potatoes. 3. Drizzle the olive oil over the potatoes. Rub the parsley, garlic, and salt into the potatoes evenly. 4. Place the potatoes in the cooking tray and cook on the Bake function for 35 to 40 minutes at 365 degrees F. 5. Serve with a dipping sauce of your choices, such as sour cream or fresh parsley. 6. Enjoy!

Per serving: Calories 213; Fat 4g; Sodium 2336mg; Carbs 39; Fiber 2g; Sugars 1g; Protein 4g

Herbs de Provence Mushrooms

Prep time: 10 minutes | Cook time: 32 minutes | Serves: 4

1 tablespoon butter	2 pounds' fresh mushrooms, quartered
2 teaspoons Herbs de Provence	2 tablespoons white wine
½ teaspoon garlic powder	

1. In a frying pan, mix the butter, herbs de Provence, wine, and garlic powder over medium-low heat and stir fry for about 2 minutes. 2. Add in the mushrooms and remove from the heat. 3. Transfer the mushroom mixture to the cooking tray. Put in the Air Fryer and cook on Bake mode for 30 minutes at 365 degrees F. 4. Serve and enjoy.

Per serving: Calories 218; Fat 3.8g; Sodium 555mg; Carbs 31.3; Fiber 2g; Sugars 1g; Protein 5.4g

Olives and Broccoli with Parmesan Cheese

Prep time: 5 minutes | Cook time: 19 minutes | Serves: 4

2 pounds' broccoli, stemmed and cut into 1-inch florets	2 tablespoons olive oil
⅓ cup Kalamata olives halved and pitted	Salt and ground black pepper, as required
¼ cup Parmesan cheese, grated	2 teaspoons fresh lemon zest, grated

1. Preheat the air fryer to 400 degrees F on Air Fry mode and oil the cooking tray. 2. Broccoli should be cooked for around 4 minutes and drained adequately. 3. Mix the broccoli, oil, salt, and black pepper in a large mixing basin, and toss well to coat. 4. Cook for around 15 minutes with broccoli in the cooking tray on Air Fry mode. 5. Toss in the olives, lemon zest, and cheese before serving.

Per serving: Calories 169; Fat 10.2g; Sodium 254mg; Carbs 16g; Fiber 1g; Sugar 3.9g; Protein 8.5g

Sweet Potatoes Noodles with Butternut Squash

Prep time: 5 minutes | Cook time: 55 minutes | Serves: 2

Squash:	⅛ teaspoon sea salt
3 cups chopped butternut squash	Veggies:
2 teaspoons extra light olive oil	5-6 Brussels sprouts
	5 fresh shiitake mushrooms
	2 cloves garlic

½ teaspoon black sesame seeds	1 teaspoon sesame oil
½ teaspoon white sesame seeds	1 teaspoon onion powder
A few sprinkles of ground pepper	1 teaspoon garlic powder
A small pinch of red pepper flake	¼ teaspoon sea salt
1 tablespoon extra light olive oil	Noodles:
	1 bundle sweet potato vermicelli
	2-3 teaspoons low-sodium soy sauce

1. Begin by soaking potato vermicelli in water for at least 2 hours. 2. Heat the air fryer to 380 degrees F in advance. 3. Drizzle olive oil over the squash and season with salt and pepper on a baking sheet with edges. On the pan, thoroughly combine all ingredients. 4. Cook for 30 minutes on Roast mode, tossing and turning the squash halfway through. 5. Chop the Brussels sprouts and remove the stems from the mushrooms. 6. Chop the garlic, and mix the vegetables. 7. Add garlic powder, onion powder, sesame seeds, red pepper flakes, salt, and pepper after drizzling sesame and olive oil over the mixture. 8. Take 15 minutes of roasting vegetables on Roast mode. 9. Put the noodles in a small saucepan with just enough water to cover them while the vegetable roast. 10. Bring water to a rolling boil and boil noodles for about 8 minutes. 11. Drain noodles and combine with squash and veggies in a large bowl. 12. Drizzle with soy sauce, sprinkle with sesame seeds, and serve.

Per serving: Calories 409; Fat 15.6g; Sodium 1124mg; Carbs 69.3g; Fiber 12.2g; Sugar 1g; Protein 8.8g

Simple Flat Bread

Prep time: 5 minutes | Cook time: 7 minutes | Serves: 2

1 cup shredded mozzarella cheese	1 ounce full-fat cream cheese softened
¼ cup almond flour	

1. Microwave the cheese for 30 seconds to melt it. Blend in the almond flour until it's completely smooth. 2. Toss in the cream cheese, and then resume mixing until form a dough. If necessary, knead with moist hands. 3. Divide the dough into two halves and layout between 2 sheets of parchment paper to a thickness of 14 inches. 4. Place the flatbreads in the cooking tray after covering them with parchment paper. If necessary, work in bunches. 5. Cook for 7 minutes at 400 degrees F on Air Fry Mode. At the halfway point, flip once more. Serve.

Per serving: Calories 296; Fat 22.6g; Sodium 654mg; Carb 3.3g; Fiber 1g; Sugar 1g; Protein 16.3g

Spicy Firm Tofu

Prep time: 5 minutes | Cook time: 25 minutes | Serves: 4

16 ounces' firm tofu, pressed and cubed	1 teaspoon sriracha
1 tablespoon vegan oyster sauce	½ teaspoon shallot powder
1 tablespoon tamari sauce	½ teaspoon porcini powder
1 teaspoon cider vinegar	1 teaspoon garlic powder
1 teaspoon pure maple syrup	1 tablespoon sesame oil
	2 tablespoons golden flaxseed meal

1. Combine the tofu, oyster sauce, tamari sauce, vinegar, maple syrup, sriracha, shallot powder, porcini powder, garlic powder, and sesame oil in a large mixing bowl. Allow 30

minutes for marinating. 2. Toss the marinated tofu and flax-seed meal together. 3. Cook for 10 minutes on Bake mode at 365 degrees F, then flip and cook for another 12 minutes.

Per serving: Calories 173; Fat 13g; Sodium 456mg; Carbs 5g; Fiber 1g; Sugar 3g; Protein 8g

Fully Creamy Cabbage

Prep time: 10 minutes | Cook time: 20 minutes | Serves: 2

½ green cabbage head, chopped	Salt and black pepper to taste
½ yellow onion, chopped	½ cup whipped cream
	1 tablespoon cornstarch

1. In the cooking tray of the air fryer, place the cabbage and onion. 2. Add cornstarch, cream, salt, and pepper to a mixing bowl, mix them well and pour over cabbage mix. 3. Cook for 20 minutes at 400 degrees F on Air Fry mode. 4. Serve.

Per serving: Calories 208; Fat 10g; Sodium 476mg; Carbs 16g; Fiber 3g; Sugar 2g; Protein 5g

Artichokes and Olives with Tomato Sauce

Prep time: 20 minutes | Cook time: 15 minutes | Serves: 4

14 ounces canned artichoke hearts, drained	2 cups black olives, pitted
½ cup tomato sauce	3 garlic cloves; minced
	1 tablespoon. olive oil
	1 teaspoon. garlic powder

1. Toss the olives with the artichokes and the other ingredients in the air fryer pan, toss, place in the fryer, and cook at 400 degrees F for 15 minutes on Air Fry Mode. 2. Serve the mixture by dividing it among plates.

Per serving: Calories 180; Fat 4g; Sodium 498mg; Carbs 5g; Fiber 3g; Sugar 2g; Protein 6g

Parmesan Asparagus in Lemon Juice

Prep time: 17 minutes | Cook time: 12 minutes | Serves: 4

1-pound asparagus, trimmed	2 tablespoons olive oil
3 garlic cloves; minced	Juice of 1 lemon
3 tablespoons Parmesan, grated	A pinch of salt and black pepper

1. Take a bowl, mix the asparagus with the ingredients, and toss. 2. Put the asparagus in your cooking tray and cook at 400 degrees F for 12 minutes on Air Fry mode. Divide between plates and serve!

Per serving: Calories 175; Fat 5g; Sodium 398mg; Carbs 4g; Fiber 2g; Sugar 1g; Protein 8g

Pecan Brownies

Prep time: 30 minutes | Cook time: 20 minutes | Serves: 6

¼ cup chopped pecans	½ cup blanched finely ground almond flour.
¼ cup low carb sugar-free chocolate chips	½ cup powdered erythritol
¼ cup unsalted butter; softened.	2 tablespoons unsweetened cocoa powder
1 large egg.	½ teaspoon Baking powder.

1. Combine almond flour, erythritol, cocoa powder, and baking powder in a large mixing basin. Combine the butter an egg in another bowl. 2. Preheat the air fryer to 400 degrees F and set the timer for 20 minutes on Air Fry mode. A toothpick inserted in the center should clean when the dish is thoroughly cooked. Allow 20 minutes for cooling and firming.

Per serving: Calories 215; Fat 18.9g; Sodium 490mg; Carbs 21.8g; Fiber 2.8g; Sugar 2g; Protein 4.2g

Cheese Endives with Lemon Zest

Prep time: 20 minutes | Cook time: 15 minutes | Serves: 4

4 endives, trimmed	2 tablespoons Olive oil
¼ cup goat cheese, crumbled	1 teaspoon Lemon zest, grated
1 tablespoon Lemon juice	A pinch of salt and black pepper
2 tablespoons Chives; chopped.	

1. Toss the endives with the remaining ingredients, except the cheese and chives, in a large mixing basin. 2. Place the endives in the basket of your air fryer and cook for 15 minutes at 380 degrees F on Roast mode. 3. Distribute the corn among the plates. 4. Serve with a sprinkling of chives and cheese on top.

Per serving: Calories 140; Fat 4g; Sodium 378mg; Carbs 5g; Fiber 3g; Sugar 2g; Protein 7g

Buffalo Cauliflower

Prep time: 20 minutes | Cook time: 15 minutes | Serves: 3

1 medium head cauliflower	1 ½ teaspoons maple syrup
2 teaspoons avocado oil	¼ teaspoon sea salt
3 tablespoons red hot sauce	1 tablespoon cornstarch or arrowroot starch
2 tablespoons nutritional yeast	

1. Preheat your air fryer to 365 degrees F on Bake mode. 2. Except for the cauliflower, combine all ingredients in a mixing basin. 3. To mix them, stir them together. Add the cauliflower to the mixing basin and toss to coat it evenly. 4. Place half of the cauliflower in the air fryer and cook for 15 minutes, occasionally shaking until desired consistency is achieved. 5. Repeat with the remaining cauliflower, but reduce the Cooking Time to 10 minutes. Refrigerate the cauliflower for 3-4 days, firmly wrapped. Return to the air fryer for 1-2 minutes to reheat until crisp.

Per serving: Calories 248; Fat 20g; Sodium 476mg; Carbs 13g; Fiber 2g; Sugar 2g; Protein 4g

Crispy Onion Rings

Prep time: 5 minutes | Cook time: 20 minutes | Serves: 3

½ cup almond flour	1 egg, beaten
¾ cup coconut milk	1 tablespoon baking powder
1 big white onion, sliced into rings	1 tablespoon smoked paprika
	Salt and pepper to taste

1. Combine the almond flour, baking powder, smoked paprika, salt, and pepper in a mixing bowl. 2. Combine the eggs and coconut milk in a separate dish. 3. In a separate bowl, soak the onion pieces in the egg mixture. 4. Using the almond flour mixture, coat the onion pieces. 5. Fill the air fryer basket halfway with the batter. Adjust the temperature to 400 degrees F and set the timer for 15 minutes on Air Fry mode. Select Start to begin preheating. 6. To ensure uniform frying, turn the food when the air fryer indicates "turn Food." 7. Once done, serve and enjoy!

Per serving: Calories 217; Fat 17g; Sodium 334mg; Carbs 2g; Fiber 6g; Sugar 0g; Protein 5g

Brussels Sprout with Caesar Dressing

Prep time: 5 minutes | Cook time: 16 minutes | Serves: 2

2 tablespoons Parmesan, freshly grated
½ pound Brussels sprouts, thinly sliced
1 teaspoon garlic powder
1 tablespoon extra-virgin olive

oil
Caesar dressing for dipping
Freshly ground black pepper to taste
Kosher salt to taste

1. Combine the oil, Brussels sprouts, garlic powder, and Parmesan in a large mixing bowl. Toss everything together well. Add salt and pepper to season. 2. In the cooking tray, place the sprouts that have been coated. 3. Place in the air fryer. Select temp of air fryer to 365 degrees F and time for 8 minutes on Air Fry mode. Cook for another 8 minutes, occasionally tossing, until the sprouts are crisp and golden brown. 4. Serve with a sprinkling of Parmesan cheese on top. Serve with Caesar salad for dipping.
Per serving: Calories 202; Fat 12.32g; Sodium 330mg; Carbs 15.9g; Fiber 2g; Sugar 4.18g; Protein 6.89g

Herbed Potatoes

Prep time: 10 minutes | Cook time: 15 minutes | Serves: 4

3 tablespoons vegetable oil
4 yellow baby potatoes, quartered
2 teaspoons dried rosemary, minced
1 tablespoon minced garlic

1 teaspoon ground black pepper
¼ cup chopped parsley
1 tablespoon fresh lime or lemon juice
1 teaspoon salt

1. Combine the potatoes, garlic, rosemary, oil, pepper, and salt in a large mixing basin. Make a thorough mix. 2. Set the seasoned potatoes on the cooking tray and place them in the air fryer. Cook for 15 minutes at 400 degrees F on Air Fry mode. 3. Check if the potatoes are fully cooked. 4. Remove it from the air fryer and set it on a serving plate after it has finished cooking. 5. Lemon juice and parsley are sprinkled on top. 6. Warm the dish before serving.
Per serving: Calories 201; Fat 10.71g; Sodium 592.97mg; Carbs 22.71g; Fiber 3.5g; Sugar 1.32g; Protein 3.34g

Yummy Stuffed Mushrooms

Prep time: 5 minutes | Cook time: 15 minutes | Serves: 3

3 portobello mushrooms
1 teaspoon garlic
1 medium onion
3 tablespoons grated mozzarella cheese
2 slices of chopped ham

1 tomato
Green pepper
½ teaspoon sea salt
¼ teaspoon pepper
1 tablespoon olive oil

1. Tomato, pepper, onion, garlic, and ham should be diced or chopped. 2. Remove the stems from the mushrooms after they have been washed and dried. Drizzle with olive oil and leave aside for the time being. 3. Pepper, salt, cheese, tomato, onion, garlic, bell peppers, and ham should all be combined. Fill the mushroom caps with the mixture. 4. Select Air Fry mode and set the temperature to 400 degrees F. Once preheated, place the food and cook for 8 minutes in the air fryer. 5. Serve alongside your favorite main course.
Per serving: Calories 271; Fat 18.3g; Sodium 398mg; Carbs 8g; Fiber 2g; Sugar 2g; Protein 19g

Green Beans with Sesame Seeds

Prep time: 5 minutes | Cook time: 8 minutes | Serves: 4

1 tablespoon reduced-sodium soy sauce or tamari
½ tablespoon Sriracha sauce
4 teaspoons toasted sesame oil, divided

12 ounces (340 g) trimmed green beans
½ tablespoon toasted sesame seeds

1. Whisk the Sriracha sauce, soy sauce, and 1 teaspoon sesame oil in a small bowl until smooth. Remove from the equation. 2. Toss the green beans with the remaining sesame oil in a large mixing basin until thoroughly coated. 3. Arrange the green beans in the cooking tray. 4. Select Air Fry mode, set the temperature to 400 degrees F, and time to 8 minutes. When the air fryer indicates "Add Food," place the food and cook. 5. When the air fryer indicates "turn Food," stir the green beans. 6. When the green beans are done, they should be lightly browned and soft. Transfer to a plate from the air fryer. Toss the green beans in the sauce that has been made. Serve with toasted sesame seeds sprinkled over the top.
Per serving: Calories 214; Fat 2.8g; Sodium 445mg; Carbs 0.1g; Fiber 0g; Sugar 0g; Protein 9.8g

Tomato and Black Beans in Vegetable Broth

Prep time: 15 minutes | Cook time: 20 minutes | Serves: 6

1 tablespoon olive oil
1 medium onion, diced
3 garlic cloves, minced
1 cup vegetable broth
3 cans of black beans, drained and rinsed

2 cans of diced tomatoes
2 chipotle peppers, chopped
2 teaspoons cumin
2 teaspoons chili powder
1 teaspoon dried oregano
½ teaspoon salt

1. Take 3 minutes over medium heat, and sauté the garlic and onions in olive oil. 2. Stir in the remaining ingredients while scraping the bottom of the pan to avoid sticking. 3. Fill a dish halfway with the mixture. Cover with a layer of aluminum foil. 4. Select "Bake" mode, set the time to 20 minutes, and adjust the temperature to 365 degrees F. 5. When the air fryer indicates "Add Food," place the food and cook for 20 minutes. 6. When ready, plate up and serve immediately.
Per serving: Calories 82; Fat 5.66g; Sodium 46mg; Carbs 6.3g; Fiber 2.4g; Sugar 2g; Protein 1.5g

Potatoes and Zucchinis

Prep time: 10 minutes | Cook time: 45 minutes | Serves: 4

2 potatoes, peeled and cubed
4 carrots, cut into chunks
1 head broccoli, cut into florets
4 zucchinis, sliced thickly

Salt and ground black pepper to taste
¼ cup olive oil
1 tablespoon dry onion powder

1. In a cooking tray, add all the ingredients and combine well. 2. Select "Bake" mode. 3. Set the temperature at 365 degrees F. 4. Set the cooking time to 45 minutes. Cook ensuring the vegetables are soft and the sides have browned before serving.
Per serving: Calories 201; Fat 10.71g; Sodium 592.97mg; Carbs 22.71g; Fiber 3.5g; Sugar 2g; Protein 3.34g

Easy-to-Prepared Veggies

Prep time: 10 minutes | Cook time: 6 minutes | Serves: 4

1 large zucchini, sliced

1 cup cherry tomatoes, halved

1 parsnip, sliced
1 green pepper, sliced
1 carrot, sliced
1 teaspoon mixed herbs
1 teaspoon mustard

1 teaspoon garlic purée
6 tablespoons olive oil
Salt and ground black pepper
to taste

1. Preheat the air fryer to 400 degrees F (204 degrees Celsius). 2. Combine all the ingredients in a bowl, and coat the vegetables well. 3. Select "Air Fry" mode, set the temperature to 400 degrees F, and cook time to 6 minutes. 4. Cook until the vegetables are tender and browned. 5. Serve immediately.
Per serving: Calories 229; Fat 1.6g; Sodium 189mg; Carbs 45.5g; Fiber 5.6g; Sugars 3.5g; Protein 7.8g

Red Potatoes Cubes

Prep time: 5 minutes | Cook time: 20 minutes | Serves: 4

6 red potatoes cut into 1-inch cubes
3 garlic cloves, minced
Salt

Pepper
1 teaspoon chopped chives
1 tablespoon extra-virgin olive oil

1. Combine the potatoes, garlic, salt & pepper to taste, chives, and olive oil in a sealable plastic bag. To coat the potatoes, seal the bag and shake it. 2. Select Air Fry mode. Cook the potatoes for 10 minutes at 400 degrees F. 3. Shake the basket in the air fryer after opening it. Cook for a further 10 minutes. 4. Cool before serving.
Per serving: Calories 257; Fat 4g; Sodium 58mg; Carbs 52g; Fiber 6g; Sugar 5g; Protein 6g

Cauliflower Rice with Peas

Prep time: 25 minutes | Cook time: 20 minutes | Serves: 5

2½ cups riced cauliflower (1 head cauliflower if making your own)
2 teaspoons sesame oil, divided
1 medium green bell pepper, chopped

1 cup peas
1 cup diced carrots
½ cup chopped onion
Salt
Pepper
1 tablespoon soy sauce
2 medium eggs, scrambled

1. If you want to create your own riced cauliflower, use a cheese grater with medium holes to shred the head of cauliflower. Alternatively, chop the cauliflower head into florets and pulse in a food processor until it resembles rice. 2. Coat the bottom of a barrel pan with 1 teaspoon of sesame oil. 3. Combine the riced cauliflower, green bell pepper, peas, carrots, and onion in a large mixing basin. Drizzle the last 1 teaspoon of sesame oil over the veggies and toss to combine. Season it to taste with salt and pepper. 4. Fill the barrel pan halfway with the mixture. Select Air Fry mode. Cook the food for 10 minutes at 400 degrees F. 5. Remove the barrel pan from the air fryer. Add the scrambled eggs and a drizzle of soy sauce. To mix, stir everything together. 6. Serve warm.
Per serving: Calories 81; Fat 4g; Sodium 280mg; Carbs 9g; Fiber 4g; Sugar 0g; Protein 5g

Veggies Medley

Prep time: 5 minutes | Cook time: 15 minutes | Serves: 4

1 head broccoli, chopped (about 2 cups)
2 medium carrots, cut into 1-inch pieces
Salt
Pepper

Cooking oil
1 zucchini, cut into 1-inch chunks
1 medium bell pepper, thinly sliced and seeded

1. Combine the broccoli and carrots in a large mixing basin. To taste, season it with salt and pepper. Cooking oil is sprayed over the surface. 2. In the cooking tray, place the broccoli and carrots. Select Air Fry mode, set the time to 6 minutes, and the temperature to 400 degrees F. When the air fryer indicates "Add Food," place the cooking tray in the air fryer and cook. 3. In a mixing dish, combine the zucchini and red pepper. To taste, season it with salt and pepper. Spray with cooking oil. 4. Combine the zucchini and red pepper with broccoli and carrots. Cook for additional 6 minutes. 5. Cool before serving.
Per serving: Calories 47; Fat 1g; Sodium 80mg; Carbs 10g; Fiber 3g; Sugar 0g; Protein 2g

Panko Asparagus

Prep time: 15 minutes | Cook time: 6 minutes | Serves: 4

2 egg whites
¼ cup water
¼ cup plus 2 tablespoons grated Parmesan cheese, divided
¾ cup panko bread crumbs

¼ teaspoon salt
12 ounces (340 g) fresh asparagus spears, woody ends trimmed
Cooking spray

1. Whisk the egg whites and water together in a small bowl until slightly frothy. Combine ¼ cup of Parmesan cheese, bread crumbs, and salt in a separate shallow dish. 2. After dipping the asparagus in the egg white, roll it in the cheese mixture to coat it thoroughly. 3. Arrange the asparagus spears in a single layer in the air fry basket, allowing space between them. Using cooking spray, spritz the asparagus. 4. Select Air Fry, set temperature to 400 degrees F (204ºC), and set time to 6 minutes. When the air fryer indicates "Add Food," place the food and cook until it is golden brown and crunchy. 5. Serve immediately with the remaining 2 tablespoons of cheese.
Per serving: Calories 246; Fat 2.8g; Sodium 875mg; Carbs 0.1g; Fiber 0g; Sugar 0g; Protein 10.8g

Cheesy Eggplant

Prep time: 15 minutes | Cook time: 20 minutes | Serves: 4

1 medium eggplant, peeled
2 eggs
½ cup all-purpose flour
¾ cup Italian bread crumbs
2 tablespoons grated Parmesan cheese
Salt

Pepper
¾ cup marinara sauce
½ cup shredded Parmesan cheese
½ cup shredded mozzarella cheese

1. Cut the eggplant into ½-inch thick circles. To dry the eggplant thoroughly, blot it using paper towels. You may also sweat off the moisture by sprinkling it with a teaspoon salt. 2. Beat the eggs in a small bowl. In a separate small bowl, put the flour. Mix the bread crumbs, grated Parmesan cheese, and salt & pepper to taste in a third small bowl. 3. Cooking oil should be sprayed into the cooking tray. 4. Each eggplant round should be floured first, dipped in eggs, and last in the bread crumb mixture. 5. In the cooking tray, place the eggplant rounds. Do not stack the items. Cook in batches if possible. Cooking oil should be sprayed on the eggplant. Select Air Fry mode. Cook for 7 minutes at 400 degrees F. 6. Activate the air fryer. 7. Remove the cooked eggplant from the air fryer and repeat steps 5 and 6 with the rest of the eggplant. 8. Let the dish cool for a while before serving.
Per serving: Calories 310; Fat 9g; Sodium 844mg; Carbs 42g; Fiber 7g; Sugar 5g; Protein 16g

Glazed Carrot Sticks

Prep time: 5 minutes | Cook time: 18 minutes | Serves: 4

3 medium-size carrots, cut
into 2-inch × ½-inch sticks
1 tablespoon orange juice
2 teaspoons balsamic vinegar
1 teaspoon maple syrup
1 teaspoon avocado oil
½ teaspoon dried rosemary
¼ teaspoon sea salt
¼ teaspoon lemon zest

1. Sprinkle the carrots in a baking pan with balsamic vinegar, orange juice, maple syrup, avocado oil, sea salt, rosemary, and lemon zest. Toss thoroughly. 2. Select Roast, set the temperature to 380 degrees F, and time to 18 minutes. Cook the carrots until they are beautifully caramelized and soft; during the cooking period, stir the carrots several times. 4. Serve immediately.
Per serving: Calories 209; Fat 2.8g; Sodium 454mg; Carbs 0.1g; Fiber 0g; Sugar 0g; Protein 11.8g

Simple Fried Asparagus

Prep time: 5 minutes | Cook time: 10 minutes | Serves: 2

Nutritional yeast
Olive oil nonstick spray
1 bunch of asparagus

1. After washing the asparagus, remove the thick, woody ends. 2. Using an olive oil spray, lightly coat the asparagus and sprinkle with yeast. 3. Arrange the asparagus in a single layer on the air fryer rack/basket. 4. Select Air Fry mode. Adjust the temperature to 400 degrees F and set the timer to 8 minutes, and cook.
Per serving: Calories 17; Fat 8g; Sodium 367mg; Carbs 2g; Fiber 0g; Sugar 0g; Protein 9g

Squash Croquettes

Prep time: 5 minutes | Cook time: 17 minutes | Serves: 4

⅓ butternut squash, peeled
and grated
⅓ cup all-purpose flour
2 eggs, whisked
4 cloves garlic, minced
1½ tablespoons olive oil
1 teaspoon fine sea salt
⅓ teaspoon freshly ground
black pepper or more to taste
⅓ teaspoon dried sage
A pinch of ground allspice

1. Using parchment paper, line the air fry basket. Remove from the equation. 2. Combine all ingredients in a mixing bowl and whisk until thoroughly mixed. 3. To make the squash croquettes, follow these steps: Drop tablespoons of the squash mixture onto a lightly floured surface with a tiny cookie scoop and roll into balls with your palms. Place them in the cooking tray to cook. 4. Select Air Fry, set temperature to 400 degrees F (204ºC), and set time to 17 minutes. 5. When the squash croquettes are done, they should be golden brown. Transfer to a platter and serve warm.
Per serving: Calories 216; Fat 3.8g; Sodium 435mg; Carbs 0.1g; Fiber 0g; Sugar 0g; Protein 10.8g

Cinnamon Squash Halves

Prep time: 5 minutes | Cook time: 15 minutes | Serves: 4

1 medium acorn squash,
halved crosswise and deseeded
1 teaspoon coconut oil
1 teaspoon light brown; Sugar
Few dashes of ground cinnamon
Few dashes of ground nutmeg

1. Rub the sliced sides of the acorn squash with coconut oil on a clean work area. Sprinkle the cinnamon, nutmeg, and brown sugar over the top. 2. Place the squash halves cut-side up in the cooking tray. 3. Put the cooking tray into the air fryer. 4. Select Air Fry, set temperature to 400 degrees F (204ºC), and set time to 15 minutes. 5. After cooking, the squash halves should be soft when poked in the center with a paring knife. Remove the air fryer basket from the grill. Rest it for 5–10 minutes before serving.
Per serving: Calories 290; Fat 1.8g; Sodium 546mg; Carbs 0.1g; Fiber 2g; Sugar 2g; Protein 10.8g

Golden Potatoes

Prep time: 5 minutes | Cook time: 20 minutes | Serves: 4

2 cups sliced frozen potatoes,
thawed
3 cloves garlic, minced
Pinch salt
Freshly ground black pepper,
to taste
¾ cup heavy cream

1. In a baking pan, toss the potatoes with salt, garlic, and black pepper until equally covered. Over the top, pour the heavy cream. 2. Select the Roast mode, set the temperature to 380 degrees F (193ºC), and set the time to 15 minutes. 3. Cook until the potatoes are soft and golden brown. If necessary, check for doneness and bake for additional 5 minutes. Remove the food from the air fryer and serve immediately.
Per serving: Calories 236; Fat 2.8g; Sodium 445mg; Carbs 0.1g; Fiber 0g; Sugar 0g; Protein 10.8g

Oat and Quinoa Burgers

Prep time: 10 minutes | Cook time: 10 minutes | Serves: 4

½ cup cooked and cooled quinoa
1 cup rolled oats
2 eggs, lightly beaten
¼ cup white onion, minced
¼ cup feta cheese, crumbled
Salt and ground black pepper,
as required
Olive oil cooking spray

1. Mix all ingredients in a large mixing bowl. 2. Form the ingredients into 4 equal-sized patties. 3. Spray the patties lightly with cooking spray. 4. Select "Air Fry" mode and set the temperature to 400 degrees F. 5. Place the patties in the oiled cooking tray and cook for 10 minutes. 6. Halfway through cooking, flip the patties. 7. Remove the patties from the air fryer and place them on a serving dish. 8. Serve warm.
Per serving: Calories 215; Fat 6.6g; Sodium 423mg; Carbs 28.7g; Fiber 3.7g; Sugar 1.1g; Protein 9.9g

Broccoli with Tofu

Prep time: 15 minutes | Cook time: 15 minutes | Serves: 2

8 ounces block of firm tofu,
pressed and cubed
1 small head of broccoli, cut
into florets
1 tablespoon canola oil
1 tablespoon nutritional yeast
¼ teaspoon dried parsley
Salt and ground black pepper,
as required

1. Mix the tofu, broccoli, and the remaining ingredients in a bowl. 2. Select "Air Fry" mode. 3. Set the cooking time to 15 minutes. 4. Set the temperature at 400 degrees F. 5. Open the lid when the device indicates "Add Food." 6. Place the tofu mixture in the cooking tray that has been oiled and placed in the air fryer. 7. While cooking, flip the tofu mixture. 8. When the cooking time is up, remove the lid and serve immediately.
Per serving: Calories 206; Fat 13.1g; Sodium 720mg; Carbs 12.7g; Fiber 5.4g; Sugar 2.6g; Protein 15g

Breaded Broccoli Gratin

Prep time: 5 minutes | Cook time: 14 minutes | Serves: 2

⅓ cup; Fat-free milk	coli florets
1 tablespoon all-purpose or gluten-free flour	6 tablespoons shredded Cheddar cheese
½ tablespoon olive oil	2 tablespoons panko bread crumbs
½ teaspoon ground sage	
¼ teaspoon kosher salt	1 tablespoon grated Parmesan cheese
⅛ teaspoon freshly ground black pepper	Olive oil spray
2 cups roughly chopped broc-	

1. Using olive oil spray, coat a baking dish. 2. Whisk the milk, olive oil, flour, salt, sage, and pepper in a medium mixing bowl. Toss the broccoli florets with the bread crumbs, Parmesan cheese, and Cheddar cheese. 3. Fill the baking dish halfway with the broccoli mixture. 4. Select Bake mode, set the temperature to 365 degrees F, and set the time to 14 minutes. Place the food in when the air fryer indicates "Add Food." 5. When the broccoli is done, the top should be golden brown and the broccoli soft. Serve warm.
Per serving: Calories 246; Fat 2.8g; Sodium 435mg; Carbs 0.1g; Fiber 0g; Sugar 0g; Protein 10.8g

Green Beans

Prep time: 10 minutes | Cook time: 20 minutes | Serves: 2

1 (10-ounce) bag frozen cut green beans	gar
	Salt and ground black pepper, as required
¼ cup nutritional yeast	
3 tablespoons balsamic vine-	

1. Toss the green beans with the nutritional yeast, vinegar, salt, and black pepper in a mixing bowl to coat well. 2. Select "Air Fry" mode, set the time to 20 minutes, and the temperature to 400 degrees F. 3. Put the green beans in when the air fryer indicates "Add Food." 4. Serve right away after the cooking time is complete.
Per serving: Calories 115; Fat 1.3g; Sodium 344mg; Carbs 18.5g; Fiber 9.3g; Sugar 1.8g; Protein 11.3g

Parmesan Cauliflower Fritters

Prep time: 10 minutes | Cook time: 7 minutes | Serves: 8

½ cup chopped parsley	cheese
1 cup Italian breadcrumbs	1 egg
⅓ cup shredded mozzarella cheese	2 minced garlic cloves
	3 chopped scallions
⅓ cup shredded sharp cheddar	1 head of cauliflower

1. Cauliflower should be cut into florets. Rinse them well, pat them dry, and then transfer them to a food processor and pulse for 20-30 seconds, or until the mixture resembles rice. 2. In a mixing bowl, combine cauliflower rice with the remaining ingredients. 3. Form 15 patties out of the mixture using your hands. If necessary, add additional breadcrumbs. 4. Spritz patties with olive oil and arrange in a cooking tray. 5. Select the Air Fry option. Set temperature 400 degrees F, and set time to 14 minutes, flipping after 7 minutes.
Per serving: Calories 209; Fat 17g; Sodium 333mg; Carbs 7g; Fiber 1g; Sugar 0.5g; Protein 6g

Mayo Zucchini and Carrot

Prep time: 10 minutes | Cook time: 20 minutes | Serves: 4

1 tablespoon grated onion	¼ teaspoon prepared horse-radish
2 tablespoons butter, melted	
½ pound carrots, sliced	¼ teaspoon salt
1-½ zucchinis, sliced	¼ teaspoon ground black pepper
¼ cup water	
¼ cup mayonnaise	¼ cup Italian bread crumbs

1. Spray the cooking tray lightly with cooking spray. Toss in the carrots. Select Air Fry mode. Cook at 400 degrees F for 8 minutes. Cook for another 5 minutes after adding the zucchini. 2. Meanwhile, combine the pepper, salt, horseradish, onion, mayonnaise, and water. Pour into the vegetable pan. Toss well to coat. 3. Melted butter and bread crumbs are combined in a small basin. Sprinkle over the vegetables. 4. Select Air Fry Mode. Set temperature 400 degrees F, and set time to 10 minutes; cook until tops are lightly browned. 5. Serve and enjoy.
Per serving: Calories 223; Fat 17g; Sodium 443mg; Carbs 9g; Fiber 1g; Sugar 0.5; Protein 2.7g

Jalapeño Cheese Balls

Prep time: 10 minutes | Cook time: 12 minutes | Serves: 12

4 ounces' cream cheese	½ cup bread crumbs
⅓ cup shredded mozzarella cheese	2 eggs
	½ cup all-purpose flour
⅓ cup shredded cheddar cheese	Salt
	Pepper
2 jalapeños, finely chopped	Cooking oil

1. Combine the cream cheese, mozzarella, cheddar, and jalapenos in a medium mixing basin. Mix thoroughly. 2. Form the cheese mixture into 1-inch-thick balls. It's best to use a tiny ice cream scoop. 3. Freeze the cheese balls for 15 minutes after placing them on a sheet pan. This step will aid in preserving the cheese balls' form when cooking. 4. Cooking oil should be sprayed on the air fryer basket. Add the bread crumbs to a bowl. Beat the eggs in a separate small bowl. Mix the flour, salt, and pepper in a third small bowl to taste. Take the frozen cheese balls out of the freezer. The cheese balls should be dipped in flour, eggs, and bread crumbs. 5. In the air fryer, place the cheese balls. Cooking oil is sprayed over the surface. Select Air Fry mode. Cook for 8 minutes at 400 degrees F temperature. 6. When the air fryer indicates "turn Food," turn the cheese balls carefully. Cook for another 4 minutes. Allow cooling before serving.
Per serving: calories 96; Fat 6g; Sodium 354mg; Carbs 4g; Fiber 0g; Sugar 0g; Protein 4g

Jalapeño Coins

Prep time: 10 minutes | Cook time: 5 minutes | Serves: 2

1 egg	Pinch of onion powder
2-3 tablespoons Coconut flour	Pinch of Cajun seasoning (optional)
1 sliced and seeded jalapeno	
Pinch of garlic powder	Pinch of pepper and salt

1. Stir all of the dry ingredients in a large mixing bowl. 2. Dry the jalapeño slices with a paper towel. Coins should be dipped in an egg wash before being dipped in the dry mixture. Toss to coat thoroughly. 3. Place coated jalapeño slices in the cooking tray. Olive oil is sprayed over the surface. 4. Select Air Fry Mode, set the temperature to 400 degrees F, and time to 5 minutes. 5. When the air fryer indicates "Add Food," place the cooking tray in the air fryer. Cook only until the bacon is crispy. 6. Serve.
Per serving: Calories 128; Fat 8g; Sodium 290mg; Carbs 9g; Fiber 0g; Sugar 0g; Protein 7g

Stuffed Bells with Cheese

Prep time: 10 minutes | Cook time: 30 minutes | Serves: 3

1 (7 ounces) can of whole green chile peppers, drained	½ (8 ounces) can of tomato sauce
1 egg beaten	¼ pound Monterey jack cheese, shredded
1 tablespoon all-purpose flour	¼ pound longhorn or cheddar cheese, shredded
½ (5 ounces) can evaporate milk	¼ cup milk

1. Spray an air fryer baking pan lightly with cooking spray. Distribute the chilies evenly and top with cheddar and jack cheese. 2. In a mixing dish, combine flour, milk, and eggs. Pour the sauce over the chiles. 3. Select the Bake option, set the time to 20 minutes, and the temperature to 365 degrees F. When the air fryer indicates "Add Food," place the food in and cook. 4. Serve with a dollop of tomato sauce on top. 5. Cook again at 365 degrees F for 10 minutes, or until the tops are gently browned. 6. Serve and enjoy.

Per serving: Calories 392; Fat 27.6g; Sodium 435mg; Carbs 5g; Fiber 1g; Sugar 1g; Protein 23.9g

Healthy Zucchini and Squash Casserole

Prep time: 5 minutes | Cook time: 30 minutes | Serves: 4

1 egg	cheese
5 saltine crackers, or as needed, crushed	1 ½ teaspoons white; Sugar
	½ teaspoon salt
2 tablespoons bread crumbs	¼ onion, diced
½ pound yellow squash, sliced	¼ cup biscuit baking mix
½ pound zucchini, sliced	¼ cup butter
½ cup shredded cheddar	

1. Spray a cooking tray lightly with cooking spray. Combine the onion, zucchini, and yellow squash in a large mixing bowl. Cover pan with foil and cook at 400 degrees F for 15 minutes or until tender on Air Fry mode. 2. Combine the salt, sugar, egg butter, baking mix, and cheddar cheese in a mixing bowl. Mix thoroughly. Crumbled crackers are folded in, and bread crumbs should be sprinkled on top. 3. Cook it at 400 degrees F for 15 minutes on Air Fry mode, or until the tops are gently browned. 4. Serve and enjoy.

Per serving: Calories 285; Fat 20.5g; Sodium 654mg; Carbs 11g; Fiber 2g; Sugar 3g; Protein 8.6g

Avocado Fingers

Prep time: 10 minutes | Cook time: 10 minutes | Serves: 4

½ cup panko breadcrumbs	and sliced
½ teaspoon salt	Liquid from 1 can of white beans or aquafaba
1 pitted Haas avocado, peeled	

1. Toss the breadcrumbs and salt together in a small dish until thoroughly mixed. 2. Dredge the avocado slices in the breadcrumb mixture first, then in the aquafaba. 3. Arrange the avocado slices in a cooking tray. 4. Select Air Fry mode, set the time to 10 minutes, and adjust the temperature to 400 degrees F. When the air fryer indicates "Add Food," place the food in and cook. 5. When the air fryer indicates "turn Food," turn the food. 6. Once done, serve and enjoy.

Per serving: Calories 51; Fat 7.5g; Sodium 443mg; Carbs 9g; Fiber 2g; Sugar 2g; Protein1.39g

Onion Rings with Cayenne Pepper

Prep time: 10 minutes | Cook time: 10 minutes | Serves: 4

1 large Spanish onion	¾ cup panko bread crumbs
½ cup buttermilk	½ teaspoon baking powder
2 eggs, lightly beaten	½ teaspoon cayenne pepper, to taste
¾ cup unbleached all-purpose flour	Salt

1. Cut your onion into ½ broad rings and divide them. Smaller chunks can be thrown away or used in other dishes. 2. Whisk the eggs and buttermilk in a large mixing basin, then put aside. 3. Combine flour, pepper, bread crumbs, and baking powder in a separate basin. 4. Dip a full ring in the buttermilk with a big spoon, then drag it through the flour mixture on both sides to thoroughly coat the ring. 5. Fill the cooking tray with the mixture. Select Air Fry mode. Adjust the temperature to 400 degrees F and the timer to 10 minutes. When the air fryer indicates "Add Food," place the food in and cook, shaking halfway through.

Per serving: Calories 225; Fat 3.8g; Sodium 780mg; Carbs 19g; Fiber2.4g; Sugar 3g; Protein19g

Butternut Squash Fries

Prep time: 5 minutes | Cook time: 10 minutes | Serves: 8

1 pinch of salt	2 teaspoons Cinnamon
1 tablespoon Powdered unprocessed; Sugar	1 tablespoon Coconut oil
½ teaspoon Nutmeg	10 ounces pre-cut butternut squash fries

1. Pour all items into a plastic bag. Coat the fries in the other ingredients until they are completely covered, and the sugar has dissolved. 2. Arrange the coated fries in a cooking tray. Select Air fry mode. Adjust the temperature to 400 degrees F, and set time to 10 minutes. Cook until the bacon is crispy.

Per serving: Calories 175; Fat 8g; Sodium 339mg; Carbs 9g; Fiber 2g; Sugar 2g; Protein1g

Peas and Mushrooms

Prep time: 15 minutes | Cook time: 15 minutes | Serves: 4

½ cup soy sauce	powder
4 tablespoons maple syrup	½ teaspoon ground ginger
4 tablespoons rice vinegar	16 ounces cremini mushrooms, halved
4 garlic cloves, finely chopped	
2 teaspoons Chinese 5 spice	½ cup frozen peas

1. Combine soy sauce, maple syrup, vinegar, garlic, spice powder, and ground ginger in a mixing bowl. Remove from the equation. 2. Place the mushrooms in a single layer in a greased baking pan. 3. Select "Air Fry" mode. 4. Set the temperature to 400 degrees F for 15 minutes. 5. After 10 minutes of cooking, in the pan, add the peas and vinegar mixture and stir to combine. 6. Serve hot.

Per serving: Calories 132 Cal; Fat 0.3g; Sodium 1100 mg; Carbs 25 g; Fiber 2.4 g; Sugar 15.4g; Protein 6.1g

Oyster Mushrooms with Buttermilk

Prep time: 30 minutes | Cook time: 15 minutes | Serves: 2

1 ½ cups all-purpose flour	1 teaspoon each salt, pepper, garlic powder, onion powder, smoked paprika, cumin
2 heaping cups of oyster mushrooms	
1 tablespoon oil	1 cup buttermilk

1. Clean the mushrooms and combine them with the butter-

milk in a large mixing dish. Allow 15 minutes for marinating. 2. In a large mixing basin, combine the flour and spices. Remove the mushrooms from the buttermilk and set them aside (keep the buttermilk). Dip each mushroom in the flour mixture, brush off excess flour, dip again in the buttermilk, and then again in the flour (short: wet> dry> wet> dry). 3. Select the Air Fry mode, and set the temperature to 400 degrees F. 4. Place the mushrooms in a cooking tray, leaving space between each mushroom. Allow 5 minutes of cooking before brushing both sides with a bit of oil to enhance browning. Cook for 5–10 minutes more until golden brown and crispy.

Per serving: Calories 345 kcal; Fat 10g; Sodium 543mg; Carbs 57 g; Fiber 9g; Sugar 7g; Protein 13 g

Veggies with Rice

Prep time: 20 minutes | Cook time: 18 minutes | Serves: 4

2 cups cooked white rice	1 large egg, lightly beaten
1 tablespoon vegetable oil	½ cup frozen peas, thawed
2 teaspoons sesame oil, toasted and divided	½ cup frozen carrots, thawed
1 tablespoon water	1 teaspoon soy sauce
Salt and ground white pepper, as required	1 teaspoon Sriracha sauce
	½ teaspoon sesame seeds, toasted

1. Combine the rice, vegetable oil, 1 teaspoon of sesame oil, water, salt, and white pepper in a large mixing basin. 2. Place the rice mixture in the pan that has been prepared. 3. Select "Air Fry" mode. 4. Set the temperature to 400 degrees F for 12 minutes. 5. Stir the rice mixture once halfway through. 6. Remove the baking pan from the air fryer and place the beaten egg over the rice. 7. Select "Air Fry" mode. 8. Adjust the temperature to 380 degrees F and set the time to 6 minutes. 9. Stir in the peas and carrots after 4 minutes. 10. Meanwhile, combine soy sauce, Sriracha sauce, sesame seeds, and the remaining sesame oil in a mixing bowl. 11. Fill a serving dish halfway with the rice mixture. 12. Serve with the sauce drizzled over the top.

Per serving: Calories 438; Fat 8.6g; Sodium 980mg; Carbs 78 g; Fiber 2.7 g; Sugar 1.9g; Protein 9.5 g

Onion Tortilla Wrap

Prep time: 5 minutes | Cook time: 15 minutes | Serves: 4

1 small red bell pepper, chopped	4 large tortillas
1 small yellow onion, diced	4 pieces of commercial vegan nuggets, chopped
1 tablespoon water	Mixed greens for garnish
2 cobs grilled corn kernels	

1. Water sauté the vegan nuggets with the onions, bell peppers, and corn kernels in a pan over medium heat. Remove from the equation. 2. Fill the corn tortillas with the filling. 3. Select Air Fry Mode. Adjust the temperature to 400 degrees F, and set time to 15 minutes. Cook until the tortilla wraps are crispy. 4. Serve with mixed greens on top.

Per serving: Calories 548; Fat 20.7g; Sodium 480mg; Carbs 0 g; Fiber 0g; Sugar 0g; Protein 46 g

Crispy Sweet Potatoes Fries

Prep time: 5 minutes | Cook time: 37 minutes | Serves: 4

2 tablespoons sweet potato fry seasoning mix	Seasoning Mix:
2 tablespoons olive oil	2 tablespoons salt
2 sweet potatoes	1 tablespoon cayenne pepper
	1 tablespoon dried oregano

1 tablespoon fennel	2 tablespoons coriander

1. Sweet potatoes should be peeled and sliced on both ends. Each potato should be cut lengthwise in half and then crosswise to form 4 pieces. 2. Each potato piece should be sliced into 2-3 slices before being sliced into fries. 3. Combine the spice mix components in a blender and add the salt. 4. Toss the potato chunks in the olive oil, then season with the spice mix and toss to coat well. 5. Fries should be placed on the cooking tray. 6. Select Air Fry Mode, set the temperature to 400 degrees F, and time to 27 minutes. Press the Start button to begin preheating. 7. When the air fryer indicates "Add Food," put it in the cooking tray. 8. Turn the fries and cook for 10-12 minutes until the fries are golden.

Per serving: Calories 89; Fat 14g; Sodium 454mg; Carbs 10g; Fiber 2g; Sugar 3g; Protein 8 g

Breaded and Buttered Cauliflower

Prep time: 5 minutes | Cook time: 15 minutes | Serves: 2

Cauliflower:	Buffalo coating:
1 cup Panko breadcrumbs	¼ cup Vegan buffalo sauce
1 teaspoon salt	¼ cup Melted vegan butter
4 cup Cauliflower florets	

1. Add the melted butter to a microwave-safe bowl and stir in the buffalo sauce. 2. Each cauliflower floret should be dipped into the buffalo mixture and well coated. Hold the floret over a bowl until it stops leaking. 3. Combine breadcrumbs and salt in a mixing bowl. 4. Place dipped florets in the cooking tray after dredging them in breadcrumbs. Select Air Fry mode. Set temp to 400 degrees F and set the timer for 15 minutes. They're ready to eat once they've slightly browned. 5. Serve with a keto dipping sauce of your choice.

Per serving: Calories 194; Fat 17g; Sodium 390mg; Carbs 15g; Fiber 2g; Sugar 3; Protein 10g

Spicy Tofu Peppers

Prep time: 5 minutes | Cook time: 15 minutes | Serves: 4

¼ cup chickpea flour	1 (15-ounce) package tofu, firm or extra-firm
¼ cup arrowroot (or cornstarch)	Cooking oil spray (sunflower, safflower, or refined coconut)
1 teaspoon sea salt	Asian Spicy Sweet Sauce, optional
1 teaspoon granulated garlic	
½ teaspoon freshly grated black pepper	

1. Combine the flour, arrowroot, salt, garlic, and pepper in a medium mixing basin. To mix, stir everything together thoroughly. 2. Cut the tofu into cubes (no need to press—alright, it's if it's a little wet!). Pour the flour mixture over the cubes. Toss well to coat. Toss the tofu one more with the oil. (The spray aids the coating's adhesion to the tofu.) 3. Spray the oil into the cooking tray. Spray the tofu tops in a single layer on the cooking tray (you may need to do this in 2 batches depending on the size of your appliance). Select Air Fry mode. Adjust the temperature to 400 degrees F and cook for 8 minutes. Remove the cooking tray from the machine and re-oil it. 4. Turn the pieces over or gently toss them. Spray again with oil and cook for another 7 minutes until golden brown and crisp. 5. Serve immediately, with or without the Asian Spicy Sweet Sauce.

Per serving: Calories 148; Fat 5g; Sodium 473mg; Carbs 14g; Fiber 1g; Sugar 4g; Protein 11g

Vegetable Mix

Prep time: 5 minutes | Cook time: 35 minutes | Serves: 4

1 tablespoon chopped tarragon leaves	1-pound yellow squash
½ teaspoon white pepper	1-pound zucchini
1 teaspoon salt	6 teaspoons olive oil
	½ pound carrots

1. Squash and zucchini should be stemmed and rooted before being cut into 34-inch half-moons. Carrots should be peeled and sliced into 1-inch pieces. Toss carrot chunks with 2 tablespoons olive oil until well coated. 2. Set the temperature to 400 degrees F and the timer to 5 minutes in the air fryer on Air Fry mode. 3. While the carrots are cooking, pour the remaining olive oil over the squash and zucchini, seasoning with pepper and salt. Toss well to coat. 4. When the timer for the carrots goes off, add the squash and zucchini. Cook for 30 minutes, tossing 2-3 times during the cooking time. 5. Remove the vegetables and mix with tarragon after they're done. Warm it up before serving.

Per serving: Calories 122; Fat 9g; Sodium 602mg; Carbs 0 g; Fiber 0g; Sugar 0g; Protein 6 g

Zucchini Chips with Lemon Aioli

Prep time: 15 minutes | Cook time: 10 minutes | Serves: 5

For the zucchini chips:	For the lemon aioli:
2 medium zucchinis	½ cup mayonnaise
2 eggs	½ tablespoon olive oil
⅓ cup bread crumbs	Juice of ½ lemons
⅓ cup grated Parmesan cheese	1 teaspoon minced garlic
Salt	Salt
Pepper	Pepper
Cooking oil	

1. To make the zucchini chips: 2. Using a knife or mandolin, slice the zucchini into thin chips (approximately ⅛ inch thick). 3. Beat the eggs in a small bowl. Combine the bread crumbs, Parmesan cheese, and salt & pepper to taste in a separate small bowl. 4. Cooking oil should be sprayed into the cooking tray. 5. Dip the zucchini slices in the eggs 1 at a time, then in the bread crumb mixture. You may also use a spoon to sprinkle the bread crumbs on the zucchini slices. 6. In the cooking tray, arrange the zucchini chips but do not stack them. 7. Place in the air fryer—Cook in batches. Spray the chips with cooking oil from a distance (otherwise, the breading may fly off). Select Air Fry mode at 400 degrees F and Cook for 10 minutes. 8. Remove the cooked zucchini chips from the air fryer, and then repeat with the remaining zucchini. 9. To make the lemon aioli: 10. Combine the mayonnaise, olive oil, lemon juice, and garlic in a small bowl while the zucchini is frying and seasoned with salt and pepper. In a large mixing bowl, blend all the ingredients until they are entirely mixed. 11. Allow the zucchini to cool before serving with the aioli.

Per serving: Calories 192; Fat 13g; Sodium 490mg; Carbs 20g; Fiber 4 g; Sugar 5g; Protein 6 g

Himalayan Kale Chips

Prep time: 5 minutes | Cook time: 10 minutes | Serves: 6

¼ teaspoon Himalayan salt	Avocado oil
3 tablespoons yeast	1 bunch of kale

1. Pat the kale dry with paper towels after rinsing it. 2. Tear the leaves of the kale into big chunks. 3. In a dish, spritz the kale pieces with avocado oil until they are glossy. Season the kale pieces with a pinch of salt and a pinch of yeast. 4. Toss the kale leaves together with your hands. 5. Set the temperature to 400 degrees F and the timer to 5 minutes after pouring half of the kale mixture into the cooking tray on Air Fry mode. Remove half of the kale and repeat with the other half.

Per serving: Calories 55; Fat 10g; Sodium 390mg; Carbs 0 g; Fiber 0g; Sugar 0g; Protein 1 g

Spicy Baby Carrots, Broccoli and Cauliflower

Prep time: 5 minutes | Cook time: 18 minutes | Serves: 4

1 cup baby carrots	1 tablespoon Italian seasoning
1 cup broccoli florets	Salt and ground black pepper,
1 cup cauliflower florets	as required
1 tablespoon olive oil	

1. Add all ingredients to a bowl and stir them well. 2. Arrange the veggies in the cooking tray. 3. Place the drip pan in the air fryer's cooking chamber. 4. Select Roast mode, and set the temperature to 380 degrees F and time to 18 minutes. Press the Start button to begin preheating. 5. When the air fryer indicates "Add Food," place the cooking tray in it and cook. 6. When the air fryer indicates "turn Food," you can open it and turn the veggies to cook them evenly. 7. Serve.

Per serving: Calories 66; Fat 4.7g; Sodium 540mg; Carbs 5.7g; Fiber 1g; Sugar 1g; Protein 1.4g

Cream Potato Pieces

Prep time: 5 minutes | Cook time: 20 minutes | Serves: 4

2 gold potatoes, cut into medium pieces	Salt and black pepper to taste
1 tablespoon olive oil	3 tablespoons sour cream

1. Toss all of the ingredients in a baking dish that fits your air fryer. 2. Select Air Fry mode. 3. Place the dish in the air fryer and cook for 20 minutes at 400 degrees F. 4. Serve as a side dish by dividing the mixture across plates.

Per serving: Calories 201; Fat 8; Sodium 450mg; Carbs 18; Fiber 9; Sugar 4g; Protein 5g

Mayo Brussels Sprout

Prep time: 5 minutes | Cook time: 15 minutes | Serves: 4

1 pound Brussels sprouts, trimmed and halved	6 teaspoons olive oil
Salt and black pepper to taste	½ cup mayonnaise
	2 tablespoons garlic, minced

1. Combine the sprouts, salt, pepper, and oil in your air fryer and stir thoroughly. 2. Select Air Fry mode. 3. Cook the sprouts for 15 minutes at 400 degrees F. 4. Transfer to a mixing bowl and combine with the mayonnaise and garlic. 5. Serve as a side dish by dividing the mixture across plates.

Per serving: Calories 202; Fat 6 8; Sodium 443mg; Carbs 12; Fiber 2g; Sugar 2g; Protein 8g

Trimmed Green Beans and Walnuts

Prep time: 5 minutes | Cook time: 25 minutes | Serves: 4

1½ pounds green beans, trimmed	½ pound shallots, chopped
Salt and black pepper to taste	¼ cup walnuts, chopped
	2 tablespoons olive oil

1. Toss all of the ingredients in the cooking tray of your air fryer. 2. Select Air Fry mode. 3. Cook the food for 25 minutes

at 400 degrees F. 4. Serve as a side dish by dividing the mixture across plates.

Per serving: Calories 182; Fat 3g; Sodium 543mg; Carbs 11g; Fiber 6g; Sugar 3g; Protein 5g

Mushroom Mix

Prep time: 5 minutes | Cook time: 15 minutes | Serves: 4

1-pound button mushrooms, halved	1 teaspoon Italian seasoning
2 tablespoons parmesan cheese, grated	A pinch of salt and black pepper
	3 tablespoons butter, melted

1. Toss all the ingredients in a pan that fits your air fryer. 2. Select Air Fry mode. 3. Place the pan in the air fryer and cook for 15 minutes at 365 degrees F. 4. Serve the mixture by dividing it among plates.

Per serving: Calories 194; Fat 4g; Sodium 420mg; Carbs 14g; Fiber 4g; Sugar 4g; Protein 7g

Buttery Squash Fritter

Prep time: 5 minutes | Cook time: 17 minutes | Serves: 4

⅓ cup all-purpose flour	⅓ butternut squash, peeled and grated
⅓ teaspoon freshly ground black pepper or more to taste	2 eggs, well whisked
⅓ teaspoon dried sage	1 teaspoon fine sea salt
4 cloves garlic, minced	A pinch of ground allspice
1 ½ tablespoons olive oil	

1. In a mixing basin, thoroughly combine all ingredients. 2. Select Air Fry mode. 3. Set temp of the air fryer to 400 degrees F and set the timer for 17 minutes; cook until the fritters are golden brown; serve immediately.

Per serving: Calories 152; Fat 10g; Sodium 540mg; Carbs 9.4g; Fiber 2g; Sugars 0.3g; Protein 5.8g

Herby Potatoes

Prep time: 5 minutes | Cook time: 17 minutes | Serves: 4

1 teaspoon crushed dried thyme	½ tablespoon crushed dried rosemary
1 teaspoon ground black pepper	3 potatoes, peeled, washed, and cut into wedges
2 tablespoons olive oil	½ teaspoon seasoned salt

1. Place the potatoes in the cooking tray and sprinkle with olive oil. 2. Select the Air Fry option, and set the temperature to 400 degrees F and time to 17 minutes. 3. When the air fryer indicates "Add Food," place the cooking tray in it and cook. 4. Season to taste and serve warm with your favorite salad on the side.

Per serving: Calories 208; Fat 7g; Sodium 540; Carbs 33.8g; Fiber 5g; Sugars 2.5g; Protein 3.6g

Sweet Potato Salad

Prep time: 5 minutes | Cook time: 20 minutes | Serves: 2

2 sweet potatoes, peeled and cut into wedges	¼ teaspoon coriander, ground
Salt and black pepper to taste	4 tablespoons mayonnaise
2 tablespoons avocado oil	½ teaspoon cumin, ground
½ teaspoon curry powder	A pinch of ginger powder
	A pinch of cinnamon powder

1. Toss the sweet potato wedges with salt, pepper, coriander, curry powder, and oil in the cooking tray of your air fryer. 2. Select Air Fry mode. 3. Cook for 20 minutes at 400 degrees F, flipping once. 4. Add the mayonnaise, cumin, ginger, and cinnamon to the potatoes in a mixing bowl. 5. Toss and serve as a salad side dish.

Per serving: Calories 190; Fat 5; Sodium 480mg; Carbs 14; Fiber 8; Sugar 5; Protein 5g

Sweet Potatoes with Tamarind Paste

Prep time: 5 minutes | Cook time: 22 minutes | Serves: 4

⅓ teaspoon white pepper	1 ½ tablespoons maple syrup
1 tablespoon butter, melted	2 teaspoons tamarind paste
½ teaspoon turmeric powder	1 ½ tablespoons fresh lime juice
5 garnet sweet potatoes, peeled and diced	1 ½ teaspoon ground allspice

1. Toss all ingredients in a mixing basin until sweet potatoes are thoroughly covered. 2. Select the Air Fry option. 3. Cook for 12 minutes at 400 degrees F in your air fryer. 4. Stop the air fryer and toss one more—Cook for a further 10 minutes at temp 400 degrees F.

Per serving: Calories 103; Fat 9g; Sodium 620mg; Carbs 4.9g; Fiber 1g; Sugars 1.2g; Protein 1.9g

Frizzled Leek

Prep time: 5 minutes | Cook time: 45 minutes | Serves: 6

½ teaspoon porcini powder	2 large-sized dishes with ice water
1 ½ cups rice flour	
1 tablespoon vegetable oil	2 teaspoons onion powder
3 medium-sized leeks, slice into julienne strips	Fine sea salt and cayenne pepper to taste

1. Drain thoroughly after soaking the leeks in cold water for about 25 minutes. 2. In a resealable bag, combine the rice flour, salt, cayenne pepper, onions powder, and porcini powder. Toss in the celery and give it a good shake to coat. 3. Drizzle the seasoned leeks with vegetable oil. 4. Select the Air Fry option. 5. Air fry for 18 minutes at 400 degrees F, turning halfway during the cooking time. Serve with homemade mayonnaise or your favorite dipping sauce. Enjoy!

Per serving: Calories 291; Fat 6g; Sodium 390mg; Carbs 53.3g; Fiber 7g; Sugars 4.3g; Protein 5.7g

Yummy Mushrooms with Tahini Sauce

Prep time: 5 minutes | Cook time: 20 minutes | Serves: 5

½ tablespoon tahini	⅓ teaspoon freshly cracked black pepper
½ teaspoon turmeric powder	
⅓ teaspoon cayenne pepper	1 ½ tablespoons vermouth
2 tablespoons lemon juice, freshly squeezed	1 ½ tablespoons olive oil
1 teaspoon kosher salt	1 ½ pound Cremini mushrooms

1. Toss the mushrooms with olive oil, turmeric powder, salt, black pepper, and cayenne pepper in a mixing bowl. 2. Select the Air Fry option. 3. Cook for 9 minutes at 400 degrees F in your air fryer. 4. Stop your air fryer, give it a nice toss, and continue to cook for another 10 minutes. 5. Meanwhile, whisk together the lemon juice, vermouth, and tahini until smooth. Warm mushrooms are served with tahini sauce.

Per serving: Calories 372; Fat 4g; Sodium 470mg; Carbs 80g; Fiber 10g; Sugars 2.6g; Protein 11.2g

Jack Cauliflower Bites

Prep time: 5 minutes | Cook time: 24 minutes | Serves: 2

⅓ teaspoon shallot powder	½ teaspoon garlic salt
1 teaspoon ground black pepper	¼ cup Pepper Jack cheese, grated
1 ½ large-sized heads of cauliflower, broken into florets	1 ½ tablespoons vegetable oil
¼ teaspoon cumin powder	⅓ teaspoon paprika

1. Cook cauliflower for 5 minutes in a pot of salted water. Drain the cauliflower florets and place them in a baking dish after that. 2. Toss the cauliflower florets with the other ingredients in a large mixing bowl. 3. Select the Roast option. 4. Set temp to 380 degrees F and roast for 16 minutes. When the air fryer indicates "turn Food," turn the food. 5. Enjoy!
Per serving: Calories 271; Fat 23g; Sodium 490mg; Carbs 8.9g; Fiber 2g; Sugars 2.8g; Protein 9.8g

Pickle Spears

Prep time: 5 minutes | Cook time: 15 minutes | Serves: 6

⅓ cup milk	⅓ cup all-purpose flour
1 teaspoon garlic powder	½ teaspoon shallot powder
2 medium-sized eggs	2 jars of sweet and sour pickle spears
1 teaspoon fine sea salt	
⅓ teaspoon chili powder	

1. Using a kitchen towel, pat the pickle spears dry. After that, get two mixing bowls. 2. In a mixing dish, whisk together the egg and milk. Combine all dry ingredients in a separate bowl. 3. Toss the pickle spears in the flour mixture first, then coat them in the egg/milk combination. Finally, dredge them in the flour mixture again for a final coating. 4. Select the Roast option. 5. At 380 degrees F, roasted battered pickles for 15 minutes. Enjoy!
Per serving: Calories 58; Fat 2g; Sodium 444mg; Carbs 6.8g; Fiber 4g; Sugars 0.9g; Protein3.2g

Buttered Squash Bites

Prep time: 5 minutes | Cook time: 23 minutes | Serves: 8

2 teaspoons fresh mint leaves, chopped	flakes
⅓ cup brown; Sugar	2 tablespoons melted butter
1 ½ teaspoons red pepper chili	3 pounds of winter squash, peeled, seeded, and cubed

1. Combine the following ingredients in a large mixing bowl. 2. Select the Roast option. 3. In an air fryer, roast the squash bits for 30 minutes at 380 degrees F, rotating once or twice. Serve with a dipping sauce prepared from scratch.
Per serving: Calories 113; Fat 3g; Sodium 349mg; Carbs 22.6g; Fiber 5g; Sugars 4.3g; Protein 1.6g

Panko Broccoli Croquettes

Prep time: 5 minutes | Cook time: 45 minutes | Serves: 6

1 ½ cups Monterey Jack cheese	1 teaspoon cayenne pepper
1 teaspoon dried dill weed	½ teaspoon kosher salt
⅓ teaspoon ground black pepper	1 cup Panko crumbs
3 eggs, whisked	½ cups broccoli florets
	⅓ cup Parmesan cheese

1. In a food processor, blitz the broccoli florets until they're finely crumbed. After that, mix the broccoli with the remaining ingredients. 2. Roll the mixture into tiny balls and store them in the fridge for about 30 minutes. 3. Select the Air Fry option. 4. Set Temp of the air fryer to 400 degrees F and set the timer for 14 minutes; cook until the broccoli croquettes are golden brown, and serve immediately.
Per serving: Calories 246; Fat 14g; Sodium 430mg; Carbs 15g; Fiber 2g; Sugars 1.6g; Protein 14.5g

Cauliflower Cake

Prep time: 5 minutes | Cook time: 45 minutes | Serves: 6

2 teaspoons chili powder	1 ⅓ cups tortilla chip crumbs
1 ½ teaspoons kosher salt	½ teaspoon crushed red pepper flakes
1 teaspoon dried marjoram, crushed	3 eggs, whisked
½ cups cauliflower, broken into florets	1 ½ cups Queso Cotija cheese, crumbled

1. In a food processor, blitz the cauliflower florets until they're crushed and the size of rice. Combine the cauliflower "rice" with the remaining ingredients. 2. Refrigerate for 30 minutes after rolling the cauliflower mixture into small balls. 3. Select the Air Fry option. 4. Set temp to the air fryer to 400 degrees F and set the timer for 14 minutes; cook until the balls are golden brown, and serve immediately.
Per serving: Calories 190; Fat 14g; Sodium 449mg; Carbs 4.7g; Fiber 1g; Sugars 1.3g; Protein 11.5g

Carrot and Sweet Potato Croquettes

Prep time: 5 minutes | Cook time: 15 minutes | Serves: 4

⅓ cup Swiss cheese, grated	3 carrots, trimmed and grated
⅓ teaspoon fine sea salt	½ teaspoon freshly cracked black pepper
⅓ teaspoon baking powder	3 sweet potatoes, grated
⅓ cup scallions, finely chopped	⅓ cup all-purpose flour
½ tablespoon fresh basil, finely chopped	2 small eggs, lightly beaten

1. Using a paper towel, wipe dry shredded sweet potatoes and carrots. 2. In the above order, combine the potatoes and carrots with the remaining ingredients. Then, using 1 ½ teaspoons of the vegetable mixture, form the balls. 3. Then, using your fingers, carefully flatten the individual ball. Using a nonstick frying spray, spritz the croquettes. 4. Select the Bake option. 5. Bake your croquettes at 365 degrees F for 13 minutes, working in batches. Serve with tomato ketchup and mayonnaise on the side.
Per serving: Calories 206; Fat 5g; Sodium 520mg; Carbs 32g; Fiber 2g; Sugars 5.7g; Protein 8.3g

Manchego and Potato Patties

Prep time: 5 minutes | Cook time: 15 minutes | Serves: 8

1 cup Manchego cheese, shredded	2 cups scallions, finely chopped
1 teaspoon paprika	2 pounds Russet potatoes, peeled and grated
1 teaspoon freshly ground black pepper	2 tablespoons canola oil
½ tablespoon fine sea salt	2 teaspoons dried basil

1. Add all the ingredients to a large mixing bowl. Then, using your hands, form the balls. To form the patties, flatten the balls. 2. Select the Bake option. 3. Bake your patties for 10 minutes at 365 degrees F. 4. Bon appétit!
Per serving: Calories 191; Fat 8.7g; Sodium 540mg; Carbs 22g; Fiber 4g; Sugars 1.4g; Protein 7g

Herb Stuffed Mushrooms

Prep time: 5 minutes | Cook time: 15 minutes | Serves: 3

3 garlic cloves, minced
1 teaspoon ground black pepper, or more to taste
⅓ cup seasoned breadcrumbs
1½ tablespoons fresh mint, chopped

1 teaspoon salt, or more to taste
1½ tablespoons melted butter
3 medium-sized mushrooms, cleaned, stalks removed

1. Mix all of the above ingredients, minus the mushrooms, in a mixing bowl to prepare the filling. 2. Then, stuff the mushrooms with the prepared filling. Select Air Fry mode. 3. Air fry stuffed mushrooms at 400 degrees F for about 12 minutes. Taste for doneness and serve at room temperature as a vegetarian appetizer.

Per serving: Calories 290; Fat 14.7g; Sodium 540mg; Carbs 13.4g; Fiber 2g; Sugars 3.3g; Protein 28g

Air-Fried Brussels Sprouts Pieces

Prep time: 5 minutes | Cook time: 20 minutes | Serves: 4

1 pound Brussels Sprouts ends trimmed and cut into bite-sized pieces
1 tablespoon balsamic vinegar

1 tablespoon Olive oil
Salt and ground black pepper, as required

1. Toss the ingredients in a mixing bowl to coat them evenly. 2. Attach the lid to the rotisserie basket with the Brussels Sprouts. Place it in the air fryer. 3. Select "Air Fry" and set the temperature to 400 degrees F. Press "Start" after setting the timer to 20 minutes. 4. When the air fryer indicates "On," touch Rotate button to start rotisserie cooking. 5. When the display shows "End," carefully remove the food. Serve hot.

Per serving: Calories 80; Fat 3.9g; Sodium 390mg; Carbs 10.3g; Fiber 1g; Sugar 2g; Protein 3.9g

Spiced Cauliflower

Prep time: 5 minutes | Cook time: 12 minutes | Serves: 4

1 large head cauliflower, cut into bite-size florets
1 tablespoon Olive oil
2 tablespoons Garlic powder

Salt and ground black pepper, as required
1 tablespoon butter melted
⅔ c warm buffalo sauce

1. Toss cauliflower florets with oil, garlic powder, salt, and black pepper in a large mixing basin to coat. 2. Arrange the cauliflower florets in a single layer on the oiled cooking tray. 3. Place the drip pan in the air fryer. Select "Air Dry" and set the temperature to 400 degrees F. Press "Start" after setting the timer for 12 minutes. 4. Insert the cooking tray when the display says "Add Food." 5. Coat the cauliflower florets in buffalo sauce when the display says "turn Food." 6. Remove the tray from the air fryer when the cooking time is over. Serve hot.

Per serving: Calories 102; Fat 9g; Sodium 534mg; Carbs 5.2g; Fiber 2g; Sugar 2g; Protein 1.7g

Carrot Omelet

Prep time: 5 minutes | Cook time: 20 minutes | Serves: 4

2 small eggs, lightly beaten
⅓ teaspoon freshly cracked black pepper
⅓ cup Colby cheese, grated
½ tablespoon fresh dill, finely

chopped
½ tablespoon garlic paste
⅓ cup onion, finely chopped
⅓ cup all-purpose flour
3 medium-sized carrots,

trimmed and grated
2 teaspoons fine sea salt
3 medium-sized celery stalks,

trimmed and grated
⅓ teaspoon baking powder

1. Remove the excess liquid from the carrots and celery by squeezing them on a paper towel. 2. In the order listed above, combine the vegetables with the other ingredients. 1 tablespoon of the veggie mixture was used to form the balls. 3. Then, carefully flatten each ball using your palm or a broad spatula. Using a nonstick frying spray, spritz the croquettes. 4. Select the Bake option. 5. Set temp to 365 degrees F and bake the veggie cakes in a single layer for 17 minutes. Serve with sour cream on the side.

Per serving: Calories142; Fat 6g; Sodium 380mg; Carbs 15.8g; Fiber 2g; Sugars 3g; Protein 7.2g

Green Beans and Carrots Sticks

Prep time: 5 minutes | Cook time: 10 minutes | Serves: 3

½ pound of Green beans trimmed
½ pound Carrots peeled and cut into sticks

1 tablespoon Olive oil
Salt and ground black pepper, as required

1. Add all ingredients to a mixing bowl and toss them well. 2. Attach the lid to the rotisserie basket and add the veggies. In the Air Fryer, arrange the drip pan. 3. Select "Air Fry," set the temperature to 400 degrees F and time to 10 minutes. 4. Touch Strat to begin. When the display shows "On," touch Rotate to begin rotisserie cooking. 5. Once done, carefully remove the food. Serve hot.

Per serving: Calories 94; Fat 4.8g; Sodium 380mg; Carbs 12.7g; Fiber 4g; Sugar 3g; Protein 2g

Cumin Potatoes and Bell Peppers

Prep time: 5 minutes | Cook time: 25 minutes | Serves: 2

2 cups Water
5 Russet potatoes, peeled and cubed
½ tablespoon extra-virgin olive oil
½ onion chopped
½ jalapeño pepper chopped
1 large bell pepper, seeded

and chopped
¼ teaspoon Dried oregano crushed
¼ teaspoon Garlic powder
¼ teaspoon Ground cumin
¼ teaspoon Red chili powder
Salt and ground black pepper, as required

1. Combine the water and potatoes in a large mixing basin and leave them aside for 30 minutes. Drain the water well and wipe dry with paper towels. 2. Toss the potatoes with the oil in a mixing dish to evenly coat them. 3. Arrange the potato cubes on the cooking tray that has been oiled. In the air fryer, place the drip pan. 4. Select "Air Dry" and set the temperature to 400 degrees F. Press "Start" after setting the timer for 5 minutes. Place the tray in the center when the display says "Add Food." 5. Do not flip the food when the display says "Turn Food." Remove the tray from the air fryer when the cooking time is up. 6. Toss the potato cubes with the other ingredients in a large mixing basin until evenly coated. Place the vegetable mixture in an equal layer on the oiled baking sheet. Select "Air Dry" and set the temperature to 400 degrees F. Press "Start" after setting the timer for 20 minutes. 7. Place the food in the center when the display says "Add Food." Turn the veggies when the display says "Turn Food." 8. Remove the tray from the air fryer when the cooking time is up. Serve immediately.

Per serving: Calories 216; Fat 2.2g; Sodium 590mg; Carbs 45.7g; Fiber 3g; Sugar 7g; Protein 5g

Glazed Vegetables

Prep time: 5 minutes | Cook time: 20 minutes | Serves: 4

2 ounces' cherry tomatoes	6 tablespoons olive oil divided
1 large parsnip, peeled and chopped	3 tablespoons Honey
1 large carrot, peeled and chopped	1 teaspoon Dijon mustard
	1 teaspoon mixed dried herbs
1 large zucchini, chopped	1 teaspoon Garlic paste
1 green bell pepper, seeded and chopped	Salt and ground black pepper, as required

1. Coat a baking dish with cooking spray that will fit in the air fryer. 2. Drizzle 3 tablespoons of oil over the veggies in the prepared baking dish. Place the drip pan in the cooking chamber of the air fryer. 3. Select "Air Dry" and set the temperature to 400 degrees F. Press "Start" after setting the timer for 15 minutes. 4. Place the baking dish in the center of the air fryer when the display says "Add Food." Meanwhile, combine the remaining oil, honey, mustard, herbs, garlic, salt, and black pepper in a mixing bowl. 5. Turn the veggies when the display says "Turn Food." 6. Remove the baking dish from the air fryer when the cooking time is over. 7. Add the honey mixture to the baking dish and stir until well combined. Select "Air Fry" once more, then set the temperature to 400 degrees F. Press "Start" after setting the timer for 5 minutes. 8. Turn the veggies when the display says "Turn Food." 9. Remove the baking dish when the cooking time is up. Serve hot.

Per serving: Calories 285; Fat 21.4g; Sodium 448mg; Carbs 25.9g; Fiber 3g; Sugar 5g; Protein 2.1g

Spicy Tofu and Cauliflower

Prep time: 5 minutes | Cook time: 15 minutes | Serves: 2

7 ounces' firm tofu, pressed and cubed	¼ teaspoon dried parsley
	1 teaspoon ground turmeric
½ small head cauliflower, cut into florets	¼ teaspoon paprika
1 tablespoon canola oil	Salt and ground black pepper, as required
1 tablespoon nutritional yeast	

1. Combine the tofu, cauliflower, and the remaining ingredients in a mixing bowl. 2. In a prepared baking pan, place the tofu mixture. 3. In the Air Fryer, place the drip pan. Select "Air Dry" and set the temperature to 400 degrees F. Press "Start" after setting the timer to 15 minutes. 4. Place the cooking tray in the center when the display says "Add Food." 5. Turn the tofu mixture when the display says "Turn Food." 6. Remove the tray from the air fryer when the cooking time is up. Serve hot.

Per serving: Calories 170; Fat 11.6g; Sodium 420mg; Carbs 8.3g; Fiber 3g; Sugar 1g; Protein 11.9g

Garlic Veggies

Prep time: 5 minutes | Cook time: 19 minutes | Serves: 5

1 tablespoon olive oil	1 small onion, sliced
1 tablespoon garlic minced	¼ cup balsamic vinegar
1 cup cauliflower florets	1 teaspoon red pepper flakes
1 cup broccoli florets	salt and ground black pepper, as required
1 cup zucchini, sliced	
½ cup yellow squash, sliced	¼ cup Parmesan cheese, grated
½ cup fresh mushrooms, sliced	

1. Toss all ingredients in a bowl, except the cheese, to coat well. 2. Fill the prepared baking tray halfway with the vege-table mixture. Place the drip pan in the Air Fryer's bottom. 3. Select "Air Dry" and set the temperature to 400 degrees F. Set the timer for 18 minutes and hit the "Start" button. 4. Place the cooking tray in the center when the display says "Add Food." 5. Turn the veggie mixture when the display says "Turn Food." 6. After 16 minutes of cooking, evenly sprinkle the cheese over the veggies. 7. Remove the tray from the Air fryer when the cooking time is up. Serve hot.

Per serving: Calories 102; Fat 6.2g; Sodium 380mg; Carbs 6.6g; Fiber 1g; Sugar 2g; Protein 6.6g

Stuffed Eggplant Halves

Prep time: 5 minutes | Cook time: 20 minutes | Serves: 2

4 small eggplants, halved lengthwise	as required
	1 tablespoon Cottage cheese
1 teaspoon fresh lime juice	¼ green bell pepper seeded and chopped
1 teaspoon vegetable oil	
1 small onion chopped	1 tablespoon Tomato paste
¼ teaspoon garlic chopped	1 tablespoon fresh cilantro chopped
½ small tomato chopped	
salt and ground black pepper,	

1. Carefully cut a lengthwise slice from one side of each eggplant. Scoop off the flesh from each eggplant with a tiny spoon, leaving a thick shell. 2. Place the eggplant flesh in a mixing basin. Drizzle the lime juice over the eggplants evenly. 3. Arrange the eggplants on the cooking tray that has been oiled. In the air fryer, place the drip pan. 4. Select "Air Dry" and set the temperature to 400 degrees F. Press "Start" after setting the timer for 3 minutes. 5. Place the frying rack in the center when the display says "Add Food." 6. Do not flip the food when the display says "Turn Food." 7. Meanwhile, heat the oil in a pan over medium heat and cook the onion and garlic for 2 minutes. Sauté for 2 minutes with the eggplant flesh, tomato, salt, and black pepper—Cook for 1 minute after adding the cheese, bell pepper, tomato paste, and cilantro. Remove the pan with the vegetable mixture from the heat. 8. Remove the eggplants from the air fryer after the cooking time is over. Place the cooked eggplants on a dish and fill with the vegetable mixture. Each one should be closed with the sliced portion. 9. Arrange the eggplants on the cooking tray that has been oiled. Select "Air Fry" once more, then set the temperature to 400 degrees F. Press "Start" after setting the timer for 8 minutes. 10. Place the frying rack in the center when the display says "Add Food." Do not flip the food when the display says "Turn Food." 11. When cooking time is complete, remove the eggplants from the air fryer. Serve hot.

Per serving: Calories 131; Fat 2g; Sodium 324mg; Carbs 27.8g; Fiber 5g; Sugar 8g; Protein 5.1g

Mozzarella Vegetable Loaf

Prep time: 5 minutes | Cook time: 1 hour and 30 minutes | Serves: 4

14 ounces' vegetable broth – 1 (14½-ounce) can	minced
	½ cup cooked brown rice
¾ cup brown lentils –rinsed	1 cup mozzarella cheese shredded
1 tablespoon olive oil	
1 ¾ cups carrots peeled and shredded	1 large egg
	1 large egg white
1 cup fresh mushrooms chopped	salt and ground black pepper, as required
1 cup onion chopped	2 tablespoons tomato paste
1 tablespoon fresh parsley minced	2 tablespoons water
1 tablespoon fresh basil	

1. Bring the broth to a boil in a saucepan over medium-high heat. Return to a boil after adding the lentils. 2. Reduce the heat to low and cook for about 30 minutes, covered. Remove the pan from the heat and set it aside to cool for a few minutes. 3. Meanwhile, heat the oil in a large pan over medium heat and cook the carrots, mushrooms, and onion for 10 minutes. Turn off the heat, add the herbs to the saucepan, and stir well. 4. Place the vegetable mixture in a large mixing dish and set it aside to cool. 5. After the lentils, rice, cheese, egg, egg white, and spices have cooled, combine the lentils, rice, cheese, egg, egg white, and seasonings with the lentils. 6. Combine the tomato paste and water in a small bowl. Fill a greased parchment paper-lined loaf pan halfway with the batter, then top with the water mixture. In the air fryer, place the drip pan. 7. Select "Bake" and set the temperature to 365 degrees F. Set the timer for 50 minutes and hit the "Start" button. 8. Place the loaf pan over the drip pan when the display says "Add Food." 9. Remove the pan from the air fryer after the cooking time is up and set it aside for approximately 10 minutes before slicing. Invert the bread carefully onto the wire rack. Serve by slicing into preferred sizes.
Per serving: Calories 2299; Fat 5.1g; Sodium 489mg; Carbs 33.4g; Fiber 6g; Sugar 5g; Protein 12.8g

Vegetable and White Rice

Prep time: 5 minutes | Cook time: 18 minutes | Serves: 4

2 cups cooked white rice	½ cup frozen peas thawed
1 tablespoon vegetable oil	½ cup frozen carrots thawed
2 tablespoons sesame oil toasted and divided	1 teaspoon soy sauce
1 tablespoon water	1 teaspoon Sriracha sauce
salt and ground white pepper, as required	½ teaspoon sesame seeds toasted
1 large egg lightly beaten	2 tablespoons fresh parsley chopped

1. Coat a baking dish with cooking spray that will fit in the air fryer. 2. Combine the rice, vegetable oil, 1 teaspoon sesame oil, water, salt, and white pepper in a large mixing basin. 3. Place the rice mixture in an equal layer in the prepared baking dish. In the air fryer, place the drip pan. 4. Select "Air Dry" and set the temperature to 380 degrees F. Press "Start" after setting the timer to 12 minutes. 5. Place the baking dish in the air fryer when the display says "Add Food." Stir the rice mixture when the display says, "turn Food." 6. Remove the baking dish from the air fryer when the cooking time is over. 7. Pour the beaten egg evenly over the rice. Select "Air Dry" and set the temperature to 400 degrees F. Set the timer for 2 minutes and hit the "Start" button. 8. Place the baking dish in the air fryer when the display says "Add Food." Stir the rice mixture when the display says, "turn Food." 9. Remove the baking dish from the air fryer when the cooking time is up. 10. Add the peas and carrots to the baking dish and toss to mix. Select "Air Fry" once more, then set the temperature to 400 degrees F. Set the timer for 4 minutes and hit the "Start" button. Place the baking dish in the air fryer when the display says "Add Food." 11. Stir the rice mixture when the display says, "turn Food." Meanwhile, combine soy sauce, Sriracha sauce, sesame seeds, and the remaining sesame oil in a mixing bowl. 12. Remove the baking dish from the air fryer when the cooking time is up. Fill a serving dish halfway with the rice mixture. Drizzle the sauce over the top and serve with a parsley garnish.
Per serving: Calories 458; Fat 8.6g; Sodium 435mg; Carbs 78g; Fiber 4g; Sugar 9g; Protein 9.5g

Spicy Macaroni

Prep time: 5 minutes | Cook time: 25 minutes | Serves: 4

2 cups Cheddar cheese shredded and divided	2 cups heavy whipping cream
1 teaspoon cornstarch	2 cups dry macaroni

1. Combine 1 ½ cups of cheese and cornstarch in a mixing dish and stir well. Remove from the equation. 2. Combine the remaining cheese, whipping cream, and macaroni in a separate dish and stir well. 3. Fill a baking dish with the macaroni mixture and place it in the air fryer. Cover the baking dish that will fit in the air fryer with a piece of foil. Place the drip pan in the Air Fryer. 4. Select "Air Dry" and set the temperature to 400 degrees F. Press "Start" after setting the timer for 25 minutes. 5. Place the baking dish in the air fryer when the display says "Add Food." Do not flip the food when the display says, "turn Food." 6. After 15 minutes, remove the foil and top the macaroni mixture with cornstarch. 7. When cooking time is complete, remove the baking dish from the air fryer. Serve warm.
Per serving: Calories 593; Fat 41.6g; Sodium 354mg; Carbs 34.8g; Fiber 6g; Sugar 8g; Protein 20.8g

Baked Beans

Prep time: 10 minutes | Cook time: 15 minutes | Serves: 4

1 28-ounce can of baked beans	¼ cup ketchup
14 ounces canned red kidney beans, boiled lightly	1 tablespoon yellow mustard
½ cup bacon, cooked and chopped	1 tablespoon Worcestershire sauce
⅓ cup onion, finely chopped	1 tablespoon apple cider vinegar
¼ cup brown; Sugar	1 tablespoon honey

1. Place all ingredients in a circular pan on the baking tray. 2. Select Air Fry mode. 3. Set the temp of the air fryer to 400 degrees F and time to 15 minutes. 4. When it says "Add Food," place the cooking tray in the air fryer. When the cooking time is up, remove it from the air fryer. Warm the dish before serving.
Per serving: Calories 472; Fat 17.4g; Sodium 365mg; Carbs 64g; Fiber 5g; Sugar 9g; Protein 20g

Zucchini Stuffed Green Pepper

Prep time: 5 minutes | Cook time: 25 minutes | Serves: 3

3 green bell peppers, tops, and seeds removed	
1 medium-sized onion, diced	1 teaspoon Chinese 5-spice
1 carrot, thinly diced	1 tablespoon olive oil
1 small cauliflower, shredded	3 tablespoons of any soft cheese
1 teaspoon garlic powder	
1 teaspoon coriander	1 zucchini, thinly diced
1 teaspoon mixed spices	¼ yellow pepper, thinly diced

1. In a pan over medium heat, cook the onion with olive oil. 2. Combine the cauliflower and spices in a large mixing bowl. Cook for 5 minutes, stirring occasionally. 3. Cook for 5 minutes after adding the veggies (carrot, zucchini, and yellow pepper). 4. Fill one spoonful of soft cheese into each green pepper. 5. The cauliflower mixture should then be stuffed into them. 6. Select Air Fry mode. 7. Cook the stuffed peppers in the air fryer for 15 minutes at 400 degrees F.
Per serving: Calories 272; Fat 12.7g; Sodium 483mg; Carbs 26g; Fiber 4g; Sugar 7g; Protein 17g

Halibut in Red Wine Vinegar

Prep time: 5 minutes | Cook time: 12 minutes | Serves: 2

2 (5-ounce) halibut fillets
2 garlic cloves, minced
1 teaspoon fresh rosemary, minced

1 tablespoon olive oil
1 tablespoon red wine vinegar
⅛ teaspoon hot sauce

1. Combine all ingredients in a big resealable bag. To mix, seal the bag and shake it thoroughly. Refrigerate for at least 30 minutes to marinate. Shake off the excess marinade from the fish fillets in the bag. Place the halibut fillets on a greased baking sheet. 2. In the air fryer, arrange the pan. Select "Bake" and set the temperature to 365 degrees F. Press "Start" after setting the timer for 12 minutes. 3. Place the cooking tray in the center when the display says "Add Food." 4. Remove the tray from the air fryer when the cooking time is up. Serve hot.
Per serving: Calories 223; Fat 10.4g; Sodium 546mg; Carbs 1g; Fiber 0g; Sugar 0g; Protein 30g

Tasty Brussels Sprout

Prep time: 5 minutes | Cook time: 10 minutes | Serves: 2

½ pound Brussels sprouts, cut in half
½ tablespoon oil

½ tablespoon unsalted butter, melted

1. Sprouts should be rubbed with oil. 2. Place the ingredients in the cooking tray. 3. Select Air Fry mode. 4. Cook for 10 minutes at 400 degrees F. At the halfway point, stir once more. 5. Remove the cooking tray from the machine and brush it with melted butter. 6. Serve.
Per serving: Calories 90; Fat 6.1g; Sodium 543mg; Carbs 4g; Fiber 2g; Sugar 1g; Protein 2.9g

Herbs de Provence Asparagus

Prep time: 5 minutes | Cook time: 10 minutes | Serves: 4

1 bunch of fresh asparagus
1 ½ teaspoons herbs de Provence
Fresh lemon wedge (optional)

1 tablespoon olive oil or cooking spray
Salt and pepper to taste

1. Trim the hard ends of the asparagus and wash it. Drizzle olive oil over asparagus and season with salt and pepper. 2. Select Roast mode. 3. Cook the asparagus in the air fryer for 6-10 minutes at 380 degrees F. 4. Drizzle lemon juice over the roasted asparagus.
Per serving: Calories 46; Fat 3g; Sodium 234mg; Carbs 1g; Fiber 0g; Sugar 0g; Protein 2g

Fresh Broccoli

Prep time: 5 minutes | Cook time: 10 minutes | Serves: 4

1 teaspoon herbs de Provence seasoning (optional)
4 cups fresh broccoli

1 tablespoon olive oil
Salt and pepper to taste

1. Drizzle or spritz the broccoli with olive oil and the remaining ingredients, and season well. 2. Select Air Fry mode. 3. Cook for 5-8 minutes at 400 degrees F after spraying the cooking tray with cooking oil. 4. When the display shows "turn Food," turn the broccoli.
Per serving: Calories 61; Fat 4g; Sodium 453mg; Carbs 4g; Fiber 1g; Sugar 1g; Protein 3g

Cheddar Vegetables Quesadillas

Prep time: 20 minutes | Cook time: 20 minutes | Serves: 4

4 sprouted whole-grain flour tortillas (6-in.)
1 cup sliced red bell pepper
4 ounces reduced-fat Cheddar cheese, shredded
1 cup sliced zucchini
1 cup canned black beans, dry out and rinsed (no salt)
Cooking spray
2 ounces plain 2% reduced-fat

Greek yogurt
1 teaspoon lime zest
1 tablespoon fresh juice (from 1 lime)
¼ teaspoon ground cumin
2 tablespoons chopped fresh cilantro
½ cup dry-out refrigerated Pico de Gallo

1. Place tortillas on a work surface, sprinkle 2 tablespoons of shredded cheese over half of each tortilla, and top with ¼ cup of red pepper slices, zucchini slices, and black beans each tortilla. The remaining ½ cup of cheese should be equally distributed. 2. To make half-moon-shaped quesadillas, fold tortillas in half, gently cover with cooking spray, then fasten with toothpicks. 3. Cooking sprays the cooking tray lightly. Select Air Fry mode. 4. Cook 2 quesadillas in the basket at 400 degrees F for 10 minutes, until tortillas are golden brown and slightly crispy, cheese has melted, and veggies have softened somewhat. When the display shows "turn Food", turn the food. 5. Repeat with the rest of the quesadillas. 6. In a small bowl, combine yogurt, juice, zest, and cumin. Each quesadilla should be cut into wedges and topped with cilantro. 7. 1 tablespoon cumin cream and 2 tablespoons Pico de Gallo are served on the side.
Per serving: Calories 291; Fat 8g; Sodium 420mg; Carbs 36g; Fiber 5g; Sugar 4g; Protein 17g

Mushroom Poppers

Prep time: 30 minutes | Cook time: 20 minutes | Serves: 8

1-pound fresh whole button mushrooms
½ teaspoon kosher salt
3 tablespoons ⅓-less-fat cream cheese,
¼ cup all-purpose flour
Softened 1 jalapeño chili, seeded and minced
Cooking spray
¼ teaspoon black pepper
1 cup panko breadcrumbs

1 large egg, lightly beaten
¼ cup buffalo-style hot sauce
2 tablespoons chopped fresh chives
½ cup low-fat buttermilk
½ cup plain; Fat-free yogurt
2 ounces' blue cheese, crumbled (about ½ cup)
3 tablespoons apple cider vinegar

1. Remove the stems from the mushroom caps, cut the stems, and set aside the caps. Combine the chopped mushroom stems, cream cheese, jalapeno, salt, and pepper in a mixing bowl. Fill each mushroom cap with about 1 teaspoon of the mixture, forming a smooth ball with the filling. 2. Put the panko in one bowl, the flour in another, and the eggs in a third. Coat the mushrooms in flour, then dip them in the egg mixture and panko, pushing them down to adhere. Cooking spray the mushrooms well.
Select Air Fry mode. 3. Cook for 20 minutes at 400 degrees F with half of the mushrooms in the cooking tray. Place the sautéed mushrooms in a large mixing basin. 4. Drizzle buffalo sauce over the mushrooms, tossing to coat, and top with chives.
Per serving: Calories 133; Fat 4g; Sodium 444mg; Carbs 16g; Fiber 2g; Sugar 3g; Protein 7g

Yummy Haddock

Prep time: 5 minutes | Cook time: 10 minutes | Serves: 3

½ cup flour
½ teaspoon Paprika
1 egg, beaten
¼ cup mayonnaise

4 ounces salt and vinegar potato chips, crushed finely
2 pounds' haddock fillet cut into 6 pieces

1. Combine the flour and paprika in a small bowl. In a second shallow bowl, whisk together the egg and mayonnaise. Place the crumbled potato chips in a third shallow dish. 2. Coat the fish pieces in the flour mixture, then the egg mixture, and the potato chips. Arrange the chunks of fish on two baking pans. 3. In the air fryer, arrange the pan. Select "Air Dry" and set the temperature to 400 degrees F. Press "Start" after setting the timer for 10 minutes. After that, cook. 4. When the display says "turn Food," don't turn the food; instead, move the cooking trays around. 5. Remove the trays from the air fryer when the cooking time is up. Serve hot.
Per serving: Calories 456; Fat 22.7g; Sodium 530mg; Carbs 40.9g; Fiber 4g; Sugar 11g; Protein 43.5g

Yummy Vegetables Cup

Prep time: 10 minutes | Cook time: 15 minutes | Serves: 4

Nonstick cooking spray
4 large eggs
1 cup diced veggies of choice
1 cup shredded cheese

4 tablespoons half and half
1 tablespoon chopped cilantro
Salt and Pepper

1. 4 ramekins, greased 2. In a large mixing bowl, combine the eggs, veggies, half of the cheese, half and half, cilantro, and salt and pepper. Divide the mixture amongst the ramekins in a medium bowl. 3. Select Air Fry mode. 4. Place the ramekins in the cooking tray and cook for 12 minutes at 400 degrees F. 5. The leftover cheese should be sprinkled on top of the cups. 6. Set the air fryer to 400 degrees F and cook for 2 minutes until the cheese has melted.
Per serving: Calories 195; Fat 12g; Sodium 435mg; Carbs 7g; Fiber 2g; Sugar 1g; Protein 13g

Refresh Steamed Veggies

Prep time: 5 minutes | Cook time: 10 minutes | Serves: 4

½ pound broccoli fresh
½ pound cauliflower fresh
1 tablespoon Olive oil

¼ teaspoon seasoning
⅓ cup water

1. Mix the veggies, olive oil, and spices in a medium mixing bowl. 2. To avoid smoke, fill the air fryer base with ⅓ cups of water. 3. Fill the cooking tray with veggies. 4. Select Air Fry mode. 5. Cook for 7-10 minutes at 400 degrees F. 6. Give the veggies a good shake halfway through the cooking time.
Per serving: Calories 65; Fat 4g; Sodium 345mg; Carbs 7g; Fiber 2g; Sugar 1g; Protein 3g

Mushroom Onion Frittata with Feta

Prep time: 15 minutes | Cook time: 15 minutes | Serves: 4

3 whole eggs
2 cups sliced button mushrooms
½ red onions

1 tablespoon Olive oil
1 tablespoon crumbled feta
1 pinch salt

1. Half a red onion, peeled and sliced into 14-inch thin slices 2. After washing the button mushrooms, cut them into 14-inch thin slices. 3. Place a skillet over medium heat, add the olive oil, and cook the onions and mushrooms until they are soft. Remove the onions and mushrooms from the heat and let them cool on a kitchen towel. 4. In a mixing bowl, crack three eggs and whisk thoroughly and vigorously. 5. Spray the pan with oil by gently coating the outside and bottom of a 6-ounce ramekin. 6. Pour the eggs into the ramekin, add ¼ cup of the onion and mushroom combination, followed by the cheese. 7. Select Air Fry mode. 8. Set temp to 400 degrees F and time to 12 minutes. 9. Once done, serve and enjoy!
Per serving: Calories 90; Fat 4.5g; Sodium 444mg; Carbs 8g; Fiber 2g; Sugar 1g; Protein 13g

Toothsome Brussels Sprouts

Prep time: 5 minutes | Cook time: 20 minutes | Serves: 8

Brussels sprout cut into 2 halves
1 ½ tablespoons vegetable oil

½ teaspoon salt
2 tablespoons honey
1 tablespoon gochujang

1. Whisk together the honey, gochujang, vegetable oil, and salt in a bowl. Remove 1 tablespoon of the sauce and set it aside, then add the Brussels sprouts to the mixing bowl and toss until well combined. 2. Select Air Fry mode. 3. Place the Brussels sprouts in your air fryer, set the temperature to 400 degrees F, and cook for 15 minutes. Halfway through the cooking time, shake the food, and place the bowl away when the timer goes off. 4. Decrease the temperature to 390 degrees F and cook for another 5 minutes after the timer goes off. 5. After 5 minutes, transfer the sprouts to a bowl and mix in the saved sauce.
Per serving: Calories 128; Fat 4g; Sodium 345mg; Carbs 20g; Fiber 2g; Sugar 7g; Protein 3g

Less-Spice Sweet Carrots

Prep time: 10 minutes | Cook time: 10 minutes | Serves: 4

3 pounds' carrots, peeled and chopped into 1-inch pieces
¼ tablespoon salt

2 tablespoons brown; Sugar
2 tablespoons melted butter

1. In a mixing dish, combine peeled and diced carrots, melted butter, brown sugar, and salt, and stir well until the carrots are thoroughly coated. 2. Select Roast mode. 3. Pour the coated mixture into an air fryer-safe bowl, place it in the air fryer, and set temp to 380 degrees F and time to 10 minutes. 4. Cook for 10 minutes at 380 degrees F, stirring halfway through. 5. Your delicious carrot is ready to eat.
Per serving: Calories 210; Fat 11g; Sodium 275mg; Carbs 17g; Fiber 3g; Sugar 1g; Protein 4g

Roasted Carrots

Prep time: 10 minutes | Cook time: 20 minutes | Serves: 4

3 pounds of medium-sized carrots (washed and peeled)
¼ cup grated parmesan cheese
Fresh chopped parsley (optional)

2 tablespoons olive oil
½ teaspoon paprika
½ teaspoon garlic powder
Salt and pepper (to taste)

1. Toss peeled and diced carrots with olive oil, garlic powder, and paprika in a large mixing dish. 2. Select Air Fry mode. 3. Cook for 10 minutes at 380 degrees F in a cooking tray, then shake and cook for another 10 minutes at the same temperature. 4. When the carrots are done, sprinkle with parsley and parmesan cheese, and season with pepper and salt to taste.
Per serving: Calories 119; Fat 6g; Sodium 390mg; Carbs 17g; Fiber 1g; Sugar 1g; Protein 1g

Yummy Broccoli Casserole

Prep time: 5 minutes | Cook time: 25 minutes | Serves: 4

1 cup diced ham	½ teaspoon garlic salt
1 (14-ounce) bag of frozen broccoli	½ teaspoon onion powder
4 ounces' cream cheese, softened	½ teaspoon dried basil
	½ teaspoon smoked paprika
½ cup plain full-fat Greek yogurt	¼ teaspoon rosemary
	¼ teaspoon thyme
¼ cup mayonnaise	½ cup shredded cheese
	½ cup crushed pork rinds

1. Set aside a 6-inch soufflé dish sprayed with nonstick cooking spray. 2. In a large mixing bowl, toss the ham, broccoli, cream cheese, yogurt, mayonnaise, garlic salt, onion powder, basil, smoked paprika, rosemary, and thyme. 3. Select Air Fry mode. 4. Fill an oiled pan halfway with batter and top with grated cheese and shredded rinds. Cook for 25 minutes at 400 degrees F, or until golden and bubbling on top.

Per serving: Calories 273; Fat 17.4g; Sodium 444mg; Carbs 9.7g; Fiber 4g; Sugar 1.5g; Protein 17.4g

Indian-Style Cauliflower

Prep time: 5 minutes | Cook time: 15 minutes | Serves: 4

240ml vegetable stock	⅓ teaspoon turmeric
180ml light coconut milk	¼ teaspoon salt
½ teaspoon garam masala	350g cauliflower florets
1 teaspoon mild curry powder	200g sweet corn kernels
1 teaspoon garlic puree	3 scallions

1. Combine the vegetable stock, light coconut milk, garam masala, mild curry powder, garlic puree, turmeric, and salt in a large mixing bowl. 2. Combine the cauliflower, sweet corn, and scallions in a large mixing bowl. Toss them in until they're evenly covered. 3. Place in a plate and cook for 12-15 minutes at 400 degrees F on Air Fry mode in the Air Fryer.

Per serving: Calories 166; Fat 4g; Sodium 222mg; Carbs 29g; Fiber 3g; Sugar 1g; Protein 4g

Potatoes and Tofu

Prep time: 10 minutes | Cook time: 45 minutes | Serves: 4

1 onion	1 tablespoon fresh basil
½ tablespoon olive oil	1 teaspoon Thai peppers
2 tablespoons lime juice & zest	226g small potatoes
400ml coconut milk	1 teaspoon coarse sea salt
2 tablespoons red curry	1 teaspoon sea salt
2 tablespoons fish sauce	1 teaspoon red curry
1 tablespoon brown; Sugar	Olive oil spray
1 tablespoon fresh mint	400g tofu
	1 teaspoon red curry

1. Spray the potatoes with cooking oil, then season with 1 teaspoon salt and 1 teaspoon red curry. 2. Select Air Fry mode, set the time to 14 minutes and the temperature to 400 degrees F. 3. Toss the potatoes for about 7 minutes and cook for another 7 minutes; after the potatoes are crispy, remove them from the pan. 4. Place paper towels on top and below your tofu to dry them. Allow tofu to dry for 10 minutes after pressing it down with something heavy. Cut the tofu into small pieces. 1 teaspoon red curry, dipped in tofu. 5. Place the tofu in your air fryer, and cook it for additional 8 minutes at 400 degrees F. 6. Cut the onion, basil, and mint into tiny squares to create the sauce. Then, heat ½ tablespoon of oil in a separate pan, add the onions and sauté until transparent. Bring the coconut milk to a boil, then add the curry, fish sauce, and brown sugar to

taste. Simmer for 10 to 15 minutes after adding the potatoes to the pan. 7. Stir in the lime juice, lime zest, and tofu until everything is thoroughly combined. Stir the mint and basil into the mixture once more. Season it with salt and pepper to taste.

Per serving: Calories 341; Fat 25g; Sodium 433mg; Carbs 22g; Fiber 2g; Sugar 6g; Protein 11g

Lime Halibut Fillets

Prep time: 5 minutes | Cook time: 20 minutes | Serves: 4

4 halibut fillets	Salt and pepper to taste
1 egg, beaten	1 tablespoon parsley, chopped
1 lemon, sliced	

1. Toss the halibut fillets with the lemon juice. 2. Combine the lemon slices, salt, pepper, and parsley in a food processor. 3. Coat the fillets in this mixture and dip them into a beaten egg. 4. Select Air Fry mode. 5. Cook the fillets in your air fryer for 15 minutes at 400 degrees F.

Per serving: Calories 48; Fat 1g; Sodium 334; Carbs 2.5g; Fiber 1g; Sugar 0g; Protein 9g

Cheesy Vegetables Quesarito

Prep time: 5 minutes | Cook time: 10 minutes | Serves: 4

2 large gluten-free tortillas	1 to 2 tablespoons spicy almond sauce
4 tablespoons Vegan Queso (divided)	1 tablespoon cashew cream or dairy-free sour cream
2 to 3 tablespoons grated cheese	added ingredients
3 tablespoons meaty crumbles	fresh baby spinach, fresh bell peppers
3 to 4 tablespoons of simple Spanish rice	roasted red peppers

1. Place the first tortilla on the prep surface flat. 2. Using a knife, cut approximately an inch from the second tortilla's edge, create one smaller tortilla, and set it aside. 3. Spread the vegan queso in a circle the size of the smaller tortilla around the center of the first tortilla. 4. 3 tablespoons of grated cheese, evenly distributed throughout the tiny circle (1 tablespoon grated cheese). Top the queso/cheese circle with the smaller second tortilla, pressing down slightly. 5. Spoon a line of meaty crumbles down the center of the second smaller tortilla, then top with Spanish rice, tangy cream sauce, and cashew cream/sour cream. 6. Fold and roll the tortilla securely with care. 1 tablespoon grated cheese, set aside, is used to secure the edge. In the cooking tray, place the burrito cheese sealed side down. 7. Select Air Fry mode. 8. Air Fry at 400 degrees F for 6-7 minutes, or until golden and crisp.

Per serving: Calories 514; Fat 18g; Sodium 543mg; Carbs 13g; Fiber 4g; Sugar 1.9g; Protein 22g

Thai-Style Noodles with Peppers

Prep time: 1 hour and 15 minutes | Cook time: 20 minutes | Serves: 6

1kg of shirataki noodles	150g water chestnuts
6 tablespoons soy sauce	1 teaspoon coriander paste
½ tablespoon fish sauce	1 tablespoon of lime juice
1 teaspoon sesame oil	1 teaspoon lemongrass paste
½ teaspoon garlic powder	1 tablespoon of rice wine vinegar
350g tofu	
150g snow peas	350g napa cabbage
1 red pepper	2 medium carrots
1 green pepper	4 green onions
100g mushrooms	6 tablespoons Thai green cur-

ry paste

1. To begin, prepare the veggies by thinly slicing the peppers, mushrooms, and water chestnuts. The carrots and cabbage must be shredded, and the green onions must be finely chopped. Save it for a later date. 2. In a large mixing bowl, combine the noodles with 500 mL boiling water and 1 tablespoon soy sauce. Remove from the equation. 3. To prepare a marinade, combine 3 tablespoons of soy sauce, fish sauce, sesame oil, and garlic powder. 4. Cut the tofu into bite-size chunks and add it to the marinade, carefully combining the ingredients thoroughly. Remove from the equation. 5. To create the stir-fry vegetables, combine the snow peas, peppers, mushrooms, and water chestnuts in a bowl. Remove from the equation. 6. Combine the coriander paste, lime juice, lemongrass paste, 4 teaspoons Thai green curry paste, and 2 tablespoons rice vinegar to make the dressing. Remove from the equation. 7. Combine the shredded cabbage, carrots, and chopped green onion to form the veg foundation. Remove from the equation. 8. Select Air Fry as your cooking mode. 9. Set the air fryer to 400 degrees F and lightly coat the cooking tray in frying oil. 10. Transfer the marinated tofu to the cooking tray; cook for 12 to 13 minutes, turning halfway through cooking. Set aside with a plate on top to keep them warm after they're done. 11. Combine the remaining marinade, 2 teaspoons rice vinegar, 2 tablespoons soy sauce, and 2 tablespoons Thai green curry paste in an Air Fryer-safe dish, then add the stir-fry vegetables and spray with cooking oil. Cook for 5 minutes. 12. Allow the noodles to air dry. 13. Combine the noodles, dressing, tofu cubes, stir-fry vegetables, and veg base in a large mixing dish. Toss with tongs to combine everything.

Per serving: Calories 183; Fat 6.1g; Sodium 342mg; Carbs 22.7g; Fiber 5g; Sugar 3g; Protein 9.9g

Mexican Taco Bowl

Prep time: 2 minutes | Cook time: 10 minutes | Serves: 2

Burrito-Sized Flour Tortilla   Cooking Spray

1. Spray the tortilla on both sides with cooking spray. 2. Fold a piece of foil twice the size of the tortilla wrap and lay it on top of the tortilla wrap. 3. Put it in the Air Fryer with a somewhat smaller bowl inside to help weigh it down. 4. Select Air Fry mode. 5. Cook the tortilla for 5 minutes at 400 degrees F. 6. Remove the bowl and continue to Air Fry for 2 minutes more. 7. Fill the burrito bowl with your favorite salad toppings.

Per serving: Calories 220; Fat 20g; Sodium 444mg; Carbs 84g; Fiber 9g; Sugar 12g; Protein 21g

Ratatouille with Bell Peppers

Prep time: 25 minutes | Cook time: 30 minutes | Serves: 4

½ Small eggplants	2 oregano sprigs
1 zucchini	5 garlic clove
1 medium tomato	½ teaspoon of salt
½ large yellow bell pepper	½ teaspoon of pepper
½ large red bell peppers	1 tablespoon of olive oil
½ onions	1 tablespoon of white wine
1 cayenne pepper	1 teaspoon of vinegar
5 basil sprigs	

1. Cube the zucchini, tomato, bell peppers, onion, and cayenne. The basil and oregano leaves should then be steamed and chopped. 2. In a large mixing bowl, combine the eggplant, zucchini, tomato, bell peppers, onions, cayenne, basil, oregano, garlic, salt, and pepper. Drizzle with the oil, wine, and vinegar combination. 3. Select Air Fry mode. Set temp to 400 degrees F. 4. Pour the veggie mixture into a baking dish that will fit inside your air fryer. Cook for 8 minutes in the air fryer with the baking dish. Cook for another 8 minutes once the first 8 minutes are up. Stir once more and continue to simmer until the veggies are soft, about another 10 minutes, stirring every 5 minutes.

Per serving: Calories 79; Fat 3.8g; Sodium 544mg; Carbs 10.2g; Fiber 2g; Sugar 2g; Protein 2.1g

Buttery Carrots

Prep time: 10 minutes | Cook time: 15 minutes | Serves: 4

½ cup butter, melted	2-pound bag baby carrots
½ cup brown; Sugar	

1. Combine the butter, brown sugar, and carrots in a mixing basin. 2. Select Air Fry mode, set the time to 15 minutes and the temperature to 400 degrees F. 3. Open the lid when the device beeps to indicate "Add Food." 4. Place the carrots in one cooking tray that has been oiled and placed in the air fryer. Cook for 15 minutes. 5. Serve warm.

Per serving: Calories 312; Fat 23.2g; Sodium 349mg; Carbs 27.1 g; Fiber 2g; Sugar 9g; Protein 1 g

Spicy Carrot and Spinach Stew

Prep time: 15 minutes | Cook time: 35 minutes | Serves: 4

4 teaspoons butter, melted and divided	1-pound zucchinis, sliced
¼ pound carrots, peeled and sliced	1 tablespoon fresh basil, chopped
	Salt and ground black pepper

1. Combine 2 teaspoons of butter and carrots in a mixing bowl. 2. Select Air Fry mode, set the temperature to 400 degrees F, and time to 35 minutes. 3. To begin, press the Start button. 4. Open the lid when the device beeps to indicate "Add Food." 5. Arrange the carrots in a cooking tray that has been oiled and placed in the air fryer, then cook. 6. Meanwhile, combine the remaining butter, zucchini, basil, salt, and black pepper in a large mixing bowl. 7. Place the zucchini mixture in the tray with the carrots after 5 minutes of cooking. 8. Toss the vegetable mixture 2-3 times during the cooking. 9. Serve hot.

Per serving: Calories 64; Fat 4g; Sodium 398mg; Carbs 6.6 g; Fiber 2g; Sugar 1g; Protein 1.7 g

Sweet Potatoes and Broccoli Bowl

Prep time: 15 minutes | Cook time: 20 minutes | Serves: 4

2 medium sweet potatoes, peeled and cut into 1-inch cubes	florets
1 head broccoli cut in 1-inch	1 tablespoon vegetable oil
	Salt and ground black pepper

1. Whisk all ingredients in a large mixing basin and toss well to combine. 2. Select Roast mode, adjust the temperature to 380 degrees F, and set the time to 20 minutes. 3. Place the carrots in the oiled cooking tray, place them in the air fryer, and cook. 4. Meanwhile, combine the remaining butter, zucchini, basil, salt, and black pepper in a large mixing bowl. 5. Place the zucchini mixture in the basket with the carrots after 5 minutes of cooking and cook for the remaining minutes. Serve hot.

Per serving: Calories 170; Fat 7.1g; Sodium 334mg; Carbs 25.2 g; Fiber 3g; Sugar 4g; Protein 2.9g

Olives with Broccoli Florets

Prep time: 15 minutes | Cook time: 15 minutes | Serves: 6

1½ pounds broccoli head stemmed and cut into 1-inch florets
2 tablespoons olive oil
Salt and ground black pepper
⅓ cup Kalamata olives halved
and pitted
2 teaspoons fresh lemon zest, grated
¼ cup Parmesan cheese, grated

1. Add the broccoli to a pan of boiling water and simmer for 3-4 minutes. 2. Dry the broccoli well. 3. Toss the broccoli, oil, salt, and black pepper in a mixing bowl to coat well. 4. Select Air Fry mode. 5. Set temp to 400 degrees F and time to 15 minutes. 6. To begin, press the Start button. 7. Open the lid when the device beeps to indicate that it has warmed. 8. Place the broccoli in the cooking tray that has been oiled and placed in the air fryer. 9. Toss the broccoli florets after 8 minutes of cooking. Transfer the broccoli to a large bowl and stir in the olives, lemon zest, and cheese. 10. Serve immediately.

Per serving: Calories 100; Fat 6.6g; Sodium 302mg; Carbs 8.1 g; Fiber 2g; Sugar 9g; Protein 4.6g

Crunchy Veggies with Chili Sauce

Prep time: 10 minutes | Cook time: 15 minutes | Serves: 2

260g of mixed vegetables, e.g., Bell peppers, cauliflower, mushrooms, zucchini, baby corn
20g of cornstarch
20g of all-purpose flour
½ teaspoon garlic powder
½ teaspoon red chili powder
½ teaspoon black pepper powder
1 teaspoon salt
1 teaspoon olive oil
2 tablespoons soy sauce
1 tablespoon chili sauce
1 tablespoon ketchup
1 tablespoon vinegar
1 teaspoon brown sugar
1 tablespoon sesame oil
1 teaspoon sesame seeds

1. Cauliflower should be cut into tiny florets. Cut the mushrooms in half and cube the bell peppers. Carrots and zucchini should be cut into rounds. 2. Combine the all-purpose flour, cornstarch, garlic powder, bell pepper powder, red chili powder, and salt in a mixing bowl to form the batter. 3. Mix in a teaspoon of oil until the batter is smooth and lump-free. 4. In a large mixing bowl, combine the veggies and ensure they are equally covered. 5. Select Air Fry mode. 6. Set the tempo of the air fryer to 400 degrees F (200 degrees Celsius). 7. Cook for 10 minutes with the veggies in the cooking tray. 8. Heat a tablespoon of oil and finely sliced garlic in a saucepan until an aroma develops. Soy sauce, chili sauce, tomato ketchup, vinegar, brown sugar, and black pepper are added. 9. Cook the sauce for 1 minute, add the Air Fried vegetables and mix well. Make sure the vegetables are evenly coated. 10. Sprinkle the sesame seeds and sesame oil over the vegetables.

Per serving: Calories 236; Fat 10.5g; Sodium 354mg; Carbs 32.2g; Fiber 2g; Sugar 8g; Protein 4.6g

Salty Tofu

Prep time: 20 minutes | Cook time: 20 minutes | Serves: 2

450g tofu
¾ teaspoon sea salt
¾ teaspoon ground white pepper
2 pinches of Chinese spice powder
1 teaspoon sugar
1 tablespoon canola
1 tablespoon cornstarch
3 ½ tablespoons rice flour
3 garlic cloves
1 serrano chile
1 large scallion

1. Toss tofu with ¼ teaspoon salt and cut into bite-size pieces. Place paper towels on top of the wet and allow to dry. 2. ¼ teaspoon salt, ⅛ teaspoon pepper, Chinese spice, and sugar are combined in a bowl. Half of the mixture should be placed in a bowl with cornstarch and rice flour. 3. Coat the tofu in 1 tablespoon canola oil before coating it in the seasoned flour and starch mixture. Select Bake mode. 4. Place the tofu in the cooking tray and cook for 15 minutes at 365 degrees F, tossing halfway during the cooking period. 5. 2 tablespoons of canola oil, garlic, chili, and scallions in a pan while cooking. Cook for about half a minute until fragrant. 6. Add the tofu to the wok and then sprinkle the remaining salt, pepper, Chinese spice, and Sugar mixture. Cook for 1 to 2 minutes, making sure to stir continuously.

Per serving: Calories 466; Fat 30.9g; Sodium 444mg; Carbs 31.6g; Fiber 9g; Sugar 7g; Protein 21.5g

Cauliflower Cooked in Vegetable Broth

Prep time: 10 minutes | Cook time: 10 minutes | Serves: 4

3 pounds' cauliflower
1 tablespoon olive oil
½ cup vegetable broth
1 teaspoon red pepper flakes,
crushed
Salt to taste
1 tablespoon fresh lemon juice

1. Select the Roast mode, set the time to 8 minutes, and the temperature to 380 degrees F. Season the cauliflower with salt and red pepper flakes in a bowl. 2. Drizzle with lemon juice and olive oil. 3. Transfer the mixture to the cooking tray after stirring in the vegetable broth. 4. When it says "Add Food," place the cooking tray in the air fryer. 5. When cooking is up, remove the food from the air fryer. Warm the dish before serving.

Per serving: Calories 87; Fat 5.2g; Sodium 448mg; Carbs 8.6g; Fiber 2g; Sugar 2g; Protein 3.9g

Easy Broccoli Florets

Prep time: 5 minutes | Cook time: 10 minutes | Serves: 3

1-pound broccoli florets
1 tablespoons butter
Salt and black pepper to taste

1. Select Roast mode, set the time to 7 minutes, and the temperature to 380 degrees F. Season the Brussels sprouts with black pepper and salt. 2. Butter the broccoli and place it on the baking pan. 3. When it says "Add Food," put the cooking tray in the air fryer. 4. When the cooking time is up, remove the food from the air fryer. Serve warm.

Per serving: Calories 119; Fat 8.2g; Sodium 554mg; Carbs 10.1g; Fiber 2g; Sugar 2g; Protein 4.3g

Spicy Tomato Halves

Prep time: 10 minutes | Cook time: 10 minutes | Serves: 2

3 tomatoes, halved
Olive oil cooking spray
Salt and ground black pepper
1 tablespoon fresh basil, chopped

1. Spray the cut sides of the tomato halves equally with cooking spray. 2. Salt, black pepper, and basil to taste. 3. Select Air Fry mode. 4. Set temp to 350 degrees F and time to 10 minutes. 5. To begin, press the Start button. 6. Open the lid when the device beeps to indicate that it has warmed. 7. Arrange the tomatoes in the cooking tray and cook them. 8. Serve warm.

Per serving: Calories 34; Fat 0.4g; Sodium 334mg; Carbs 7.2

g; Fiber 1g; Sugar 1.9g; Protein 1.7g

Buttered Asparagus

Prep time: 10 minutes | Cook time: 10 minutes | Serves: 3

2 pounds' fresh asparagus, trimmed	1 tablespoon butter, melted
1 tablespoon Parmesan cheese, grated	1 teaspoon garlic powder
	Salt and ground black pepper

1. Combine the asparagus, cheese, butter, garlic powder, salt, and black pepper in a mixing bowl. 2. Select Air Fry mode. 3. Set temp to 400 degrees F and time to 10 minutes. 4. To begin, press the Start button. Open the lid when the device beeps to indicate that it has warmed. 5. Place the vegetable mixture in a greased cooking tray and cook it. Serve hot.
Per serving: Calories 73; Fat 4.4g; Sodium 332mg; Carbs 6.6 g; Fiber 2g; Sugar 2.7g; Protein 4.2g

Balsamic Almond Asparagus

Prep time: 15 minutes | Cook time: 10 minutes | Serves: 3

1-pound asparagus	Salt and ground black pepper
1 tablespoon olive oil	⅓ cup almonds, sliced
1 tablespoon balsamic vinegar	

1. Combine the asparagus, oil, vinegar, salt, and black pepper in a mixing bowl. 2. Select Air Fry mode. 3. Set temp to 400 degrees F and time to 6 minutes. 4. To begin, press the Start button. 5. Open the lid when the device beeps to indicate that it has warmed. 6. Place the vegetable mixture in a greased cooking tray and cook it. 7. Serve with the almonds.
Per serving: Calories 173; Fat 14.8g; Sodium 442mg; Carbs 8.2 g; Fiber 2g; Sugar 2.2g; Protein 5.6g

Buttery Squash with Cilantro

Prep time: 15 minutes | Cook time: 20 minutes | Serves: 4

1 medium squash, peeled, seeded, and cut into chunk	Salt and ground black pepper
1 teaspoon cumin seed	1 tablespoon olive oil
⅛ teaspoon garlic powder	1 tablespoon pine nut
⅛ teaspoon chili flakes, crushed	1 tablespoon fresh cilantro, chopped

1. Combine the squash, spices, and oil in a mixing basin. 2. Select Air Fry mode. 3. Set temp to 400 degrees F and time to 20 minutes. 4. To begin, press the Start button. 5. Open the lid when the device beeps to indicate that it has warmed. 6. Place the squash pieces in a cooking tray that has been oiled and placed in the air fryer. 7. Serve immediately with pine nuts and cilantro on top.
Per serving: Calories 191; Fat 7g; Sodium 520mg; Carbs 34.3 g; Fiber 7g; Sugar 9g; Protein 3.7g

Feta Tomatoes with Pesto

Prep time: 15 minutes | Cook time: 15 minutes | Serves: 4

3 large heirloom tomatoes are cut into ½-inch thick slices.	½-inch thick slices.
1 cup pesto	½ cup red onions, sliced thinly
8 ounces' feta cheese, cut into	1 tablespoon olive oil

1. Put a dollop of pesto on each tomato slice. Drizzle oil over each tomato slice and top with a feta slice and onion. 2. Select Air Fry mode. 3. Set temp to 400 degrees F and time to 14 minutes. 4. Place the tomatoes in a cooking tray that has been oiled and placed in the air fryer. 5. Serve warm.
Per serving: Calories 480; Fat 41.9g; Sodium 330mg; Carbs 13 g; Fiber 2g; Sugar 2.9g; Protein 15.4g

Curry Cauliflower Florets

Prep time: 5 minutes | Cook time: 20 minutes | Serves: 4

1 small cauliflower head, cut into florets	boiling water and dried
1 tablespoon pine nut, toasted	1 teaspoon curry powder
1 tablespoon raisin soak in	½ teaspoon sea salt
	3 tablespoons olive oil

1. Toss the items together in a mixing basin. 2. Select Air Fry mode. 3. Set temp to 400 degrees F and time to 15 minutes. 4. Cook for 15 minutes in the cooking tray with the cauliflower mixture.
Per serving: Calories 264; Fat 26g; Sodium 441mg; Carbs 8g; Fiber 1g; Sugar 1.9g; Protein 2g

Hot Potatoes

Prep time: 10 minutes | Cook time: 20 minutes | Serves: 2

¾ pound potatoes, peeled and cubed	Salt and black pepper to taste
1 tablespoon olive oil	½ tablespoon hot paprika
	½ cup Greek yogurt

1. Place the potatoes in a dish and cover them with water. Set aside for 10 minutes. Drain and wipe dry before transferring to a new bowl. 2. Toss the potatoes with salt, pepper, paprika, and half of the oil. 3. Select Air Fry mode. 4. Place the potatoes in the cooking tray and cook for 20 minutes at 400 degrees F. 5. Whisk the yogurt, salt, pepper, and the remaining oil in a mixing bowl. 6. Serve potatoes on plates with yogurt dressing drizzled over them.
Per serving: Calories 170; Fat 3g; Sodium 338mg; Carbs 20g; Fiber 4g; Sugar 3.6g; Protein 5g

Cherry Potatoes and Green Beans

Prep time: 10 minutes | Cook time: 15 minutes | Serves: 2

8 ounces' cherry tomatoes	1 tablespoon olive oil
8 ounces of green beans	Salt and black pepper to taste

1. Combine cherry tomatoes, green beans, olive oil, salt, and pepper in a mixing dish. Mix well. 2. Select Air Fry mode. 3. Cook for 15 minutes at 400 degrees F. Shake it once. 4. Serve.
Per serving: Calories 162; Fat 6g; Sodium 441mg; Carbs 8g; Fiber 2g; Sugar 1g; Protein 9g

Potatoes and Brussels Sprout

Prep time: 10 minutes | Cook time: 8 minutes | Serves: 2

¾ pound Brussels sprouts, washed and trimmed	2 teaspoons bread crumbs
½ cup new potatoes, chopped	Salt and black pepper to taste
	2 teaspoons butter

1. Combine Brussels sprouts, potatoes, bread crumbs, salt, pepper, and butter in a mixing bowl. Mix thoroughly. 2. Select Air Fry mode. 3. Cook for 8 minutes at 400 degrees F. 4. Serve.
Per serving: Calories 152; Fat 3g; Sodium 412mg; Carbs 17g; Fiber 1g; Sugar 2g; Protein 4g

Garlic Tomatoes

Prep time: 10 minutes | Cook time: 15 minutes | Serves: 2

2 big tomatoes, halved and
inside scooped out
Salt and black pepper to taste

½ tablespoon olive oil
2 cloves garlic, minced
¼ teaspoon thyme, chopped

1. In the cooking tray, mix tomatoes with thyme, garlic, oil, salt, and pepper, and mix well. 2. Select Air Fry mode. 3. Cook at 400 degrees F for 15 minutes. 4. Serve.
Per serving: Calories 112; Fat 1g; Sodium 220mg; Carbs 4g; Fiber 1g; Sugar 1g; Protein 4g

Leek Halves

Prep time: 10 minutes | Cook time: 7 minutes | Serves: 2

2 leeks, washed, ends cut, and
halved
Salt and black pepper to taste

½ tablespoon butter, melted
½ tablespoon lemon juice

1. Season leeks with salt and pepper after rubbing them with melted butter. 2. Select Air Fry mode. 3. Place it in the air fryer and cook for 7 minutes at 400 degrees F. 4. Place on a serving plate. Serve with a squeeze of lemon juice.
Per serving: Calories 100; Fat 4g; Sodium 442mg; Carbs 6g; Fiber 1g; Sugar 1g; Protein 2g

Sweet Potatoes with Parmesan Cheese

Prep time: 5 minutes | Cook time: 25 minutes | Serves: 4

2 large sweet potatoes, peeled
and sliced
1 teaspoon olive oil
1 tablespoon white balsamic

vinegar
1 teaspoon dried thyme
¼ cup grated Parmesan cheese

1. Toss the sweet potato pieces with olive oil in a large mixing basin. 2. Toss the salad with balsamic vinegar and thyme once more. 3. Toss the potatoes with the Parmesan cheese to coat them. 4. Select Roast mode. Set temp to 380 degrees F and timer to 25 minutes. 5. Roast the sweet potato slices in batches in the cooking tray for 18 to 23 minutes, turning them once during cooking, until soft. 6. Carry on with the remaining sweet potato slices in the same manner. Serve right away.
Per serving: Calories 100; Fat 3g; Sodium 132mg; Carbs 15g; Fiber 1g; Sugar 3g; Protein 4g

Lemon Artichokes

Prep time: 15 minutes | Cook time: 45 minutes | Serves: 2

2 lemons
2 artichokes
1 teaspoon kosher salt

2 garlic head
1 teaspoon olive oil

1. Artichokes' edges should be cut off. 2. Using a knife, cut the lemon in half. 3. Garlic cloves should be coarsely chopped after peeling the garlic head. 4. Then, in the artichokes, add the chopped garlic. 5. Olive oil and kosher salt should be drizzled over the artichokes. 6. The lemon juice should then be squeezed into the artichokes. 7. Wrap the artichokes in foil and set them aside. 8. Select Air fry mode. 9. Set temp to 400 degrees F and timer to 45 minutes. 10. Cook for 45 minutes in the air fryer with the wrapped artichokes. 11. Remove the foil and serve the artichokes. 12. Enjoy.
Per serving: Calories 133; Fat 5; Sodium 449mg; Carbs 21.7; Fiber 9.7; Sugar 4g; Protein 6g

Asparagus in Chicken Stock

Prep time: 10 minutes | Cook time: 6 minutes | Serves: 2

1 teaspoon sesame oil
11 ounces' asparagus
1 teaspoon chicken stock

½ teaspoon ground white pepper
3 ounces Parmesan

1. Asparagus should be washed and chopped coarsely. 2. Combine the chopped asparagus, chicken stock, and freshly ground white pepper in a mixing bowl. 3. Then drizzle the sesame oil over the veggies and shake them. 4. In the cooking tray, place the asparagus. 5. Select Air Fry mode. 6. Set temp to 400 degrees F and timer to 6 minutes. 7. Cook the vegetables for 4 minutes at 400 degrees F. 8. In the meantime, grate the Parmesan cheese. 9. When the time is up, lightly shake the asparagus and top it with shredded cheese. 10. Cook the asparagus for another 2 minutes at 400 degrees F. 11. Transfer the cooked asparagus to the serving dishes after that. 12. Serve and taste it.
Per serving: Calories 189; Fat 11.6; Sodium 552mg; Carbs 7.9; Fiber 3.4; Sugar 1.9mg; Protein 17.2g

Corns on Cobs

Prep time: 10 minutes | Cook time: 10 minutes | Serves: 2

2 fresh corn on cobs
2 teaspoons butter
1 teaspoon salt

1 teaspoon paprika
¼ teaspoon olive oil

1. Rub the corn on cobs with salt and paprika. 2. Then drizzle olive oil over the corn on the cobs. 3. In the cooking tray, place the corn on the cobs. 4. Select Air Fry mode. 5. Set temp to 400 degrees F and timer to 10 minutes. 6. Cook the corn for 10 minutes on the cobs. 7. When the timer goes off, place the corn on the cobs in the serving dishes and gently massage with the butter. 8. Serve the dish right away. 9. Enjoy.
Per serving: Calories 122; Fat 5.5; Sodium 441mg; Carbs 17.6; Fiber 2.4; Sugar 4g; Protein 3.2

Green Beans and Onion

Prep time: 10 minutes | Cook time: 12 minutes | Serves: 2

11 ounces of green beans
1 tablespoon onion powder
1 tablespoon olive oil

½ teaspoon salt
¼ teaspoon chili flakes

1. Carefully wash the green beans and set them in the basin. 2. Onion powder, salt, chili flakes, and olive oil are sprinkled over the green beans. 3. Carefully shake the green beans. 4. Select Air Fry mode. 5. Set temp to 400 degrees F and timer to 12 minutes. 6. Cook the green beans for 8 minutes in the air fryer. 7. After that, give the green beans a good shake and cook for another 4 minutes at 400 degrees F. 8. Shake the green beans when the timer goes off. 9. Serve the side dish and enjoy.
Per serving: Calories 1205; Fat 7.2; Sodium 442mg; Carbs 13.9; Fiber 5.5; Sugar 4g; Protein 3.2g

Mashed Potatoes with Half-and-Half

Prep time: 10 minutes | Cook time: 15 minutes | Serves: 2

2 potatoes
2 tablespoons fresh dill,
chopped

1 teaspoon butter
½ teaspoon salt
¼ cup half-and-half

1. Place the potatoes in the air fryer after properly rinsing them. 2. Select Air Fry mode. 3. Set temp to 400 degrees F and timer to 15 minutes. 4. Cook the potatoes for 15 minutes. 5. Remove the potatoes from the air fryer after that. 6. Peel the potatoes. 7. Use a fork to mash the potatoes thoroughly. 8. Then season with salt and chopped fresh dill. 9. Gently stir in the butter and half-and-half. 10. Blend the ingredients well with the hand blender. 11. When the mashed potatoes are done, serve them right away. Enjoy.
Per serving: Calories 211; Fat 5.7; Sodium 440mg; Carbs 36.5; Fiber 5.5; Sugar 7g; Protein 5.1g

Palatable Potatoes with Italian Seasoning

Prep time: 15 minutes | Cook time: 20 minutes | Serves: 2

3 medium potatoes, scrubbed
½ teaspoon kosher salt
1 tablespoon Italian seasoning
⅓ cup cream
½ teaspoon ground black pepper

1. Cut the potatoes into slices. 2. In the cooking tray, make a layer of sliced potato. 3. Season the potato layer using kosher salt and ground black pepper. 4. Make the second layer of the potato and season it with Italian seasoning after that. 5. Place the cream on top of the last layer of sliced potato. 6. Select Air Fry mode. 7. Set temp to 400 degrees F and timer to 20 minutes. 8. Cook for 20 minutes with the scalloped potato. 9. Allow the scalloped potato to cool to room temperature. Enjoy.
Per serving: Calories 269; Fat 4.7g; Sodium 541mg; Carbs 52.6 g; Fiber 7.8 g; Sugar 2g; Protein 5.8g

Swiss Chard

Prep time: 10 minutes | Cook time: 10 minutes | Serves: 2

3 ounces Cheddar cheese, grated
10 ounces' Swiss chard
3 tablespoons cream
1 tablespoon sesame oil
Salt and pepper to taste

1. Swiss chard should be washed and chopped coarsely. 2. Season the Swiss chard with salt and freshly ground white pepper. 3. Carefully stir it. 4. Sprinkle the sesame oil over the Swiss chard and mix gently with two spatulas. 5. Cook for 6 minutes in the air fryer basket with chopped Swiss chard. 6. Select Air Fry mode. 7. Set temp to 400 degrees F and timer to 10 minutes. 8. After 3 minutes of cooking, give it a good shake. 9. After that, pour the cream into the air fryer basket and stir it around. 10. Cook the food for a further 3 minutes. 11. Cook for a further 2 minutes after adding the shredded cheese. 12. After this, transfer the meal onto the serving plates. Enjoy.
Per serving: Calories 272; Fat 22.3g; Sodium 330mg; Carbs 6.7 g; Fiber 2.5 g; Sugar 2g; Protein 13.3g

Spicy Acorn Squash Wedges

Prep time: 10 minutes | Cook time: 18 minutes | Serves: 2

11 ounces Acorn squash
½ teaspoon salt
1 tablespoon olive oil
½ teaspoon chili pepper
½ teaspoon paprika

1. Cut the acorn squash into serving wedges. 2. Salt, olive oil, chili pepper, and paprika are sprinkled over the slices. 3. Gently massage the wedges. 4. Select Air Fry mode, set the temperature to 400 degrees F, and the timer to 18 minutes. 5. Cook for 18 minutes in the cooking tray with acorn squash wedges. 6. After 9 minutes of cooking, flip the wedges to the other side. 7. Serve the hot prepared food. Enjoy.
Per serving: Calories 125; Fat 7.2g; Sodium 448mg; Carbs 16.7 g; Fiber 2.6 g; Sugar 6g; Protein 1.4g

Honey Carrots

Prep time: 7 minutes | Cook time: 12 minutes | Serves: 2

1 cup baby carrot
½ teaspoon salt
½ teaspoon white pepper
1 tablespoon honey
1 teaspoon sesame oil

1. Toss the tiny carrots with sesame oil, salt, and white pepper. 2. Transfer the young carrot to the air fryer basket after shaking it. 3. Select Air Fry mode. 4. Set temp to 400 degrees F and timer to 12 minutes. 5. Cook for 10 minutes with the veggies. 6. After that, drizzle honey over the veggies and give them a good shake. 7. Cook for 2 minutes before serving. 8. After that, give the veggies a good shake and serve right away. 9. Enjoy.
Per serving: Calories 83; Fat 2.4g; Sodium 338mg; Carbs 16 g; Fiber 2.6 g; Fiber 2g; Protein 0.6g

Cauliflower Fritter with Greek Yogurt

Prep time: 5 minutes | Cook time: 10 minutes | Serves: 4

1 large chopped into florets cauliflower
1 tablespoon of Greek yogurt
1 tablespoon of flour
½ teaspoon of ground turmeric
½ teaspoon of ground cumin
½ teaspoon of ground paprika
½ teaspoon of ground coriander
½ teaspoon of salt
½ teaspoon of black pepper

1. Combine the Greek yogurt, flour, and the remaining spices in a large mixing basin. 2. Toss in the cauliflower florets until they are well coated. 3. Spray half of the cauliflower florets in your cooking tray with nonstick cooking spray. 4. Select Air Fry mode. 5. Set temp to 400 degrees F and timer to 10 minutes. 6. Cook for 10 minutes, or until golden brown and crispy, shaking it every 5 minutes. (Do the same with the other half.) 7. Serve and enjoy!
Per serving: Calories 120; Fat 4g; Sodium 336mg; Carbs 14g; Fiber 3.4g; Sugar 4g; Protein 7.5g

Extra-Firm Tofu

Prep time: 5 minutes | Cook time: 50 minutes | Serves: 4

1 block pressed and sliced into 1-inch cubes of extra-firm tofu
1 tablespoon soy sauce
1 teaspoon seasoned rice vinegar
2 teaspoons toasted sesame oil
1 tablespoon cornstarch

1. Toss the tofu, soy sauce, seasoned rice vinegar, and sesame oil in a bowl until thoroughly combined. 2. Allow it to marinate for 30 minutes in the refrigerator. 3. Toss the tofu mixture with the cornstarch until it is well coated. 4. Spray the interior of your cooking tray with nonstick cooking spray and place the tofu inside. 5. Select Air Fry mode. 6. Set temp to 400 degrees F and temp to 20 minutes. 7. Cook it at 400 degrees F for 20 minutes, shaking it after 10 minutes. 8. Serve and enjoy!
Per serving: Calories 80; Fat 5.8g; Sodium 441mg; Carbs 3g; Fiber 1.2g; Sugar 2g; Protein 5g

Lemony Broccoli

Prep time: 10 minutes | Cook time: 15 minutes | Serves: 4

1 large head of fresh broccoli
1 teaspoon olive oil
1 tablespoon lemon juice

1. Rinse and pat dry the broccoli. Remove the florets and set them aside. Broccoli stems can also be used; cut them into 1″ piece and peel them. 2. Toss the broccoli with olive oil and lemon juice in a large mixing basin until evenly covered. 3. Select the Roast option. Set temp to 380 degrees F and time to 14 minutes. 4. In batches, roast the broccoli for 10 to 14 minutes until crisp, tender, and lightly browned around the edges. Carry on with the rest of the broccoli. Serve right away.
Per serving: Calories 63; Fat 2g; Sodium: 50mg; Carbs: 10g; Fiber 4g; Sugar 2g; Protein 4g

Simple Bell Peppers

Prep time: 5 minutes | Cook time: 20 minutes | Serves: 4

4 bell peppers, any colors, stemmed, seeded, membranes removed, and cut into 4ths
1 teaspoon olive oil
4 garlic cloves, minced
½ teaspoon dried thyme

1. Drizzle the peppers with olive oil and place them on the cooking tray. 2. Select the Roast option. Set temp to 380 degrees F and time to 20 minutes. 3. After 15 minutes of cooking, top the vegetables with garlic and thyme. Roast for another 3 to 5 minutes, or until the vegetables are soft. Serve right away.
Per serving: Calories 36; Fat 1g; Sodium 21mg; Carbs 5g; Fiber 2g; Sugar 1g; Protein 1g

Delicious Zucchini Chips

Prep time: 5 minutes | Cook time: 10 minutes | Serves: 4

2 thinly sliced zucchinis
1 beaten egg
½ cup panko breadcrumbs
½ cup grated Parmesan cheese
Salt and black pepper

1. Prepare your zucchini by thinly slicing it on a mandolin or with a knife. 2. Dry the zucchini chips with a towel. 3. The eggs should then be added to a bowl and well beaten. Then, combine the breadcrumbs, Parmesan cheese, salt, and black pepper in a separate dish. 4. Dredge the zucchini chips in the egg, then top with the Parmesan-breadcrumb mixture. 5. Place the battered zucchini chips in your cooking tray and coat them with nonstick cooking spray. 6. Select Air Fry mode. 7. Cook it for 8 minutes at 400 degrees F. 8. Gently take it from the air fryer and season it with another teaspoon of salt. Serve and have fun!
Per serving: Calories 100; Fat 6g; Sodium 410mg; Carbs 9g; Fiber 1.8g; Sugar 1g; Protein 4g

Husk-less Corns

Prep time: 5 minutes | Cook time: 10 minutes | Serves: 4

4 ears of husk-less corn
1 tablespoon olive oil
1 teaspoon salt
1 teaspoon black pepper

1. Olive oil, salt, and black pepper are sprayed on the ears of corn. 2. Select Air Fry mode. 3. Place it in your air fryer and cook it at 400 degrees F for 10 minutes. 4. Serve and have fun!
Per serving: Calories 100; Fat 1g; Sodium 441mg; Carbs 22g; Fiber 3g; Sugar 4g; Protein 3g

Sweet Carrots

Prep time: 5 minutes | Cook time: 12 minutes | Serves: 1

3 cups chopped into ½-inch pieces of carrots
1 tablespoon olive oil
1 tablespoon honey
1 tablespoon brown sugar
Salt and black pepper

1. Add the carrot chunks, olive oil, honey, brown sugar, salt, and black pepper to a mixing bowl and toss until well combined. 2. Add the seasoned glazed carrots to it and place them in your cooking tray. 3. Select Air Fry mode. 4. Cook it at 400 degrees F for 12 minutes, then shake it after 6 minutes. Serve and have fun!
Per serving: Calories 90; Fat 3.5g; Sodium 447mg; Carbs 13g; Fiber 2g; Sugar 3g; Protein 1g

Chunk Eggplants

Prep time: 5 minutes | Cook time: 20 minutes | Serves: 4

2 thinly sliced or chopped into chunks eggplants
1 teaspoon salt
1 teaspoon black pepper
1 cup rice flour
1 cup white wine

1. In a mixing bowl, combine the rice flour and white wine and whisk until smooth. 2. Stir in the salt and black pepper once more. 3. Remove any extra batter from the eggplant slices or pieces after dredging them. 4. Select Air Fry mode. 5. Set temp to 400 degrees F and timer to 20 minutes. 6. Use a nonstick cooking spray to coat the cooking tray. 7. Place the eggplant slices or chunks in the air fryer and cook for 15 to 20 minutes until golden brown and crispy, shaking the pan regularly. 8. Remove it from the air fryer carefully and set it aside to cool. Serve and have fun!
Per serving: Calories 380; Fat 15g; Sodium 380mg; Carbs 51g; Fiber 6.1g; Sugar 2g; Protein 13g

Cauliflower with Chopped Turkey Fillet

Prep time: 10 minutes | Cook time: 15 minutes | Serves: 6

2 pounds' cauliflower
2 eggs
1 teaspoon salt
½ teaspoon ground paprika
4 ounces' turkey fillet, chopped

1. Cauliflower should be washed, chopped, and left aside. 2. Crack the eggs in a separate dish and whisk them well. 3. Stir in the salt and paprika powder. 4. Select Air Fry mode. 5. Set temp to 400 degrees F and timer to 15 minutes. 6. Cook the chopped turkey for 4 minutes at 400 degrees F in the cooking tray, stirring halfway through. 7. After that, stir in the cauliflower that has been chopped. 8. Cook the turkey/cauliflower combination at 400 degrees F for another 6 minutes, stirring halfway through. 9. Then gently pour the whisked egg mixture and stir it in. 10. Continue to cook the cauliflower hash at 400 degrees F for another 5 minutes. 11. Allow the cauliflower hash to cool before transferring it to serving dishes. Serve and take pleasure in.
Per serving: Calories 143; Fat 9.5g; Sodium 337mg; Carbs 4.5 g; Fiber 2 g; Sugar 4g; Protein 10.4g

Almond Asparagus

Prep time: 10 minutes | Cook time: 5 minutes | Serves: 2

9 ounces' asparagus
1 teaspoon almond flour
1 tablespoon almond flakes
¼ teaspoon salt
1 teaspoon olive oil

1. Combine the almond flour and flakes in a large mixing bowl and whisk thoroughly. 2. Season the asparagus with salt and olive oil. 3. Gently shake it to coat it in the almond flour mixture. 4. Select Air Fry mode. 5. Cook the asparagus in the cooking tray for 5 minutes at 400 degrees F, stirring halfway through. 6. Allow cooling slightly before serving.

Per serving: Calories 143; Fat 11g; Sodium 446mg; Carbs 8.6g; Fiber 4.6 g; Sugar 3g; Protein 6.4g

Yummy Zucchini in Chicken Stock

Prep time: 7 minutes | Cook time: 8 minutes | Serves: 2

A zucchini	1 teaspoon oregano
½ teaspoon ground black pepper	1 tablespoon chicken stock
	½ teaspoon coconut oil

1. Prepare the zucchini by chopping it into pieces. 2. Combine the ground black pepper and oregano in a mixing bowl and whisk well. 3. Sprinkle the spice mixture over the zucchini chunks and toss thoroughly. 4. After that, pour the chicken stock over the veggies. 5. Select Air Fry mode, set the temperature to 400 degrees F, and time to 8 minutes. 6. When the display shows "Add Food," place the food with the coconut oil in the air fryer and cook. Turn the food when the display shows "turn Food." 7. Serve immediately on serving plates.

Per serving: Calories 30; Fat 1.5g; Sodium 545mg; Carbs 4.3g; Fiber 1.6g; Sugar 2g; Protein 1.4g

Onion and Sweet Potatoes

Prep time: 10 minutes | Cook time: 15 minutes | Serves: 4

2 sweet potatoes, peeled	1 teaspoon olive oil
1 red onion, peeled	¼ cup almond milk
1 white onion, peeled	

1. Cut the onions and sweet potatoes into cubes. 2. Drizzle the olive oil over the sweet potatoes. 3. Select Air Fry mode. 4. Cook the sweet potatoes for 5 minutes at 400 degrees F. 5. Stir in the sweet potatoes, followed by the chopped onions. 6. Pour in the almond milk and give it a good swirl. 7. Cook the mixture for another 10 minutes at 400 degrees F. 8. Allow the mixture to cool slightly before serving.

Per serving: Calories 56; Fat 4.8g; Sodium 453mg; Carbs 3.5 g; Fiber 0.9 g; Sugar 1g; Protein 0.6 g

Savory Eggplants

Prep time: 10 minutes | Cook time: 20 minutes | Serves: 2

12 ounces' eggplants	per
½ teaspoon cayenne pepper	½ teaspoon cilantro
½ teaspoon ground black pep-	½ teaspoon ground paprika

1. Cut the eggplants into cubes after rinsing them. 2. Cayenne and ground black pepper should be sprinkled over the eggplant cubes. 3. Toss with cilantro and paprika powder. 4. Allow for a 10-minute rest period after thoroughly stirring the mixture. 5. The eggplants should then be brushed with olive oil and placed on the cooking tray. 6. Select the Roast option. 7. Cook the eggplants at 380 degrees F for 20 minutes, stirring halfway through. 8. Serve the eggplant cubes straight away!

Per serving: Calories 67; Fat 2.8g; Sodium 382mg; Carbs 10.9 g; Fiber 6.5 g; Sugar 2g; Protein 1.9

Air-Fired Garlic Head

Prep time: 5 minutes | Cook time: 10 minutes | Serves: 4

1-pound garlic head	1 teaspoon thyme
1 tablespoon olive oil	

1. Cut the garlic head's ends and set it in the cooking tray. 2. Then drizzle olive oil and thyme over the garlic head. 3. Select Air Fry mode. 4. Cook the garlic head for 10 minutes at 400 degrees F. 5. The garlic head should be tender and fragrant after cooking. 6. Serve right away.

Per serving: Calories 200; Fat 4.1g; Sodium 413mg; Carbs 37.7 g; Fiber 2.5 g; Sugar 2g; Protein 7.2 g

Yummy Asparagus Wraps

Prep time: 10 minutes | Cook time: 5 minutes | Serves: 4

12 ounces' asparagus	3 ounces' turkey fillet, sliced
½ teaspoon ground black pepper	¼ teaspoon chili flakes

1. Season the asparagus with chili flakes and ground black pepper. 2. Carefully mix everything. 3. Place the asparagus in the cooking tray after wrapping it with the sliced turkey fillet. 4. Cook the asparagus for 5 minutes at 400 degrees F, rotating halfway through. 5. Allow 2 minutes for the wrapped asparagus to cool before serving.

Per serving: Calories 133; Fat 9g; Sodium 482mg; Carbs 3.8 g; Fiber 1.9 g; Sugar 1g; Protein 9.8 g

Coconut Yams

Prep time: 10 minutes | Cook time: 8 minutes | Serves: 2

2 yams	1 teaspoon coconut oil
1 tablespoon fresh dill	½ teaspoon minced garlic

1. Wash the yams thoroughly before cutting them in half. 2. After sprinkling the yam halves with coconut oil, massage with the minced garlic. 3. Select Air Fry mode. 4. Cook the yams for 8 minutes at 400 degrees F. 5. After that, lightly mash the yams with a fork and top with the fresh dill. 6. Serve the yams right away.

Per serving: Calories 25; Fat 2.3g; Sodium 421mg; Carbs 1.2 g; Fiber 0.2 g; Sugar 1g; Protein 0.4 g

Honey White Onions

Prep time: 10 minutes | Cook time: 20 minutes | Serves: 2

2 large white onions	1 teaspoon water
1 tablespoon raw honey	1 tablespoon paprika

1. Peel the onions and chop them into a cross shape using a knife. 2. Then, mix the raw honey and water in a separate bowl and whisk well. 3. Stir in the paprika until it is completely smooth. 4. Sprinkle the onions with the honey mixture and place them in the air fryer basket. 5. Select the Roast option. 6. At 380 degrees F, cook the onions for 16 minutes. 7. The onions should be tender. 8. Serve the sautéed onions on individual serving dishes.

Per serving: Calories 102; Fat 0.6g; Sodium 451mg; Carbs 24.6g; Fiber 4.5g; Sugar 1g; Protein 2.2g

Garlic Slices

Prep time: 10 minutes | Cook time: 8 minutes | Serves: 4

1 teaspoon coconut oil
½ teaspoon dried cilantro
¼ teaspoon cayenne pepper

12 ounces' garlic cloves, peeled

1. Cayenne pepper and dried cilantro should be sprinkled over the garlic cloves. 2. Combine the garlic and spices in a mixing bowl, then add to the cooking tray. 3. Select Roast mode. 4. Cook the garlic in the coconut oil for 8 minutes at 380 degrees F, stirring halfway through. 5. Transfer the garlic cloves to serving dishes after they've finished cooking.

Per serving: Calories 137; Fat 1.6g; Sodium 425mg; Carbs 28.2g; Fiber 1.8g; Sugar 2g; Protein 5.4g

Hot Cauliflower Bites

Prep time: 5 minutes | Cook time: 20 minutes | Serves: 4

1 large chopped into florets cauliflower head
1 beaten eggs

⅔ cup cornstarch
2 tablespoons melted butter
¼ cup hot sauce

1. Add the eggs and cornstarch to a large mixing basin and thoroughly whisk them together. 2. Add the cauliflower and gently toss it in the butter until it is completely covered. Shake off any excess batter and put it aside. 3. Spray your cooking tray with nonstick cooking spray and add the cauliflower bits, working in batches if necessary. 4. Select Air Fry mode. 5. Set temp to 400 degrees F and timer to 20 minutes. 6. Cook the cauliflower bits for 15 to 20 minutes, or until golden brown in color and crispy in texture, shaking periodically. 7. Then, thoroughly combine the melted butter and spicy sauce in a small mixing dish. 8. Once the cauliflower bites are done, remove them from your air fryer and place them into a large bowl. Pour the buffalo sauce over the cauliflower bites and toss them until it is adequately covered. 9. Serve and enjoy!

Per serving: Calories 240; Fat 5.5g; Sodium 442mg; Carbs 37g; Fiber 6.3g; Sugar 7g; Protein 8.8g

Cayenne Artichokes

Prep time: 10 minutes | Cook time: 13 minutes | Serves: 4

2 pounds' artichokes
1 tablespoon coconut oil
1 tablespoon water

½ teaspoon minced garlic
¼ teaspoon cayenne pepper

1. Trim the artichokes' ends, drizzle them with water and massage them with chopped garlic. 2. Sprinkle with cayenne pepper and coconut oil. 3. Wrap the artichokes in foil and put them in the cooking tray afterward. 4. Select Air fry mode. 5. Cook at 400 degrees F for 10 minutes. 6. Remove the artichokes from the foil and continue to cook for another 3 minutes at 400 degrees F. 7. Allow cooling slightly before transferring the cooked artichokes to serving dishes. 8. Serve.

Per serving: Calories 83; Fat 3.6g; Sodium 440mg; Carbs 12.1g; Fiber 6.2g; Sugar 2g; Protein 3.7g

Onion and Mushroom Hat

Prep time: 10 minutes | Cook time: 5 minutes | Serves: 2

12 ounces' mushroom hats
¼ cup fresh dill, chopped
¼ teaspoon onion, chopped

olive oil, for cooking
¼ teaspoon turmeric

1. Combine the chopped dill and onion in a mixing bowl. 2. Stir in the turmeric until evenly distributed throughout the mixture. 3. After that, add the olive oil and stir until everything is well combined. 4. Then spoon the dill mixture into the mushroom hats and set them in the cooking tray. 5. Select Air Fry mode. 6. Cook the mushrooms for 5 minutes at 400 degrees F. 7. Allow time for the veggies to cool to room temperature before serving.

Per serving: Calories 73; Fat 3.1g; Sodium 339mg; Carbs 9.2g; Fiber 2.6g; Sugar 2g; Protein 6.6g

Yams with Parsley

Prep time: 10 minutes | Cook time: 10 minutes | Serves: 5

2 pounds' yams
1 teaspoon olive oil
2 tablespoons almond milk

¾ teaspoon salt
1 teaspoon dried parsley

1. Peel and cut the yams. 2. Sprinkle the salt and dry parsley over the diced yams in the cooking tray. 3. Stir in the olive oil until everything is well combined. 4. Select Air Fry mode. 5. Cook the yams for 10 minutes at 400 degrees F, stirring twice throughout the process. 6. When the yams are done, use a hand blender to puree them until smooth. 7. Stir in the almond milk gently. 8. Serve and have fun!

Per serving: Calories 120; Fat 1.8g; Sodium 229mg; Carbs 25.1g; Fiber 3.6g; Sugar 2g; Protein 1.4g

Coconut Cauliflower Rice

Prep time: 10 minutes | Cook time: 12 minutes | Serves: 4

14 ounces' cauliflower heads
1 tablespoon coconut oil

1 tablespoon fresh parsley, chopped

1. Wash the cauliflower heads well before chopping them into rice-sized pieces. 2. Pour the coconut oil over the cauliflower in the air fryer. 3. Select Air Fry mode. 4. Cook for 10 minutes at 400 degrees F, stirring constantly. 5. Then mix in the fresh parsley well. 6. Cook the cauliflower rice for another 2 minutes at 400 degrees F. 7. After that, mix the cauliflower rice lightly and serve it right away.

Per serving: Calories 55; Fat 3.5g; Sodium 443mg; Carbs 5.4g; Fiber 2.5g; Sugar 2g; Protein 2g

Paprika Cabbage

Prep time: 15 minutes | Cook time: 15 minutes | Serves: 4

15 ounces' cabbage
¼ teaspoon salt

¼ cup chicken stock
½ teaspoon paprika

1. Sprinkle the cabbage with salt and paprika before shredding it. 2. Allow the cabbage to sit for 10 minutes after stirring it. 3. Then, add the chicken stock to the cabbage in the cooking tray. 4. Select Air Fry mode. 5. At 400 degrees F, cook the cabbage for 15 minutes, stirring halfway through. 6. It's done when the cabbage is tender. 7. Serve immediately while the food is still warm.

Per serving: Calories 132; Fat 2.1g; Sodium 449mg; Carbs 32.1g; Fiber 3g; Sugar 2g; Protein 1.78g

Garlic Baba Ghanoush

Prep time: 10 minutes | Cook time: 25 minutes | Serves: 8

1 ½ pounds eggplant, diced	¼ cup tahini
4 tablespoons olive oil	Coarse sea salt and ground
1 medium head of garlic	pepper, to taste
1 tablespoon fresh lemon juice	1 teaspoon smoked paprika
1 tablespoon lemon zest	

1. 2 tablespoons olive oil, tossed with the eggplant. Place the garlic head on a square of aluminum foil and fold the foil up and around it. Arrange eggplant and garlic into the cooking tray of the air fryer. 2. Place the drip pan at the bottom of the cooking chamber. Using the display panel, select Air Fry, adjust the temperature to 350 degrees F and the time to 20 minutes, then touch Start. 3. When the display indicates "Add Food," insert one cooking tray in the top position. 4. When the display indicates "turn Food," turn the food. 5. When the time is up, carefully remove them from the cooking tray. 6. Once done, add the remaining 2 tablespoons of olive oil to the bowl of your food processor and pulse until creamy and smooth.

Per serving: Calories 128; Fat 11.2g; Sodium 11mg; Carbs 7.1g; Fiber 3.9g; Sugar 2.7g; Protein 2.2g

Cayenne Green Bean Fries

Prep time: 10 minutes | Cook time: 15 minutes | Serves: 5

2 medium eggs	½ teaspoon cayenne pepper
½ cup flour	Sea salt
1 cup breadcrumbs	Ground black pepper to taste
½ cup Parmesan cheese, grated	1 teaspoon garlic powder
	1-pound fresh green beans

1. In a small dish, whisk the eggs; add the flour and stir to incorporate. 2. Combine the breadcrumbs, cheese, and seasonings in another shallow bowl. Roll the green beans in the breadcrumb/cheese mixture after dipping them in the egg mixture. 3. Arrange green beans on the cooking tray. 4. Place the drip pan at the bottom of the cooking chamber. Using the display panel, select Air Fry, adjust the temperature to 400 degrees F and the time to 10 minutes, then touch Start. 5. When the display indicates "Add Food," insert one cooking tray in the top position. 6. When the display indicates "turn Food," turn the food. 7. When the time is up, carefully remove them from the cooking tray. 8. Once done, serve and enjoy!

Per serving: Calories 196; Fat 3.8g; Sodium 215mg; Carbs 32.3g; Fiber 4.5g; Sugar 2.9g; Protein 9g

Salty Butter Roasted Almonds

Prep time: 10 minutes | Cook time: 20 minutes | Serves: 9

1 ½ cups raw almonds	Himalayan pink salt, to taste
2 teaspoons butter, softened	

1. Mix almond with other ingredients 2. Arrange almonds into the cooking tray. 3. Place the drip pan at the bottom of the cooking chamber. Using the display panel, select Roast, adjust the temperature to 350 degrees F and the time to 15 minutes, then touch Start. 4. When the display indicates "Add Food," insert one cooking tray in the top position. 5. When the time is up, carefully remove them from the cooking tray. 6. Once done, serve and enjoy.

Per serving: Calories 99; Fat 8.8g; Sodium 6mg; Carbs 3.4g; Fiber 2g; Sugar 0.7g; Protein 3.4g

Parmesan Eggplant Chips

Prep time: 10 minutes | Cook time: 20 minutes | Serves: 7

1-pound eggplant, sliced	Sea salt
2 large eggs	Ground black pepper to taste
½ cup Parmesan cheese, grated	1 teaspoon smoked paprika
	½ teaspoon onion powder
1 clove of garlic, minced	½ teaspoon mustard powder

1. Using kitchen towels, pat the eggplant dry. 2. In a small dish, whisk together the eggs and the remaining ingredients. Combine the eggplant slices and the egg mixture in a mixing bowl. Arrange eggplant into the cooking tray of the air fryer. 3. Place the drip pan at the bottom of the cooking chamber. Using the display panel, select Air Fry, adjust the temperature to 370 degrees F and the time to 15 minutes, then touch Start. 4. When the display indicates "Add Food," insert one cooking tray in the top position 5. When the display indicates "turn Food," turn the food. 6. When the time is up, carefully remove them from the cooking tray. 7. Once done, serve and enjoy.

Per serving: Calories 46; Fat 2.1g; Sodium 40mg; Carbs 4.5g; Fiber 2.5g; Sugar 2.5g; Protein 3.2g

Chinese-Style Dumplings

Prep time: 10 minutes | Cook time: 15 minutes | Serves: 5

1-pound cooked ham, chopped	1 medium carrot, diced
2 garlic cloves, minced	3 scallion stalks, chopped
1 teaspoon fresh ginger, peeled and grated	1 (12-ounce) package of wonton wrappers
2 tablespoons soy sauce	1 tablespoon sesame oil

1. Combine the cooked ham, garlic, ginger, soy sauce, carrot, and scallions in a mixing bowl. 2. Fill wonton wrappers halfway with the mixture. 3. Each wonton should be folded in half. Bring the two ends of the wonton together by bringing them up. Brush each wonton with sesame oil after pinching the edges. Arrange wontons into the cooking tray of the air fryer. 4. Place the drip pan at the bottom of the cooking chamber. Using the display panel, select Air Fry, adjust the temperature to 380 degrees F and the time to 10 minutes, then touch Start. 5. When the display indicates "Add Food," insert one cooking tray in the top position. 6. When the display indicates "turn Food," turn the food. 7. When the time is up, carefully remove them from the cooking tray. 8. Once done, serve and enjoy!

Per serving: Calories 387; Fat 11.6g; Sodium 1943mg; Carbs 45.9g; Fiber 3.1g; Sugar 0.9g; Protein 22.5g

Cheese Broccoli Dip

Prep time: 10 minutes | Cook time: 10 minutes | Serves: 8

1-pound broccoli florets
2 teaspoons olive oil
2 scallion stalks, chopped
1 garlic clove, minced
¼ cup cilantro leaves, chopped

1 lime, squeezed
Sea salt
Ground black pepper to taste
¼ cup cream cheese

1. Using olive oil, toss the broccoli florets. 2. Arrange broccoli florets into the cooking tray of the air fryer. 3. Place the drip pan at the bottom of the cooking chamber. Using the display panel, select Air Fry, adjust the temperature to 350 degrees F and the time to 6 minutes, then touch Start. 4. When the display indicates "Add Food," insert one cooking tray in the top position. 5. When the display indicates "turn Food," turn the food. 6. When the time is up, carefully remove them from the cooking tray. 7. Combine the roasted broccoli and the remaining ingredients in a blender until smooth and creamy. 8. Once done, serve and enjoy.

Per serving: Calories 59; Fat 3.9g; Sodium 41mg; Carbs 5.3g; Fiber 5.3g; Sugar 1.8g; Protein 2.3g

Parmesan Baby Carrots

Prep time: 10 minutes | Cook time: 25 minutes | Serves: 4

1 ½ pounds of baby carrots
¼ cup butter
1 teaspoon garlic powder
½ cup parmesan cheese, grated

2 tablespoons tortilla chips, crushed
Kosher salt and cayenne pepper, to taste
1 teaspoon dried parsley flakes

1. In a mixing dish, combine all of the ingredients. 2. Arrange baby carrots on the cooking tray of the air fryer. 3. Place the drip pan at the bottom of the cooking chamber. Using the display panel, select Air Fry, adjust the temperature to 380 degrees F and the time to 20 minutes, then touch Start. 4. When the display indicates "Add Food," insert one cooking tray in the top position. 5. When the display indicates "turn Food," turn the food. 6. When the time is up, carefully remove them from the cooking tray. 7. Once done, serve and enjoy

Per serving: Calories 201; Fat 12.8g; Sodium 253mg; Carbs 20.3g; Fiber 5.8g; Sugar 8.1g; Protein 3.1g

BBQ Little Sausages

Prep time: 10 minutes | Cook time: 15 minutes | Serves: 5

1 pound smoked little sausages
1 cup barbecue sauce
1 red chili pepper, chopped

1. Combine all ingredients in a mixing dish and stir well. Arrange sausages on the cooking tray of the air fryer. 2. Place the drip pan at the bottom of the cooking chamber. Using the display panel, select Air Fry, adjust the temperature to 380 degrees F and the time to 10 minutes, then touch Start. 3. When the display indicates "Add Food," insert one cooking tray in the top position. 4. When the display indicates "turn Food," turn the food. 5. When the time is up, carefully remove them from the cooking tray. 6. Once done, serve and enjoy.

Per serving: Calories 282; Fat 14.1g; Sodium 1252mg; Carbs 19.3g; Fiber 0.3g; Sugar 14.1g; Protein 14.3g

Paprika Sweet Potato Fries

Prep time: 10 minutes | Cook time: 20 minutes | Serves: 5

1-pound sweet potatoes, peeled and cut into sticks
2 tablespoons olive oil
1 teaspoon garlic powder
1 teaspoon smoked paprika

Kosher salt and freshly cracked black pepper, to taste

1. Mix the sweet potatoes with the remaining ingredients. 2. Arrange sweet potato fries into the cooking tray of the air fryer. 3. Place the drip pan at the bottom of the cooking chamber. Using the display panel, select Air Fry, adjust the temperature to 380 degrees F and the time to 15 minutes, then touch Start. 4. When the display indicates "Add Food," insert one cooking tray in the top position. 5. When the display indicates "turn Food," turn the food. 6. When the time is up, carefully remove them from the cooking tray. 7. Once done, serve and enjoy.

Per serving: Calories 158; Fat 5.8g; Sodium 8mg; Carbs 25.3g; Fiber 4g; Sugar 0.6g; Protein 1.5g

Japanese Cheese Korokke

Prep time: 10 minutes | Cook time: 15 minutes | Serves: 5

1-pound mashed potatoes
Kosher salt and ground black pepper, to taste
3 ounces' ham, chopped
1 cup cheese, shredded

1 cup flour
4 eggs, whisked
1 cup breadcrumbs
2 teaspoons olive oil

1. In a large mixing bowl, thoroughly incorporate all ingredients. 2. Form the mixture into equal-sized balls and arrange them in a single layer in the cooking tray of the air fryer. 3. Place the drip pan at the bottom of the cooking chamber. Using the display panel, select Air Fry, adjust the temperature to 350 degrees F and the time to 15 minutes, then touch Start. 4. When the display indicates "Add Food," insert one cooking tray in the top position. 5. When the display indicates "turn Food," turn the food. 6. When the time is up, carefully remove them from the cooking tray. 7. Once done, serve and enjoy.

Per serving: Calories 436; Fat 16.8g; Sodium 773mg; Carbs 50.5g; Fiber 1.9g; Sugar 1.8g; Protein 20.4g

Palatable Chicken Drumettes

Prep time: 10 minutes | Cook time: 15 minutes | Serves: 5

2 pounds of chicken drumettes
1 teaspoon smoked paprika
Kosher salt and ground black pepper, to taste
1 teaspoon cayenne pepper
1 tablespoon ancho chile pepper

1 teaspoon onion powder
1 teaspoon garlic powder
1 tablespoon brown sugar
1 teaspoon mustard powder
2 tablespoons butter
2 ounces' gorgonzola cheese, crumbled

1. Toss the remaining ingredients with the chicken wings. 2. Arrange chicken wings into the cooking tray of the air fryer. 3. Place the drip pan at the bottom of the cooking chamber. Using the display panel, select Air Fry, adjust the temperature to 350 degrees F and the time to 15 minutes, then touch Start. 4. When the display indicates "Add Food," insert one cooking tray in the top position. 5. When the display indicates "turn Food," turn the food. 6. When the time is up, carefully remove them from the cooking tray. 7. Once done, serve and enjoy.

Per serving: Calories 204; Fat 15.3g; Sodium 329mg; Carbs 3.7g; Fiber 0.7g; Sugar 2.1g; Protein 12.9g

Smoky Carrot Dip

Prep time: 10 minutes | Cook time: 25 minutes | Serves: 7

1 ½ pounds carrots, trimmed and sliced	1 teaspoon Dijon mustard
3 teaspoons olive oil	Sea salt
2 cloves garlic, minced	Ground black pepper to taste
1 teaspoon lime zest	¼ cup tahini
1 teaspoon lemon juice	½ teaspoon ground cumin
	½ teaspoon turmeric powder

1. In a mixing bowl, toss the carrots with olive oil. 2. Arrange carrots on the cooking tray of the air fryer. 3. Place the drip pan at the bottom of the cooking chamber. Using the display panel, select Air Fry, adjust the temperature to 350 degrees F and the time to 15 minutes, then touch Start. 4. When the display indicates "Add Food," insert one cooking tray in the top position. 5. When the display indicates "turn Food," turn the food. 6. When the time is up, carefully remove them from the cooking tray 7. Once done, Combine the carrots and the remaining ingredients in a blender until smooth and creamy. 8. Serve and enjoy

Per serving: Calories 111; Fat 6.7g; Sodium 85mg; Carbs 11.9g; Fiber 3.3g; Sugar 4.9g; Protein 2.4g

Cajun Zucchini Chips

Prep time: 10 minutes | Cook time: 20 minutes | Serves: 7

1 large egg, beaten	mix
1 cup breadcrumbs	1-pound zucchini, thinly sliced
½ cup Pecorino cheese, grated	2 teaspoons olive oil
1 tablespoon Cajun seasoning	

1. In a shallow bowl, whisk the egg. Combine the breadcrumbs, cheese, and seasoning mix in a shallow bowl. 2. Dip the zucchini slices into the beaten egg. Then, dredge the zucchini slices into the breadcrumb mixture. Arrange zucchini fries into the cooking tray of the air fryer 3. Place the drip pan at the bottom of the cooking chamber. Using the display panel, select Air Fry, adjust the temperature to 370 degrees F and the time to 10 minutes, then touch Start. 4. When the display indicates "Add Food," insert one cooking tray in the top position. 5. When the display indicates "turn Food," turn the food and brush them with olive oil. 6. When the time is up, carefully remove them from the cooking tray. 7. Once done, serve and enjoy.

Per serving: Calories 153; Fat 6g; Sodium 1490mg; Carbs 16.7g; Fiber 4.2g; Sugar 2.5g; Protein 7.6g

Chili Party Mix

Prep time: 10 minutes | Cook time: 20 minutes | Serves: 9

1 cup miniature pretzels	½ cup butter, melted
2 cups corn Chex	2 teaspoons cayenne pepper
2 cups wheat Chex	Kosher salt, to taste
1 cup peanuts	1 teaspoon garlic powder
1 cup almonds	1 teaspoon chili powder

1. Mix all the ingredients 2. Arrange party min into the cooking tray of air fryer 3. Place the drip pan at the bottom of the cooking chamber. Using the display panel, select Roast, adjust the temperature to 320 degrees F and the time to 15 minutes, then touch Start. 4. When the display indicates "Add Food," insert one cooking tray in the top position. 5. When the time is up, carefully remove them from the cooking tray. 6. Once done, before serving, let the party mix cool fully. Keep your party mix fresh for up to three months in an airtight container. Enjoy!

Per serving: Calories 321; Fat 24g; Sodium 223mg; Carbs 22.9g; Fiber 5.2g; Sugar 3.4g; Protein 8.6g

Herbed Walnuts

Prep time: 10 minutes | Cook time: 20 minutes | Serves: 9

2 cups raw walnuts	2 tablespoons nutritional yeast
2 tablespoons olive oil	Sea salt and cayenne pepper to taste
1 teaspoon dried thyme	
1 teaspoon dried rosemary	

1. Mix all the ingredients 2. Arrange walnuts into the cooking tray of the air fryer. 3. Place the drip pan at the bottom of the cooking chamber. Using the display panel, select Roast, adjust the temperature to 320 degrees F and the time to 15 minutes, then touch Start. 4. When the display indicates "Add Food," insert one cooking tray in the top position 5. When the display indicates "turn Food," turn the food. 6. When the time is up, carefully remove them from the cooking tray. 7. Once done, serve and enjoy.

Per serving: Calories 187; Fat 17.7g; Sodium 2mg; Carbs 3.5g; Fiber 2.3g; Sugar 0.3g; Protein 7g

Turmeric Brussel Sprout Chips

Prep time: 10 minutes | Cook time: 10 minutes | Serves: 2

2 cups Brussel sprouts, trimmed and separated into leaves	Coarse salt and red pepper flakes, to taste
2 teaspoons olive oil	½ teaspoon smoked paprika
	½ teaspoon turmeric powder

1. Mix all the ingredients 2. Arrange potato fries into the cooking tray of the air fryer. 3. Place the drip pan at the bottom of the cooking chamber. Using the display panel, select Air Fry, adjust the temperature to 350 degrees F and the time to 15 minutes, then touch Start. 4. When the display indicates "Add Food," insert one cooking tray in the top position 5. When the display indicates "turn Food," turn the food. 6. When the time is up, carefully remove them from the cooking tray. 7. Once done, serve and enjoy.

Per serving: Calories 81; Fat 5.1g; Sodium 22mg; Carbs 8.7g; Fiber 3.6g; Sugar 2g; Protein 3.1g

Spicy Potato Chips

Prep time: 10 minutes | Cook time: 20 minutes | Serves: 4

1-pound russet potatoes, peeled and sliced	to taste
2 teaspoons olive oil	1 teaspoon ancho chili pepper flakes
Sea salt and cayenne pepper	

1. Toss the potato slices with the remaining ingredients. 2. Arrange potato slices into the cooking tray of the air fryer 3. Place the drip pan at the bottom of the cooking chamber. Using the display panel, select Air Fry, adjust the temperature to 400 degrees F and the time to 15 minutes, then touch Start. 4. When the display indicates "Add Food," insert one cooking tray in the top position. 5. When the display indicates "turn Food," turn the food. 6. When the time is up, carefully remove them from the cooking tray. 7. Once done, serve and enjoy.

Per serving: Calories 99; Fat 2.5g; Sodium 7mg; Carbs 18g; Fiber 2.8g; Sugar 1.4g; Protein 1.9g

Beet Chickpeas Hummus Dip

Prep time: 10 minutes | Cook time: 25 minutes | Serves: 6

2 beets, peeled and diced
1 tablespoon olive oil
1 can chickpeas, drained
¼ cup tahini
2 teaspoons lemon juice
2 cloves garlic, peeled and

sliced
1 teaspoon ground cumin
½ teaspoon ground bay leaf
Kosher salt and ground black
pepper, to taste

1. 1 tablespoon of olive oil, tossing the beets until nicely coated. Arrange potato fries into the cooking tray of the air fryer. 2. Place the drip pan at the bottom of the cooking chamber. Using the display panel, select Air Fry, adjust the temperature to 400 degrees F and the time to 20 minutes, then touch Start. 3. When the display indicates "Add Food," insert one cooking tray in the top position. 4. When the display indicates "turn Food," turn the food. 5. When the time is up, carefully remove them from the cooking tray. 6. Once done, combine the roasted beets and the remaining ingredients in a blender. Enjoy!

Per serving: Calories 328; Fat 14.8g; Sodium 69mg; Carbs 39.3g; Fiber 11.2g; Sugar 9.5g; Protein 13.3g

Easy Parsnip Fries

Prep time: 10 minutes | Cook time: 20 minutes | Serves: 4

1-pound parsnip, cut into
matchsticks
2 teaspoons extra-virgin olive
oil

½ teaspoon garlic powder
½ teaspoon smoked paprika
Kosher salt and ground black
pepper, to taste

1. Toss the parsnip with the remaining ingredients. 2. Arrange parsnip into the cooking tray of the air fryer. 3. Place the drip pan at the bottom of the cooking chamber. Using the display panel, select Air Fry, adjust the temperature to 390 degrees F and the time to 15 minutes, then touch Start. 4. When the display indicates "Add Food," insert one cooking tray in the top position. 5. When the display indicates "turn Food," turn the food. 6. When the time is up, carefully remove them from the cooking tray. 7. Once done, serve and enjoy.

Per serving: Calories 107; Fat 2.7g; Sodium 12mg; Carbs 20.8g; Fiber 5.7g; Sugar 5.6g; Protein 1.5g

Mustard Chicken Winglets

Prep time: 10 minutes | Cook time: 15 minutes | Serves: 5

1 ½ pounds chicken winglets
2 tablespoons olive oil
4 cloves garlic, pressed
1 teaspoon mustard powder

1 teaspoon chili powder
Kosher salt and ground black
pepper to season

1. Arrange chicken winglets into the cooking tray of the air fryer. 2. Place the drip pan at the bottom of the cooking chamber. Using the display panel, select Air Fry, adjust the temperature to 375 degrees F and the time to 15 minutes, then touch Start. 3. When the display indicates "Add Food," insert one cooking tray in the top position. 4. When the display indicates "turn Food," turn the food. 5. When the time is up, carefully remove them from the cooking tray. 6. Once done, serve and enjoy.

Per serving: Calories 260; Fat 18.1g; Sodium 81mg; Carbs 1.3g; Fiber 0.3g; Sugar 0.1g; Protein 24.9g

Greek Pita Chips

Prep time: 10 minutes | Cook time: 10 minutes | Serves: 4

2 large pitas, cut into triangles
1 tablespoon extra-virgin olive
oil

1 teaspoon Greek seasoning
blend
Coarse sea salt, to taste

1. Toss the remaining ingredients with the pita triangles. 2. Arrange pita triangles into the cooking tray of the air fryer 3. Place the drip pan at the bottom of the cooking chamber. Using the display panel, select Air Fry, adjust the temperature to 350 degrees F and the time to 15 minutes, then touch Start. 4. When the display indicates "Add Food," insert one cooking tray in the top position. 5. When the display indicates "turn Food," turn the food. 6. When the time is up, carefully remove them from the cooking tray. 7. Once done, serve and enjoy

Per serving: Calories 113; Fat 3.9g; Sodium 226mg; Carbs 16.7g; Fiber 0.7g; Sugar 0.4g; Protein 2.7g

Cheese Broccoli

Prep time: 10 minutes | Cook time: 15 minutes | Serves: 7

1-pound broccoli florets
2 teaspoons olive oil
crumbled feta cheese, as needed
¼ cup cream of onion soup
1 teaspoon cayenne pepper

1 teaspoon garlic powder
Kosher salt
Freshly ground black pepper,
to taste
½ cup Parmesan cheese, grated

1. Using olive oil, toss the broccoli florets. Arrange potato fries into the cooking tray of the air fryer. 2. Place the drip pan at the bottom of the cooking chamber. Using the display panel, select Air Fry, adjust the temperature to 400 degrees F and the time to 6 minutes, then touch Start. 3. When the display indicates "Add Food," insert one cooking tray in the top position. 4. When the display indicates "turn Food," turn the food. 5. When the time is up, carefully remove them from the cooking tray. 6. Once done, combine the roasted broccoli, feta cheese, onion soup, and spices in a blender until smooth and creamy. Pour the sauce into a lightly buttered casserole dish. 7. Select the "Broil" setting and top the sauce with parmesan cheese. Broil the sauce until the cheese has completely melted. 8. serve and enjoy.

Per serving: Calories 56; Fat 3.1g; Sodium 144mg; Carbs 5.3g; Fiber 1.9g; Sugar 1.5g; Protein 3.2g

Egg Cauliflower Tots

Prep time: 10 minutes | Cook time: 15 minutes | Serves: 5

1-pound cauliflower, grated
1 cup Mexican cheese blend,
shredded
½ cup all-purpose flour
1 teaspoon baking powder
1 tablespoon butter, at room
temperature

2 eggs, whisked
2 scallion stalks, chopped
1 cup tortilla chips, crushed
½ teaspoon cayenne pepper
Kosher salt and ground black
pepper, to taste

1. Combine all of the ingredients thoroughly. 2. Make equal-sized balls out of the mixture. Arrange balls into the cooking tray of the air fryer. 3. Place the drip pan at the bottom of the cooking chamber. Using the display panel, select Air Fry, adjust the temperature to 350 degrees F and the time to 10 minutes, then touch Start. 4. When the display indicates "Add Food," insert one cooking tray in the top position. 5. When the display indicates "turn Food," turn the food. 6. When the time is up, carefully remove them from the cooking tray. 7. Once done, serve and enjoy.

Onion Fried Dill Pickles

Prep time: 10 minutes | Cook time: 15 minutes | Serves: 5

1 large egg, beaten	Sea salt and freshly cracked
½ cup all-purpose flour	black pepper to season
½ teaspoon onion powder	2 large dill pickles, sliced into
1 teaspoon garlic powder	rounds

1. In a small dish, whisk the eggs; add the flour and spices; stir to incorporate. Using your pickles, dredge them in the egg mixture. 2. Arrange Dill Pickles into the cooking tray of the air fryer. 3. Place the drip pan at the bottom of the cooking chamber. Using the display panel, select Air Fry, adjust the temperature to 350 degrees F and the time to 15 minutes, then touch Start. 4. When the display indicates "Add Food," insert one cooking tray in the top position. 5. When the display indicates "turn Food," turn the food. 6. When the time is up, carefully remove them from the cooking tray. 7. Once done, serve and enjoy.

Per serving: Calories 68; Fat 1.2g; Sodium 667mg; Carbs 11.3g; Fiber 1.1g; Sugar 0.9g; Protein 2.8g

Crunchy Nut Pretzel Mix

Prep time: 10 minutes | Cook time: 15 minutes | Serves: 10

2 cups pretzel sticks	perature
2 cups oat cereal	1 tablespoon brown sugar
1 cup almonds	1 teaspoon garlic powder
1 cup walnuts	1 teaspoon smoked paprika
1 cup pine nuts	Coarse sea salt, to taste
½ cup butter, at room tem-	

1. Mix all the ingredients. 2. Arrange party mix into the cooking tray of the air fryer. 3. Place the drip pan at the bottom of the cooking chamber. Using the display panel, select Air Fry, adjust the temperature to 350 degrees F and the time to 15 minutes, then touch Start. 4. When the display indicates "Add Food," insert one cooking tray in the top position. 5. When the display indicates "turn Food," turn the food. 6. When the time is up, carefully remove them from the cooking tray. 7. Once done, serve and enjoy.

Per serving: Calories 377; Fat 31.1g; Sodium 301mg; Carbs 20.4g; Fiber 3.6g; Sugar 2.5g; Protein 8.9g

Pepper Beetroot Chips

Prep time: 10 minutes | Cook time: 10 minutes | Serves: 2

2 medium-size red beets,	1 teaspoon cayenne pepper
peeled and sliced	Kosher salt
2 teaspoons olive oil	Freshly ground black pepper,
½ teaspoon mustard powder	to taste

1. Mix all the ingredients in the bowl. 2. Arrange beet chips into the cooking tray of the air fryer. 3. Place the drip pan at the bottom of the cooking chamber. Using the display panel, select Air Fry, adjust the temperature to 350 degrees F and the time to 15 minutes, then touch Start. 4. When the display indicates "Add Food," insert one cooking tray in the top position. 5. When the display indicates "turn Food," turn the food. 6. When the time is up, carefully remove them from the cooking tray. 7. Once done, serve and enjoy.

Per serving: Calories 87; Fat 5.2g; Sodium 66mg; Carbs 9.3g; Fiber 2.1g; Sugar 6.9g; Protein 1.8g

Bell Pepper Bean Dip

Prep time: 10 minutes | Cook time: 20 minutes | Serves: 9

4 bell peppers	
2 teaspoons olive oil	cheese, grated
1 cup canned or boiled red	1 tablespoon freshly squeezed
beans	lemon juice
2 tablespoons fresh basil	2garlic cloves, peeled and
leaves	chopped
2 tablespoons fresh parsley	Kosher salt and ground black
leaves	pepper, to taste
1 tablespoon fresh mint leaves	¼ cup tahini
4 tablespoons Pecorino	

1. Using olive oil, toss the bell peppers. Arrange bell peppers into a cooking tray of the air fryer. 2. Place the drip pan at the bottom of the cooking chamber. Using the display panel, select Roast and adjust the temperature to 350 degrees F and the time to 15 minutes, then touch Start. 3. When the display indicates "Add Food," insert one cooking tray in the top position. 4. When the display indicates "turn Food," turn the food. 5. When the time is up, carefully remove them from the cooking tray. 6. Once done, in a food processor bowl, combine the roasted peppers and the remaining ingredients. Blend the mixture until it is creamy and smooth.

Per serving: Calories 266; Fat 10.6g; Sodium 135mg; Carbs 33g; Fiber 8.2g; Sugar 5.7g; Protein 13.1g

Peanut Chicken Egg Rolls

Prep time: 0 minutes | Cook time: 10 minutes | Serves: 4

4 egg roll wrappers	½ cup peanut butter
2 cup rotisserie chicken,	2 tablespoon sesame oil
shredded	¼ cup fresh lime juice
¼ cup Thai peanut sauce	2 tablespoons soy sauce
1 medium carrot, thinly sliced	1½ teaspoon crushed red pep-
3 green onions, chopped	per flakes
¼ red bell pepper, julienned	1 tablespoon rice wine vinegar
Non-stick cooking; Spray	1 tablespoon honey
For the sauce:	¼ teaspoon ground ginger
¾ cup light coconut milk	

1. In a blender, combine the sauce ingredients and puree for 1 minute, or until smooth. 2. In a small bowl, toss the chicken with the prepared sauce. 3. On a clean surface, spread out the egg roll wrappers. Place ¼ bell peppers, onions, and carrots in the bottom third of each roll wrapper. 12 cups of the chicken mixture should be spooned over the vegetables. 4. Then, using water, moisten the wrapper's outside edges. Roll tightly by folding the wrapping sides toward the center. 5. Spray both sides of the prepared egg roll with cooking spray. Arrange rolls into the cooking tray of the air fryer. 6. Place the drip pan at the bottom of the cooking chamber. Using the display panel, select Air Fry, adjust the temperature to 390 degrees F and the time to 10 minutes, then touch Start. 7. When the display indicates "Add Food," insert one cooking tray in the top position. 8. When the display indicates "turn Food," turn the food. 9. When the time is up, carefully remove them from the cooking tray. 10. Once done, serve and enjoy.

Per serving: Calories 556; Fat 40.4g; Sodium 853mg; Carbs 39.8g; Fiber 5.5g; Sugar 11.3g; Protein 14.9g

Salty Russet Potato Chips

Prep time: 10 minutes | Cook time: 20 minutes | Serves: 4

1-pound russet potatoes, sliced
2 teaspoons olive oil
Coarse sea salt, to taste

1 tablespoon dried rosemary, chopped

1. Mix the potato slices with the remaining ingredients. 2. Arrange potato chips into a cooking tray of the air fryer. 3. Place the drip pan at the bottom of the cooking chamber. Using the display panel, select Air Fry, then adjust the temperature to 350 degrees F and the time to 15 minutes; touch Start to begin preheating. 4. When the display indicates "Add Food," insert one cooking tray in the top position. 5. When the display indicates "turn Food," turn the food. 6. When the time is up, carefully remove them from the cooking tray. 7. Once done, serve and enjoy.

Per serving: Calories 101; Fat 2.6g; Sodium 67mg; Carbs 18.3g; Fiber 3.1g; Sugar 1.3g; Protein 2g

Jelly Sausage Meatballs

Prep time: 10 minutes | Cook time: 20 minutes | Serves: 5

1-pound beef sausage, crumbled
2 tablespoons fresh herbs,

chopped
2 ounces' grape jelly

1. Combine the sausage and herbs in a mixing dish and stir well. Then, using a tiny scoop, place mounds of the mixture in a single layer onto the prepared pan. 2. Arrange meatballs into the cooking tray of the air fryer. 3. Place the drip pan at the bottom of the cooking chamber. Using the display panel, select Air Fry, adjust the temperature to 350 degrees F and the time to 15 minutes, then touch Start. 4. When the display indicates "Add Food," insert one cooking tray in the top position. 5. When the display indicates "turn Food," turn the food. 6. When the time is up, carefully remove them from the cooking tray. 7. Once done, top them with grape jelly. Select Broil, adjust the time to 05 minutes using the display panel, then touch Start. 8. Once done, serve and enjoy.

Per serving: Calories 376; Fat 32.9g; Sodium 732mg; Carbs 6.3g; Fiber 0.3g; Sugar 2.8g; Protein 12.6g

Coconut Onion Rings

Prep time: 15 minutes | Cook time: 8 minutes | Serves: 4

1 large onion, cut into ½-inch thick rings
3 tablespoons coconut flour
Salt, as required
2 large eggs

⅔ cup pork rinds
3 tablespoons blanched almond flour
½ teaspoon paprika
½ teaspoon garlic powder

1. Combine the coconut flour and salt on a shallow plate. 2. Add the eggs to a second shallow dish and lightly beat them. 3. Combine the pork rinds, almond flour, and spices in a third shallow dish. 4. Coat the onion rings in the flour mixture, then dip them in the egg whites before coating them in the pork rind mixture. Arrange onion rings into both cooking trays of the air fryer. 5. Place the drip pan at the bottom of the cooking chamber. Using the display panel, select Air Fry, adjust the temperature to 400 degrees F and the time to 15 minutes, then touch Start. 6. When the display indicates "Add Food," insert one cooking tray in the top position and another in the bottom position. 7. When the display indicates "turn Food," do not turn the food but switch the position of the cooking trays. When the time is up, carefully remove them from the cooking

tray. 8. Once done, serve and enjoy.

Per serving: Calories 180; Fat 10.2g; Sodium 323mg; Carbs 9g; Fiber 3.7g; Sugar 1.9g; Protein 13.9g

Butter Sandwich with Cheese Slices

Prep time: 10 minutes | Cook time: 10 minutes | Serves: 2

3 tablespoons butter, softened
4 white bread slices

2 cheddar cheese slices

1. Spread a liberal amount of butter on each slice of bread. 2. Place 2 bread pieces, buttered side down, on a baking sheet. 3. 1 piece of cheese should be placed on top of each buttered bread slice. 4. Cover with buttered side up the remaining bread slices. 5. Arrange the sandwich into the cooking tray of the air fryer. 6. Place the drip pan at the bottom of the cooking chamber. Using the display panel, select Air Fry, adjust the temperature to 375 degrees F and the time to 10 minutes, then touch Start to begin preheating. 7. When the display indicates "Add Food," insert one cooking tray in the top position. 8. When the display indicates "turn Food," turn the food. 9. When the time is up, carefully remove them from the cooking tray. 10. Once done, serve and enjoy

Per serving: Calories 307; Fat 27.1g; Sodium 425mg; Carbs 9.4g; Fiber 0.4g; Sugar 0.8g; Protein 8.2g

Corn Dogs

Prep time: 14 minutes | Cook time: 15 minutes | Serves: 4

2 uncured all-beef hot dogs, sliced in half lengthwise
bamboo skewers
½ cup all-purpose flour
2 large eggs, lightly beaten

1½ cups very finely crushed cornflakes cereal
Cooking Spray
Yellow mustard and ketchup, to taste

1. Cut each half of a hot dog into two equal pieces. 1 end of each hot dog component should be skewered with a craft stick or bamboo skewer. 2. In a small bowl, beat the eggs. To a second one, add the flour. To a third one, add cornflakes. 3. Using flour, dredge each hot dog and shake off the excess. Dip in beaten egg and let excess fall off. Coat with cornflakes crumbs equally. 4. Arrange corn dogs into the cooking tray of the air fryer. 5. Place the drip pan at the bottom of the cooking chamber. Using the display panel, select Air Fry, adjust the temperature to 375 degrees F and the time to 10 minutes, then touch Start. 6. When the display indicates "Add Food," insert one cooking tray in the top position. 7. When the display indicates "turn Food," turn the food. 8. When the time is up, carefully remove them from the cooking tray. 9. Once done, serve and enjoy.

Per serving: Calories 153; Fat 7.3g; Sodium 320mg; Carbs 11.8g; Fiber 0.4g; Sugar 0.5g; Protein 8.1g

Parmesan Potato Slices

Prep time: 10 minutes | Cook time: 30 minutes | Serves: 2

2 large red potatoes
2 teaspoons salt
4 garlic cloves, minced

2 tablespoons parmesan, more for serving

1. Using a mandolin, thinly slice the potatoes. 2. In a basin, combine the water and salt. Soak for 30 minutes with the cut potatoes. Drain and rinse thoroughly. Allow to air dry. 3. In a clean bowl, toss the potatoes with the garlic and parmesan. Arrange potato slices into a cooking tray of the air fryer. 4. Place the drip pan at the bottom of the cooking chamber.

Using the display panel, select Air Fry, adjust the temperature to 350 degrees F and the time to 25 minutes, then touch Start. 5. When the display indicates "Add Food," insert one cooking tray in the top position. 6. When the display indicates "turn Food," turn the food. 7. When the time is up, carefully remove them from the cooking tray. 8. Once done, serve and enjoy.

Per serving: Calories 375; Fat 6.6g; Sodium 2684mg; Carbs 61.8g; Fiber 6.4g; Sugar 3.8g; Protein 16.9g

Garlic Edamame

Prep time: 5 minutes | Cook time: 10 minutes | Serves: 2

2 cups fresh edamame	Garlic salt, to taste
Olive oil spray	

1. Arrange edamame into the cooking tray of the air fryer Spray with olive oil evenly, and season with garlic and salt. 2. Place the drip pan at the bottom of the cooking chamber. Using the display panel, select Air Fry, adjust the temperature to 350 degrees F and the time to 1 minute, then touch Start. 3. When the display indicates "Add Food," insert one cooking tray in the top position. 4. When the display indicates "turn Food," turn the food. 5. When the time is up, carefully remove them from the cooking tray. 6. Once done, serve and enjoy.

Per serving: Calories 379; Fat 17.1g; Sodium 38mg; Carbs 28g; Fiber 10.7g; Sugar 0g; Protein 33.2g

Tasty Kale Chips

Prep time: 7 minutes | Cook time: 15 minutes | Serves: 2

1 batch curly kale, washed and patted dry, stems removed	¼ teaspoon sea salt
2 teaspoons olive oil	⅛ teaspoon ground black pepper
1 tablespoon nutritional yeast	

1. In a medium mixing basin, combine the kale leaves. Combine the olive oil, yeast, salt, and pepper in a mixing bowl. Gently mix with your hands until everything is uniformly coated. Arrange kale chips into a cooking tray of the air fryer. 2. Place the drip pan at the bottom of the cooking chamber. Using the display panel, select Air Fry, adjust the temperature to 390 degrees F and the time to 10 minutes, then touch Start. 3. When the display indicates "Add Food," insert one cooking tray in the top position. 4. When the display indicates "turn Food," turn the food. 5. When the time is up, carefully remove them from the cooking tray. 6. Once done, serve and enjoy.

Per serving: Calories 82; Fat 5.4g; Sodium 256mg; Carbs 6.7g; Fiber 3.1g; Sugar 1.1g; Protein 4.4g

Oregano Olives

Prep time: 10 minutes | Cook time: 5 minutes | Serves: 4

2 cups olives	½ teaspoon dried oregano
2 teaspoon garlic, minced	Salt and Pepper
2 tablespoons olive oil	

1. Add olives and remaining ingredients into the bowl and stir well. 2. Arrange olives into the cooking tray of the air fryer. 3. Place the drip pan at the bottom of the cooking chamber. Using the display panel, select Air Fry, adjust the temperature to 300 degrees F and the time to 5 minutes, then touch Start. 4. When the display indicates "Add Food," insert one cooking tray in the top position. 5. When the display indicates "turn Food," turn the food. 6. When the time is up, carefully remove them from the cooking tray. 7. Once done, serve and enjoy.

Per serving: Calories 280; Fat 28.4g; Sodium 1153mg; Carbs 9.6g; Fiber 4.5g; Sugar 0.1g; Protein 1.4g

Pepper-Nut Mix

Prep time: 10 minutes | Cook time: 5 minutes | Serves: 2

2 cups mixed nuts	1 teaspoon ground cumin
1 tablespoon olive oil	1 teaspoon pepper
¼ teaspoon cayenne	1 teaspoon salt

1. In a bowl, add all ingredients and stir well. 2. Arrange mixed nuts into the cooking tray of the air fryer. 3. Place the drip pan at the bottom of the cooking chamber. Using the display panel, select Roast, adjust the temperature to 350 degrees F and the time to 5 minutes, then touch Start. 4. When the display indicates "Add Food," insert one cooking tray in the top position. 5. When the time is up, carefully remove them from the cooking tray. 6. Once done, serve and enjoy.

Per serving: Calories 953; Fat 88.2g; Sodium 1606mg; Carbs 33.3g; Fiber 8.5g; Sugar 6.4g; Protein 22.7g

Smoked Paprika Chickpeas

Prep time: 10 minutes | Cook time: 12 minutes | Serves: 4

2 ounces can of chickpeas, rinsed, drained, and pat dry	½ teaspoon chili powder
½ teaspoon smoked paprika	1 tablespoon olive oil
¼ teaspoon cayenne	Salt and Pepper

1. Toss the chickpeas with chili powder, cayenne, pepper, paprika, oil, and salt in a large mixing basin. Arrange chickpeas into the cooking tray of the air fryer. 2. Place the drip pan at the bottom of the cooking chamber. Using the display panel, select Roast, adjust the temperature to 350 degrees F and the time to 12 minutes, then touch Start. 3. When the display indicates "Add Food," insert one cooking tray in the top position. 4. When the display indicates "turn Food," turn the food. 5. When the time is up, carefully remove them from the cooking tray. 6. Once done, serve and enjoy.

Per serving: Calories 49; Fat 3.8g; Sodium 46mg; Carbs 3.6g; Fiber 0.9g; Sugar 0.1g; Protein 0.9g

Homemade Apple Chips

Prep time: 10 minutes | Cook time: 15 minutes | Serves: 2

One apple, cored and thinly sliced	½ teaspoon cinnamon powder
	1 tablespoon stevia

1. Toss apple slices with stevia and cinnamon in the cooking tray of your air fryer. 2. Place the drip pan at the bottom of the cooking chamber. Using the display panel, select Air Fry, adjust the temperature to 390 degrees F and the time to 10 minutes, then touch Start. 3. When the display indicates "Add Food," insert one cooking tray in the top position. 4. When the display indicates "turn Food," turn the food. 5. When the time is up, carefully remove them from the cooking tray. 6. Once done, serve and enjoy.

Per serving: Calories 40; Fat 0g; Sodium 0mg; Carbs 10.9g; Fiber 2.5g; Sugar 8.4g; Protein 0g

Easy-to-Prepared Walnuts

Prep time: 10 minutes | Cook time: 05 minutes | Serves: 6

2 cups walnuts
1 teaspoon olive oil

Salt and Pepper

1. Toss the walnuts, oil, pepper, and salt in a mixing bowl. Arrange walnuts into the cooking tray of the air fryer. 2. Place the drip pan at the bottom of the cooking chamber. Using the display panel, select Roast, adjust the temperature to 350 degrees F and the time to 05 minutes, then touch Start. 3. When the display indicates "Add Food," insert one cooking tray in the top position. 4. When the time is up, carefully remove them from the cooking tray. 5. Once done, serve and enjoy.

Per serving: Calories 264; Fat 25.4g; Sodium 1mg; Carbs 4.1g; Fiber 2.8g; Sugar 0.5g; Protein 10g

Savory Avocado Chips

Prep time: 10 minutes | Cook time: 15 minutes | Serves: 3

1 avocado, pitted, peeled, and sliced
Salt and pepper

½ cup vegan bread crumbs
A drizzle of olive oil

1. Combine bread crumbs, salt, and pepper in a mixing basin. 2. Brush avocado slices with oil and bread crumbs before serving. Arrange avocado slices into the cooking tray of the air fryer. 3. Place the drip pan at the bottom of the cooking chamber. Using the display panel, select Roast, adjust the temperature to 350 degrees F and the time to 15 minutes, then touch Start. 4. When the display indicates "Add Food," insert one cooking tray in the top position. 5. When the time is up, carefully remove them from the cooking tray. 6. Once done, serve and enjoy.

Per serving: Calories 248; Fat 18.7g; Sodium 136mg; Carbs 18.8g; Fiber 5.3g; Sugar 1.5g; Protein 3.9g

Simple-Fried Potato Fries

Prep time: 15 minutes | Cook time: 16 minutes | Serves: 2

½ pound potatoes, peeled and cut into ½-inch thick sticks lengthwise

1 tablespoon olive oil
Salt and ground black pepper, as required

1. Toss all ingredients in a large mixing bowl until well combined. 2. Arrange the potato sticks onto a cooking tray of the air fryer. 3. Place the drip pan at the bottom of the cooking chamber. Using the display panel, select Air Fry, adjust the temperature to 400 degrees F and the time to 16 minutes, then touch Start. 4. When the display indicates "Add Food," insert one cooking tray in the top position. 5. When the display indicates "turn Food," turn the food. 6. When the time is up, carefully remove them from the cooking tray. 7. Once done, serve and enjoy.

Per serving: Calories 138; Fat 7.1g; Sodium 84mg; Carbs 17.8g; Fiber 2.7g; Sugar 1.3g; Protein 1.9g

Ranch Chickpeas

Prep time: 10 minutes | Cook time: 17 minutes | Serves: 6

1 (15-ounce) can of chickpeas, rinsed, drained, and pat dry
1 teaspoon olive oil

1 tablespoon dry ranch seasoning mix

1. Place the chickpeas on a baking sheet and spread them out evenly. 2. Place the drip pan at the bottom of the cooking

chamber. Using the display panel, select Roast and adjust the temperature to 390 degrees F and the time to 17 minutes, then touch Start to begin preheating. 3. When the display indicates "Add Food," insert one cooking tray in the top position. 4. When the display indicates "turn Food," turn the food. 5. When the time is up, carefully remove them from the cooking tray. 6. Once done, toss in the ranch seasoning and toss well to coat. Serve cold.

Per serving: Calories 268; Fat 5.1g; Sodium 197mg; Carbs 43g; Fiber 12.7g; Sugar 7.3g; Protein 13.9g

Turmeric Banana Chips

Prep time: 10 minutes | Cook time: 10 minutes | Serves: 2

3 large raw bananas, peeled
1 teaspoon turmeric powder for soaking
3 tablespoons coconut oil

2 teaspoons salt
2 teaspoons turmeric powder
1 medium bowl of water

1. In a dish of water, combine turmeric and salt. Soak the peeled bananas for 5-10 minutes in the water. Dry the bananas and slice them thinly on a mandolin. 2. In a bowl, combine the coconut oil and 2 teaspoons of turmeric. Toss in the sliced bananas and toss well to coat. 3. Arrange banana slices into the cooking tray of the air fryer. 4. Place the drip pan at the bottom of the cooking chamber. Using the display panel, select Air Fry, adjust the temperature to 350 degrees F and the time to 15 minutes, then touch Start. 5. When the display indicates "Add Food," insert one cooking tray in the top position. 6. When the display indicates "turn Food," turn the food. 7. When the time is up, carefully remove them from the cooking tray. 8. Once done, serve and enjoy.

Per serving: Calories 361; Fat 211g; Sodium 2384mg; Carbs 47.8g; Fiber 5.7g; Sugar 25g; Protein 2.3g

Celery Chicken Wings

Prep time: 05 minutes | Cook time: 10 minutes | Serves: 8

½ teaspoon celery salt
½ teaspoon bay leaf powder
¼ teaspoon allspice
2 pounds of chicken wings
½ teaspoon ground black pep-

per
½ teaspoon paprika
¼ teaspoon dry mustard
¼ teaspoon cayenne pepper

1. Mix celery salt, bay leaf powder, paprika, dry mustard, black pepper, cayenne pepper, and allspice in a mixing bowl. Coat the wings in this mixture thoroughly. Arrange wings into the cooking tray of the air fryer. 2. Place the drip pan at the bottom of the cooking chamber. Using the display panel, select Air Fry, adjust the temperature to 390 degrees F and the time to 10 minutes, then touch Start. 3. When the display indicates "Add Food," insert one cooking tray in the top position. 4. When the display indicates "turn Food," turn the food. 5. When the time is up, carefully remove them from the cooking tray. 6. Once done, serve and enjoy.

Per serving: Calories 217; Fat 8.4g; Sodium 98mg; Carbs 0.3g; Fiber 0.1g; Sugar 0g; Protein 32.9g

Thin Banana Chips

Prep time: 10 minutes | Cook time: 10 minutes | Serves: 4

4 bananas, peeled and sliced into thin pieces

A drizzle of olive oil
Pepper

1. In your mixing bowl, place banana slices, sprinkle with oil, season with pepper, and toss to coat. Arrange banana chips

into the cooking tray of the air fryer. 2. Place the drip pan at the bottom of the cooking chamber. Using the display panel, select Air Fry, adjust the temperature to 350 degrees F and the time to 10 minutes, then touch Start. 3. When the display indicates "Add Food," insert one cooking tray in the top position. 4. When the display indicates "turn Food," turn the food. 5. When the time is up, carefully remove them from the cooking tray. 6. Once done, serve and enjoy.

Per serving: Calories 135; Fat 3.9g; Sodium 1mg; Carbs 27g; Fiber 3.1g; Sugar 14.3g; Protein 1.9g

Roasted Raw Almonds

Prep time: 10 minutes | Cook time: 25 minutes | Serves: 6

½ cup raw almonds	½ teaspoon cumin
½ teaspoon cayenne	½ teaspoon chili powder
¼ teaspoon onion powder	½ teaspoon sea salt
¼ teaspoon dried basil	melted butter, as needed
½ teaspoon garlic powder	

1. Add almonds and remaining ingredients into the mixing bowl and stir well. 2. Arrange almonds into the cooking tray of the air fryer. 3. Place the drip pan at the bottom of the cooking chamber. Using the display panel, select Roast, adjust the temperature to 350 degrees F and the time to 25 minutes, then touch Start. 4. When the display indicates "Add Food," insert one cooking tray in the top position. 5. When the display indicates "turn Food," turn the food. 6. When the time is up, carefully remove them from the cooking tray. 7. Once done, serve and enjoy.

Per serving: Calories 176; Fat 15.4g; Sodium 853mg; Carbs 5.8g; Fiber 1.5g; Sugar 11.3g; Protein 14.9g

Basil Crackers

Prep time: 10 minutes | Cook time: 10 minutes | Serves: 6

½ teaspoon baking Powder	¼ teaspoon basil, dried
Salt and black pepper to the taste	1 garlic clove, minced
One and ¼ cups whole wheat flour	2 tablespoons vegan basil pesto
	2 tablespoons olive oil

1. Combine flour, salt, pepper, baking powder, garlic, cayenne, basil, pesto, and oil in a prepared basin and whisk until a dough forms. Arrange spread the dough into the cooking tray of the air fryer. 2. Place the drip pan at the bottom of the cooking chamber. Using the display panel, select Bake, adjust the temperature to 325 degrees F and the time to 05 minutes, then touch Start. 3. When the display indicates "Add Food," insert one cooking tray in the top position. 4. When the time is up, carefully remove them from the cooking tray. 5. Once done, serve and enjoy.

Per serving: Calories 77; Fat 6.4g; Sodium 27mg; Carbs 4.7g; Fiber 0.9g; Sugar 0.3g; Protein 1.2g

Beets Chips with Chives

Prep time: 10 minutes | Cook time: 20 minutes | Serves: 4

4 medium beets, peeled and cut into skinny slices	Cooking; Spray
1 tablespoon chives, chopped	Salt and pepper

1. Arrange beet chips in the cooking tray of your air fryer and grease with cooking oil; spray, salt, and black pepper. Place the drip pan at the bottom of the cooking chamber. Using the display panel, select Roast, then adjust the temperature to 350

degrees F and the time to 15 minutes; touch Start to begin preheating. 2. When the display indicates "Add Food," insert one cooking tray in the top position. 3. When the time is up, carefully remove them from the cooking tray. 4. Once done, serve and enjoy.

Per serving: Calories 30; Fat 0.1g; Sodium 52mg; Carbs 6.8g; Fiber 1.5g; Sugar 5.3g; Protein 1.2g

Chili Bean Burger

Prep time: 10 minutes | Cook time: 25 minutes | Serves: 6

1 ¼ cup rolled oats	¼ teaspoon chipotle chili powder
3 oz. black beans, rinsed and drained	1 tablespoon soy sauce
¾ cup of salsa	½ teaspoon garlic powder
¼ teaspoon chili powder	

1. In a food processor, pulse the oats until they are powdery. 2. Pulse in the remaining ingredients until they're well blended. 3. Refrigerate for 15 minutes after transferring to a bowl. 4. Make burger patties out of the mixture. Arrange burger patties into the cooking tray of the air fryer. 5. Place the drip pan at the bottom of the cooking chamber. Using the display panel, select Air Fry, adjust the temperature to 375 degrees F and the time to 15 minutes, then touch Start. 6. When the display indicates "Add Food," insert one cooking tray in the top position. 7. When the display indicates "turn Food," turn the food. 8. When the time is up, carefully remove them from the cooking tray. 9. Once done, serve and enjoy.

Per serving: Calories 53; Fat 0.7g; Sodium 350mg; Carbs 10.1g; Fiber 2.1g; Sugar 1.3g; Protein 2.6g

Veggie Spring Rolls

Prep time: 10 minutes | Cook time: 25 minutes | Serves: 8

2 cups cabbage, chopped	1 teaspoon coconut aminos
2 yellow onions, chopped	2 tablespoons olive oil
1 carrot, chopped	10 vegan spring roll sheets
½ red bell pepper, chopped	Cooking spray
1-inch piece ginger, grated	2 tablespoons Corn flour mixed with 1 tablespoon of water
8 garlic cloves, minced	
Salt and pepper	

1. Heat the oil in a pan over medium-high heat, then add the cabbage, onions, carrots, bell pepper, ginger, pepper and amino, garlic, and salt, mix to combine, and simmer for 4 minutes. 2. Each spring roll sheet should be cut into four parts. 3. Place 1 tablespoon in a small bowl. Place the veggie mix in one corner, roll it up, and fold the sides. 4. Carry with the rest of the rolls in the same manner. Arrange rolls into the cooking tray of air fryer 5. Place the drip pan at the bottom of the cooking chamber. Using the display panel, select Air Fry, adjust the temperature to 350 degrees F and the time to 10 minutes, then touch Start. 6. When the display indicates "Add Food," insert one cooking tray in the top position. 7. When the display indicates "turn Food," turn the food. 8. When the time is up, carefully remove them from the cooking tray. 9. Once done, serve and enjoy.

Per serving: Calories 102; Fat 3.9g; Sodium 82mg; Carbs 13.8g; Fiber 1.5g; Sugar 1.7g; Protein 1.5g

Cauliflower Crackers with Cashew Cheese

Prep time: 10 minutes | Cook time: 20 minutes | Serves: 12

1 big Cauliflower head, florets separated and riced	1 tablespoon flax meal mixed with 1 tablespoon water
½ cup cashew cheese, shredded	1 teaspoon Italian seasoning
	Salt and pepper

1. Transfer cauliflower to a mixing bowl and season with salt, pepper, cashew cheese, flax meal, and Italian seasoning; stir well, then distribute into an air fryer-safe rectangle pan. Arrange the pan into the cooking tray of the air fryer. 2. Place the drip pan at the bottom of the cooking chamber. Using the display panel, select Bake, adjust the temperature to 350 degrees F and the time to 15 minutes, then touch Start. 3. When the display indicates "Add Food," insert one cooking tray in the top position. 4. When the time is up, carefully remove them from the cooking tray. 5. Once done, Cut into medium crackers.

Per serving: Calories 12; Fat 0.8g; Sodium 9mg; Carbs 1g; Fiber 0.4g; Sugar 0.3g; Protein 0.5g

Sriracha Tomato-Avocado Rolls

Prep time: 20 minutes | Cook time: 10 minutes | Serves: 4

10 rice paper wrappers	4 tablespoons sriracha
3 avocados, sliced	2 tablespoons sugar
1 tomato, diced	1 tablespoon rice vinegar
Salt and pepper	2 tablespoons sesame oil
1 tablespoon olive oil	

1. In a mixing basin, mash the avocados. 2. Toss in the tomatoes with a pinch of salt and pepper. 3. Mix thoroughly. 4. Arrange the rice paper wrappers in a pleasing pattern. 5. Place a scoop of the mixture on top. 6. Roll and water-seal the edges. Arrange rolls into the cooking tray of the air fryer. 7. Place the drip pan at the bottom of the cooking chamber. Using the display panel, select Air Fry, adjust the temperature to 350 degrees F and the time to 05 minutes, then touch Start. 8. When the display indicates "Add Food," insert one cooking tray in the top position 9. When the display indicates "turn Food," turn the food. 10. When the time is up, carefully remove them from the cooking tray. 11. Once done, Mix the rest of the ingredients. 12. Serve and enjoy.

Per serving: Calories 481; Fat 32.7g; Sodium 223mg; Carbs 45.8g; Fiber 8.5g; Sugar 8.3g; Protein 4.9g

Cheese Cream Dip

Prep time: 10 minutes | Cook time: 25 minutes | Serves: 12

4 garlic cloves, minced	shredded
2 ounces Asiago cheese, shredded	1-ounce cream cheese softened
1 cup mozzarella cheese,	1 cup sour cream

1. In a mixing bowl, combine all ingredients and stir until well blended. 2. Fill the baking dish halfway with the mixture. Arrange the pan into the cooking tray of the air fryer. 3. Place the drip pan at the bottom of the cooking chamber. Using the display panel, select Bake, adjust the temperature to 350 degrees F and the time to 25 minutes, then touch Start. 4. When the display indicates "Add Food," insert one cooking tray in the top position. 5. When the time is up, carefully remove them from the cooking tray. 6. Once done, serve and enjoy.

Per serving: Calories 74; Fat 6.6g; Sodium 89mg; Carbs 1.3g; Fiber 0g; Sugar 0g; Protein 2.7g

Spiced Brussels Sprouts

Prep time: 10 minutes | Cook time: 12 minutes | Serves: 4

1 pound Brussels sprouts, cut stems, and halved	¼ teaspoon paprika
¼ cup parmesan cheese, grated	¼ teaspoon chili powder
	½ teaspoon garlic powder
1 tablespoon olive oil	Salt and Pepper

1. Place Brussels sprouts in an air fryer cooking tray with the remaining ingredients, except the cheese, and place the air fryer. 2. Place the drip pan at the bottom of the cooking chamber. Using the display panel, select Air Fry, adjust the temperature to 350 degrees F and the time to 12 minutes, then touch Start. 3. When the display indicates "Add Food," insert one cooking tray in the top position. 4. When the display indicates "turn Food," turn the food. 5. When the time is up, carefully remove them from the cooking tray. 6. Once done, Top with parmesan cheese, serve, and enjoy.

Per serving: Calories 87; Fat 4.4g; Sodium 46mg; Carbs 10.8g; Fiber 4.5g; Sugar 2.3g; Protein 4.9g

Cumin Chickpeas Snack

Prep time: 10 minutes | Cook time: 20 minutes | Serves: 4

4 ounces canned chickpeas, drained	1 tablespoon olive oil
	1 teaspoon smoked paprika
½ teaspoon cumin, ground	Salt and pepper

1. Toss chickpeas with oil, paprika, cumin, salt, and pepper in a mixing bowl to coat. Arrange Chickpeas on the cooking tray of the air fryer. 2. Place the drip pan at the bottom of the cooking chamber. Using the display panel, select Roast, adjust the temperature to 390 degrees F and the time to 10 minutes, then touch Start. 3. When the display indicates "Add Food," insert one cooking tray in the top position. 4. When the time is up, carefully remove them from the cooking tray. 5. Once done, serve and enjoy.

Per serving: Calories 136; Fat 5.3g; Sodium 7mg; Carbs 17.8g; Fiber 5.2g; Sugar 3.1g; Protein 5.9g

Sweet Banana Bread

Prep time: 15 minutes | Cook time: 20 minutes | Serves: 8

1 ⅓ cups flour	3 bananas, peeled and sliced
⅔ cup sugar	½ cup milk
1 teaspoon baking Soda	½ cup olive oil
1 teaspoon baking powder	1 teaspoon salt
1 teaspoon ground cinnamon	

1. Combine all of the ingredients in the bowl of a stand mixer and combine well. 2. Grease a loaf pan and set it aside. 3. Place the mixture in the pan that has been prepared. Arrange the loaf pan into the cooking tray of the air fryer. 4. Place the drip pan at the bottom of the cooking chamber. Using the display panel, select Bake, adjust the temperature to 330 degrees F and the time to 20 minutes, then touch Start. 5. When the display indicates "Add Food," insert one cooking tray in the top position. 6. When the time is up, carefully remove them from the cooking tray. 7. Once done, allow 10 minutes for the pan to cool on a wire rack. 8. Before slicing, carefully transfer the bread onto a wire rack to cool. 9. Cut the bread into the size slices you want.

Per serving: Calories 295; Fat 13.3g; Sodium 458mg; Carbs 44g; Fiber 1.9g; Sugar 22.8g; Protein 3.9g

Mustard Corn Fritters

Prep time: 15 minutes | Cook time: 10 minutes | Serves: 4

¼ cup ground cornmeal
¼ cup flour
¼ teaspoon garlic powder
¼ teaspoon onion powder
¼ teaspoon paprika
Salt and pepper
½ teaspoon baking; Powder

¼ cup parsley, chopped
1 cup corn kernel mixed with
3 tablespoons almond milk
2 cups fresh corn kernels
4 tablespoons mayonnaise
2 teaspoons grainy mustard

1. Mix the cornmeal, flour, salt, garlic powder, onion powder, pepper, baking powder, paprika, and parsley in a large mixing bowl. 2. In a food processor, combine the corn kernels and almond milk. 3. Use salt and pepper to taste. 4. Pulse until everything is combined correctly. 5. Add the corn kernels to the mix. 6. Place in a mixing basin and stir in the cornmeal mixture. 7. In the air fryer pan, pour a tiny amount of batter. Arrange the pan into the cooking tray of air fryer 8. Place the drip pan at the bottom of the cooking chamber. Using the display panel, select Bake, adjust the temperature to 350 degrees F and the time to 10 minutes, then touch Start. 9. When the display indicates "Add Food," insert one cooking tray in the top position. 10. When the time is up, carefully remove them from the cooking tray. 11. Once done, Serve with mayonnaise mustard dip.

Per serving: Calories 185; Fat 6.3g; Sodium 172mg; Carbs 31g; Fiber 3.5g; Sugar 3.6g; Protein 4.1g

Cheese-Onion Dip

Prep time: 10 minutes | Cook time: 35 minutes | Serves: 12

½ cup mayonnaise
1 small onion, diced
4 ounces' cream cheese, cubed
1 ½ cups mozzarella cheese,

shredded
1 ½ cups cheddar cheese,
shredded

1. In a mixing bowl, combine all ingredients and stir until well blended. 2. Pour the mixture into the baking dish that has been prepared. Arrange the pan into the cooking tray of the air fryer. 3. Place the drip pan at the bottom of the cooking chamber. Using the display panel, select Bake, adjust the temperature to 400 degrees F and the time to 35 minutes, then touch Start. 4. When the display indicates "Add Food," insert one cooking tray in the top position. 5. When the time is up, carefully remove them from the cooking tray. 6. Once done, serve and enjoy.

Per serving: Calories 140; Fat 11.9g; Sodium 207mg; Carbs 3.8g; Fiber 0.1g; Sugar 1g; Protein 5.9g

Zucchini Chips

Prep time: 10 minutes | Cook time: 30 minutes | Serves: 6

3 zucchinis, thinly sliced
Salt and black pepper to the
taste

2 tablespoons olive oil
2 tablespoons balsamic vinegar

1. In a mixing bowl, combine all ingredients and stir until well blended. 2. Pour the mixture into the baking dish that has been prepared. Arrange zucchini slices into the cooking tray of the air fryer. 3. Place the drip pan at the bottom of the cooking chamber. Using the display panel, select Air Fry, adjust the temperature to 350 degrees F and the time to 30 minutes, then touch Start. 4. When the display indicates "Add Food," insert one cooking tray in the top position. 5. When the display indicates "turn Food," turn the food. 6. When the

time is up, carefully remove them from the cooking tray. 7. Once done, serve and enjoy.

Per serving: Calories 57; Fat 4.4g; Sodium 10mg; Carbs 3.3g; Fiber 1.1g; Sugar 1.7g; Protein 1.2g

Creamy Crab Dip

Prep time: 10 minutes | Cook time: 20 minutes | Serves: 6

2 ounces' crab lump meat
1 tablespoon mayo
¼ teaspoon salt
⅛ teaspoon paprika
1 tablespoon green onion,
sliced
¼ cup sour cream
4 teaspoons bell pepper, diced

1 tablespoon butter, softened
2 ounces' cream cheese, softened
1 teaspoon parsley, chopped
¼ cup mozzarella cheese,
shredded
4 teaspoons onion, chopped

1. Cream cream cheese, butter, sour cream, and mayonnaise in a mixing bowl until smooth. 2. Stir in the remaining ingredients thoroughly. 3. Fill the greased baking dish halfway with the mixture. Arrange the pan into the cooking tray of the air fryer. 4. Place the drip pan at the bottom of the cooking chamber. Using the display panel, select Bake, adjust the temperature to 350 degrees F and the time to 20 minutes, then touch Start. 5. When the display indicates "Add Food," insert one cooking tray in the top position. 6. When the time is up, carefully remove them from the cooking tray. 7. Once done, serve and enjoy.

Per serving: Calories 118; Fat 9.3g; Sodium 224mg; Carbs 7.8g; Fiber 1.5g; Sugar 4.4g; Protein 3.7 g

Tofu Cube-Onion Balls

Prep time: 10 minutes | Cook time: 35 minutes | Serves: 6

1 small yellow onion, chopped
1 cup Arborio rice
1 tablespoon olive oil
1 cup veggie stock
2 ounces' tofu, cubed
¼ cup sun-dried tomatoes,

chopped
1 ½ cups bread crumbs
Marinara sauce for serving
A drizzle of olive oil
Salt
Pepper

1. 1 tablespoon of butter, heated in a pan. Over medium heat, heat the oil, add the onion, stir, and cook for 5 minutes. 2. Stir in the rice, stock, salt, and pepper, cook for 20 minutes on low heat, then spread out on a baking sheet to cool. 3. Toss the rice with the tomatoes and half of the bread crumbs in a mixing bowl. 4. Form 12 balls, poke a hole in each one, load with tofu cubes, and remolds. 5. Dredge them in the remaining bread crumbs, place all the balls in the air fryer, and sprinkle with oil. Arrange balls into the cooking tray of the air fryer. 6. Place the drip pan at the bottom of the cooking chamber. Using the display panel, select Air Fry, adjust the temperature to 380 degrees F and the time to 10 minutes, then touch Start. 7. When the display indicates "Add Food," insert one cooking tray in the top position. 8. When the display indicates "turn Food," turn the food. 9. When the time is up, carefully remove them from the cooking tray. 10. Once done, serve and enjoy

Per serving: Calories 297; Fat 4.9g; Sodium 314mg; Carbs 49g; Fiber 3.1g; Sugar 4.3g; Protein 7g

Fried Basil Ravioli

Prep time: 15 minutes | Cook time: 8 minutes | Serves: 4

½ cup panko breadcrumbs
1 teaspoon garlic powder
1 teaspoon dried oregano
1 teaspoon dried basil
2 teaspoon nutritional yeast flakes

¼ cup aquafaba liquid
Cooking Spray
½ cup marinara sauce
Salt and pepper
Ravioli, as needed

1. On a dish, toss the breadcrumbs, salt, pepper, garlic powder, oregano, basil, and nutritional yeast flakes. 2. Pour the aquafaba liquid into a separate bowl. 3. After dipping each ravioli in the liquid, coat it with the breadcrumb mixture. Arrange ravioli on the cooking tray of the air fryer. 4. Place the drip pan at the bottom of the cooking chamber. Using the display panel, select Air Fry, adjust the temperature to 390 degrees F and the time to 6 minutes, then touch Start. 5. When the display indicates "Add Food," insert one cooking tray in the top position. 6. When the display indicates "turn Food," turn the food. 7. When the time is up, carefully remove them from the cooking tray. 8. Once done, serve and enjoy.
Per serving: Calories 175; Fat 6.7g; Sodium 536mg; Carbs 19.8g; Fiber 4g; Sugar 6.7g; Protein 5.9g

Cheese Onion Dip

Prep time: 10 minutes | Cook time: 20 minutes | Serves: 8

1 ½ onion, chopped
½ teaspoon garlic powder
1 ½ cup Swiss cheese, shredded
1 cup mozzarella cheese,

shredded
1 cup cheddar cheese, shredded
1 ½ cup mayonnaise
Salt and Pepper

1. In a mixing bowl, combine all ingredients and stir until well blended. 2. Pour the mixture into the baking dish that has been prepared. Arrange the pan into the cooking tray of the air fryer 3. Place the drip pan at the bottom of the cooking chamber. Using the display panel, select Roast, adjust the temperature to 350 degrees F and the time to 15 minutes, then touch Start. 4. When the display indicates "Add Food," insert one cooking tray in the top position. 5. When the time is up, carefully remove them from the cooking tray. 6. Once done, serve and enjoy.
Per serving: Calories 325; Fat 25.4g; Sodium 47mg; Carbs 14g; Fiber 0.5g; Sugar 4.1g; Protein 10.9g

Garlic Spinach with Cheeses

Prep time: 10 minutes | Cook time: 25 minutes | Serves: 12

3 ounces frozen spinach, defrosted & chopped
1 cup sour cream
2 cups cheddar cheese, shred-

ded
2 ounces' cream cheese
1 teaspoon garlic salt

1. In a mixing dish, combine all ingredients and stir thoroughly. 2. Fill the baking dish halfway with the mixture. Arrange the pan into the cooking tray of the air fryer. 3. Place the drip pan at the bottom of the cooking chamber. Using the display panel, select Bake, adjust the temperature to 350 degrees F and the time to 25 minutes, then touch Start. 4. When the display indicates "Add Food," insert one cooking tray in the top position. 5. When the time is up, carefully remove them from the cooking tray. 6. Once done, serve and enjoy.
Per serving: Calories 13; Fat 11.9g; Sodium 147mg; Carbs 1.6g; Fiber 0.2g; Sugar 0.2g; Protein 5.9g

Garlicky Cauliflower Florets

Prep time: 10 minutes | Cook time: 20 minutes | Serves: 4

2cups cauliflower florets
2 garlic cloves, chopped
4 tablespoons olive oil

½ teaspoon cumin powder
½ teaspoon salt

1. Toss all of the ingredients together in a large mixing bowl. 2. Add all ingredients into the large bowl and toss well. 3. Arrange cauliflower florets into the cooking tray of the air fryer. 4. Place the drip pan at the bottom of the cooking chamber. Using the display panel, select Air Fry, adjust the temperature to 400 degrees F and the time to 20 minutes, then touch Start. 5. When the display indicates "Add Food," insert one cooking tray in the top position. 6. When the display indicates "turn Food," turn the food. 7. When the time is up, carefully remove them from the cooking tray. 8. Once done, serve and enjoy.
Per serving: Calories 136; Fat 14.1g; Sodium 306mg; Carbs 3.3g; Fiber 1.3g; Sugar 1.2g; Protein 1.1g

Jalapeno Spinach Dip

Prep time: 10 minutes | Cook time: 35 minutes | Serves: 6

4 ounces frozen spinach, thawed and drained
2 teaspoon jalapeno pepper, minced
½ cup onion, diced
½ cup cheddar cheese, shredded

½ cup mozzarella cheese, shredded
2 oz. cream cheese
2 teaspoons garlic, minced
½ cup Monterey jack cheese, shredded
½ teaspoon salt

1. In a mixing bowl, combine all ingredients and stir until well blended. 2. Fill a 1-quart casserole dish halfway with the mixture. 3. Arrange the casserole dish into the cooking tray of the air fryer. 4. Place the drip pan at the bottom of the cooking chamber. Using the display panel, select Bake, adjust the temperature to 350 degrees F and the time to 35 minutes, then touch Start. 5. When the display indicates "Add Food," insert one cooking tray in the top position 6. When the time is up, carefully remove them from the cooking tray. 7. Once done, serve and enjoy.
Per serving: Calories 123; Fat 9.8g; Sodium 360mg; Carbs 2.4g; Fiber 0.7g; Sugar 0.6g; Protein 6.9g

Zucchini Mushroom Pizza

Prep time: 15 minutes | Cook time: 15 minutes | Serves: 4

4 large Portobello mushrooms, stems, and gills removed
1 teaspoon balsamic vinegar
4 tablespoons pasta sauce
1 clove of garlic, minced
3 oz. zucchini, chopped
4 olives, sliced

2 tablespoons sweet red pepper, diced
1 teaspoon dried basil
½ cups hummus
Fresh basil, minced
Salt
Pepper

1. Season the mushrooms with salt and pepper after coating them with balsamic vinegar. 2. Fill each mushroom with pasta sauce. 3. Garlic should be minced and sprinkled on top. Arrange mushrooms into the cooking tray of the air fryer. 4. Place the drip pan at the bottom of the cooking chamber. Using the display panel, select Air Fry, adjust the temperature to 350 degrees F and the time to 15 minutes, then touch Start. 5. When the display indicates "Add Food," insert one cooking tray in the top position 6. When the display indicates "turn Food," turn the food. Take the mushrooms out and top with zucchini, olives, and peppers. Season with salt, pepper, and

basil. 7. When the time is up, carefully remove them from the cooking tray. 8. Once done, serve and enjoy.
Per serving: Calories 114; Fat 4.1g; Sodium 263mg; Carbs 15.4g; Fiber 4.5g; Sugar 4.3g; Protein 6.9g

Tasty Polenta Biscuits

Prep time: 10 minutes | Cook time: 25 minutes | Serves: 4

4 ounces cooked polenta roll, cold	1 tablespoon olive oil

1. Brush the polenta slices with olive oil after cutting them into the medium. Arrange polenta biscuits into the cooking tray of the air fryer. 2. Place the drip pan at the bottom of the cooking chamber. Using the display panel, select Air Fry, adjust the temperature to 350 degrees F and the time to 25 minutes, then touch Start. 3. When the display indicates "Add Food," insert one cooking tray in the top position. 4. When the display indicates "turn Food," turn the food. 5. When the time is up, carefully remove them from the cooking tray. 6. Once done, serve and enjoy.
Per serving: Calories 120; Fat 3.5g; Sodium 85mg; Carbs 4.3g; Fiber 0.3g; Sugar 0.3g; Protein 0.6g

Salsa Cream Dip

Prep time: 10 minutes | Cook time: 15 minutes | Serves: 6

16 ounces' cream cheese, softened	ded
3 cups cheddar cheese, shred-	1 cup sour cream
	½ cup hot salsa

1. Combine the ingredients in a mixing basin and stir until just blended before pouring into the baking dish. Arrange the baking pan cooking tray of the air fryer. 2. Place the drip pan at the bottom of the cooking chamber. Using the display panel, select Bake, adjust the temperature to 350 degrees F and the time to 15 minutes, then touch Start. 3. When the display indicates "Add Food," insert one cooking tray in the top position. 4. When the time is up, carefully remove them from the cooking tray. 5. Once done, serve and enjoy.
Per serving: Calories 272; Fat 4.4g; Sodium 314mg; Carbs 49g; Fiber 3.1g; Sugar 4.3g; Protein 7g

Fired Chicken Breast Cubes

Prep time: 5 minutes | Cook time: 20 minutes | Serves: 4

1-pound chicken breast, boneless, skinless, cubed	crumbs
½ teaspoon ground pepper	2 tablespoon panko bread-crumbs
¼ teaspoon kosher salt	2 tablespoon grated Parmesan cheese
¼ teaspoon seasoned salt	
2 tablespoon plain bread-	2 tablespoons olive oil

1. Set aside the chicken after seasoning it with pepper, kosher, and seasoned salt. Pour olive oil into a bowl. Crumbs and Parmesan cheese should be combined in a separate bowl. 2. Coat the chicken pieces with oil, then roll them in the breadcrumb mixture. Arrange chicken Nuggets into the cooking tray of the air fryer. 3. Place the drip pan at the bottom of the cooking chamber. Using the display panel, select Air Fry, adjust the temperature to 350 degrees F and the time to 15 minutes, then touch Start. 4. When the display indicates "Add Food," insert one cooking tray in the top position. 5. When the display indicates "turn Food," turn the food. 6. When the time is up, carefully remove them from the cooking tray. 7. Once done, serve and enjoy

Per serving: Calories 257; Fat 13.1g; Sodium 472mg; Carbs 5g; Fiber 0.5g; Sugar 0.3g; Protein 29g

Sweet Potato and Beans Dip

Prep time: 10 minutes | Cook time: 15 minutes | Serves: 10

2 ounces canned garbanzo beans, drained	½ teaspoon cumin, ground
1 cup sweet potatoes, peeled and chopped	2 tablespoons water
	1 tablespoon olive oil
¼ cup sesame paste	2 tablespoons lemon juice
garlic cloves, minced	Salt
	White pepper

1. Arrange sweet potatoes on the cooking tray of the air fryer. 2. Place the drip pan at the bottom of the cooking chamber. Using the display panel, select Roast, adjust the temperature to 350 degrees F and the time to 15 minutes, then touch Start. 3. When the display indicates "Add Food," insert one cooking tray in the top position. 4. When the time is up, carefully remove them from the cooking tray. 5. Cool them down, peel them in your food processor, and pulse well. 6. Add sesame paste, garlic, beans, lemon juice, cumin, water, oil, salt, and pepper, pulse again, divide into bowls and serve cold.
Per serving: Calories 89; Fat 5.1g; Sodium 20mg; Carbs 9.4g; Fiber 2g; Sugar 0.8g; Protein 2.5 g

Spiced Potato Halves

Prep time: 5 minutes | Cook time: 30 minutes | Serves: 4

1.5 pounds of potatoes, halved	2 tablespoons olive oil
3 garlic cloves, grated	1 teaspoon salt
1 tablespoon minced fresh rosemary	¼ teaspoon freshly ground pepper

1. Combine potatoes, garlic, rosemary, olive oil, salt, and pepper in a mixing bowl and toss thoroughly. 2. Arrange potatoes on the cooking tray of the air fryer. 3. Place the drip pan at the bottom of the cooking chamber. Using the display panel, select Air Fry, adjust the temperature to 360 degrees F and the time to 20 minutes, then touch Start. 4. When the display indicates "Add Food," insert one cooking tray in the top position. 5. When the display indicates "turn Food," turn the food. 6. When the time is up, carefully remove them from the cooking tray. 7. Once done, serve and enjoy
Per serving: Calories 184; Fat 7.4g; Sodium 592mg; Carbs 28.1g; Fiber 4.5g; Sugar 2g; Protein 3.1g

Ranch Baby Potato Halves

Prep time: 10 minutes | Cook time: 20 minutes | Serves: 2

½ pound baby potatoes, wash and cut in half	¼ teaspoon dill
	¼ teaspoon garlic powder
¼ teaspoon parsley	¼ teaspoon chives
¼ teaspoon paprika	¼ teaspoon onion powder
½ tablespoon olive oil	Salt to taste

1. Add all ingredients into the bowl and toss well. 2. Arrange potatoes on the cooking tray of the air fryer. 3. Place the drip pan at the bottom of the cooking chamber. Using the display panel, select Air Fry, adjust the temperature to 400 degrees F and the time to 20 minutes, then touch Start. 4. When the display indicates "Add Food," insert one cooking tray in the top position. 5. When the display indicates "turn Food," turn the food. 6. When the time is up, carefully remove them from the cooking tray. 7. Once done, serve and enjoy.
Per serving: Calories 99; Fat 3.7g; Sodium 90mg; Carbs 14.8g; Fiber 3g; Sugar 0.3g; Protein 3.1g

Old Bay Cauliflower Florets

Prep time: 10 minutes | Cook time: 15 minutes | Serves: 4

1 medium cauliflower head, cut into florets
½ teaspoon old bay seasoning
¼ teaspoon paprika
¼ teaspoon cayenne
¼ teaspoon chili powder
1 tablespoon garlic, minced
Salt and Pepper
3 tablespoons olive oil

1. In a bowl, toss cauliflower with the remaining ingredients. 2. Arrange cauliflower into the cooking tray of the air fryer. 3. Place the drip pan at the bottom of the cooking chamber. Using the display panel, select Air Fry, adjust the temperature to 400 degrees F and the time to 15 minutes, then touch Start. 4. When the display indicates "Add Food," insert one cooking tray in the top position. 5. When the display indicates "turn Food," turn the food. 6. When the time is up, carefully remove them from the cooking tray. 7. Once done, serve and enjoy.
Per serving: Calories 111; Fat 10.7g; Sodium 102mg; Carbs 4.4g; Fiber 1.8g; Sugar 1.6g; Protein 1.5g

Spiced Chicken Wings

Prep time: 10 minutes | Cook time: 40 minutes | Serves: 4

2 pounds of chicken wings
1 cup soy sauce, divided
½ cup brown sugar
½ cup apple cider vinegar
2 tablespoons fresh garlic, minced
2 tablespoons fresh ginger,
minced
2 tablespoons cornstarch
1 teaspoon finely ground black pepper
2 tablespoons cold water
1 teaspoon sesame seeds

1. Pour ½ cup soy sauce into a mixing dish with chicken wings. Dry out and pat dry after 20 minutes in the refrigerator. Arrange chicken wings into the cooking tray of the air fryer. 2. Place the drip pan at the bottom of the cooking chamber. Using the display panel, select Air Fry, adjust the temperature to 350 degrees F and the time to 15 minutes, then touch Start. 3. When the display indicates "Add Food," insert one cooking tray in the top position. 4. When the display indicates "turn Food," turn the food. 5. When the time is up, carefully remove them from the cooking tray. 6. Once done, stir sugar, half cup soy sauce, vinegar, ginger, garlic, and black pepper in a pan over medium heat. Cook until the sauce has somewhat reduced, about 4 to 6 minutes. 7. In a bowl, dissolve 2 tablespoons of cornstarch in cold water, then whisk the slurry into the sauce for 2 minutes, or until it thickens. Drizzle the sauce over the wings and top with sesame seeds.
Per serving: Calories 545; Fat 17.4g; Sodium 430mg; Carbs 25.8g; Fiber 0.7g; Sugar 17.3g; Protein 66.6g

Cumin Potato Tots

Prep time: 10 minutes | Cook time: 12 minutes | Serves: 10

2 cups sweet potato puree
½ teaspoon cumin
½ teaspoon coriander
½ cup breadcrumbs
Cooking Spray
½ teaspoon salt
Mayonnaise

1. In a mixing dish, combine all of the ingredients. 2. Make balls out of the mixture. 3. Arrange the ingredients on the air fryer pan. 4. Oil is sprayed over the surface. Arrange balls into the cooking tray of the air fryer 5. Place the drip pan at the bottom of the cooking chamber. Using the display panel, select Air Fry, adjust the temperature to 390 degrees F and the time to 15 minutes, then touch Start. 6. When the display indi-

cates "Add Food," insert one cooking tray in the top position. 7. When the display indicates "turn Food," turn the food. 8. When the time is up, carefully remove them from the cooking tray. 9. Once done, serve and enjoy.
Per serving: Calories 77; Fat 0.4g; Sodium 194mg; Carbs 15.8g; Fiber 1.1g; Sugar 3.1g; Protein 1.9g

Honey Chickpeas

Prep time: 10 minutes | Cook time: 12 minutes | Serves: 4

1 (15-ounce) can of chickpeas, rinsed, drained, and pat dry
1 tablespoon olive oil
½ teaspoon ground cinnamon
1 tablespoon honey
Salt and Pepper

1. Spread chickpeas in the air fryer cooking tray. 2. Place the drip pan at the bottom of the cooking chamber. Using the display panel, select Air Fry, adjust the temperature to 375 degrees F and the time to 12 minutes, then touch Start. 3. When the display indicates "Add Food," insert one cooking tray in the top position. 4. When the display indicates "turn Food," turn the food. 5. When the time is up, carefully remove them from the cooking tray. 6. Combine cinnamon, honey, oil, pepper, and salt in a large mixing basin. Toss in the chickpeas thoroughly. Once done, serve and enjoy.
Per serving: Calories 173; Fat 4.7g; Sodium 318mg; Carbs 28.6g; Fiber 4.9g; Sugar 4.3g; Protein 5.3g

Simple Parsnips and Sweet Potatoes Sticks

Prep time: 10 minutes | Cook time: 30 minutes | Serves: 4

4 parsnips, cut into thin sticks
2 sweet potatoes, cut into sticks
4 carrots, cut into sticks
2 tablespoons rosemary,
chopped
2 tablespoons olive oil
A pinch of garlic powder
Salt and pepper

1. Toss the parsnips, sweet potatoes, and carrots in a bowl with the oil, garlic powder, salt, pepper, and rosemary. 2. Arrange vegetables on the cooking tray of the air fryer. 3. Place the drip pan at the bottom of the cooking chamber. Using the display panel, select Air Fry, adjust the temperature to 350 degrees F and the time to 15 minutes, then touch Start. 4. When the display indicates "Add Food," insert one cooking tray in the top position. 5. When the display indicates "turn Food," turn the food. 6. When the time is up, carefully remove them from the cooking tray. 7. Once done, serve and enjoy.
Per serving: Calories 279; Fat 7.8g; Sodium 63mg; Carbs 52g; Fiber 11.5g; Sugar 9.8g; Protein 3.4g

Garlicky Potato Wedges

Prep time: 10 minutes | Cook time: 15 minutes | Serves: 4

2 medium potatoes, cut into wedges
¼ teaspoon garlic powder
½ teaspoon paprika
1 ½ tablespoons olive oil
⅛ teaspoon cayenne
1 teaspoon sea salt
¼ teaspoon pepper

1. Soak potato wedges for 30 minutes in water. 2. Drain thoroughly and dry thoroughly with a paper towel. 3. Toss the potato wedges with the other ingredients in a bowl. Arrange potatoes wedges into the cooking tray of the air fryer. 4. Place the drip pan at the bottom of the cooking chamber. Using the display panel, select Air Fry, adjust the temperature to 400 degrees F and the time to 15 minutes, then touch Start. 5. When the display indicates "Add Food," insert one cooking tray in the top position. 6. When the display indicates "turn Food,"

turn the food. 7. When the time is up, carefully remove them from the cooking tray. 8. Once done, serve and enjoy.

Per serving: Calories 120; Fat 5.4g; Sodium 475mg; Carbs 17.1g; Fiber 2.7g; Sugar 1.3g; Protein 1.9g

Veggie Wontons with Chili Sauce

Prep time: 10 minutes | Cook time: 10 minutes | Serves: 10

Cooking Spray	1 tablespoon chili sauce
½ cup white onion, grated	1 teaspoon garlic powder
½ cup mushrooms, chopped	Salt
½ cup carrot, grated	30 wonton wrappers
¾ cup red pepper, chopped	Water
¾ cup cabbage, grated	

1. In a pan, spray some oil. 2. Cook the onion, mushrooms, carrot, red pepper, and cabbage in the pan over medium heat until soft. 3. Combine the chili sauce, garlic powder, salt, and pepper in a mixing bowl. 4. Allow it to cool for a few minutes before serving. 5. On top of the wrappers, place a scoop of the mixture. 6. Fold and seal the corners with water. Arrange potatoes and Wontons into the cooking tray of the air fryer. 7. Place the drip pan at the bottom of the cooking chamber. Using the display panel, select Air Fry, adjust the temperature to 320 degrees F and the time to 7 minutes, then touch Start. 8. When the display indicates "Add Food," insert one cooking tray in the top position. 9. When the display indicates "turn Food," turn the food. 10. When the time is up, carefully remove them from the cooking tray. 11. Once done, serve and enjoy.

Per serving: Calories 296; Fat 2g; Sodium 571mg; Carbs 58.4g; Fiber 2.3g; Sugar 1.3g; Protein 10g

Crispy Breaded Cauliflower Florets

Prep time: 10 minutes | Cook time: 10 minutes | Serves: 4

1-pound cauliflower florets	1 teaspoon garlic, crushed
1 extra-large egg, whisked	Sea salt
1 tablespoon Dijon mustard	Ground black pepper to taste
1 tablespoon soy sauce	1 cup seasoned breadcrumbs

1. Dry the cauliflower florets with a paper towel. In a small dish, whisk the egg. Combine the other ingredients in another bowl. The cauliflower florets should be dipped in the whisked egg. The cauliflower florets should then be rolled in the breadcrumb mixture. Arrange cauliflower florets into the cooking tray of the air fryer. 2. Place the drip pan at the bottom of the cooking chamber. Using the display panel, select Air Fry, adjust the temperature to 380 degrees F and the time to 10 minutes, then touch Start. 3. When the display indicates "Add Food," insert one cooking tray in the top position. 4. When the display indicates "turn Food," turn the food. 5. When the time is up, carefully remove them from the cooking tray. 6. Once done, serve and enjoy.

Per serving: Calories 159; Fat 2.9g; Sodium 519mg; Carbs 26.3g; Fiber 4.2g; Sugar 4.6g; Protein 7.9g

Homemade Potato Chips

Prep time: 30 minutes | Cook time: 30 minutes | Serves: 4

4 potatoes, scrubbed, peeled, and cut into thin strips	2 teaspoons rosemary, chopped
A pinch of sea salt	1 tablespoon olive oil

1. Combine potato chips, salt, and oil in a mixing dish and toss to coat. 2. Arrange potato chips into a cooking tray of the

air fryer. 3. Place the drip pan at the bottom of the cooking chamber. Using the display panel, select Air Fry, adjust the temperature to 330 degrees F and the time to 30 minutes, then touch Start. 4. When the display indicates "Add Food," insert one cooking tray in the top position. 5. When the display indicates "turn Food," turn the food. 6. When the time is up, carefully remove them from the cooking tray. 7. Once done, serve and enjoy.

Per serving: Calories 179; Fat 3.8g; Sodium 72mg; Carbs 33.8g; Fiber 5.4g; Sugar 2.5g; Protein 3.6g

Delicious Corn Tortilla Chips

Prep time: 10 minutes | Cook time: 15 minutes | Serves: 4

4 corn tortillas, each cut into triangles	Salt and pepper
	1 tablespoon olive oil

1. Brush the tortilla chips with the oil, and set them aside. Arrange tortilla chips into the cooking tray of the air fryer. 2. Place the drip pan at the bottom of the cooking chamber. Using the display panel, select Air Fry, adjust the temperature to 350 degrees F and the time to 15 minutes, then touch Start. 3. When the display indicates "Add Food," insert one cooking tray in the top position. 4. When the display indicates "turn Food," turn the food. 5. When the time is up, carefully remove them from the cooking tray. 6. Once done, serve and enjoy.

Per serving: Calories 82; Fat 4.4g; Sodium 11mg; Carbs 10.8g; Fiber 1.5g; Sugar 0.3g; Protein 1.4g

Chicken Stuffed Mushrooms

Prep time: 10 minutes | Cook time: 30 minutes | Serves: 8

40 mushrooms, clean & remove stems	1 cup cheddar cheese, shredded
1 teaspoon garlic, crushed	2 cups chicken, cooked & chopped
¼ cup hot sauce	Pepper
½ cup mayonnaise	Salt
4 ounces' cream cheese, softened	

1. Arrange mushrooms onto the cooking tray of the air fryer. 2. Place the drip pan at the bottom of the cooking chamber. Using the display panel, select Bake, adjust the temperature to 400 degrees F and the time to 15 minutes, then touch Start. 3. When the display indicates "Add Food," insert one cooking tray in the top position. 4. When the time is up, carefully remove them from the cooking tray. 5. Once done, remove mushrooms from the fryer and let them cool completely. 6. Combine chicken, ¾ cup cheddar cheese, cream cheese, mayonnaise, spicy sauce, garlic, pepper, and salt in a mixing bowl. Fill each mushroom with the chicken mixture and top with the remaining ingredients.; 7. Arrange mushrooms into the cooking tray of the air fryer. 8. Place the drip pan at the bottom of the cooking chamber. Using the display panel, select Air Fry, adjust the temperature to 350 degrees F and the time to 15 minutes, then touch Start. 9. When the display indicates "Add Food," insert one cooking tray in the top position. 10. When the display indicates "turn Food," turn the food. 11. When the time is up, carefully remove them from the cooking tray. 12. Once done, serve and enjoy.

Per serving: Calories 237; Fat 15.9g; Sodium 471mg; Carbs 7.3g; Fiber 0.9g; Sugar 2.7g; Protein 17.8g

Onion Mozzarella Sticks with Marinara Sauce

Prep time: 40 minutes | Cook time: 15 minutes | Serves: 4

1 package of mozzarella sticks cut in half	¼ cup fine dry breadcrumbs
¼ cup mayonnaise	½ teaspoon onion powder
1 large egg	½ teaspoon garlic powder
¼ cup all-purpose flour	1 cup marinara sauce

1. Make the breading by whisking together mayonnaise and egg in a mixing dish, then adding bread crumbs, onions, garlic, and flour. 2. Roll the frozen sticks in the mayo-egg mixture to coat them before passing them through the flour in six groups. Before putting it in the air fryer, ensure it's free of excess flour. 3. Arrange Mozzarella Sticks into the cooking tray of the air fryer. 4. Place the drip pan at the bottom of the cooking chamber. Using the display panel, select Bake, adjust the temperature to 350 degrees F and the time to 15 minutes, then touch Start. 5. When the display indicates "Add Food," insert one cooking tray in the top position. 6. When the time is up, carefully remove them from the cooking tray. 7. Once done, serve and enjoy.

Per serving: Calories 366; Fat 18.6g; Sodium 1816mg; Carbs 36.1g; Fiber 3.8g; Sugar 7.2g; Protein 13.9g

Egg Almond Balls with Cheeses

Prep time: 10 minutes | Cook time: 10 minutes | Serves: 4

2 eggs	shredded
½ teaspoon baking Powder	½ cup cheddar cheese, shredded
½ cup almond flour	
¼ cup parmesan cheese, shredded	Pepper
¼ cup mozzarella cheese,	Salt

1. In a mixing dish, whisk the eggs until they are well beaten. 2. Mix in the other ingredients until everything is nicely mixed. 3. Form 8 balls out of the cheese mixture and lay them on a parchment-lined baking sheet. Arrange balls into the cooking tray of the air fryer 4. Place the drip pan at the bottom of the cooking chamber. Using the display panel, select Bake, adjust the temperature to 400 degrees F and the time to 10 minutes, then touch Start. 5. When the display indicates "Add Food," insert one cooking tray in the top position. 6. When the time is up, carefully remove them from the cooking tray. 7. Once done, serve and enjoy

Per serving: Calories 180; Fat 14.6g; Sodium 185mg; Carbs 3.8g; Fiber 1.5g; Sugar 0.7g; Protein 10.4g

Cheesy Pepper Chicken Dip

Prep time: 10 minutes | Cook time: 30 minutes | Serves: 8

2 cups chicken, cooked & shredded	1 ½ cups cheddar cheese, shredded
1 bell pepper, chopped	2 ounces' cream cheese, softened
⅓ cup basil pesto	
½ cup ricotta cheese	

1. Cream cream cheese, pesto, 1 cup cheddar cheese, and ricotta cheese in a mixing basin until thoroughly blended. 2. Add the bell pepper and shredded chicken and mix well. Pour mixture into the prepared baking dish, spread evenly, and top with remaining ingredients. 3. Arrange the pan into the cooking tray of the air fryer. 4. Place the drip pan at the bottom of the cooking chamber. Using the display panel, select Bake,

adjust the temperature to 350 degrees F and the time to 30 minutes, then touch Start. 5. When the display indicates "Add Food," insert one cooking tray in the top position. 6. When the time is up, carefully remove them from the cooking tray. 7. Once done, serve and enjoy.

Per serving: Calories 189; Fat 11.8g; Sodium 194mg; Carbs 2.4g; Fiber 0.2g; Sugar 0.9g; Protein 17.9g

Bacon Stuffed Mini Peppers

Prep time: 10 minutes | Cook time: 12 minutes | Serves: 12

12 mini sweet peppers, sliced in half, remove membranes & seeds	4 bacon slices, cooked and chopped
1 teaspoon Worcestershire sauce	½ teaspoon garlic powder
	2 tablespoon green onions, sliced
½ cup cheddar cheese, shredded	4 ounces' cream cheese

1. Combine cream cheese, green onions, garlic powder, bacon slices, cheddar cheese, and Worcestershire sauce in a small mixing bowl until well blended. 2. Fill each pepper half with the cream cheese mixture. Arrange the stuffed peppers on the baking sheet. 3. Place the drip pan at the bottom of the cooking chamber. Using the display panel, select Bake, adjust the temperature to 400 degrees F and the time to 12 minutes, then touch Start. 4. When the display indicates "Add Food," insert one cooking tray in the top position. 5. When the time is up, carefully remove them from the cooking tray. 6. Once done, serve and enjoy.

Per serving: Calories 125; Fat 7.9g; Sodium 211mg; Carbs 9.6g; Fiber 1.9g; Sugar 6.2g; Protein 5.8g

Buttered Spinach Meatballs

Prep time: 10 minutes | Cook time: 18 minutes | Serves: 10

1 egg	½ cup parmesan cheese, grated
1-pound sausage, casings removed	
1 teaspoon garlic, chopped	½ cup mozzarella cheese, shredded
½ onion, chopped	1 teaspoon salt
1 cup spinach, chopped	

1. In a mixing bowl, combine all ingredients and stir until well blended. 2. Make little balls out of the dough and lay them on a cooking tray coated with parchment paper. 3. Place the drip pan at the bottom of the cooking chamber. Using the display panel, select Air Fry, adjust the temperature to 350 degrees F and the time to 15 minutes, then touch Start. 4. When the display indicates "Add Food," insert one cooking tray in the top position. 5. When the display indicates "turn Food," turn the food. 6. When the time is up, carefully remove them from the cooking tray. 7. Once done, serve and enjoy.

Per serving: Calories 172; Fat 13.9g; Sodium 603mg; Carbs 0.8g; Fiber 0.2g; Sugar 0.3g; Protein 10.8g

Cinnamon Churro Bites

Prep time: 15 minutes | Cook time: 20 minutes | Serves: 4

1 cup water	3 large eggs
1 teaspoon unsalted butter	2 teaspoons ground cinnamon
1 cup all-purpose flour	4 ounces chopped dark chocolate
½ cup granulated sugar	
1 teaspoon vanilla extract	¼ cup sour cream

1. Bring butter, water, and 1 teaspoon sugar to a boil, then reduce to low heat and leave to simmer for a few minutes. 2.

Add the flour and mix with a sturdy wooden spoon until the flour smells toasted. Place the ingredients in a large mixing basin. 3. With the same wooden spoon, whip the flour mixture until it has slightly cooled, then add the vanilla extract. 4. Add and stir the eggs one at a time, ensuring that each is thoroughly combined before moving on to the next. 5. Place the dough in a zip-top bag and set aside an hour to rest. Prepare the cinnamon sugar and chocolate sauce in the meantime. 6. In a microwave-safe bowl, combine the cinnamon and the remaining ½ cup sugar and heat for 2 minutes, or until everything is melted. Arrange Churro Bites into the cooking tray of the air fryer. 7. Place the drip pan at the bottom of the cooking chamber. Using the display panel, select Bake, adjust the temperature to 375 degrees F and the time to 15 minutes, then touch Start. 8. When the display indicates "Add Food," insert one cooking tray in the top position. 9. When the time is up, carefully remove them from the cooking tray. 10. Once done, the churros with cinnamon and sugar coat them. 11. Serve and enjoy.

Per serving: Calories 458; Fat 16.4g; Sodium 92mg; Carbs 67.7g; Fiber 2.4g; Sugar 40.1g; Protein 10.6g

Almond Sausage Balls with Pepper Jerk Cheese

Prep time: 10 minutes | Cook time: 20 minutes | Serves: 6

1 egg	2 tablespoons butter, melted
1-pound breakfast sausage, casing removed	1 cup pepper jack cheese, shredded
1 teaspoon baking powder	¼ teaspoon salt
1 cup almond flour	

1. Add all ingredients into the large bowl and mix until well combined. 2. Make small balls from the mixture 3. Arrange balls into the cooking tray of the air fryer 4. Place the drip pan at the bottom of the cooking chamber. Using the display panel, select Bake, adjust the temperature to 350 degrees F and the time to 20 minutes, then touch Start. 5. When the display indicates "Add Food," insert one cooking tray in the top position. 6. When the time is up, carefully remove them from the cooking tray. 7. Once done, serve and enjoy.

Per serving: Calories 427; Fat 36.8g; Sodium 730mg; Carbs 4.5g; Fiber 2g; Sugar 0.7g; Protein 20.7g

Ranch Spinach Dip

Prep time: 10 minutes | Cook time: 25 minutes | Serves: 16

2 cups spinach, washed & chopped	½ cup red pepper, diced
¼ cup parmesan cheese, grated	¼ cup green onion, sliced
1 ½ cups mozzarella cheese	½ cup mayonnaise
1 teaspoon ranch seasoning	½ cup sour cream
	2 ounces' cream cheese

1. In a pan over medium heat, cook spinach until it has wilted. Squeezed all the juice out of the spinach. 2. In a mixing bowl, combine the spinach, 1 cup of mozzarella cheese, and the remaining ingredients until well blended. 3. Pour the mixture into the baking dish and evenly distribute it. The remaining mozzarella cheese should be sprinkled on top. Arrange the baking dish into the cooking tray of the air fryer. 4. Place the drip pan at the bottom of the cooking chamber. Using the display panel, select Bake, adjust the temperature to 350 degrees F and the time to 25 minutes, then touch Start. 5. When the display indicates "Add Food," insert one cooking tray in the top position. 6. When the time is up, carefully remove them

from the cooking tray. 7. Once done, serve and enjoy.

Per serving: Calories 68; Fat 5.8g; Sodium 104mg; Carbs 2.8g; Fiber 0.2g; Sugar 0.7g; Protein 1.7g

Tasty Buffalo Chicken Dip

Prep time: 10 minutes | Cook time: 20 minutes | Serves: 12

2 cups chicken breast, cooked & diced	ded
2 green onions, sliced	1 teaspoon garlic powder
1 cup mozzarella cheese, shredded	⅔ cup sour cream
1 cup cheddar cheese, shred-	⅔ cup buffalo sauce
	2 ounces' cream cheese, softened

1. Mix the chicken, green onion, ½ cup mozzarella cheese, ½ cup cheddar cheese, garlic powder, sour cream, buffalo sauce, and cream cheese. 2. Fill the baking dish halfway with the mixture and top with the remaining cheese. Arrange the baking dish into the cooking tray of the air fryer. 3. Place the drip pan at the bottom of the cooking chamber. Using the display panel, select Air Fry, adjust the temperature to 350 degrees F and the time to 20 minutes, then touch Start. 4. When the display indicates "Add Food," insert one cooking tray in the top position. 5. When the time is up, carefully remove them from the cooking tray. 6. Once done, serve and enjoy

Per serving: Calories 110; Fat 8.3g; Sodium 156mg; Carbs 1.3g; Fiber 0.2g; Sugar 0.2g; Protein 7.4g

Easy Artichoke Dip

Prep time: 10 minutes | Cook time: 40 minutes | Serves: 8

14 ounces can of artichoke hearts, drained & chopped	1 cup parmesan cheese, shredded
1 tablespoon garlic, minced	1 cup mayonnaise

1. In a baking dish, combine all ingredients and stir thoroughly. 2. Arrange the baking dish on the cooking tray of the air fryer. 3. Place the drip pan at the bottom of the cooking chamber. Using the display panel, select Air Fry, adjust the temperature to 350 degrees F and the time to 40 minutes, then touch Start. 4. When the display indicates "Add Food," insert one cooking tray in the top position. 5. When the display indicates "turn Food," turn the food. 6. When the time is up, carefully remove them from the cooking tray. 7. Once done, serve and enjoy

Per serving: Calories 142; Fat 10.6g; Sodium 403mg; Carbs 10g; Fiber 1.7g; Sugar 2.7g; Protein 2.3g

Mexican Cheese Dip

Prep time: 10 minutes | Cook time: 30 minutes | Serves: 10

½ cup salsa	1 cup sour cream
3 cups cheddar cheese, shredded	15 ounces' cream cheese, softened

1. In a baking dish, combine all ingredients and stir thoroughly. 2. Arrange the baking dish on the cooking tray of the air fryer. 3. Place the drip pan at the bottom of the cooking chamber. Using the display panel, select Bake, adjust the temperature to 350 degrees F and the time to 30 minutes, then touch Start. 4. When the display indicates "Add Food," insert one cooking tray in the top position. 5. When the time is up, carefully remove them from the cooking tray. 6. Once done, serve and enjoy.

Per serving: Calories 338; Fat 30.8g; Sodium 427mg; Carbs 3.4g; Fiber 0.2g; Sugar 0.7g; Protein 12.7g

Perfect Ricotta Cheese Dip

Prep time: 10 minutes | Cook time: 20 minutes | Serves: 6

2 cups ricotta cheese	shredded
3 tablespoons olive oil	½ cup mozzarella cheese,
2 garlic cloves, minced	shredded
2 teaspoons fresh thyme	Pepper
1 lemon zest	Salt
¼ cup parmesan cheese,	

1. In a mixing bowl, combine all ingredients and stir until well blended. 2. Pour the mixture into the baking dish. 3. Arrange the pan into the cooking tray of the air fryer. 4. Place the drip pan at the bottom of the cooking chamber. Using the display panel, select Bake, adjust the temperature to 375 degrees F and the time to 20 minutes, then touch Start. 5. When the display indicates "Add Food," insert one cooking tray in the top position. 6. When the time is up, carefully remove them from the cooking tray. 7. Once done, serve and enjoy.

Per serving: Calories 190; Fat 14.3g; Sodium 156mg; Carbs 5.8g; Fiber 0.4g; Sugar 0.5g; Protein 10.7g

Crispy Almond Fried Artichoke Hearts

Prep time: 10 minutes | Cook time: 18 minutes | Serves: 5

15 ounces can of artichoke	ed
hearts, drained & quartered	½ teaspoon garlic powder
¼ cup almond flour	¼ cup butter, melted
¼ cup parmesan cheese, grat-	

1. Pat dry artichoke hearts with a paper towel. 2. Mix the melted butter and garlic powder in a small bowl. 3. In a separate bowl, mix parmesan cheese and almond flour. 4. Dip each quartered artichoke heart in melted butter and coat with parmesan cheese. 5. Arrange artichoke into the cooking tray of the air fryer. 6. Place the drip pan at the bottom of the cooking chamber. Using the display panel, select Air Fry, adjust the temperature to 400 degrees F and the time to 18 minutes, then touch Start. 7. When the display indicates "Add Food," insert one cooking tray in the top position. 8. When the display indicates "turn Food," turn the food. 9. When the time is up, carefully remove them from the cooking tray. 10. Once done, serve and enjoy.

Per serving: Calories 144; Fat 12.3g; Sodium 355mg; Carbs 5.7g; Fiber 3.5g; Sugar 1g; Protein 3.2g

Tuna Muffins with Celery

Prep time: 10 minutes | Cook time: 20 minutes | Serves: 8

2 large eggs	shredded
1 can tuna, flaked	¼ cup sour cream
1 teaspoon cayenne pepper	¼ cup mayonnaise
1 celery stalk, chopped	Pepper
1 ½ cups cheddar cheese,	Salt

1. Whisk the eggs and the remaining ingredients in a mixing dish. 2. Fill the silicone muffin tins halfway with the batter. 3. Arrange the muffin tin into the cooking tray of the air fryer. 4. Place the drip pan at the bottom of the cooking chamber. Using the display panel, select Bake, adjust the temperature to 350 degrees F and the time to 15 minutes, then touch Start. 5. When the display indicates "Add Food," insert one cooking tray in the top position. 6. When the time is up, carefully remove them from the cooking tray. 7. Once done, serve and enjoy.

Per serving: Calories 190; Fat 14.1g; Sodium 237mg; Carbs 2.6g; Fiber 0.1g; Sugar 0.7g; Protein 13.1g

Almond-Asparagus Fries

Prep time: 10 minutes | Cook time: 10 minutes | Serves: 6

4 eggs, lightly beaten	¾ cup almond flour
1-pound asparagus, trimmed	1 cup parmesan cheese, grated
& poke using a fork	Pepper
¼ teaspoon baking; Powder	Salt
¼ teaspoon cayenne pepper	

1. Season asparagus spears with salt and pepper and set aside for 30 minutes on a plate. 2. Combine parmesan cheese, cayenne pepper, and almond flour in a shallow basin. 3. In a separate shallow bowl, whisk the eggs thoroughly. 4. Asparagus stalks are dipped in eggs and then coated in a parmesan cheese concoction. 5. Arrange asparagus spears into the cooking tray of the air fryer. 6. Place the drip pan at the bottom of the cooking chamber. Using the display panel, select Air Fry, adjust the temperature to 400 degrees F and the time to 10 minutes, then touch Start. 7. When the display indicates "Add Food," insert one cooking tray in the top position. 8. When the display indicates "turn Food," turn the food. 9. When the time is up, carefully remove them from the cooking tray. 10. Once done, serve and enjoy.

Per serving: Calories 152; Fat 11g; Sodium 114mg; Carbs 6.4g; Fiber 3.1g; Sugar 2.2g; Protein 9.9g

Asiago Zucchini Chips

Prep time: 10 minutes | Cook time: 15 minutes | Serves: 8

2 medium zucchinis, sliced	4 tablespoons olive oil
into rounds	¼ teaspoon smoked paprika
¾ teaspoon garlic powder	Pepper
⅔ cup Asiago cheese, grated	salt

1. Toss zucchini with garlic powder, paprika, oil, pepper, and salt in a mixing bowl until evenly covered. 2. Arrange the zucchini slices on the baking sheet and cover them with grated cheese. Arrange zucchini into the cooking tray of the air fryer. 3. Place the drip pan at the bottom of the cooking chamber. Using the display panel, select Air Fry, adjust the temperature to 375 degrees F and the time to 15 minutes, then touch Start. 4. When the display indicates "Add Food," insert one cooking tray in the top position. 5. When the display indicates "turn Food," turn the food. 6. When the time is up, carefully remove them from the cooking tray. 7. Once done, serve and enjoy.

Per serving: Calories 77; Fat 7.8g; Sodium 53mg; Carbs 1.9g; Fiber 0.6g; Sugar 0.9g; Protein 1.2g

Mustard Zucchini-Almond Patties

Prep time: 10 minutes | Cook time: 30 minutes | Serves: 8

2 eggs	1 tablespoon Dijon mustard
2 cups shredded zucchini,	1 tablespoon mayonnaise
squeeze out all liquid	1 cup almond flour
1 teaspoon dried chili flakes	¼ cup onion, chopped
½ cup parmesan cheese, grat-	Pepper
ed	Salt

1. In a mixing bowl, combine all ingredients and stir until well blended. 2. Make patties out of the mixture and set them on a cooking tray. 3. Arrange patties into the cooking tray of the air fryer. 4. Place the drip pan at the bottom of the cooking chamber. Using the display panel, select Bake, adjust the temperature to 400 degrees F and the time to 30 minutes, then touch Start. 5. When the display indicates "Add Food," insert one cooking tray in the top position. 6. When the time is up,

carefully remove them from the cooking tray. 7. Once done, serve and enjoy.

Per serving: Calories 116; Fat 9.2g; Sodium 471mg; Carbs 7.3g; Fiber 0.9g; Sugar 2.7g; Protein 17.8g

Garlicky Mushrooms

Prep time: 10 minutes | Cook time: 12 minutes | Serves: 4

1-pound mushrooms, clean & stems removed	1 teaspoon garlic, minced
⅛ teaspoon garlic powder	1 tablespoon olive oil
2 tablespoons chives, sliced	⅛ teaspoon pepper
	⅛ teaspoon kosher salt

1. Toss the mushrooms with the remaining ingredients in a large mixing basin until evenly coated. 2. Place the mushrooms on the cooking tray. 3. Place the drip pan at the bottom of the cooking chamber. Using the display panel, select Bake, adjust the temperature to 400 degrees F and the time to 12 minutes, then touch Start. 4. When the display indicates "Add Food," insert one cooking tray in the top position. 5. When the time is up, carefully remove them from the cooking tray. 6. Once done, serve and enjoy.

Per serving: Calories 71; Fat 3.8g; Sodium 156mg; Carbs 4.4g; Fiber 1.3g; Sugar 2g; Protein 3.7g

Savoury Brussels Sprout Halves

Prep time: 10 minutes | Cook time: 35 minutes | Serves: 6

2 cups Brussels sprouts, halved	¼ teaspoon onion powder
¼ teaspoon chili pepper	¼ cup olive oil
¼ teaspoon garlic powder	¼ teaspoon salt

1. Toss all of the ingredients together in a large mixing basin. 2. Place the Brussels sprouts on the baking sheet. 3. Arrange Brussels sprouts into the cooking tray of the air fryer. 4. Place the drip pan at the bottom of the cooking chamber. Using the display panel, select Air Fry, adjust the temperature to 400 degrees F and the time to 35 minutes, then touch Start. 5. When the display indicates "Add Food," insert one cooking tray in the top position 6. When the display indicates "turn Food," turn the food. 7. When the time is up, carefully remove them from the cooking tray. 8. Once done, serve and enjoy

Per serving: Calories 86; Fat 8.5g; Sodium 104mg; Carbs 2.9g; Fiber 1.1g; Sugar 0.7g; Protein 1g

Cream Cheese Dip

Prep time: 10 minutes | Cook time: 20 minutes | Serves: 12

2 ounces' cream cheese, softened	1 tablespoon garlic, minced
4.5 ounces Asiago cheese, shredded	1 cup mozzarella cheese, shredded
1 cup sour cream	¼ teaspoon onion powder

1. Mix all ingredients in a mixing bowl and stir until well combined. 2. Fill the buttered baking dish halfway with the mixture. 3. Arrange the baking dish into the cooking tray of the air fryer. 4. Place the drip pan at the bottom of the cooking chamber. Using the display panel, select Bake, adjust the temperature to 350 degrees F and the time to 20 minutes, then touch Start. 5. When the display indicates "Add Food," insert one cooking tray in the top position. 6. When the time is up, carefully remove them from the cooking tray. 7. Once done, serve and enjoy.

Per serving: Calories 68; Fat 5.8g; Sodium 104mg; Carbs

2.8g; Fiber 0.2g; Sugar 0.7g; Protein 1.7g

Lemon Ricotta Dip

Prep time: 10 minutes | Cook time: 15 minutes | Serves: 6

1 cup ricotta cheese, shredded	shredded
1 tablespoon lemon juice	2 tablespoons olive oil
¼ cup parmesan cheese, grated	1 teaspoon garlic, minced
	Pepper
½ cup mozzarella cheese,	Salt

1. Mix all ingredients in a mixing bowl and stir until well combined. 2. Fill the buttered baking dish halfway with the mixture. 3. Arrange the baking dish into the cooking tray of the air fryer. 4. Place the drip pan at the bottom of the cooking chamber. Using the display panel, select Bake, adjust the temperature to 400 degrees F and the time to 15 minutes, then touch Start. 5. When the display indicates "Add Food," insert one cooking tray in the top position. 6. When the time is up, carefully remove them from the cooking tray. 7. Once done, serve and enjoy.

Per serving: Calories 109; Fat 8.6g; Sodium 104mg; Carbs 2.5g; Fiber 0g; Sugar 0.2g; Protein 5.8g

Swiss Onion Dip

Prep time: 10 minutes | Cook time: 40 minutes | Serves: 8

1 cup mozzarella cheese, shredded	2 onions, chopped
1 cup cheddar cheese, shredded	1 ½ cups Swiss cheese, shredded
1 ½ cups mayonnaise	Pepper
	Salt

1. Whisk all ingredients in a mixing bowl and stir until well combined. 2. Fill the buttered baking dish halfway with the mixture. Arrange the baking dish into the cooking tray of the air fryer. 3. Place the drip pan at the bottom of the cooking chamber. Using the display panel, select Bake, adjust the temperature to 350 degrees F and the time to 40 minutes, then touch Start. 4. When the display indicates "Add Food," insert one cooking tray in the top position. 5. When the time is up, carefully remove them from the cooking tray. 6. Once done, serve and enjoy

Per serving: Calories 327; Fat 25.7g; Sodium 482mg; Carbs 14.5g; Fiber 0.6g; Sugar 4.3g; Protein 10.7g

Brussels Sprout Chips

Prep time: 10 minutes | Cook time: 10 minutes | Serves: 4

2 Brussels sprouts split leaves	¼ teaspoon pepper
2 tablespoons olive oil	½ teaspoon salt
¼ teaspoon garlic powder	

1. Toss the Brussels sprouts with the oil, garlic, pepper, and salt in a mixing bowl. 2. Arrange Brussels sprouts on a cooking tray. 3. Place the drip pan at the bottom of the cooking chamber. Using the display panel, select Air Fry, adjust the temperature to 350 degrees F and the time to 10 minutes, then touch Start. 4. When the display indicates "Add Food," insert one cooking tray in the top position 5. When the display indicates "turn Food," turn the food. 6. When the time is up, carefully remove them from the cooking tray. 7. Once done, serve and enjoy.

Per serving: Calories 80; Fat 7.2g; Sodium 302mg; Carbs 4.5g; Fiber 0g; Sugar 1.7g; Protein 1.5g

Mini Calzones

Prep time: 25 minutes | Cook time: 12 minutes | Serves: 8

1 cup pizza sauce	1-ounce shredded mozzarella
pizza dough, as needed	cheese
All-purpose flour	1-ounce sliced pepperoni

1. Roll out the pizza dough on a lightly floured surface until it's a quarter-inch thick. Cut ten dough rounds with the 3-inch cutter or a glass and place them on a baking sheet tray. 2. Gather the dough scraps, reroll them, and repeat the process to make more rounds. 3. 2 tablespoon sauce, 1 tablespoon pepperoni, and 1 tablespoon cheese on each round. Working with one dough at a time, fold it in half and pinch the corners to seal it. Once each calzone is sealed, crimp the edges and seal it more. Arrange Mini Calzones into the cooking tray of the air fryer. 4. Place the drip pan at the bottom of the cooking chamber. Using the display panel, select Air Fry, adjust the temperature to 375 degrees F and the time to 12 minutes, then touch Start. 5. When the display indicates "Add Food," insert one cooking tray in the top position. 6. When the display indicates "turn Food," turn the food. 7. When the time is up, carefully remove them from the cooking tray. 8. Once done, serve and enjoy.

Per serving: Calories 368; Fat 20g; Sodium 468mg; Carbs 39.5g; Fiber 2.9g; Sugar 1.1g; Protein 7.1g

Broccoli Tots with Italian Seasoning

Prep time: 10 minutes | Cook time: 16 minutes | Serves: 4

1 egg	2 cups broccoli rice, cooked
2 tablespoons almond flour	1 teaspoon Italian seasoning
2 cups cheddar cheese, shredded	Pepper
	Salt

1. Add all ingredients into the mixing bowl and mix until well combined. 2. Make small balls from the mixture and place them on a cooking tray. 3. Arrange balls into the cooking tray of the air fryer. 4. Place the drip pan at the bottom of the cooking chamber. Using the display panel, select Air Fry, adjust the temperature to 400 degrees F and the time to 15 minutes, then touch Start. 5. When the display indicates "Add Food," insert one cooking tray in the top position. 6. When the display indicates "turn Food," turn the food. 7. When the time is up, carefully remove them from the cooking tray. 8. Once done, serve and enjoy.

Per serving: Calories 322; Fat 24.4g; Sodium 535mg; Carbs 8.2g; Fiber 1.4g; Sugar 1.1g; Protein 17.7g

Almond Baked Broccoli Florets

Prep time: 10 minutes | Cook time: 15 minutes | Serves: 4

2 large eggs	ed
3 ½ cups broccoli florets	½ cup almond flour
½ teaspoon garlic powder	1 tablespoon unsweetened almond milk
¼ cup cheddar cheese, grated	
½ cup parmesan cheese, grat-	¼ teaspoon salt

1. Whisk the egg and almond milk together in a small bowl and set aside. 2. Combine almond flour, garlic powder, parmesan cheese, and salt in a separate basin. 3. After dipping the broccoli florets in the egg mixture, coat them with the almond flour. 4. Sprinkle cheddar cheese over the breaded broccoli florets and Arrange them on the cooking tray of the air fryer. 5. Place the drip pan at the bottom of the cooking chamber. Using the display panel, select Bake, adjust the temperature

to 400 degrees F and the time to 15 minutes, then touch Start. 6. When the display indicates "Add Food," insert one cooking tray in the top position. 7. When the time is up, carefully remove them from the cooking tray. 8. Once done, serve and enjoy.

Per serving: Calories 184; Fat 12.9g; Sodium 288mg; Carbs 9g; Fiber 3.6g; Sugar 2.2g; Protein 11.8g

Crispy Sweet Onion Rings

Prep time: 10 minutes | Cook time: 25 minutes | Serves: 4

2 eggs	½ teaspoon pepper
2 large sweet onions, cut into rings	½ teaspoon salt
	1 ½ cups almond flour
½ teaspoon garlic powder	Thyme

1. Combine almond flour, garlic powder, thyme, pepper, and salt in a mixing bowl. 2. Whisk the eggs in a separate basin. 3. After dipping the onion ring in the egg mixture, coat it with the almond flour. 4. Place the onion ring on the cooking tray that has been greased. 5. Place the drip pan at the bottom of the cooking chamber. Using the display panel, select Air Fry, adjust the temperature to 400 degrees F and the time to 25 minutes, then touch Start. 6. When the display indicates "Add Food," insert one cooking tray in the top position. 7. When the display indicates "turn Food," turn the food. 8. When the time is up, carefully remove them from the cooking tray. 9. Once done, serve and enjoy.

Per serving: Calories 303; Fat 23.3g; Sodium 325mg; Carbs 16.5g; Fiber 6.2g; Sugar 4.9g; Protein 12.7g

Crunchy Cashews

Prep time: 10 minutes | Cook time: 15 minutes | Serves: 4

1 cup cashews, soak in water overnight	2 tablespoons cinnamon

1. Drain the cashews thoroughly and dry them with a paper towel. 2. Sprinkle cinnamon over the cashews on the cooking tray. 3. Place the drip pan at the bottom of the cooking chamber. Using the display panel, select Roast, adjust the temperature to 350 degrees F and the time to 15 minutes, then touch Start. 4. When the display indicates "Add Food," insert one cooking tray in the top position. 5. When the time is up, carefully remove them from the cooking tray. 6. Once done, serve and enjoy. Store in an air-tight container.

Per serving: Calories 205; Fat 15.9g; Sodium 6mg; Carbs 13.5g; Fiber 2.8g; Sugar 1.8g; Protein 5.4g

Ginger Turkey Meatballs

Prep time: 10 minutes | Cook time: 25 minutes | Serves: 6

1-pound ground turkey	2 tablespoons fresh mint, chopped
¼ teaspoon pepper	
½ teaspoon ground coriander	¼ cup bell pepper, diced
1 ½ teaspoons ginger, grated	½ cup onion, diced
1 teaspoon ground cumin	½ teaspoon sea salt
2 tablespoons red curry paste	

1. In a mixing bowl, combine all ingredients and stir until well blended. 2. Form small balls from the beef mixture and lay them on a parchment-lined baking sheet. 3. Arrange balls into the cooking tray of the air fryer. 4. Place the drip pan at the bottom of the cooking chamber. Using the display panel, select Air Fry, adjust the temperature to 350 degrees F and the time to 25 minutes, then touch Start to begin preheating.

5. When the display indicates "Add Food," insert one cooking tray in the top position. 6. When the display indicates "turn Food," turn the food. 7. When the time is up, carefully remove them from the cooking tray. 8. Once done, serve and enjoy.

Per serving: Calories 177; Fat 5.8g; Sodium 104mg; Carbs 2.8g; Fiber 0.2g; Sugar 0.7g; Protein 1.7g

Cauliflower Popcorn

Prep time: 10 minutes | Cook time: 15 minutes | Serves: 6

1 medium cauliflower head, cut into florets	¾ cup almond flour
⅔ cup water	Pepper
	Salt

1. Fill a mixing basin halfway with cauliflower florets. 2. Toss the cauliflower florets with water, almond flour, pepper, and salt. 3. Arrange cauliflower florets on a cooking tray lined with parchment paper. Place the drip pan at the bottom of the cooking chamber. Using the display panel, select Air Fry, adjust the temperature to 400 degrees F and the time to 15 minutes, then touch Start. 4. When the display indicates "Add Food," insert one cooking tray in the top position. 5. When the display indicates "turn Food," turn the food. 6. When the time is up, carefully remove them from the cooking tray. 7. Once done, serve and enjoy.

Per serving: Calories 115; Fat 7.1g; Sodium 70mg; Carbs 10.4g; Fiber 5g; Sugar 0.7g; Protein 1.7g

Tasty Cauliflower Muffins

Prep time: 10 minutes | Cook time: 15 minutes | Serves: 6

1 cup cheddar cheese, shredded	eggs whites
½ cup cauliflower rice	Pepper
	Salt

1. In a mixing bowl, combine all ingredients and stir until well blended. 2. Fill a mini silicone muffin pan halfway with the mixture. 3. Arrange the muffin pan into the cooking tray of the air fryer. 4. Place the drip pan at the bottom of the cooking chamber. Using the display panel, select Bake, adjust the temperature to 400 degrees F and the time to 15 minutes, then touch Start. 5. When the display indicates "Add Food," insert one cooking tray in the top position. 6. When the time is up, carefully remove them from the cooking tray. 7. Once done, serve and enjoy.

Per serving: Calories 83; Fat 6.4g; Sodium 160mg; Carbs 0.9g; Fiber 0g; Sugar 0.5g; Protein 5.6g

Herbed Mushrooms

Prep time: 10 minutes | Cook time: 15 minutes | Serves: 4

1-pound mushrooms	1 garlic clove, minced
1 tablespoon basil, minced	½ tablespoon vinegar
1 teaspoon rosemary, chopped	Pepper
1 teaspoon thyme, chopped	Salt

1. Toss all of the ingredients together in a large mixing basin. 2. Arrange mushrooms into the cooking tray of the air fryer. 3. Place the drip pan at the bottom of the cooking chamber. Using the display panel, select Air Fry, adjust the temperature to 350 degrees F and the time to 15 minutes, then touch Start. 4. When the display indicates "Add Food," insert one cooking tray in the top position. 5. When the display indicates "turn Food," turn the food. 6. When the time is up, carefully remove them from the cooking tray. 7. Once done, serve and enjoy.

Per serving: Calories 28; Fat 0.4g; Sodium 46mg; Carbs 4.4g; Fiber 1.4g; Sugar 2g; Protein 3.7g

Baked Broccoli Nuggets

Prep time: 10 minutes | Cook time: 20 minutes | Serves: 4

2 egg whites	ded
2 cups broccoli florets, chopped	¼ cup almond flour
1 cup cheddar cheese, shred-	¼ teaspoon garlic powder
	⅛ teaspoon salt

1. In a mixing bowl, combine all ingredients and stir until well blended. 2. Place 20 scoops on a baking sheet and lightly press into nugget shapes. Place the drip pan at the bottom of the cooking chamber. Using the display panel, select Bake, adjust the temperature to 350 degrees F and the time to 20 minutes, then touch Start. 3. When the display indicates "Add Food," insert one cooking tray in the top position. 4. When the time is up, carefully remove them from the cooking tray. 5. Once done, serve and enjoy.

Per serving: Calories 179; Fat 13g; Sodium 207mg; Carbs 5.1g; Fiber 0g; Sugar 0.2g; Protein 5.8g

Cumin Carrot Fries

Prep time: 10 minutes | Cook time: 15 minutes | Serves: 2

½ pound carrots, peeled and cut into 4-inch-long pieces	¼ teaspoon cumin
¼ teaspoon paprika	½ tablespoon olive oil
	¼ teaspoon salt

1. In a large bowl, add all ingredients and toss until well coated. 2. Arrange carrot fries into the cooking tray of the air fryer. 3. Place the drip pan at the bottom of the cooking chamber. Using the display panel, select Air Fry, adjust the temperature to 400 degrees F and the time to 15 minutes, then touch Start. 4. When the display indicates "Add Food," insert one cooking tray in the top position. 5. When the display indicates "turn Food," turn the food. 6. When the time is up, carefully remove them from the cooking tray. 7. Once done, serve and enjoy.

Per serving: Calories 78; Fat 3.6g; Sodium 369mg; Carbs 11.5g; Fiber 2.9g; Sugar 5.6g; Protein 1g

Feta Jalapeno Poppers

Prep time: 10 minutes | Cook time: 13 minutes | Serves: 4

4 jalapeno peppers, sliced in half and deseeded	4 ounces' feta cheese, crumbled
¼ teaspoon chili powder	Pepper
½ teaspoon garlic, minced	Salt
2 tablespoons salsa	

1. Combine the cheese, salsa, chili powder, garlic, pepper, and salt in a small mixing bowl. 2. Fill each jalapeño half with cheese mixture and set on the cooking tray. 3. Place the drip pan at the bottom of the cooking chamber. Using the display panel, select Air Fry, adjust the temperature to 350 degrees F and the time to 13 minutes, then touch Start. 4. When the display indicates "Add Food," insert one cooking tray in the top position. 5. When the display indicates "turn Food," turn the food. 6. When the time is up, carefully remove them from the cooking tray. 7. Once done, serve and enjoy.

Per serving: Calories 84; Fat 6.3g; Sodium 772mg; Carbs 2.9g; Fiber 2.9g; Sugar 0.8g; Protein 4.4g

Spinach Dip with Chestnuts

Prep time: 10 minutes | Cook time: 40 minutes | Serves: 8

2 ounces' cream cheese, softened
1 cup mayonnaise
1 cup cheddar cheese, grated
1 cup frozen spinach, thawed,
and squeeze out all liquid
¼ teaspoon garlic powder
½ cup onion, minced
⅓ cup water chestnuts, drained and chopped

1. In a mixing bowl, combine all ingredients and stir until well blended. 2. Fill the oiled baking dish halfway with the bowl mixture. 3. Arrange the baking dish into the cooking tray of the air fryer. 4. Place the drip pan at the bottom of the cooking chamber. Using the display panel, select Bake, adjust the temperature to 300 degrees F and the time to 35 minutes, then touch Start. 5. When the display indicates "Add Food," insert one cooking tray in the top position. 6. When the time is up, carefully remove them from the cooking tray. 7. Once done, serve and enjoy.
Per serving: Calories 202; Fat 17g; Sodium 321mg; Carbs 8.7g; Fiber 0.2g; Sugar 2.3g; Protein 4.6g

Almond Zucchini Fries

Prep time: 10 minutes | Cook time: 10 minutes | Serves: 4

1 egg, lightly beaten
2 medium zucchinis, cut into fries' shape
1 teaspoon Italian seasoning
½ cup parmesan cheese, grated
½ cup almond flour
Pepper
Salt

1. In a mixing dish, crack one egg and whisk it thoroughly. 2. Combine almond flour, parmesan cheese, Italian seasoning, pepper, and salt in a shallow dish. 3. After dipping the zucchini fries in the egg, coat them with the almond flour mixture and lay them on the baking sheet. 4. Arrange zucchini fries into the cooking tray of the air fryer. 5. Place the drip pan at the bottom of the cooking chamber. Using the display panel, select Air Fry, adjust the temperature to 400 degrees F and the time to 10 minutes, then touch Start. 6. When the display indicates "Add Food," insert one cooking tray in the top position 7. When the display indicates "turn Food," turn the food. 8. When the time is up, carefully remove them from the cooking tray. 9. Once done, serve and enjoy.
Per serving: Calories 126; Fat 9.4g; Sodium 97mg; Carbs 6.6g; Fiber 2.6g; Sugar 2.4g; Protein 6.7g

Hot Chicken Cheese Dip

Prep time: 10 minutes | Cook time: 20 minutes | Serves: 6

2 cups chicken, cooked and shredded
¾ cup sour cream
2 ounces' cream cheese, softened
4 tablespoons hot sauce

1. In a mixing basin, combine all ingredients and stir until well blended. 2. Fill the buttered baking dish halfway with the mixture. 3. Arrange the baking dish into the cooking tray of the air fryer. 4. Place the drip pan at the bottom of the cooking chamber. Using the display panel, select Bake, adjust the temperature to 325 degrees F and the time to 20 minutes, then touch Start. 5. When the display indicates "Add Food," insert one cooking tray in the top position. 6. When the time is up, carefully remove them from the cooking tray. 7. Once done, serve and enjoy.
Per serving: Calories 166; Fat 10.8g; Sodium 326mg; Carbs 1.7g; Fiber 0g; Sugar 0.2g; Protein 15.7g

Baked Eggplant Chips

Prep time: 5 minutes | Cook time: 20 minutes | Serves: 4

1 eggplant, cut into 1-inch slices
½ teaspoon Italian seasoning
1 teaspoon paprika
2 tablespoons olive oil
⅛ teaspoon cayenne
½ teaspoon red pepper
1 teaspoon garlic powder

1. Toss all of the ingredients together in a mixing basin. 2. Arrange the eggplant slices on a cooking tray. 3. Place the drip pan at the bottom of the cooking chamber. Using the display panel, select Air Fry, adjust the temperature to 375 degrees F and the time to 20 minutes, then touch Start. 4. When the display indicates "Add Food," insert one cooking tray in the top position. 5. When the display indicates "turn Food," turn the food. 6. When the time is up, carefully remove them from the cooking tray. 7. Once done, serve and enjoy.
Per serving: Calories 99; Fat 7.5g; Sodium 3mg; Carbs 8.7g; Fiber 4.5g; Sugar 4.5g; Protein 1.5g

Cheese Spinach Dip

Prep time: 10 minutes | Cook time: 35 minutes | Serves: 6

2 ounces frozen spinach, thawed, drained & chopped
2 ounces' cream cheese, softened
¼ teaspoon black pepper
1 teaspoon onion powder
½ cup Asiago cheese, shredded
½ cup parmesan cheese, grated
2 garlic cloves, minced
½ cup mayonnaise
¼ teaspoon salt

1. Combine all ingredients (excluding spinach) in a mixing bowl and stir until well blended. 2. Mix in the spinach until everything is nicely mixed. 3. Fill the baking dish halfway with the mixture. 4. Arrange the baking dish into the cooking tray of the air fryer. 5. Place the drip pan at the bottom of the cooking chamber. Using the display panel, select Bake, adjust the temperature to 350 degrees F and the time to 35 minutes, then touch Start. 6. When the display indicates "Add Food," insert one cooking tray in the top position. 7. When the time is up, carefully remove them from the cooking tray. 8. Once done, serve and enjoy.
Per serving: Calories 130; Fat 11.1g; Sodium 322mg; Carbs 6.1g; Fiber 0.3g; Sugar 1.7g; Protein 2.7g

Spicy Salmon Bites

Prep time: 10 minutes | Cook time: 12 minutes | Serves: 4

1-pound salmon fillets, boneless and cubes
½ teaspoon chili powder
2 teaspoons olive oil
Pepper
Salt

1. Toss all of the ingredients together in a mixing bowl. Arrange salmon cubes onto the cooking tray. 2. Place the drip pan at the bottom of the cooking chamber. Using the display panel, select Air Fry, adjust the temperature to 350 degrees F and the time to 12 minutes, then touch Start. 3. When the display indicates "Add Food," insert one cooking tray in the top position. 4. When the display indicates "turn Food," turn the food. 5. When the time is up, carefully remove them from the cooking tray. 6. Once done, serve and enjoy.
Per serving: Calories 171; Fat 9.4g; Sodium 92mg; Carbs 0.2g; Fiber 0.1g; Sugar 0g; Protein 22g

Creamy Turkey Dip

Prep time: 10 minutes | Cook time: 25 minutes | Serves: 6

1-pound turkey breast, skinless, boneless, and minced	1 cup tomatoes, chopped
2 shallots, chopped	1 tablespoon garlic, minced
1 tablespoon olive oil	Pepper
¼ cup heavy cream	Salt

1. In a large mixing basin, combine all ingredients and stir until well blended. 2. Fill the buttered baking dish halfway with the mixture. 3. Arrange the baking dish into the cooking tray of the air fryer. 4. Place the drip pan at the bottom of the cooking chamber. Using the display panel, select Bake, adjust the temperature to 380 degrees F and the time to 25 minutes, then touch Start. 5. When the display indicates "Add Food", insert one cooking tray in the top position. 6. When the time is up, carefully remove them from the cooking tray. 7. Once done, serve and enjoy

Per serving: Calories 126; Fat 5.5g; Sodium 798mg; Carbs 5.5g; Fiber 0.8g; Sugar 3.5g; Protein 14.3g

Coriander Mushroom Caps

Prep time: 10 minutes | Cook time: 15 minutes | Serves: 4

1-pound mushroom caps	¼ teaspoon onion powder
1 garlic clove, minced	¼ teaspoon cayenne
½ tablespoon vinegar	Pepper
½ teaspoon ground coriander	Salt
¼ teaspoon garlic powder	

1. Toss all of the ingredients together in a large mixing bowl. 2. Arrange mushrooms into the cooking tray of the air fryer. 3. Place the drip pan at the bottom of the cooking chamber. Using the display panel, select Air Fry, adjust the temperature to 350 degrees F and the time to 15 minutes, then touch Start. 4. When the display indicates "Add Food," insert one cooking tray in the top position 5. When the display indicates "turn Food", turn the food. 6. When the time is up, carefully remove them from the cooking tray. 7. Once done, serve and enjoy. 8. Spread mushrooms onto the cooking tray.

Per serving: Calories 27; Fat 0.3g; Sodium 46mg; Carbs 4.3g; Fiber 1.2g; Sugar 2.1g; Protein 3.7g

Creamy Shrimp Dip

Prep time: 10 minutes | Cook time: 8 minutes | Serves: 6

1-pound shrimp, peeled, deveined, and chopped	1 cup heavy cream
1 teaspoon chili powder	2 tablespoons olive oil

1. In a mixing bowl, combine all ingredients and stir until well blended. 2. Fill the buttered baking dish halfway with the mixture. Arrange the baking dish into the cooking tray of the air fryer. 3. Place the drip pan at the bottom of the cooking chamber. Using the display panel, select Bake, adjust the temperature to 380 degrees F and the time to 8 minutes, then touch Start. 4. When the display indicates "Add Food", insert one cooking tray in the top position. 5. When the time is up, carefully remove them from the cooking tray. 6. Once done, serve and enjoy.

Per serving: Calories 200; Fat 13.4g; Sodium 197mg; Carbs 2g; Fiber 0.2g; Sugar 0.1g; Protein 17.7g

Cajun Zucchini Slices

Prep time: 10 minutes | Cook time: 16 minutes | Serves: 2

1 ¼ cup zucchini slices	Pepper
1 teaspoon Cajun seasoning	Salt
1 tablespoon olive oil	

1. Combine zucchini slices, oil, Cajun seasoning, pepper, and salt in a mixing bowl. 2. Arrange zucchini slices onto the cooking tray. 3. Place the drip pan at the bottom of the cooking chamber. Using the display panel, select Air Fry, adjust the temperature to 370 degrees F and the time to 16 minutes, then touch Start. 4. When the display indicates "Add Food," insert one cooking tray in the top position. 5. When the display indicates "turn Food," turn the food. 6. When the time is up, carefully remove them from the cooking tray. 7. Once done, serve and enjoy.

Per serving: Calories 71; Fat 7.1g; Sodium 110mg; Carbs 2.4g; Fiber 0.8g; Sugar 1.2g; Protein 0.9g

Ranch Chicken Wings

Prep time: 10 minutes | Cook time: 20 minutes | Serves: 4

1 pound of chicken wings	soning
2 tablespoons. olive oil	3 garlic cloves, minced
1 ½ tablespoons. ranch sea-	

1. Toss chicken wings with garlic, oil, and ranch seasoning. 2. Arrange chicken wings onto the cooking tray. 3. Place the drip pan at the bottom of the cooking chamber. Using the display panel, select Air Fry, adjust the temperature to 360 degrees F and the time to 20 minutes, then touch Start. 4. When the display indicates "Add Food", insert one cooking tray in the top position. 5. When the display indicates "turn Food", turn the food. 6. When the time is up, carefully remove them from the cooking tray. 7. Once done, serve and enjoy.

Per serving: Calories 286; Fat 15.4g; Sodium 503mg; Carbs 0.7g; Fiber 0.1g; Sugar 0g; Protein 33g

Toothsome Beef Meatballs

Prep time: 10 minutes | Cook time: 15 minutes | Serves: 4

1 pound of ground beef	1 tablespoon almond flour
1 cup olives, pitted and chopped	1 tablespoon chives, chopped
1 tablespoon oregano, chopped	Pepper
	Salt

1. In a mixing bowl, combine all ingredients and stir until well blended. 2. Make little meatballs out of the mixture. Arrange meatballs into the cooking tray of the air fryer. 3. Place the drip pan at the bottom of the cooking chamber. Using the display panel, select Air Fry, adjust the temperature to 350 degrees F and the time to 15 minutes, then touch Start. 4. When the display indicates "Add Food," insert one cooking tray in the top position. 5. When the display indicates "turn Food," turn the food. 6. When the time is up, carefully remove them from the cooking tray. 7. Once done, serve and enjoy.

Per serving: Calories 263; Fat 11.7g; Sodium 407mg; Carbs 3.3g; Fiber 1.8g; Sugar 0.1g; Protein 35.2g

Parmesan Carrot Fries

Prep time: 10 minutes | Cook time: 15 minutes | Serves: 4

4 carrots, peeled and cut into fries
2 tablespoons parmesan cheese, grated
2 tablespoons olive oil
Pepper
Salt

1. Toss the carrots in a large mixing bowl with the remaining ingredients. 2. Arrange carrots fries onto the cooking tray of the air fryer. 3. Place the drip pan at the bottom of the cooking chamber. Using the display panel, select Air Fry, adjust the temperature to 350 degrees F and the time to 15 minutes, then touch Start. 4. When the display indicates "Add Food," insert one cooking tray in the top position. 5. When the display indicates "turn Food," turn the food. 6. When the time is up, carefully remove them from the cooking tray. 7. Once done, serve and enjoy.

Per serving: Calories 130; Fat 9.4g; Sodium 97mg; Carbs 6.6g; Fiber 2.6g; Sugar 2.4g; Protein 6.7g

Almond Broccoli Balls with Cilantro

Prep time: 10 minutes | Cook time: 30 minutes | Serves: 4

2 cups broccoli florets
¼ cup onion, minced
1 cup cheddar cheese, shredded
½ cup almond flour
2 eggs, lightly beaten
1 teaspoon Cajun seasoning
1 garlic clove, minced
2 tablespoons fresh cilantro, chopped
Pepper
Salt

1. Add broccoli into the boiling water and cook until tender. 2. Drain broccoli well and transfer in food processor and process until minced. Transfer to the bowl. 3. Add remaining ingredients and mix until just combined. 4. Arrange balls into the cooking tray of the air fryer. 5. Place the drip pan at the bottom of the cooking chamber. Using the display panel, select Air Fry, adjust the temperature to 400 degrees F and the time to 30 minutes, then touch Start. 6. When the display indicates "Add Food," insert one cooking tray in the top position. 7. When the display indicates "turn Food," turn the food. 8. When the time is up, carefully remove them from the cooking tray. 9. Once done, serve and enjoy.

Per serving: Calories 245; Fat 18.7g; Sodium 273mg; Carbs 7.5g; Fiber 2.9g; Sugar 1.9g; Protein 14.2g

Basil Pesto Poppers

Prep time: 10 minutes | Cook time: 15 minutes | Serves: 6

3 jalapeno peppers, halved and remove seeds
½ cup cheddar cheese, shredded
ded
¼ cup cream cheese
3 tablespoons basil pesto

1. Combine pesto, cheese, and cream cheese in a mixing bowl. 2. Fill each half of a jalapeño with the pesto cheese mixture. Arrange jalapeno into the cooking tray of the air fryer. 3. Place the drip pan at the bottom of the cooking chamber. Using the display panel, select Air Fry, adjust the temperature to 400 degrees F and the time to 15 minutes, then touch Start. 4. When the display indicates "Add Food," insert one cooking tray in the top position. 5. When the display indicates "turn Food," turn the food. 6. When the time is up, carefully remove them from the cooking tray. 7. Once done, serve and enjoy.

Per serving: Calories 75; Fat 6.6g; Sodium 271mg; Carbs 0.9g; Fiber 0.3g; Sugar 0.3g; Protein 3.2g

Parsley Turkey Meatballs

Prep time: 10 minutes | Cook time: 25 minutes | Serves: 6

1 egg, lightly beaten
1-pound ground turkey
1 teaspoon garlic powder
1 ½ tablespoons olive oil
¾ cup parmesan cheese, grated
¼ cup fresh parsley, chopped
½ teaspoon cayenne
1 teaspoon paprika
1 teaspoon onion powder
½ teaspoon salt

1. Add all ingredients into the mixing bowl and mix until well combined. 2. Make small balls from the meat mixture. 3. Arrange meatballs into the cooking tray of the air fryer. 4. Place the drip pan at the bottom of the cooking chamber. Using the display panel, select Air Fry, adjust the temperature to 400 degrees F and the time to 25 minutes, then touch Start. 5. When the display indicates "Add Food," insert one cooking tray in the top position 6. When the display indicates "turn Food," turn the food. 7. When the time is up, carefully remove them from the cooking tray. 8. Once done, serve and enjoy.

Per serving: Calories 205; Fat 13.4g; Sodium 319mg; Carbs 1.3g; Fiber 0.3g; Sugar 0.4g; Protein 23g

Garlicky Cauliflower Tots

Prep time: 10 minutes | Cook time: 18 minutes | Serves: 16

1 large egg
1 tablespoon butter
2 cups cauliflower, steamed and shredded
¼ teaspoon onion powder
¼ teaspoon garlic powder
½ cup parmesan cheese, shredded
Pepper
Salt

1. In a mixing bowl, combine all ingredients and stir until well blended. 2. To make little tots, combine all ingredients in a mixing bowl. Arrange tots into the cooking tray of the air fryer. 3. Place the drip pan at the bottom of the cooking chamber. Using the display panel, select Air Fry, adjust the temperature to 400 degrees F and the time to 18 minutes, then touch Start. 4. When the display indicates "Add Food," insert one cooking tray in the top position. 5. When the display indicates "turn Food," turn the food. 6. When the time is up, carefully remove them from the cooking tray. 7. Once done, serve and enjoy.

Per serving: Calories 17; Fat 1.2g; Sodium 33mg; Carbs 0.8g; Fiber 0.3g; Sugar 0.3g; Protein 0.9g

Sausage and Onion Rolls

Prep time: 15 minutes | Cook time: 15 minutes | Serves: 12

1 pound (454g) bulk breakfast sausage
½ cup finely chopped onion
½ cup fresh bread crumbs
½ teaspoon dried mustard
½ teaspoon dried sage
¼ teaspoon cayenne pepper
1 large egg, beaten
1 garlic clove, minced
2 sheets of frozen puff pastry, thawed
All-purpose flour for dusting

1. Break up the sausage in a medium bowl. Combine the onion, bread crumbs, mustard, sage, cayenne pepper, egg, and garlic in a large mixing bowl. 2. Half the sausage mixture and cover each half tightly in plastic wrap. Refrigerate for 5 to 10 minutes before serving. 3. On a lightly floured work surface, place the pastry sheets. To smooth out the dough, lightly roll it out. 4. Take one of the sausage packages out of it and roll it into a long roll. Remove the plastic wrap from the sausage and place it 1 inch from one of the long ends of the puff pastry. 5. To seal the pastry, roll it around the sausage and pinch the sides together. Continue with the remaining pastry sheet

and meat. 6. Cut the logs into lengths of about 1½ inches. Place the sausage rolls cut-side down in the baking pan. Place the baking pan into the cooking tray of the air fryer. 7. Using the display panel, select Roast, adjust the temperature to 350 degrees F and the time to 10 minutes, then touch Start. 8. When the display indicates "Add Food," insert one cooking tray at the bottom-most position. 9. When the program is complete, remove the food and allow 5 minutes to cool before serving.

Per serving: Calories 94; Fat 20.3g; Sodium 374mg; Carbs 16.2g; Fiber 0.8g; Sugar 1g; Protein 7.6g

Dehydrated Bacon Slices

Prep time: 03 minutes | Cook time: 4 hours and 10 minutes | Serves: 4

6 slices bacon	2 tablespoons rice vinegar
3 tablespoons light brown sugar	2 tablespoons chili paste
	1 tablespoon soy sauce

1. Mix brown sugar, rice vinegar, chili paste, and soy sauce in a mixing bowl. 2. Mix in the bacon slices until they are all equally coated. 3. Place in the refrigerator for up to 3 hours or until ready to dehydrate. 4. After that, arrange the bacon on the cooking tray. 5. Place the drip pan in the bottom of the cooking chamber and insert one cooking tray in the top-most position. 6. Using the display panel, select DEHYDRATE, adjust the temperature to 160 degrees F and the time to 4 hours, then touch START. 7. When the Dehydrate program is complete, remove it from the tray and set it aside to cool for 5 minutes before serving.

Per serving: Calories 212; Fat 13.2g; Sodium 976mg; Carbs 10.3g; Fiber 0g; Sugar 8.7g; Protein 11.3 g

Bacon Roasted Jalapeño Poppers

Prep time: 15 minutes | Cook time: 15 minutes | Serves: 8

6 ounces (170g) of cream cheese at room temperature	deseeded and sliced in half lengthwise
4 ounces (113g) shredded Cheddar cheese	2 slices of cooked bacon, chopped
1 teaspoon chili powder	¼ cup panko bread crumbs
12 large jalapeño peppers,	1 tablespoon butter, melted

1. Mix the cream cheese, Cheddar cheese, and chili powder in a medium mixing bowl. Fill the jalapeño halves with the cheese mixture and lay them on the cooking tray. 2. Combine the bacon, bread crumbs, and butter in a small mixing basin. Over the jalapeño halves, sprinkle the mixture. 3. Place the drip pan at the bottom of the cooking chamber. Using the display panel, select Roast, adjust the temperature to 375 degrees F and the time to 15 minutes, then touch Start to begin preheating. 4. When the display indicates "Add Food," insert one cooking tray at the bottom-most position. 5. When the Roast program is complete, remove the tray from the air fryer, then let the poppers cool for 5 minutes before serving.

Per serving: Calories 193; Fat 16.2g; Sodium 850mg; Carbs 5g; Fiber 1.1g; Sugar 1.1g; Protein 7.7 g

Slices Choco-Hazelnut Spread

Prep time: 10 minutes | Cook time: 6 hours | Serves: 3

2 large oranges, cut into ⅛-inch-thick slices	½ teaspoon ground cinnamon
½ teaspoon ground star anise	1 tablespoon Choco-hazelnut spread

1. Dash seasonings on the orange slices. 2. Place the drip pan in the bottom of the cooking chamber and insert one cooking tray in the mid-most position. 3. Using the display panel, select Dehydrate, then adjust the temperature to 140 degrees F and the time to 6 hours, then touch Start. 4. When the Dehydrate program is complete, remove it from the tray and set it aside to cool for 5 minutes before serving. 5. Serve with chocolate hazelnut spread.

Per serving: Calories 90; Fat 2.2g; Sodium 3mg; Carbs 18.2g; Fiber 3.3g; Sugar 14.7g; Protein 1.5 g

Spicy and Sweet Walnut

Prep time: 05 minutes | Cook time: 15 minutes | Serves: 4

1 pound (454g) of walnut halves and pieces
½ cup granulated sugar
3 tablespoons vegetable oil
1 teaspoon cayenne pepper
½ teaspoon fine salt

1. Soak the walnuts for a minute or two in a big dish of boiling water. The walnuts should be drained. 2. To coat well, add the sugar, vegetable oil, and cayenne pepper. In the cooking tray, spread the walnuts in a single layer. Place the drip pan in the bottom of the cooking chamber and insert one cooking tray in the mid-most position. 3. Using the display panel, select Roast, adjust the temperature to 325 degrees F and the time to 15 minutes, then touch Start. When the display indicates "Add Food," insert one cooking tray in the bottom-most position. 4. When the Roast program is complete, remove it from the tray and set it aside to cool for 5 minutes before serving. Sprinkle the nuts with the salt.

Per serving: Calories 925; Fat 84.2g; Sodium 291mg; Carbs 37.3g; Fiber 12.3g; Sugar 25.7g; Protein 20.1 g

Mini Pork Burgers

Prep time: 05 minutes | Cook time: 25 minutes | Serves: 4

500g Minced pork	Spices
Salt	1 egg
Ground pepper	1 tablespoon grated bread
Garlic Powder	Mini Bread for Burgers
Fresh parsley	

1. Add salt, pepper, garlic powder, a tablespoon of chopped fresh parsley, and a teaspoon of spices to the ground beef. 2. To make the meat more uniform, toss an egg and one or two teaspoons of breadcrumbs. Whisk all ingredients in a large mixing bowl and stir well until everything is properly combined. 3. Cover it with transparent plastic wrap and chill it for at least half an hour or more. It will be simpler when you've handled the meat and shaped it into a hamburger. 4. Remove the meat after the time has passed. Remove it from the paper that encircles the container and begin molding and shaping the little burger. 5. Place the burger patties in the cooking tray of the air fryer in a single layer. 6. Place the drip pan at the bottom of the cooking chamber. Using the display panel, select Air Fry, adjust the temperature to 325 degrees F and the time to 15 minutes, then touch Start. 7. When the display indicates "Add Food," insert both cooking trays in the top-most position. 8. When the display indicates "turn Food," turn the food. 9. When the hash burger patties are cooked, carefully remove them from the cooking tray.

Per serving: Calories 198; Fat 5.5g; Sodium 127mg; Carbs 0.8g; Fiber 0.2g; Sugar 0.3g; Protein 34.3 g

Coconut Turkey-Onion Meatballs

Prep time: 10 minutes | Cook time: 15 minutes | Serves: 8

2 pounds of ground turkey
½ cup coconut flour
1 tablespoon fresh ginger, grated
1 teaspoon garlic, minced
2 tablespoons fresh cilantro,

chopped
2 tablespoons green onion, sliced
2 eggs, lightly beaten
1 tablespoon sesame oil
1 teaspoon sea salt

1. In a mixing bowl, combine all ingredients and stir until well blended. 2. Make little meatballs out of the mixture. 3. Arrange meatballs into the cooking tray of the air fryer. 4. Place the drip pan at the bottom of the cooking chamber. Using the display panel, select Air Fry, adjust the temperature to 400 degrees F and the time to 15 minutes, then touch Start. 5. When the display indicates "Add Food," insert one cooking tray in the top position. 6. When the display indicates "turn Food," turn the food. 7. When the time is up, carefully remove them from the cooking tray. 8. Once done, serve and enjoy.
Per serving: Calories 259; Fat 15.4g; Sodium 373mg; Carbs 1.3g; Fiber 0.5g; Sugar 0.2g; Protein 32.7g

Honey Roasted Carrots

Prep time: 05 minutes | Cook time: 20 minutes | Serves: 4

1 tablespoon honey, raw
3 cups baby carrots
1 tablespoon olive oil

Sea salt & black pepper to taste

1. Put all the ingredients in a bowl, and spread them into the cooking tray of the air fryer. 2. Place the drip pan at the bottom of the cooking chamber. Using the display panel, select Roast, adjust the temperature to 390 degrees F and the time to 20 minutes, then touch Start. 3. When the display indicates "Add Food," insert both cooking trays in the top-most position. 4. When the hash carrots are cooked, carefully remove them from the cooking tray.
Per serving: Calories 68; Fat 3.5g; Sodium 50mg; Carbs 9.8g; Fiber 1.9g; Sugar 7.3g; Protein 0.4 g

Veggie Wonton Steamed Pot Stickers

Prep time: 20 minutes | Cook time: 10 minutes | Serves: 30

½ cup finely chopped cabbage
2 teaspoons low-sodium soy sauce
2 tablespoons cocktail sauce
30 wonton wrappers
¼ cup finely chopped red bell

pepper
3 tablespoons water, and more for brushing the wrappers
2 green onions, finely chopped
1 egg, beaten

1. In a small mixing bowl, combine the cabbage, bell pepper, chives, egg cocktail sauce, and soy sauce. 2. 1 teaspoon of the filling should be placed in the center of each wonton wrapper. Cover the filling by folding the wrap in half. Using water, moisten the edges and seal them. You can use your fingers to fold the edges of the wrapper to resemble the restaurant stickers. Water should be brushed on them. 3. Put pot-stickers into two cooking trays. 4. Place the drip pan in the bottom of the cooking chamber and insert one cooking tray in the top-most position and one tray in the middle position. 5. Using the display panel, select Air Fry, adjust the temperature to 325 degrees F and the time to 10 minutes, then touch Start. 6. When the display indicates "Add Food," insert both cooking trays in the top-most position and one tray in the middle. 7. When the

display indicates "turn Food," turn the food and rotate the tray means middle one place into the top and top one place into the middle. 8. When the Air Fry program is complete, remove it from the tray and set it aside to cool for 5 minutes before serving. Sprinkle the nuts with the salt.
Per serving: Calories 101; Fat 0.6g; Sodium 268mg; Carbs 19.9g; Fiber 0.7g; Sugar 1g; Protein 3.4 g

Green Nachos with Oregano

Prep time: 15 minutes | Cook time: 10 minutes | Serves: 6

8 ounces (227g) of tortilla chips
3 cups shredded Monterey Jack cheese, divided
2 (7oz/198g) cans chopped green chilies, drained
1 (8oz/227g) can tomato sauce

¼ teaspoon dried oregano
¼ teaspoon granulated garlic
¼ teaspoon freshly ground black pepper
Pinch cinnamon
Pinch cayenne pepper

1. In the cooking tray of the air fryer, arrange the tortilla chips in a single layer, close together. 1-½ cup of cheese should be over the chips. 2. Arrange the green chilies as equally as possible on top of the cheese. The remaining 1-½ cup of cheese should be sprinkled on top. 3. Place the drip pan at the bottom of the cooking chamber. Using the display panel, select Roast, adjust the temperature to 375 degrees F and the time to 10 minutes, then touch Start. 4. When the display indicates "Add Food," insert one cooking tray in the bottom-most position. 5. When the Roast program is complete, remove the tray from air fryer 6. In a separate bowl, combine the remaining sauce ingredients. 7. sprinkle the sauce over them. Serve warm.
Per serving: Calories 306; Fat 18.3g; Sodium 574mg; Carbs 20g; Fiber 3.1g; Sugar 2.7g; Protein 16.6g

Dill Zucchini-Onion Cakes

Prep time: 10 minutes | Cook time: 10 minutes | Serves: 8

Cooking Spray
½ cup dill, chopped
1 egg
½ cup whole wheat flour
Salt and black pepper to the

taste
1 yellow onion, chopped
2 garlic cloves, minced
3 zucchinis, grated

1. Combine zucchinis, garlic, onion, flour, salt, pepper, egg, and dill in a mixing dish and whisk well. Form small patties from this mixture and spray with cooking spray. Arrange patties into the cooking tray of the air fryer. 2. Place the drip pan at the bottom of the cooking chamber. Using the display panel, select Air Fry, adjust the temperature to 370 degrees F and the time to 6 minutes, then touch Start. 3. When the display indicates "Add Food," insert one cooking tray in the top position. 4. When the display indicates "turn Food," turn the food. 5. When the time is up, carefully remove them from the cooking tray. 6. Once done, serve and enjoy.
Per serving: Calories 62; Fat 0.9g; Sodium 22mg; Carbs 11.6g; Fiber 1.5g; Sugar 1.9g; Protein 3.8g

Shrimp Muffins

Prep time: 10 minutes | Cook time: 26 minutes | Serves: 6

1 spaghetti squash, peeled and halved
2 tablespoons mayonnaise
1 cup mozzarella, shredded
8 ounces' shrimp, peeled, cooked, and chopped
1 and ½ cups panko
1 teaspoon parsley flakes
1 garlic clove, minced
Salt and black pepper to the taste
Cooking; Spray

1. Arrange squash into the cooking tray of the air fryer 2. Place the drip pan at the bottom of the cooking chamber. Using the display panel, select Roast, adjust the temperature to 350 degrees F and the time to 15 minutes, then touch Start. 3. When the display indicates "Add Food," insert one cooking tray in the top position 4. When the time is up, carefully remove them from the cooking tray, then set them to cool before scraping the flesh into a basin. Stir in the salt, pepper, parsley flakes, panko, shrimp, mayo, and mozzarella. 5. Spray a muffin tray that suits your air fryer; 6. Arrange the muffins tray into the cooking tray of the air fryer 7. Place the drip pan at the bottom of the cooking chamber. Using the display panel, select Bake, adjust the temperature to 350 degrees F and the time to 10 minutes, then touch Start. 8. When the display indicates "Add Food," insert one cooking tray in the top position. 9. When the time is up, carefully remove them from the cooking tray. 10. Enjoy!

Per serving: Calories 138; Fat 3.2g; Sodium 185mg; Carbs 15.6g; Fiber 0g; Sugar 0.3g; Protein 11.8g

Vanilla Pâte à Choux

Prep time: 05 minutes | Cook time: 15minutes | Serves: 6

2 tablespoons coconut oil, melted	1 teaspoon vanilla extract
	3 cups all-purpose flour
2 tablespoons Aquafaba	¼ teaspoon ground cinnamon

1. Combine the coconut oil, Aquafaba, and vanilla with the paddle attachment. Add the flour and cinnamon in a slow, steady stream. 2. Knead the dough for about 3 minutes, then cover it with a clean dish towel and let it rise in a warm location for 1 hour. 3. Cut the dough into 24 squares after rolling it out. 4. Place the squares in a baking pan that has been lightly oiled. Place the drip pan at the bottom of the cooking chamber. 5. Using the control panel, select Air Fry, adjust the temperature to 360 degrees F and the time to 15 minutes, then touch Start. 6. When the display indicates "Add Food," place the pan on the cooking tray in the center. 7. When displaying "turn Food," turn the food and cook them. 8. Serve with toppings of choice, and enjoy!

Per serving: Calories 269; Fat 5.1g; Sodium 1mg; Carbs 47.9g; Fiber 1.8g; Sugar 0.3g; Protein 6.5 g

Coconut and Blueberry Cookies

Prep time: 05 minutes | Cook time: 15 minutes | Serves: 6

1 egg	½ teaspoon ground cinnamon
½ cup coconut sugar	½ cup all-purpose flour
¼ cup coconut oil	½ cup coconut flour
4 tablespoons coconut milk	½ teaspoon baking powder
½ teaspoon pure vanilla extract	A pinch of kosher salt
1 teaspoon crystallized ginger	½ cup blueberries

1. Set aside a muffin tray that has been sprayed with nonstick cooking spray. 2. After properly mixing the dry ingredients, incorporate the wet components. Combine the wet and dry ingredients in a mixing bowl and stir until thoroughly combined. Combine the berries and fold them in. Place the muffin tray into the cooking tray. 3. Place the drip pan at the bottom of the cooking chamber. Using the control panel, select Bake, then adjust the temperature to 330 degrees F and the time to 15 minutes or until tender and lightly caramelized, then touch Start. 4. When the display indicates "Add Food," place the cooking tray in the center position. 5. Serve and enjoy!

Per serving: Calories 357; Fat 18.8g; Sodium 41mg; Carbs 47.1g; Fiber 2g; Sugar 25.2g; Protein 3.7 g

Lime Vanilla Cheesecake

Prep time: 05 minutes | Cook time: 25 minutes | Serves: 9

Crust:	½ cup double cream
8 ounces Oreos, crushed	4 large eggs
6 tablespoons unsalted butter, softened	A pinch of kosher salt
	A pinch of grated nutmeg
½ teaspoon ground cinnamon	2 tablespoons freshly squeezed
Filling:	key lime juice
20 ounces of cream cheese	½ teaspoon coconut extract
1 cup granulated sugar	½ teaspoon vanilla extract

1. Mix all the crust ingredients; press the crust into a baking pan. Place the drip pan at the bottom of the cooking chamber. 2. Using the control panel, select Bake, then adjust the temperature to 400 degrees F and the time to 6 minutes, then touch Start. 3. When the display indicates "Add Food," place the cooking tray in the center. 4. When time is up, open the unit and allow it to cool on wire racks. 5. Using an electric mixer, whip the cream cheese, sugar, and double cream until fluffy; add one egg at a time and continue to beat until creamy; mix in the salt, nutmeg, and key lime juice, coconut extract, and vanilla extract. 6. Pour the topping mixture on top of the crust, place the baking pan into a cooking tray of your air fryer and place the drip pan in the bottom of the cooking chamber. 7. Using the control panel, select Bake, then adjust the temperature to 390 degrees F and the time to 15 minutes, then touch Start. 8. When the display indicates "Add Food," place the cooking tray in the center. 9. Allow your cheesecake to chill in your refrigerator before serving. Enjoy!

Per serving: Calories 533; Fat 39.6g; Sodium 421mg; Carbs 43.4g; Fiber 1.4g; Sugar 22.8g; Protein 8.8 g

Baked Nut and Apples

Prep time: 05 minutes | Cook time: 15 minutes | Serves: 4

4 large apples	½ teaspoon ground cardamom
½ cup old-fashioned rolled oats	½ teaspoon ground cinnamon
	¼ teaspoon ground nutmeg
¼ cup walnuts, chopped	⅛ teaspoon kosher salt
2 tablespoons coconut oil	2 tablespoons raisins
¼ cup brown sugar	

1. Remove the stem and seeds from the apples with a paring knife, leaving deep holes. 2. Combine the remaining ingredients in a mixing dish and stir well. Fill the apples with the filling. 3. Put the apples in a cooking tray of the air fryer and place the drip pan at the bottom of the cooking chamber. 4. Using the control panel, select Air Fry, adjust the temperature to 350 degrees F and the time to 15 minutes, then touch Start. 5. When the display indicates "Add Food," place the cooking tray in the center. 6. Close the door. 7. When time ends, carefully remove the apple and serve.

Per serving: Calories 311; Fat 12.6g; Sodium 6mg; Carbs 51.4g; Fiber 7.4g; Sugar 34.8g; Protein 4 g

Cardamom Berry Crisp

Prep time: 05 minutes | Cook time: 15 minutes | Serves: 8

1 cup frozen mixed berries	½ cup sugar
1 teaspoon crystallized ginger	½ teaspoon ground cardamom
½ cup rolled oats	½ teaspoon ground cinnamon
½ cup all-purpose flour	¼ cup soy butter
2 large eggs, beaten	

1. Toss the berries with the crystallized ginger in a lightly oiled baking pan. 2. Combine all remaining ingredients in a mixing bowl until creamy and homogeneous. 3. Place a few teaspoons of batter on the fruit layer. 4. Place the drip pan at the bottom of the cooking chamber. Using the control panel, select Air Fry, then adjust the temperature to 360 degrees F and the time to 15 minutes until the topping is golden brown, then touch Start. 5. When the display indicates "Add Food," place the cooking tray in the center. 6. Close the door. 7. When time ends, carefully remove from the unit and serve.

Per serving: Calories 129; Fat 2.2g; Sodium 22mg; Carbs

24.6g; Fiber 1.5g; Sugar 14.8g; Protein 3.4 g

Vanilla Brownie with Sultanas

Prep time: 05 minutes	Cook time: 15 minutes	Serves: 8
1 cup all-purpose flour	1 cup sugar
1 cup unsweetened cocoa powder	A pinch of salt
	A pinch of grated nutmeg
⅓ cup butter	2 eggs, beaten
2 ounces' dark chocolate	1 teaspoon vanilla paste
2 ounces Sultanas (soaked in 2 tablespoons of rum)	¼ teaspoon ground anise

1. Brush a baking pan with nonstick cooking spray oil; set it aside. 2. Mix the dry ingredients; now, thoroughly combine the wet ingredients. Add the wet mixture to the dry mixture and mix until everything is well incorporated. 3. Place the drip pan at the bottom of the cooking chamber. Using the control panel, select Bake, adjust the temperature to 330 degrees F and the time to 15 minutes, then touch Start. 4. When the display indicates "Add Food," place the cooking tray in the center. 5. Serve and enjoy

Per serving: Calories 332; Fat 12.2g; Sodium 103mg; Carbs 55.1g; Fiber 4.5g; Sugar 36.8g; Protein 5.8g

Honey Orange Pecans

Prep time: 05 minutes	Cook time: 15 minutes	Serves: 8
½ pound pecan halves	½ cup honey
1 egg white	1 teaspoon ground cinnamon
1 tablespoon fresh orange juice	A pinch of grated nutmeg
	A pinch of coarse sea salt
2 tablespoons brown sugar	

1. In a mixing dish, toss all the ingredients. 2. Place the drip pan at the bottom of the cooking chamber. Using the control panel, select Roast, adjust the temperature to 320 degrees F and the time to 10 minutes, then touch Start. 3. When the display indicates "Add Food," place the cooking tray in the center. 4. Close the door. 5. When time ends, carefully remove from the unit and serve.

Per serving: Calories 274; Fat 20.2g; Sodium 38mg; Carbs 24.1g; Fiber 3.5g; Sugar 20.8g; Protein 3.8 g

Coconut Banana Bread

Prep time: 05 minutes	Cook time: 15 minutes	Serves: 6
3 overripe bananas, peeled and mashed	perature
	½ cup granulated sugar
½ cup self-raising flour	½ cup coconut oil, melted
1 teaspoon baking powder	¼ teaspoon ground cardamom
3 medium eggs, at room tem-	½ teaspoon ground cinnamon

1. Set aside a baking pan that has been sprayed with nonstick cooking spray. 2. Combine the dry ingredients in a large mixing bowl; thoroughly combine the wet ingredients in a separate mixing bowl. Combine the wet and dry ingredients in a mixing bowl and stir until thoroughly combined. 3. Place the baking pan into a cooking tray of the air fryer. 4. Place the drip pan at the bottom of the cooking chamber. Using the control panel, select Bake, adjust the temperature to 330 degrees F and the time to 15 minutes, then touch Start. 5. When the display indicates "Add Food," place the cooking tray in the center.

Per serving: Calories 343; Fat 20.7g; Sodium 32mg; Carbs 38.9g; Fiber 2g; Sugar 24.1g; Protein 4.5g

Cinnamon Pineapple Rings

Prep time: 05 minutes	Cook time: 15 minutes	Serves: 3
1 large egg	½ teaspoon ground cinnamon
½ cup desiccated coconut	4 tablespoons powdered sugar
A pinch of kosher salt	6 canned pineapple rings

1. Beat the large egg until pale and frothy. Add in the coconut, salt, cinnamon, and powdered sugar. 2. Dip the pineapple rings into the egg mixture and put them into the cooking tray of the air fryer. 3. Place the drip pan at the bottom of the cooking chamber. Using the control panel, select Air Fry, adjust the temperature to 340 degrees F and the time to 10 minutes, then touch Start. 4. When the display indicates "Add Food," place the cooking tray in the center.

Per serving: Calories 261; Fat 5.1g; Sodium 80mg; Carbs 55.5g; Fiber 5.6g; Sugar 43.3g; Protein 4.2g

Vanilla Oatmeal Bars

Prep time: 05 minutes	Cook time: 15 minutes	Serves: 7
1 cup whole wheat flour	½ cup brown sugar
1 cup old-fashioned oats	2 medium eggs, beaten
½ teaspoon baking powder	1 teaspoon vanilla paste
½ teaspoon baking soda	¼ teaspoon sea salt
1 stick butter, melted	

1. In a large mixing bowl, stir together all the dry ingredients. In another bowl, mix the wet ingredients. 2. Add the wet mixture to the dry ingredients and stir to combine well. 3. Press the batter onto a parchment-lined baking pan and put the baking pan into a cooking tray of the air fryer. 4. Place the drip pan at the bottom of the cooking chamber. Using the control panel, select Bake, adjust the temperature to 360 degrees F and the time to 15 minutes, then touch Start. 5. When the display indicates "Add Food," place the cooking tray in the center. 6. Let it sit on a wire rack for 20 minutes before slicing and serving.

Per serving: Calories 316; Fat 15.1g; Sodium 277mg; Carbs 39.5g; Fiber 1.6g; Sugar 17.3g; Protein 5g

Baked Plums with Almond Topping

Prep time: 05 minutes	Cook time: 15 minutes	Serves: 4
8 fresh plums, pitted and halved	8 teaspoons ground almonds
	8 teaspoons coconut sugar
2 teaspoons coconut oil	

1. Top the plum halves with the remaining ingredients. And put them into the cooking tray of the air fryer. 2. Place the drip pan at the bottom of the cooking chamber. Using the control panel, select Air Fry, adjust the temperature to 350 degrees F and the time to 10 minutes, then touch Start. 3. When the display indicates "Add Food," place the cooking tray in the center. 4. Serve at room temperature and enjoy!

Per serving: Calories 316; Fat 15.1g; Sodium 277mg; Carbs 39.5g; Fiber 1.6g; Sugar 17.3g; Protein 5g

Mini Pies with Blueberry Jam

Prep time: 05 minutes | Cook time: 10 minutes | Serves: 6

12 ounces refrigerated pie crust

½ cup blueberry jam
1 teaspoon pure vanilla extract

1. Using a nonstick spray, coat six standard-size muffin cups. 2. Make six squares out of your dough. Place the dough pieces in the muffin cups and press them down. 3. Between the muffin cups, divide the blueberry jam and vanilla extract. Place muffin cup into the cooking tray of the air fryer. 4. Place the drip pan at the bottom of the cooking chamber. Using the control panel, select Bake, adjust the temperature to 350 degrees F and the time to 10 minutes, then touch Start. 5. When the display indicates "Add Food," place the cooking tray in the center.

Per serving: Calories 295; Fat 13.1g; Sodium 295mg; Carbs 44.5g; Fiber 0g; Sugar 8.1g; Protein 2.4g

Pistachio Cheese-Stuffed Apricots

Prep time: 05 minutes | Cook time: 10 minutes | Serves: 3

½ cup mascarpone cheese, at room temperature
¼ cup honey

¼ cup pistachios shelled and finely chopped
9 apricots, pitted and halved

1. thoroughly combine the mascarpone cheese, honey, and pistachios in a mixing bowl. Divide the mixture between the apricot halves. Place the apricot into the cooking tray of the air fryer. 2. Place the drip pan at the bottom of the cooking chamber. Using the control panel, select Air Fry, adjust the temperature to 330 degrees F and the time to 10 minutes, then touch Start. 3. When the display indicates "Add Food," place the cooking tray in the center. 4. Serve at room temperature and enjoy!

Per serving: Calories 235; Fat 8.4g; Sodium 64mg; Carbs 37.4g; Fiber 2.6g; Sugar 33.1g; Protein 7.1g

Almond Chocolate Lava Cake

Prep time: 05 minutes | Cook time: 10 minutes | Serves: 4

2 large eggs
½ stick butter softened
4 ounces' dark chocolate chunks
½ cup brown sugar
A pinch of kosher salt

A pinch of grated nutmeg
½ teaspoon ground cinnamon
2 tablespoons cocoa powder
4 tablespoons almond flour
4 ramekins, sprayed with non-stick spray

1. Whisk the eggs and sugar together until they are foamy. Mix in the other ingredients until everything is well combined. 2. Pour the batter into the ramekins that have been prepared and place them into the cooking tray. 3. Place the drip pan at the bottom of the cooking chamber. Using the control panel, select Air Fry, adjust the temperature to 375 degrees F and the time to 10 minutes, then touch Start. 4. When the display indicates "Add Food," place the cooking tray in the center. 5. Serve warm.

Per serving: Calories 385; Fat 27.4g; Sodium 161mg; Carbs 38.4g; Fiber 5.5g; Sugar 29.5g; Protein 7.2g

Maple Syrup Toast Sticks

Prep time: 05 minutes | Cook time: 15 minutes | Serves: 3

2 large eggs
¼ cup milk
2 tablespoons half-and-half

2 tablespoons butter, melted
1 teaspoon vanilla extract
1 teaspoon ground cinnamon

6 slices of day-old bread, cut into sticks

2 tablespoons maple syrup

1. Whisk the eggs, milk, half-and-half, butter, vanilla, and cinnamon in a mixing dish. 2. Dip all the sticks of bread in this mixture. 3. Place the drip pan at the bottom of the cooking chamber. Using the control panel, select Bake, adjust the temperature to 390 degrees F and the time to 10 minutes, then touch Start. 4. When the display indicates "Add Food," place the cooking tray in the center. 5. Drizzle the French toast with maple syrup and enjoy!

Per serving: Calories 319; Fat 14.7g; Sodium 396mg; Carbs 35.9g; Fiber 1.4g; Sugar 13.3g; Protein 9.3g

Chocolate Hazelnut Biscuits

Prep time: 05 minutes | Cook time: 15 minutes | Serves: 6

1 can (16-ounce) refrigerated buttermilk biscuits
2 tablespoons butter, melted

½ cup chocolate hazelnut spread

1. Separate the biscuits and place them on parchment paper. Brush them with melted butter. Put biscuits into the cooking tray of the air fryer. 2. Place the drip pan at the bottom of the cooking chamber. Using the control panel, select Air Fry, adjust the temperature to 340 degrees F and the time to 15 minutes, then touch Start. 3. When the display indicates "Add Food," place the cooking tray in the center position 4. Dip the warm biscuits into the chocolate hazelnut spread and enjoy!

Per serving: Calories 186; Fat 12.2g; Sodium 136mg; Carbs 18.9g; Fiber 0.8g; Sugar 13.3g; Protein 2.2g

Lemon Cheesecake with Raspberries

Prep time: 05 minutes | Cook time: 25 minutes | Serves: 9

Crust:
1½ cups cracker crumbs
6 tablespoons unsalted butter, softened
2 tablespoons honey
½ teaspoon ground cardamom
½ teaspoon ground cinnamon
¼ teaspoon kosher salt
Filling:
20 ounces of cream cheese at room temperature

½ cup sour cream
1 cup granulated sugar
4 large eggs
2 tablespoons corn flour
1 teaspoon vanilla extract
1 teaspoon lemon zest, grated
1 tablespoon freshly squeezed lemon juice
Topping:
1 cup raspberries

1. Mix all the crust ingredients; press the crust into a baking pan and put the baking pan into a cooking tray of the air fryer. 2. Place the drip pan at the bottom of the cooking chamber. Using the control panel, select Bake, adjust the temperature to 400 degrees F and the time to 6 minutes, then touch Start. 3. When the display indicates "Add Food," place the cooking tray in the center. 4. When time is up, open the door of the air fryer and put out the cooking tray. 5. Using an electric mixer, whip the cream cheese, sour cream, and sugar until fluffy; add one egg at a time and continue to beat until creamy; mix in the corn flour, vanilla extract, lemon zest, and lemon juice. 6. Pour the topping mixture on top of the crust. Place the drip pan at the bottom of the cooking chamber. 7. Using the control panel, select Bake, adjust the temperature to 390 degrees F and the time to 15 minutes, then touch Start. 8. When the display indicates "Add Food," place the cooking tray in the center. 9. Allow your cheesecake to cool completely; top the cheesecake with fresh or frozen raspberries. Enjoy!

Per serving: Calories 512; Fat 37.3g; Sodium 433mg; Carbs 38g; Fiber 1.3g; Sugar 27.5g; Protein 9.1g

Baked Pears with Honey

Prep time: 05 minutes | Cook time: 15minutes | Serves: 4

4 ripe pears	1 teaspoon vanilla extract
4 tablespoons butter, melted	½ cup old-fashioned rolled oats
¼ teaspoon sea salt	¼ cup almonds, chopped
½ teaspoon ground cardamom	¼ cup brown sugar
1 teaspoon ground cinnamon	2 tablespoons honey
¼ teaspoon grated nutmeg	

1. Remove the stem and seeds from the pears with a paring knife, leaving deep holes. 2. Combine the remaining ingredients in a mixing dish and stir well. Fill the pears with the filling and place pears into a cooking tray of the air fryer. 3. Place the drip pan at the bottom of the cooking chamber. Using the control panel, select Bake, adjust the temperature to 350 degrees F and the time to 15 minutes, then touch Start. 4. When the display indicates "Add Food," place the cooking tray in the center. 5. serve at room temperature. Enjoy!

Per serving: Calories 512; Fat 37.3g; Sodium 433mg; Carbs 38g; Fiber 1.3g; Sugar 27.5g; Protein 9.1g

Chocolate Cranberry Brownies

Prep time: 05 minutes | Cook time: 15 minutes | Serves: 4

½ cup all-purpose flour	½ teaspoon ground cinnamon
¼ cup butter	¼ teaspoon ground anise
½ cup brown sugar	2 eggs, well-beaten
½ cup cocoa powder	2 ounces' cranberries
1 teaspoon vanilla extract	

1. Set aside a muffin tray that has been sprayed with nonstick cooking spray. 2. After properly mixing the dry ingredients, incorporate the wet components. 3. Combine the wet and dry ingredients in a mixing bowl and stir until thoroughly combined. Fold in the cranberries using a spatula. 4. Put the muffin tin into the cooking tray. Place the drip pan at the bottom of the cooking chamber. Using the control panel, select Bake, adjust the temperature to 350 degrees F and the time to 15 minutes, then touch Start. 5. When the display indicates "Add Food," place the cooking tray in the center. 6. When baked, let the food cool for a while and enjoy!

Per serving: Calories 294; Fat 15.3g; Sodium 120mg; Carbs 37.4g; Fiber 4.3g; Sugar 18.7g; Protein 6.5g

Fried Banana Slices

Prep time: 05 minutes | Cook time: 8 minutes | Serves: 1

1 large banana, peeled and sliced	1 teaspoon ground cinnamon
1 tablespoon peanut oil	½ teaspoon ground cardamom

1. Toss the banana slices with the remaining ingredients. 2. Put the banana into a cooking tray. Place the drip pan at the bottom of the cooking chamber. Using the control panel, select Air Fry, adjust the temperature to 350 degrees F and the time to 5 minutes, then touch Start. 3. When the display indicates "Add Food," place the cooking tray in the center. 4. When showing the message "turn Food," turn the food. 5. Close the door. 6. When time ends, carefully remove from the unit and serve.

Per serving: Calories 249; Fat 14.1g; Sodium 2mg; Carbs 33.6g; Fiber 5g; Sugar 16.7g; Protein 1.7g

Coconut Bread Slice

Prep time: 05 minutes | Cook time: 15 minutes | Serves: 2

2 teaspoons butter	½ teaspoon ground cinnamon
2 large eggs	⅓ cup brown sugar
2 tablespoons coconut milk	4 slices of thick white bread
½ teaspoon vanilla extract	

1. Whisk the butter, eggs, coconut milk, vanilla, cinnamon, and sugar in a mixing dish. 2. Dip all the slices of bread in this mixture. And place them into the cooking tray. 3. Place the drip pan at the bottom of the cooking chamber. Using the control panel, select Air Fry, adjust the temperature to 390 degrees F and the time to 10 minutes, then touch Start. 4. When the display indicates "Add Food," place the cooking tray in the center. 5. When showing the message "turn Food," turn the food and cook for 5 minutes. 6. Close the door. 7. When time ends, carefully remove from the unit and serve.

Per serving: Calories 295; Fat 12.1g; Sodium 256mg; Carbs 37.6g; Fiber 1.3g; Sugar 25.4g; Protein 9.1g

Cinnamon Waffle Sticks

Prep time: 05 minutes | Cook time: 6 minutes | Serves: 4

4 (4-inch) frozen waffles, cut into thirds	1 tablespoon cinnamon powder
4 teaspoons butter, softened	2 tablespoons agave syrup

1. Place waffles into the cooking tray. Place the drip pan at the bottom of the cooking chamber. 2. Using the control panel, select Air Fry, adjust the temperature to 350 degrees F and the time to 6 minutes, then touch Start. 3. When the display indicates "Add Food," place the cooking tray in the center. 4. When showing the message "turn Food," just turn the food. 5. Toss the waffle sticks with the butter, cinnamon, and agave syrup and serve immediately. Enjoy!

Per serving: Calories 246; Fat 10.8g; Sodium 414mg; Carbs 34.6g; Fiber 5g; Sugar 5g; Protein 5g

Ginger Pear and Raisin Crisp

Prep time: 05 minutes | Cook time: 15 minutes | Serves: 8

2 large pears, peeled, cored, and chopped	Topping:
¼ cup golden raisins	½ cup rolled oats
½ teaspoon ground cinnamon	½ cup all-purpose flour
½ teaspoon ground cardamom	½ cup butter softened
⅛ teaspoon grated nutmeg	5 tablespoons brown sugar
1 teaspoon crystallized ginger	¼ cup vanilla extract
½ cup brown sugar	2 large eggs, well-beaten

1. In a lightly oiled baking pan, toss the pears with the raisins, cinnamon, cardamom, nutmeg, ginger, and sugar. 2. Mix the oats, flour, butter, brown sugar, and vanilla in a mixing bowl. Then mix in the eggs until they are smooth and uniform. 3. Drop tablespoons of the batter onto the pear layer. And place them into the cooking tray of the air fryer. 4. Place the drip pan at the bottom of the cooking chamber. Using the control panel, select Air Fry, adjust the temperature to 360 degrees F and the time to 12 minutes, then touch Start. 5. When the display indicates "Add Food," place the cooking tray in the center. 6. Serve at room temperature or well chilled. Enjoy!

Per serving: Calories 241; Fat 13.8g; Sodium 103mg; Carbs 28.6g; Fiber 2.4g; Sugar 16g; Protein 3.5g

Almond Brownie

Prep time: 05 minutes | Cook time: 15 minutes | Serves: 6

¼ cup all-purpose flour
¼ cup almond meal
⅔ cup granulated sugar
½ cup cocoa powder
½ teaspoon baking powder

A pinch of kosher salt
A pinch of grated nutmeg
⅓ cup coconut oil, melted
2 eggs, beaten

1. Set aside a baking pan that has been sprayed with nonstick cooking spray. 2. In a mixing bowl, combine the dry ingredients; next, completely incorporate the wet ingredients. Combine the wet and dry ingredients in a mixing bowl and stir until thoroughly combined. And place them into the cooking tray of the air fryer. 3. Place the drip pan at the bottom of the cooking chamber. Using the control panel, select Bake, adjust the temperature to 330 degrees F and the time to 15 minutes, then touch Start. 4. When the display indicates "Add Food," place the cooking tray in the center. 5. Close the door. 6. When time ends, carefully remove from the unit and serve.
Per serving: Calories 267; Fat 16.6g; Sodium 50mg; Carbs 31.3g; Fiber 2.8g; Sugar 22.7g; Protein 4.5g

Chocolate Almond Cake with Prunes

Prep time: 05 minutes | Cook time: 15 minutes | Serves: 7

½ cup all-purpose flour
½ cup almond meal
1 teaspoon baking powder
3 medium eggs
½ cup sour cream

⅔ cup sugar
½ cup coconut oil
2 ounces' prunes, pitted and chopped
⅓ cup cocoa powder

1. Set aside a baking pan that has been sprayed with nonstick cooking spray. 2. Combine the dry ingredients first, then the wet components. Combine the wet and dry ingredients in a mixing bowl and stir until thoroughly combined. Place the baking pan into the cooking tray of the air fryer. 3. Place the drip pan at the bottom of the cooking chamber. Using the control panel, select Bake, adjust the temperature to 330 degrees F and the time to 15 minutes, then touch Start. 4. When the display indicates "Add Food," place the cooking tray in the center.
Per serving: Calories 369; Fat 24.9g; Sodium 37mg; Carbs 35.9g; Fiber 2.9g; Sugar 22.7g; Protein 6.2g

Vanilla Candied Walnuts

Prep time: 05 minutes | Cook time: 10 minutes | Serves: 6

2 cups raw walnut halves
¼ cup brown sugar
½ teaspoon coarse sea salt

1 teaspoon ground cinnamon
1 teaspoon vanilla extract
1 egg white, whisked

1. In a mixing dish, toss all the ingredients. And spread into the cooking tray. 2. Place the drip pan at the bottom of the cooking chamber. Using the control panel, select Roast, adjust the temperature to 330 degrees F and the time to 10 minutes, then touch Start. 3. When the display indicates "Add Food," place the cooking tray in the center. 4. Serve.
Per serving: Calories 286; Fat 24.6g; Sodium 168mg; Carbs 10.5g; Fiber 3g; Sugar 6.5g; Protein 10.5g

Honey Nut Granola Bars

Prep time: 05 minutes | Cook time: 15 minutes | Serves:
7½ cup almond meal

1 cup rolled oats
½ cup packed dates pitted

½ cup raisins
¼ cup honey
¼ teaspoon coarse sea salt
½ teaspoon ground almonds
¼ cup almond butter (or pea-

nut butter)
½ cup walnuts, roughly chopped (or peanuts)
1 teaspoon vanilla extract

1. Combine all of the dry ingredients in a large mixing basin. Combine the wet ingredients in a separate bowl. 2. Stir the wet liquid into the dry ingredients until everything is thoroughly combined. 3. Place the batter in a baking pan lined with parchment paper. Arrange the baking pan into the cooking tray. 4. Place the drip pan at the bottom of the cooking chamber. Using the control panel, select Bake, adjust the temperature to 330 degrees F and the time to 15 minutes until golden brown, then touch Start. 5. When the display indicates "Add Food," place the cooking tray in the center. 6. Let it sit on a wire rack for 20 minutes before slicing and serving.
Per serving: Calories 195; Fat 8.6g; Sodium 68mg; Carbs 27.5g; Fiber 2.8g; Sugar 16.5g; Protein 5g

Cardamom Banana Cake

Prep time: 05 minutes | Cook time: 15 minutes | Serves: 6

¾ cup cake flour
¾ cup caster sugar
½ cup butter, melted
2 medium eggs, beaten
½ teaspoon almond extract
½ teaspoon vanilla extract

¼ teaspoon ground cardamom
⅓ teaspoon crystallized ginger
¼ cup Greek-style yogurt
2 overripe bananas, peeled and mashed

1. Set aside a baking pan that has been sprayed with nonstick cooking spray. 2. Combine the dry ingredients in a large mixing bowl; thoroughly combine the wet ingredients in a separate mixing bowl. Combine the wet and dry ingredients in a mixing bowl and stir until thoroughly combined. Arrange the baking pan into the cooking tray. 3. Place the drip pan at the bottom of the cooking chamber. Using the control panel, select Bake, adjust the temperature to 330 degrees F and the time to 15 minutes until golden brown, then touch Start. 4. When the display indicates "Add Food," place the cooking tray in the center. 5. Close the door. 6. When time ends, carefully remove from the unit and serve.
Per serving: Calories 344; Fat 17.1g; Sodium 130mg; Carbs 46.2g; Fiber 1.5g; Sugar 30g; Protein 4.1g

Apple Oats Cups

Prep time: 05 minutes | Cook time: 12minutes | Serves: 4

2 large apples, peeled, cored, and diced
4 tablespoons granulated sugar
½ teaspoon ground cinnamon
½ teaspoon ground cardamom
½ teaspoon ginger, peeled and minced
Topping:

1 cup all-purpose flour
1 cup old-fashioned oats
½ cup brown sugar
2 tablespoons maple syrup
1 teaspoon ground cinnamon
¼ teaspoon grated nutmeg
⅛ teaspoon kosher salt
½ stick butter

1. Set aside ramekins that have been sprayed with nonstick cooking spray. 2. Combine the apples, granulated sugar, cinnamon, cardamom, and ginger in a mixing bowl; divide the mixture among ramekins. 3. In a mixing bowl, combine the flour, oats, sugar, maple syrup, cinnamon, nutmeg, salt, and butter. Mix until the mixture is smooth and homogeneous. 4. Place a few teaspoons of batter on the fruit layer. 5. Arrange ramekins into the cooking tray 6. Place the drip pan at the bottom of the cooking chamber. Using the control panel,

select Bake, adjust the temperature to 360 degrees F and the time to 12 minutes until golden brown, then touch Start. 7. When the display indicates "Add Food," place the cooking tray in the center. 8. Close the door. 9. When time ends, carefully remove from the unit and serve.

Per serving: Calories 327; Fat 9g; Sodium 59mg; Carbs 59.9g; Fiber 3.9g; Sugar 31.9g; Protein 4.2g

Banana Bites

Prep time: 05 minutes | Cook time: 10 minutes | Serves: 3

1 large egg, beaten	¼ teaspoon ground cloves
½ cup rice flour	2 tablespoons coconut sugar
½ cup breadcrumbs	2 medium bananas, peeled and
½ teaspoon ground cinnamon	sliced
¼ teaspoon grated nutmeg	

1. Mix the egg and rice flour thoroughly in a mixing bowl. Mix the other ingredients in a separate bowl until well blended. 2. Dredge each banana slice in the flour mixture. Roll them in the breadcrumb mixture after that. Arrange the banana on the cooking tray. 3. Place the drip pan at the bottom of the cooking chamber. Using the control panel, select Air Fry, adjust the temperature to 350 degrees F and the time to 10 minutes until golden brown, then touch Start. 4. When the display indicates "Add Food," place the cooking tray in the center. 5. When displaying the message "turn Food," turn the banana slice. 6. Close the door. 7. When time ends, carefully remove the banana and serve.

Per serving: Calories 294; Fat 3.4g; Sodium 156mg; Carbs 60.9g; Fiber 3.8g; Sugar 19g; Protein 7g

Honey-Roasted Peaches

Prep time: 05 minutes | Cook time: 12minutes | Serves: 4

4 teaspoons coconut oil	¼ teaspoon kosher salt
4 tablespoons honey	4 large ripe peaches, pitted
1 tablespoon rum	and halved
1 teaspoon pure vanilla extract	4 tablespoons Greek yogurt
½ teaspoon ground anise	

1. In a mixing bowl, thoroughly combine the coconut oil, honey, rum, vanilla, anise, and salt. Divide the filling between the peaches. 2. Arrange peaches into the cooking tray 3. Place the drip pan at the bottom of the cooking chamber. Using the control panel, select Roast, adjust the temperature to 350 degrees F and the time to 12 minutes until golden brown, then touch Start. 4. When the display indicates "Add Food," place the cooking tray in the center. 5. Garnish the roasted peaches with Greek yogurt and serve at room temperature. 6. Enjoy!

Per serving: Calories 265; Fat 8.6g; Sodium 214mg; Carbs 25.5g; Fiber 0g; Sugar 25.4g; Protein 20.2g

Walnut Cheesecake

Prep time: 05 minutes | Cook time: 25 minutes | Serves: 10

Crust:	24 ounces' cream cheese, at
1 cup cracker crumbs	room temperature
½ cup ground walnuts	8 ounces Greek-style yogurt
1 stick butter, melted3 table-	1 cup granulated sugar
spoons honey	1 teaspoon vanilla paste
½ teaspoon ground cardamom	3 extra-large eggs, at room
½ teaspoon ground cinnamon	temperature
Filling:	

1. Mix all the crust ingredients; press the crust into a baking pan. 2. Arrange the baking pan on the cooking tray. 3. Place the drip pan at the bottom of the cooking chamber. Using the control panel, select Bake, adjust the temperature to 400 degrees F and the time to 6 minutes until golden brown, then touch Start. 4. When the display indicates "Add Food," place the cooking tray in the center. 5. When time is up, open the air fryer door and put out the baking pan, and allow it to cool on wire racks. 6. Whip the cream cheese, yogurt, granulated sugar, and vanilla paste until frothy with an electric mixer; add one egg at a time and whisk until creamy. 7. Fill the crust with the filling mixture. Place the drip pan at the bottom of the cooking chamber. Using the control panel, select Bake, adjust the temperature to 390 degrees F and the time to 15 minutes until golden brown, then touch Start. 8. When the display indicates "Add Food," place the cooking tray in the center. 9. Allow your cheesecake to cool completely before serving. Enjoy!

Per serving: Calories 520; Fat 40g; Sodium 350mg; Carbs 32.5g; Fiber 0.6g; Sugar 26.4g; Protein 11.2g

Cardamom Carrot Cupcakes with Almonds

Prep time: 05 minutes | Cook time: 15 minutes | Serves: 6

1 cup self-raising flour	and grated
½ cup granulated sugar	2 tablespoons almond milk
2 tablespoons maple syrup	2 medium eggs, beaten
1 teaspoon ground cinnamon	1 stick butter, melted
½ teaspoon ground cardamom	2 tablespoons almonds,
¼ teaspoon grated nutmeg	chopped
2 medium carrots, trimmed	

1. Set aside a muffin tray that has been sprayed with nonstick cooking spray. 2. After properly mixing the dry ingredients, incorporate the wet components. Combine the wet and dry ingredients in a mixing bowl and stir until thoroughly combined. Combine the berries and fold them in. Arrange the muffin tin into the cooking tray. 3. Place the drip pan at the bottom of the cooking chamber. Using the control panel, select Bake, adjust the temperature to 330 degrees F and the time to 15 minutes, then touch Start. 4. When the display indicates "Add Food," place the cooking tray in the center. 5. Close the door. 6. When time ends, carefully remove muffins and serve.

Per serving: Calories 345; Fat 19.2g; Sodium 145mg; Carbs 40.5g; Fiber 1.6g; Sugar 22.4g; Protein 4.9g

Tasty Chocolate Almond Croissants

Prep time: 05 minutes | Cook time: 15minutes | Serves: 4

1 can (8-ounce) refrigerated	rum
crescent rolls	¼ cup almonds, chopped
½ cup chocolate spread	1 large egg, whisked
¼ cup raisins soaked in dark	

1. Make eight triangles out of the crescent rolls. Spread chocolate spread, raisins, and almonds on each triangle. They should be rolled up and placed in the baking pan. 2. Brush each croissant with the whisked egg. 3. Arrange the baking pan into the cooking tray of the air fryer. 4. Place the drip pan at the bottom of the cooking chamber. Using the control panel, select Air Fry, adjust the temperature to 350 degrees F and the time to 15 minutes, then touch Start. 5. When the display indicates "Add Food," place the cooking tray in the center. 6. Close the door. 7. When time ends, carefully remove crescent rolls and serve.

Per serving: Calories 159; Fat 8.6g; Sodium 130mg; Carbs 16.7g; Fiber 1.3g; Sugar 9.2g; Protein 4.4g

Cinnamon Tortilla Chips

Prep time: 05 minutes | Cook time: 10 minutes | Serves: 2

2 (8-inch) whole-wheat tortillas, cut into triangles
2 tablespoons brown sugar

1 teaspoon ground cinnamon
2 tablespoons butter, softened

1. Toss the tortilla pieces with the remaining ingredients. 2. Arrange the tortilla chips into the cooking tray of the air fryer. 3. Place the drip pan at the bottom of the cooking chamber. Using the control panel, select Air Fry, adjust the temperature to 330 degrees F and the time to 10 minutes, then touch Start. 4. When the display indicates "Add Food," place the cooking tray in the center. 5. When the message "turn Food" appears, turn the fritters and cook for more minutes. 6. Close the door. 7. When time ends, carefully remove the tortilla and serve.
Per serving: Calories 191; Fat 12.2g; Sodium 95mg; Carbs 20.7g; Fiber 2.1g; Sugar 9g; Protein 1.6 g

Almond Oats Energy Bars

Prep time: 05 minutes | Cook time: 15 minutes | Serves: 8

1 cup old-fashioned rolled oats
1 cup almond meal
½ cup brown sugar
2 tablespoons honey
1 ½ teaspoons baking powder
¼ teaspoon salt

½ teaspoon ground cinnamon
½ cup peanut butter
½ cup almond milk
2 eggs
1 teaspoon vanilla extract
2 ounces dried cranberries

1. Combine all of the dry ingredients in a large mixing basin. Combine the wet ingredients in a separate bowl. 2. Stir the wet liquid into the dry ingredients until everything is thoroughly combined. Fold in the cranberries using a spatula. 3. Place the batter in a baking pan lined with parchment paper. Arrange the baking pan into the cooking tray of the air fryer. 4. Place the drip pan at the bottom of the cooking chamber. Using the control panel, select Bake, adjust the temperature to 360 degrees F and the time to 15 minutes, then touch Start. 5. When the display indicates "Add Food," place the cooking tray in the center. 6. Let it sit on a wire rack for 20 minutes before slicing and serving.
Per serving: Calories 308; Fat 19.4g; Sodium 179mg; Carbs 27.5g; Fiber 4.1g; Sugar 16.4g; Protein 9.9g

Banana Walnuts Muffins

Prep time: 05 minutes | Cook time: 15 minutes | Serves: 6

1 cup all-purpose flour
½ cup walnuts, ground
½ teaspoon baking powder
1 teaspoon baking soda
¼ teaspoon kosher salt
3 large overripe bananas,

mashed
½ cup granulated sugar
2 tablespoons honey
2 eggs, beaten
½ cup coconut oil

1. Set aside a muffin tin that has been sprayed with nonstick cooking spray. 2. Combine the dry ingredients in a large mixing bowl; thoroughly combine the wet ingredients in a separate mixing bowl. Combine the wet and dry ingredients in a mixing bowl and stir until thoroughly combined. 3. Arrange the muffins tins into a cooking tray of the air fryer. 4. Place the drip pan at the bottom of the cooking chamber. Using the control panel, select Bake, adjust the temperature to 330 degrees F and the time to 15 minutes, then touch Start. 5. When the display indicates "Add Food," place the cooking tray in the center. 6. Close the door. 7. When time ends, carefully remove muffins and serve.

Per serving: Calories 405; Fat 26g; Sodium 330mg; Carbs 43.7g; Fiber 2.7g; Sugar 32.1g; Protein 5.9g

Peach Crumble Cake

Prep time: 05 minutes | Cook time: 15 minutes | Serves: 6

½ cup old-fashioned oats
¼ cup almond meal
½ teaspoon baking powder
A pinch of sea salt
¼ cup butter, cold
3 large peaches, peeled, pitted, and diced

½ teaspoon ground anise
1 teaspoon ginger, peeled and ground
1 teaspoon ground cinnamon
¼ cup brown sugar
1 tablespoon honey

1. Combine the oats, almond meal, baking powder, salt, and butter in a large mixing bowl. Mix until the mixture is smooth and homogeneous. 2. In a lightly greased baking pan, press the mixture. Place the peaches on the crust after tossing them with the remaining ingredients. 3. Arrange the baking tin on the cooking tray of the air fryer. 4. Place the drip pan at the bottom of the cooking chamber. Using the control panel, select Bake, adjust the temperature to 330 degrees F and the time to 12 minutes, then touch Start. 5. When the display indicates "Add Food," place the cooking tray in the center.
Per serving: Calories 312; Fat 12.6g; Sodium 35mg; Carbs 48.7g; Fiber 2.8g; Sugar 31.1g; Protein 3.9g

Spiced Pumpkin Cupcakes

Prep time: 05 minutes | Cook time: 15 minutes | Serves: 6

1 ½ cups all-purpose flour
1 teaspoon baking powder
½ teaspoon baking powder
A pinch of sea salt
1 teaspoon pumpkin spice mix

¼ cup butter, at room temperature
½ cup brown sugar
2 eggs, beaten
1 cup pumpkin puree

1. Set aside a muffin tray lined with parchment paper. 2. After properly mixing the dry ingredients, incorporate the wet components. Combine the wet and dry ingredients in a mixing bowl and stir until thoroughly combined. Combine the berries and fold them in. 3. Arrange the baking tin on a cooking tray of the air fryer. 4. Place the drip pan at the bottom of the cooking chamber. Using the control panel, select Bake, adjust the temperature to 330 degrees F and the time to 15 minutes, then touch Start. 5. When the display indicates "Add Food," place the cooking tray in the center.
Per serving: Calories 263; Fat 9.6g; Sodium 82mg; Carbs 38.7g; Fiber 2g; Sugar 13.3g; Protein 5.6g

Apple Cream Cheese Rolls

Prep time: 20 minutes | Cook time: 12 minutes | Serves: 4

1 ½ cups tart apples, peeled, cored, and chopped
¼ cup light brown sugar
1 ¼ teaspoons ground cinnamon, divided

½ teaspoon corn starch
4 egg roll wrappers
¼ cup cream cheese softened
Olive oil cooking spray
1 tablespoon sugar

1. Combine the apples, brown sugar, 1 teaspoon of cinnamon, and corn starch in a small mixing dish. 2. Place one egg roll wrapper on a clean, flat surface. 3. Spread 1 tablespoon of cream cheese over the roll, leaving a 1-inch border. 4. Place 13 cups of apple mixture directly below the center of one wrapper's corner. 5. Fold the bottom corner of the envelope over the filling. 6. Moisten the remaining wrapper edges with your fingers. 7. Over the filling, fold the side corners toward the center. 8. Roll the egg roll tightly and seal the tip with

your fingertips. 9. Repeat the process using the remaining wrappers, cream cheese, and filling. 10. Spray the rolls with the cooking spray and place them on a cooking tray of the air fryer. 11. Place the drip pan at the bottom of the cooking chamber. Using the control panel, select Air Fry, adjust the temperature to 400 degrees F and the time to 12 minutes, then touch Start. 12. When the display indicates "Add Food," place the cooking tray in the center. 13. When the display shows "turn Food," turn the rolls and spray with the cooking spray. 14. Meanwhile, combine the sugar and remaining cinnamon in a shallow dish. 15. Remove the cooking tray from the unit after the cooking time is up. 16. Serve the hot egg rolls with the sugar mixture.

Per serving: Calories 236; Fat 4.1g; Sodium 154mg; Carbs 49.9g; Fiber 5.9g; Sugar 29.2g; Protein 3.4g

Cinnamon Donuts

Prep time: 15 minutes | Cook time: 6 minutes | Serves: 8

½ cup granulated sugar	flaky biscuits
1 tablespoon ground cinnamon	Olive oil cooking spray
1 (16.3-ounce) can of large	4 tablespoons unsalted butter, melted

1. Using parchment paper, line a baking sheet. 2. Combine the sugar and cinnamon on a small plate. Remove from the equation. 3. Remove the biscuits from the can and separate them carefully. 4. Place the biscuits on the prepared baking sheet and cut holes in the center of each biscuit with a 1-inch-round biscuit cutter. 5. Place four donuts in a single layer on the air fryer's lightly oiled cooking tray. 6. Place the drip pan at the bottom of the cooking chamber. Using the control panel, select Air Fry, adjust the temperature to 350 degrees F and the time to 6 minutes, then touch Start. 7. When the display indicates "Add Food," place the cooking tray in the center. 8. When the display shows "turn Food," turn the donuts. 9. Remove the tray from the unit after the cooking time is up. 10. Brush the warm doughnuts with melted butter before coating them in cinnamon sugar. 11. Carry on with the remaining doughnuts in the same manner. 12. Warm the dish before serving.

Per serving: Calories 289; Fat 14.3g; Sodium 590mg; Carbs 36.7g; Fiber 1.4g; Sugar 15.3g; Protein 3.9 g

Almond Chocolate Pastry

Prep time: 20 minutes | Cook time: 10 minutes | Serves: 4

8 ounces frozen puff pastry, thawed	plus more for topping
4 tablespoons hazelnut spread	1 egg, beaten
4 teaspoons slivered almonds	1 tablespoon water
	2 tablespoons turbinado sugar

1. Unfold the puff pastry on a lightly floured work surface. 2. Cut the puff pastry into four squares. 3. Apply 1 tablespoon of hazelnut spread on each square and sprinkle with almonds. 4. Moisten the edges of each pastry with damp fingers and fold it into a rectangular shape. 5. To seal the edges, use a fork to press them together. 6. Whisk together the egg and 1 tablespoon of water in a small bowl. 7. Apply an egg wash to the tops of each pastry and sprinkle with turbinado sugar, then a few slivered almonds. 8. Place the pastries on two cooking trays. 9. Place the drip pan at the bottom of the cooking chamber. Using the control panel, select Air Fry, adjust the temperature to 330 degrees F and the time to 10 minutes, then touch Start. 10. When the display indicates "Add Food," place the cooking tray in the top position. and another in the bottom. 11. When the display shows "turn Food," do not turn the food but switch the position of the cooking trays. 12. When cooking time is complete, remove the trays from the unit and serve warm.

Per serving: Calories 452; Fat 29.6g; Sodium 168mg; Carbs 40.5g; Fiber 1.6g; Sugar 14.5g; Protein 7.1g

Strawberry Jam Roll

Prep time: 20 minutes | Cook time: 25 minutes | Serves: 6

1 tube full-sheet crescent roll dough	½ cup fresh strawberries, hulled and chopped
4 ounces' cream cheese, softened	1 cup confectioner's sugar
¼ cup strawberry jam	2-3 tablespoons of cream

1. Unroll the crescent roll dough sheet onto a clean, flat surface. 2. Microwave the cream cheese for about 20-30 seconds in a microwave-safe bowl. 3. Remove from microwave and continue to stir until the mixture is creamy and smooth. 4. Spread the cream cheese, then the strawberry jam, over the dough sheet. 5. Now, equally distribute the strawberry chunks across the top. 6. Roll the dough from the short side and pinch the seam to seal it. 7. Place a greased parchment paper on top of the cooking tray. 8. Carefully curve the rolled pastry into a horseshoe shape and arrange it onto the prepared cooking tray. 9. Place the drip pan at the bottom of the cooking chamber. Using the control panel, select Air Fry, adjust the temperature to 350 degrees F and the time to 25 minutes, then touch Start. 10. When the display indicates "Add Food," place the cooking tray in the center. 11. When the display shows "turn Food," turn the rolls and spray with the cooking spray. 12. Meanwhile, combine the sugar and remaining cinnamon in a shallow dish. 13. Remove the tray from the unit when the cooking time is up and place it on a cooling rack. 14. Meanwhile, combine the confectioner's sugar and cream in a mixing basin. 15. Serve the cream mixture over the chilled rolls.

Per serving: Calories 338; Fat 13.6g; Sodium 341mg; Carbs 48.7g; Fiber 0.2g; Sugar 4.8g; Protein 4.2g

Honey Apple Rings

Prep time: 05 minutes | Cook time: 10minutes | Serves: 5

2 medium eggs	¼ teaspoon ground anise
½ cup all-purpose flour	4 tablespoons honey
½ cup almond meal	¾ cup buttermilk
½ teaspoon baking powder	3 large apples, cored, peeled, and cut into rings
A pinch of kosher salt	
½ teaspoon ground cinnamon	

1. Beat the eggs until pale and frothy. Add flour, almond meal, baking powder, salt, cinnamon, anise, honey, and buttermilk. 2. Dip the apple rings into the egg, then into the flour mixture, and arrange the apple into the cooking tray of the air fryer. 3. Place the drip pan at the bottom of the cooking chamber. Using the control panel, select Air Fry, adjust the temperature to 360 degrees F and the time to 10 minutes, then touch Start. 4. When the display indicates "Add Food," place the cooking tray in the center. 5. When displaying "turn Food," turn the apple and cook for 3 more minutes. 6. Let it sit on a wire rack to cool before serving.

Per serving: Calories 262; Fat 7.2g; Sodium 97mg; Carbs 46.5g; Fiber 4.9g; Sugar 30.1g; Protein 7.2g

Coconut Walnut Blondies

Prep time: 05 minutes | Cook time: 15 minutes | Serves: 7

1 cup all-purpose flour
½ cup coconut flour
1 teaspoon baking powder
1 stick butter, melted
½ cup brown sugar
2 large eggs, well-beaten
1 teaspoon vanilla extract
A pinch of grated nutmeg
A pinch of kosher salt
½ cup walnuts, chopped

1. Set aside a baking pan that has been sprayed with nonstick cooking spray. 2. In a mixing bowl, combine the dry ingredients; next, completely incorporate the wet ingredients. Combine the wet and dry ingredients in a mixing bowl and stir until thoroughly combined. 3. arrange the baking pan into the cooking tray of the air fryer. 4. Place the drip pan at the bottom of the cooking chamber. Using the control panel, select Bake, adjust the temperature to 330 degrees F and the time to 15 minutes, then touch Start. 5. When the display indicates "Add Food," place the cooking tray in the center position

Per serving: Calories 303; Fat 20.1g; Sodium 143mg; Carbs 25.8g; Fiber 1.5g; Sugar 10.1g; Protein 6.2g

Sheet Roll Oreos

Prep time: 15 minutes | Cook time: 4minutes | Serves: 9

1 crescent sheet roll
9 Oreo cookies

1. Place the sheet of crescent roll dough onto a flat surface and unroll it. 2. With a knife, cut the dough into nine even squares. 3. Wrap each cookie in 1 dough square completely. 4. Arrange the Oreos onto a cooking tray. 5. Place the drip pan at the bottom of the cooking chamber. Using the control panel, select Air Fry, adjust the temperature to 360 degrees F and the time to 4 minutes, then touch Start. 6. When the display indicates "Add Food," place the cooking tray in the center. 7. When the display shows "turn Food," turn the Oreos. 8. When cooking time is complete, remove the tray from the unit and serve warm.

Per serving: Calories 137; Fat 6.4g; Sodium 237mg; Carbs 17.1g; Fiber 0.3g; Sugar 6.8g; Protein 2.3g

Chocolate Brownies

Prep time: 15 minutes | Cook time: 15 minutes | Serves: 4

½ cup all-purpose flour
¾ cup sugar
6 tablespoons unsweetened cocoa powder
¼ teaspoon baking powder
¼ teaspoon salt
¼ cup unsalted butter, melted
2 large eggs
1 tablespoon vegetable oil
½ teaspoon vanilla extract

1. Grease a 7-inch baking pan generously. Set aside. 2. In a bowl, add all the ingredients and mix until well combined. 3. Place the mixture into the prepared baking pan, and smooth the top surface with the back of a spoon. 4. Place the drip pan at the bottom of the cooking chamber. Using the control panel, select Air Fry, adjust the temperature to 330 degrees F and the time to 15 minutes, then touch Start. 5. When the display indicates "Add Food," place the cooking tray in the center. 6. When the display shows "turn Food," do nothing but wait for it after 10 seconds to automatically resume cooking. 7. Remove the pan from the unit after the cooking time is up and lay it on a wire rack to cool entirely before cutting. 8. Cut the brownie into squares of your choice and serve.

Per serving: Calories 385; Fat 18.6g; Sodium 266mg; Carbs 54.3g; Fiber 3.1g; Sugar 38g; Protein 6.5g

Luscious Cake

Prep time: 15 minutes | Cook time: 25 minutes | Serves: 6

½ package yellow cake mix
½ (3.4-ounce) package Jell-O instant pudding
2 eggs
¼ cup vegetable oil
¼ cup water
¼ cup dark rum

1. Whisk all ingredients in a mixing bowl and beat with an electric mixer until well blended. 2. In the bottom of a greased 8-inch pan, place parchment paper. 3. Arrange a piece of foil around the cake pan now. 4. Place the mixture in the prepared baking pan and smooth the top with the back of a spoon. 5. Place the drip pan at the bottom of the cooking chamber. Using the control panel, select Bake, adjust the temperature to 325 degrees F and the time to 30 minutes, then touch Start. 6. When the display indicates "Add Food," place the cooking tray in the center. 7. When the cooking time is up, take the pan out of the air fryer and set it on a wire rack to cool for about 10 minutes. 8. Before cutting, carefully turn the cake onto a wire rack to cool. 9. Serve by slicing into preferred sizes.

Per serving: Calories 315; Fat 14.9g; Sodium 613mg; Carbs 36.5g; Fiber 0.4g; Sugar 16.5g; Protein 3.5g

Blueberry Cobbler

Prep time: 15 minutes | Cook time: 20 minutes | Serves: 6

For Filling:
2½ cups fresh blueberries
1 teaspoon vanilla extract
1 teaspoon fresh lemon juice
1 cup sugar
1 teaspoon flour
1 tablespoon butter, melted
For Topping:
1¾ cups all-purpose flour
6 tablespoons sugar
4 teaspoons baking powder
1 cup milk
5 tablespoons butter
For Sprinkling:
2 teaspoons sugar
¼ teaspoon ground cinnamon

1. To make the filling, place all the filling ingredients in a mixing dish and stir until well blended. 2. Combine the flour, baking powder, and sugar in a separate large mixing bowl. 3. Mix in the milk and butter until you have a crumpy mixture. 4. To sprinkle, combine the sugar and cinnamon in a small basin. 5. Place the blueberry mixture in the bottom of a greased pan and equally cover it with the flour mixture. 6. Evenly sprinkle the cinnamon sugar on top. 7. Place the drip pan at the bottom of the cooking chamber. Using the control panel, select Bake, adjust the temperature to 320 degrees F and the time to 20 minutes, then touch Start. 8. When the display indicates "Add Food," place the cooking tray in the center. 9. When cooking time is complete, remove the pan from the unit and place it onto a wire rack to cool for about 10 minutes before serving.

Per serving: Calories 459; Fat 12.6g; Sodium 105mg; Carbs 84g; Fiber 2.7g; Sugar 53.3g; Protein 5.5g

Baked Oats Apples

Prep time: 5 minutes | Cook time: 15 minutes | Serves: 2

2 Pink Lady apples
1 teaspoon butter, melted
½ teaspoon cinnamon
Whipped cream for serving
For the Topping:
⅓ cup old-fashioned oats
1 tablespoon butter, melted
¼ cup raisins
¼ nuts of choice
1 tablespoon maple syrup
1 teaspoon whole wheat flour
½ teaspoon cinnamon

1. Remove the apples' core, stem, and seeds by cutting them in half. Brush the sliced sides of the apples with butter, then

sprinkle with cinnamon. 2. In a small dish, combine the topping ingredients, then spread the mixture over the apple halves. 3. Put the halves into the cooking tray. 4. Place the drip pan at the bottom of the cooking chamber. Using the control panel, select Bake, adjust the temperature to 350 degrees F and the time to 15 minutes, then touch Start. 5. When the display indicates "Add Food," place the cooking tray in the center. 6. When cooking time is complete, remove the apple from the unit and place it onto a wire rack to cool for about 10 minutes before serving. 7. Serve warm with whipped cream.
Per serving: Calories 425; Fat 15.6g; Sodium 20mg; Carbs 65.8g; Fiber 8.5g; Sugar 32.3g; Protein 8.2g

Cinnamon Cheese Rolls

Prep time: 05 minutes	Cook time: 10 minutes	Serves: 6

For the Rolls:
2 tablespoons melted butter, plus more for brushing
⅓ cup packed brown sugar
½ teaspoon ground cinnamon
1 pinch of kosher salt
All-purpose flour for surface
1 (8-ounce) tube refrigerated
Crescent rolls
For the Glaze:
2 ounces' cream cheese, softened
½ cup powdered sugar
1 tablespoon whole milk, plus more if needed

1. Line a cooking tray with parchment paper and oil it with butter. 2. Cream the butter, cinnamon, brown sugar, and salt in a mixing bowl until light and fluffy. 3. On a floured board, roll out the crescent rolls in one piece. Fold the dough in half by pinching the seams. It should be rolled out into a 9x7-inch rectangle. 4. Leave a 14-inch border around the dough while applying the butter mixture. Starting at the long edge, roll the dough into a log and cut it crosswise into six pieces. 5. Cut side up, and place the pieces in the cooking tray. Place the drip pan at the bottom of the cooking chamber. 6. Using the control panel, select Bake, adjust the temperature to 350 degrees F and the time to 10 minutes, then touch Start. 7. When the display indicates "Add Food," place the cooking tray in the center. 8. When cooking time is complete, remove the rolls from the unit and place them onto a wire rack to cool for about 10 minutes before serving. 9. Whisk the powdered sugar, cream cheese, and milk in a bowl. If it's too thin, add milk – 1 teaspoon at a time – to thin the glaze. 10. Drip the glaze over the warm rolls and serve.
Per serving: Calories 363; Fat 15.5g; Sodium 383mg; Carbs 49.1g; Fiber 0.7g; Sugar 20.5g; Protein 5.7g

Hazelnut Croissants

Prep time: 05 minutes	Cook time: 15 minutes	Serves: 4

1 can (8-ounce) refrigerated crescent rolls
2 tablespoons almond butter (or peanut butter)
3 ounces' hazelnuts, finely chopped
½ cup chocolate syrup

1. Make eight triangles out of the crescent rolls. Spread almond butter and hazelnuts on each triangle. They should be rolled up and placed in the baking pan. Arrange baking pan into cooking tray 2. Place the drip pan at the bottom of the cooking chamber. Using the control panel, select Air Fry, adjust the temperature to 340 degrees F and the time to 15 minutes until golden brown, then touch Start. 3. When the display indicates "Add Food," place the cooking tray in the center. 4. When cooked, remove from the air fryer. 5. Drizzle the warm croissants with chocolate syrup and enjoy!
Per serving: Calories 294; Fat 3.4g; Sodium 156mg; Carbs 60.9g; Fiber 3.8g; Sugar 19g; Protein 7g

Blueberry Muffins

Prep time: 14 minutes	Cook time:17 minutes	Serves: 3

1 egg
⅓ cup sugar
½ cup oil
2 tablespoons water
¼ teaspoon vanilla extract
1 teaspoon lemon zest
⅔ cup flour
½ teaspoon baking powder
1 pinch of salt
½ cup blueberries

1. Mix the wet ingredients and the zest in a mixing bowl. Remove from the equation. 2. In a separate bowl, combine all of the dry ingredients. Combine the dry and wet ingredients in a mixing bowl. To blend, whisk everything together thoroughly. 3. Line 1 cup of oven-safe ramekins with parchment muffin papers. Scoop the batter into the paper with an ice cream scoop. 4. Arrange ramekins into the cooking tray. 5. Place the drip pan at the bottom of the cooking chamber. Using the control panel, select Bake, adjust the temperature to 350 degrees F and the time to 15 minutes, then touch Start. 6. When the display indicates "Add Food," place the cooking tray in the center. 7. When cooking time is complete, remove the muffins from the unit and place them onto a wire rack to cool for about 10 minutes before serving.
Per serving: Calories 543; Fat 38.1g; Sodium 73mg; Carbs 47.6g; Fiber 1.4g; Sugar 24.3g; Protein 4.9g

Almond Vanilla Cheesecake

Prep time: 20 minutes	Cook time: 20 minutes	Serves: 4

For the Crust:
1 tablespoon melted butter
½ cup almond flour
¼ teaspoon cinnamon
⅛ teaspoon cardamom
1 tablespoon brown sugar
For the Cheesecake:
8 ounces' cream cheese
1 egg
½ teaspoon pure vanilla extract
½ teaspoon cinnamon
¼ teaspoon cardamom
3 tablespoons brown sugar

1. For a 4-inch small spring form pan, cut a circle of parchment paper and set it inside the pan. Cooking spray the paper and the pan. 2. Mix the flour, butter, cinnamon, cardamom, and brown sugar in a mixing bowl. 3. Fill the prepared pan halfway with the prepared mixture and push it down. 4. Place the drip pan at the bottom of the cooking chamber. Using the control panel, select Bake, adjust the temperature to 350 degrees F and the time to 5 minutes, then touch Start. 5. When the display indicates "Add Food," place the cooking tray in the center. 6. When cooking time is complete, remove the pan from the unit and place it onto a wire rack to cool for about 10 minutes 7. Mix the cream cheese, vanilla, egg, cardamom, cinnamon, and brown sugar in a bowl with an electric mixer. 8. Without overfilling the pan, spoon the cream mixture on top of the almond crust, leaving a bit of room on top. 9. Place the drip pan at the bottom of the cooking chamber. Using the control panel, select Bake, adjust the temperature to 300 degrees F and the time to 15 minutes, then touch Start. 10. When the display indicates "Add Food," place the cooking tray in the center. 11. When cooking time is complete, remove the pan from the unit, place it onto a wire rack to cool for about 10 minutes, and put it in the fridge for 3-5 hours. 12. Remove from the pan and serve with whipped cream and a dash of cinnamon.
Per serving: Calories 331; Fat 30.8g; Sodium 204mg; Carbs 8.4g; Fiber 1.7g; Sugar 2.9g; Protein 8.8g

Chocolate Lava Cake

Prep time: 05 minutes | Cook time: 10 minutes | Serves: 3

4 ounces' semi-sweet chocolate bar, broken into pieces
6 tablespoons unsalted butter,
cut into pieces
3 tablespoons all-purpose
flour

1 egg yolk from a large egg
½ teaspoon vanilla extract
1 large egg
3 tablespoons white sugar
1 pinch of salt

1. Set aside three 6-ounce ramekins that have been greased with butter. 2. Microwave the chocolate and butter for 1 minute, stirring every 30 seconds, until thoroughly melted. Remove from the equation. 3. In a separate bowl, whisk the egg, vanilla, egg yolk, and sugar with an electric mixer until thoroughly combined. 4. Then, add and toss the flour, choco-late mixture, and salt until everything is thoroughly blended. Fill each of the prepared ramekins halfway with the mixture. In the cooking tray, place the ramekins. 5. Place the drip pan at the bottom of the cooking chamber. Using the control pan-el, select Bake, adjust the temperature to 370 degrees F and the time to 10 minutes, then touch Start. 6. When the display indicates "Add Food," place the cooking tray in the center. 7. When cooking time is complete, allow cooling in the ra-mekins for 1 minute. 8. Using a butter knife, loosen the cake from the ramekin and turn it over onto a plate. 9. Serve imme-diately and enjoy.
Per serving: Calories 510; Fat 37.1g; Sodium 240mg; Carbs 42.7g; Fiber 2.3g; Sugar 33.3g; Protein 4.1g

Sweet Apple Coconut Fritters

Prep time: 05 minutes | Cook time: 10 minutes | Serves: 4

½ cup self-rising flour
½ cup coconut flour
1 cup sour cream
½ cup granulated sugar

1 teaspoon ground cinnamon
½ teaspoon ground cardamom
1 large apple, peeled, cored,
and grated

1. Nonstick oil should be used to grease a baking pan. 2. Combine all ingredients in a mixing dish and stir well. Form the mixture into equal-sized fritters and lay them on the bak-ing sheet. 3. Arrange the baking pan into the cooking tray of the air fryer. 4. Place the drip pan at the bottom of the cook-ing chamber. Using the control panel, select Air Fry, adjust the temperature to 330 degrees F and the time to 10 minutes, then touch Start. 5. When the display indicates "Add Food," place the cooking tray in the center. 6. When the message "turn Food" appears, turn the fritters and cook for more minutes. 7. Dust your fritters with confectioners' sugar, if desired, and serve immediately!
Per serving: Calories 312; Fat 12.6g; Sodium 35mg; Carbs 48.7g; Fiber 2.8g; Sugar 31.1g; Protein 3.9g

Vanilla Semolina Pudding

Prep time: 10 minutes | Cook time: 20 minutes | Serves: 4

2 ounces' semolina
2½ cups milk

1 teaspoon pure vanilla extract
½ cup caster sugar

1. In a medium mixing bowl, combine the semolina and 2 cups milk. Mix everything until you get a smooth paste. Add the remaining milk, vanilla essence, and caster sugar gradual-ly. Mix until everything is well blended. 2. Transfer to a bak-ing dish and arrange into the cooking tray. 3. Place the drip pan at the bottom of the cooking chamber. Using the control panel, select Air Fry, adjust the temperature to 300 degrees

F and the time to 20 minutes, then touch Start. 4. When the display indicates "Add Food," place the cooking tray in the center. 5. When the message "turn Food" appears, wait 10 seconds until it resumes cooking. 6. When cooking time is complete, allow to cool in. Serve either warm or cold.
Per serving: Calories 209; Fat 2.6g; Sodium 58mg; Carbs 41.5g; Fiber 0.7g; Sugar 30.3g; Protein 5.8g

Glazed Donuts

Prep time: 10 minutes | Cook time: 15 minutes | Serves: 14

1 ¼ cups all-purpose flour,
plus more for working surface
2 tablespoons granulated sugar
1 teaspoon baking powder
¼ teaspoon table salt

4 tablespoons cold butter, cut
into pieces
⅓ cup whole milk
Cooking spray
1 cup powdered sugar
3 tablespoons water

1. Mix the all-purpose flour, salt, baking powder, and sugar in a mixing bowl. Cut the butter into the flour until it resembles coarse cornmeal and is well mixed. Stir in the milk until the dough can be formed into a ball. 2. Knead the dough for 30 seconds on a floured surface until it is smooth and forms a co-hesive ball. Cut into 14 pieces that are of the same size. Each one should be rolled into a smooth ball. 3. Place the drip pan at the bottom of the cooking chamber. Using the control pan-el, select Air Fry, adjust the temperature to 350 degrees F and the time to 10 minutes, then touch Start. 4. When the display indicates "Add Food," place the cooking tray in the center. 5. When the message "turn food" appears, turn the donuts. When cooking time is up, remove it from the cooking tray and cool onto a wire rack. 6. Whisk the water and powdered sugar together in a mixing bowl until smooth. Roll the cooked dough balls in the glaze to evenly coat them. To dry, place on a wire rack. For each ball, repeat the process.
Per serving: Calories 114; Fat 3.6g; Sodium 69mg; Carbs 19.2g; Fiber 0.3g; Sugar 10.3g; Protein 1.5g

Strawberry Scones

Prep time: 05 minutes | Cook time: 15 minutes | Serves: 4

1 ¾ cups self-raising flour
¼ cup butter
¼ cup caster sugar
4 tablespoon milk
vanilla essence, to taste

2 cups diced strawberries
¼ cup fresh strawberries
4 tablespoons whipped cream
1 tablespoon strawberry jam

1. Combine the flour, butter, and sugar in a mixing dish. To make breadcrumbs, rub the butter into the flour until it resem-bles breadcrumbs. To make a soft dough, add enough milk and vanilla extract. 2. Divide into four equal parts. Form the dough into four equal balls and flatten them slightly. Put them on a baking sheet and bake them. 3. Place the baking pan into the cooking tray. 4. Place the drip pan at the bottom of the cooking chamber. Using the control panel, select Bake, adjust the temperature to 360 degrees F and the time to 10 minutes, then touch Start. 5. When the display indicates "Add Food," place the cooking tray in the center. 6. Remove from the air fryer and let the scones cool on a cooling rack. 7. Cut in half and fill with strawberry jam, whipped cream, and some fresh strawberries. Serve and enjoy!
Per serving: Calories 442; Fat 17.6g; Sodium 96mg; Carbs 65.6g; Fiber 2.9g; Sugar 16.3g; Protein 7.1g

Buttered Shortbread Sticks

Prep time: 15 minutes | Cook time: 12 minutes | Serves: 10

⅓ cup caster sugar
1 ⅔ cups plain flour
¾ cup butter

1. Combine the sugar and flour in a mixing bowl. 2. Mix in the butter until you have a smooth dough. 3. Make ten equal-sized sticks out of the dough. 4. Prick the sticks lightly with a fork. 5. Place the sticks in the baking pan that has been lightly oiled. 6. Place the baking pan into the cooking tray. 7. Place the drip pan at the bottom of the cooking chamber. Using the control panel, select Air Fry, adjust the temperature to 355 degrees F and the time to 12 minutes, then touch Start. 8. When the display indicates "Add Food," place the cooking tray in the center. 9. When the display shows "turn Food," just wait 10 seconds until it resumes cooking. 10. Place the baking pan onto a wire rack to cool for about 5-10 minutes. 11. Now, invert the shortbread sticks onto a wire rack to cool completely.
Per serving: Calories 223; Fat 14g; Sodium 99mg; Carbs 22.6g; Fiber 0.6g; Sugar 6.7g; Protein 2.3g

Strawberry Cake

Prep time: 05 minutes | Cook time: 30 minutes | Serves: 4

¼ cup butter, melted
1 cup powdered Erythritol
1 teaspoon strawberry extract
12 egg whites
2 teaspoons cream of tartar
A pinch of salt

1. Combine the egg whites and cream of tartar in a mixing bowl. 2. Whip the egg whites with a hand mixer until they are white and fluffy. 3. Whisk in the other ingredients, excluding the butter, for another minute. 4. Fill a baking dish halfway with the mixture. Place the baking pan into the cooking tray. 5. Place the drip pan at the bottom of the cooking chamber. Using the control panel, select Bake, adjust the temperature to 400 degrees F and the time to 30 minutes, then touch Start. 6. When the display indicates "Add Food," place the cooking tray in the center. 7. When cooking time is complete, remove the baking pan from the unit and place it onto a wire rack to cool for about 10 minutes before serving. 8. Drizzle with melted butter once cooled.
Per serving: Calories 160; Fat 11.7g; Sodium 221mg; Carbs 61.8g; Fiber 0g; Sugar 60.8g; Protein 10.9g

Banana Slices with Sesame Seeds

Prep time: 15 minutes | Cook time: 15 minutes | Serves: 8

4 medium ripe bananas, peeled
⅓ cup rice flour, divided
2 tablespoons all-purpose flour
2 tablespoons corn flour
2 tablespoons desiccated coconut
½ teaspoon baking powder
½ teaspoon ground cardamom
1 pinch of salt
Water, as required
¼ cup sesame seeds

1. Mix 2 tablespoons of rice flour, all-purpose flour, cornmeal, coconut, baking powder, cardamom, and salt in a bowl until well combined. 2. Mix in the water gradually until a thick, homogeneous dough forms. 3. Place the remaining rice flour in a separate basin. 4. Add the sesame seeds to a third bowl. 5. Each banana should be split in half lengthwise and then into two segments. 6. Dip the banana slices in the coconut mixture, then top with the remaining rice flour, sesame seeds, and a pinch of salt. 7. Place the banana slices into the cooking tray. 8. Place the drip pan at the bottom of the cooking chamber. Using the control panel, select Air Fry, adjust the temperature to 390 degrees F and the time to 15 minutes, then touch Start. 9. When the display indicates "Add Food," place the cooking tray in the center. 10. When the display shows "Turn Food," turn the banana slice. 11. Remove the tray from the unit after the cooking time is up. 12. Serve.
Per serving: Calories 164; Fat 7.2g; Sodium 24mg; Carbs 24.6g; Fiber 3.6g; Sugar 7.8g; Protein 2.7g

Lemon Apple Pie

Prep time: 05 minutes | Cook time: 10 minutes | Serves: 4

½ teaspoon vanilla extract
1 beaten egg
1 large apple, chopped
1 Pillsbury Refrigerator pie crust
1 tablespoon butter
1 tablespoon ground cinnamon
1 tablespoon raw sugar
2 tablespoons sugar
2 teaspoons lemon juice
Baking spray

1. Using cooking spray, lightly coat a baking pan. Cover the bottom and sides of the pan with the pie crust. 2. Combine cinnamon, lemon juice, vanilla, sugar, and apples in a mixing dish. Pour over the pie crust. 3. Butter slices should be placed on top of the apples. 4. The other pie crust should be used to cover the apples. The tops of the pies should be pierced with a knife. 5. Sprinkle sugar over the beaten egg on top of the crust. 6. Wrap foil around the dish. 7. Pour the baking pan into the cooking tray. Place the drip pan at the bottom of the cooking chamber. Using the control panel, select Bake, adjust the temperature to 390 degrees F and the time to 10 minutes, then touch Start. 8. When the display indicates "Add Food", place the cooking tray in the center. 9. When cooking time is complete, remove the baking pan from the unit and place it onto a wire rack to cool for about 10 minutes before serving.
Per serving: Calories 110; Fat 5.2g; Sodium 57mg; Carbs 14.5g; Fiber 2.3g; Sugar 9.4g; Protein 2.1g

Almond Chocolate Cake

Prep time: 05 minutes | Cook time: 45 minutes | Serves: 9

½ cup hot water
1 teaspoon vanilla
¼ cup olive oil
½ cup almond milk
1 egg
½ teaspoon Salt
¾ teaspoon baking soda
¾ teaspoon baking powder
½ cup unsweetened cocoa powder
2 cups almond flour
1 cup brown sugar

1. Combine all of the dry ingredients in a large mixing basin. Then add the wet ingredients and mix well. Last but not least, add boiling water. 2. No worries, the batter will be thin. 3. In a cake pan, pour the batter. Cover with aluminum foil and poke holes in it. 4. Pour the baking pan into the cooking tray. Place the drip pan at the bottom of the cooking chamber. Using the control panel, select Bake, adjust the temperature to 390 degrees F and the time to 35 minutes, then touch Start. 5. When the display indicates "Add Food," place the cooking tray in the center. Discard foil and then bake another 10 minutes. 6. When cooking time is complete, remove the baking pan from the unit and place it onto a wire rack to cool for about 10 minutes before serving.
Per serving: Calories 302; Fat 22.4g; Sodium 247mg; Carbs 24.8g; Fiber 4.6g; Sugar 17.8g; Protein 7.8g

Chocolate Almond Soufflé

Prep time: 05 minutes | Cook time: 15 minutes | Serves: 2

2 tablespoons Almond flour
½ teaspoon vanilla
3 tablespoons sweetener
2 separated eggs
¼ cup melted coconut oil
3 ounces' semisweet chocolate, chopped

1. Brush ramekins with coconut oil and sweetener. 2. Melt the coconut oil and chocolate together in a double boiler. 3. Combine the egg yolks, vanilla, and sweetener in a mixing bowl. Make sure there are no lumps when you add the flour. 4. Whisk the egg whites until stiff peaks form, then fold them into the chocolate mixture. 5. Pour batter into ramekins and place them into the cooking tray. 6. Place the drip pan at the bottom of the cooking chamber. Using the control panel, select Bake, adjust the temperature to 330 degrees F and the time to 14 minutes, then touch Start. 7. When the display indicates "Add Food," place the cooking tray in the center. 8. When cooking time is complete, remove the cooking tray from the unit and place it onto a wire rack to cool for about 10 minutes. 9. Serve with powdered sugar dusted on top.

Per serving: Calories 419; Fat 31g; Sodium 364mg; Carbs 32.3g; Fiber 3.2g; Sugar 18.6g; Protein 7g

Fried Brandy Peaches

Prep time: 130 minutes | Cook time: 15 minutes | Serves: 4

4 ripe peaches (½ a peach = 1 serving)
1½ cups flour
Salt
2 egg yolks
¾ cup cold water
1½ tablespoons olive oil
2 tablespoons brandy
4 egg whites
Cinnamon

1. Mix the flour, egg yolks, and salt in a mixing dish. Stir in the water gradually, then add the brandy. Set aside the mixture for 2 hours and 45 minutes while preparing something. 2. In a big pot of water, boil the peaches and carve an X on the bottom of each one. Fill a big dish halfway with water and ice while the water is heating up. Each peach should be cooked for about a minute before being placed in the ice bath. The skins should now fall away from the peach. Mix the egg whites into the butter mixture after beating them. To coat each peach, dip it into the mixture. 3. Pour the coated peach into the cooking tray. Place the drip pan at the bottom of the cooking chamber. Using the control panel, select Air Fry, adjust the temperature to 360 degrees F and the time to 10minutes, then touch Start. 4. When the display indicates "Add Food," place the cooking tray in the center. 5. When the display shows "turn Food," turn the peaches slice. 6. When cooking time is complete, remove the baking pan from the unit and place it onto a wire rack to cool for about 10 minutes before serving. 7. Prepare a plate with the cinnamon, and roll the peaches in the mixture.

Per serving: Calories 468; Fat 22.4g; Sodium 78mg; Carbs 50.8g; Fiber 3.9g; Sugar 14.4g; Protein 11.2g

Crispy Bananas

Prep time: 10 minutes | Cook time: 10 minutes | Serves: 2

1 large egg
¼ cup cornstarch
¼ cup plain bread crumbs
3 bananas halved crosswise
Cooking oil
Chocolate sauce

1. Beat the egg in a small bowl. Place the cornstarch in a separate bowl. 2. In a third bowl, combine the breadcrumbs. 3.

The bananas should be dipped in cornstarch, egg, and breadcrumbs. Spray the cooking tray with cooking oil. Place the bananas in the cooking tray and spray them with cooking oil. 4. Place the drip pan at the bottom of the cooking chamber. Using the control panel, select Air Fry, adjust the temperature to 360 degrees F and the time to 5 minutes, then touch Start. 5. When the display indicates "Add Food," place the cooking tray in the center. 6. When displaying "turn Food," turn the banana. Transfer the bananas to plates. 7. Drizzle the chocolate sauce over the bananas and serve.

Per serving: Calories 392; Fat 11.1g; Sodium 179mg; Carbs 70.2g; Fiber 6.2g; Sugar 22.6g; Protein 8.1g

Banana Muffins with Chocolate Chips

Prep time: 05 minutes | Cook time: 25 minutes | Serves: 12

¾ cup whole wheat flour
¾ cup plain flour
¼ cup cocoa powder
¼ teaspoon baking powder
1 teaspoon baking soda
¼ teaspoon salt
2 large bananas, peeled and
mashed
1 cup sugar
⅓ cup canola oil
1 egg
½ teaspoon vanilla essence
1 cup mini chocolate chips

1. Combine flour, cocoa powder, baking powder, baking soda, and salt in a mixing dish. 2. Mix the bananas, sugar, oil, egg, and vanilla extract in a separate bowl and beat well. 3. Slowly add the flour mixture to the egg mixture, mixing just until incorporated. 4. Chocolate chunks should be folded in. Grease 12 muffin molds. 5. Transfer the mixture into prepared muffin molds evenly and put it into the cooking tray. 6. Place the drip pan at the bottom of the cooking chamber. Using the control panel, select Bake, adjust the temperature to 345 degrees F and the time to 25 minutes, then touch Start. 7. When the display indicates "Add Food," place the cooking tray in the center. 8. When time is up, muffin molds and keep on a wire rack to cool for about 10 minutes. 9. Carefully turn on a wire rack to cool completely before serving.

Per serving: Calories 191; Fat 7.2g; Sodium 164mg; Carbs 31.3g; Fiber 1.2g; Sugar 20.6g; Protein 2.2g

Cinnamon Apple Pies

Prep time: 10 minutes | Cook time: 15 minutes | Serves: 4

4 tablespoons butter
6 tablespoons brown sugar
1 teaspoon ground cinnamon
2 medium Granny Smith apples, diced
1 teaspoon cornstarch
2 teaspoons cold water
½ (14 ounces) package pastry
to get a 9-inch double-crust pie
cooking spray
½ tablespoon grapeseed oil
¼ cup powdered sugar
1 teaspoon milk, or more as required

1. In a skillet, combine the apples, butter, brown sugar, and cinnamon. Cook for 5 minutes over medium heat or until apples has softened. 2. Cornstarch should be dissolved in cold water. Cook, constantly stirring, until the sauce thickens, about 1 minute. While preparing the crust, remove the apple pie filling from the heat and set it aside to cool. 3. Unroll the pie crust on a lightly floured board and lightly roll it out to level the surface. Cut the dough into small rectangles so that two can be cooked simultaneously in the air fryer. Repeat with the remaining crust, rolling back a few pieces of dough if necessary until you have eight equal rectangles. 4. Wet the outside corners of four rectangles with water, then fill the center with apple filling, about 12 inches from the edges. Roll out the remaining rectangles so that they are slightly larger than the ones that will be served. Place these

rectangles on top of the filling, and use a fork to seal the edges. 4 Tiny slits should be cut in the tops of the cupcakes. 5. Spray the cooking tray of an air fryer with cooking spray. Brush the tops of 2 tablespoons with grapeseed oil and then move the cupcakes to the cooking tray of the air fryer using a spatula. 6. Place the drip pan at the bottom of the cooking chamber. Using the control panel, select Bake, adjust the temperature to 385 degrees F and the time to 8 minutes, then touch Start. 7. When the display indicates "Add Food," place the cooking tray in the center. 8. Mix the milk powder and sugar in a small bowl. Brush frosting over hot cakes and allow to dry. Drink the pops warm or at room temperature.

Per serving: Calories 342; Fat 18.8g; Sodium 189mg; Carbs 45g; Fiber 3.2g; Sugar 32.6g; Protein 1.2g

Banana Chocolate Muffins

Prep time: 05 minutes | Cook time: 20 minutes | Serves: 2

⅓ cup oil	3 teaspoons yeast
⅓ pound brown sugar	½ pound chocolate and hazel-
3 ripe bananas	nut cream
½ pound flour	

1. Chop the bananas after peeling them. Place them in a bowl and use a fork to fry them. Stir in the oil and sugar until everything is well combined. 2. Mix in the flour with the sprinkled yeast until you have a homogeneous dough. 3. Place muffin tins on a plate and fill them halfway with batter. Stir 1 teaspoon of cocoa cream in with a toothpick until thoroughly blended. Pour the muffin tins into the cooking tray. 4. Place the drip pan at the bottom of the cooking chamber. Using the control panel, select Bake, adjust the temperature to 360 degrees F and the time to 20 minutes, then touch Start. 5. When the display indicates "Add Food," place the cooking tray in the center. 6. When cooking time is complete, remove the muffin tins from the unit and place them onto a wire rack to cool for about 10 minutes before serving.

Per serving: Calories 779; Fat 39.3g; Sodium 23mg; Carbs 105.5g; Fiber 6.7g; Sugar 59.8g; Protein 7.8g

Buttered Churros

Prep time: 08 minutes | Cook time: 15 minutes | Serves: 4

¼ cup butter	2 eggs
½ cup milk	¼ cup white sugar
1 pinch salt	½ teaspoon ground cinnamon
½ cup flour	

1. In a saucepan over medium-high heat, melt the butter. After that, add the milk and the salt. Reduce heat to low and bring to a slow boil, constantly stirring with a wooden spoon. All of the flour should be added at the same time. Stir the contents together until it comes together. 2. Remove from the fire and set aside 5-7 minutes to cool. With a wooden spoon, stir in the eggs until the choux paste comes together. 3. Spoon dough into a pastry bag fitted with a large star tip-pipe dough pieces directly into the cooking tray. 4. Place the drip pan at the bottom of the cooking chamber. Using the control panel, select Air Fry, adjust the temperature to 340 degrees F and the time to 5 minutes, then touch Start. 5. When the display indicates "Add Food," place the cooking tray in the center. 6. When the display shows "turn food," no action is required. 7. Meanwhile, mix the sugar and cinnamon in a small bowl and then pour them onto a dish. 8. When done, remove the fried churros from the air fryer and roll them out of the cinnamon and sugar mixture.

Per serving: Calories 253; Fat14.5g; Sodium 166mg; Carbs 26.3g; Fiber 0.6g; Sugar 14.6g; Protein 5.5g

Spicy Pecans Crumb Cake

Prep time: 05 minutes | Cook time: 65 minutes | Serves: 2

For the Topping:	1 cup whole milk
2 cups pecans	½ stick unsalted butter, melted
2 sticks of unsalted butter melted	2 teaspoons pure vanilla extract
¾ cup light brown sugar	½ teaspoons baking powder
½ cup granulated sugar	1 teaspoon salt
2 ⅔ cups all-purpose flour	For the Glaze:
½ teaspoon ground cardamom	½ cup confectioners' sugar
½ teaspoon salt	2 tablespoons unsalted butter,
For the Cake:	melted
3 cups all-purpose flour	2 teaspoons whole milk
¼ cup sugar	½ teaspoon pure vanilla extract
2 large eggs	

1. Grease the cooking tray with butter. Add the pecans to the cooking tray. 2. Place the drip pan at the bottom of the cooking chamber. Using the control panel, select Roast, adjust the temperature to 350 degrees F and the time to 8 minutes, then touch Start. 3. When the display indicates "Add Food," place the cooking tray in the center. 4. When time is up, open the unit door, chop the pecans, and set them aside. 5. In a medium mixing bowl, combine the melted butter, light brown sugar, granulated sugar, cardamom, flour, chopped pecans, and salt. Mix thoroughly. 6. Mix the flour, baking powder, sugar and salt in a separate bowl. 7. Whisk together the eggs, milk, melted butter, and vanilla extract in a separate bowl. Combine the wet and dry ingredients and pour into the oiled baking dish. Top with a coating of pecans crumbs. 8. Place the drip pan at the bottom of the cooking chamber. Using the control panel, select Bake, adjust the temperature to 350 degrees F and the time to 55 minutes, then touch Start. 9. When the display indicates "Add Food," place the cooking tray in the center. 10. When time is up, open the unit door and cool the cake for 10 minutes. 11. Meanwhile, in a separate bowl, whisk together the glaze ingredients and pour over the cooled cake.

Per serving: Calories 216; Fat 16g; Sodium 364mg; Carbs 17g; Fiber 3.2g; Sugar 18.6g; Protein 1g

Lemon Peach Cobbler

Prep time: 05 minutes | Cook time: 50 minutes | Serves: 8

8 fresh peaches, peeled and sliced	½ cup sugar
½ cup packed light brown sugar	2 tablespoons lemon juice
	1 teaspoon grated ginger
¼ cup cornstarch	1 teaspoon baking powder
½ cup butter, melted	1 teaspoon lemon zest
1 ¼ cups all-purpose flour	2 tablespoons milk
	½ teaspoon salt

1. Combine the peaches, brown sugar, cornstarch, lemon juice, and ginger in a large mixing bowl. Mix thoroughly until the cornstarch is completely dissolved. Fill the oiled baking pan halfway with this mixture. 2. Combine flour, sugar, baking powder, lemon zest, and salt in a separate basin. Slowly drizzle in the milk and butter. 3. Pour the mixture over the peaches in the cooking tray. 4. Place the drip pan at the bottom of the cooking chamber. Using the control panel, select Bake, adjust the temperature to 350 degrees F and the time to 45 minutes, then touch Start. 5. When the display indicates "Add Food," place the cooking tray in the center. 6. When time is up, open the door and cool the peaches for 10 minutes.

Per serving: Calories 333; Fat 12.2g; Sodium 236mg; Carbs 54.3g; Fiber 3g; Sugar 35.6g; Protein 3.7g

Ginger Apple Cider Donuts

Prep time: 10 minutes | Cook time: 25 minutes | Serves: 18

2 cups apple cider
3 cups all-purpose flour
½ cup packed light brown sugar
½ cup cold milk
One stick of unsalted butter, grated
2 teaspoons baking powder
1 teaspoon ground cinnamon

1 teaspoon ground ginger
½ teaspoon baking soda
½ teaspoon kosher salt
¼ cup all-purpose flour
8 tablespoons unsalted butter, melted
1 cup granulated sugar
1 teaspoon ground cinnamon

1. Preheat a skillet over medium heat. Bring 2 cups apple cider to a boil and cook for 12 minutes. Allow cooling before serving. 2. Whisk flour, light brown sugar, baking powder, baking soda, cinnamon, ginger, and salt in a mixing dish. Mix thoroughly. 3. Toss the flour mixture with the grated butter. Mix everything thoroughly, form a well in the center, and pour the apple cider and milk. To make the dough, thoroughly combine all ingredients. 4. On a floured surface, knead the dough for about 5 minutes. Make a 9x13-inch rectangle out of it, about 12 inches thick. 5. Cut donuts out of the dough with a doughnut cutter and lay them on a baking sheet. Refrigerate for 30 minutes before serving. 6. Combine the granulated sugar and cinnamon in a mixing bowl. Melt the butter in a separate bowl. 7. Add donuts to the cooking tray. 8. Place the cooking tray at the bottom of the cooking chamber. Using the control panel, select Air Fry, adjust the temperature to 375 degrees F and the time to 12 minutes, then touch Start. 9. When the display indicates "Add Food," place the cooking tray in the center. 10. When the message shows "turn Food," turn the donuts. 11. When the time is up, open the unit and cool the donuts on the wire rack for 10 minutes. 12. Dip cooked donuts in the melted butter, then in the cinnamon mixture.

Per serving: Calories 131; Fat 0.6g; Sodium 104mg; Carbs 29.3g; Fiber 0.7g; Sugar 12.6g; Protein 2.4g

Apple Custard

Prep time: 10 minutes | Cook time: 45 minutes | Serves: 6

1 cup brown sugar
1 cup all-purpose flour
½ cup 2% milk
2 cups boiling water
3 apples, peeled and chopped

2 teaspoons baking powder
½ teaspoon ground cinnamon
2 tablespoons butter, cubed
½ teaspoon salt

1. Combine flour, baking powder, sugar, cinnamon, and salt in a mixing dish. 2. Combine the milk and apples in a mixing bowl. Mix thoroughly and pour into a prepared cooking tray. 3. Butter the dough and roll it out. Fill the pot halfway with boiling water. 4. Place the drip pan at the bottom of the cooking chamber. Using the control panel, select Bake, adjust the temperature to 400 degrees F and the time to 45 minutes, then touch Start. 5. When the display indicates "Add Food," place the cooking tray in the center. 6. When time is up, open the unit and set it aside to cool for 15 minutes. Serve with ice cream.

Per serving: Calories 272; Fat 4.7g; Sodium 243mg; Carbs 56.9g; Fiber 3.4g; Sugar 36g; Protein 3.2g

Cream Cinnamon Rolls

Prep time: 10 minutes | Cook time: 10 minutes | Serves: 6

⅓ cup packed brown sugar
⅓ cup all-purpose flour for

surface
8-ounce tube refrigerated

Crescent rolls
2 tablespoons melted butter, plus more for brushing
½ teaspoon ground cinnamon
A pinch of salt

2 ounces' cream cheese, softened
½ cup powdered sugar
1 tablespoon milk

1. Line the cooking tray with parchment paper and grease with butter. 2. Mix the butter, brown sugar, cinnamon, and salt in a mixing dish. On a floured surface, roll out the crescent rolls. 3. Roll up the rolls with the butter mixture on top and seam the edges. Place the rolls in the cooking tray, leaving some room between them. 4. Place the drip pan at the bottom of the cooking chamber. Using the control panel, select Air Fry, adjust the temperature to 350 degrees F and the time to 10 minutes, then touch Start. 5. When the display indicates "Add Food," place the cooking tray in the center. 6. When displaying "turn Food," turn the roll. 7. When time's up, open the unit and set aside rolls for cool for 15 minutes. 8. Meanwhile, combine cream cheese, powdered sugar, and milk in a separate bowl. Spread glaze over the cinnamon rolls.

Per serving: Calories 312; Fat 15.4g; Sodium 383mg; Carbs 38.5g; Fiber 0.3g; Sugar 20.5g; Protein 4.3g

Homemade Lava Cake

Prep time: 10 minutes | Cook time: 10 minutes | Serves: 4

3½ ounce unsalted butter
3½ ounce dark chocolate, chopped

2 eggs
1½ tablespoon self-rising flour
3½ tablespoons sugar

1. 4 oven-safe ramekins, greased and floured 2. Melt the chocolate and butter in a microwave-safe bowl for 3 minutes, stirring regularly to avoid burning. 3. Whisk the eggs and sugar together in a separate bowl until foamy. Pour in the chocolate mixture that has melted. 4. Mix in the flour thoroughly. Fill the ramekins with this mixture. Place them into the Air Fry cooking tray. 5. Place the drip pan at the bottom of the cooking chamber. Using the control panel, select Bake, adjust the temperature to 375 degrees F and the time to 10 minutes, then touch Start. 6. When the display indicates "Add Food," place the cooking tray in the center. 7. When times up, open the unit and set aside rolls for cool for 5 minutes.

Per serving: Calories 392; Fat 29.7g; Sodium 193mg; Carbs 27.7g; Fiber 0.9g; Sugar 23.6g; Protein 5.2g

Banana Choco Brownies

Prep time: 05 minutes | Cook time: 30 minutes | Serves: 12

2 cups almond flour
2 teaspoons baking powder
½ teaspoon baking powder
½ teaspoon baking soda
½ teaspoon salt
1 over-ripe banana

3 large eggs
½ teaspoon stevia powder
¼ cup coconut oil
1 tablespoon vinegar
⅓ cup almond flour
⅓ cup cocoa powder

1. In a food processor, add all ingredients and pulse until well incorporated. 2. Fill a baking dish halfway with the mixture. Place the baking dish into the cooking tray. 3. Place the drip pan at the bottom of the cooking chamber. Using the control panel, select Bake, adjust the temperature to 350 degrees F and the time to 30 minutes, then touch Start. 4. When the display indicates "Add Food," place the cooking tray in the center. 5. When cooking time is complete, remove the baking pan from the unit and place it onto a wire rack to cool for about 10 minutes before cutting and serving.

Per serving: Calories 135; Fat 10.9g; Sodium 53mg; Carbs 8.5g; Fiber 3.2g; Sugar 2g; Protein 5 g

Allspice Donuts

Prep time: 05 minutes | Cook time: 05 minutes | Serves: 8

1 pinch of allspice	⅓ cup granulated sweetener
4 tablespoons dark brown sugar	3 tablespoons melted coconut oil
½ to 1 teaspoon cinnamon	1 can biscuits

1. Mix allspice, sugar, sweetener, and cinnamon. 2. Take out biscuits from the can, and with a circle cookie cutter, cut holes from the centers, and place them into the cooking tray. 3. Place the drip pan at the bottom of the cooking chamber. Using the control panel, select Air Fry, adjust the temperature to 350 degrees F and the time to 5 minutes, then touch Start. 4. When the display indicates "Add Food," place the cooking tray in the center. 5. When cooking time is complete, remove the cooking tray from the unit and place it onto a wire rack to cool for about 10 minutes. Use a brush to coat the donuts with melted coconut oil and dip each into the sugar mixture. 6. Serving.

Per serving: Calories 151; Fat 8.1g; Sodium 331mg; Carbs 18.3g; Fiber 0.5g; Sugar 5.4g; Protein 1.8g

Lemon Cheesecake Egg Rolls

Prep time: 10 minutes | Cook time: 20 minutes | Serves: 8

1 block (16 ounces) of cream cheese, at room temperature	1 egg, beaten
8½ ounces fig jam	1 tablespoon water
15 ready-made egg roll wrappers, refrigerated	¾ cup sugar
2 tablespoons unsalted butter, melted	1 teaspoon ground cinnamon
	1 tablespoon lemon juice
	1 teaspoon vanilla extract

1. In an electric mixer, combine the sugar, cream cheese, lemon juice, and vanilla extract. Whip on medium speed until well mixed. Fill a pastry bag with the mixture. 2. Place an egg roll wrapper on a work surface and pipe 2 tablespoons of cream cheese into the center, followed by 1 tablespoon of jam. 3. Brush the roll's edge with egg and water mix. Spray the wrap with cooking spray before folding and rolling it. Add them to the Air Fry cooking tray. 4. Place the drip pan at the bottom of the cooking chamber. Using the control panel, select Air Fry, adjust the temperature to 370 degrees F and the time to 7 minutes, then touch Start. 5. When the display indicates "Add Food," place the cooking tray in the center. 6. When shown the message "turn Food," turn the roll. 7. When times up, open the unit and set aside rolls for cool for 15 minutes. 8. Meanwhile, combine sugar and cinnamon in a bowl. Brush the cooked egg rolls with butter and sprinkle with the cinnamon mix.

Per serving: Calories 547; Fat 19.7g; Sodium 629mg; Carbs 84.7g; Fiber 2g; Sugar 32.6g; Protein 13.2g

Brazilian Pineapple

Prep time: 10 minutes | Cook time: 10 minutes | Serves: 4

1 pineapple, peeled, cored, and sliced	2 teaspoons ground cinnamon
½ cup brown sugar	3 tablespoons butter, melted

1. In a mixing dish, combine brown sugar and cinnamon. Remove from the equation. 2. Brush the pineapple slices with butter and sprinkle with the cinnamon mixture on a platter. 3. In the Air Fryer cooking tray, place the pineapples. Place the drip pan at the bottom of the cooking chamber. Using the control panel, select Air Fry, adjust the temperature to 400 degrees F and the time to 10 minutes, then touch Start. 4. When the display indicates "Add Food," place the cooking tray in the center. 5. When shown the message "turn Food," turn the pineapple Brush with more butter. 6. When times up, open the unit and set aside pineapples to cool for 15 minutes.

Per serving: Calories 169; Fat 8.7g; Sodium 67mg; Carbs 24.1g; Fiber 1.2g; Sugar 21.6g; Protein 0.4g

Chocolate Walnut Blondies

Prep time: 10 minutes | Cook time: 35 minutes | Serves: 12

1 cup butter, melted	chunks
2 cups packed brown sugar	2 eggs
2 cups all-purpose flour	2 teaspoons vanilla extract
½ cup ground walnuts	1 teaspoon baking powder
1 cup walnuts, chopped, toasted	⅛ teaspoon baking soda
1 cup semisweet chocolate	A pinch of salt

1. Grease a baking dish and set it aside. Mix the butter, brown sugar, and vanilla extract in a mixing basin. 2. Add and stir the eggs one at a time. Combine flour, baking powder, crushed walnuts, baking soda, and salt in a separate bowl. 3. Combine the chopped walnuts and chocolate chunks in a mixing bowl. Spread on the food that has been prepared. 4. Place the drip pan at the bottom of the cooking chamber. Using the control panel, select Bake, adjust the temperature to 350 degrees F and the time to 35 minutes, then touch Start. 5. When the display indicates "Add Food," place the cooking tray in the center. 6. When times up, open the unit and set aside Blondies on the cooling rack for 15 minutes.

Per serving: Calories 346; Fat 19.7g; Sodium 371mg; Carbs 40.4g; Fiber 0.9g; Sugar 23.6g; Protein 4.5g

Vanilla Blueberry Bars

Prep time: 10 minutes | Cook time:40 minutes | Serves: 24

1 ⅓ cups butter, softened	¼ teaspoon salt
⅔ cup sugar	3 cups blueberries
½ teaspoon vanilla extract	1 cup sugar
3 ¾ cups all-purpose flour	3 tablespoons cornstarch
1 egg	

1. Cream the butter, sugar, and salt in a mixing bowl until light and fluffy. 2. Mix in the egg and vanilla extract thoroughly. Gradually add the flour, mixing well after each addition. Form the dough into a ball, wrap it in plastic wrap, and chill for 2-8 hours. 3. Using nonstick cooking spray, grease a baking dish. 4. Preheat a saucepan over medium-high heat. Combine the blueberries, sugar, and cornstarch in a mixing bowl. Bring to a boil, reduce to low heat and keep stirring until the sauce thickens. Turn off the heat and set aside to cool. 5. Roll out the dough on a working surface. Freeze for 10 minutes after shaping into a rectangle. 6. Place one rectangle on top of the filling in the baking dish. Place the remaining rectangle over the filling and cut it into strips. 7. Place the drip pan at the bottom of the cooking chamber. Using the control panel, select Bake, adjust the temperature to 375 degrees F and the time to 35 minutes, then touch Start. 8. When the display indicates "Add Food," place the cooking tray in the center. 9. When the time is up, open the unit and set aside bars on the cooling rack for 15 minutes

Per serving: Calories 199; Fat 10.7g; Sodium 99mg; Carbs 24g; Fiber 1g; Sugar 7.4g; Protein 2.5g

Cream Potato Bars

Prep time: 10 minutes | Cook time: 50 minutes | Serves: 24

1 package of white cake mix	3 eggs, divided
1 cup chopped pecans, toasted	14 ounce sweetened condensed milk, divided
½ cup cold butter, cubed	
8 ounces' cream cheese, softened	3 cups sweet potatoes, cooked and mashed
½ cup sugar	2 teaspoons pumpkin pie spice

1. Using nonstick cooking spray, grease a baking pan. 2. Combine cake mix, pecans, and butter in a mixing basin. Place the mixture in the baking dish. 3. Cream the cream cheese, sugar, 1 egg, and 2 tablespoons of milk in a separate bowl. 4. Combine the sweet potatoes, 2 eggs, remaining milk, and pie spice in a mixing bowl. This mixture should be poured on top of the pecan mixture. Add a spoonful of cream cheese on top. 5. Place the drip pan at the bottom of the cooking chamber. Using the control panel, select Bake, adjust the temperature to 350 degrees F and the time to 45 minutes, then touch Start. 6. When the display indicates "Add Food," place the cooking tray in the center. 7. When times up, open the unit and set aside for cooling rack for 15 minutes. Cut into bars before serving.

Per serving: Calories 275; Fat 13.2g; Sodium 231mg; Carbs 36.2g; Fiber 1.2g; Sugar 25.6g; Protein 4.3g

Brownies with Chocolate Chips

Prep time: 10 minutes | Cook time: 30 minutes | Serves: 24

1 package fudge brownie mix	pepper
¾ cup dark chocolate chips	½ cup canola oil
2 teaspoons ground cinnamon	¼ cup water
1 teaspoon ground ancho chili	2 eggs

1. Combine the brownie mix, cinnamon, and chili pepper in a large mixing bowl. Fill a glass jar halfway with the mixture and top with chocolate chips. 2. Grease a baking dish and set it aside. Whisk together the oil, eggs, and water in a separate basin. Stir in the chocolate mixture well. 3. In a greased baking dish, spread the batter. Place baking dish into cooking tray 4. Place the drip pan at the bottom of the cooking chamber. Using the control panel, select Bake, adjust the temperature to 350 degrees F and the time to 25 minutes, then touch Start. 5. When the display indicates "Add Food," place the cooking tray in the center. 6. When times up, open the unit and set aside Brownies on the cooling rack for 15 minutes.

Per serving: Calories 75; Fat 6g; Sodium 13mg; Carbs 5.7g; Fiber 0.3g; Sugar 3.6g; Protein 0.9g

Vanilla Chocolate Chip Blondies

Prep time: 10 minutes | Cook time: 35 minutes | Serves: 4

2 cups all-purpose flour	1 teaspoon baking soda
¾ cup packed brown sugar	1 teaspoon salt
¾ cup sugar	¾ cup canola oil
1 cup semisweet chocolate chips	2 eggs
	1 teaspoon vanilla extract

1. Combine the flour, brown sugar, sugar, chocolate chips, baking soda, and salt in a bowl. 2. Grease a baking dish and set it aside. Whisk together the oil, eggs, and water in a separate basin. Stir in the chocolate mixture well. 3. In a greased baking dish, spread the batter. 4. Place baking dish into cooking tray 5. Place the drip pan at the bottom of the cooking chamber. Using the control panel, select Bake, adjust the temperature to 350 degrees F and the time to 35 minutes,

then touch Start. 6. When the display indicates "Add Food," place the cooking tray in the center. 7. When the time is up, open the unit and set aside Blondies on the cooling rack for 15 minutes

Per serving: Calories 906; Fat 32.4g; Sodium 936mg; Carbs 148.7g; Fiber 4.9g; Sugar 92.6g; Protein 9.2g

Raspberry Almond Crumble

Prep time: 10 minutes | Cook time: 40 minutes | Serves: 12

2 cups raspberries, frozen	1 teaspoon salt
¼ cup butter softened	3 egg whites
¾ cup sugar	1 cup sugar
¾ cup 2% milk	½ cup boiling water
2 ¼ cups all-purpose flour	⅓ cup almonds, sliced
2 eggs, room temperature	⅛ teaspoon cream of tartar
2 teaspoons baking powder	¼ teaspoon almond extract

1. Using nonstick cooking spray, grease a baking dish. In a mixing dish, cream together the butter and sugar until creamy. Continue to whisk in the eggs. 2. In a separate basin, combine flour, baking powder, and salt. Mix in the cream mixture and the milk thoroughly. 3. Spread the frozen berries in the baking dish after folding them. 4. Place the drip pan at the bottom of the cooking chamber. Using the control panel, select Bake, adjust the temperature to 350 degrees F and the time to 30 minutes, then touch Start. 5. When the display indicates "Add Food," place the cooking tray in the center. 6. When times up, open the unit and set aside for cooling rack for 15 minutes. 7. In a heatproof bowl, whisk together the egg whites, sugar, and cream of tartar. Place the bowl over a pot of boiling water. Remove it from the stove and whip it on high until stiff peaks form. 8. Spread the icing over the cake and fold in the almond essence. Almonds should be sprinkled on top.

Per serving: Calories 211; Fat 5.3g; Sodium 251mg; Carbs 36.6g; Fiber 2g; Sugar 14.3g; Protein 5g

Vanilla Carrot Cake

Prep time: 10 minutes | Cook time: 60 minutes | Serves: 12

2 cups all-purpose flour	2 teaspoons ground cinnamon
2 cups sugar	1 teaspoon baking soda
1½ cups canola oil	1 teaspoon vanilla extract
2 cups carrots, grated	A pinch of salt
1 cup pineapple, crushed	6 ounces' cream cheese, softened
1 cup sweetened coconut, shredded	
1 cup nuts, chopped	3 cups confectioners' sugar
3 eggs	6 tablespoons butter, softened
	1 teaspoon vanilla extract

1. In a mixing bowl, combine flour, sugar, cinnamon, baking soda, salt, eggs, carrots, and vanilla. Stir everything together thoroughly. 2. Combine the pineapple, coconut, and chopped nuts in a mixing bowl. Place the mixture in a baking pan that has been sprayed with nonstick cooking spray. 3. Place the drip pan at the bottom of the cooking chamber. Using the control panel, select Bake, adjust the temperature to 350 degrees F and the time to 60 minutes, then touch Start. 4. When the display indicates "Add Food," place the cooking tray in the center. 5. When times up, open the unit and set aside for cooling rack for 15 minutes. 6. Meanwhile, beat the cream cheese and butter until fluffy. Add confectioner's sugar and vanilla and mix until smooth. Spread this frost on top of the cooled cake.

Per serving: Calories 786 Fat 47.4g; Sodium 305mg; Carbs 87.7g; Fiber 3g; Sugar 36.7g; Protein 7.2g

Tasty Pineapple Orange Cake

Prep time: 10 minutes | Cook time: 25minutes | Serves: 15

1 package yellow cake mix	20-ounce crushed pineapple, undrained
11 ounces' mandarin oranges, undrained	1-ounce sugar-free instant vanilla pudding mix
4 egg whites	8-ounce reduced-fat whipped topping
½ cup unsweetened applesauce	

1. In a bowl, beat the oranges, egg whites, and applesauce on low speed using a hand mixer. In a baking dish sprayed with nonstick cooking spray, pour the dough. 2. Place the drip pan at the bottom of the cooking chamber. Using the control panel, select Bake, adjust the temperature to 350 degrees F and the time to 30 minutes, then touch Start. 3. When the display indicates "Add Food," place the cooking tray in the center. 4. When the time is up, open the unit and set aside for cooling rack for 15 minutes. 5. Combine the topping ingredients in a separate bowl and spread over the cooled cake. 6. Refrigerate the cake for 60 minutes.
Per serving: Calories231; Fat 7.5g; Sodium 287mg; Carbs 38.9g; Fiber 1.2g; Sugar 24.6g; Protein 3.3g

Chocolate Vanilla Strawberry Cobbler

Prep time: 10 minutes | Cook time: 40 minutes | Serves: 12

1 cup butter, cubed, melted	4 cups fresh strawberries, quartered
1½ cups self-rising flour	2 cups boiling water
2 ¼ cups sugar, divided	Whipped cream
¾ cup 2% milk	1 teaspoon vanilla extract
⅓ cup baking cocoa	

1. To oil a baking dish, melt the butter. 2. Combine flour, 1 cup sugar, milk, and vanilla in a separate basin. Mix thoroughly. 3. In a separate bowl, combine the cocoa and the remaining sugar. 4. Pour the cocoa mixture into the baking dish. On top of that, pour boiling water. 5. Place the drip pan at the bottom of the cooking chamber. Using the control panel, select Bake, adjust the temperature to 350 degrees F and the time to 40 minutes, then touch Start. 6. When the display indicates "Add Food," place the cooking tray in the center. 7. When the time is up, open the unit and set aside for cooling rack for 15 minutes. 8. Serve the cake with whipped cream.
Per serving: Calories 392; Fat 19.7g; Sodium 122mg; Carbs 55.5g; Fiber 2.2g; Sugar 40.6g; Protein 3.2g

Gingerbread with Lemon Cream

Prep time: 10 minutes | Cook time: 40 minutes | Serves: 20

1 cup shortening	½ cup sugar
1 cup sugar	1 cup half-and-half cream
1 cup molasses	2 large egg yolks, beaten
2 eggs	2 teaspoons cornstarch
3 cups all-purpose flour	2 tablespoons butter
½ teaspoons baking soda	4 tablespoons lemon juice
1 teaspoon ground ginger	1 teaspoon grated lemon zest
1 teaspoon ground cinnamon	1 dash nutmeg
1 cup hot water	1 dash salt
A pinch of salt	

1. Grease a baking dish and set it aside. Set aside a bowl containing shortening, sugar, molasses, and eggs. 2. Flour, baking powder, baking soda, cinnamon, ginger, and salt should all be mixed together. In a separate bowl, thoroughly combine the ingredients. 3. Alternate adding the flour mixture to the molasses mixture with hot water, stirring until dough forms.

Place the dough on the prepared baking sheet. 4. Place the drip pan at the bottom of the cooking chamber. Using the control panel, select Bake, adjust the temperature to 350 degrees F and the time to 40 minutes, then touch Start. 5. When the display indicates "Add Food," place the cooking tray in the center position 6. Meanwhile, in a small saucepan over medium-high heat, combine all of the ingredients for the lemon sauce except the egg yolks, butter, lemon juice, and zest. Remove from heat once the sauce has thickened. 7. Return the mixture to the pan and stir well, adding a little of the hot filling to the egg yolks. 8. Bring to a boil, then reduce to a simmer for 2 minutes. Remove the pan from the heat. Combine the butter, lemon juice, and zest in a separate bowl. 9. Serve the cake with a dollop of lemon cream.
Per serving: Calories 392; Fat 19.7g; Sodium 122mg; Carbs 55.5g; Fiber 2.2g; Sugar 40.6g; Protein 3.2g

Vanilla Pumpkin Cheesecake

Prep time: 10 minutes | Cook time: 45 minutes | Serves: 24

1½ cups gingersnaps, crushed	1 teaspoon ground cinnamon
¼ cup butter, melted	1 teaspoon vanilla extract
40 ounces' cream cheese, softened	5 eggs, beaten
1 cup sugar	1 pinch of ground nutmeg
15-ounce solid-pack pumpkin	Maple syrup

1. Using nonstick cooking spray, grease a baking pan. 2. In a mixing bowl, combine the gingersnaps crumbs and butter; press this mixture into the bottom of the baking pan. 3. In a separate dish, beat cream cheese and sugar with a hand mixer until smooth. 4. Combine the pumpkin, cinnamon, vanilla, and eggs in a mixing bowl. Low-speed drumming Sprinkle nutmeg on top of the mixture and pour it over the crust. Place the drip pan in the bottom of the cooking chamber. Using the control panel, select Bake then adjust the temperature to 350 degrees F and the time to 45 minutes then touch Start. 5. When the display indicates "Add Food", place the cooking tray in the center position. 6. When times up, open the unit and set aside for cooling rack for 15 minutes Slice the cake.
Per serving: Calories 246; Fat 19.6g; Sodium 185mg; Carbs 13.5g; Fiber 0.6g; Sugar 10.1g; Protein 5.1g

Nutmeg Bread Pudding

Prep time: 10 minutes | Cook time: 40 minutes | Serves: 2

1 cup cinnamon-raisin bread, cubed	3 tablespoons brown sugar
1 egg	1 tablespoon butter, melted
⅔ cup 2% milk	½ teaspoon ground cinnamon
⅓ cup raisins	¼ teaspoon ground nutmeg
	A pinch of salt

1. Using nonstick cooking spray, grease a baking pan. 2. Bread cubes should be placed in the baking pan. Whisk together the egg, milk, brown sugar, butter, cinnamon, nutmeg, and salt in a mixing dish. Mix thoroughly. 3. Set aside for 15 minutes after adding the raisins and pouring the mixture over the cubed bread. Place the drip pan at the bottom of the cooking chamber. Using the control panel, select Bake, adjust the temperature to 350 degrees F and the time to 40 minutes, then touch Start. 4. When the display indicates "Add Food," place the cooking tray in the center. 5. When the time is up, open the unit and set it aside for cooling.
Per serving: Calories 325; Fat 10.7g; Sodium 294mg; Carbs 51.5g; Fiber 1.2g; Sugar 33.6g; Protein 8.2g

Chocolate Croissant Pudding

Prep time: 10 minutes | Cook time: 60 minutes | Serves: 15

6 croissants, at least 1-day-old
1 cup semisweet chocolate chips
5 eggs
12 egg yolks
5 cups half-and-half cream
1½ cups sugar
1½ teaspoons vanilla extract
1 tablespoon coffee liqueur

1. Using nonstick cooking spray, grease a baking pan. 2. Bread cubes should be placed in the baking pan. Whisk together the egg, milk, brown sugar, butter, cinnamon, nutmeg, and salt in a mixing dish. Mix thoroughly. 3. Set aside for 15 minutes after adding the raisins and pouring the mixture over the cubed bread. 4. Place the drip pan at the bottom of the cooking chamber. Using the control panel, select Bake, adjust the temperature to 350 degrees F and the time to 60 minutes, then touch Start. 5. When the display indicates "Add Food," place the cooking tray in the center position 6. When the time is up, open the unit and set it aside for cooling.
Per serving: Calories 432; Fat 24.3g; Sodium 260mg; Carbs 46.5g; Fiber 1.5g; Sugar 31.6g; Protein 8.6g

Chocolate Tiramisu Cheesecake

Prep time: 10 minutes | Cook time: 45 minutes | Serves: 12

32 ounces' cream cheese, softened
12 ounces' vanilla wafers
1 cup sugar
1 cup sour cream
5 teaspoons of instant coffee
3 tablespoons hot water
4 eggs, beaten
1 cup whipped cream topping
1 tablespoon cocoa powder

1. Using nonstick cooking spray, grease a baking dish. With a mixing bowl, dissolve 2 teaspoons of coffee granules in 2 tablespoons of boiling water. 2. Half wafers should be layered at the bottom of the baking sheet, and 1 tablespoon of coffee mix should be brushed on top. 3. Combine the sour cream cheese and sugar in a mixing bowl and beat until smooth. Continue to beat at moderate speed after adding the eggs. Half of the filling should be set aside. 4. Remaining coffee granules should be dissolved in the remaining water and added to half of the filling. Fill the wafers with the filling. 5. On top of it, layer the remaining wafers, brush with the coffee mixture, and spread the other half of the filling. Place the drip pan at the bottom of the cooking chamber. Using the control panel, select Bake, adjust the temperature to 350 degrees F and the time to 45 minutes, then touch Start. 6. When the display indicates "Add Food," place the cooking tray in the center position 7. When times up, open the unit and set aside for cooling rack for 15 minutes. 8. Spread whipped topping on top and slice.
Per serving: Calories 527; Fat 37.3g; Sodium 350mg; Carbs 41.5g; Fiber 0.7g; Sugar 28g; Protein 9.8g

Zesty Almond Muffins with Swerve

Prep time: 10 minutes | Cook time: 15 minutes | Serves: 6

2 eggs, separated
1 teaspoon baking powder
1½ cups almond flour
1 lemon juice
1 lemon zest, grated
3 tablespoon Swerve
¼ cup heavy cream

1. Combine egg yolks, heavy cream, Sweetener, lemon zest, lemon juice, almond flour, and baking powder in a mixing bowl until well blended. 2. Egg whites should be whisked until soft peaks form in a separate basin. 3. Slowly incorporate the egg whites into the egg yolk mixture. 4. Fill the silicone muffin tins halfway with the batter. Arrange muffin cup into the cooking tray. 5. Place the drip pan at the bottom of the cooking chamber. Using the control panel, select Bake, adjust the temperature to 350 degrees F and the time to 15 minutes, then touch Start. 6. When the display indicates "Add Food," place the cooking tray in the center. 7. When the time is up, open the unit and set it aside for cooling. 8. Serve and enjoy.
Per serving: Calories 206; Fat 17.3g; Sodium 26mg; Carbs 8.7g; Fiber 3.3g; Sugar 1.6g; Protein 8.1g

Almond Chocolate Chip Muffins

Prep time: 10 minutes | Cook time: 12 minutes | Serves: 6

3 eggs
½ cup unsweetened chocolate chips
1 tablespoon Swerve
1 teaspoon baking powder
1 cup almond flour
1½ cups mozzarella cheese, shredded

1. Whisk eggs and shredded cheese together in a mixing dish until well mixed. 2. Mix in the Swerve, baking powder, and almond flour until thoroughly combined. 3. Fold in the chocolate chips thoroughly. 4. Fill the silicone muffin tins halfway with the batter. Place muffin tin into cooking tray 5. Place the drip pan at the bottom of the cooking chamber. Using the control panel, select Bake, adjust the temperature to 400 degrees F and the time to 12 minutes, then touch Start. 6. When the display indicates "Add Food," place the cooking tray in the center position 7. When the time is up, open the unit and set it aside for cooling. 8. Serve and enjoy.
Per serving: Calories 293; Fat 23.5g; Sodium 81mg; Carbs 10.5g; Fiber 4.5g; Sugar 0.8g; Protein 11.4 g

Almond Chia Blondies

Prep time: 10 minutes | Cook time: 20minutes | Serves: 16

1 cup almond butter
3 tablespoons water
1 tablespoon ground chia seeds
¼ teaspoon salt
¼ cup dark chocolate chips
½ teaspoon baking soda
1 teaspoon vanilla
½ cup coconut sugar

1. Combine ground chia seeds and water in a large mixing dish. Allow sitting for 5 minutes after thoroughly stirring. 2. Combine the almond butter, baking soda, vanilla, coconut sugar, and salt in a mixing bowl. Stir everything together thoroughly. Fold in the chocolate chips thoroughly. 3. In a greased baking dish, pour the batter. 4. Place the drip pan at the bottom of the cooking chamber. Using the control panel, select Bake, adjust the temperature to 350 degrees F and the time to 20 minutes, then touch Start. 5. When the display indicates "Add Food," place the cooking tray in the center position. 6. When the time is up, open the unit and set it aside for cooling. 7. Slice and serve.
Per serving: Calories 47; Fat 1.6g; Sodium 74mg; Carbs 8.2g; Fiber 0.8g; Sugar 7.1g; Protein 0.6g

Healthy Flax Chia Muffins

Prep time: 10 minutes | Cook time: 35 minutes | Serves: 6

2 tablespoons coconut flour
20 drops of liquid stevia
¼ cup almond flour
½ cup ground flax
2 tablespoons ground chia
¼ cup water
¼ teaspoon vanilla
¼ teaspoon baking soda
½ teaspoon baking powder
1 teaspoon cinnamon

1. 6 tablespoons of water and crushed chia seeds in a small basin, set aside after thoroughly mixing. 2. Combine ground flax, baking soda, baking powder, cinnamon, coconut flour, and almond flour in a large mixing bowl. 3. Stir the chia seed mixture, vanilla, water, and stevia. 4. Fill the silicone muffin tins halfway with the batter. Place the drip pan at the bottom of the cooking chamber. Using the control panel, select Bake, adjust the temperature to 350 degrees F and the time to 35 minutes, then touch Start. 5. When the display indicates "Add Food," place the cooking tray in the center position 6. When the time is up, open the unit and set it aside for cooling. 7. Serve and enjoy.

Per serving: Calories 99; Fat 6.8g; Sodium 63mg; Carbs 7.9g; Fiber 6g; Sugar 0.5g; Protein 4.2 g

Easy Protein Choco Brownies

Prep time: 10 minutes | Cook time: 35 minutes | Serves: 4

½ cup almond butter, melted	2 tablespoons unsweetened cocoa powder
1 scoop of vanilla protein powder	1 cup bananas, overripe

1. In a blender, combine all ingredients and blend until smooth. 2. Fill the oiled baking dish halfway with the mixed mixture. 3. Place the drip pan at the bottom of the cooking chamber. Using the control panel, select Bake, adjust the temperature to 350 degrees F and the time to 35 minutes, then touch Start. 4. When the display indicates "Add Food," place the cooking tray in the center position 5. When the time is up, open the unit and set it aside for cooling. 6. Serve and enjoy.

Per serving: Calories 80, Fat 1.6g; Sodium 14mg; Carbs 10.6g; Fiber 2.2g; Sugar 4.8g; Protein 8.1g

Protein Pumpkin Muffins

Prep time: 10 minutes | Cook time: 15 minutes | Serves: 20

2 scoops of vanilla protein powder	½ cup pumpkin puree
½ cup almond flour	½ cup almond butter
½ cup coconut oil	1 tablespoon cinnamon
	1 teaspoon baking powder

1. Combine all dry ingredients in a large mixing basin and stir thoroughly. 2. Combine the wet and dry ingredients in a mixing bowl and stir until completely blended. 3. Fill the silicone muffin tins halfway with the batter. 4. Place the drip pan at the bottom of the cooking chamber. Using the control panel, select Bake, adjust the temperature to 350 degrees F and the time to 15 minutes, then touch Start. 5. When the display indicates "Add Food," place the cooking tray in the center position. 6. When the time is up, open the unit and set it aside for cooling. 7. Serve and enjoy.

Per serving: Calories 80, Fat 1.6g; Sodium 14mg; Carbs 10.6g; Fiber 2.2g; Sugar 4.8g; Protein 8.1g

Strawberry Almond Muffins

Prep time: 10 minutes | Cook time: 20 minutes | Serves: 12

3 eggs	1 teaspoon cinnamon
⅔ cup strawberries, diced	2 teaspoons baking powder
1 teaspoon vanilla	2½ cups almond flour
½ cup Swerve	⅓ cup heavy cream
5 tablespoons butter, melted	¼ teaspoon Himalayan salt

1. Combine butter and swerve in a mixing basin. Whisk together the eggs, cream, and vanilla extract until foamy. 2. Combine almond flour, cinnamon, baking powder, and salt in

a sifter. 3. Mix in the almond flour mixture with the wet ingredients until everything is completely blended. Fold in the strawberries thoroughly. 4. Fill the silicone muffin tins halfway with the batter. Pour the mixture into the 12 silicone muffin molds. Place silicone muffin molds into the cooking tray. 5. Place the drip pan at the bottom of the cooking chamber. Using the control panel, select Bake, adjust the temperature to 350 degrees F and the time to 15 minutes, then touch Start. 6. When the display indicates "Add Food," place the cooking tray in the center. 7. When the time is up, open the unit and set it aside for cooling. 8. Serve and enjoy.

Per serving: Calories 208, Fat 18.8g; Sodium 63mg; Carbs 6.4g; Fiber 2.8g; Sugar 1.3g; Protein 6.6g

Allspice Pecan Muffins

Prep time: 10 minutes | Cook time: 20minutes | Serves: 12

4 eggs	1½ cups almond flour
¼ cup almond milk	½ cup pecans, chopped
2 tablespoons butter, melted	½ teaspoon ground cinnamon
½ cup swerve	2 teaspoons allspice
1 teaspoon psyllium husk	1 teaspoon vanilla
1 tablespoon baking powder	

1. In a mixing bowl, whisk the eggs, almond milk, vanilla, sweetener, and butter until creamy. 2. Mix in the other ingredients until fully blended. 3. Fill the silicone muffin tins halfway with the mixture. Pour the mixture into the 12 silicone muffin molds. Place silicone muffin molds into the cooking tray. 4. Place the drip pan at the bottom of the cooking chamber. Using the control panel, select Bake, adjust the temperature to 350 degrees F and the time to 15 minutes, then touch Start. 5. When the display indicates "Add Food," place the cooking tray in the center. 6. When the time is up, open the unit and set it aside for cooling. 7. Serve and enjoy.

Per serving: Calories 139, Fat 12g; Sodium 39mg; Carbs 5.4g; Fiber 2.6g; Sugar 0.8g; Protein 5.1g

Almond Blueberry Muffins

Prep time: 10 minutes | Cook time: 20 minutes | Serves: 12

3 large eggs	½ teaspoon vanilla
¾ cup blueberries	⅓ cup unsweetened almond milk
1½ teaspoons baking powder	
½ cup Swerve	⅓ cup coconut oil, melted
2½ cups almond flour	

1. Combine almond flour, baking powder, and erythritol in a large mixing basin. 2. Combine the coconut oil, vanilla, eggs, and almond milk in a mixing bowl. Lastly, fold in the blueberries. 3. Fill the silicone muffin tins halfway with the mixture. Pour the mixture into the 12 silicone muffin molds. Place silicone muffin molds into the cooking tray. 4. Place the drip pan at the bottom of the cooking chamber. Using the control panel, select Bake, adjust the temperature to 350 degrees F and the time to 15 minutes, then touch Start. 5. When the display indicates "Add Food," place the cooking tray in the center. 6. When the time is up, open the unit and set it aside for cooling. 7. Serve and enjoy.

Per serving: Calories 211, Fat 19.1g; Sodium 23mg; Carbs 6.9g; Fiber 2.8g; Sugar 1.9g; Protein 6.7g

Flourless Chocolate Cake

Prep time: 10 minutes | Cook time: 30 minutes | Serves: 12

3 large eggs
1 tablespoon vanilla
½ cup unsweetened cocoa powder
¾ cup coconut sugar

½ cup butter
1 cup unsweetened chocolate chips
½ teaspoon sea salt

1. Set aside an 8-inch cake pan lined with parchment paper. 2. Melt the butter in a small saucepan over medium heat, add the chocolate chips and remove the pan from the heat. Stir until the chocolate chips are completely melted. 3. Whisk in the remaining ingredients until smooth. 4. Pour the batter into the cake pan that has been prepared. 5. Place the drip pan at the bottom of the cooking chamber. Using the control panel, select Bake, adjust the temperature to 375 degrees F and the time to 30 minutes, then touch Start. 6. When the display indicates "Add Food," place the cooking tray in the center position 7. When the time is up, open the unit and set it aside for cooling. 8. Slice and serve.
Per serving: Calories 161; Fat 10.4g; Sodium 167mg; Carbs 17.2g; Fiber 1.2g; Sugar 12.6g; Protein 2.6g

Chia Chocolate Cookies

Prep time: 10 minutes | Cook time: 10minutes | Serves: 20

3 tablespoons ground chia
1 cup almond flour
2 tablespoons chocolate pro-

tein powder
1 cup sunflower seed butter

1. Incorporate all ingredients in a large mixing bowl and stir to combine. 2. Make little balls out of the dough and lay them on a baking sheet coated with parchment paper. Lightly press down. 3. Place the drip pan at the bottom of the cooking chamber. Using the control panel, select Bake, adjust the temperature to 350 degrees F and the time to 10 minutes, then touch Start. 4. When the display indicates "Add Food," place the cooking tray in the center position 5. When the time is up, open the unit and set it aside for cooling. 6. Serve and enjoy.
Per serving: Calories 122; Fat 9.4g; Sodium 17mg; Carbs 5.6g; Fiber 1.1g; Sugar 0.4g; Protein 6g

Pumpkin Coconut Blondies

Prep time: 10 minutes | Cook time: 40minutes | Serves: 12

1 cup pumpkin puree
1 tablespoon pumpkin pie spice
¼ cup Erythritol
¼ cup coconut flour

½ cup tahini
1 teaspoon baking powder
1 teaspoon vanilla extract
1 tablespoon vinegar

1. Combine pumpkin, vinegar, vanilla, sweetener, and tahini in a mixing bowl. 2. Combine coconut flour, baking powder, and spices in a separate bowl. 3. Stir the dry and wet ingredients until everything is completely blended. 4. Pour the batter into an 8-inch baking pan that has been buttered. 5. Place the drip pan at the bottom of the cooking chamber. Using the control panel, select Bake, adjust the temperature to 350 degrees F and the time to 40 minutes, then touch Start. 6. When the display indicates "Add Food," place the cooking tray in the center position 7. When the time is up, open the unit and set it aside for cooling. 8. Slice and serve.
Per serving: Calories 54; Fat 4.4g; Sodium 11mg; Carbs 3g; Fiber 1.2g; Sugar 0.4g; Protein 1.6g

Vanilla Pumpkin Muffins

Prep time: 10 minutes | Cook time: 25 minutes | Serves: 10

4 large eggs
1 tablespoon baking powder
⅔ cup erythritol
½ cup almond flour
½ cup coconut flour
1 teaspoon vanilla

⅓ cup coconut oil, melted
½ cup pumpkin puree
1 tablespoon pumpkin pie spice
½ teaspoon sea salt

1. Set aside a muffin tray that has been sprayed with cooking spray. 2. Combine coconut flour, pumpkin pie spice, baking powder, erythritol, almond flour, and sea salt in a large mixing bowl. 3. Whisk together the eggs, vanilla, coconut oil, and pumpkin puree in a large mixing bowl until well blended. 4. Fill the silicone muffin tins halfway with batter. 5. Pour the mixture into the ten silicone muffin molds. Place silicone muffin molds into cooking tray 6. Place the drip pan at the bottom of the cooking chamber. Using the control panel, select Bake, adjust the temperature to 350 degrees F and the time to 25 minutes, then touch Start. 7. When the display indicates "Add Food," place the cooking tray in the center position 8. When the time is up, open the unit and set it aside for cooling. 9. Serve and enjoy.
Per serving: Calories 135, Fat 12.3g; Sodium 125mg; Carbs 19.9g; Fiber 1.3g; Sugar 16.9g; Protein 4g

Blueberry Muffins with Whipping Cream

Prep time: 10 minutes | Cook time: 25 minutes | Serves: 12

2 large eggs
½ cup fresh blueberries
1 teaspoon baking powder
5 drops stevia
¼ cup butter, melted

1 cup heavy whipping cream
2 cups almond flour
¼ teaspoon lemon zest
½ teaspoon lemon extract

1. In a mixing bowl, whisk together the eggs until well combined. 2. Toss in the remaining ingredients and stir well to incorporate. 3. Fill the silicone muffin tins halfway with batter. 4. Pour the mixture into the 12 silicone muffin molds. Place silicone muffin molds into cooking tray 5. Place the drip pan at the bottom of the cooking chamber. Using the control panel, select Bake, adjust the temperature to 350 degrees F and the time to 25 minutes, then touch Start. 6. When the display indicates "Add Food," place the cooking tray in the center position 7. When the time is up, open the unit and set it aside for cooling. 8. Serve and enjoy.
Per serving: Calories 191, Fat 17.7g; Sodium 43mg; Carbs 6.3g; Fiber 2.2g; Sugar 1.4g; Protein 5.4g

Cream Chocolate Muffins with Almond

Prep time: 10 minutes | Cook time: 30 minutes | Serves: 10

2 eggs, lightly beaten
1 cup almond flour
1 tablespoon baking powder
4 tablespoons Erythritol

½ cup cocoa powder
½ cup heavy cream
½ teaspoon vanilla
Pinch of salt

1. Combine almond flour, baking powder, Erythritol, cocoa powder, and salt in a mixing dish. 2. Whisk together the eggs, cream, and vanilla extract in a separate bowl. 3. Mix the egg mixture thoroughly into the almond flour mixture. 4. Divide the batter evenly among the ten silicone muffin tins. Place silicone muffin molds into cooking tray 5. Place the drip pan at the bottom of the cooking chamber. Using the control panel, select Bake, adjust the temperature to 350 degrees F and the time to 25 minutes, then touch Start. 6. When the display

indicates "Add Food," place the cooking tray in the center position 7. When the time is up, open the unit and set it aside for cooling. 8. Serve and enjoy.

Per serving: Calories 109, Fat 9.3g; Sodium 32mg; Carbs 11.7g; Fiber 2.5g; Sugar 6.6g; Protein 4.4g

Banana Almond Bread

Prep time: 10 minutes | Cook time: 40minutes | Serves: 12

3 large eggs
3 bananas, mashed
½ teaspoon baking powder
¼ cup coconut flour
1½ teaspoons vanilla extract
¼ cup coconut oil, melted

½ cup almond butter
⅛ cup chocolate chips
¼ teaspoon sea salt
½ teaspoon cinnamon
½ teaspoon baking soda

1. Combine bananas, vanilla, coconut oil, almond butter, and eggs in a large mixing bowl. 2. Combine all of the dry ingredients in a large mixing bowl. 3. Pour the batter into the loaf pan that has been oiled. 4. Place the drip pan at the bottom of the cooking chamber. Using the control panel, select Bake, adjust the temperature to 350 degrees F and the time to 40 minutes, then touch Start. 5. When the display indicates "Add Food," place the cooking tray in the center position 6. When the time is up, open the unit and set it aside for cooling. 7. Slice and enjoy.

Per serving: Calories 117, Fat 8g; Sodium 138mg; Carbs 9.9g; Fiber 1.2g; Sugar 4.9g; Protein 2.6g

Zucchini Chocolate Bread

Prep time: 10 minutes | Cook time: 40 minutes | Serves: 6

2 large eggs
1 cup zucchini, shredded
1 tablespoon cocoa powder
1 cup almond butter
2 tablespoons chocolate chips

½ teaspoon baking soda
1 teaspoon apple cider vinegar
1 teaspoon stevia
1 tablespoon vanilla extract
¼ teaspoon sea salt

1. Blend almond butter, sea salt, cocoa powder, vanilla, stevia, and eggs in a mixing dish for 2 minutes. 2. Fold the vinegar and soda into the batter. Add the shredded zucchini and mix well. 3. The batter should be poured into a prepared loaf pan and then topped with chocolate chips. Place the loaf pan into the cooking tray. Place the drip pan at the bottom of the cooking chamber. Using the control panel, select Bake, adjust the temperature to 350 degrees F and the time to 40 minutes, then touch Start. 4. When the display indicates "Add Food," place the cooking tray in the center position 5. When the time is up, open the unit and set it aside for cooling. 6. Slice and enjoy.

Per serving: Calories 70, Fat 4.4g; Sodium 211mg; Carbs 4.4g; Fiber 0.9g; Sugar 2.7g; Protein 3.3g

Tasty Almond Chocolate Brownie

Prep time: 10 minutes | Cook time: 10 minutes | Serves: 1

1 scoop of chocolate protein powder
1 tablespoon cocoa powder

½ teaspoon baking powder
¼ cup almond milk

1. Add baking powder, protein powder, and cocoa powder to a ramekin. Add milk and stir well. 2. Place the ramekin into the cooking tray. Place the drip pan at the bottom of the cooking chamber. Using the control panel, select Bake, adjust the temperature to 390 degrees F and the time to 10 minutes, then touch Start. 3. When the display indicates "Add Food," place the cooking tray in the center. 4. When time's up, open the door and place the baking pan on the wire rack for cooling. 5. Slice, serve and enjoy.

Per serving: Calories 207, Fat 15.8g; Sodium 92mg; Carbs 9.5g; Fiber 3.4g; Sugar 3.1g; Protein 12.4g

Vanilla Protein Mug Cake

Prep time: 10 minutes | Cook time: 10 minutes | Serves: 1

1 tablespoon almond flour
½ teaspoon baking powder
¼ teaspoon vanilla
¼ cup almond milk, unsweetened

1 scoop of vanilla protein powder
½ teaspoon cinnamon
1 teaspoon Swerve

1. In a ramekin, combine the protein powder, sweetener, cinnamon, almond flour, and baking powder. 2. Stir in the almond milk and vanilla extract well. 3. Place the ramekin into the cooking tray. Place the drip pan at the bottom of the cooking chamber. Using the control panel, select Bake, adjust the temperature to 390 degrees F and the time to 10 minutes, then touch Start. 4. When the display indicates "Add Food," place the cooking tray in the center. 5. When time's up, open the unit door and place the cake pan on the wire rack for cooling. 6. Serve and enjoy.

Per serving: Calories 351, Fat 21.4g; Sodium 141mg; Carbs 20.1g; Fiber 5.7g; Sugar 4.4g; Protein 25.9g

Luscious Chocolate Brownies

Prep time: 10 minutes | Cook time: 30 minutes | Serves: 8

3 eggs
½ cup unsweetened chocolate chips

1 teaspoon vanilla
¼ cup Truvia
½ cup butter

1. Microwave the chocolate chips and butter for 1 minute in a microwave-safe bowl. Remove the dish from the microwave and mix thoroughly. 2. Whisk together the eggs, vanilla, and sweetener in a mixing bowl until foamy. 3. Mix the melted chocolate and butter in a mixing bowl and beat until smooth. 4. In a prepared baking pan, pour the batter. 5. Place the baking pan into the cooking tray. Place the drip pan at the bottom of the cooking chamber. 6. Using the control panel, select Bake, adjust the temperature to 350 degrees F and the time to 30 minutes, then touch Start. 7. When the display indicates "Add Food," place the cooking tray in the center. 8. When time's up, open the unit door and place the baking pan on the wire rack for cooling. 9. Slice and Serve and enjoy.

Per serving: Calories 227, Fat 21.2g; Sodium 110mg; Carbs 7.3g; Fiber 2g; Sugar 0.2g; Protein 4.2g

Simple Coconut Muffins

Prep time: 10 minutes | Cook time: 12 minutes | Serves: 1

1 egg
2 teaspoons coconut flour

1 pinch of salt
1 pinch of baking soda

1. In a small bowl, mix all ingredients and pour into the greased ramekin. 2. Place the ramekin cooking tray. Place the drip pan at the bottom of the cooking chamber. Using the control panel, select Bake, adjust the temperature to 400 degrees F and the time to 12 minutes, then touch Start. 3. When the display indicates "Add Food," place the cooking tray in the center. 4. When time's up, open the door of the unit and place muffins on the wire rack for cooling. 5. Serve and enjoy.

Per serving: Calories 183, Fat 8.4g; Sodium 435mg; Carbs 16.4g; Fiber 10g; Sugar 2.3g; Protein 9.3g

Vanilla Coconut Pie with Monk Fruit

Prep time: 10 minutes | Cook time: 12 minutes | Serves: 6

2 eggs
1 cup shredded coconut
1 teaspoon vanilla
4 tablespoons butter
1½ cups coconut milk
½ cup coconut flour
½ cup monk fruit

1. In a large bowl, add all ingredients and mix until well blended. 2. Pour batter into the greased 6-inch pie dish. 3. Place the ramekin 6-inch pie dish. Place the drip pan at the bottom of the cooking chamber. Using the control panel, select Bake, adjust the temperature to 350 degrees F and the time to 12 minutes, then touch Start. 4. When the display indicates "Add Food," place the cooking tray in the center. 5. When time's up, open the unit door and place the baking pan on the wire rack for cooling. 6. Slice and Serve and enjoy.
Per serving: Calories 288, Fat 28.2g; Sodium 98mg; Carbs 7.6g; Fiber 3g; Sugar 3.7g; Protein 4.1g

Cranberry Bread Loaf

Prep time: 10 minutes | Cook time: 30 minutes | Serves: 10

1 large egg
2 egg whites
⅓ cup cassava flour
1 teaspoon vanilla
½ tablespoon vinegar
1 teaspoon stevia
3 tablespoons cranberries, chopped
½ teaspoon baking soda
½ tablespoon cinnamon
3 tablespoons butter, melted
¼ teaspoon salt

1. Whisk the egg whites and the egg in a mixing dish. 2. Combine the vanilla, vinegar, and butter in a mixing bowl. Mix thoroughly. 3. Combine the cranberries, salt, stevia, baking soda, cinnamon, and cassava flour in a large mixing bowl. Mix thoroughly. 4. Pour the batter into the loaf pan that has been oiled. Place the loaf pan into the cooking tray. 5. Place the drip pan at the bottom of the cooking chamber. Using the control panel, select Bake, adjust the temperature to 350 degrees F and the time to 25 minutes, then touch Start. 6. When the display indicates "Add Food," place the cooking tray in the center position 7. When the time is up, open the unit and set it aside for cooling. 8. Slice and enjoy.
Per serving: Calories 56, Fat 4g; Sodium 173mg; Carbs 3.3g; Fiber 0.7g; Sugar 0.2g; Protein 1.4g

Tasty Chocolate Brownies

Prep time: 10 minutes | Cook time: 15 minutes | Serves: 6

3 eggs
⅓ cup butter, melted
⅓ cup cocoa powder
½ cup Erythritol
1 cup almond flour
1 tablespoon gelatin

1. In a mixing bowl, combine all ingredients and stir until well blended. 2. Fill the silicone muffin tins halfway with the batter. 3. Place the drip pan at the bottom of the cooking chamber. Using the control panel, select Bake, adjust the temperature to 350 degrees F and the time to 15 minutes, then touch Start. 4. When the display indicates "Add Food," place the cooking tray in the center. 5. When time's up, open the door and place muffin tins on the wire rack for cooling. 6. Serve and enjoy.
Per serving: Calories 70, Fat 4.4g; Sodium 211mg; Carbs 4.4g; Fiber 0.9g; Sugar 2.7g; Protein 3.3g

Swerve Raspberry Muffins

Prep time: 10 minutes | Cook time: 35 minutes | Serves: 6

2 eggs
4 ounces' raspberries
1 teaspoon baking powder
5 ounces' almond flour
2 tablespoons coconut oil
2 tablespoons Swerve

1. Combine almond meal and baking powder in a medium mixing basin. 2. Stir in the Swerve, eggs, and oil until barely mixed. Fold in the raspberries thoroughly. 3. Fill the silicone muffin tins halfway with batter. 4. Place muffin tins into the cooking tray. 5. Place the drip pan at the bottom of the cooking chamber. Using the control panel, select Bake, adjust the temperature to 350 degrees F and the time to 35 minutes, then touch Start. 6. When the display indicates "Add Food," place the cooking tray in the center. 7. When time's up, open the door of the unit and place muffin tins on the wire rack for cooling. 8. Serve and enjoy.
Per serving: Calories 206, Fat 17.8g; Sodium 21mg; Carbs 8.4g; Fiber 3.9g; Sugar 1.7g; Protein 7.3g

Easy-to-Make Apple Bars

Prep time: 10 minutes | Cook time: 45 minutes | Serves: 8

¼ cup dried apples
¼ cup coconut butter softened
1 cup pecans
1 cup of water
1 teaspoon vanilla
2 tablespoons swerve
1½ teaspoons baking powder
1½ teaspoons cinnamon
1 tablespoon ground flax seed

1. Add all ingredients into the blender and blend until smooth. 2. Pour the blended mixture into the greased baking dish. 3. Place the baking dish into the cooking tray. 4. Place the drip pan at the bottom of the cooking chamber. Using the control panel, select Bake, adjust the temperature to 350 degrees F and the time to 45 minutes, then touch Start. 5. When the display indicates "Add Food," place the cooking tray in the center position. 6. When time's up, open the door and place the baking dish on the wire rack for cooling. 7. Slice and serve and enjoy.
Per serving: Calories 181, Fat 17.4g; Sodium 5mg; Carbs 6.8g; Fiber 3.9g; Sugar 1.9g; Protein 2.3g

Moist Almond Chocolate Cake

Prep time: 10 minutes | Cook time: 15 minutes | Serves: 8

3 eggs
⅓ cup almond milk
2 ¼ teaspoons baking powder
¼ cup cocoa powder
1½ cups almond flour
1½ teaspoons vanilla
⅓ cup erythritol
1 pinch of salt

1. Add all ingredients into the mixing bowl and mix until well combined. 2. Pour batter into the greased 8-inch cake pan. 3. Place the cake pan into the cooking tray. 4. Place the drip pan at the bottom of the cooking chamber. Using the control panel, select Bake, adjust the temperature to 350 degrees F and the time to 15 minutes, then touch Start. 5. When the display indicates "Add Food," place the cooking tray in the center. 6. When time's up, open the door and place the cake on a wire rack for cooling. 7. Slice and Serve and enjoy.
Per serving: Calories 176, Fat 14.4g; Sodium 46mg; Carbs 17.4g; Fiber 3.3g; Sugar 11.7g; Protein 7.3g

Delicious Coconut Vanilla Cake

Prep time: 10 minutes | Cook time: 40 minutes | Serves: 8

6 egg whites
½ cup Swerve
¼ cup sour cream
1 teaspoon vanilla
¼ cup coconut oil, melted
1 teaspoon baking powder
¼ cup coconut flour
1 cup almond flour
1 pinch of salt

1. Whisk together vanilla and coconut oil in a mixing bowl. Whisk in the sour cream until smooth. 2. Beat in the sweetener and egg whites one at a time until well mixed. 3. Blend in the flours, baking powder, and salt until thoroughly blended. 4. Pour the batter into the loaf pan that has been oiled. 5. Place the loaf pan into the cooking tray. 6. Place the drip pan at the bottom of the cooking chamber. Using the control panel, select Bake, adjust the temperature to 350 degrees F and the time to 40 minutes, then touch Start. 7. When the display indicates "Add Food", place the cooking tray in the center position. 8. When time's up, open the door and place the cake on a wire rack for cooling. 9. Slice and Serve and enjoy.
Per serving: Calories 70, Fat 4.4g; Sodium 211mg; Carbs 4.4g; Fiber 0.9g; Sugar 2.7g; Protein 3.3g

Swerve Raspberries Almond Cobbler

Prep time: 10 minutes | Cook time: 10 minutes | Serves: 6

1 egg, lightly beaten
1 cup raspberries, sliced
2 teaspoons swerve
1 tablespoon butter, melted
1 cup almond flour
½ teaspoon vanilla

1. In a baking dish, place cut raspberries. 2. Over the berries, sprinkle the swerve. 3. In a mixing dish, combine almond flour, vanilla, and butter. 4. Stir the egg into the almond flour mixture until everything is thoroughly combined. 5. Over the sliced raspberries, spread the almond flour mixture. Place baking dish on cooking tray. 6. Place the drip pan at the bottom of the cooking chamber. Using the control panel, select Bake, adjust the temperature to 360 degrees F and the time to 10 minutes, then touch Start. 7. When the display indicates "Add Food," place the cooking tray in the center. 8. When time's up, open the door and place the cake on the wire rack for cooling. 9. Serve and enjoy.
Per serving: Calories 148, Fat 12.1g; Sodium 24mg; Carbs 7.2g; Fiber 3.3g; Sugar 1.7g; Protein 5.2g

Tasty Espresso Coffee Cookies

Prep time: 10 minutes | Cook time: 15 minutes | Serves: 12

2 eggs, lightly beaten
¼ cup Erythritol
¼ cup brewed espresso
1 cup almond flour
½ cup ghee, melted
2 teaspoons baking powder
½ tablespoon cinnamon

1. In a mixing bowl, combine all ingredients and stir until well blended. 2. Make little cookies using the mixture and set them on a cooking tray coated with parchment paper. 3. Place the drip pan at the bottom of the cooking chamber. Using the control panel, select Bake, adjust the temperature to 350 degrees F and the time to 15 minutes, then touch Start. 4. When the display indicates "Add Food," place the cooking tray in the center. 5. When time's up, open the door and place the cake on the wire rack for cooling. 6. Serve and enjoy.
Per serving: Calories 141, Fat 13.9g; Sodium 12mg; Carbs 7.8g; Fiber 1.2g; Sugar 5.4g; Protein 3g

Spiced Apple Slices

Prep time: 10 minutes | Cook time: 10 minutes | Serves: 6

4 small apples, sliced
½ cup Swerve
2 tablespoons coconut oil,
melted
1 teaspoon apple pie spice

1. Add apple slices to a bowl, sprinkle sweetener, apple pie spice, and coconut oil over the apple, and toss to coat. 2. Transfer apple slices to the cooking tray. 3. Place the drip pan at the bottom of the cooking chamber. Using the control panel, select Air Fry, adjust the temperature to 350 degrees F and the time to 10 minutes, then touch Start. 4. When the display indicates "Add Food," place the cooking tray in the center. 5. When displaying "turn Food," turn apples. 6. When time's up, open the door and place the cake on a wire rack for cooling. 7. Serve and enjoy
Per serving: Calories 118, Fat 4.8g; Sodium 1mg; Carbs 20.9g; Fiber 3.6g; Sugar 15.7g; Protein 0.4g

Chocolate Macaroon

Prep time: 10 minutes | Cook time: 20 minutes | Serves: 20

2 eggs
¼ cup coconut oil
½ teaspoon baking powder
¼ cup unsweetened cocoa powder
3 tablespoons coconut flour
1 cup almond flour
⅓ cup unsweetened coconut, shredded
⅓ cup Erythritol
1 teaspoon vanilla
1 pinch of salt

1. Add all ingredients into the mixing bowl and mix until well combined. 2. Make small balls from the mixture and place them onto the parchment-lined cooking tray. 3. Place the drip pan at the bottom of the cooking chamber. Using the control panel, select Bake, adjust the temperature to 350 degrees F and the time to 20 minutes, then touch Start. 4. When the display indicates "Add Food," place the cooking tray in the center. 5. When time's up, open the door and place the macaroon on a wire rack for cooling. 6. Serve and enjoy.
Per serving: Calories 79, Fat 6.9g; Sodium 19mg; Carbs 7.3g; Fiber 1.8g; Sugar 4.7g; Protein 2.3g

Cream Almond Pumpkin Pie

Prep time: 10 minutes | Cook time: 30 minutes | Serves: 4

3 eggs
½ cup pumpkin puree
½ cup cream
½ cup unsweetened almond
milk
½ teaspoon cinnamon
1 teaspoon vanilla
¼ cup Swerve

1. In a large bowl, add all ingredients and whisk until smooth. 2. Pour the pie mixture into the greased baking dish. 3. Place the drip pan at the bottom of the cooking chamber. Using the control panel, select Bake, adjust the temperature to 350 degrees F and the time to 30 minutes, then touch Start. 4. When the display indicates "Add Food", place the cooking tray in the center position. 5. When time's up, open the door and place the baking pan on the wire rack for cooling. 6. Slice and enjoy.
Per serving: Calories 86, Fat 5.5g; Sodium 80mg; Carbs 4.4g; Fiber 1.3g; Sugar 2g; Protein 4.9g

Stevia Hazelnut Cookies

Prep time: 10 minutes | Cook time: 10 minutes | Serves: 16

¾ cup hazelnut flour
⅓ cup Swerve
½ cup almond flour
20 drops of liquid stevia
6 tablespoons butter, softened

1. Mix all ingredients in a mixing bowl until a soft dough forms. 2. Make little dough balls and set them on a parchment-lined baking sheet. Using a fork, flatten each ball. 3. Place the drip pan at the bottom of the cooking chamber. Using the control panel, select Bake, adjust the temperature to 350 degrees F and the time to 10 minutes, then touch Start. 4. When the display indicates "Add Food," place the cooking tray in the center position. 5. When time's up, open the door and place the cookies on the wire rack for cooling. 6. Serve and enjoy.
Per serving: Calories 92, Fat 9.3g; Sodium 31mg; Carbs 4.2g; Fiber 0.9g; Sugar 0.3g; Protein 1.6 g

Buttered Pumpkin Cookies

Prep time: 10 minutes | Cook time: 25 minutes | Serves: 6

1 egg
1 teaspoon vanilla
½ cup butter
½ cup pumpkin puree
2 cups almond flour
1 teaspoon liquid stevia
½ teaspoon pumpkin pie spice

1. Add all ingredients into the mixing bowl and mix until well combined. 2. Make small balls from the mixture and place them onto the parchment-lined cooking tray. Lightly flatten the balls using a fork. 3. Place the drip pan at the bottom of the cooking chamber. Using the control panel, select Bake, adjust the temperature to 350 degrees F and the time to 25 minutes, then touch Start. 4. When the display indicates "Add Food," place the cooking tray in the center. 5. When time's up, open the door and place muffin tins on the wire rack for cooling. 6. Serve and enjoy.
Per serving: Calories 148, Fat 12.1g; Sodium 24mg; Carbs 7.2g; Fiber 3.3g; Sugar 1.7g; Protein 5.2g

Almond-Coconut Butter Cookies

Prep time: 10 minutes | Cook time: 15 minutes | Serves: 6

1 egg
¼ cup coconut butter
9 ounces' almond butter
¼ cup Swerve
1 pinch of salt

1. Add all ingredients into the food processor and process until well combined. 2. Make small balls from the mixture and place them onto the parchment-lined cooking tray. 3. Place the drip pan at the bottom of the cooking chamber. Using the control panel, select Bake, adjust the temperature to 320 degrees F and the time to 15 minutes, then touch Start. 4. When the display indicates "Add Food," place the cooking tray in the center. 5. When time's up, open the door and place cookies on the wire rack for cooling. 6. Serve and enjoy.
Per serving: Calories 132, Fat 12g; Sodium 24mg; Carbs 4.2g; Fiber 3.3g; Sugar 1g; Protein 4g

Almond Flaxseed Muffins

Prep time: 10 minutes | Cook time: 20 minutes | Serves: 9

4 eggs, lightly beaten
½ cup erythritol
1 cup almond flour
1 cup ground flaxseed
½ cup butter, melted
1 tablespoon cinnamon
1 teaspoon nutmeg
1 teaspoon baking powder
1 pinch of salt

1. Add all ingredients into the mixing bowl and beat until well combined. 2. Divide the mixture into the nine silicone muffin molds. 3. place silicone muffin molds on the cooking tray. 4. Place the drip pan at the bottom of the cooking chamber. Using the control panel, select Bake, adjust the temperature to 350 degrees F and the time to 20 minutes, then touch Start. 5. When the display indicates "Add Food," place the cooking tray in the center. 6. When time's up, open the door and place muffin tins on the wire rack for cooling. 7. Serve and enjoy.
Per serving: Calories 262, Fat 22.1g; Sodium 124mg; Carbs 20.7g; Fiber 5.2g; Sugar 13.7g; Protein 7.6g

Cream Apple Almond Muffins

Prep time: 10 minutes | Cook time: 25 minutes | Serves: 36

4 eggs
2 tablespoons olive oil
2 tablespoons Swerve
¼ cup heavy cream
½ cup apple, peeled and diced
1 cup almond flour
½ teaspoon baking soda
1 teaspoon baking powder
1 tablespoon ground cinnamon

1. In a mixing bowl, combine all ingredients except the apple and stir until well blended. Stir in the chopped apple thoroughly. 2. Fill the silicone muffin tins halfway with the batter. 3. Place the drip pan at the bottom of the cooking chamber. Using the control panel, select Bake, adjust the temperature to 350 degrees F and the time to 25 minutes, then touch Start. 4. When the display indicates "Add Food," place the cooking tray in the center. 5. When time's up, open the door and place muffin tins on the wire rack for cooling. 6. Serve and enjoy!
Per serving: Calories 37, Fat 3.1g; Sodium 24mg; Carbs 1.5g; Fiber 0.5g; Sugar 0.5g; Protein 1.2g

Peanut Butter Choco Muffins

Prep time: 10 minutes | Cook time: 25 minutes | Serves: 8

2 eggs
⅓ cup unsweetened coconut milk
⅓ cup peanut butter
⅓ cup Swerve
1 teaspoon baking powder
⅓ cup unsweetened chocolate chips

1. Combine all dry ingredients in a mixing basin. Stir in the milk and peanut butter until everything is well combined. 2. Stir in the eggs until they are entirely smooth. Fold in the chocolate chips thoroughly. 3. Fill the silicone muffin tins halfway with the batter. 4. Place silicone muffin molds on the cooking tray. 5. Place the drip pan at the bottom of the cooking chamber. Using the control panel, select Bake, adjust the temperature to 350 degrees F and the time to 25 minutes, then touch Start. 6. When the display indicates "Add Food," place the cooking tray in the center. 7. When time's up, open the door of the unit and place muffin tins on the wire rack for cooling. 8. Serve and enjoy!
Per serving: Calories 168, Fat 14.2g; Sodium 70mg; Carbs 5.8g; Fiber 2.2g; Sugar 1.4g; Protein 5.6g

Conclusion

Instant Vortex Air Fryer Oven is a perfect choice for your kitchen. It's a dynamic apparatus that will change your way of life and make it more comfortable. It will help you to prepare tasty, juicy & crispy meals with the least effort & time. It will become your latest best partner in the kitchen and help you prepare excellent & yummy dishes for yourself and your family.

If you already have this appliance and don't know how to cook, this cookbook is ideal. I added recipes for your Instant Vortex Air Fryer Oven. The recipes are written in a way that even kids can understand. You can cook food for your family and friends on any occasion or gathering in less time. This cooking function has eight functions. You can choose your favorite option for cooking food. It will fulfill all your cooking needs. Now, you can prepare healthy and delicious food in less time. Thank you for purchasing my cookbook!

Appendix 1 Measurement Conversion Chart

WEIGHT EQUIVALENTS

US STANDARD	METRIC (APPROXIMATE)
1 ounce	28 g
2 ounces	57 g
5 ounces	142 g
10 ounces	284 g
15 ounces	425g
16 ounces (1 pound)	455 g
1.5pounds	680 g
2pounds	907g

VOLUME EQUIVALENTS (LIQUID)

US STANDARD	US STANDARD (OUNCES)	METRIC (APPROXIMATE)
2 tablespoons	1 fl.oz	30 mL
¼ cup	2 fl.oz	60 mL
½ cup	4 fl.oz	120 mL
1 cup	8 fl.oz	240 mL
1½ cup	12 fl.oz	355 mL
2 cups or 1 pint	16 fl.oz	475 mL
4 cups or 1 quart	32 fl.oz	1 L
1 gallon	128 fl.oz	4 L

VOLUME EQUIVALENTS (DRY)

US STANDARD	METRIC (APPROXIMATE)
⅛ teaspoon	0.5 mL
¼ teaspoon	1 mL
½ teaspoon	2 mL
¾ teaspoon	4 mL
1 teaspoon	5 mL
1 tablespoon	15 mL
¼ cup	59 mL
½ cup	118 mL
¾ cup	177 mL
1 cup	235 mL
2 cups	475 mL
3 cups	700 mL
4 cups	1 L

TEMPERATURES EQUIVALENTS

FAHRENHEIT (F)	CELSIUS (C) (APPROXIMATE)
225°F	107°C
250°F	120°C
75°F	135°C
300°F	150°C
325°F	160°C
350°F	180°C
375°F	190°C
400°F	205°C
425°F	220°C
450°F	235°C
475°F	245°C
500°F	260°C

Appendix 2 Recipes Index

Made in United States
Troutdale, OR
10/11/2023

13615805R00128